To Geordie,

With my ⟨...⟩

and friendly Bursmal

greetings on the occasion

of your visit to Fitzwilliam

1 June 1934.

David Bryan

Fitzwilliam College Cambridge
1869 – 1969

Fitzwilliam College Cambridge
1869 – 1969

Its history as the Non-Collegiate
Institution of the University and its beginnings
as an independent College

by

W. W. Grave

Life Fellow of Emmanuel College,
sometime Censor of Fitzwilliam House
and
Master of Fitzwilliam College

THE FITZWILLIAM SOCIETY

1983

Typeset by Lindonprint Typesetters, Cambridge
Printed in England by the Saffron Press, Saffron Walden

To

K. M. G.

Preface

This story of the Non-Collegiate Society of the University, from its beginnings to its centenary in 1969, three years after its recognition as an independent College, was undertaken on the initiative of Mr J. R. W. Alexander, in 1924 the first honorary secretary and treasurer of the Fitzwilliam Society. I have appreciated the equanimity with which the Master and Fellows of the College appeared to approve Mr Alexander's suggestion, and I am grateful for their permission to examine the minutes and other records of the Governing Body, and of its predecessor the Non-Collegiate Students Board. For virtually the whole of period covered by this History the non-collegiate body, by whatever name, was under University supervision, and I am much indebted to the Council of the Senate for leave to consult their minutes and other papers, containing as they do authoritative material not elsewhere available. My thanks are also due to the Syndics of the Cambridge University Press for permission to quote from Denys Winstanley's *Early Victorian Cambridge*.

Other sources of information have been the minutes of the Fitzwilliam Hall Trust set up by Censor Reddaway in 1921; earlier numbers of the *Cambridge Review*; the undergraduate *Fitzwilliam Magazine,* and successive volumes of the *Fitzwilliam Journal*, a monument to the industry and enthusiasm of the late Mr Guy Milner Walton, its editor for many years.

The interest of former resident members of the College was not confined to proposals, only, that its history should be written, for they also provided material help without which publication could not have contemplated. Generous grants have been made by the Fitzwilliam Society, and by its associated Trust, but even so publication would not have been feasible without the support of the College itself – willingly given at a most difficult time.

It is a pleasure, also, to acknowledge the help of friends. Amid many preoccupations, Dr Leslie Wayper, as a recent President of the Fitzwilliam Society, has found it possible to supervise the activities of a small publication committee appointed to make necessary arrangements, and in these I have been helped by the knowledge and experience of Professor Norman Pounds. I am grateful to the University Draftsman, Mr Geoffrey Hunt, for timely assistance in one particular crisis; and, like so many others, I have had the inestimable boon of being able to draw upon the remarkable knowledge of Fitzwilliam affairs possessed by Dr Raymond Kelly, recently retired from the Bursarship after nearly thirty years of service in different capacities as an officer of the House and College. To Dr Kelly and Dr Wayper my thanks are also due for the care with which they have read my typescript.

These acknowledgements would be culpably incomplete without a grateful mention of help received – and so willingly given that it became a pleasure to ask for it – from the Bursary and the General Office of the College; and, no less, of the patient courtesy of the typesetters in supplying the needs of an author with previous experience limited to the editorship of the *Cambridge University Reporter* in the now long distant past.

Cambridge
November 1982   W. W. G.

Contents

List of Illustrations

Abbreviations

(in footnotes)

A.C. Minutes	Minutes of meetings of undergraduate Amalgamated Clubs, or of their committees
D.N.B.	Dictionary of National Biography
Journal	The Journal of the Fitzwilliam Society
Magazine	The undergraduate Fitzwilliam Hall Magazine (as first entitled)
Minutes	Minutes of meetings of the Non-Collegiate Students Board
Trust Minutes	Minutes of meetings of the Council of Governors of the Fitzwilliam Hall Trust

Introduction

Widespread demand for greater educational opportunities – the University Extension Movement. Stagnation in the two senior Universities of England – their exclusiveness – appointment of Royal Commissions (1850) on Oxford and Cambridge Universities. Oxford Commissioners and 'unattached students'. Private halls (hostels) under University Reform Acts of 1854 and 1856.

When, in 1852, the Cambridge Royal Commissioners, with every appearance of asserting a self-evident truth, wrote of the desirability of extending the benefits of university education 'so as to embrace a larger number of Students than at present exists, and more proportionate to the great increase of our population and national wealth',[1] they enunciated no new principle, but lent the weight of their considerable prestige to a growing insistence on the need to bring a university education within the reach of many who, it was believed, had the capacity to profit from it, but lacked the means.

Already in the eighteenth century the exclusiveness and conservatism of the ancient universities had resulted in the establishment of Dissenting Academies which set out to provide for non-anglicans the educational opportunities denied them elsewhere; and in 1808, on the proposal of certain nonconformists and with the need for medical training particularly in mind, the establishment of a university in London was being considered. The year 1826 saw the foundation of University College which, from the beginning, in addition to providing for medical studies, laid emphasis on modern subjects, excluded theology from its curriculum, and imposed no religious tests. In 1829 King's College was founded by Royal Charter for instruction in the various branches of science (including medicine) and in the doctrines of Christianity; and in 1836 the University of London was founded, also by Royal Charter, as a body empowered to grant degrees, after examination, to students of approved institutions. The significance of the establishment of these centres of learning, with the declared intention of promoting studies virtually ignored by the older universities, did not escape notice, for in 1834 the Cambridge Senate, Regents and Non-

---

[1] *Report of Her Majesty's Commissioners appointed to enquire into the State, Discipline, Studies, and Revenues of the University and Colleges of Cambridge: together with The Evidence, and an Appendix* (London, 1852), pp. 143–144.

Regents alike, approved by substantial majorities a petition to Parliament against the proposal to constitute London University a degree
granting body.[1]

Nor was this all, for the time had come when it was no longer
thought adequate that opportunities denied by Oxford and Cambridge
should be supplied elsewhere; and it was repeatedly urged that the two
Universities should themselves become more responsive to the needs of
the times; and in the early 1830s their effective exclusion of dissenters
was made the point of attack. In April 1834 a Bill dispensing with religious tests in English universities, whether for matriculation or for admission to degrees except those in Divinity, was carried in the House
of Commons, but thrown out in the Lords. The tests were not finally
abolished until 1871, but this marked the beginning of the campaign
against discrimination on religious grounds, and it was followed three
years later by the introduction of a Bill in the House of Lords for the
appointment of a Commission of Enquiry into the working of the
statutes and the application of the revenues of the halls and colleges of
Oxford and Cambridge. This Bill, also, was rejected, but it conveyed
more than a hint that the time might come when the national Government might take an interest, perhaps an unwelcome interest, in the
affairs of the national universities.

The widespread demands for greater opportunities for university
education were part of what came to be known as the University
Extension Movement, a term which in its early days bore a more general connotation than when it was used to describe work done, in the
first instance by the University of Cambridge, under the aegis of University Extra-mural Departments in organizing educational courses in
large centres of population for members of the working classes. Here in
Cambridge it may be supposed that something more than passing
interest will have been aroused when there was laid, in 1846, before
the Hebdomadal Board of the University of Oxford an Address upon
the Extension of University Education ('influentially signed', as they
said there) whose authors desired particularly to find means of increasing the supply of candidates for Holy Orders by 'rendering academical
education accessible to the sons of parents whose incomes are too
narrow for the scale of expenditure at present prevailing among the
junior members of the University of Oxford', and suggested that this
should be done by enlarging existing colleges or, if necessary, by the
foundation of new ones. A committee of the Board appointed to consider the Address, after observing that they were concerned that help

[1]   D. A. Winstanley, *Early Victorian Cambridge* (C.U.P., 1940; reprint 1955), p. 89, footnote.

should be given to many more of the sons of the higher classes of the community whatever their destination in life, rejected the suggestion that new colleges should be 'established or existing ones extended, and recommended the provision of exhibitions to be awarded, not on grounds of literary merit, but of character and economical habits, for the direct purpose of aiding those, and only those, who needed such assistance. This recommendation seems to have found favour – a somewhat leisurely favour – for seven years later the Hebdomadal Board, possibly smarting under the strictures of the Oxford Royal Commissioners, agreed to propose that a sum of £20,000 should be reserved for the purpose. It appears, however, that the Board quickly regained their poise, for they rescinded the proposal, and never put it to Convocation.[1]

During the first half of the nineteenth century the University of Cambridge had made considerable efforts to put its house in order.

> There had certainly [wrote Denys Winstanley] been great progress during the previous fifty years: the Mathematical Tripos had been much improved, the Classical Tripos and the Voluntary Theological Examination had been established, and Professors were for the most part conscientiously performing their duties. But much remained to be done. The ease with which it was possible for all but the greatest dullards to obtain an ordinary degree, the omission to require candidates for admission to pass a University entrance examination, the very restricted range of subjects which undergraduates were encouraged to study, the inability of the Professors to attract hearers, and the medieval character of many of the statutes of the University and the colleges, were some of the evils which called out for remedy. But as many of them could not be cured unless the colleges were willing to sacrifice a measure of their influence and independence, the outlook was not promising.[2]

There were not wanting signs that outside the precincts not only was the future of the two Universities regarded with misgiving, but that such improvements as they claimed to have made were judged unimpressive, and in July 1848 a memorial was presented to the Prime Minister (Lord John Russell), urging that as the Universities were incapable of reforming themselves a commission should be appointed to enquire into their affairs. The Prime Minister took no immediate action on the memorial, but when, three years later, Mr James

---

[1] The *Report* of the Hebdomadal Board's Committee, together with the *Address*, is included as an Appendix to the second of six reports handed by Dr H. G. Liddell to the Select Committee on the Oxford and Cambridge Education Bill (1867). See also pp. 15–17.

[2] *Early Victorian Cambridge*, p. 197.

Heywood,[1] who was believed to have been largely responsible for it, tried again, and announced his intention of proposing in the House of Commons an address to the Crown, praying for the appointment of a commission of enquiry 'into the state of the Universities and Colleges of Oxford, Cambridge and Dublin', the Prime Minister took the matter into his own hands, and announced that if Mr Heywood would withdraw his motion he himself would advise the Crown that a Royal Commission should be appointed. This was bad enough; far worse was Lord John Russell's scarcely veiled belief that the Royal Commission might recommend urgently needed reforms to which effect could be given only by legislation. Not only was the University faced with the prospect of a Royal Commission, but with the spectre of a Statutory Commission to follow.

Two commissions were appointed, in identical terms, 'for the purpose of enquiring into the State, Discipline, Studies, and Revenues of Our University of Oxford (Cambridge) and of all and singular the Colleges in Our said University'[2] The commissions were issued on 31 August 1850, and the Commissioners were required to report within two years of their appointment, 'or sooner, if the same can reasonably be'.

While the Reports are of consuming interest to students of university history, they also have for us an especial significance in that they are the first, in modern times, to pose the question whether admission to either University must necessarily be conditional upon membership of a college. In the event, the Oxford Commissioners recommended the adoption of the non-collegiate principle; and, as the Cambridge Commissioners did not, it is in the Oxford Report that the arguments in its favour are to be sought.

Among the large number of matters on which the Commissioners invited the opinion of all Heads of colleges, all Professors and public officers of the University, and of other eminent persons who might be in a position to offer advice, one was set forth as follows:

---

[1] A persistent critic of the two ancient Universities, and particularly of their discrimination against those who were not members of the Established Church. At Trinity College he was twelfth *Senior Optime* in 1833, but as a dissenter did not graduate until 1857, after the passing of the Cambridge Reform Act of the previous year. He was Member of Parliament for North Lancashire from 1847–57. (See also Venn, *Alumni Cantabrigienses*, part II, 1752–1900 (C.U.P., 1947) vol. iii, p. 354.)

[2] See *Reports*, pp. iii, iv. In identical terms, save there were seven Oxford Commissioners, and five for Cambridge. The Secretary to the Oxford Commissioners was named, but the Cambridge Commissioners were left to appoint their own.

6. The means of extending the benefits of the University to a larger number of Students,

(1) By the establishment of new Halls, whether as independent societies, or in connexion with Colleges;

(2) By permitting Undergraduates to lodge in private houses more generally than at present;

(3) By allowing Students to become Members of the University, and to be educated in Oxford under due superintendence, but without subjecting them to the expenses incident to connexion with a College or Hall;

(4) By admitting persons to Professorial lectures, and authorising the Professors to grant certificates of attendance, without requiring any further connexion with the University.[1]

Of these four possibilities, the Commissioners favoured the third. After observing that they had no wish to encourage the admission of poor men to the University just because they were poor, and saying also that they did not believe that a wider use of lodging houses would reduce the cost of residence – they would expect 'Collegians' to take their expensive habits with them wherever they resided – they expressed their views on this third proposition at some length.

While they admitted that to many this proposal seemed a dangerous change in the Oxford system, the Commissioners saw in it many advantages: no great capital outlay would be needed, and the scheme would offer greater opportunities than any other to a much poorer class of student, hitherto kept out of Oxford by its expense. For such 'University students', as they called them, there would be no college fees, no need for caution money, no purchase of furniture, no payments to college servants, and no contribution to the upkeep of college fabric. Each would be free to seek out the cheapest tolerable lodging he could find, and there would be nothing to prevent him from ordering his affairs as economically as he could contrive, without the comparison or comment which life in a college might invite. The Commissioners believed that for such men the cost of a four year degree course could be kept down to £200, including money for clothes and pocket money, but not for board during vacations. Many critics of the plan had expressed alarm at the effect on University discipline of the presence of unattached students living in lodgings without proper supervision, but the Commissioners were of the opinion that there was less to fear in Oxford from the young men they were seeking to admit than there was to fear for them. They would lack the means of indulgence; they would

---

[1] *Report*, 'Evidence', part I, p. 2.

be 'reading men', and not idlers; and it might even be hoped that their success in the Schools would provide a much needed stimulus in the University at large. Their lodgings would be subject to licence, and they themselves would be as amenable to University discipline as members of colleges. There was no reason to suppose that their residence in lodgings would be any less satisfactory in Oxford than it was in Scotland, or, indeed, in Cambridge, even if in Oxford it should prove impossible to match the extremes of thrift practised, as they had been told, in some Scottish universities.

It seemed to the Commissioners that this scheme was free from obstacles in the way of the others they were considering, and that it retained many of their most practicable features. Accordingly they recommended its adoption. There was widespread agreement that the benefits of university education should be extended to many who had been excluded; and the Commissioners thought that the University itself would benefit from their admission. They had heard from witnesses that it was not only lack of means that kept men away, but a fear among parents that the atmosphere of the place was positively harmful; and they hoped that the presence in the University of men of the kind they wished to see admitted might, in time at least, discourage the prevalent extravagance of life and thought.

The Report contains forty-seven recommendations, of which twenty-nine are described as affecting, particularly, the University, and eighteen the colleges. Of the former, the tenth relates to University Extension, and the Commissioners declare it to be one of the two most important:

> 10. That the provision of the Statutes, by which all Members of the University are obliged to belong to some College or Hall, as also that by which Colleges and Halls are obliged to have all their rooms accessible through one common gate, should be annulled; and that liberty be given for the extension of the University, as well by the foundation of Halls as by permitting Members of the University, under due superintendence, to live in private lodgings, without connexion with a College or Hall.[1]

Such was the recommendation of the Oxford Commissioners in April 1852. The Cambridge Commissioners did not report until 30 August (with one day to spare), but a hint was given in the interval of their probable attitude on the issue of non-collegiate membership, and of the very different attitude of the Prince Consort, who, since his election as Chancellor of the University in 1847, had taken a lively

---

[1] *Report*, p. 257.

interest in its proceedings. One of the Cambridge Commissioners was Adam Sedgwick, Woodwardian Professor of Geology, who had been appointed the Chancellor's Secretary for University affairs, and so had more opportunities than most of knowing the Chancellor's mind. In an engaging letter written to his niece in July 1852 from Osborne, he says:

> I found that the Prince greatly admired the Oxford *Report*. He seemed to like the idea, there started, of mixing the foreign and the English systems. The Oxford Commission suggest a plan of admitting any numbers who like to come, without belonging to any college, or being under the ordinary restraints of academic discipline – just as at Edinburgh and the foreign universities. I told the Prince, honestly, that we should not recommend this plan. Each system might do by itself, but the two would never, we thought, work well together. I think he was a little disappointed at this; for 'tis just the part of the Oxford *Report* that has been puffed up by the bellows of *The Times*, and of the whole daily press; and he evidently does not wish us to fall behind Oxford ... He has studied the Oxford *Report* from end to end, which is more than I have done, or mean to do. I read it in the way in which Jack Horner ate pie.[1]

Like their counterparts in Oxford, the Cambridge Commissioners addressed a series of questions to the principal administrative officers of the University, to the Professors, the Heads and Tutors of colleges, and other persons, not all resident, whose views they thought might be of assistance to them. With the main body of the Report we have no immediate concern; its general tenor is far more kindly than that of the Oxford Commissioners. The Commissioners noted that the University and some of the colleges had done much to set their house in order, and in some instances where they felt constrained to recommend further improvements they were of the opinion that the University and the colleges alike, hampered as they were by ancient statutes, might need the help of legislation to remove obstacles in the path of reform which, on their own initiative, they had begun to tread. The Commissioners also suggested that, if the Government should contemplate further reforms, it might be convenient if the principles upon which they should be based were laid down in an Act of Parliament. This had been said before; and the urbanity of the Commissioners' phraseology did not disguise the possibility of the appointment of a Statutory Commission – hitherto a cloud no bigger than a man's hand in a light blue sky – with the coercive powers feared by many in the University.

In framing their enquiries the Cambridge Commissioners made no

---

[1]   J. W. Clark and T. McKenny Hughes, *Life and Letters of Adam Sedgwick* (2 vols., C.U.P., 1890), vol. II, p. 223.

specific mention of the possibility of admitting to the University men who were not also members of a college, but three of the questions have some bearing on the admission of students, in the Oxford phrase, of narrow means:

> 1. Does it appear to you practicable, consistently with what is due to the habits of those classes of society in this country to which Students usually belong, to diminish very materially the necessary expenses of a residence in College? ...
>
> 8. What provision is made in your College for the maintenance or assistance of poor Students? ... Is it, in your opinion, expedient to afford such aid in the education of Students, on the ground of poverty alone, without regard to merit and superior attainments? ... What would be the effect, as far as your observation would enable you to judge, of the establishment of a Hall or College for poor students only, who should be educated and maintained on the lowest practicable scale of expenditure? ...
>
> 15. Do any of the students of your College reside in lodgings in the town? To what regulations are the keepers of such lodgings subject, and are those regulations, in your opinion, generally observed? Are you disposed to think that Students in the town are under less rigorous control or exposed to greater temptations than those who are within the College? ...[1]

On question 1 the general opinion was that necessary expenses could not be significantly reduced, though some correspondents stress the word 'necessary'. From the answers to question 8 it appears that sizarships were the main source of assistance for poor students, and their number is given as 143 at twelve of the colleges. There is insufficient evidence in the *Report* for any calculation of the average value of a sizarship: the highest figure mentioned in correspondence was £70 (Trinity College), and the lowest £12 (Pembroke College). The Commissioners make much of the case of a sizar at St John's whose college bills for ten terms exceeded by only £19 the amount derived from his college awards. They felt bound to add that he paid a further sum of £111 for private tuition; and that as a very distinguished student his case might be exceptional; but, even so, they had grounds for thinking that other men in a similar position might have enjoyed corresponding advantages.[2]

There was almost no support for the making of grants on the ground of poverty alone, and very little for the establishment of halls or colleges for poor men, though one correspondent made an exception in favour of such a hall confined to theological students. The replies to

[1] *Report*, 'Evidence on Expenses and Tuition', p. 140.
[2] *Report*, p. 196.

question 15 reveal considerable uncertainty whether students were under more effective supervision in college than in lodgings, and virtually nobody was unwilling for men to be put in lodgings if a college had more students than could be accommodated within its walls. In the absence of any specific enquiry by the Commissioners, there is little reference to the possibility of non-collegiate residence, but it is recommended in two replies which appear to contemplate arrangements similar to those adopted some years later for private hostels.[1]

On this question of non-collegiate membership the views of the Commissioners are definite and succinct: 'It has been contended that it would be desirable to ... revert to the ancient practice so far as to allow of matriculated Students of the University, not attached to any College or Hall ... and we are of opinion that it would not be expedient to adopt any change of that nature in the present system of the University. It appears to us that one of the most striking and valuable characteristics of our English Universities is to be found in the domestic system of their education, by which habits of order and moral control are most satisfactorily obtained.' They quote with approval the evidence of Dr Philpott, Master of St Catharine's Hall: 'It seems to be one of the advantages of the present system of admission and residence in Colleges, that students of different classes of society and of different means and circumstances are brought to associate together during their residence at the University, and the good effect of this arrangement upon both the higher and lower classes of students is very obvious, and produces permanent results.'[2] The Commissioners conclude, therefore, that the two systems of collegiate and unattached students are hardly compatible with one another, and that great difficulties would be experienced in blending them together, if a non-collegiate body were recognized, and attained any considerable size.

On the matter of residence kept in lodgings, which, unlike Oxford, Cambridge had permitted extensively for many years, the Commissioners did not wish to recommend that the practice should cease, but thought that there was much to be said for the establishment of affiliated halls, under direct college control.[3]

As we have seen, the Commissioners were prepared to accept the general proposition that the University should take more students, but they do not appear to have had in mind that this should be brought

[1] *Report*, 'Evidence on Expenses and Tuition', pp. 151, 216.
[2] *Report*, p. 143.
[3] In the Michaelmas term of 1851, of 1923 undergraduates in residence 736 were in Lodgings. *Report*, p. 145.

about by the admission, particularly, of poor men, hitherto excluded by lack of means. They deplore unnecessary expense; they offer a number of reasons for the difficulty of controlling expense by regulation, and they, indeed, agree with an opinion, which they quote, that it was undesirable to impose greater restraint than was already exercised, on the grounds that this might deprive the men of opportunities of learning wisdom, through experience, in the management of their affairs. They admit their inability to offer, beyond one or two relatively minor suggestions, any practical recommendations on the subject, and add that they trust that their recommendation on the limitation of private tuition may considerably reduce the cost of education in the University. They also believe that if the curriculum could be broadened so as to excite greater interest among the students, this too might induce among them more diligence, and less extravagant habits.

At Oxford the Hebdomadal Board lost no time in appointing, in June 1852, a committee to consider their Commissioners' recommendations. The committee, in a Report presented to the Board in December and published in 1853, found little in them to commend. They disapproved of suggestions for the establishment of independent halls, and for the licensing of lodgings unconnected with colleges, although they were willing to contemplate the setting up of affiliated halls.[1]

In Cambridge the Chancellor asked the Vice-Chancellor for a 'statement of the steps which the University had taken with regard to the report', and passed on the information to the Prime Minister on 4 March 1853; but neither the Report of the Hebdomadal Board's committee nor the communication from the Vice-Chancellor of Cambridge can have dispelled the opinion entertained in Government circles that progress in the Universities was being unacceptably slow, and that, as the Cambridge Commissioners had hinted, they needed help from Parliament if obstacles in the way of reform were to be overcome. In April Lord John Russell, after informing the House of Commons that the Government intended to give the Universities themselves time to effect improvements, thought it well to specify certain principles on which action was needed; and among them included the need for the Universities to be able to admit students without requiring them to be members of colleges. After an interval of some months the Home Secretary (Lord Palmerston) in a letter to the Chancellor again referred to those matters to which the Government attached particular importance. Of these the second was:

---

[1] C.E. Mallet, *A History of the University of Oxford*, vol. III (O.U.P., 1927), p. 318.

The adoption of measures which might enable the Universities, without weakening the proper securities for discipline, to extend the benefits of training to a greater number of students, whether in connexion or not with colleges and halls, and also to diminish the relative disadvantages which now attach within colleges and halls to students of comparatively limited means.[1]

As Lord Palmerston also asked what reforms the University and the colleges intended to adopt, and what assistance they needed from Parliament to give effect to them, the Vice-Chancellor asked for the appointment of a Syndicate to prepare a reply. The Syndicate's task was a difficult one, for while it would have been very convenient if they could have framed a reply drawing suitable attention to improvements made in the recent past, and – no less – to reforms likely to prove acceptable to Government and University alike in the immediate future, for this there was no abundance of material. And in the matter of poor and unattached students the Syndicate's difficulty was increased by the opposition of most of the colleges, who declared that discipline would certainly be impaired by the presence in the University of men not under college supervision. Furthermore, they said, admission of men in this way was unnecessary, in the light of the moderate scale of college charges, and the fact that their awards were open for competition. Under the heading of University Extension, therefore, the Syndicate had little option but to give reasons why the University should not permit students to reside and graduate without being members of any college; and for this part of their draft material was at hand in the *Report* of the Cambridge Commissioners, with which members of the Syndicate affirmed their concurrence, only adding a suggestion that, where colleges did not possess means of erecting further buildings of their own, they might nevertheless be able to accommodate more students in hired houses in the town. The Syndicate's Report on this and other matters was unanimously approved by the Senate on 17 January 1854.

There was little here to persuade the politicians that the University had made, or was likely to make, good use of the opportunities for reform allowed by Lord John Russell nine months previously; and on 17 March 1854 the Government brought in a Bill for the Good Government of the University of Oxford and the Colleges therein, very largely drafted by Mr W. E. Gladstone, then member for the University, which proposed in the University changes so sweeping that an enthusiastic ob-

---

[1] D. A. Winstanley, *Early Victorian Cambridge,* p. 275.

server was moved to declare that the years which included the University Reform Bill had seen more improvement in the temper and the teaching of Oxford than the three centuries that went before.[1] On the matter of the admission of unattached students, it was to be sixteen years, in spite of the recommendation of the Commissioners, before Oxford admitted them, and a year longer before non-collegiate students came to Cambridge, and only then under pressure from outside; but the Oxford Act of 1854 made the first tentative moves in that direction by authorizing the establishment of private halls in the University; and a similar Act of 1856 included provision for private hostels in Cambridge, though not, apparently, at the suggestion of those members of the University who prepared a preliminary draft of the Bill for the guidance of Ministers.

Under the Cambridge Act, any member of the University of such standing and qualifications as might be required by statute would be entitled, by licence to be obtained from the Vice-Chancellor, to open his residence, if it was within a mile and a half of Great St Mary's, for the reception of students who should be matriculated and admitted to all the privileges of the University without being of necessity entered as members of any college. In the Lent term of 1857 the Council of the Senate (which had in the previous November replaced the *Caput Senatus*) devoted the greater part of four consecutive meetings to the business of preparing draft statutes for the regulation of hostels, and on 13 February approved for submission to the Senate on 5 March five separate Graces, one for each statute.[2] The Graces were opposed on the grounds that they did not require the Principal of a hostel to be a member of the Senate (and therefore also of the Church of England), and did not, like the Oxford statutes, provide for the instruction of the students, for Public Prayer, or indeed for any recognition of religion;[3] and although the point was made that this reflected not so much a difference of policy between the two Universities as a difference in the Acts of Parliament on which their statutes were based, three of the five Graces – the three that mattered – failed to secure Senate approval.

Winstanley quotes a letter written on 13 March by the Vice-Chancellor to the Chancellor's private secretary saying that he had that day consulted the Council of the Senate about a revision of the Hostel

[1] Mark Pattison (Mallet, *op. cit.*, p. 330).
[2] Minutes of the Council of the Senate, vol. 1, 1856–58. Minutes of 2,6,9,13,20 February 1857 (University Archives).
[3] Flysheet, dated 3 March 1857, by H. J. Hotham, Fellow of Trinity College. Cavendish College, Selwyn College, Hostels, Camb. Univ. Reg. 104, University Archives.

Statutes, in view of the objections expressed by members of the Senate, and that the Council had decided not to alter them.[1] The minutes of the Council do not allude to this consultation, but a note in the Registrary's hand – 'The Council then abandoned the Hostels.' – appears to suggest that they had enough of them, at least for the time being; and, in any event, they had no need to make alterations, for the 1856 Act, which had given the University and the colleges until 1 January 1958 to amend their statutes so as to give effect to necessary reforms, had also provided that if this were not done the Commissioners themselves would do the amending; and the statutes for hostels approved by the Queen in Council on 31 July 1858 were to all intents and purposes identical with those rejected by the Senate in the first place.[2]

[1] *Early Victorian Cambridge*, p. 318.
[2] Camb. Univ. Reg. 104, University Archives.

CHAPTER I

The 'Non-Collegiate' Debate

Small importance of hostels in Cambridge. University extension in Oxford – proposals for residence in lodgings there 'with or without connexion with Colleges'. Oxford and Cambridge Education Bill (1867). Cambridge Syndicate on existing provision for poor students – rejection of its proposals (May 1868). Second Syndicate to consider admission of students not members of any college (December 1868) – its Report approved – amendment of University Statutes by Queen in Council 13 May 1869. Appointment of members of Non-Collegiate Students Board.

Statutorily the recognition of hostels represented a half-way house between a University whose members must all belong to a college and a University which allowed non-collegiate membership for all qualified students who preferred it; but in practice the result of the Council's labours was unimpressive, for their only immediate outcome was the opening in the Michaelmas term 1859 by Dr G. M. Humphry of Downing College, Surgeon to Addenbrooke's Hospital and Lecturer to the University in Human Anatomy,[1] of his houses at 56 and 57 Trumpington Street as a hostel for medical students. There were five who matriculated at Michaelmas 1859, four a year later, and that was all.[2] Of the nine, five graduated as migrants to colleges, and of these only two obtained a Cambridge medical qualification. After 1862 Dr Humphry's hostel no longer appears in the *University Calendar*, and shortly afterwards it was suggested that it had closed through lack of pupils. There were then no hostels under the 1858 statutes until 1884, when the Rev. William Ayerst, Master of Arts of Caius College and Rector of Hungarton in Leicestershire, opened one in his own name.[3]

[1] Professor of Anatomy 1866–83, of Surgery 1883–1903. Fellow of King's College in 1884. The observant pedestrian may still wonder whether the sealed-up street door of number 57 is a relic of the time when the two houses together served as an undergraduate hostel.

[2] *University Calendar* 1860, 1861, 1862.

[3] Ayerst Hostel, which throughout its existence appears in the *University Calendar* as 'Ayerst Hall', at first consisted of a single house (number 9) in Queen Anne Terrace on the south side of Parker's Piece. Its declared object was 'to enable theological and other students to keep their terms at Cambridge at the same cost as at the younger universities and at theological colleges, thereby bringing the expense of education at this University within the limits of moderate professional incomes'. At the beginning of the Michaelmas term 1884, Mr Ayerst had obtained a Vice-Chancellor's licence for number 8 also, and in a Directory for 1887 he is shown as occupying numbers 1,4,5,7,8,9. He applied unsuccessfully in May 1886, and again in 1889, for Public Hostel status under arrangements approved in 1882 for New Institutions for Academical Education (under which Selwyn College and Cavendish College were shortly afterwards recognized). In 1893 he sold his leasehold property in

The introduction of hostels cannot, therefore, be said to have done much to make the University more readily accessible to poor students, and although matriculations as a whole increased substantially in the 1860s, there is little evidence of a corresponding increase in the admission of a class of applicants hitherto excluded by lack of means. In Oxford, however, the advocates of University extension were still active, and on 16 November 1865 a meeting of graduates was held in Oriel College, under the chairmanship of the Provost, 'to consider the question of the extension of the University, with a view especially to the education of persons needing assistance and desirous of admission into the Christian ministry'; and by a resolution passed at that meeting a committee was nominated with representatives of twenty-two colleges and halls, which in its turn appointed six sub-committees to consider and report on various plans for University extension. Of these sub-committees, one, whose Chairman was Dr H. G. Liddell, Dean of Christ Church, was asked 'to consider the expediency of allowing undergraduates to reside in lodgings, whether with or without connexion with colleges, and to recommend provision for securing their discipline and tuition'. The Report of this sub-committee, with others, was published in the following year;[1] and its recommendations foreshadow the arrangements adopted shortly afterwards by both Universities for their non-collegiate students.

Queen Anne Terrace, and, in the hope that he might further his plans for the eventual foundation of a college, acquired a freehold site on Mount Pleasant in the parish of St Giles, where 'on May 31, 1893, the memorial stone of new buildings … was laid by the Master of Corpus Christi College'. In 1895 he built six additional sets of rooms.

From a statement dated 18 August 1896, prepared for private circulation, it appears that after unsuccessful attempts to raise money, and after receiving advice that on his retirement there was no prospect that 'the college' could be continued, Mr Ayerst accepted an offer to purchase his property, and closed the Hostel. He adds 'Through the kindness of St Catharine's College I am allowed to tell our members that they may obtain permission to write themselves of that College, without forfeiture of the privileges set forth in the prospectus of Ayerst Hall.'

Throughout the twelve years of its existence the Hostel had, on average, just under thirty undergraduate members in residence. Numbers began to fall in 1893, and in the year 1895/96 there were twenty-two. The purchasers of the Mount Pleasant property were the Council of St Edmund's House, the first of the 'Attached Houses' whose men, if they wished to sit for the degree examinations of the University, were enrolled as non-collegiate students under the supervision of the Non-collegiate Students Board.

(See University Calendars for the years 1885–1896/97, and University Library, Cambridge Papers FM 251. Also University Archives, 'hostels (private)', Camb. Univ. Reg. 104, for details of protracted deliberations of the Council of the Senate, advised by the Proctorial Syndicate, on the desirability of more effective supervision of such hostels, which in a Report, dated 14 January 1889 (*University Reporter*, 1889–89 p. 343), the Council recommended should thenceforth be known as 'Private Hostels'.)

[1] *Oxford University Extension* (Macmillan, 1866).

The sub-committee believed that the students whom the advocates of University extension had in mind belonged to a different class from those who had hitherto sought admission to Oxford, and that their main task was to provide academic status and instruction for poor men seeking to be ordained, to practise in the law or in medicine, or to go into business. As the extent of the demand could be ascertained by experiment only, it would be prudent to proceed with as little outlay and as little risk as possible, in order that the minimum of loss should be incurred in the event of failure. The cheapest and simplest expedient would undoubtedly be the relaxation of the requirement that residence must be kept in a college. On the matter of expense, the sub-committee estimated that the average total of annual college charges (fixed fees, and kitchen and buttery bills) was about £100, and about half this sum might be saved by a careful student living in independent lodgings. Also, such a student would not need to pay an appreciable part of a sum of about £60 for initial expenses which, although it was mostly refunded at the end of residence, had to be found in the interval. With regard to discipline, there were small grounds for apprehension, for the men could not afford, and by habit would not wish, to be disorderly. Regular attendance at chapel and lectures was more likely to be secured in college than in lodgings, and in college there was likely to be what the sub-committee described as 'less positive temptation to immorality'; but they drew attention to the experience of Cambridge, which had shewn that residence in lodgings need not be harmful, and suggested that with a system of supervision on the Cambridge pattern the regulation of lodgings in Oxford could be very different from what it had hitherto been. As for chapel, it would be perfectly possible to have morning prayers in the University church for those unattached students who were members of the Church of England. On the provision of instruction, if the number of the students were small there would surely be graduates of the University willing to give lectures for a small fee, and if numbers should be large the University itself might feel justified in providing teaching staff. The character and the circumstances of the students would be such that compulsory attendance at lectures would be unnecessary. Lastly, the point was made, in reply to those who maintained that men in independent lodgings would be deprived of the social advantages of college life, that the question at issue was how young men who, as things were, could not come to Oxford at all might be enabled to do so, even if they might have to be content with something less than the best. In any event, some would be likely to better themselves by winning college scholarships.

Accordingly, the sub-committee recommended

I. That a delegacy, with a paid secretary, be appointed, whose duty it shall be –

(1) To grant licenses to ... (suitable) students to reside in lodgings, with or without connection with a college or hall, provided ... their parents or guardians sanction the proposal; and to report the names of such students to the Vice-Chancellor.

(2) To grant licenses to any (suitable) persons applying to keep lodging houses for the purpose of receiving such students, provided ... their accommodation is sufficient, and their rent reasonable; and to report the names of such lodging-house keepers to the Vice-Chancellor.

II. That this delegacy have all the authority over these students which a college has over its members, and also full power over the lodging-house keepers; and that it should frame rules for the management of the houses, and the discipline of the students.

III. That the secretary's salary be provided by a small fee on every license so granted.

IV. That University tutors be appointed as the academical guardians of the unattached students and the medium of communication with their parents, but not necessarily to take part in their instruction; and that a reasonable fee be paid by each unattached student. That the tutor have the power of entering the lodgings of his pupils whenever he thinks proper.

After the publication of the sub-committees' Reports, but before their recommendations could be adopted, there were again warnings that if the Universities did not move of their own accord they might be required to do so by Parliament. Minute 3 of a meeting of the Council of the Senate (in Cambridge) held on 25 March 1867 reads:

> The Vice-Chancellor said that his attention had been called to three Bills which had been brought into the House of Commons; (1) by Mr Coleridge and Mr Grant Duff[1] to provide for the abolition of Religious Tests in connection with Academical Degrees and Offices in the University of Oxford, the provisions of which Bill it is proposed to extend to the University of Cambridge when the said Bill is considered in Committee; (2) by Professor Fawcett and Mr Bouverie[2] 'to repeal certain portions of the Act of Uniformity relating to Fellows of Colleges'; (3) by Mr Ewart, Mr Neate

---

[1] John Duke Coleridge (1820–94). Fellow of Exeter College, Oxford. Liberal Member of Parliament for Exeter 1865–73. Lord Chief Justice 1873.
　　Mountstuart Elphinstone Grant Duff (1829–96). Liberal Member of Parliament for Elgin Burghs 1857–81.

[2] Henry Fawcett (1833–84). Fellow of Trinity Hall 1856. Liberal Member of Parliament for Brighton 1865; for Hackney 1874. Professor of Political Economy 1863.
　　Edward Pleydell-Bouverie (1818–89). Trinity College. Liberal Member of Parliament for Kilmarnock 1844–74.

and Mr Pollard Urquhart[1] 'to extend the Benefits of Education in the Universities of Oxford and Cambridge to Students not belonging to any College or Hall'. A memorial signed by 59 members of the Senate had been sent to the Vice-Chancellor in favour of a Petition against the first Bill, and one signed by 61 against the second. A conversation took place, and the Vice-Chancellor was requested to prepare petitions against the first two Bills, to be considered at the next meeting.[2]

The first two Bills are not our immediate concern. The Petitions were duly brought to the Council, approved by large majorities of the Senate, and laid before Parliament. They are, nevertheless, of indirect interest because the attitude of those members of the University who opposed the removal of the disabilities still suffered by the Dissenters was also to raise difficulty, when the time came, in the way of the Council's plans for a non-collegiate organization.

Mr Ewart's Bill, on the other hand, bore directly on the question of university extension, and the Vice-Chancellor was asked to enquire of Mr Walpole and Mr Selwyn[3] about its probable effect upon the University if it became law. On 4 April he informed the Council that Mr Selwyn had said that there was to be a meeting of the University members with a view to some joint action, and on 10 June he reported that Mr Selwyn had recommended a Petition against the Bill, and also thought that some members of the University should appear before a Select Committee (to which the Bill had been referred after its second reading on 5 June). By nine votes to two the Council decided against a Petition. On 11 June they appointed a committee of their own number 'to watch

---

[1] William Ewart (1798–1869). A classical graduate of Oxford (Christ Church) in 1821, he had been Newdigate Prizeman in the previous year. He was first elected to Parliament in 1828 as member for Blechingley, and then represented Liverpool (his birthplace) and Wigan almost continuously until 1841, when he became the member for Dumfries burghs, and sat for that constituency until he retired from public life in 1868. Throughout his life an advanced Liberal, he campaigned vigorously against the excessive rigour of the law, and was a strenuous, and frequently successful, initiator of measures designed to benefit the working classes. The movement for university extension was very fortunate in having an advocate so persistent, and of such high standing.

    Charles Neate (1806–79). Fellow of Oriel College 1828. Drummond Professor of Political Economy at Oxford 1857–62. Liberal Member of Parliament for Oxford City 1857, and 1863–68.

    William Pollard Urquhart (1815–71). Trinity College (B.A. 1938, as William Pollard). Liberal Member of Parliament for Westminster 1852–57, and 1859–71.

[2] University Archives. The Council minutes to which reference is made in this chapter are to be found in vol. III (Jan. 1864 – Dec. 1868), and IV (Jan. 1869 –   ).

[3] Spencer Horace Walpole (1808–98). Trinity College. Conservative Member of Parliament for Midhurst 1846. University Burgess 1856–82. Home Secretary (thrice).

    Charles Jasper Selwyn (1813–69). Trinity College. Commissary 1855–58. University Burgess (Conservative) 1859–68. Solicitor General 1867. Lord of Appeal 1868.

the progress of several Bills now before Parliament, and to report if necessary'. On 2 November the Vice-Chancellor drew the Council's attention to the 'Report on the Evidence given before the Select Committee on the Oxford and Cambridge Universities Bill 1867', and also to the subject of the two Bills brought into Parliament in the last session by Mr Coleridge and Mr Bouverie respectively; and the Council discussed, apparently inconclusively, whether a Syndicate should be appointed to consider these questions. Two days later the Council received a Report, dated 19 October, from their committee appointed on 11 June. On Mr Ewart's Bill the committee informed the Council (what they already knew) that it had been referred to a Select Committee of twenty-one members with power to examine witnesses. Several resident and non-resident members of the University had appeared before the committee, and their evidence had been printed in a Blue Book which the Council had received.[1] It appears that the Council thought that other witnesses might with advantage also have been examined,

---

[1] Oxford and Cambridge Universities Education Bill, University Library, Cam. a. 867.1. The twenty-one members of the committee, who included, in addition to Mr Ewart, Mr Gladstone, Mr Selwyn, Professor Fawcett, Mr Pollard-Urquhart, and Mr Grant Duff, had been nominated by the end of June, and on 24 July the Solicitor General was added to their number. During the month of July two petitions were referred to the committee – one against the Bill, from the Clergy of the Framland Deanery (in the Archdeaconry of Leicester), and one, in favour, from the Leicestershire Association of Baptist Congregations. By the end of the month the committee had taken evidence from twenty-one witnesses, of whom 13 were from Oxford and 7 from Cambridge, proportions which may have provoked the opinion expressed in the Council of the Senate that it might have been advantageous if more had been invited. The seven Cambridge residents who appeared before the committee were

    Dr Bateson, Master of St John's College (previously Bursar)
    Mr J. L. Hammond, Bursar of Trinity College (previously Tutor)
    Rev. Robert Burn, Tutor of Trinity College
    Rev. Henry Latham, Tutor of Trinity Hall
    Mr H. J. Roby, Fellow and Classical Lecturer of St John's College
    Rev. W. M. Campion, Tutor of Queens' College
    Mr G. D. Liveing, Professor of Chemistry, Fellow, and formerly Lecturer, of St John's College

These witnesses were, in general, sympathetic to the objects of the Bill, provided, as Mr Campion said, they could be achieved without interference with University discipline; and this, as Mr Campion also said, he thought could be done.

By the end of July the committee had decided that it would not be possible to complete their hearing of evidence bearing on the Bill before Parliament rose, and on 31 July they reported it to the House without amendment. This is the last mention of the Bill as an item of parliamentary business, but the Select Committee's Minutes of Evidence Taken contain much information of very great interest on the educational policy, and practice, of the two Universities and their colleges in the middle of the nineteenth century. The committee included, among a number of Appendices to their Report, a paper supplied by Mr Hammond on the necessary annual expenses of different classes of undergraduates at Trinity College, and the Reports of the Oxford Sub-Committees on University Extension, handed in by Dr Liddell, Dean of Christ Church.

but Parliament had been prorogued without the Bill being called.

Just how immediate was the effect of Mr Ewart's Bill is not easy to determine with certainty. One authority has no doubt on the point:[1] 'In 1867 he proposed a measure of University reform which led to the admission of unattached students'; and the editor of *The Times* appears to have been of same opinion, for a leading article declares:

> [Yet] it is only within the last three or four years that the question of receiving non-collegiate students in lodging-houses has been fairly reconsidered at either University. The example was set by Oxford, where the rule compelling all Undergraduate members of Colleges to reside within the walls sensibly aggravated the College monopoly. A great variety of plans was started and canvassed by a number of sub-committees; but, as usual, with no practical result, until a Bill for the removal of both restrictions was introduced by Mr Ewart into the House of Commons. The publication and reception of a special Report, containing a remarkable body of evidence, by the Select Committee on this Bill have acted like a charm in opening the eyes of both Universities.[2]

The University, which had every reason to remember the Cambridge Reform Act of 1856 and the effects of consequent legislation, could not have been unaware of the growing volume of public opinion, shared by many of its resident members, in favour of the removal of such of the old restrictions as were still retained, and it may have seemed no longer prudent, on the question of non-collegiate membership, to shelter behind the authority of the Cambridge Royal Commissioners, who had pronounced against the idea. However all this may have been, the Council of the Senate lost little time. On 18 November they carried without a division a motion proposed by the Master of St Peter's College (Dr H. W. Cookson) and seconded by Mr E. H. Perowne, of Corpus Christi College, 'That a Grace be offered to the Senate to appoint a Syndicate to consider the provisions existing at present in the University for the education of poor students, and whether those provisions may with advantage be extended, and in what manner, and to report to the Senate from time to time till the end of the ensuing Lent Term'. The Council then nominated the Vice-Chancellor and sixteen other persons to be members of the Syndicate. The Registrary's Grace (Grace 2 of 28 November) passed the Senate without a division:

> 2 *Placeat vobis ut* DOMINUS PROCANCELLARIUS, Dr. COOKSON *Coll. Div. Pet. Præfectus*, Dr. CORRIE *Coll. Jes. Præfectus*, Dr. BATESON *Coll. Div. Joh.*

---

[1] *D.N.B.* (1889), vol. xviii, p. 91.
[2] *The Times*, 28 March 1868.

Præfectus, Dr. LIGHTFOOT *Professor Hulseanus*, Magr. CLARK *Orator Publicus*, Professor LIVEING, Magr. PARKINSON *e Coll. Div. Joh.*, Magr. CAMPION *e Coll. Reginali*, Magr. E. H. PEROWNE *e Coll. Corp. Chri.*, Magr. PHEAR *e Coll. Emman.*, Magr. LATHAM *ex Aul. SS. Trin.*, Magr. GUNSON *e Coll. Chri.*, Magr. TODHUNTER *e Coll. Div. Joh.*, Magr. FERRERS *e Coll. Gon. et Cai.*, Magr. R. BURN *e Coll. SS. Trin.*, et Magr. H. A. MORGAN *e Coll. Jes. Syndici vestri constituantur qui, considerato quomodo eorum quorum res familiaris impensis academicis minus sufficiat educationi ad hoc tempus in academia provisum sit, deliberent utrum alia aliqua ratione pluribus ejusmodi alumnis in academia erudiendis commode provideri possit, et ad vos de tempore in tempus referant ante finem termini proximi quadragesimalis.*[1]

However various may have been the motives of the Council in setting up a Syndicate to advise the University on the admission of poor undergraduates, and whatever difficulties they encountered by the way, there is no doubt about the quality, or the breadth of experience, of their nominees for appointment to it. Four members of the Syndicate had been Senior Wranglers, and three Senior Classics. Its Chairman was the Vice-Chancellor, and of three other Heads of Colleges two were previous Vice-Chancellors. W. G. Clark was Public Orator, and Dr Bateson had been his predecessor. Four members of the Syndicate were, or had been, Professors, some of unusual distinction; ten were past or present tutors of colleges; and there were former Proctors and members of the Lodging-Houses Syndicate.

The Council also seem to have adopted the policy – no doubt in the hope that some differences might be resolved within the Syndicate itself – of nominating members from different political camps. Dr Bateson was a life-long liberal; while of Mr Perowne, who did not change noticeably with the years, it has been said that the period of his mastership of Corpus (1879–1906) coincided with important reforms in University and college administration, against nearly all of which he strenuously protested.[2]

The minutes of the Syndicate's meetings, apparently kept by the Vice-Chancellor as Chairman (Dr W. H. Thompson, Master of Trinity), are to be found in what became the first Minute Book of the Non-Collegiate Students Board. The Syndicate was convened on 9 December 1867, and approved a proposal by Mr Parkinson, seconded by Mr Latham, 'that it is desirable to obtain an accurate statement of the number and value of the Scholarships and Exhibitions at the several

[1] Camb. Univ. Reg. 60,1, University Archives. See also Syndicate Minutes, 9 December 1867.
[2] J. P. T. Bury, *History of Corpus Christi College 1822–52* (C.U.P. printed for the College, 1952), p. 86.

Colleges in the University, specifying the amount annually awarded to (a) persons commencing residence (1) with and (2) without Examination and (b) persons who have kept two or more terms either (1) after or (2) irrespective of an Examination: as well as of the average number of sizars within the last (say) 3 years and the estimated value of such sizarships'. On 16 December the Vice-Chancellor circulated to Heads of Colleges a questionnaire designed to elicit this information.

The Syndicate, presumably in order to allow time for answers to come in, did not meet again until 12 February, but neither in the minutes of that meeting nor in any others is there any reference to the questions or to answers received. On the same day, after much discussion, they approved without a division a proposal by Dr Bateson, that they should proceed to consider regulations for the admission to the University of students who would not be members of any college; and, for his pains, Dr Bateson was requested to submit a list of rules to the Syndicate at their next meeting. On 15 February he read them his proposed regulations, which were discussed at that meeting, and again on 26 February and 7 March, without substantial amendment, when the Syndicate agreed, with three abstentions, to sign a Report to the University,[1] after rejecting by eleven votes to two a proposal by Mr Perowne, supported by Dr Corrie, for the omission at the end of the preamble to the Report of the words 'which the Syndicate recommend to the Senate for its adoption.[2]

The Council received the Report (see below) on 12 March, and agreed that it should be discussed in the Arts School[3] on 24 March. On 13 March it was circulated by the Vice-Chancellor, with an invitation to members of the Senate to attend the Discussion.

THE SYNDICATE appointed by GRACE of the SENATE, 28 *November, 1867,* ... beg leave to report to the Senate:

That they are of opinion that the benefits of Education in the University might be extended to an increased number of such Students as are contemplated by the Grace, by admitting a greater number of Sizars in Colleges, and by offering facilities for the admission of Students to reside in the University, who may not be Members of any College or Hostel.

The first method must be left to the discretion of the several Colleges, and the Syndicate desire to state that a very large addition has been made to the emoluments attainable by persons *in statu pupillari* by the changes which have been recently carried into effect.

---

[1] Camb. Univ. Reg. 60,2, University Archives. The members of the Syndicate who abstained were Dr Cookson, Dr Corrie, and Mr Perowne.
[2] Syndicate Minutes, 7 March 1868.
[3] At present, Lecture Room 4 in the Old Schools.

The second method may in the opinion of the Syndicate be provided for by the subjoined regulations, which the Syndicate recommend to the Senate for its adoption:

1. THAT with the view of admitting to residence in the University Students who may not be members of any College or Hostel, application shall be made to the Crown for its sanction to such changes in the Statutes of the University as may be necessary for that purpose.

2. That an Officer shall be appointed by the University, to be called CENSOR[1], whose duty shall be to superintend and maintain the good order and discipline of all such students, and to assist the Officers of the University in maintaining good order and due obedience to all academical regulations.

3. That the Censor shall, after careful inquiry with respect to moral character admit as a non-collegiate Student any person whom he may consider a fit and proper person to become a Member of the University; provided always that no Student who has at any time commenced residence as a Member of any College in the University shall be capable of admission by the Censor unless he produce to the Censor, under the hand and seal of the Head of the College or his *locum tenens*, and counter-signed by the Vice-Chancellor, a certificate in the following form:

I A. B. Master of C. College, hereby certify that D. E., who has resided in this College as stated below, conducted himself during the whole of that time in a satisfactory manner, and is in my judgment a fit and proper person to reside as a non-Collegiate Student in the University.

A. B.

Residence kept.   Master of C. College.
Approved.
F.G.   *V.C.*

4. That it shall be the duty of the Censor to record the date of admission of every such Student, to register his daily residence within the University, and to grant certificates of the same, to present such Students for University Examination, and to offer the proper supplicats for their Degrees.

5. That the Censor shall be appointed by Grace of the Senate for the period of three years only.

6. That at the expiration of that time, or on the occurrence of a vacancy in the office at an earlier period, a fresh election shall be made in like manner and so on from time to time, the retiring Censor being always capable of re-election.

7. If it shall be proved to the satisfaction of the Vice-Chancellor and the six persons elected and acting in accordance with Section 4, Chapter VII. of the Statutes of the University, that the Censor has been wilfully neglect-

[1] See also p. 44 n.

ful of his duties, or guilty of gross or habitual immorality, it shall be competent to the Vice-Chancellor and the said six persons to admonish the Censor, or to deprive him of his office, as the case may seem to them to require; and if the sentence of deprivation be thus passed upon him, the office of Censor shall thereupon become ipso facto void; but in every case, whether of admonition or of deprivation, an appeal to the University shall be allowed in accordance with the provisions of Chapter VIII. of the Statutes of the University.

8. That the Stipend of the Censor shall in the first instance be £100 per annum, payable out of the University Chest, but that such Stipend shall increase until it reach £250 per annum, as the receipts from the yearly payments of non-Collegiate Students, hereinafter provided, may allow of such increase.

9. That all non-Collegiate Students shall reside in lodgings licensed by the Lodging-House Syndicate, it being competent for the Syndicate to grant a special license for any such Student on the application of the Censor.

10. That all the rules prescribed by authority of the University or of the Lodging-House Syndicate for the government of Lodging-House Keepers shall be enforced in the case of non-Collegiate Students, *the Censor* or the *Censor's Servant* being substituted, as the case may require, for *the Officer of the College* or *the Porter*.

11. If any non-Collegiate Student shall be guilty of gross misconduct or immorality, the Censor shall be empowered, with the consent of the Vice-Chancellor, signified after hearing the accused, to remove the name of such Student from the list of Members of the University.

12. That every non-Collegiate Student shall pay to the University Chest at the commencement of every term of residence, until he has been admitted to a Degree, the sum of thirty-five shillings. That such payment shall be payable in advance, and that no Student whose terminal payment shall be in arrear shall be considered as resident in the University. That every non-Collegiate Student shall pay to the University the same fees and dues as he would have been liable to pay, had he been a Member of a College, the fee payable at Matriculation being fifteen shillings. He shall also pay to the Censor a fee of one guinea on admission to any Degree after the first.

Before the Discussion only one flysheet seems to have been issued, over the signature of Mr A. F. Torry, of St John's College.[1] He was against the Report. He did not believe that the students to be admitted under its provisions could save more than £20 a year; he dwelt on their loss of college amenities and of the possibility of winning college awards, and suggested that the University's degree course might be

---

[1]   University Archives, Camb. Univ. Reg. 60,7.

made less expensive by permitting candidates who had obtained a certain standard in the Oxford or Cambridge Local Examinations to count their first term of residence as their fourth. If it were thought undesirable that a two year course should lead to the same degree as the normal course of three years, the degrees could no doubt bear different names.

The Discussion, here reproduced in the form of an account published in the *Cambridge Chronicle*, was opened by the Vice-Chancellor, who remarked on the circumstances which led to the Syndicate's appointment. It would have been helpful if there had been a fuller statement of what he said, for the precise reason why the Council moved for the Syndicate's appointment just when they did remains a matter of some conjecture.

The report of the Special Syndicate recommending the extension of University education to persons whose means would not permit them to enter a college, and the appointment of a Censor to superintend them, was printed in our last number. A meeting to discuss the subject was held in the Arts' School, on Tuesday last, the Vice-Chancellor presiding; the attendance was large, and included the Masters of Christ's, Clare, St John's, and St Catharine's; Professors Babington, Lightfoot, Stokes, Liveing; Messrs Luard, Campion, E. H. Perowne, Reyner, Prescott, Bonney, Russell, Todhunter, W. S. Smith, H. Sidgwick, G. F. Browne, Markby, Potts, Dale, Ferrers, Hotham, Croft, Vansittart, Holmes, H. Latham, Dodd, Besant, T. P. Hudson &c.

The Vice-Chancellor said that they were met to discuss a very important report on the admission of poor scholars to the University, under more favourable circumstances than at present existed. The Vice-Chancellor remarked on the circumstances that gave rise to the Syndicate being appointed.

Mr Reyner, St John's, would scorn to enter into the details of this report which he with many others abhorred. He would speak of the main features of the report. Nothing more was to be required of these men than attendance at examinations; there was to be a Censor to admit and direct these students, and interfere in gross cases of immorality. This was the whole scheme; then as to the principle of the scheme it was infidel. It was a scheme to admit members to this University, who would in no way be brought into contact with religion; they would be simply students seeking a degree here. The apparent motive of the scheme was one of base expediency, a motive which actuated Pontius Pilate *populo satisfacere*; he would not say *populus*, but *plebs* – the *plebs* of newpapers and magazines, which advocated infidelity to make themselves sell – the *plebs* of philosophers, falsely so called. Lastly, it was the scheme urged by Political Dissenters whom he classed with the *plebs* of the whole population of England. As to orthodox godly Dissenters they would only support it in ignorance, as, for instance, the Wesleyan Methodists; no man would condemn this scheme for a godless education more than John Wesley. It was a scheme for informing the mind and the mind only; a scheme for furnishing the mind with unsanctified knowledge. He could not believe that Cambridge would accept the scheme – that its colleges which had been the mainstay of religion in this country would tolerate so godless a proposal. Attempts were now being made to damage the Church, and secularise the Universities with more show of success than ever before, and let no man support this scheme with the idea that it would satisfy those who urged it. If we were to have godless the infidel education, let it be forced upon us from without, but let not the University itself take the initiatory step.

Mr E. H. Perowne, Corpus, explained why he had not signed the report. Their function was to consider how a larger number of poor students could be admitted than at present. On reading the report, he saw no provision whatever for these students – no allusion to them – no notice of certificates of poverty, or any other means of knowing that candidates for admission were the persons intended. The provision made in this report was as much for the rich as for the poor. As to the Censor, there was no single word as to his social or academical position. 'He might be my gyp', said Mr Perowne, 'and certainly a college porter would not regard £100 a year as a large salary.' He should deprecate as strongly as the last speaker had done the adoption of this scheme as it was; and he thought that of late they had yielded a good deal too much to outward pressure. He thought the Senate should consider what was best for its students, and that they should be willing to stand up in defence of a great principle, that this was a religious institution, and that whatever else we did, we could in no respect cease to recognise that this was a place of Christian education.

The Master of St John's said this was the first time he had heard of any of the difficulties suggested by Mr Reyner. Those who had not signed the report had never raised in the Syndicate any difficulties about the Church of England, or secular as against religious education. He would just remind the meeting that it was competent to anyone properly qualified to open a hostel tomorrow. Dr Humphry did, in fact, open one, and if it had gone on he supposed Dr Humphry would have been entirely responsible for the religious education of the students therein. He should think they might safely trust the Senate, in whom the appointment was to be vested, to elect a suitable person as Censor. The real security in such cases was the party to whom the appointment was intrusted. He was sorry to hear Mr Reyner use language which in his cooler moments he would possibly regret ('No!' from Mr Reyner). Well, he (Dr Bateson) would hope so still; but whether or no, there were words of charity that might possibly obtain a hearing. They should bear in mind that the University is open to all parties; and was it a satisfactory state of things that, on the entry of a Jew or a Roman Catholic, they should have to discuss whether they should be obliged to attend

William Henry Bateson, D.D., Master of St John's College, 1857–81;
first Chairman of the Non-Collegiate Students Board, 1869–76

chapel services? Was it not far more decorous to leave the matter to the discretion of the college authorities, as was, he believed, the case in some instances at present; and were there not other modes of divine service within the reach of various persons? He did not contemplate that any of the difficulties would arise that had been conjured up in connection with this scheme. He was persuaded that there was a considerable class that would avail themselves of its advantages. It had been said that these would be a despised class of students; but he did not think so, for they were far more prone to consider in Cambridge what a man was than who he was. He was quite sure that a diligent student would receive the encouragement of his elders, and he did not believe there was that mean spirit amongst the undergraduates that would induce them to reject the society of a student simply because he was poor (applause). The extravagance so much complained of had a social rather than a general origin, and it was to remedy this that this scheme had been introduced. One reason of that extravagance was that undue credit was given; and that was given to a man because he was a member of a college, as the tradesmen knew that they could exercise a moral pressure upon their debtors through the college authorities. They would have no means of doing this upon the men admitted under this scheme, and the men would not have any inducement to live beyond their means. The excessive expenses in hall arose from the fact that men dining in society frequently ordered things because their neighbours did so. They had reduced the price of dinner at St John's; but how many dined at the minimum rate? Men ordered extras in the shape of ''sizings'', whereas if they dined at home they would have no such luxury. If they gave the men the chance of the exercise of prudence and frugality in the attainment of the advantages the University set before them, they would exercise them, but were not so likely to do so while they lived gregariously, as the expenses arose from the social condition of the place. Oxford had passed a similar scheme. The qualification of poverty did find its way into the scheme there, and was the only part of it that was rejected.

Mr Bonney thought that if anything could show that our scheme of education was imperfect, it was the tone of the speech which opened the debate. Mr Bonney supported the report, and said that from careful calculations he found that a student by this scheme might save £40 a year, which he could not save if in college, though he would give up much, of course, in the way of social and educational advantages. The class of men, he thought, who would be most benefited by this scheme was that of men who intended taking orders in the Church of England, and whom it was most important to educate here, instead of letting them go to narrower institutions. The saving on dinner in the aggregate would amount to something considerable. He hoped the University would adopt this or a similar scheme, and no doubt the result would be the addition of a large number of well-conducted and religious young men.

The Master of Christ's hoped to see the report become the law of the University; he approved of it for what it contained and for what it omitted. He could see nothing wrong in the University trying to embrace within her those poor men who could not afford to enter a college, though of course they must be careful not to stamp with their degrees men who were unworthy of them. He had listened with much pain to the remarks of Mr Reyner, and he instanced the case of his own college to show that Roman Catholics, Jews, and Orientals had been admitted, and that they had conducted themselves exceedingly well, being of course excused chapel. He had no difficulty with them at all, though he appreciated as well as anybody the benefits of keeping up the public worship of the college chapel. He thought this was a plain practical scheme, and the Syndicate had done well in keeping clear of the college in their recommendations. He suggested that it was worth while to consider whether the lodging-house Syndicate should not be more fully organised. He hoped the Senate would accept the report.

Mr Dodd, Magdalene, in opposing the report, urged that it did not meet the objects for which the Syndicate was appointed – it did not require that a man should be poor who availed himself of the scheme, nor did it make it necessary that he should receive instruction, whilst the words of the grace appointing the Syndicate were – 'quorum res familiaris impensis academicis minus sufficiat educationi ad hoc tempus in academia provisum sit, deliberent utrum alia aliqua ratione pluribus ejusmodi alumnis in academia erudiendis commode provideri possit'. The Syndicate had not done what it was told to do, and it had done what it was not told to do. To adopt the report was blindly to alter the University statutes. He entirely concurred with the remarks of his friend Mr Reyner on godless education.

Mr Campion, Queens', supported the report, and replied to the objection that poverty was nowhere stipulated in the report: the Syndicate were told to draw up a scheme of which a poor man might avail himself, not one of which no one else could avail himself. He did not see how attendance on religious worship could be enforced; and there was nothing new in this principle because the Hostel Statute, which had now long been in existence, made no stipulation as to religious worship, and it was competent even for a man not a member of the Senate to keep one of these Hostels – the keeper need only be a Master of Arts. Mr Campion said he had as strong a feeling on religious points as other members of the Senate; but he did not admire the principle of forcing people into our particular branch of the Church. This was no doubt a 'place of sound learning' – and a 'place of sound learning and religious education', but only to those who could pay for it; the principle was simply that of 'No penny, no pater-noster'. There was no doubt that a man could live cheaper separate from a college, and therefore the college religious attendance must be abandoned in the case of these men. The Syndicate had felt that it was no duty of theirs to put out even a moral pressure on the colleges to devote their funds to these poor students, and however he and others might desire to see the colleges encourage such men, yet it must not be forgotten that the colleges were independent corporations, and must not be subjected to pressure as to the application of their funds. No one had, as far as he saw, objected to the admission of students to the University without being members of colleges. *Mr Luard* accepted very readily the challenge, and said that he objected. The men who would avail themselves of the scheme would not be very intellectual, as the vast amount given away every year before residence would enable most persons of any ability to gain something; and then he supposed that they would be very poor. But mainly Mr Luard objected to the practical absence of all discipline, which under this scheme would exist; it would give admission to men who would probably be the greatest offenders against academic discipline. If this kind of reform was forced upon the University, let them take it and make the best of it, but let them not forget that they had a duty to perform to themselves, to their successors, and to the University, and this was no part of their duty.

Mr Holmes, Clare, remarked that there appeared to be no proposal whatever in the report which met the educational requirements of these men.

Mr Vansittart, Trinity, followed on the same side, and recounting the arguments, expressed great doubt whether the presence of the class proposed would be beneficial to the place. The question required more time for consideration, especially with respect to the Censor.

Mr Torry, John's, who had issued a paper shewing the minimum expenses of St John's, spoke against the scheme, and urged that the social education and improvement which very many derived from contact with their fellow-students in college would not be acquired by these non-collegiate students. Mr Torry spoke against the growing tendency to yield to external pressure.

Professor Liveing thought this scheme would increase the number of men coming to college, and that was one reason why he supported it. An opinion prevailed outside that the style of life here unfitted men for their callings afterwards; and he thought this scheme might give rise to a more frugal and inexpensive style of life in college, and thus remove an objection which at present was on the increase. The University staff of Professors could not give these men every instruction, but the majority of the students would be older men, or men who had received some training and could educate themselves; there would, no doubt, be some requiring assistance, and these could go to a private tutor in a class at a small individual cost, or to the college lectures for a small payment – these lectures not being now always very fully attended.

Mr Henry Sidgwick, Trinity, thought it better to open the University to poor men of no great talent than to give them Sizarships in the colleges. There could be no doubt whatever of the great saving that men could make under this system, and he apprehended no difficulty as to non-collegiate men obtaining instruction.

Mr Russell, John's, quoted the opinion of the Royal Commission that a collegiate and a non-collegiate system were scarcely compatible with each other in the same University. The system ought not to be accepted because it made the University responsible for a charge that it had no means adequately to fulfil – namely, to superintend in a large town like this any great number of students, under the control of no college. Whatever might be said about older men availing themselves of the scheme, Cambridge might in a few years have what now prevailed at the German Universities. He thought the Syndicate had not attended to the terms of the question which had been referred to them, which was instruction for persons of inadequate means; and under their scheme the principle that men who came here for education should be under religious influences could not be maintained.

At the conclusion of Mr Russell's remarks the meeting broke up.[1]

The speakers at the Discussion made few points that had not been made already on a number of occasions in Oxford or Cambridge, to the Royal Commissioners of 1850, or in connexion with proposals for private halls or hostels, or to Mr Ewart's Select Committee, but there is here evidence enough of hostility in some quarters towards a proposal which in retrospect appears to have done little harm to any University institution then in being. It is not difficult to recognize the force of Mr Bonney's opening remark, or to understand the surprise expressed by the author of a later flysheet at what he there described as 'the amenities of clerical controversy'.[2]

It is no wonder that at the Council's meeting held on 2 April 'a conversation took place' on the Syndicate's Report; but the Council were not to be hurried, and postponed any decision until the Easter term. On 20 April they decided to propose a Grace (approved by the Senate on 28 April) for the reappointment of the Syndicate until the end of the term; and after further discussion on 30 April they sent the Report back for such revision as might seem proper. On 7 May the Report was again before the Council with the information that it had been reconsidered by the Syndicate, but not altered; and the Council finally agreed without a division, on a proposal by Professor Liveing, that the Report should, in effect, be divided into two parts, each to be the subject of a Grace, the first for the approval of Regulation 1 of the Report on the policy of admitting non-collegiate students, and the second for the approval of the remaining regulations for the working of the scheme if the policy should be accepted in principle. The Report was then re-

[1] *Cambridge Chronicle,* 28 March 1868.
[2] Mr J. B. Pearson. See also p. 32.

issued by the Vice-Chancellor in its new form,[1] with a note that Graces for the confirmation of its two parts would be submitted to the Senate on 20 May. Whereupon Dr Corrie and the Hon. Latimer Neville,[2] joined by Mr Perowne and Registrary Luard, whose tenure of high administrative office did not, it seems, require him to maintain an appearance of impartiality, gave notice of *non placet*, on the grounds that the scheme made no provision for '1. Attendance on Religious Worship 2. Instruction in Religion 3. Superintendence of a tutor *in loco parentis* 4. Secular instruction in Lectures or otherwise, and 5. Education in the best sense of the word.' On 16 May there appeared Mr Pearson's flysheet[3] in which he expresses his surprise at the extent to which the whole matter was regarded as a mainly religious question when, as it seemed to him, the point at issue was one of money – whether the University was ready to modify its arrangements so as to enable people to come to it who could not afford to pay the ruling prices. Finally, on 18 May, Mr Perowne said at greater length by himself what he had said in company four days earlier.[4]

At the Congregation on 20 May, the voting was relatively heavy, and on the Grace that mattered it was close, for the first Grace was rejected by 88 votes to 82, and the second by 84 to 60.[5]

The Council's efforts to extend the University had so far resulted, after much deliberation of statutes, in the opening of one hostel, disbanded after three years when it had recruited a total of nine medical students, and in the rejection by the Senate of their proposals for the admission as members of the University of undergraduates who had no connexion with a college. In the Michaelmas term of 1868 the Council returned to the charge, and on 16 November Dr Bateson gave notice of a motion 'That application be made to the Crown for power to make such changes in the University Statutes as may be necessary to authorize the admission of students to the University who may not be members of any college'. The minutes are not informative, for they

[1] Camb. Univ. Reg. 60,4, University Archives. Council Minutes of 12 March, of 2, 20, 30 April, and of 7 May all give 7 March as the date of the Syndicate's Report. The Graces give it as 13 March, which was the date of the Vice-Chancellor's notice promulgating the Report. There is no doubt that all the references are meant to be to the Syndicate's first Report received by the Council on 12 March, and modified only by its division into two parts by the Council.

[2] Master of Magdalene College 1853–1904. For the fly-sheet, see Camb. Univ. Reg. 60,8, University Archives.

[3] *Ibid.*, 60,6.

[4] *Ibid.*, 60,5.

[5] Minutes of the Council of the Senate (vol. III), Graces for 20 May 1868 (University Archives).

merely record that the motion was withdrawn after discussion for some time; and the Council, in spite of their earlier rebuff, resolved by twelve votes to two to approve the appointment of a new Syndicate 'to consider the best means of introducing students as members of the University who are not members of Colleges, and the alterations which it is desirable to make in the University Statutes for this purpose'.

On 30 November they agreed to nominate, in two groups of six, the following persons for appointment as members (it being assumed that the Vice-Chancellor would preside): Dr Cookson, Dr Bateson, Dr Lightfoot, Mr Burn, Mr Pike, of Downing College, and Mr King, of Jesus College; and Messrs Prescott, of Corpus Christi College, Latham, of Trinity Hall, Porter, of St Peter's College, Ellis, of Sidney Sussex College, Pattrick of Magdalene College, and Mr J. R. Pearson. The appointments were approved on 10 December, with the substitution of Mr T. P. Hudson, of Trinity College, for Mr Burn, who declined to serve.[1]

The minutes of this second Syndicate,[2] kept by the Vice-Chancellor as Chairman (Dr Edward Atkinson, Master of Clare), show that their first meeting was held on 15 December, but that as attendance was small no business was done. They did not meet again until 8 February, when they discussed general principles on which a scheme for the admission of non-collegiate students might be based, but recorded no decision. On 15 February they resolved

(1) by ten votes in favour, one member being neutral, that it was desirable that a Syndicate should be appointed, with powers to be determined, to admit non-collegiate students;

(2) by seven votes in favour, four members being neutral, that it should be the duty of the proposed Syndicate to ensure that the students were enabled to find out proper means of instruction;

(3) that it should be the duty of the Syndicate to provide for the superintendence of the students and the maintenance of good order among them;[3]

(4) that the Syndicate should have power to admit, after careful enquiry as to his moral character, any student whom they might deem suitable for admission to the University.

On 22 February, the Syndicate further resolved (5) that the proposed Syndicate, either collectively or by some of its members or officers, should have power to rusticate or expel, or visit with less serious

---

[1] Occasional Syndicates 1868–9, part 1, University Archives.
[2] *Ibid.*
[3] Where no vote is mentioned, agreement was without a division.

punishment, any student guilty of misconduct, or to remove a student's
name from the list of members of the University for any grave and sufficient cause;

(6) that the operation of the scheme should be limited to five
years;

(7) that while it was desirable that the scheme should be self-
supporting the University should indemnify the Syndicate against loss
to a maximum of £100 p.a.;

(8) that the Syndicate should appoint one or more salaried
officers to record, and under their authority to certify, residence, to
present for degrees, and to do such other things as the Syndicate might
determine;

(9) by eight votes to four, one member being neutral, that the
Syndicate should provide as far as possible for the attendance of students at public worship, but not so as to interfere with the convictions
of any who were not members of the Church of England;

(10) that the fees to be paid by the students should be those
proposed by the former Syndicate;

(11) that the proposed Syndicate should consist of nine persons, with power to choose their own chairman.

Of these resolutions, listed in the Syndicate's minutes, those numbered 1, 3, 4, 5, 8, and 11 appear to be aimed at the transfer to an
elected body (which the Report recommended should be not a Syndicate, but a Board) of responsibilities which the Report of the first
Syndicate had laid upon the Censor. There is a similar shift of duties in
Clause 12 of the second Report (see below), which relates to applications for specially licensed lodgings. Resolution 2 was designed to meet
allegations made at the discussion of the earlier Report, that it made no
provision for the instruction of students who would be outside the college system, and Resolution 9 seems to take account of Mr Reyner's
reproaches about the 'godlessness' of the first proposals. Resolution 6,
which is imprecise, may have served to conciliate those who feared an
indefinite extension of arrangements that they did not want at all, and
Resolution 7, while it appears to be financially helpful to the scheme,
could be thought by some to impose a wise limit on the amount of the
University's assistance. And Resolution 10 did not prevent the Syndicate from increasing to £3, payable to the Board, the sum of £1.1.0
payable to the Censor, hitherto proposed as a charge to the students for
any degree after their first. Finally, the second Report excluded from
admission as a non-collegiate student any graduate of the University, a
restriction which may well reflect apprehension in some colleges that

their graduates might find attractions in the non-collegiate scheme; it also prescribed that in the absence of its prolongation by Grace of the Senate no student should be admitted under its provisions after 1 October 1873.

On 22 February the Syndicate asked the Masters of St Peter's and St John's Colleges, respectively, to draft a scheme for the admission of non-collegiate students, and a Petition to the Queen in Council for the necessary amendment of University Statutes.[1] There is no further reference to the Report in the minutes of the Syndicate, which end with the meeting held on 22 February. There can have been little further discussion of the draft, of which the proposed scheme constituted Part I and the draft amendment of statutes Part II, for the Vice-Chancellor promulgated the Report,[2] signed by all the members of the Syndicate, and here subjoined, on 1 March, when he also announced that it would be discussed in the Arts School on March 6. Clearly he did not wish for more delay.

Report of the Syndicate appointed by the ... Grace of the Senate which was approved December 10, 1968:–

The Syndicate have carefully considered the questions referred to them and have prepared the following Scheme for the admission of Students as members of the University who are not members of any College or Hostel. They have also prepared for the sanction of the Crown a form of Statute to enable the University to make rules for the admission, government, discipline, instruction, residence and graduation of such Students. They recommend these for the approval of the Senate.

I. *Scheme for Non-Collegiate Students.*

1. There shall be a Board for admitting and superintending Students who shall be Members of the University without being Members of any College, to consist of nine Members of the Senate to be elected by Grace.[3]

---

[1]   There appears to have been some uncertainty over the instructions given to Dr Bateson; for the Syndicate's minute was amended. In its earlier form he was asked to draft, not a Petition to the Queen in Council but, for inclusion in a Petition in due course, an amendment of statute such as would be needed if the Syndicate's proposals for non-collegiate students of the University were to be adopted. There is no evidence that Dr Bateson prepared the Petition which was to cause difficulty for the Council.

[2]   Camb. Univ. Reg. 60,10, University Archives.

[3]   Recommendation 1 of the scheme as it appears in the Report differs in two respects from the Syndicate's proposals as they are recorded in their minutes. The body which is to superintend the non-collegiate students is given the title of 'Board' instead of 'Syndicate'; and it is to consist not of 'nine persons', but of nine members of the Senate; its membership being limited, therefore, to members of the Church of England.

2. Of the said nine Members three shall retire by rotation on the 20th November in every year, and their places shall be supplied by three other Members of the Senate elected by Grace, the retiring Members being re-eligible.

3. The order of rotation shall be that of priority of election.

4. In the case of a vacancy occurring by the death of a Member or otherwise a new Member shall be elected as soon as possible to supply the vacant place, and the person so elected shall continue to be a Member of the Board for the same period as that during which the person, whose substitute he is, would have continued.

5. Three of the persons first elected shall hold office till the 20th Nov., 1871, three till the 20th Nov. 1872, and three till the 20th Nov. 1873.

6. The Members of the Board shall elect their own Chairman, to hold office for a year, or for such other period as the Board, by a Resolution of a majority of the whole body, shall prescribe. Four Members shall form a quorum (the Chairman or his deputy formally appointed by the Board being one) and the Chairman (or his deputy as the case may be) shall have a second or casting vote.

7. If any Member of the Board be absent from every Meeting held in any one Term, his place on the Board shall be *ipso facto* vacant.

8. The Board shall be empowered to entrust particular duties to Committees of their own Members or to their Chairman or to any officers appointed by them.

9. The Board shall be empowered, after careful enquiry with respect to moral character, to admit as a non-collegiate Student any person whom they may consider a fit and proper person to become a Member of the University; provided always that no Student who has at any time commenced residence as a Member of any College in the University shall be capable of admission by the Board unless he produce under the hand and seal of the Head of the College or his *locum tenens*, a certificate in the following form:

I A. B. Master of   C. College, hereby certify that D. E., who has resided in this College as stated below, conducted himself during the whole of that time in a satisfactory manner, and is in my judgment a fit and proper person to reside as a non-Collegiate Student in the University.

A. B.

(L.S.)   Master of C. College.

Residence kept.

10. No Graduate of the University shall be admitted as a Non-Collegiate Student under these Regulations.

11. All the Rules prescribed either by the Statutes of the University or by Graces of the Senate for the Matriculation and Examination of Students who are members of Colleges, and for their proceeding to Degrees, shall also apply to Non-Collegiate Students, the Chairman of the Board or his deputy being substituted for the Head of a College or his *Locum Tenens*, and

the Officer of the Board, hereinafter directed to be appointed, being sub-stituted for the Prælector; and, subject to this Regulation, Non-Collegiate Students shall be entitled to be matriculated, examined and admitted to Degrees in the same manner, and with the same status and privileges as Students who are members of Colleges.

12. All Non-Collegiate Students shall reside in lodgings licensed by the Lodging-House Syndicate, it being competent for the Syndicate to grant a special license for any such Student on the application of the Board.

13. All the rules prescribed by authority of the University or of the Lodging-House Syndicate for the government of Lodging-House Keepers shall be enforced in the case of Non-Collegiate Students, *the Officer of the Board* or *the Officer's Servant* being substituted, as the case may require, for *the Officer of the College* or *the Porter.*

14. Every Non-Collegiate Student shall pay to the Board at the commencement of every Term of residence, until he has been admitted to a Degree the sum of Thirty-five Shillings; and he shall further pay to the Board for the University the same quarterly Capitation Tax as he would have been liable to pay had he been a member of a College. Such sums shall be payable in advance, and no Student whose payments shall be in arrear shall be considered as resident in the University. He shall also pay to the Board a fee of Three Guineas on admission to any Degree after the first.

15. The fee payable to the University at Matriculation shall be Fifteen Shillings. Other fees and dues to the University shall be the same as for members of Colleges.

16. It shall be the duty of the Board,

(1) To make provision for superintending and maintaining the good order and discipline of such Students, and for their paying due obedi-ence to all academical regulations.

(2) To take care that such Students are informed as to the means of instruction within their reach in the University, and to see that they are advised as to their studies and conduct.

(3) To make provision as far as may be practicable for due atten-dance of such Students on Public Worship, yet so as not to interfere with the religious convictions of persons who are not members of the Church of England.

(4) To appoint one or more Officers with Salaries whose duties shall be to record the date of admission of every such Student, to register his daily residence within the University, to present such Students for Matriculation and for University Examination, to offer the proper Supplicats and Certificates for their Degrees, under the sanction of the Board, to present them for their Degrees and to perform such other functions as the Board may determine.

(5) To keep an account of all Receipts and Payments connected with the operation of this Scheme, to hold an Audit at least once a year, and

to deliver annually to the Vice-Chancellor a Summary of the Accounts for publication with the other Accounts of the University; the Board being guaranteed a sum not exceeding £100 per annum from the Chest to meet any expenditure which may be incurred beyond the receipts.

17. The Board shall have power either collectively or by a Committee of its Members or by one or more of its Officers to expel or rusticate or visit with less serious punishment any Student guilty of misconduct, or to remove the name of any Student from the List of Members of the University for any grave cause which may seem to the Board to require such course: provided, however, that no Student be rusticated or expelled without the concurrence of the major part of the whole Board; and provided also that the power thus given to the Board does not in any way interfere with or hinder the jurisdiction of the Vice-Chancellor or Proctors as prescribed in Statuta Cap. 7, § 1, 2, 4, which shall apply to all Students who are not Members of Colleges as well as to those who are.

18. The foregoing Scheme shall come into operation so soon as the University shall have obtained the sanction of the Crown to make such changes in the Statutes of the University as are necessary for the purpose; but no Student shall be admitted under its provisions after the First of October, 1873, and no Student shall continue a Member of the University under its provisions after the end of the Easter Term, 1877, unless the University, by Grace of the Senate, shall prolong the period during which this Scheme shall continue in operation.

II. *Application to the Crown.*

An application shall be made to the Crown for its sanction to the following Statute.

"Notwithstanding anything expressed or contained in the Statutes of the University

"framed and sanctioned in accordance with the provisions of the Act of Parliament

"19 and 20 Vict. cap. 88 it shall be lawful for the University to admit as Students

"and to confer Degrees upon any persons who may not be Members of any College

"or Hall or of any Hostel and to frame from time to time such rules as may be

"deemed expedient for the government, discipline, instruction and residence of such

"Students as well as for their temporary or permanent removal from the University

"if at any time such removal should appear to be necessary or expedient."

Such were the proposals by which the new Syndicate sought to allay the fears of those who had seen, or had professed to see, in the admission of students with no college connexion a moral danger to the rest of the University and a lowering of its academic standards. It is possible that some also saw, or thought they saw, a threatened diversion of eligible candidates for admission to colleges, some of which admitted very few students at that time.[1]

At the Discussion on 6 March twelve speakers took part.[2] The only root and branch objector was Registrary Luard, for even Mr Perowne was prepared to concede that the second scheme was an improvement on the first, and made certain suggestions for its further improvement which seemed to imply that he was regarding its adoption as within the realm of practical politics. By this time the corresponding scheme at Oxford was in being, and the Registrary, who believed that the Oxford numbers had been exaggerated, had heard that it was a failure; and suggested that Cambridge should await further particulars before starting on an amended scheme of its own. The Master of St John's was ready with the Oxford figures – thirty-eight, with three who had joined colleges, none having been sent away – and also seemed to imply that the publicity given to Mr Ewart's Bill had caused the Council to move when they did.

On 8 March the Vice-Chancellor reported the Discussion to the Council, who thereupon approved separate Graces for submission to the Senate, for the approval of Parts I and II of the Syndicate's Report. The Grace for Part I was opposed, but passed safely by 65 votes to 4, and there was no opposition to the second Grace for the approval of Part II.[3] There now remained one last step for the Council to take – the preparation for submission to the Senate of a Petition to the Queen in Council for the approval of the amending Statute set forth in the second part of the Syndicate's Report, and approved by the Senate on 13 March. The Council, however, were not yet out of the wood, for in drafting the Petition for submission to the Senate on 18 March, the Vice-Chancellor or his advisers inserted in the draft Statute, approved by the Senate, an additional clause which, so far as residential requirements for the B.A. degree were concerned, would have had the effect – unintentional, no doubt – of placing non-collegiate undergraduates in a more favourable position than the members of colleges. Dr James Cartmell, Master of Christ's, must have been waiting in the wings, for he very quickly issued a flysheet pointing out the effect of the Council's new draft, and announced that the Grace for its approval would be

[1]   In 1874 five colleges each admitted fewer than ten freshmen.
[2]   *The Times*, 8 March 1869.
[3]   University Papers, 1866–73, University Archives.

opposed.[1] On the day of the Congregation the Council withdrew the Grace, and sought expert advice on the preparation of an alternative draft. Their final deliberations are recorded in Minute 6 of their meeting of 8 April: 'An amended form of Statute, empowering the University to make regulations for the admission, discipline &c. of non-collegiate students had been prepared by Mr Denman and Mr Druce.[2] Some alterations were made in it by the Council and, amongst others, after a division of four to three, that the members of the Board or Syndicate should not necessarily be members of the Senate. The Statute was finally adopted and a Grace approved for fixing the Seal to a Petition to the Queen in Council to sanction it.' In form the statute is very different from that approved by the Senate when it passed Part II of the Syndicate's Report, but it appears to have met the objection raised by Dr Cartmell, and there is no record of any objection when the Grace for its approval passed the Senate on 15 April. Nevertheless, this last episode in the Council's lengthy efforts to obtain approval for the admission of non-collegiate students remains something of an administrative curiosity. The second Syndicate had proposed the constitution of a Board consisting of members of the Senate, but they did not insist on Senate membership for the officer of the Board who was to perform for the non-collegiate students the functions of a college praelector; and these dispositions received Senate approval. The draft statute finally adopted by the Council and sanctioned by the Senate on 15 April, apparently without discussion, did not limit membership of the Board to members of the Senate, but did require Senate membership of the officer of the Board. In the event, the matter was not to be important for much longer, because in 1871, with the passing of the Universities Tests Abolition Act, membership of the Senate ceased to be limited to members of the Church of England.

The Council's final draft Statute, which gave the Privy Council, at least, very little trouble, for they approved it within a month, read as follows:

'1. Notwithstanding anything expressed or contained in the statutes of the University framed and sanctioned in accordance with the provisions of the Act of Parliament, 19 and 20 Vict., c. 88, it shall be lawful for the University to admit as Students to matriculate and to confer degrees on persons who may not be members of any College or Hall or of any Hostel.

---

1   Camb. Univ. Reg. 60,12 (1), University Archives.
2   The Council were clearly anxious to avoid further misadventures over the Petition, for both were University Counsel. The Hon. George Denman (1819–96) was Fellow of Trinity College, and Mr George Druce (1821(?)–69) of Peterhouse. Each had been Senior Classic, Denman in 1842, and Druce in 1843.

'2. The functions assigned to the Head or Prælector of a College, or to the Principal of a Hostel in cap. I, sec. 3, and cap. III, sec. 1, of the said statutes so framed and sanctioned as aforesaid shall be exercised in respect of such Students by a Member or Members of the Senate who shall be specially appointed from time to time for that purpose, but the said statutes shall in all other respects be deemed to apply and extend to such Students as well as others.

'3. In addition to the provisions of the said statutes the University shall have power from time to time to frame and enforce such Rules as may be deemed expedient for the admission, government, discipline, and instruction of such Students, and for the payments to be made by them.

'4. The University shall have power to make special provision for the temporary or permanent removal from the University of any such Student if at any time such removal shall appear necessary or expedient, anything contained in the said statutes notwithstanding.

'5. The University shall have power from time to time to appoint a Board or Syndicate, to consist of such persons as may be determined by Grace of the Senate for the purpose of exercising and carrying into effect the powers and provisions of this statute, or any of them, subject to such Rules and Regulations as the University may from time to time prescribe, and all the acts of the Board for such purposes shall be deemed to be acts of the University.[1]

At their meeting on 17 May 1869 the Council of the Senate agreed to nominate, for appointment by the Senate, as members of the Board under the scheme for the admission of non-collegiate students (until 20 November in their respective years):

Dr Bateson, Master of St John's College, Mr J. E. Prescott, of Corpus Christi College, and Mr Thomas Markby, of Trinity College (1873); Professor Humphry, Mr J. H. Hamblin Smith, of Gonville and Caius College, and Mr J. B. Pearson, of St John's College (1872); and Professor Lightfoot, Mr R. B. Somerset, of Trinity College, and Mr F. Pattrick, of Magdalene College (1871).

Again, the Council appear to have taken considerable care in choosing their nominees, and to have selected members of the Senate whose experience would be likely to assist the Board in dealing with the problems which they might have to face. Dr Bateson had played a prominent part in the preparation of the scheme, and was in sympathy with its objects. Mr Prescott had been a member of the second Syndicate whose Report had been finally accepted. Dr Humphry was the only resident member of the University who had been Principal of a hostel, whose members were not obliged to belong to a college; Mr Pearson

[1] Camb. Univ. Reg. 60,14, University Archives.

had taken an eminently sensible interest in the scheme since its inception, and had served on the second Syndicate. Dr Lightfoot was a member of the Council, had been on both Syndicates, and, in earlier years, had been a tutor of Trinity College. Mr Pattrick was also a tutor, and a member of the Lodging-Houses Syndicate. Three of the nominees were newcomers to the scheme. Mr Thomas Markby had taken high classical honours in 1846. He was not a Fellow, and although he does not appear to have been prominent in University affairs, he, like Dr Lightfoot, was a member of the Non-Gremials Examination Syndicate, which suggests an interest in the work of University extension. Mr Hamblin Smith, a graduate of 1850, when he was a Wrangler and was in the second class of the Classical Tripos, had been selected while still an undergraduate at Caius to compose a Latin ode in commemoration of the five hundredth anniversary of its foundation.[1] He was a prominent private tutor in the subjects of the examination for the Ordinary B.A. degree. Of Mr Somerset much more will be heard; but it is not likely ever to be known whether somebody on the Council, in putting his name forward, regarded him as a likely 'officer of the Board'.

On 20 May the Council, having been informed that Mr Pattrick was unwilling to serve, agreed to nominate Mr E. H. Perowne, whose knowledge of the scheme, by this time, must have been as complete as his lack of sympathy with its aims. The Council's nominations were approved by the Senate on 27 May.[2]

---

[1] Known as 'Big Smith', which, if it be taken literally, will not surprise any who remember the impressive figure of his nephew R. Hamblin Smith (Peterhouse), Esquire Bedell from 1913 to 1936.

[2] Minutes, 2 June 1869.

CHAPTER II

The First Censorship

First meeting of the Non-Collegiate Students Board on 2 June 1869 – appointment of Chairman – arrangements for admission and superintendence of students – title and duties of 'officer of the Board' – appointment as first Censor of R. B. Somerset, of Trinity College. Academic dress of undergraduates – their courses of study – first admissions for Michaelmas term 1869. Censor's *Reports* to the Board – attendance of students at religious services – their social isolation – need for meeting place, and for library. Non-collegiate scheme made permanent (May 1873) – rooms in 31 Trumpington Street. Cavendish College. Need for scholarships and exhibitions – Clothworkers' Company. Stricter regulation of academic standing for examinations. *Report* of Board of 23 October 1876 – loss of best men to colleges – memorial to Cambridge Commissioners (1880). Illness of Censor – his resignation (October 1881) – appointment of F. G. Howard, of Trinity College.

The Board first met on 2 June 1869, all the members being present except Mr Perowne. Their first recorded act was to appoint Dr Bateson as their Chairman (for one year) – a most suitable choice, in view of his standing in the University, and of what he had done to bring the scheme into being. They also decided that meetings should, whenever possible, be in the Council Room.[1]

Five meetings were held in the month of June, at which certain immediately necessary arrangements were made. It was resolved

1) that each candidate for admission as a non-collegiate student shall produce a testimonial to character, with a reference to two respectable persons, and also, if not twenty-one years of age, a statement from the parent or guardian that the applicant has his permission to reside at the University as a non-collegiate student;

2) that immediately after residence has commenced the officers of the Board shall enquire from each student what place of religious worship he is accustomed to attend, and shall report the name and lodging of each non-collegiate student to the Parochial Minister in whose parish he resides;

3) that each student shall make returns of the studies he is pursuing, and of the lectures he is attending, or the instruction he is receiving.[2]

---

[1] The present general office of the General Board of the Faculties, on the ground floor in the Old Schools. See also Willis and Clark, *The Architectural History of the University of Cambridge*, vol. IV (1886).

[2] Minutes, 2 June 1869. No students' Reports have survived.

On 3 June the Board met again, all the members being present. They decided to appoint an officer to be called Censor, who should act as their Secretary. His tenure would be for five years, at an annual stipend of £100, to 'cover all ordinary expenses except printing'. They also resolved

> That his duties embrace all correspondence with applicants for admission; making personal acquaintance with the students on commencing residence; advising them as to their course of study and general superinten-.dence of their conduct; the receipt of the fees prescribed by the Senate as payable to the Board and the keeping of the accounts of all receipts and payments: collecting and laying before the Board once a term the returns to be made by the students of the studies they are pursuing, and of the lectures they are attending or the instruction they are receiving; and preparing and presenting to the Board every term a report of the operation of the Scheme.[1]

At the beginning of each term the Censor was to appoint a deputy, subject to the agreement of the Board, to act for him in any illness or absence from Cambridge, and he was not to be away for more than three days during term without leave, to be obtained beforehand or afterwards. Finally, it was agreed that the Censor might be a member

---

[1] Minutes, 3 June 1869. In choosing their officer's name the Board followed the first Syndicate's recommendation that there should be a 'Censor, whose duty it shall be to superintend and maintain the good order and discipline of all such students, and to assist the officers of the University in maintaining good order and due obedience to all academical regulations'. The second Syndicate had laid these wider responsibilities upon the Board, and without assigning him a name had proposed for its officer duties more closely akin to those of a College Praelector. The intentions of those who framed the University Statute for Non-Collegiate Students are, however, sufficiently plain, for they equate the functions of the officer of the Board with those of the Principal of a hostel, as these are prescribed in the Statute *De officio principalis hospitii:*
> Principalis moribus et pietati scholarium suorum sedulo invigilet, improbos autem, immodestos et inertes coerceat atque corrigat. Ab hospitio ne absit, nisi alium probatum a cancellario sibi substituerit, cui, absente se, regimen hospitii et vicem suam gerendam committat. Si contegerit ut in quemquam e suis animadversum sit ab officiariis academiae, his opem praestet, semperque obsecundet quicquid auctoritate academica ad bene conformandos mores praescriptum fuerit.
> Nothing is said about the choice of the name; but Cambridge may well have taken over the title then recently adopted in Oxford, where, furthermore, it was already borne by two officers in Christ Church, with similar functions. The Board's officer accordingly became known as Censor of Non-Collegiate Students; and this remained his official title until 1935, when the University approved a change of statute whereby the community of resident non-collegiate students was designated 'Fitzwilliam House', with a consequential change in the description of the office of Censor, and W. S. Thatcher, appointed Censor of Non-Collegiate Students in 1924, was first given the new title of 'Censor of Fitzwilliam House' in the University's list of administrative officers in the Michaelmas term of 1935. (See also p. 221).

of the Board, although it is not possible to say whether, in arriving at this decision, the Board had any particular person in mind. The Board met again on 5 June, and their minute reads: 'At a meeting ... held this day for the election of a Censor to discharge duties defined in the preceding minutes, Mr R. B. Somerset of Trinity College, was elected.' The minutes do not record the names of those present.

Mr Somerset appears to have been well qualified for his appointment. He came to Trinity College from Manchester Grammar School in 1852 at the age of eighteen. He was made a Sub-sizar of the College on 25 October, Sizar in 1853 and Scholar in 1855. In 1857 he was thirty-ninth Wrangler, and was in the second class of the Classical Tripos. In the same year he took his B.A. degree, and his M.A. in 1860. He became a Fellow of Trinity in 1859, and held his fellowship for ten years. He was Junior Dean of Trinity from 1866 to 1869, and was a College Preacher. He served as Junior Proctor for the year 1868/69.[1] In 1868 he became Vicar of St Michael's, and so remained until his resignation in 1875.[2] On 30 March 1869 he married Miss Frances Brocklehurst of Macclesfield,[3] and in that year his address was given as Trumpington Road.[4] In 1872 he was living at 17 Brookside,[4] but these addresses may have been one and the same.

Having elected a Censor, the Board gave some thought to the pattern of the gown to be worn by the non-collegiate students, and decided that they would adopt the gown formerly worn by the members of Dr Humphry's hostel, this being 'a B.A. gown, without strings, opened at the sleeves, with two narrow strips of velvet, costing, when new, two guineas'. The matter was quickly resolved, but it seems surprising that there was no objection to the adoption of a gown so nearly resembling that worn by Bachelors of Arts.

At the two remaining meetings of the term, held on 11 and 15 June, the Board discussed and approved a pamphlet containing information which would be needed by applicants for admission as non-collegiate students. It names the members of the Board, gives directions about application, about the keeping of residence, and the fees to be paid to the University and to the Board. It announces that non-collegiate students, like others, will be admitted to the University Library and Museums, and to Professors' lectures. It adds that it is already known

[1] *University Calendar 1868–69*; also W. W. Rouse Ball and J. A. Venn, *Admissions to Trinity College, Cambridge*, vol. V, 1851 to 1900 (1913).
[2] *Cambridge Chronicle*, 3 April 1875.
[3] *The Times*, 1 April 1869.
[4] *Information relating to Non-Collegiate Students in the University of Cambridge*, June 1869; also Crockford, *Clerical Directory 1872*.

that some college lectures will be open to them, and on this promises further information as soon as may be after the beginning of the coming Michaelmas term. The Board are careful to repeat – what had been a matter of so much heart searching throughout all the discussions about the scheme – that every student, at the request of the Censor, must make a written report as to the place of worship he attends, his studies and the lectures he is attending and the instruction he is receiving.

Then, having completed their dispositions for the conduct of business by authorizing the Chairman and the Censor to admit students during the long vacation (on the understanding that 'the application of any applicant of a doubtful character should be brought before them before admission'), the Board rested from their labours until the Michaelmas term.[1]

It will make for a clearer understanding of references to the academic performances of the students, and of the Board's decisions in administering the University's regulations and their own, if some account is here given of the degree courses offered by the University at the time of the setting up of the non-collegiate institution.

Every student was required to reside during two-thirds of each of nine terms – about twenty-two weeks in each of the three academical years. Matriculation, for which there was no examination, could be in an undergraduate's first, second, or third term of residence. A student's choice of examinations depended on whether he was reading for a pass degree, or for honours.

For pass degree men, the examinations were

(a) The *Previous Examination*, held towards the end of the Michaelmas terms, normally open to men in their third term of residence at least, but exceptionally in their second. Another examination was held in the Lent term for those who had previously failed, or been absent for approved reasons.

(b) A *General Examination*, held towards the end of the Easter term, and again in November, open to students who, having passed the Previous Examination, were in their fifth term at least.

(c) For students in their ninth term at least, who had passed the Previous Examination and the General Examination, either a *Special Examination* in Theology, if during one term they had satisfactorily attended a course of professorial lectures and had passed an examination paper in some branch of Moral or Natural Science, or a *Special Examination* in Moral Science, Law and Modern History, Natural

[1] Minutes, 11 June 1869.

Science, or Mechanism and Applied Science, if they had satisfactorily attended during one term a course of professorial lectures on the subject of their choice. Special Examinations were held in the Easter term and at the end of the Michaelmas term.

The subjects in the Previous and General Examinations were mathematical or classical, except for Paley's *Evidences* in the first, and the *Acts of the Apostles* (but, even so, in Greek) in the second. In the Special Examinations in Theology, Moral Science and Law periods for study or practical work were prescribed, in Natural Science there was a choice between Chemistry, Geology, Botany, and Zoology (including Anatomy and Physiology); and in Mechanism and Applied Science candidates were required to offer limited fields of Mechanics and Hydrostatics, Hydraulics, Heat, Electronics and Magnetism.

For honours, besides the Previous Examination there was an *Additional Examination in Mathematics*, held at the times of the Previous Examination, in the subjects Algebra, Trigonometry and Mechanics (all elementary) and then, for candidates who had passed these examinations and were in their ninth term at least, there was a Tripos (or more than one) in Mathematics, Classics, Moral Science, Natural Science, or Law and Modern History. Of these Tripos examinations the last three were held towards the end of the Michaelmas term, the first in January and the second at the end of February. Detailed syllabuses were published in the *University Calendar*.

Shortly after the admission of the first non-collegiate students certain changes were made in these arrangements. In 1874, while the subjects remained substantially unaltered, the Previous Examination was divided. Part I consisted of the classical subjects, and Part II of the rest. Examinations in both parts were held in the first week of December, and late in the Easter term, and they were open to candidates in their second or later term of residence. From 1871 candidates in the Special Examination in Theology were no longer required to pass an examination paper in a subject in Moral or Natural Science, but in other Special Examinations were required to supply evidence of approved attendance during one term at a single course of lectures by a Professor in their subjects. In 1871, also, the History section of the Special Examination in Moral Sciences was transferred to the Special Examination in Law.

For honours candidates a Theological Tripos was introduced in 1874, and in 1875 the Law and Modern History Tripos was divided into two separate examinations.

The University did little to provide instruction for its degree courses. With audiences of widely differing ability, the Professors' lectures could hardly fail, on the one hand, to be unexciting for the best men or, on the other, above the heads of the rest; and it is not unlikely that one of the reasons for the requirement that the poll men should attend professorial lectures as a condition of admission to some of their degree examinations was a wish to secure for the Professors audiences that they might otherwise not have attracted. The undergraduate was taught by the staff of his college, or by private tutors, and the wealthier colleges were best able to provide teaching. If a man's needs could not be supplied by his college, either from its own resources or in association with others, he would be likely to incur the expense of private tuition; and this was to be a source of much concern to those who were responsible for superintending the studies of the non-collegiate students.

From the minutes of the Non-Collegiate Students Board it appears that, with little delay or difficulty, its members settled into a routine in the conduct of their business, which in those first years was seldom disturbed, or relieved, by unusual problems or events. There was no rule about the frequency of Board meetings, which were usually held two or three times a term, at dates which suggest that they were not regularly spaced out or fixed in advance, but were convened by the Chairman when sufficient business had accumulated, or when particular matters needed attention. Of nine members rarely more than six attended, and no meeting was held in the Long Vacation.

At the first meeting of the Michaelmas term 1869, the Chairman and the Censor reported that, under the authority given them by the Board, they had accepted for admission the first two non-collegiate students (T. H. F. Bee and F. T. Prince), and at that meeting four other applications were approved, one from a member of St John's College (H. J. Mason). The first group of eight students admitted in time to keep that term by residence was completed a fortnight later, when two more candidates were accepted, one of them from Queens'. The names of these men are recorded in a list of non-collegiate students of the early years, which gives the approximate dates of their admission, their terms kept, and the dates of the termination of their non-collegiate courses, whether by graduation, migration, or otherwise.[1] No personal files have been preserved, and probably none were kept, of students who matriculated before the beginning of Mr Thatcher's censorship, but a note by Registrary Luard on this first group gives some particulars of their circumstances, and some indication, therefore, of the kind of

[1]   Register of Non-collegiate Students, No. 1, College Archives.

The First VIII (1869). A note by the Registrary

man who at that time might be expected to seek non-collegiate membership of the University.[1] Mr Somerset also mentions these men in his first Report to the Board (see p.54). Their examination results can hardly have encouraged him, for of the eight three graduated, the first

[1] University Papers 1868–83, no. 224+, University Archives.

being H. J. Mason, who had matriculated from St John's in 1868, and after becoming a non-collegiate student in the following year took his B.A. degree in 1872. T. H. F. Bee graduated B.A. in 1873; and by virtue of his place in the alphabet was the first non-collegiate student to matriculate, and in 1873 the first to graduate, without having previously been a member of a college. T. S. Little did well, but he did not stay. Born on 8 July 1845 at Kilkenny, he came to Cambridge from Queen's College, Liverpool, and during his first year was elected a Whewell Scholar in International Law, and transferred as Sub-sizar to Trinity College in the Michaelmas term of 1970. He was in the first class of the Law and History Tripos in 1972, became Sizar in this year, took his B.A. degree in 1873, and his M.A. in 1890. The remaining five members of the group fell by the wayside.

Early in the Michaelmas term 1869 the Board agreed to enquire of colleges whether any of their lectures could be opened to the non-collegiate students and, if so, on what terms. They added that already, at the end of the preceding Easter term, two colleges had offered admission for a very small fee, and also mentioned that four Oxford colleges had agreed to admit unattached students to their lectures. In December the Censor reported that his men would be admitted to lectures in Christ's College, in Trinity, St John's and Trinity Hall, but not at Corpus, St Peter's, or Sidney Sussex, or, for that term at least, at Downing. By the end of the Lent term he was able to add that King's College had approved admission on conditions to be arranged, and there, so far as the minutes go, the matter rests, except that a year later the Board agreed that the Censor should prepare and print a list of available lectures, with fees so far as it had been possible to ascertain them.

Another step taken by the Board at an early stage was to ask the Censor to issue, at the end of the scheme's first year, a short account of the courses leading to the B.A. degree, and to send it with extracts from his Report for the Easter term 1870, and the Information sheet previously prepared, to 'Mayors of Towns and any public institutions to which it may be likely to be of interest'.[1] The Board may have been influenced by the Censor's own suggestion in his terminal Report that, the first year having passed, it might be desirable to call further attention to the opportunities offered by the scheme of obtaining a university education and a degree at moderate cost.

In their early years certain topics appear frequently in the Board's

---

[1] Minutes, 20 June 1870.

minutes – admissions are reported regularly or brought up for decision (and comparatively rarely refused), as are applications to the Lodging-Houses Syndicate for specially licensed lodgings.

Applications for admission [says a Board minute of 7 December, 1869] from Mr John Jackson, now Headmaster of the Guildhall Commercial School, Bury St Edmund's, and from Rev. J. L. Brereton,[1] on behalf of his son, aged 14 years, were considered. Mr Jackson was admitted on the understanding stated in the margin.

The marginal note reads:

Mr Jackson allowed to keep the first three terms by intermittent residence while holding his present office at Bury St Edmund's, if possible. He is to reside continuously at the beginning and end of each of these terms, and during the middle of the terms to reside at Cambridge from Friday to Monday in each week. Less periods of residence are thought not to be within the spirit of the rule. After these three terms it is understood that Mr Jackson will reside without intermission.

The minute continues

Mr Brereton was admitted on the understanding that during the first part of his residence he would be placed under the supervision of Mr Thompson, Headmaster of the Devon County School, now keeping terms at Jesus College, and that when he should cease to be under Mr Thompson's care, the Board should be specially satisfied as to his being placed under proper supervision.

At their next meeting the Board gave instructions for an application to be made to the Lodging-Houses Syndicate that leave should be given for Brereton to reside with Mr Thompson at 13 Trumpington Road, in a house hired by Brereton's father for the purpose.

Another application, received by the Board at their meeting on 11 October 1870, illustrates the extent of their willingness to do everything they reasonably could to accommodate their regulations to the circumstances of individual applicants:

An application not accompanied as yet by the required testimonial, from Herbert Rees Philipps, formerly a pensioner of Trinity College, now a clerk in the India Office, for admission with leave to keep residence while retaining his appointment at the India Office and frequently going thither during the day, was discussed; and it was considered that his application should be agreed to if before the next meeting satisfactory testimony to his character should be forthcoming from Trinity College.

[1] Subsequently Chairman of the Directors of the County College Association, which, in 1873, founded Cavendish College. See also p. 63.

The Board duly confirmed their approval of Mr Philipps's application; but not, it seems, without further thought; for the Censor in a
marginal note is careful to record the conditions under which it was
given:

> Mr Philipps ... undertook, while counting continuous residence by nights
> for at least two thirds of each term, to give *at least* six weeks in each year
> of complete daily residence, *exclusive of Sundays*, in periods of about a fort-
> night terminally.

By the following Easter term, however, these requirements had been
found irksome, for the matter is again before the Board:

> The Censor having made reference to the minute of October 17, 1870,
> note, respecting Herbert Rees Philipps, a non-collegiate student, who had
> recently gained the Porson Prize for Greek Iambic Verse,[1] and having
> stated that he believed it would be a great relief to Mr Philipps to be
> allowed to keep this term by sleeping in Cambridge on alternate nights
> during the week and by residence on Sundays, without the fortnight of
> complete daily residence proposed in his application for admission, it was
> agreed that this permission should be given him. [In the draft minutes as
> they were submitted for the Board's approval there follow the words 'in
> consideration of his having gained the Porson Prize'; but it was clearly felt
> that this was not a circumstance that should be recorded as having influ-
> enced the Board's decision, and the words are, with some appearance of
> emphasis, deleted.]

One of the Censor's duties was to register the presence of men in
Cambridge in order that he might be able to certify that they had kept
terms by residence. They were required to call on him at specified
times and write their names in a book kept for the purpose. At first the
Censor had no office unless it were at his home, and the men were told
to sign their names within certain time limits in specified places such as
'a room in Free School Lane', 'a room in St John's', or 'Mr Peck's
shop'.[2] The book had to be signed on five days in each week if the week
was to count for residence. This must have been a tiresome rule,

---

[1]   Philipps, who matriculated in the Michaelmas term 1865 from Trinity College and kept
three terms there, became a non-collegiate student in the Michaelmas term 1870. He
appears not to have read for honours in Classics, but was admitted to the (Ordinary) B.A.
degree in the Easter term 1873, with a first class in the Special Examination in Botany. He
was Porson Prizeman in 1871 and 1872. *The Historical Register of the University of Cambridge*
(1917), p. 317, in error gives as Prizeman in both years Henry Rees Philipps, brother of
Herbert, who was admitted as a non-collegiate student in the Easter term 1873, and
migrated to Downing College in the Lent term 1876.

[2]   '*Memories of Sixty Years*' (anon.) in *Journal*, April 1930, p. 13. Mr Peck's shop, now Messrs
Savory and Moore's, needs no further description; and of the room in Free School Lane

although something of the sort was doubtless unavoidable in the circumstances, and there came before the Board repeated applications for
the allowance of a week's residence to men whose names appeared in
the lists on fewer than five days out of seven. Each term the Board was
asked to fix the date of the men's return to Cambridge after the ensuing
vacation, and it is surprising to find that the first day of residence in the
Lent term was sometimes as late as 30 January. Another associated
matter was the subject of a discussion, on one occasion only, on the
effect of an *absit* on a student's residence if he used it to be away from
Cambridge from Saturday to Monday 'as is allowed at at least one
College'. The Board were unanimous that they could not be so accommodating, and ruled that such absence would need to be covered by an
exeat, with a consequential break in the tally of nights kept.[1]

All in all, a reading of the Board's early minutes leaves an impression
that its members were asked to devote considerable time to relatively
unimportant matters which might have been delegated to their officer,
but it may well be that they felt it incumbent upon them to be able personally to assure a still apprehensive University that the fears aroused
by the proposals to bring to it a class of students not under the superintendence of any college were not so well grounded as had been
thought. Certainly the Board were acting in the spirit of the recommendations of the second Syndicate's Report, which placed on their
shoulders the responsibility for many matters which the first Syndicate
had left to the Censor.

There were certain duties that the Board were particularly careful to
require the Censor to perform. They themselves had been charged to
see that the students were advised about their studies, and to provide,
subject to safeguards against undesirable persuasion, for their 'due
attendance on Public Worship'. These instructions they passed on to
the Censor, adding riders of their own that he, in his turn, should

there is no further trace; but through the diligence and courtesy of Mr W. T. Thurbon,
lately Bursar's Clerk in the College, it has been possible to identify with reasonable certainty the 'room in St John's'.

In a letter, dated 27 May 1891, to Mr Huddleston the Rev. Isaac Wodhams (B.A. 1876),
then Headmaster of Magdalen College School in Brackley, refers to himself as 'one who
came up when the only place where we could meet was a room in Dr Pearson's suite at St
John's, for the purpose of signing our names'. In the same issue of the *Journal* (p. 18), Mr
Huddleston relates how 'J. B. Pearson, Fellow of St John's, and subsequently Bishop of
Newcastle, Australia, at the very outset took charge of the Students who used to meet in his
rooms'. Mr Pearson had been a strong supporter of the admission of non-collegiate students
to the University (see also pp. 32, 33, 41), and was one of the original members of the Non-
Collegiate Students Board. From the College records it appears that from 1867 until 1876
he occupied rooms at F5 in the Third Court.

[1] Minutes, 20 June 1870.

enquire of the students as to the places of worship they were accustomed to attend, and obtain from them reports about their lectures and the instruction they were receiving. These matters figured prominently in the Censor's terminal Reports to the Board.[1]

As a source of detailed information about the students, their academic progress, and, so far as it was possible for them to have one, their corporate life, the Reports are of considerable interest. The first Report of all, communicated to the Board on 7 December 1869, is a brief summary of the reception given to the scheme by the world at large, and of the work of the eight students. It also contains the only reference to an instruction by the Board that the Censor should communicate the names and addresses of his men to the parochial ministers in whose parishes they were living.

> The first duty imposed on me by the Board [says the Censor] was to circulate the paper of *Information relating to Non-Collegiate Students* sanctioned at a meeting held June 15, 1869. I sent this paper to the principal London and Provincial English Journals as well as to those published at Edinburgh, Glasgow, Dublin and Belfast. I believe it was printed in a fair number of these; others mentioned it and referred inquirers to me.
>
> I have received written applications for information from fifty-eight persons, half of them reaching me before the end of July. A few of these simply asked for the paper of information; five imagined the new class of students would be non-resident; the majority were very careful in their inquiries about the whole cost of living at the University. Only three wished to know what Exhibitions or Scholarships would be open to them. Many of my correspondents gave no information about themselves; but eleven were Schoolmasters of Middle Class or National Schools. Three seemed to be hesitating between this mode of residence at the University, and residence at a Theological College as a preliminary to ordination.
>
> Besides these written applications (of which fourteen were followed by further correspondence) I have had a few visits from persons who came to make their inquiries on the spot.
>
> Eight students were admitted in time to keep this term. Two of these had been members of Colleges. Of the six freshmen three were professional men previously resident in the town. These have not been receiving any regular instruction, but have been devoting some time to the study of the subjects of the Previous Examination. The other three freshmen have been attending lectures at Christ's College. I have reason to hope they will all study seriously some of the subjects prescribed for Honours Examinations. One of the Junior Sophs has been attending the instruction of a private tutor, as well as some Professors' lectures; the other, being engaged as

[1] College Archives.

an Assistant at a School, has not received any instruction.

By direction of the Board I gave notice of the names and residences of the students to the parochial ministers in whose parishes they reside; in several cases I know that the students were called on in consequence of this notice. Six of the students state that they attend parish Churches, the other two a Wesleyan Chapel. They have all conducted themselves with due regularity, and all have kept, or may have kept before December 17, the required amount of residence for the Term.

In accordance with a resolution adopted by the Board on the 23rd October, 1869, a circular was sent to Heads and Tutors of Colleges, asking them whether any Lectures in their Colleges would be open to Non-Collegiate Students. I have received several answers, but others may yet be expected.

There is good reason to believe that the numbers of the students will increase, and at present there are no applications which confirm the apprehension that students will choose this mode of residence as giving more opportunity for a life of mere amusement than residence in a College. All those who apply are of mature age, or are designed by their friends to be under the charge of persons of trustworthy age and character.

I may remark that scarcely any of the applicants are boys at schools. The eleven schoolmasters whom I have mentioned were interested in the Scheme on their own account, not on account of pupils.

Fifteen months later in another Report (his fifth) Mr Somerset is able to give some account of the academic performance of the twenty-one men in residence. Their attendance at religious services again is the subject of comment (although in less detail than subsequently), and he has much to say about the attitude of the men themselves to non-collegiate status. He writes:

Since the time of my last report there has been but little change in the number or the position of the students. The lists of the General Examination for the Ordinary Degree and the Previous Examination last term included some of the students under your charge: in the former there were four candidates, of whom two failed; in the latter, of eleven candidates, (one of whom only appeared *pro forma*) eight were approved, three of them in the additional as well as the ordinary subjects. In the 2nd Previous Examination, just concluded, the three who did not pass the Examination in December presented themselves again, and two were approved. Of the two who failed in the General Examination one is a medical student who had not been attending sufficiently to the subjects of the Examination; the other was employed in tuition. The one student who has failed twice in the Previous Examination is a person of great moral excellence, and will probably pass in December, if permitted to go on. One freshman has availed himself of the recent regulation allowing him to present himself at the

Examination in his second term, and has passed in the additional as well as the ordinary subjects.

In estimating the number of graduates to be expected from coming examinations, it is to be noticed that three of the successful candidates at the Previous Examination, having been previously members of Colleges, have preferred to join Colleges again. Another student has returned to the College to which he had belonged, after less than one term … The number of those who have completed the residence for this term under your superintendence is twenty-one.

An examination of the reports of the students now presented to you shews that three have been reading for Mathematical Honours; one for Law Honours; three have been engaged in Medical Study; two have been preparing for Special Examinations for the B.A. Degree; two for the General Examination for the same; ten for the Previous Examination, some of them with some additional work. Only seven have availed themselves of any public lectures, three of these having attended lectures in Colleges: seven appear to have received no instruction. As to religious worship, twelve mention single parish Churches as attended by them, another has "given attendance, with one exception, at the University Service at St Mary's Church". Another has "preferred King's College Chapel" as his place of religious worship. Another mentions the Wesleyan Chapel and a Sunday School: four of them mention two parish Churches or more; and one carefully enumerates twelve Churches where he has attended services during the term.

Speaking generally, the students now in residence seem to me to be a well-conducted body of men, fairly occupied in the work of the University: some of them are backward in attainments, and there are few who shew any great promise of future distinction in the University, but I believe the great majority will pass the Ordinary Examinations with credit, and be benefited by their residence at the University.

The great drawback to their position is still the smallness of their numbers, which seems in several ways to isolate them unduly. They have not hitherto been much brought together, and as they live at considerable distances from one another, they are hardly likely to find themselves associating with each other as members of one body, unless they form clubs, or secure a common room at which to meet freely, or in some other way have more frequent occasions of meeting than they have hitherto had.

This want of social union among them seems to me to have diminished for most of them the chance of forming associations with members of Colleges. Very few of those who have not themselves been members of Colleges seem to have so much acquaintance with other students as I believe to be desirable even for the poorest. In a few cases this is readily accounted for by personal peculiarities together with want of the school connection which introduces so many freshmen at once to a circle of friendly acquaintances. But there are at least some who suffer from the undue separation of

Non-Collegiate from College Students, and from the unnecessary disper-
sion of the Non-Collegiate Students themselves. Probably an undue sensi-
tiveness makes them unwilling to avail themselves, as far as they might, of
the liberality of the Colleges, by attending their Lectures and Chapel services.

They are inclined to shrink from benefiting by institutions provided for
others, partly because they have nothing to offer in return, partly because
they think, rightly or wrongly, that other students regard them with cold-
ness. They would feel more confidence in their position if they had some
institution which might afford visible proof of their being one body, and if
they had some advantages, however small, of which a share might be extended to other students.

It would probably be premature at present to attempt to arrange any lectures expressly (I do not say, exclusively) for these students. Besides the
smallness of the classes we could form, our pecuniary resources are not
sufficient to provide for anything effective in the way of separate lectures.
One wish expressed by a number of the students I propose to meet next
term by conducting a short morning service for them at St Michael's
Church. Another wish may be regarded less favourably by some members
of the Board. It is for a large club room (or two rooms) which might be
used, by any of themselves, or by other students, on payment of a moderate subscription. I do not think such a club room, after its first establishment need involve greater expenditure than the majority of them would be
willing and able to meet. But at present there are not students enough to
meet the first expenses without help, and the funds at the disposal of the
Board might be unduly strained if they were made to meet any such claim.

I believe it to be important for the future growth of the body, possibly
even for your work being maintained long enough to have a fair chance of
being developed by supplementary institutions, that in some way the students should have rather more than most of them have hitherto had of the
social advantages of residence at the University.

On 19 June 1875 Mr Somerset presented his eighteenth Report, remarkable for the detail with which he informs his Board of the courses
of study undertaken by his men, of their examination results, and,
again, of the 'places of religious worship' they attended (the fractions
applying, presumably, to some whose allegiance was divided). Mr
Somerset's punctilious observance of the regulations that required him
to see that the Board were informed about these matters suggests that
those responsible for the scheme still felt it essential to be in a position
to refute, from their personal knowledge, any allegation that the
presence of a body of undergraduates not amenable to college control
constituted a moral danger to the rest of the University, and an unacceptable lowering of its academic standards.

I beg leave to report [says Mr Somerset] that this term sixty-six students commenced residence, whose aims, as declared by themselves in their reports for this term, may be thus described:

43 were preparing for the Previous Examination in one or more of its parts

11 were preparing for the General Examination for the Ordinary B.A. Degree

3 were preparing for the Special Examination in Theology for the Ordinary B.A. Degree

3 were preparing for the Special Examination in Chemistry (two of these being medical students)

1 was preparing for the Special Examination in History

1 was preparing for the 2nd M.B. Examination and Natural Sciences Tripos

1 was preparing for the Theological Tripos

1 was preparing for the Mathematical Tripos

1 was preparing for the Historical Tripos

1 was preparing for the Natural Sciences Tripos

The places of religious worship attended are approximately represented by the following numbers:—

16 students attended All Saints Church

13 students attended St Michael's Church

3 students attended St Paul's Church

4 students attended Great St Andrew's Church

4 students attended Great St Mary's Church

1 student attended St Barnabas's Church

2½ students attended Holy Trinity Church

2½ students attended St Sepulchre Church

1 student attended St Benet's Church

1 student attended St Clement's Church

1 student attended St Mark's Church

1 student attended Grantchester Church

2 students attended St Giles's Church

2 students attended Christ Church

2 students attended Little St Mary's Church

3 students attended Baptist Chapels

2 students attended Roman Catholic Chapels

1 student attended Wesleyan Chapels

1 student attended Primitive Methodist Chapels

1 student attended Congregational Chapels

1 student attended King's College Chapel

1 student attended University Sermon alone

College Lectures on Greek Testament and the Classical and Mathematical subjects of the Previous Examination and of the General Examination for the Ordinary B.A. Degree have been attended by 15 (by 3 of those without payment); College Lectures on Theology by 3, and partly by another; Professor Seeley's lectures and classes by 4; Professor Liveings's lectures and practical instruction by 2; Mr Michael Foster's by 2; Professor C. C. Babington's by one; Dr Westcott's lectures by 2; Medical Lectures and Hospital Practice by 3.

For private instruction three depended on the (provisional) County College; twelve had recourse to undergraduates; four to Bachelor of Arts, seventeen to tutors of older standing (not all these accepting the fees).

The results of examinations held this Term, as far as they concern Non-Collegiate Students, are summed up thus:–

Previous Examination

Part II	Five in first Class
	Thirteen in second Class
	Ten rejected
Part I	Seven in first Class
	Ten in second Class
	Four rejected

General Examination for Ordinary B.A. Degree

| One in first Class |
| Two in second Class |
| Four in third Class |
| One in fourth Class |
| Two rejected |

Special Examination in Chemistry

| One in first Class |
| One in second Class |
| One rejected |

Special Examination in History

| One in second Class |

Special Examination in Theology

| One in second Class |
| Two rejected |

This last result confirms the impression I had formed that for this examination something more is needed than to indicate to the students the lectures open to them. I hope this deficiency may be in some degree supplied next year by efforts of mine.

Some of the failures in the Previous Examination and in the General Examination are such as seem to call for some notice; and perhaps the Board will be willing to lay down some general rules as to the number of times a student may have the option of presenting himself for each of these examinations.

I believe it to be desirable that the library provided for the use of the students should be augmented as opportunity occurs.

Although the Board were not required by regulation to submit reports to the Senate on the progress of the scheme for non-collegiate students, they did so from time to time. Their first Report was made on 17 October, 1870,[1] and gives an account of their stewardship during the first year. Brief but informative, it is signed by all the members of the Board and reads:

> The Board for admitting and superintending Non-Collegiate Students desire to make known to the University the following extracts from a Report made to them by the Censor in the last Easter Term.
>
> The third term of the operation of the Scheme for admitting Non-Collegiate Students has not been marked by any noticeable incident. There has been a slight increase in the number of the Students; nineteen will have kept the Term, one commenced but did not complete the residence for the Term, and two have been non-resident altogether. Hitherto the results of the new Scheme have been satisfactory, if not very considerable. The Students have been well-conducted and generally speaking studious, and it has been proved by experience that it is possible for an undergraduate to live in Cambridge as cheaply as in many other towns. In one case the whole cost of board and lodging (including washing, cooking, and all attendance) has averaged not more than a guinea a week during residence, the Student residing only the necessary time for keeping the Terms. College Lectures, in increasing number, are open to the attendance of the Students, and in several cases a disposition has been shewn to afford gratuitous instruction privately to Students in needy circumstances. The great drawback to the position of the Students at present is their social isolation, which is felt on account of the smallness of their number, and will be diminished as the numbers increase in successive years.
>
> There is every reason to expect a gradual, if not a rapid, increase of number. But at present a decided majority of those who are attracted by the Scheme are students of more advanced age than is usual in those who commence residence in Colleges. Such publicity as was given to the Scheme last year by means of newspapers has not produced many letters of inquiry from either the masters or the parents of boys still at school, though it may have interested both classes in the Scheme in a general way...
>
> One of the students has been elected to one of Dr Whewell's International Law Scholarships and will therefore become a member of Trinity College.
>
> Annexed is an abstract of the accounts of the Board for the year ending at Midsummer, 1870.

[1] Camb. Univ. Reg. 60, 16, University Archives.

Payments				Receipts			
	£	s.	d.		£	s.	d.
To the University Press	9	0	0	1869, Michaelmas Term,			
For stationery ...		10	0	Eight Students' pay-			
To the Censor,				ments to the Board,			
stipend for one year				thirtyfive shillings			
ended Midsummer,				each ...	14	0	0
1870	100	0	0	1870, Lent Term.			
				Seventeen Students'			
				payments to the Board	29	15	0
				1870, Easter Term.			
				Twenty Students' pay-			
				ments to the Board	35	0	0
				Deficiency to balance	30	15	0
	109	10	0		109	10	0

On April 22, 1873 the Board reported again[1] – as they were obliged to do, for they were not empowered to admit students after 1 October 1873 unless the scheme should be prolonged by Grace of the Senate. They reported satisfactory progress, and recommended that the operation of the scheme be made permanent; and after a Discussion on 1 May at which no comment was made, their recommendation was approved by Grace 1 of 15 May 1873.

A year later the Board agreed that it was desirable that they should report to the Senate annually, but after their next Report on 30 April 1874 they did not do so, for there are no more than three Reports during the remainder of Mr Somerset's censorship – those dated 23 October 1876, 12 November 1878, and (a special Report on Fees) 19 November 1879.

These Reports reveal a pattern of development in the first ten years or so of the non-collegiate system which soon made apparent the strengths and the weaknesses which were to be characteristic of the scheme in its later years. From the beginning the Board were satisfied that they could achieve a principal object of the scheme by making a university education possible at a substantially reduced cost, and they were soon able to show that this was being done. Thanks to the assistance of some of the colleges, the provision of instruction for the men had not raised any insuperable problems; but there was early evidence of the migration which was to be a very real handicap to the non-collegiate institution for forty years or more; for already in 1870 the winner of a Whewell Scholarship in International Law had moved to Trinity College at the end of his first year. By April 1873, when the

[1] *University Reporter*, Easter term 1873, p. 23.

Board were recommending that the scheme should be made permanent, they reported that of ninety men admitted since the scheme
began twenty-three had become members of colleges; and although
gradually increasing numbers were beginning to remove the sense of
social isolation which had been a regular theme of the Censor's first
Reports, the lack of premises where the men could meet was a serious
obstacle to corporate activities. It may well be supposed that the members of the Board were greatly interested, at their meeting on 18
November 1873, in an offer of three unfurnished rooms in a house in
Trumpington Street for use as an office. The offer was then declined,
on account of the high rent (£55) proposed, but in the following term
'it was agreed that the Board should accept the agreement made by the
Censor with Mr Peck, chemist, of Trumpington Street for their hiring
of certain rooms in a house belonging to him, and situated opposite the
Fitzwilliam Museum; these rooms to be furnished by the Board, and in
part painted and prepared, for the use of the Censor and of the students
under the control of the Censor. The rent to be £40 a year. The Board
not to pay any rates or taxes.'[1] There is a marginal note that the Board
thought that £100 might be spent upon furniture if that was necessary.
In a Report to the Senate on 30 April 1874, this most important acquisition is recorded in these terms: 'The Board have now been able to
secure convenient rooms at 31 Trumpington Street, for the transaction
of the Censor's business; and to meet the expense of furnishing them
by a sum which has been allowed to accumulate from the fees paid by
the students for supervision. One room of considerable dimensions is
assigned during a large part of the day to the students themselves, to
serve the purpose of a reading room, and as a place in which they may
hold meetings. It is believed that the want of a common centre, which
has hitherto been felt, may thus in a fair degree be supplied.'[2]

The financial prospects of the new scheme were not unpromising.
With eight men in the first year a deficit was inevitable, but it was kept
down to £30.15.0. In the second year, with twenty men, the deficit was
£6.14.6, and this was the last occasion that any call was made on the
annual subvention of £100 which the University had undertaken to
provide in case of need. By the exercise of the most rigid economy, the
Board had been able to show, in their accounts for the year 1878/9, an

[1] Minutes, 29 January 1874.
[2] University Reporter, 1873–74, p. 371. Of these rooms, all on the first floor, two facing
Trumpington Street were occupied by the Censor and his clerk, and were later thrown into
one to form a Students' Common Room. The large room at the back, which was also used
for lectures, was converted in 1937 into a Staff Parlour.

31 and 32 Trumpington Street (1887)

accumulated balance of just over £450, with annual stipends of £350 to the Censor, of £75 to the Assistant Censor, and of £50 to their Clerk; furthermore, with the help of a grant of £50 from the University they had made a modest beginning in the provision of a library.

The Board also received quite unforeseen, but by no means negligible, assistance from another quarter.

In 1873 a company was formed called The County College Association Limited, whose objects were 'to combine and assist certain efforts that are being made in the various Counties of England to extend and raise the standard of Middle Class Education, and for that purpose to purchase and hold and occupy certain buildings and lands at Cambridge or elsewhere, and to erect thereon one or more College or Colleges upon a proprietary basis.'[1] With the general approval of the Senate, given by Grace 3 of 1 May 1873, a county college, subsequently named Cavendish College after the Chancellor of the University, was estab-

1 Memorandum of Association (Cambridge Papers FM 101, University Library).

lished in Cambridge in temporary accommodation at Norwich House in Panton Street, for the purpose of 'enabling students somewhat younger than the ordinary undergraduate to pass through a university course and obtain a university degree; of training in the art of teaching those students who wish to become schoolmasters; and of securing the greatest possible economy in cost as well as in time.'[1] The College was designed to accommodate 300 students, with such staff and servants as might be necessary, at an estimated cost of £50,000 for the site and buildings, with a further £10,000 for furnishings. Students were to be admitted at the age of 16, they would in due course all reside in College, and residence would be for two-thirds of the year, at an annual charge of £84; of which it was calculated that not more than £40 would be needed for board and lodging, and £30 for tuition and University fees, the remaining £14 being available for reserves and shareholders' dividends. This is not the place to follow the fortunes of Cavendish College. In 1876 it moved to a splendid site on the Hills Road – where Homerton College now is – even if, at the time of its recognition as a public hostel within the University, the Senior Proctor[2] found the prospect of an evening expedition from the centre of the town less rewarding than subsequent generations of undergraduates. The interest of the Non-collegiate Students Board in this matter lay in the fact that between 1873 and November 1882, when as a public hostel the College acquired the right to present candidates for matriculation, to enter them for University examinations and present them for degrees, the undergraduates of Cavendish College entered the University as non-collegiate students and paid to the Board a terminal residence fee of £1.15.0.[3] Over the period of nine years or so the Board thus received additional revenue of the order of £1,500, at small cost to themselves, because the undergraduates at Cavendish College were in effect under the superintendence of the College staff, even if their admission was subject to the formal approval of the Board.[4] This fortunate arrangement came to an end in 1883. In 1891 Cavendish College was obliged to close down through lack of numbers, and its story remains a melancholy episode in the history of the University Extension movement.

At about this time there was another, and more unusual, move to en-

---

[1] Memorandum of Association. Norwich House, now numbered 65 Panton Street, at the junction of Norwich Street with Panton Street, had been built in 1867.

[2] Oscar Browning, of King's College. See Discussion of the (amended) Report of the Council on New Institutions, *University Reporter*, 1881–82, p. 534.

[3] £1.10.0 from the Lent term 1880.

[4] There were similar arrangements for Selwyn College, but only for the Michaelmas term 1882, before its recognition as a public hostel on 8 February 1883.

large the field of the University's activity in the form of a proposal from Mr J. B. Allen, Headmaster of the Perse School, that his boarders might while still at the school be made eligible for admission as non-collegiate students. As by the terms of its Scheme of Government boys might not remain at the School beyond the end of the term in which they became nineteen years old, they would, if the Board should look with favour on his proposal, need to be admitted to the University rather younger than was usual, and he was therefore seeking an extension to his boys of the privileges granted to the students of Cavendish College, although he was careful to add that the number of his candidates was likely to be very small. The Headmaster continued: 'All I desire from you is permission that any of my pupils who have resided in my house a reasonable time – say two years at least – shall, if they desire to obtain the B.A. degree earlier than usual, and if I consider them qualified to enter the University, be allowed to matriculate whilst still under my roof.' He supposes that most of the boys would leave after they had passed the General Examination, and spend one further year in lodgings of their own.

The Board received the Headmaster's letter, dated 25 October 1880, at their meeting on 27 October, and resolved that it be brought to them at their next meeting, and be circulated for their consideration beforehand. After another postponement on 30 November, they agreed on 10 December to inform Mr Allen that acceptance of his proposal would introduce a new principle into the working of their scheme, and that they were not at liberty to do this without an express direction from the Senate. They added that they were 'not prepared to move the Senate in the matter'.[1]

The Non-Collegiate Students Board very soon felt the lack of scholarships and exhibitions which might serve to stimulate recruitment, encourage undergraduates in residence, and, not least, discourage the migration of their best men. As early as 29 January 1871 the Censor reported that he had heard that the Oxford Delegacy had urged the City Companies to open to unattached students the awards which they had founded for members of the Oxford Colleges, and the Board at once agreed to make similar representation. Two months later the Censor had no definite information on the subject; there is no further reference to it until the Michaelmas Term 1874, when he informed the Board that in the Long Vacation he had heard from the Clerk to the Clothworkers' Company that his Court proposed to provide each year

[1] Minutes, 10 December 1880.

an exhibition of the value of £50, preferably to a candidate in the Physical Sciences, which would be tenable for three years by a non-collegiate student, but would be forfeited on migration to a college.[1] The company's offer was accepted on 15 October, and arrangements were put in hand for an examination in January 1875, open to candidates who had not begun residence or, being resident, had not kept more than one term. The first Clothworkers' Exhibition – indeed the first exhibition of any kind awarded by the Board – was divided between two candidates, presumably of equal merit;[2] and this decision to divide the award appears to have been unfortunate, for one of the exhibitioners, after keeping four terms, accepted an offer of a scholarship at a college. Two years later the Board again split the award, with a similar result.

The establishment of these exhibitions was announced in the Board's Report, dated 23 October 1876, to the Senate.[3] In the same Report they affirm that the non-collegiate system has enabled students to come to the University at greatly reduced cost, and add that for some of their undergraduates the annual expenses incurred in Cambridge have not exceeded £50. These include board, lodging, washing, fire and lighting; dues to the University and to the Board, fees for college lectures and the cost of books that are ordinarily necessary. The importance which the Board will have attached to the Company's Exhibitions may readily be appreciated in the light of this information about expenses, for in those days the annual emoluments of an exhibitioner will have gone a long way towards meeting his expenses in Cambridge for the whole of an academic year.

By the Easter term 1875, the performance of some of the men in their examinations had caused the Censor, and at the Censor's prompting the Board, to feel the need of regulations prescribing limits of standing for candidates for degree examinations. For examinations leading to the pass degree, for which half the undergraduates in the University still read, such limits were virtually non-existent; and the Board must have felt that in a community admitted to membership of the University under arrangements specifically designed to enable its members to follow a degree course with the minimum of expense, it was desirable that too leisurely a progress should be discouraged. Accordingly, at the beginning of the following Michaelmas term the Cen-

---

[1]   Minutes, 7 October 1874.
[2]   H. J. H. Fenton and E. F. Taylor. Fenton migrated to Christ's College, and in 1878 was in the first class in the Natural Sciences Tripos. See also pp. 75, 76, 77. Taylor was in the second class.
[3]   *University Reporter*, 1876–77, p. 61.

sor submitted draft regulations to the Board, and at the end of the term their Chairman promulgated the following statement:

I. Ordered by the Board that if any student have failed, except for some cause approved by the Board,
(1) at the end of five terms from the commencement of his residence, to pass one part of the Previous Examination;
(2) at the end of seven terms from the commencement of his residence, to pass both parts of the Previous Examination; or
(3) at the end of nine terms from the commencement of his residence, to pass the General Examination for the Ordinary B.A. Degree or the Examination in the Additional Subjects required from candidates for Honours, he shall forthwith cease to reside in the University; and that he shall not be allowed to continue a Non-Collegiate Student unless within twelve months he pass the examination necessary under the foregoing order to entitle him to resume his residence.

Ordered also that, except for some cause to be approved by the Board, no student who is not *bona fide* a candidate for Honours be allowed to reside in the University beyond the end of the tenth term from the commencement of his residence, or be allowed to remain a Non-Collegiate Student unless he have passed the examinations necessary for his Degree within twelve months from the end of the said tenth term.

II. Ordered by the Board that every student who wishes to reside in Cambridge during any term which he is not keeping as a term of residence for a degree must obtain leave to do so from the Board through the Censor, whether his ordinary home be in Cambridge or elsewhere.[1]

These limits of standing cannot be regarded as strict, but in his Report at the end of the Easter term 1877 the Censor informs the Board that they have 'reduced considerably' the number of those who had been allowed to remain on the books as nominal students, and that although he has removed some names with regret he is satisfied that in the majority of cases removal has been desirable.

Shortly after the Board had adopted these new rules for the standing of candidates for examinations, they reported rather more comprehensively than usual on the examination results obtained by their men. In their Report to the Senate of 23 October 1876 they state:

The whole number of students who have resided in the University under the supervision of the Board previously to this term is 203. Of these
28 have proceeded to at least the B.A. degree, remaining non-collegiate students (six of them having obtained places in Honours Triposes):

[1] Minutes, 4 December 1875.

36 have left the University without having completed the course for a degree:

84 have become members of the Colleges:

55 now remain on the list of non-collegiate undergraduates.

Of the whole number, 24 had previously been members of the Colleges, and of these 9 again entered Colleges.

Of the 84 students who by entering Colleges passed from under the supervision of the Board, 20 have obtained honourable distinctions in their Colleges or in the University; one has become a Fellow of a College.[1]

From information in the College Archives it has been possible to identify by name the 203 men to whom the Board refer,[2] and thus to follow through to their completion, or their abandonment, the courses of the migrants, and of those who at the time of this Report were still on the Board's roll of undergraduates. Of the 203 men who, at one time or another, had been under the Board's supervision before the beginning of the Michaelmas term 1876, 103 left for a college,[3] and of these 95 graduated. Of the 100 who did not join a college, 48 graduated. Of the total of 203, therefore, who during the first seven years of the non-collegiate system had at one time or another been under the supervision of the Board, 143 completed a degree course, the remainder having given it up, for whatever reason, or having failed in their final examination. The loss of so many of his most promising men was a source of growing anxiety to the Censor, who, shortly before the Board's statement to the University had unburdened himself in a Report of his own, describing the problem and doing what he could to suggest a solution to it.

The numbers of students [he writes] who have during the last three years passed from under your supervision by becoming members of Colleges, have been respectively 9, 21, 26, the last number including two who have migrated since the beginning of this term. It appears to me that during the last two years the numbers have been unduly large. Some of the students leave us for good reasons; in some cases, however, the reasons seem to be unsatisfactory. Persons who have undoubtedly found the pecuniary arrangements of the scheme more suitable to them than those of Colleges, have continued with us as long as they could without preventing their ultimate admission to a College, and then, without any change in their

---

[1] *University Reporter*, 1876–77, p. 60. The college Fellow was James Ward, elected at Trinity in 1875. He became Sc.D. in 1887, and Professor of Mental Philosophy and Logic in 1897.

[2] Register of Non-Collegiate Students No. 1, College Archives.

[3] No account is taken of a small number (9) of students who became non-collegiate after a period of residence as members of a college, and subsequently returned to a college, the same or another.

pecuniary circumstances having occurred, and without any inducement of superior instruction being to be gained by the change, have incurred the higher expenses of a College for the last two or three terms and for the degree, in order to secure, before going out into the world, a status which they were sure of finding universally known and recognized. Those who thus graduate as members of Colleges thenceforward move in the world outside of the University in that character; the scheme under which they have mainly resided loses its natural representatives in the places from which new students should come; and the degree lists contain but few of the names by which a more general attention to the existence of the scheme might be excited.

Even when these graduates are desirous of making known by personal effort the opportunity which the scheme affords to those whose circumstances hinder them from entering upon a College Course, they can do little to recommend it when in their own persons they have gone out of their natural course to exchange their connection with it for the ordinary position of College graduates, under the impression that that was necessary to success in the world. Without entering into undesirable details, I cannot prove that there is a solid foundation for my opinion, that this desire to shake off a connection which may possibly be challenged is the chief motive, in many cases, for migration; but I have the testimony both of some who have gone and of some who have remained to the same effect. Without a wish to discourage the natural and honest desire to join a college for the sake of its real advantages, I regret that the stream of fashion has during the last two years set so strongly in that direction as to remove some who, I think, ought not to have gone, and to unsettle some who, after all, have remained with us. I have some reason to think that the stream will not be so strong in the coming year; but of this I cannot speak with confidence.

These observations may justify my suggesting that it would be in my opinion most useful if exhibitions of moderate value could be provided, to be awarded for proficiency in the subjects on which the Previous and General Examinations directly bear. If, for example, in each year one or two such exhibitions were offered for competition to candidates, who, already being non-collegiate students, had passed the Previous Examination and either the Additional Subjects Examination, or the General Examination, the questions set being a little more difficult or advanced than those of the examinations already passed, but nearly confined to the same subjects, it seems likely that the offer of such rewards on these terms might afford a stimulus which would be felt by a fair proportion of the students during the first one or two years of their time of residence; and after they were awarded, they might probably have a further value in fixing as non-collegiate students to the time of the degree (with a position recognized as not less honourable than that of mere members/pensioners of Colleges) men of energy and character whose success would give weight to their example. The importance generally attributed to exhibitions offered for competition (beyond their direct value) leads me to think that any such offered to Non-Collegiate Students might recommend the scheme to popular opinion; and if the exhibitions were small in value, their smallness would be compensated for by their being offered for subjects not specially requiring an expensive previous training, as well as by their being offered to men whose necessary expenses are so small.

Even if such exhibitions were provided only for a short term of years, their indirect effects might be considerable. I do not know how to find donors of sufficient funds, but if the Board were able to provide enough from other sources to give fair continuity to a system of moderate exhibitions of this kind, I am assured that a friend of mine would be ready to contribute thirty pounds a year for at least five years. This would be available either for exhibitions, or for the expenses of the examination.[1]

The disabilities which the Board felt themselves to be suffering were the subject of direct representation to the Cambridge Commissioners appointed under the Universities of Oxford and Cambridge Act of 1877. In February 1878 the Secretaries to the commission sent to the Vice-Chancellor a statement of the main University purposes for which, in the Commissioners' views, provision would need to be made, and made it plain that one of the sources of the necessary funds would be contributions made by the colleges from their revenues. The Commissioners included in their list of requirements 'Additional buildings for museums, laboratories, libraries, lecture rooms and other rooms for University business'.[2] Under the Act the University and the colleges were given until the end of 1878 to amend their statutes, if they chose to do so in the light of its provisions, and thereafter any necessary statutes were to be framed by the Commissioners themselves.

It seems reasonable to suppose that the Censor had concluded that accommodation for non-collegiate students might be regarded as coming under the heading of 'other rooms for University business' to which the Commissioners' letter had referred; and it may well be that he had also heard that the Oxford Commissioners had generous proposals in mind for the benefit of the unattached students there.[3] He would cer-

---

[1] Censor's Report to the Non-Collegiate Students Board 6 June 1876, College Archives. For a casual reference from a 'receiving' college, see G. G. Coulton, *Fourscore Years* (C.U.P., 1943), p. 111. An undergraduate at St Catharine's from 1877 to 1881, Dr Coulton writes: '...the College had in my time from 50 to 52 undergraduates. A notable proportion had begun as non-collegiate students, whom our tutors had admitted for their last year to jump off from the College'.

[2] *University Reporter*, 1877–88, p. 350.

[3] The University of Oxford was to provide an annual sum of £400 as a contribution towards the stipend of the Censor (or Censors), and £600 for tuition and scholarships or exhibitions for the students. Further, the University, as soon as its resources should permit, was to make available not less than £7,000 for offices, a library, and other buildings.

tainly know that by the end of 1878 there had been no fresh statutory provision by the University for its non-collegiate students, and when after nearly two more years he had heard nothing of any action by the Commissioners he did what he could to bring the matter to a head, and consulted the Board, whose minute reads:

> Mr Somerset mentioned that he had on November 25th asked a question of one of the University Commissioners on the omission of any Statutes for Non-collegiate Students from the Statutes proposed by the Commissioners for the University, and had been advised to communicate at once with the Secretary to the Commissioners. He therefore wrote to Mr Browne, the Secretary, expressing the desire of some members of the Board that the attention of the Commissioners should be invited to the omission, and on November 27th received a reply on the part of the Commissioners, suggesting that the Board should at its meeting today frame a Representation to the Commissioners, setting forth the wishes of the Board, and adding that the Commissioners would be able to consider such a Representation in the course of this week. After some consideration a draft Representation was agreed to, and it was understood that, after it had been revised by Mr Somerset, it should be signed on behalf of the Board by Mr Gunson, Deputy Chairman, and Mr Somerset, and forwarded to the Secretary of the Commissioners.[1]

The 'Representation', dated 30 November 1880 and reproduced below, was duly sent; but it appears to have had no effect, for there is no further reference to it in the minutes of the Board; and there was certainly no alteration of the University Statute for Non-Collegiate Students. It summarizes the principal events of the earliest years of the scheme, draws attention to the difficulties encountered by those responsible for its working, makes suggestions for their alleviation, and pays tribute where tribute is due.

> Memorial from the Board for Admitting and Superintending Non-Collegiate Students to the Cambridge University Commissioners
> November 30th 1880
> *A Statute* was confirmed by order of Her Majesty in Council, May 13, 1869, to enable the University to admit as Students, matriculate, and confer Degrees on, persons who may not be members of any College or Hall or of any Hostel. *A Scheme* had already been provisionally sanctioned by Grace of the Senate, dated March 13, 1869, providing for the admission of such students, and *this Board* was constituted on May 27, 1869, and shortly afterwards framed Regulations and appointed an officer under the designation of Censor. On the 22nd of April, 1873, the Board reported to the Senate

[1] Minutes, 30 November 1880.

the result of their work till then, and on their recommendation the Scheme was made permanent.

The progress made in later years has not disappointed the expectation on the ground of which the Board recommended that the Scheme should be made permanent. The numbers of undergraduate Students resident in the University under the care of the Board in the several terms since their work began are shewn in the following table:

	LENT	EASTER	MICHAELMAS
1869	–	–	8
1870	17	20	19
1871	22	20	23
1872	26	25	43
1873	43	40	55
1874	61	60	65
1875	66	60	60
1876	58	58	75
1877	80	72	98
1878	100	94	120
1879	117	119	154
1880	149	143	166

In the later years these numbers included such as were resident at an institution which since it has occupied its own building has borne the name of Cavendish College. Excluding the students thus living together, the remaining numbers were, in the several terms:

1873	–	–	54
1874	58	56	62
1875	63	57	56
1876	52	52	66
1877	63	57	79
1878	81	74	94
1879	86	88	99
1880	94	91	93

The number of students admitted in the several years bears a higher proportion to the total number in residence than in the University generally. This is chiefly due to the migration of a large proportion of the Students into Colleges before the end of their course, a migration not compensated by any considerable number coming from the Colleges. The whole number of the students admitted by the Board who have resided in the University under its care is 557. Of these only 41 had previously kept any residence, 36 in Colleges at Cambridge and 5 at the University of Oxford. Of the whole number, 223 have passed from the care of the Board to enter Colleges (including 20 out of the 41 just mentioned); 75 have graduated as Non-Collegiate Students; 79 have left the University without graduating; 4 have died; and the remainder (176) are still on the list of the undergraduates under the care of the Board. The majority of the Students are persons of the ordinary age of College undergraduates and live in licensed Lodgings; in almost every case they enter the University in this way for the sake of greater economy, and many of those who have afterwards entered Colleges, as well as of those who have remained to graduate as Non-Collegiate Students, have declared that they would not have ventured to enter the University originally in any other way. From returns collected on several occasions by the Censor it has appeared likely that the average expenditure of these students in Cambridge (including private tuition, where it has been had, and vacation residence in a few cases, but not clothes, travelling, or cost of living elsewhere in vacations) was between £70 and £80 a year, while a few scarcely exceeded £50 a year. The Board has addressed Reports to the Senate, expressing its satisfaction with the general conduct of its students, and its conviction that the Scheme which it administers provides a safe and convenient mode of residence in the University for a considerable class. The degree of success already attained has not cost much to the University in the way of direct contributions. During the first two years deficiencies, together amounting to £37.9s.6d. were made up from the University Chest, and in 1874 a grant of £50 was made by Grace of the Senate in aid of the formation of a small library for the use of the Students; otherwise the only pecuniary help afforded by the University has consisted in its receiving from these Students the same matriculation fee as from Sizars of Colleges. No accommodation has been provided in any University building for the business of the Board. For several years the Censor made such provision as he could out of a gross income assigned to him of £100 per annum; more lately the Board has been able, while increasing the stipend of its officer, and providing for him some assistance, to hire also rooms in a private house which have been tolerably convenient for temporary use; but they do not afford opportunity for assembling the majority of the students at any one time, and if regular Lectures or frequent Examinations were instituted by the Board they must be held elsewhere, or the students be shut out to an inconvenient extent from their present use of the reading room and library. The Board think it unsuitable that they should permanently depend on the use of such hired rooms for carrying on the business entrusted to them by the University; and their own income from fees, diminished as this is likely to be by the withdrawal of the Students of Cavendish College from their connection with the Board, seems insufficient to enable them to provide an adequate building for themselves.

At present, besides the instruction provided by the University itself, and the Inter-Collegiate Lectures offered by many of the Colleges, chiefly in subjects of Honours Examinations to the whole University, the Board has been enabled by the special kindness of several Colleges to send its students to Lectures on the more elementary branches of University Study. Foremost in giving this help is Christ's College, which has for very small fees admitted these students to almost all its Lectures; and Emmanuel College has also given considerable assistance in this way. For many students these Lectures have been suitable and sufficient; but if the Board had the means it might with advantage establish at least some elementary Lectures and more systematic examinations.

The only College Emoluments now open to the competition of Non-Collegiate Students, as such, are Scholarships at Trinity College restricted to Moral Sciences and certain Scholarships at Downing College. In Natural Sciences Scholarships at Trinity and Christ's Colleges, which were more than once gained by Non-Collegiate Students are now closed. The Company of Clothworkers in the City of London gives annually by open competition one Exhibition of £52.10s. a year for three years, to be held by an Unattached Student of the University of Oxford or a Non-Collegiate Student of this University, and recently every student has preferred Cambridge. The same Company now gives annually an Exhibition for three years of £30 a year to a Non-Collegiate Student of Cambridge nominated by the Censor with the approval of the Board.[1] There are no other special emoluments for such students.

Under these circumstances the Board desire to express to the Commissioners their opinion that it would be advantageous that a new Statute should be framed for the University, empowering it

(1) to admit as students, matriculate and confer Degrees on persons who may not be members of any College or Hall, or of any Hostel, as is provided in the present Statute; and

(2) to accept endowments to be applied in providing a suitable building or in payment of Teachers or other officers, or in establishing small Exhibitions or Scholarships for such students.

They also venture to suggest that a College Statute might empower the Governing Body of each College to make gifts to the University for the purposes above mentioned, if it should seem fit to them to do so, without prejudice to other interests provided for in the Statutes.

Signed on behalf of the Board

W. M. Gunson, Deputy Chairman

R. B. Somerset, Censor[2]

The Memorial tells how nearly half of the men matriculated by the Board before the end of 1880 had gone on to become members of colleges; but the subsequent careers of these men are not on this account

---

[1]　A modification of the original system of awards.

[2]　College Archives. The Memorial is copied in Mr Somerset's hand at the end of the book of his Reports to the Board for 1869–81. The original, which has also been kept, was returned to Mr Somerset's successor, with a letter dated 18 September 1886, by the Rev. G. F. Browne, secretary to the Commissioners. 'Long ago', he writes, 'Somerset asked if he could have the representation made to the Commissioners by your Board. In making a clearance, I have found it. It is quite at your service, or his, to do what you like with.'

irrelevant to any assessment of the success of the non-collegiate scheme as a whole in its earliest years.

It may be assumed that, with very few exceptions, the men who entered the University as non-collegiate students did so either because they believed that they could not afford the expense of college membership, or because they could not get into a college. If they had not come to Cambridge under the scheme, they would not have come at all. It is therefore legitimate to take into account not only the records of those who graduated as non-collegiate students, but also of those who, having contrived to get to the University as such, then discovered ways of demonstrating at closer quarters, by their academic performance (or other prowess), their worthiness of acceptance by a college, and, on occasion, their suitability for college awards. Whereas of the men admitted by Mr Somerset between 1869 and 1881, no more than two were placed in the first class in a Tripos examination while they were still non-collegiate students,[1] there were twenty, in one or more examinations, among those who had been admitted to a college. Nor was this early success belied in the men's subsequent careers. Of twenty-eight of Mr Somerset's migrants (if eight are included who, for whatever reason, were not first class Tripos men) twelve occupied posts of professorial rank in Universities or comparable institutions; thirteen proceeded to Cambridge doctorates in Law, Science, Letters, or Music; eight were elected to the Royal Society, and one to the British Academy. Pre-eminent was Charles Scott Sherrington, who came into residence from Ipswich School in 1879, and kept three terms as a non-collegiate student before his admission to Caius College in October 1880. In the fullness of time he was to be Professor of Physiology at Liverpool, and then at Oxford, President of the Royal Society from 1920 to 1925, in 1924 a member of the Order of Merit, and Nobel Prizeman in Medicine and Physiology in 1932.

Particulars of the distinctions gained by this group of men are given below.

Class I in Tripos Examinations

Ambridge, F. J.	Joh.	M.S. 1874
Bellars, William	Trin.	M.S. 1879
Brough, Joseph	Down.	M.S. 1880; Law 1881
Carnegie, C. E.	Cai.	N.S.I 1884; II 1886
Evans, C. S.	Cla.	N.S.I 1882; II 1883
Fenton, H. J. H.	Chr.	N.S.I 1877
Hall, Leonard	Joh.	Sixteenth Wrangler 1881
Hickson, S. J.	Down.	N.S.I 1881

---

[1] R. H. Harris (Theology, 1880); E. W. Reid (Natural Sciences I, 1882).

Class I in Tripos Examinations (continued)

Little, T. S.	Trin.	Law & History 1872
Morrison, J. T. J.	Chr.	N.S.I 1882
Reid, E. W.	Non-Coll.	N.S.I 1882; H. Cav. N.S.II 1883
Ryan, John	King's	N.S.I 1882; II 1883
Schneider, G.A.S.	Cai.	Theol. 1882
Scott, Alexander	Trin.	N.S. 1878
Sherrington, C. S.	Cai.	N.S.I 1881; II 1883
Small, E. W.	Chr.	N.S.I 1882; II 1883
Ward, H. M.	Chr.	N.S. 1879
Ward, James	Trin.	M.S. 1874
Williams, Thomas	Joh.	Theol. 1878
Winter, W. H.	Cla.	Twenty-sixth Wrangler 1882

Professors (and the like)

Bose, J. C.	Chr.	Physical Science, Presidency College, Calcutta
Barclay Smith, Edward	Down.	Anatomy, London
Bridge, T. W.	Trin.	Botany and Zoology, Birmingham
Brough		Political Economy, Univ. Coll. of North Wales, Aberystwyth
Hickson, S. J.		Zoology, Manchester
Morrison, J. T. J.		Forensic Medicine, Birmingham
Reid, E. W.	Down.	Physiology, Univ. Coll. of Dundee
Ryan, John		Mechanics and Engineering, Univ. Coll. of Bristol
Scott, Alexander	Pet.	Director Scientific Research, British Museum
Sherrington, C. S.		Physiology, Liverpool, and Oxford
Ward, H. M.		Botany, Cambridge
Ward, James		Mental Philosophy and Logic, Cambridge

Cambridge Doctorates

LL.D.	Brough		1891
	Sewell, J. T. B.	Down.	1897
	Sydenham Jones, T. R.	Joh.	1897
	Whittaker, C. D.	Sid.	1904
Sc.D.	Bridge		1896
	Fenton		1906
	Reid	Down.	1905
	Scott		1907
	Sherrington		1904
	Ward, H. M.		1892
	Ward, James		1887
Litt.D.	Budge, E. A. T. W.	Chr.	1891
Mus.D.	Somervell, Arthur	King's	1904

Fellows of the Royal Society

Bose	1920
Bridge	1903
Fenton	1899
Hickson	1895
Reid	1898
Scott	1898
Sherrington	1893
Ward, H. M.	1888

Fellow of the British Academy*

Ward, James	1902

*Founded in 1901

Of the above, who all came first to the University as non-collegiate students, Fenton, Sherrington, and Hickson (whose son was among the earliest of the Fellows of Fitzwilliam House in 1963) were elected Honorary Fellows of their colleges. Bose (1917), Budge (1920), and Somervell (1929) were knighted, and Sherrington (1922) was made G.B.E.[1]

Not included in this talented group – he did not even take a Tripos, nor did he migrate – the name of George Turner comes nevertheless to mind as an outstanding example of the sort of man for whom entry to the University was made possible by the non-collegiate scheme. Already medically qualified (L.R.C.S., M.R.C.P.) he came in search of a Cambridge medical degree. 'I was 34 years old when I entered at Cambridge;' he wrote some years afterwards, 'I had been in practice for years, was the Father of a family and had lost my wife, so my University life was rather different from that of the ordinary run of students. I was then Medical Officer of Health for the Combined Districts of Herts and Essex, and lectured on Hygiene at Guy's. I was living at Broxbourne, and used to catch the 10.10 train, get to Cambridge, run to my rooms, run a mile to sign the book in Trumpington Street, get my breakfast, catch the 8.20 train to my district... I could not keep my terms regularly; some times only one in twelve months, and after I had passed all the examinations I still had four terms to keep. It was most annoying.'

In 1895 Turner was appointed Medical Officer of Health of Cape Colony, and in 1901 of the Transvaal, but his most notable achievements were in fields far outside his official duties – in the Rinderpest Research Station at Kimberley, as adviser on sanitation to the British Army in the South African War, and at the Pretoria Leper Asylum. In

[1] I am indebted to Dr S. G. Fleet, of Downing College, for drawing my attention to Sir Charles Sherrington's early non-collegiate membership of the University. For Fenton, Scott, and Ryan, who began their Cambridge careers as Clothworkers' Exhibitioners, see also pp. 541–2.

all three he did work of high distinction and the greatest practical value, until his retirement in 1908, when he returned to the United Kingdom to continue his search for a cure for leprosy; and after three or four years discovered that he had contracted the disease. He died in 1915, but some two years previously his work was recognized by the offer of a knighthood, made, it was said, on the personal initiative of the King.[1]

Shortly after the submission of their Memorial, the Non-Collegiate Students Board received from Mr Somerset a letter, dated 17 January, 1881, in which, as he said, he desired to explain to them the circumstances which compelled him to seek leave of absence for the remainder of the Lent term, and suggested, in the event of his application being approved, that Mr Howard, who as Assistant Censor had signed *exeats* in December and had made himself responsible for correspondence during the Christmas vacation, should assume the whole of the Censor's duties, except those relating to finance and the certification of residence, which would be undertaken by Mr Rose (a member of the Board). The Board agreed, and also appointed Mr Howard to be Deputy Censor, at a stipend of £75, for a period which they clearly expected to include the Easter vacation. The shortness of the notice given to the Board suggests that Mr Somerset's application for leave of absence had been made for reasons of health, and it appears that the term's rest effected no permanent improvement, for on 11 October he submitted his resignation from the censorship, specifically on health grounds. The Board accepted the resignation, to take effect as soon as a successor could be appointed, and directed their Chairman to convey to Mr Somerset the following resolution:

> In accepting Mr Somerset's resignation the Board desire to place on record their regret for the cause which has necessitated his retirement and their grateful sense of his services. They wish here to recognise that it is due to his discretion and zeal as Censor from the commencement of the operation of the 'Scheme for Non-Collegiate Students' that this Scheme has been brought to its present satisfactory footing, and to express further their feeling that whilst through his retirement the Board lose the services of a valued Officer their students will have to regret the loss of a judicious, kind and considerate friend.[2]

The Board then resolved that Mr Howard should be asked to be Deputy Censor for the term, Mr Somerset being relieved of all respon-

---

[1] For a fuller note on the career of Sir George Turner, entitled 'Another Father Damien', see *Journal*, 1975, pp. 15–21.

[2] Minutes, 11 October 1881.

sibility, and agreed that a notice of the vacancy should be sent to all persons on the Electoral Roll, to *The Times*, and the *University Reporter*, in the following terms:

> The Board for admitting and superintending Non-Collegiate Students are about to elect a Censor in the place of the Rev. R. B. Somerset, who has signified his intention of resigning his office. The appointment will be in the first instance for one year and may be renewed from year to year. The person elected will be expected to enter upon his duties at the end of the present term. The duties of the Censor are generally similar in kind to the duties of a College Tutor. The Board offer for the first year a stipend of £250.
>
> Candidates for the office, who must be graduates of the University of M.A. standing at least, are requested to send their names to the Chairman of the Non-Collegiate Students Board, Emmanuel College Lodge, on or before Friday, October the twenty-first.[1]

The closing date for the receipt of applications, and the date on which a new Censor was to take up his duties, suggest not only that the Board were anxious to avoid delay, but that some members, at least, had in mind a candidate whom they thought to be not only suitable but quickly available.

Thirteen applications were received; and at a meeting held on 24 October in the Lodge of Emmanuel College, attended by eight members of the Board, Mr Howard (Assistant Censor since 1877) was elected Censor for one year from the end of the term.[2] Born in Grantchester on 6 December 1843, he went from St Paul's School to Trinity College as Sub-sizar in 1862, and was twenty-sixth Wrangler in 1866. He held a curacy in Grantchester for some years until 1875. Appointed Chaplain of Trinity College in 1873, he served the University as Secretary of the Lodging-Houses Syndicate, and as Additional Pro-Proctor for four years from 1878, when that office was created at least in part on account of the greatly increased number of undergraduates living in licensed lodgings.[3]

---

[1] *University Reporter*, 1881–82, p. 48.

[2] In the University Archives (Camb. Univ. Reg. 60,31) is a copy of a communication to members of the Board, giving the names of the applicants, with a note that of seven votes cast (Mr Somerset presumably abstained) four were for Mr Howard, and three for Mr Oscar Browning, of King's College.

There are conflicting accounts of the effective date of Mr Howard's appointment. The Board's notice of the vacancy expects the person appointed to enter upon his duties 'at the end of the present term'; on 24 October they announce his appointment from that day; and, some years later, a memorial medallion (see p. 89) describes him as Censor from 1882 to 1889.

[3] Report of the Proctorial Syndicate, dated 17 May 1878. *University Reporter*, 1877–78, p. 538.

Mr Somerset's membership of the Board (he had first been elected in 1869, before he became Censor) continued until 22 January 1887, and he was its Deputy Chairman for three years from 5 December 1883. Elected to fill a casual vacancy in February 1889, he was again Deputy Chairman from January 1890, and remained a member until his death on 23 March 1891. As first Censor of the non-collegiate students his success in introducing and administering a scheme which, as the Board had affirmed in their Representation, was providing a 'safe and convenient mode of residence in the University for a considerable class', had already shown how groundless were the fears of many who had professed uneasiness at the prospect of the introduction into the University of a body of men who, on the one hand, would lack the privileges of college membership, and, on the other, would not be subject to college discipline.

CHAPTER III

A Local Habitation and the Name

Expansion of courses of instruction and of teaching staff – need for better accommodation – possible building sites – purchase by University of 31 and 32 Trumpington
Street – Fitzwilliam Hall. Persistent ill health of Censor – his death (11 December
1888). Appointment of T. F. C. Huddleston, of King's College. Death of first Censor.
Report of Board on alterations to Fitzwilliam Hall – amended and approved 8 May
1890 – appeal for funds – alterations completed 1892 – debt to University extinguished 1903. Chapel services. Indifferent success of measures to reduce migration.
Censor's failing eyesight and resignation – appointment (1907) of W. F. Reddaway,
of King's College – his appreciation of Huddleston's work.

During Mr Howard's tenure the Board took two important decisions
with the intention of improving the arrangements made for their men:
they resolved to extend the courses of instruction available to them by
the creation of lectureships, and to take active measures to improve the
accommodation at the disposal of students and staff. The cost of the
improved arrangements for teaching was met, as the cost of previous
small improvements had been met, out of recurrent income, augmented for a time at least by the fees of larger numbers of undergraduates. The Board's plans for better accommodation, however, mark the
beginning of a more venturesome policy, and a readiness to incur expenditure of a different order; but it is fair to remember that it would
not have been possible for them to think in these terms without Mr
Somerset's prudent management in the earliest years of the scheme. In
Mr Howard's and Mr Huddleston's time the Board, with some years of
successful experience behind them, were no longer content to live
from hand to mouth on exiguous annual balances; and they sought to
implement their bolder plans by appealing to the liberality of private
individuals, and by pressing their claims for help, whether by way of
loans or of outright grants, from the University. Henceforward policy
and finance became interdependent, for the Board had not only to plan
for the health of the student body, but also to persuade potential benefactors that their plans were worthy of support.

In the matter of teaching the Board decided that in each of the Lent
and Easter terms 1885 four courses of lectures should be given for Parts
I and II of the Previous Examination, and for the Mathematical and
Classical Parts of the General Examination, respectively. Three lectures weekly would be given for each course; the fee for a course

would be ten shillings, and for each course the lecturer would receive a fee of £15, with a capitation payment of five shillings.[1] Thereupon the Board appointed Mr Christopher Geldard, of Trinity College, lecturer in Mathematics, and Mr T. F. C. Huddleston of King's College, lecturer in Classics.[2] The experiment was successful, for both were reappointed annually until other duties prevented them from continuing. In 1890 Mr Huddleston was succeeded by Mr E. S. Shuckburgh, of Emmanuel College, selected from ten applicants.[3] Mr Shuckburgh held his lectureship until he died in 1906, when he was followed by Mr W. W. Walker, then lately a Fellow of Christ's.[4] Mr Geldard resigned in the Michaelmas term 1893, on becoming an inspector under the Science and Art Department of the Education Office, and was followed by Mr W. G. Bell, Fellow of Trinity Hall, and also at the time a member of the Non-Collegiate Students Board, whose post is described in the Board's minutes as that of 'Lecturer in Mathematics and Paley's *Evidences*'.[5] In the Easter term 1893 the Board had also appointed, provisionally, a lecturer in History. 'It was agreed', says the minute, 'that in the event of his obtaining a first or second class in the Historical Tripos, Mr J. H. B. Masterman, Scholar of St John's College, be invited to lecture for one year for the Board in history, at a stipend not exceeding £25 a year, provided he shall occupy rooms in the Building on such terms as may be approved by the Chairman and Censor.' Mr Masterman got his first, and took up the appointment.[6] He had kept three terms as a non-collegiate student, and had won the Chancellor's

1   Minutes, 6 December 1884. The fee was increased to 15s. in the Michaelmas term 1886.
2   *Ibid.*
3   *Ibid.*, 12 March 1890. See also *University Reporter*, 1889–90, p. 549.
4   Minutes, 11 October 1906. See also *University Reporter*, 1893–94, p. 104.
5   Minutes, 12 March 1894. See also *University Reporter*, 1893–94, p. 557.
      Eighth Wrangler in 1879, and thenceforth until his death in 1925 Fellow of Trinity Hall, and Assistant Tutor there from 1884 until 1920, Bell retained his non-collegiate lectureship until he left Cambridge in 1921 (although on his re-appointment from time to time there was no further mention of Paley's *Evidences*). A member of the Society of Friends, and known, according to Venn, as a supporter of unpopular causes, he was to enter very fully into the corporate life of the non-collegiate students, and was much in demand on their various social occasions. He was President of the Amalgamated Clubs for more than twenty-five years, was a trustee of the Clubs, and was one of three members of the teaching staff who, in a memorandum addressed to the Royal Commission of 1919, urged that some change should be made in the negative title of their non-collegiate body recognizing its predominantly collegiate character.
      In 1965 Bell's son Alan, who had taken his B.A. degree as a non-collegiate student in 1922, commissioned from Mr Kenneth Green a portrait in oils, done from a photograph, and presented it to Fitzwilliam House, where it now hangs in the Gaskoin Room in the Huntingdon Road buildings.
6   Minutes, 7 June 1893. See also *University Reporter*, 1893–94, p. 2.

medal for English Verse, before going to St John's at Michaelmas 1891. This appointment also was successful, for it was renewed for the year 1894/95, at double the stipend.[1] When, after three years as Lecturer, Mr Masterman left Cambridge, the Board advertised for a 'Lecturer in History and Essay Writing'; and their choice, from five applicants, of W. F. Reddaway, of King's College,[2] was to exercise an influence on the development of the whole non-collegiate institution that they could not then have foreseen.

This teaching staff was enlarged in the Michaelmas term 1901, when the Rev. T. W. Crafer, of Jesus College, was invited to supervise in theology, at an annual stipend of £25, guaranteed by the Board's Chairman (Mr Walter Durnford, of King's) and Mr T. C. Fitzpatrick, then of Christ's College. The renewal of the appointment, in circumstances of considerable financial difficulty, attributable in the opinion of the Censor to the South African War, was made possible by the generosity of the Rev. H. J. Carter of Duxford, who provided Mr Crafer's stipend for two further years, after which the Board were able to find it for themselves, and in 1906 to increase it to £40.[3]

On 5 December 1883 the Board, who had not reported to the Senate since 1878, had approved a more than usually comprehensive account of the progress of the non-collegiate scheme, particularly since 1875, and one of the matters to which they drew the Senate's attention was the serious disadvantage they suffered from the inadequacy of their premises.

> Since the Spring of 1874 [runs the Report] the Board has hired an office (consisting till 1880 of three, since then of four, rooms in Trumpington Street), and it has secured to itself the right of continuing its tenure till Midsummer 1886. These rooms cannot be used together for any single gathering, and some of them are inconveniently small. Even now, therefore, the limits of accommodation leave very imperfect opportunities of dealing with the students as a body. It is important to remember that the Board requires its students to conform to rules of residence as strict as Colleges generally impose on their students, and that it calls on each student to record his name at the Censor's office on five days of each week. If

---

[1] Minutes, 1 June 1894. In the following year lack of money made it necessary to reduce the stipend. (Report of the Non-Collegiate Students Board, dated 2 May 1896 – *University Reporter*, 1895–96, p. 698).

[2] Minutes, 19 November 1896. See also *University Reporter*, 1896–97, pp. 149,233.

[3] Minutes, 11 October 1901, 2 June 1903, 1 June 1906. See also *University Reporter*, 1901–02, p. 241.

Henry James Carter, of Clare College (Scholar). B.A. 1855. Vicar of St John's, Duxford, 1865–77; Rector of St Peter's with St John's, Duxford, from 1877 until his death on 24 April 1904. See also pp. 95,441.

public lectures were to be provided by the Board, or simultaneous examinations to be held, an enlarged and more convenient domicile would become imperatively necessary. The occupation of some University building
for such purposes would have the advantage of contributing to the more
distinct recognition of the status of Non-collegiate Students as members of
the University.[1]

On 10 February 1885 the Board appointed Mr Somerset, Mr Rose,
Mr Howard and Mr Huddleston as a committee to report upon sites
available for a permanent building,[2] and at a meeting on 19 May they
told the Board that after finding that various freehold sites could not be
obtained they had reason to believe that Downing College would be
willing to let a site on Regent Street on a ninety-nine year lease. The
Board agreed that an approach should be made to the College with a
view to securing the lease of a site of not less than 2,500 square feet,
for the erection of a building at a cost of not less than £2,500. On 5
November the Board received from the Bursar a reply, dated 4 August,
to the effect that the College after a long discussion on the previous
day, had decided that it did not wish to entertain the proposal.[3] The
committee were asked to make further enquiries, and on 4 May 1886
they reported that they had inspected a site at 26 Regent Street, but
that the owner (Miss Knightley) did not wish to sell, and that in any
event the area was not large enough.[4]

At the beginning of the following Michaelmas term the Censor reported the offer of nos. 18–22 in Corn Exchange Street for £2,400, but
added that this site also was unsatisfactory,[5] and the Board then resolved to ascertain whether the University would be willing to let 'one
or more of their houses on St Andrew's Hill'. On 1 November they
heard that their committee had consulted one or two members of the
Council of the Senate, who had seemed to favour the idea, but that before the committee had taken any further action the Censor had re-

---

[1] *University Reporter* 1883–84, p. 333.
[2] Minutes, 10 February 1885. Alfred Rose, Fellow and Bursar of Emmanuel College, was first
appointed to the Board in November 1878. See also p. 107.
[3] *Ibid.*, 19 May and 5 November 1885. From information supplied by the Bursar of Downing
College (Dr S. G. Fleet), it appears that the building site under discussion (with, approximately, a frontage of 54 feet, and a depth of 46 feet) is now occupied by premises numbered 56–62 (even numbers).
[4] This property, numbered 27 in successive (Spalding's) Directories, was in the neighbourhood of premises now numbered 78 and 80.
[5] Minutes, 16 October 1886. It must have been very unsatisfactory. The properties, in a congested area dominated by the recently erected Corn Exchange, were on the eastern side of
the narrow Corn Exchange Street (formerly Slaughter House Lane) about three quarters of
the way from Wheeler Street, where the numbering began, to St Andrew's Hill.

ceived a letter from Mr George Peck,[1] of 30 Trumpington Street; and
the story of the Board's negotiations with Mr Peck is told in their
Report, of 19 November 1886, addressed to the Senate:

> Since the Lent Term, 1874, the Board has rented rooms at 31, Trump-
> ington Street for the use of the Censor and of the Students, and in 1880 a
> room was built adjoining one of the others for use as a Students' Library.
> The tenure of these rooms has been by successive agreements each for
> three years, the last of which terminated at Midsummer, 1886. The situa-
> tion has always been found convenient, but the Board has already pointed
> out to the Senate, in a Report dated December 5, 1883, its need of en-
> larged accommodation.
>
> Repeated endeavours to find a convenient site elsewhere for the erection
> of suitable offices have been hitherto unsuccessful. But Mr G. Peck, the
> owner of Nos. 30, 31, 32, Trumpington Street, has offered to sell to the
> Board for the sum of three thousand pounds the houses Nos. 31 and 32, in
> the former of which the rooms now rented by the Board are contained. At
> the request of the Board, Messrs Nockolds and King, Estate Agents, of
> Saffron Walden, have inspected the property, and have recommended the
> purchase on a further condition which Mr Peck has since accepted. The
> offer thus amended includes the property in a Warehouse at the back of
> No. 31 which is used by Mr Peck, and the Library room above it, subject to
> a proviso that the tenancy of the Warehouse shall be assured to him at a
> nominal rent, so long as the adjoining property, now belonging to and
> occupied by him, is occupied or owned by any members of his family.
>
> The property is Freehold and there is no Land-tax. The area is about
> 3500 superficial feet, and the frontage to Trumpington Street is 65 ft. 10 in.
> The Buildings are for the most part in fair external repair. Considerable
> alteration would be needed eventually to adapt the interior arrangements
> of the space to the uses of the Board, but, for the present, comparatively
> small changes would add materially to the convenience afforded in the
> rooms now occupied, while rents would still accrue from the remainder of
> the premises. The tenancies are annual and the total Rent of the property,
> including the rooms occupied by the Board, is £167 per annum.
>
> The Board is able to make use of £1500 Exchequer Bills and £500 Leeds
> Corporation 3½ per cent. Stock, which it has acquired by investing sums
> saved out of its Receipts in past years. It is understood that there are legal
> difficulties in the way of raising part of the purchase money by mortgage,
> and therefore the Board, having regard to the extreme importance of per-
> manently securing this property which is so admirably situated for its pur-
> poses, suggests that the remaining £1000 should be lent by the University
> to the Board at a moderate rate of interest. It will not be necessary to com-
> plete the purchase till Midsummer, 1887, and the Board could use tempo-

---

[1] For Mr Peck's letter, dated 26 October, see Minutes, 1 November, 1886.

rarily £500 from the Caution Money in its hands, but it would be desirable that this should be replaced at the end of one year. It would be sufficient therefore if the University were to provide £500 at Midsummer, 1887, and £500 at Midsummer, 1888.

The Board therefore recommends:

1. That the Common Seal of the University be affixed to Articles of Agreement for the purchase from Mr G. Peck, at the price of £3000, of premises in Trumpington Street.

2. That for the purpose of enabling the Board to effect the purchase, the University should lend to the Board £500 at Midsummer, 1887, and £500 at Midsummer, 1888, and that the Board should pay interest to the Chest at the rate of 3½ per cent. per annum.[1]

On 16 November the Board had given instructions for a draft of their Report to be communicated to the Financial Board of the University, and after correspondence between the Secretary of that Board, the Vice-Chancellor, the Secretary of the Local Examinations and Lectures Syndicate and the Censor, it was agreed that as the University had no funds available from which a loan might be made to the Board, but was not unwilling to help in any way possible, two Graces should be submitted to the Senate on 10 February 1887; the first for the approval of the recommendations contained in the Board's Report of 19 November (as amended, see below); the second to authorize the Syndicate to advance to the University a similar capital sum, at the same rate of interest and subject to the same rate of repayment as the University's loan to the Board.[2] On 26 January the Vice-Chancellor, in informing the Censor of this arrangement, suggested that the Board should now 'complete' its Report by the inclusion of a reference to the repayment of capital, and on 29 January the Board approved an amended Report in which they added to their second recommendation the words 'and should repay the capital sum by annual instalments of not less than £50, the first instalment being paid at Midsummer 1889'.

The Report came up for discussion by the Senate on 3 February.[3] Mr Mayo, of Trinity College, would have liked the proposed purchase to include all three houses. He thought that the prospect of the Fitzwilliam Museum would be much improved if the corner of 30 Trumpington Street were rounded off. Mr Hill, of St John's, who had been a member of the Board from 1881 to 1884, did not agree that the situation of the house was very convenient. Members of the Board from his

1   University Reporter, 1886–87, p. 236.
2   Minutes, 29 January 1887, and University Reporter, 1886–87, p. 380.
3   University Reporter, 1886–87, p. 419.

end of the town found it a long way to come. Mr R. T. Wright, of Christ's College, raised a point of more substance in asking whether it was intended that the purchase should be made by the Non-collegiate Students Board; if so, he wondered whether they were able to hold real property. From the reference in the Grace to the affixing of the seal of the University, he supposed the purchase would be made by the University, and that the Board 'for the future would be of the nature of tenants of the University'. He thought this should be made clear in the Report, and the Master of Peterhouse (Dr Porter) agreed. The point was not pursued, possibly because the Vice-Chancellor, in his letter to the Censor of 26 January, had already written 'You will, of course, understand that when your purchase is made it will vest in the Chancellor, Masters and Scholars.' On February 10 both Graces passed the Senate without a division; and at the Board's meeting on 15 February it was proposed that the name Fitzwilliam Hall should be given to the premises in their occupation. After one adjournment for its further consideration this proposal was adopted at a meeting of the Board held on 26 April.[1]

By the Easter term 1887 the Board had achieved, therefore, two principal objectives which they had set before themselves at the beginning of Mr Howard's term of office – the students were no longer wholly dependent for their instruction on such college lectures as they were permitted to attend, largely at Christ's College, and they had a building of their own, although this was in need of considerable adaptation for their particular purposes. But before this work could be begun they had lost, within the space of a year or so, not only their Censor but his predecessor, who since his retirement had rendered the Board devoted service. Less than a year after his appointment, Mr Howard's indifferent health had caused him to be, temporarily, 'relieved of attending at the Rooms', and an Assistant to the Censor (Mr William Cunningham, of Trinity College, a member of the Board) was appointed for what was left of the Michaelmas term 1882.[2] A similar arrangement was made for the Lent and Easter terms 1883, when the Assistant Censor (Mr A. H. Cooke, of King's College) was made Deputy Censor;[3] and from then onwards it proved necessary, from time to time, to relieve Mr Howard of such of his duties as required his presence in the Trumpington Street building. On one occasion it was agreed that he should keep the accounts, deal with correspondence and

---

[1] Minutes, 15 February 1887. See, however, p. 127.
[2] *Ibid.*, 24 October 1882.
[3] *Ibid.*, 18 January and 23 April 1883.

write reports, Mr Cooke being made responsible for his other duties. Except for a period of three years from November 1884, when he was a Board member, and was regular in his attendance – although he was obliged to use a wheel-chair to go to his office from his home at 9 Harvey Road – it is not clear how often Mr Howard was able to get to meetings; but he appears to have played some part in the Board's business at least until May 1889. He had not kept its records since March 1884, and it may be taken as evidence of his persistent disability, and of the lack of secretarial assistance provided for him, that for more than half his censorship the Board's minutes appear to have been written up by his wife.[1] Mr Howard died on 11 December 1889, shortly after his forty-sixth birthday.

Mr Somerset, who was well qualified to judge the value of Mr Howard's work, paid tribute to his academic and administrative gifts, to his unfailing and kindly courtesy, and not least to the fortitude with which he had endured the serious illness which had assailed him in early middle age. His evident friendliness and his tact served him well in the discharge of his duties as Secretary of the University Lodging-Houses Syndicate, a new post created for the purpose of ensuring, by interview and inspection, the fitness for a licence of would-be lodging-house keepers and their premises. Mr Howard had been Assistant Censor of non-collegiate students for four years before his election as Censor in 1881.

> He entered on this office [writes Mr Somerset] with a sympathetic sense of the opportunities it offered of being a helper and a guide, and he was fitted for it by mental temper as well as by his varied experience. In fact he did attain a marked success in it. Even the test afforded by numbers shows this in part, when the necessary allowance is made for members of the two Public Hostels who had at first been counted as Non-Collegiate Students: but the surer proof is the regard with which he inspired the great body of his pupils. Those who attended his funeral on Dec. 14 must have been impressed by the large number of present and past students who even on that day presented themselves at Grantchester Church.[2]

On 24 February 1890, Mr Somerset, Mr J. W. Cartmell of Christ's College, and Mr Cunningham sent the following letter to those who, they thought, might be in sympathy with its object:

> Some of the friends of the late Rev. F. G. Howard think that a personal

---

[1] This is suggested by letters in Mrs Howard's hand, written to Mr Huddleston shortly after her husband's death (College Archives).
[2] *Cambridge Review*, 16 January 1890.

memorial of him might fitly be placed in the building in which for some years he discharged his duties as Censor of Non-College Students. They agree in the choice of a medallion portrait as the most suitable form of memorial. Mr Wiles, the Cambridge sculptor who has made some excellent portrait busts of resident members of the University, knew Mr Howard; he has been consulted and is ready to produce a medallion portrait in marble for a fee of fifty guineas. It is not proposed to make any public appeal for contributions but the present statement is being sent to you and to some others who it is thought may be glad to join in the proposed memorial. Contributions may be sent to any of the undersigned who will acknowledge the receipt and afterwards report what has been done.[1]

A statement of account addressed subsequently to subscribers (who included twenty-one students) records that a sum of £64.1.8 was collected; and in their Report to the Senate of 5 March 1891, the Board announced that the medallion, executed by Mr Henry Wiles, had been placed in the students' library.[2]

At their meeting on 14 January 1890, the Board agreed to give notice of their intention to elect a Censor, and invited applications from graduates of the University, of the standing of Master of Arts at least, to be received by the end of the month. There were ten applicants, and at a meeting on 4 February, 'after various scrutinies had been held', Mr T. F. C. Huddleston, of King's College, was elected. The Board may have found difficulty in making up their minds, for they also resolved unanimously to express their admiration of Mr Cooke's work as Assistant Censor, and their hope that he would be able to continue in it.[3]

In view of the indifference, if not worse, with which the non-collegiate institution was regarded in some University circles, the Board must have been gratified to have the opportunity of choosing between

---

[1] College Archives.
[2] *University Reporter*, 1890–91, p. 625.
[3] Minutes, 14 January 1890. See also *University Reporter*, 1889–90, pp. 374, 423.

There is a list of candidates in the minutes of the Board for 4 February 1890; and a similar list in a letter of 2 February written to the Registrary by Mr A. V. Boughey of Trinity College, and a member of the Board (University Archives, Camb. Univ. Reg. 60,45). To this list the Registrary added the dates of first degrees. There seems to have been some doubt about Mr Conybeare (of Barrington), of whom the Board's list says that his application was conditional, and Mr Boughey that he had sent in his name, 'but retires'. The names, with dates of graduation, are as follows:

Rev. G. B. Atkinson (Trin.H.1856); Mr J. Brill (Joh.1882); Mr O. Browning (King's 1860); Rev. A. H. Cooke (King's 1878); *Rev. E. Conybeare; Mr E. H. Fishbourne (Trin. 1879); Rev. F. W. Henstock (Down. 1876); Mr T. F. C. Huddleston (King's 1871); Rev. T. J. Lawrence (Down. 1872); Rev. T. B. Rowe (Joh.1856); Mr J. H. Taylor (Trin. 1868).

*Trin. 1866. In Mr Boughey's letter Mr Rowe is described as 'late Headmaster of Tonbridge'.

two such suitable applicants. Mr Huddleston had graduated in 1871 with first class honours in classics, having been Powis medallist in 1868, 1869, and 1870, and Browne medallist in 1868 and 1869. He was a Fellow of his college from 1872 to 1880, was for a time a Classical Lecturer of the college, and one of its three Bursars. Like Mr Howard, he was said also to have been a successful Secretary of the Lodging-Houses Syndicate. Mr Cooke graduated as Senior Classic in 1878. He too was Powis Medallist, was a Craven Scholar, and Chancellor's Medallist, and was remarkable for combining distinguished classical scholarship with a great enthusiasm for the Natural Sciences. He was University Curator in Zoology from 1880 to 1890, and was to proceed Sc.D. in 1914. Fellow of King's in 1880, he was Dean of the College (in company with M. R. James) from 1890 to 1893. He resigned the assistant censorship to become Tutor of King's in 1892; and from 1900 was Headmaster of Aldenham for twenty years.

On 23 March 1891, a little more than a year after he had written about his successor, with so much affection and such discernment, Mr Somerset died. A notice in the *Cambridge Review* tells of his school career, and of his undergraduate time at Trinity College, where he became a favourite pupil of Lightfoot, and a close friend of Henry Sidgwick. Of Somerset's work for his non-collegiate undergraduates the notice continues:

> Only an outline can be given of that part of his life, for which Somerset will chiefly be remembered in the University. In 1869, the new Statute establishing the Non-Collegiate system was passed, and he was appointed Censor. The scheme was entirely novel; every detail of organisation had to be created; and the whole burden of successfully developing an experiment, viewed at that time askance by not a few, rested almost solely on Somerset. Slowly by a sacrifice known only to very few, by rare tact and untiring patience, he established the system on a firm basis; accumulating its resources against the time when, after a due period of probation, it might realise the just expectations of those who founded it. Until the end his heart was in the success of this work, so well inaugurated by himself; and it was in the last few months of his life that with extreme generosity he placed himself at the head of a successful effort to free from debt the building, which in the early years of his Censorship he had found for his Students.

And, again,

> Without the common associations of a College, it may easily be imagined how his pupils rallied round the home of a man whom they recognised at once as a central support. It was not only that his liberality

was great, and that justice governed his liberality, but there was a peculiar grace, bred of sympathy and unselfishness, which won a younger man's confidence. Of the feeling of the Students towards him there is general testimony. In 1881, when ill-health forced him to resign the Censorship, one of his old pupils wrote to him, "I am thankful beyond all that words can say for the years you have served the body. I can only speak for myself, and so speak for all as for myself, that I look upon my Cambridge course with the deepest and most lasting thankfulness; and the one thing for which I shall be thankful to the end of my life is the memory of your kindness and sympathy, for all the thought and care and help you so generously gave."[1]

On 8 March 1895, the Non-Collegiate Students Board received from Mrs Somerset, and gratefully accepted, the gift of a medallion portrait in marble of her late husband, also the work of Mr Wiles, which depicts admirably those qualities of mind and heart described in Mr Huddleston's notice. First placed in the lecture room, it was moved in 1913 to the chapel, when this was fashioned out of the former library. A photograph taken in 1957 shows the two medallions (of Mr Somerset and Mr Howard) on the west wall, with the 1914–1918 memorial triptych between them.[2]

In their Report of 19 November 1886 on the purchase of the Trumpington Street houses the Board had said that whereas they were in fair condition externally, considerable interior alterations would be necessary to adapt them for their use; and on 7 March 1890 the Board approved for publication to the Senate a further Report in which, after summarizing the history of the non-collegiate scheme, particularly with regard to its accommodation, they gave details of changes proposed, and in effect sought the University's approval for two grants, one of a sum of £450 to be put towards the extinction of the debt which they had incurred in 1887, the other of an amount not exceeding £500 towards the cost of the alterations, each grant to be conditional upon the provision of matching amounts from funds at the Board's disposal.

> The first admission of Non-Collegiate Students [said the Board] was in 1869, and *Reports* have from time to time been made to the Senate.
>
> While these students have had access to the advantages provided by the University generally, and in some cases have also had the benefit of Lectures specially offered by Colleges, the Board desire to remind the Senate that the system has almost entirely borne its own expenses. The exceptions

---

[1] *Cambridge Review*, 30 April 1891.
[2] Censor's Report of 2 March 1895; *Magazine*, June 1913, p. 224; and *Journal*, December 1957, facing p. 13. See also pp. 444 and 451.

are these: during the first two years advantage was taken of a guarantee given by the University, but only to a total amount of less than £38; up to the end of 1884 the students were admitted to matriculation on payment of the same fee which was then charged to Sizars of Colleges; in 1874 the Senate made a grant of £50 for the purchase of books to form the nucleus of a Students' Library; and in 1887 a sum of £61, part of the cost attendant upon the purchase of premises in Trumpington Street, was contributed by the University.

The property referred to includes rooms which from 1874 to 1887 had been hired by the Board. During that period the Board, having regard to the urgent need of more accommodation for their Officers and Students, accumulated a portion of their yearly income, and in particular the exceptional receipts which during several years accrued from their connection with Institutions which afterwards obtained direct recognition as Public Hostels. They were by these means enabled to provide £2000 of the £3000 required for the purchase of the building, part of which they still occupy. The remaining £1000 was advanced by the University (Grace 8, Feb. 10, 1887), upon interest at $3\frac{1}{2}$% per annum, the principal to be repaid by instalments of not less than £50 a year. This will, by Midsummer, 1890, be reduced to £900...

The rooms now in use are reached by a mean and inconvenient staircase; they are a room for the Censor, a most inadequate office room for his Clerk, a Common-room for the Students, 26 ft. 9 in. by 19 ft., and a room approached through the last, 21 ft. 10 in. by 16 ft. 6 in., used both as a Library and as a Lecture-room. In view of the actual number of resident students (114)* and of the importance of encouraging them to meet in a common centre, the Board cannot consider this accommodation as other than provisional. Moreover, it is hardly possible that it should not be contrasted with that provided for Non-Collegiate Students by the University of Oxford, which, while making a large annual grant from the University Chest for their benefit, has recently erected mainly for their use a large and handsome building adjoining the Schools.

* The payments of the Students to the University Chest have been considerable. In the year 1889 the total, including Matriculation Fees, Capitation Tax, Examination and Degree Fees, was £1135.

The Board feel it to be of great importance that they should be enabled to use a larger part of their building than at present, at a much earlier date than under existing conditions they can hope to do. The obstacles are

(1) the debt to the University, the repayment of which may extend to 1908, and

(2) the cost of some necessary adaptation of the building to the requirements of the Board.

These requirements are – a Censor's Room, a Clerk's Office, two Lecture Rooms, a Library, a Common Room of adequate size and a Reading Room for the Students, Lavatories and rooms for a Porter and his wife. With a view to this accommodation, the Board have sought the advice of Professor Middleton,[1] who has kindly inspected the building and whose Report is subjoined:

To the Rev. the Provost of King's College,
Chairman of the Board of Non-Collegiate Students

Dear Sir,

At the request of the Censor of the Non-Collegiate Students I have examined the house which is the property of your Board, and I beg leave to report as follows:–

The house, which is dated 1727, is very well built, with the exception of an unimportant wing at the back on the north side, and is a very pleasing example of the simple red brick architecture which was in vogue during the early part of the last century.

In some ways, owing to the interior of the house being cut up by three staircases, it is not specially suited to the needs of the Non-Collegiate Students and the Officers of the Board, but a moderate amount of alteration will, I think, make it available for their chief necessities.

On the left hand of the chief entrance are two good rooms, which could be used by the Censors and their Clerk. The front part of the present furniture shop would make a good lecture room for 50 or 60 students. The back portion, when cut off from the lecture-room by a partition wall (being badly lighted) would be best employed as the place for lavatories and store-closets.

A comfortable small room on the first floor, looking north, might easily be made available for the students by opening out a blocked door in the side wall of the present Common Room, the lighting of which could be much improved by the use of patent reflectors.

For the sake of the beauty of the façade it is important that the original windows should be replaced, removing the present ugly shop front, and also the shop door which would then be useless.

The Attics at the south end of the house would be available as living and sleeping rooms for the Porter and his wife. There will still remain some other good rooms, which can either be let to undergraduates, or utilized for the growing needs of the body of Non-Collegiate Students.

Though no very serious structural repairs seem to be immediately needed, yet the whole house requires painting, papering and whitening throughout. The cost of this, together with the expense of some such alterations as those I have suggested, will certainly be not less than £900, not including the cost of furniture. I have however little doubt that an expen-

---

[1] Then Slade Professor of Fine Art, and Director of the Fitzwilliam Museum.

diture of from £900 to £1000 would place the main building in a good state of repair, and would render it available for its special purpose as an office and meeting-place for the Non-Collegiate students and their Censors.

The expense might be spread over several years as it would be *possible*, though not *desirable*, to carry out the work in separate portions.

I am, yours faithfully,
J. Henry Middleton
(Fitzwilliam Museum)

February 20, 1890

The Board are unwilling to ask the University for so large a grant as would itself suffice for the extinction of the debt and for the necessary alterations and improvements of the Building. But they are led to believe that help will be forthcoming from private sources if the University declares its readiness to meet any sum which may be offered with an equivalent amount, and already the sum of nearly £400 has been conditionally promised for this purpose. They think it will be convenient to deal separately with (1) the repayment of the debt and (2) the costs of altering and improving the Building. The Board therefore recommend:

I. That, if a sum of £450 be offered from private sources by Midsummer, 1890, towards extinguishing the debt of the Non-Collegiate Students Board to the University, the repayment of the remaining £450 be not required by the University (Grace 8, Feb. 10, 1887).

II. That, in the event of the debt of the Board being thus extinguished, any sums accruing from private gifts or from other external sources, or appropriated from the income of the Board, to form a fund for the adaptation of Nos. 31 and 32, Trumpington Street, to the requirements of the Board, be met with equivalent grants from the University Chest, provided the total amount of such grants shall not exceed £500.[1]
March 7, 1890

The Report came up for discussion by the Senate on 26 April, and ran into trouble. The root of the difficulty was a fear that if the Board's proposals were approved other urgent projects would, in the prevailing shortage of University funds, be bound to suffer. Possibly, also, the Board's spokesmen were a little too ready to emphasize the extent to which, as it seemed to them, the Board had met the cost of the recent purchase of the house from savings made in the running of the non-collegiate scheme in its first years. One speaker, indeed, wished to point out that, if the Board's first recommendation were approved, the University would have acquired for £450 a property worth £3,000. The Registrary could not, or would not, let this pass. In his view the sum of

[1]   *University Reporter*, 1889–90, p. 524.

£2,000 paid by the Board towards the purchase price was University money, which it could have spent in other ways if it had chosen to do so. The last speaker of all, with the air of setting a poser, but with unusual foresight, 'wished to know whether the Board was looking forward to discontinuing the non-collegiate system, and handing over the building to the University'.[1]

After the Discussion, the Council of the Senate gave the Board the opportunity of reconsidering their Report, and on 2 May the Chairman (Mr Austen Leigh, Provost of King's) wrote to the Vice-Chancellor informing him that, in view of what had been said, the Board wished to withdraw their second recommendation, but that they hoped that there might be in the future an opportunity of putting forward proposals for the improvement of their offices which would be acceptable to the Senate.[2] Their first recommendation was approved by Grace a week later.[3]

The Censor had not awaited the approval of Grace 9 of 8 May before seeking ways and means whereby the Board might be enabled, under its terms, to make its own contribution towards the extinction of the debt, and to the cost of the building work proposed. The whole amount of the Board's necessary payment towards the extinction of the debt had been received by the date when their Report was discussed by the Senate, and a 'List of those who have contributed towards the purchase and improvement of 31 and 32 Trumpington Street', included in a letter of 16 June 1890 to be sent to other possible benefactors, gives the names of the subscribers and the amounts of their subscriptions, promised or received, which had then reached a total of £616.13.0,[4] of which Mr Somerset and Mr Huddleston had given nearly one third. It appears that the attempt to raise further sums from private sources was either unsuccessful or was not vigorously pursued, for in a final list published by the Board in their Report of 12 March, 1894, although there are some changes in detail, the total of the contributions is by three shillings less than it had been four years previously. There was, however, subsequently added to it a generous gift of £100 from the Rev. H. J. Carter, of Duxford.[5]

The names of the contributors bear eloquent testimony to the quality of the support enjoyed by this modest appeal. The Censor's

1   *Ibid.*, p. 667.
2   Minutes, 2 May 1890; *University Reporter*, 1889–90, p. 676.
3   *University Reporter*, 1889–90, p. 683.
4   College Archives.
5   *University Reporter*, 1893–94, p. 649; and 1900–01, p. 643.

final list announced two anonymous gifts, and names fifty-seven subscribers. Twenty-five were, or had been, members of Trinity College.
The Duke of Devonshire (lately Chancellor of the University), the Earl
of Powis and his successor as High Steward (Lord Walsingham) are
followed by John Couch Adams, Lowndean Professor of Astronomy
and Geometry (said to have refused a knighthood in 1847, and in 1886
to have declined appointment as Astronomer Royal). Among the reigning Heads of Houses were Dr Atkinson of Clare College; Dr Montagu
Butler of Trinity, recently Vice-Chancellor; Dr Ferrer of Caius; Henry
Arthur Morgan, presumably, since his election as Master of Jesus, no
longer needing identification as 'Black Morgan'; Dr Phear of Emmanuel
College, and Dr Henry Perowne of Corpus Christi. Among future
Heads, of Selwyn College Dr F. A. Kirkpatrick, Regius Professor of
Hebrew, and subsequently Lady Margaret Professor of Divinity, with
his successor in the Mastership, the Reverend Richard Appleton; of
Queens' Herbert Edward Ryle, Hulsean Professor, afterwards Bishop
of Exeter and of Winchester, and Dean of Westminster; of Queens',
also, Frederick Henry Chase, Principal of the Cambridge Clergy Train-
ing School, later Norrisian Professor, Vice-Chancellor, and Bishop of
Ely; and of Emmanuel, William Chawner. Among others, Brooke Foss
Westcott, Regius Professor of Divinity and founder of the Clergy
Training School which took his name, had been appointed Bishop of
Durham in 1890; Mandell Creighton, in 1884 the first Dixie Professor
of Ecclesiastical History, was Bishop of Peterborough; H. M. Gwatkin,
Creighton's rival for the Dixie Chair,[1] and in 1891 his successor, was in
the first class in four Triposes – rumour had it that there would have
been more if the time-table had been more accommodating; and
F. J. A. Hort, Lady Margaret Professor, and Fellow of Emmanuel, was
acclaimed as the greatest theologian of them all. Others again, all from
Trinity College, were Arthur Cayley, Sadleirian Professor of Pure
Mathematics since 1863, past President of the Royal Society; E. C.
Clark, Regius Professor of Civil Law for forty years from 1873; F. W.
Maitland, Downing Professor of the Laws of England, pre-eminent
among the lawyers of his generation, in spite of his death at the age of
fifty-six; John Westlake, like Adams a Cornishman, Whewell Professor
of International Law; and Dr Henry Sidgwick, Knightbridge Professor
of Moral Philosophy, a founder of Newnham College, and husband of
its second Principal.

---

[1]   For Gwatkin's most generous letter to Creighton on the latter's election to the Professorship, see *Life and Letters of Mandell Creighton by his Wife*, in two volumes (Longmans, Green
and Co., 1904), vol. I, p. 245.

Mr Huddleston kept some of the replies to his appeals for help. Dr Perowne had never forgiven the Statutory Commissioners of 1877 for the introduction of a system of contribution from college revenues for University purposes, and resentment still smoulders in his letter of 19 March 1890:

> I must apologize for not answering your letter more promptly. I enclose a *small* contribution. It would have been much larger, did I not feel that the cost ought to be met by the University itself, for it has ample funds at its disposal.[1]

In a happier vein is Gwatkin's whimsy, from his home at 8 Scroope Terrace:

> Mr dear Huddleston,
>   Impudent beggars are generally reverend persons; but you are an exception, for you are impudent without being reverend.
>   You can put me down conditionally for £5, and I will pay the same when the condition is fulfilled.
>   Allnutt is a good man. He may get his first class if his Greek is up to the mark.[2]
>
> Yours truly
H. M. Gwatkin

Two former non-collegiate undergraduates are recorded as having subscribed to the appeal. One, the Rev. W. S. Houghton, Congregational Minister at Emmanuel Church from 1879 to 1891, matriculated in 1884 but did not graduate; the other, the Rev. Isaac Wodhams – whose name is unfortunately given as 'Rev. J. Woodams' – was an admirable example of the kind of man for whom the non-collegiate scheme was devised. Son of a blacksmith at Brackley in Northamptonshire, he went to Magdalen College School there, came into residence in 1873, was Treasurer of the Non-Collegiate Cricket Club in 1874, and graduated in 1876 (*Senior Optime*). Ordained deacon in 1876, and priest in 1878, he held curacies in Brackley and Northampton, and was Headmaster of his old school from 1882 till 1899. In a letter, dated 27 May 1891, he thanks Mr Huddleston for sending him the *Cambridge Review*, with its memorial notice of Mr Somerset, says that he would like to give two guineas to the appeal, and continues 'As I am carrying out improvements here, I cannot afford more, so I hope that my grati-

---

[1] College Archives.
[2] *Ibid.* Apparently it was not. S. G. J. Allnutt kept three terms as a non-collegiate student, migrated to Emmanuel College in the Michaelmas term of 1890, and was placed in the third class of Part I of the Theological Tripos in 1892.

tude for all the help that the Non-Collegiate System gave me will not be supposed to be measured by my modest contribution.'[1]

With commendable energy the Board had contrived to rid themselves of the debt which they contracted in persuading the University to purchase their premises. By 1891 they had begun to occupy part of the new accommodation by taking over the rooms let as a furniture shop, and allocating them as a temporary office and residence for the Clerk; and, although they were to receive from the University less financial aid than they had hoped, they addressed themselves to the task of adapting for its new purposes the whole of the building then in their possession. On 5 March 1891 the Board received a report from Mr W. M. Fawcett (architect in 1873 of the Cavendish Laboratory, and some years before that of the 'gothicized' windows of the dining hall and library of St Catharine's), and agreed that Messrs Kerridge and Shaw should be invited to tender for the work recommended by Mr Fawcett, of whose report no copy remains, although there is a copy of his detailed instructions to the contractors, most regrettably, however, without its accompanying drawings. On 5 June they accepted the tender, and gave instructions for 'the alteration of the front of the shop occupied by Mrs Dodd at a cost of £33.18.6', provided that the work should be finished by 15 September; and on 11 March 1892 they also agreed that Messrs Kerridge and Shaw should complete the work of alteration at a cost of not more than £1,500. The whole operation is summarized in a Report to the Senate of 12 March 1894:

> During the summer of 1892, under the superintendence of Mr W. M. Fawcett, Messrs Kerridge and Shaw of Cambridge completed the re-construction of the building. The ugly shop front and side entrance have been removed, and the original design of the façade has been in part replaced. By the demolition of a huge chimney stack, the large room on the ground floor, previously used as a furniture show room, and the entrance passage adjoining have been thrown together, and now form a large dining room divisible by a moveable partition. The kitchen and private rooms of the Custodian have been improved, and lavatories added. On the first floor, a large reading room for the use of the Students has been formed by throwing together the two rooms, once used by the Censor and the Clerk, and the passage adjoining, the new room being divided from the adjoining large room (now used as a Lecture Room) by a moveable partition. On the second floor, two rooms have been similarly thrown together, and in course of time may conveniently be used as a Library. By a rearrangement

[1]   College Archives.

Fitzwilliam Hall, the west front restored

of the roof additional accommodation has been gained in the attics. Until the debt has been extinguished, it has been thought expedient to let off some of the upper rooms, but it will probably not be long before the Board will be able to remove the Library to the second floor, and to assign, if then thought desirable, rooms to each of the three Lecturers. The payments to the Reserve Fund, now temporarily suspended, might then be renewed, so as to form a fund for the purchase in due course of the adjoining premises. A further restoration of the original façade would then complete the unity of the Building.[1]

The total cost of the alterations, as given by the Board in this same Report, was £1,639 (building £1,392, architect £73, furniture and sundries £174); and in order to help to meet it they secured, in 1892, a temporary loan of £500 from Mortlock's Bank, offered at 4% or, as they preferred, at 1% above bank rate.[2] In 1896, when they had paid off £200, the Censor applied to the Financial Board for a loan of £300; and on 10 December the Senate approved a recommendation of the Board that they should be authorized to make an advance of this amount, free of interest, the capital to be repaid before the end of 1904.[3]

In May 1887 the Non-Collegiate Students Board had agreed to place all items of receipt and expenditure connected with their new premises in a separate Fitzwilliam Hall Account (they had then only recently resolved that their building should be known as Fitzwilliam Hall). Into this account, therefore, which from time to time is also described as the Building Fund or Building Account, were paid each year sums received from the letting of rooms in the building, grants from the Board's General Account, latterly in the form of transfers of its annual surplus in years when there was a surplus. In its turn the Fitzwilliam Hall Account paid rates and taxes, and loan interest when it was due, and shouldered the burden of the debt. At Midsummer 1893, when the bills for the alterations had been settled, the debt was £824.12.8. Seven years later, at the end of a year when there had been no subvention from the General Account, which had made a loss, it stood at £250.11.8. After two more years, in one of which the Building Fund itself shewed a small deficit, the figure was £236.10.6; and it may well

1 *University Reporter*, 1893–94, p. 649. In his Report, on which this account was based, the Censor had been more specific. Instead of 'the adjoining premises', he had written 'Mr Peck's premises', and had continued 'These, with the original façade restored, might perhaps conveniently form a residence for the Censor of the next generation.'

2 Censor's Report of 1 March 1893; Report of the Board to the Senate, 12 March 1894, *University Reporter*, 1893–94, p. 649.

3 Report of the Financial Board to the Senate, dated 25 November 1896, *University Reporter*, pp. 260, (approved) 350.

be imagined that Censor Huddleston, thinking that the affair had gone on long enough, cast about for ways and means of bringing it to an end, for in the year 1902/03 gifts were received from private individuals amounting to £228.1.0, including a sum of £172 sent anonymously. Again the story is told most simply, and perhaps, even, most impressively, in the Board's figures: in the Building Fund for the year ending at Midsummer 1903 there appears, instead of the customary transfer from the General Account towards the extinction of the debt, a small but significant payment to the General Account of 14s.8d – the amount by which, after current expenses had been met, the total of the private gifts and the fund's normal income had in that year exceeded the debt that still remained.[1] By a careful husbanding of their resources the Board had made themselves masters of their building, which, with relatively small internal changes, assisted by the acquisition of a number of dwelling houses in the vicinity (and, maybe, by the neighbourliness of a tavern known as The Little Rose) was to remain the headquarters of the non-collegiate institution until, after sixty years, the time came for a move to a new site, new buildings, and, in prospect, a new status.

It will be remembered that one of the most insistent requirements at the beginning of the non-collegiate scheme was that every reasonable effort should be made to ensure the attendance of the men, as the phrase then was, 'on Public Worship'; and the Reports of the first Censor have shown how meticulously he sought to discharge this duty. Since the Easter term 1871 he had himself conducted a daily morning service at St Michael's Church, of which he was then vicar, and had continued it, with Mr Howard's help, until the end of the Easter term 1880, when he told the Board that the service had been very poorly attended, and that he hoped to transfer it to St Paul's Church, which was nearer to the lodgings of most of the students.[2] The holding of a service at St Paul's led to a request that attendance there might be used in mitigation of the troublesome rule about daily signatures at the Censor's office for the purpose of counting residence, and in the Michaelmas term 1884 the Board agreed in principle that signatures might be entered after morning chapel, provided that 'facilities should be offered to students not attending Chapel to sign at the same hour'.[3]

[1] College Archives, Accounts of the Board for Superintending Non-Collegiate Students.
[2] College Archives, Censor's Report to the Board, 23 June 1880.
[3] Minutes, 27 November 1884.

Shortly afterwards the Board also agreed that during the Lent and Easter terms 1885 students attending the week-day morning service at St Paul's Church should be allowed to sign in the vestry afterwards, and that any student should be allowed to sign in Mr Peck's shop.[1] There was a sting in the tail of this last concession, for it was to be valid only from 7.45 till 8.15 o'clock in the morning; and so the Board must have felt, for later in their same meeting the restriction was modified by a further decision that 'during the continuance of lectures students should be allowed to sign between 9 and 10 a.m., and that in consideration of the extra work thrown upon the clerk (in the office) the Censor might raise his salary to not more than £60 a year'. As the amended ruling referred merely to the continuance of lectures, and made no stipulation about attending them, Dr Reyner (who shortly after his outburst of some years earlier had proceeded to the degree of Doctor of Divinity) might well have felt, and if so would certainly have said, that the ungodly were being treated with a degree of impartiality that was quite uncalled for. As time passed similar concessions were made in respect of services elsewhere. In 1890, at the very beginning of Mr Huddleston's tenure, the Board heard with marked approval that the Council of King's College had agreed to assign places in their Chapel for the use of non-collegiate students at the weekday service, and that the Deans of the College had been asked to make arrangements whereby the students might register their attendance there.[2] In due course the Board approved similar arrangements in connexion with week-day services held in St Matthew's Church, with services in the Roman Catholic Church, and also in St Edmund's House, and for non-college students at Cheshunt House.[3] In the meantime, the Censor's Reports to the Board, from the beginning of Mr Howard's tenure, make little mention of attendance at church or chapel.

Mr Somerset had been distressed by the extent, and the effects, of migration, and it will be remembered that he had urged the establishment of exhibitions as a means of making non-collegiate status more attractive. In the year 1878/79 there had been 34 migrants out of a total, in the Michaelmas term, of 120 undergraduates in residence, including 26 at Cavendish College, whose men would be less likely to wish for a move; and in November 1879 the Board made the first of a number of alterations in their fees, with the intention of dissuading

---

[1] Minutes, 6 December 1884.
[2] *Ibid.*, 21 February 1890.
[3] Minutes, 15 March 1893 (St Matthew's Church); 12 March 1896 (Roman Catholic Church); 19 November 1900 (St Edmund's House); 21 November 1905 (Cheshunt House).

undergraduates from applying for membership of a college. When the non-collegiate scheme began, the fee payable to the Board, as distinct from fees paid through the Board to the University, had been fixed at £1.15.0 for each term of residence, and in 1879 the Board obtained authority to charge an entrance fee of £2, to reduce the terminal residence fee to £1.10.0, and, if they should see fit, to vary the amount of their fees within an overall maximum of £15.15.0 for nine terms. They were, in addition, permitted to require the payment of Caution Money of not more than £3.[1] At the same time the Board drew the attention of the Council of the Senate to a loss to the University of £4.5.0 in matriculation fees in respect of any non-collegiate student who transferred to a college, since the fee for a pensioner was £5, and for a non-collegiate student 15s. They made no recommendation, as they did not regard the matter as being within their competence, but the Council took the point, and the anomaly was adjusted.[2]

This was the beginning of a practice designed to collect fees earlier in the men's period of residence, so that migration should entail a smaller financial loss to the Board. In the Michaelmas term 1884 the entrance fee of £2 was, in effect, raised by a requirement that on admission a payment of 5s. should be made as a contribution to the maintenance of a library. In 1890 the entrance fee was doubled (to £4.10.0), and the terminal residence fee was reduced from £1.10.0 to 15s after six terms. In 1892 the entrance fee was raised to £5.5.0, while the residence fee after six terms was brought down to 10s. A year later the entrance fee was raised yet again to £6.15.0, while the residence fee remained at £1.10.0 for the first six terms, but was not charged at all thereafter. In 1895 the Censor recommended, but the Board did not agree, that the entrance fee should be raised from £6.15.0 to £9. In 1896, on the grounds that so much more was then done for the men, the University raised the permissible total of fees from £15.15.0 to £18.18.0,[3] and the terminal residence fee was raised from £1.10.0 to £1.17.0. In 1903 it was increased again to £2.4.0 for the first three terms, left unchanged for the fourth, fifth and sixth terms and, as before, not charged after that. At Easter 1904 the entrance fee was reduced from £6.15.0 to £6.6.0, the terminal fee raised from £2.4.0 to

---

[1] Report of the Board to the Senate, 19 November 1879 (*University Reporter*, 1879–80, pp. 132, (approved) 196.

[2] Report of the Council of the Senate, 5 May 1881, *University Reporter*, 1880–81, pp. 529, (discussed) 573, (approved) 589.

[3] Report of the Board to the Senate, 2 May 1896, *University Reporter*, 1895–96, pp. 696, (approved) 927.

£3.3.0 for the first three terms, reduced from £1.17.0 to £1.1.0 for the next three, and then, as before, not charged.[1]

It is difficult to judge what was the effect of these measures, for it is quite possible that matters might have been worse if they had not been taken; but by the end of the academical year 1906/07 they had failed to bring down the number of migrations to anything which the Board could be expected to regard as acceptable. From 1885 to 1907, with the exception of one unusual year (1890/91), when they fell from 27 to 14, only to rise again to 31 the year after, the proportion of migrations to the numbers in residence in any year was rarely less than a fifth and on occasion rose to more than a third. The formidable nature of the problem is made plain in Mr Huddleston's Report to the Board of February 1897 in which he says, in speaking of students who by then might be expected to have completed their degree course, 'Of the 64 students, exclusive of candidates in Music, who entered during the academical year 1893–4, 13 graduated as non-collegiate students, 30 migrated to Colleges or Hostels, 11 left the University without graduating, one died, leaving 9 undergraduates on the books.'[2]

One further expedient was adopted before the end of Mr Huddleston's censorship: in March 1907, after considering the Censor's Annual Report, the Board resolved that a migration fee of £3.3.0 should be charged to students migrating after the end of their third term.[3]

The nature of these changes, and their frequency, seem to reveal a Board anxiously, almost feverishly, groping for a way of ridding themselves of a most damaging threat to the success, as they conceived it, of their whole undertaking. Their officers were not content to acquiesce in the transfer of so many of their senior students to the colleges, and so to be a channel through which a large number of students might receive a University and college education who would not have had it any other way. As time passed, the circumstances of the setting up of the non-collegiate scheme were less clearly remembered, and those most closely associated with it, young and old, came to think of themselves as members of a body with a life of its own, and with claims on their loyalty and affection. Non-collegiate it might be, but for them its

[1] For the changes described in this paragraph, and within the Board's jurisdiction, see Minutes, 4 March 1884, 28 May 1890, 11 March 1892, 15 March 1893, 8 March 1895, 17 November 1902, 17 November 1903.
[2] College Archives, Censor's Reports to the Board, dated 20 February 1897, 20 February 1907.
[3] Minutes, 5 March 1907.

success was to be judged by its ability to acquire a collegiate way of life.

At a meeting on 30 March 1907, the Board appointed a committee 'to consult with the Censor respecting the future tenure of the Censorship and the Lectureships', and it seems likely that by then, if not before, Mr Huddleston had made it known that he would soon be compelled, by his failing eyesight, to resign his office. On 30 April the Board published a notice of the vacancy, and invited applications for election to the censorship, at a stipend of £300 a year, with a capitation allowance.[1] In spite of a rather chilly statement that the Censor elected would not be at liberty to undertake other work without the Board's permission, seventeen candidates applied, from whom three were chosen for interview on 6 June. They were the Rev. T. W. Crafer scholar of Christ's College, then of Jesus, Chaplain and Lecturer in Classics and Theology at Downing College, as well as Lecturer to the non-collegiate students; Mr W. F. Reddaway, Fellow and Lecturer in History at King's College, and since 1896 Lecturer in History to the non-collegiate students; and Dr W. W. Skeat, Fellow of Christ's College, who in 1878 had become the first Elrington and Bosworth Professor of Anglo-Saxon in the University. Dr Skeat was a scholar of the highest eminence, and although it remains surprising that the Board should have wished to interview him – he had graduated nearly fifty years previously – his, at first sight, equally surprising wish to be considered for the appointment may have been due to a wish to supplement his professorial stipend (£479.3.0 in the financial year ending 31 December 1907).[2]

Not for the first time were the Board most fortunate in being able to choose from so good a field. Mr Crafer had taken a high second class in the Classical Tripos in 1892, and a first class in the Theological Tripos two years later; Mr Reddaway was in the first class in the Historical Tripos in 1894, and both were University prizemen; and in electing Reddaway they were to add, beyond anything they could know, to their indebtedness to his College.[3] Huddleston had come from King's; so had A. H. Cooke; and Mr Austen Leigh had served the Board as Chairman for three most important years. Happily, Reddaway's own links with King's were not to be severed, for, in spite of the Board's caution-

---

[1] *University Reporter*, 1906–07, p. 817.
[2] University Accounts for the Year ended December 31, 1907. *University Reporter*, 18 March 1908, p. 39.
[3] *University Reporter*, 1906–07, p. 1055.

ary words about other work, he remained a Fellow and Lecturer of the College throughout his time as Censor, and so continued after his retirement from the censorship in 1924.

After his retirement Mr Huddleston remained in Cambridge until the academical year 1934/35, when he went to live in Dumbartonshire with his son, who had recently retired from the Foreign Service.[1] Shortly after his death, on 26 February 1936, the *Cambridge Review* published an obituary notice, undoubtedly written by his successor as Censor, even though the author's initials appear as 'W.R.F.'.

> The death of Tristram Frederick Croft Huddleston, after more than sixty years of life as a graduate among us, has broken one of the strongest links remaining between Victorian and post-war Cambridge. Until late in King George's reign he preserved the tradition of the small and intimate society, with its widespread classical culture and "general equality of fortune," which ruled the University in the days when marriage forfeited fellowships, as in his case in 1879. Shortly before his eighty-eighth birthday he delighted his friends with a small collection of his classical verses and translations.

After references to Huddleston's achievements at the Colleges of Eton and King's, the notice continues:

> Later, he acted as Lecturer to the new Non-Collegiate body, and as Inspector of University lodging-houses. But his most memorable services were rendered as Censor, from 1890 to 1907.
>
> The office was at that time one of extraordinary difficulty. The Censor must act as Tutor, Prælector, and Bursar for all the students, and contrive to pay himself, the Lecturers, and a resident clerk from fees which by Ordinance were fixed at some £18 for the whole course. In addition, Fitzwilliam House must be kept up and the balance on its purchase paid off. Financial stringency, however, was a small burden in comparison with the negative title which the new body was condemned to bear. Huddleston set out bravely to navigate a vessel in which the owners maintained a spacious leak.
>
> For seventeen years the Censor struggled with his problem, usually resigned, but always combative when the interests of his pupils were attacked. He gathered round him such helpers as E. S. Shuckburgh, W. W. Walker, T. W. Crafer, and the great-hearted W. G. Bell. To the crude endeavours of a junior colleague he was all indulgence. Aided by the gracious lady whom the Bessie Huddleston foundation at Addenbrooke's commemorates, he provided the most charming hospitality for Fitzwilliam

---

[1] He was living at 15 Selwyn Gardens in September 1932, and then appears to have moved to 12 Newnham Terrace for two years. His name is not in the Cambridge Directory (Spalding) for 1935–36.

men, especially, as an old oarsman, for the boat. His graceful speeches at Terminal Dinners are also well remembered, and his kindness to men who fell ill.

In 1907, when his sight had seriously failed, he quitted office, and soon afterwards his household was shattered by death. The war also took his gallant younger son. Yet he faced life with unbroken courage, serving many good causes, especially that of the Hospital, with an almost exuberant enthusiasm, and rejoicing in the society of his family and friends, and in the career of his elder son. When at last his square firm figure and scholar's features were seen no more Cambridge was peculiarly conscious of its loss.[1]

Reddaway's notice should not suffer from any presumptuous or unnecessary gloss, but he, in his turn, would surely have been 'all indulgence' to a suggestion that it might be amplified in two comparatively minor ways.

Of Huddleston's combativeness on behalf of his pupils there is evidence enough in a printed document inscribed in his own hand 'Volunteer Corps Controversy 1900',[2] which consists of a number of letters about the difficulties encountered by non-collegiate applicants for enlistment in the Cambridge University Rifle Volunteers. The principal correspondents were Huddleston himself and the Rev. Alfred Rose, Chairman of the Board at the time, on the one side, and Colonel H. S. Cronin, Commanding Officer of the Corps, with some subordinates, on the other. Colonel Cronin was also Dean of Trinity Hall, and he was on the Board. From a perusal of these letters, extending over a period of nearly two years, it is difficult to escape the conclusion that in the face of Huddleston's persistent efforts to discover whether there was any objection to non-collegiate applicants as such, the replies of the officers of the Corps were evasive in substance, and in manner abrupt. Huddleston made repeated attempts to obtain an unequivocal ruling; but the exchanges ended with a refusal by the Adjutant of the Corps, at a meeting with the President of Queens' College and Mr Rose, to 'offer ... any plan in the direction of giving non-collegiate students readier admission to the Corps'. Huddleston will have found even more disappointing his own Board's reluctance, at a meeting at which Colonel Cronin was present, to seek an authoritative statement that non-collegiate members of the University were eligible for membership. To some it must have seemed only too apparent that, in certain circles, the non-collegiate student was regarded as a second class citizen; but of

[1]   *Cambridge Review*, 6 March 1936.
[2]   College Archives.

their Censor's readiness to support his men when he felt that their
interests were legitimately engaged this unfortunate episode affords
ample proof. It lends, furthermore, an additional significance to a statement by Huddleston in a Report to his Board in the Lent term of 1900,
when all this was going on, that two of his first year men had joined
Mounted Corps for service in South Africa. He did not add that one,
the son of a Cambridge Master of Arts in Holy Orders, a 'marksman' in
the Port Wakefield (Australia) Corps, and a member of the South Australia cricket side, had been refused admission to the Volunteers a few
weeks before; but he returned to the subject in a later Report, in which
he told the Board that both men, on their safe return from active service, had been accepted by Queens' College.

In a lighter vein, Reddaway's description of his predecessor as 'an
old oarsman', though correct, leaves a good deal unsaid. Captain of the
School at Eton, Huddleston came up to King's in 1867, and rowed in
the College boat for ten years; and when, for seven of those years, he
stroked the boat, it rose from twenty-third place to ninth – in a year in
which the total number of King's undergraduates was twenty-four.[1]

It will be remembered that from the beginning it had been intended
that the non-collegiate scheme should be financially self-supporting.
Although the non-collegiate body was to be in effect a department of
the University, neither of the two Syndicates had recommended any
form of regular subvention from University funds; and the first Syndicate, in proposing that the stipend of the Censor should initially be
£100, added a cautious rider that although this sum might be increased,
this should only be when student numbers justified it. The sole assistance available to the Non-Collegiate Students Board was a guarantee
of not more than £100 in any year in which they made a loss.

The first book of the Accounts of the Board for superintending Non-
Collegiate Students (from Midsummer 1869 to Midsummer 1890)
reflects, from its own viewpoint, the more general history of these
early years, and occasionally affords information not to be found elsewhere.[2] The extreme simplicity, and the modest scale, of the non-collegiate scheme are apparent in the Accounts of its first year (p. 61),
which shew how completely its financial well-being depended on the
numbers of its undergraduates. In the three terms of the next year
numbers in residence rose to nineteen, twenty, and twenty, and the
deficit was reduced to £6.14.6., after which, on the normal running of
the scheme, there was for some fifty years no loss which the Board were

[1]   King's College, Annual Report of the Council, 1936.
[2]   College Archives.

unable to make good from hard won reserves. The figures for 1873/74 are the first to record expenditure on the three rooms rented by Mr Somerset in January at 31 Trumpington Street, when £105.15.3 was spent on furniture, and a sum of £25.18.2 includes for a part of the year the cost of the annual rent of £40, and the wages of a clerk (Throssell) hired at £30 a year to help the Censor in the Board's work, the whole of which he had until then done by himself. In this year, too, with sixty men in residence, the Censor's stipend was raised to £150. The year 1874/75 was notable for the receipt of a grant from the Vice-Chancellor on the University's behalf, to be put towards the beginnings of a library; and for a payment from the Clothworkers' Company of an amount of £25 for the expenses of an examination for candidates for their Exhibition, first awarded in January 1875. In the following year the Company very reasonably decided that the grant should be £15, the cost of a similar examination in Oxford. In 1876 the Board received their first fees from men (2) who had proceeded Masters of Arts,[1] for although they had no power to demand fees from a non-collegiate student proceeding in a first degree, there was no such prohibition for any degree after the first.

Thenceforward the Accounts follow an established pattern, with no more than occasional items of especial significance. They shew a steady, if moderate, increase in expenditure, made necessary, and indeed made possible, by a corresponding increase in undergraduate numbers. By the last complete year of Mr Somerset's censorship (1880/81) his stipend had by stages reached £300, and an Assistant Censor (Mr Howard), first appointed at a stipend of £50 in 1876, was being paid £75. The clerk's wages were £58, and the rent and cleaning of the Rooms, at first £40, and then £50, was raised to £55, presumably to take account of the previous year's addition to the building of a first floor room for use as a library, and known to later generations of Fitzwilliam men as their chapel. It is difficult to believe today that the cost of this addition to the building was no more than £60.

Items of smaller importance also catch the reader's eye: in the year 1872/73 Mr Spalding is paid the sum of 4s.6d for 'Signature Books for the Students', of which one survives in the College Archives, by its condition a mute witness to undergraduate irritation caused by the tiresome, but perhaps unavoidable, insistence on daily signatures as evi-

---

[1] Henry Harold Rose and Thomas Henry Found Bee, admitted respectively to the title of the M.A. degree on 7 December 1875 and 9 May 1876, were admitted to their complete degrees on 20 June 1876, the day appointed for the inauguration of Masters of Arts. In the *Ordo Senioritatis* of that date Rose's names are given as 'Edw. Harold'.

dence of residence – a rule which, although by various expedients it was made less rigid with the passage of time, was not finally rescinded until 1935.[1] In June 1874 a payment of 4s for 'escutcheons' (to a recipient whose name is undecipherable) suggests an interest in heraldry some years before the appointment of J. H. Bloom's committee by the Amalgamation Club 'to consider the question of armorial bearings'.[2] Of two consecutive items in the Accounts for 1876/77, one records a payment of 12s for the binding of the first six years of the *University Reporter* (1870–76), and the other an insurance premium of 3s, but whether the one relates to the other is not clear. 'Library and fencing of Recreation Ground' is an unusual heading in 1880/81; and elsewhere it appears that of this composite amount of £20.0.6 no more than 18s.11d found its way to the library. Mr Somerset, in 1877/78, has an entry 'Seal ... £1.5.0', which almost certainly refers to a most seemly, ivory handled, oval seal, with the device 'Non-Collegiate Students Board' now kept in the college Bursary. Lastly, in this miscellany from the very earliest years, is the admission in the year 1878/79 of a remarkable total of forty-two candidates for the degree of Bachelor of Music. There was no requirement of residence for these men, who, provided they were in a position to supply evidence of having passed the Previous Examination, or some equivalent, were admitted to the Mus. B. examination on payment to the Non-Collegiate Students Board of an admission fee of £1.15.0; and not even the Previous Examination was required of candidates over thirty years old. This last concession, however, was withdrawn with effect from the end of the Easter term 1879, and Mr Somerset, who had accepted ten candidates in the year before, was besieged by a host of applicants, most of whom will have been relatively elderly gentlemen, for whom the Previous Examination, if not a totally insuperable barrier, was nevertheless an obstacle better avoided.

By the Michaelmas term 1881 the number of men in residence was 184, of whom 80 were members of Cavendish College, and on 7 November, when Mr Somerset presented the last account of his stewardship, he was able to hand over to his successor a balance of £1,080.15.2.

Mr Somerset's Accounts are written out in his own hand, and are most carefully kept. The signatures of those members of the Board who attended the audit meetings are eminently readable – in those days legibility was evidently no occasion for reproach – and have an interest of

[1]   Minutes, 31 January 1935.
[2]   See p. 125.

their own for a reader who may fancy his ability to detect in them something of the personalities of the writers: the breezy assertiveness of J. Rawson Lumby, the fastidiousness of 'E. Hy Perowne', the demure neatness of J. B. Pearson, of St John's, whose allusion to the 'amenities of clerical controversy' pricked more than one bubble when feelings ran high over the original proposals for University Extension,[1] or the curiously laboured hand of Dr Phear, Master of Emmanuel, Vice-Chancellor in 1874 and 1875, and Chairman of the Board from 1876 until 1881.

Mr Howard, Censor from the end of the Michaelmas term 1881, took on where Mr Somerset had left off, and himself drafted the Accounts for the rest of that financial year; but here again the Accounts reflect the course of the more general history of the Board, for from Midsummer 1882 the writing is the unmistakable hand of Salmon, appointed Clerk (and general custodian) in or about April of that year; and it seems not unlikely that the change was made because of the illness which overtook Mr Howard before the end of his first year of office, from which he never fully recovered. Mr Huddleston saw no reason to make any change, and Salmon continued to keep the Accounts until Reddaway, who was appointed Censor in 1907, and had a poor opinion of clerks, made other arrangements.

After Mr Somerset's retirement, the Censor's basic stipend remained unchanged at £300, save on first appointment, but from the Lent term 1893 there was added to it a capitation allowance of 6s a term for each resident undergraduate, increased in 1907 to 7s on the appointment of W. F. Reddaway, when stipend and allowances were both paid free of income tax. The best paid lecturers were those who gave their lectures for the Previous and General Examinations, attended by men reading for a pass degree. From the fixed charge for each course, together with *per capita* payments on a varying scale, these lecturers received annual emoluments of rather more than £100. In 1902 the *per capita* payments ceased, and a lump sum of £100 was paid to Mr Shuckburgh and Mr Bell and of £60 to Mr Reddaway. From 1905 these amounts also were paid free of tax.

With the purchase of their buildings the Board became liable for rates and taxes, and in 1888 they first paid under this general heading a sum of £14.16.2; which by 1893 had increased to £30.0.8, made up of Poor Rate at £12.2.8, General District Rates at £8.8.8, Inhabited House Duty and Property Tax at £6, and Church Rate (for two years) at

[1] See p. 31.

£3.9.4. The total increased gradually, until in 1907 it was half as much again.

In 1895 the Board agreed to meet, on behalf of the Amalgamation Club, an annual duty of £1.1.0 on armorial bearings, and payments of this amount were made for twenty years.[1] It may be a matter for speculation whether this charge was properly levied in respect of arms unlawfully borne, or whether the Inland Revenue authorities were concerned, only, to prevent evasion of payment, and did not go into the question whether arms had been duly granted. The Board also made grants, as they felt able and according to the urgency of the need, to the Amalgamation Club for its general purposes – of £15 in 1886 and 1891, of £20 in 1897, and of £25 in 1901, 1902, 1906, and 1907.

'Expenses of Daily Service' is an item which first appears in 1881, when contributions were made to the funds of St Paul's Church (whose vicar from 1891 to 1917 was the Rev. H. P. Stokes, the antiquary). In 1881 a sum of £5.5.0 was given to the sexton, of £1.1.0 to the cleaner, and of £3.3.0 to the Churchwardens' Fund. Amounts of this order were repeated until 1892; thereafter they were limited to the subscription to the Churchwardens' Fund, and ceased altogether in December 1898. In the previous February Mr Huddleston had informed his Board that 'less than a quarter of the number of students now lodge in the vicinity of the Church, and one only attends the morning service, and there certifies his residence instead of at the office'.

The Accounts also throw some light on the early history of the Gibson Prize for proficiency in New Testament Greek (see also p. 461). It is first mentioned in the Accounts for the year ending at Midsummer 1890, which show that a Gibson Prize Fund received a sum of £126.8.0 (of which £1.8.0 was for interest earned on deposit), to which Mrs

---

[1] Minutes, 8 March 1895. At the beginning of his censorship, W. F. Reddaway refers to this payment, which, he says, 'enables our clubs to use heraldic devices without penalty' (*Magazine*, November 1908, p. 55).

There had been trouble at Oxford some years previously (see *University Archives* (U.P., 1867–83), 783): '*Armorial Bearings at Oxford*. At the Vice-Chancellor's Court at Oxford, on June 30th, before the Vice-Chancellor, Dr Sewell, and Dr Holland, Assessor, two undergraduates named James Campbell Vernon, of Merton College, and Charles Robert Patey, of Exeter College, were summoned by the Inland Revenue Officer for wearing and using armorial bearings without taking out a licence. Mr Vernon pleaded guilty. Mr Mallam, who appeared for the Inland Revenue authorities, had no desire to press the case unduly against the defendants, their only object being to remove the erroneous impression which prevailed amongst the undergraduates that they could wear the college crest without a licence. With regard to the charge against Mr Patey, Mr A. J. Stone, an officer of the Inland Revenue, stated that he saw the defendant in the Exeter boat, rowing bow. They made a bump, and when the boat stopped he saw the defendant put on his head a blue cap, bearing the crest of the college. Defendants were fined £5 each.'

Gibson added an amount of £5 to meet purchase charges on £100 4%
North Western Railway stock at £130.13.6. In the following year interest of £3.18.0 was received (£4 less income tax at sixpence in the
pound), and payments were made to Deighton Bell (£2.2.6), to Wilson
the bookbinder, and to Palmer for a name plate, amounting in all to
£5.5.9. No prize winner is mentioned in the Accounts, but according to
the *University Calendar* for 1890 it was divided between Preston Haigh
and Frederick Daniel Vaughan, who will have competed for it by
examination in the Easter term of that year. Thereafter the value of the
prize was fixed at £4 until the Michaelmas term of 1896. Interest for
the year ending Midsummer 1897, on the increased capital, was
£7.6.10 (net), but there was no award in the next term, and the augmented prize of £7.7.0 was first given on the result of the competition
in the Easter term of 1898.

In June 1895 the Board authorized their Chairman and the Censor to
arrange for the letting of the rooms then recently vacated by Mr
Masterman, and their Cash Book records the receipt on 7 October of a
sum of £3.19.0 from Lord Acton, who in the previous February had
been appointed Regius Professor of Modern History, and admitted
Honorary Fellow of Trinity College. Lord Acton rented his College
rooms (A2 Nevile's Court) from Michaelmas 1895, and it seems likely
that his occupation of rooms in the Trumpington Street building was
for the Long Vacation. From a scrutiny of the Board's minutes referring
to the occupants of rooms, it is virtually certain that the rooms let to
Lord Acton were those on the second floor, to the north of the main
staircase, which have since been occupied by successive Censors.

Finally, among these random gleanings from the story of the Non-
Collegiate Students Board's getting and spending, it is on record that
the cost of printed circulars, and of other items, for Mr Huddleston's
Appeal in 1890 amounted to £6.0.0 – a sum which, at one per cent of
the yield, stands in marked contrast to the expense of the more professional methods of seeking funds which have since become fashionable.

CHAPTER IV

Status Pupillaris 1869–1907

Composition of the undergraduate body – misleading examination results – the first individual clubs (1874) – amalgamation (1884) – difficulty over distinctive name – armorial bearings – colours of the clubs – their scanty membership, and persisting financial insecurity. Other corporate activities – dining, debating, and music. Foundation of Historical (1900) and Theological (1902) Societies. Continuing loss of undergraduates to the colleges – varied opinions about migration.

The scarcity of information about the background of the early non-collegiate students has already been observed, and it has also been noted that a little more is known about the first students of all, because the University Registrary made, and kept, his own comments on them.[1] After nine years, according to a Report by the Non-Collegiate Students Board to the Senate, out of 174 men admitted since the Long Vacation of 1876 four had parents ordinarily resident in the town, fifteen were curates or assistant masters in schools, and the remainder had come to the University under ordinary conditions.[2] Mr Howard's Reports do not enter into these particulars, and in 1894 the Board do little more than call attention to the fact that of 21 members of the Day Training College for Schoolmasters (established in 1891) 10 were non-collegiate undergraduates.[3] Mr Huddleston is more communicative, for in 1896 he tells the Board that of 94 men in residence there were two who were married, 13 living with parents or guardians, 7 assistants in schools, 9 members of the Day Training College, 11 curates or lay readers, 12 Indians, and 4 residing temporarily.[4] His Reports for the next two years are to much the same effect, and in 1905 the Board inform the Senate that, of a total of 90 residents, there were 2 advanced students, 7 married, 19 living with parents or guardians, 9 assistant masters, 9 members of the Day Training College, 8 lay readers at St Matthew's House, 5 living in St Edmund's House, 5 Japanese and 4 Indians.[5] These reports all suggest that among the non-collegiate undergraduates of the earlier years there were, in spite of what the Board had found in 1878, a considerable proportion who, like the schoolmasters, and, in those

[1] See p. 49
[2] *University Reporter*, 1878–79, p. 147.
[3] Report dated 12 March 1894, *University Reporter*, 1893–94, p. 649.
[4] Censor's Reports to the Board, 1882–98.
[5] Report dated 21 March 1905, *University Reporter* 1904–05, p. 766.

days, the married students, were older men or men living in communities of their own (St Edmund's House and St Matthew's), or with their parents, and so would not feel the need of the corporate activities that were regarded as an essential part of college life.

The published examination results obtained by the non-collegiate students are misleading, for it is in the class-lists that the effect of the transfer of so many of them to the colleges is most clearly seen. Academic performance throughout the University during the latter half of the nineteenth century was not what it has since become. In 1887, for instance, the number of honours graduates is said to have been 356, and of poll men 330; twenty-five years later there were more graduates, but the corresponding figures were 508 and 425.[1] In 1908 Mr J. A. Venn,[2] then of Trinity College, published statistics of degree results gained in the years 1851–1906, from which it appears that of the undergraduates who matriculated between 1848 and 1903, forty-five per cent went out in honours, thirty-four per cent were poll men, and twenty-one per cent did not graduate. Mr Venn adds that the proportion of men who went down without a degree changed very little throughout the period. One table in his paper provides a most striking illustration of the effects of migration on the non-collegiate body in the five years from 1902 to 1906.

Table D.   Total degree percentage, 1902–1906.

College	Honour	Poll	Total	Wastage
St. Catharine's	62.0	50.6	112.6	–
Downing	66.0	46.0	112.0	–
Peterhouse	63.2	44.1	107.3	–
Sidney	65.6	28.8	94.4	5.6
Queens'	49.6	40.5	90.1	9.9
Christ's	54.8	34.5	89.3	10.7
Emmanuel	54.2	35.1	89.3	10.7
King's	76.9	12.3	89.2	10.8
Selwyn H.	46.4	42.1	88.5	11.5
Caius	55.4	31.6	87.0	13.0
St. John's	54.9	30.6	85.5	14.5
Corpus	43.1	41.0	84.1	15.9
Pembroke	51.3	31.6	82.9	17.1
Jesus	49.7	31.3	81.0	19.0
Trinity	36.7	38.6	75.3	24.7

[1]   Royal Commission on Oxford and Cambridge Universities, *Appendices* (1922), p. 154.
[2]   President of Queens' College, 1932–58. See *Cambridge Review*, 23 and 30 January 1908, pp. 178, and 196.

College	Honour	Poll	Total	Wastage
Magdalene	55.3	17.6	72.9	27.1
Clare	36.5	34.8	71.3	28.7
Trinity Hall	24.3	28.1	52.4	47.6
Fitzwilliam Hall	13.4	24.0	37.4	62.6
University	46.3	32.9	79.2	20.8

The writer hesitated for some time [says Mr Venn] before allowing Table D to appear in the full glare of publicity – the reason for which hesitation will be apparent if the "total degree" column for the first three colleges be scrutinised. A percentage of over 100 in such tables as these generally requires a considerable amount of explanation, but it is hoped that the following will satisfy most critics. In the first place there is no denying the fact that the matriculations at Peterhouse, St Catharine's and Downing during the five years 1899–1903 were 68, 79, and 50, and it is equally certain that the corresponding degrees were 73, 89, and 56. But there is surely a subtle connection between the abnormal wastage at Fitzwilliam Hall of 62 per cent and the excess of degrees over matriculations at these three colleges in question. It is a well-known feature of the non-collegiate system that their students are as a body men to whom a degree is of the utmost and vital importance; and it is equally well-known that the authorities at this Board are constantly lamenting the loss by migration to smaller Colleges of their best men prior to degree-taking.

Whether the connexion between the abnormal wastage at Fitzwilliam Hall and the excess of degrees over matriculations at St Catharine's, Downing and Peterhouse is best described as 'subtle' is possibly a matter of opinion, but it is of no great importance now, and there are one or two comments which may perhaps be added by way of further explanation. Men who transferred to a college in mid-course would already have been matriculated as non-collegiate students, and would not be matriculated again. They would therefore not appear in their college's list of matriculations, but, if they passed their examinations, would be included among its graduates. If, therefore, in any year the number of migrant graduates of a particular college were to exceed the number of its men who did not graduate, it would be possible for that college to shew a number of graduates greater than the number of men whom it had presented for matriculation three years earlier. It seems clear that this happened at St Catharine's, Downing and Peterhouse; and it is probable that the same kind of thing occurred at other colleges, though not to the same extent, and the cumulative effect of this improvement in degree results elsewhere is matched by the statistical distortion in Mr Venn's table, which lists more than sixty per cent of the intake of non-collegiate students over five years as 'wasted'. The table is also misleading in that it suggests that in five years there was no 'wastage' at the three colleges, which is inconceivable.[1] The scale of these transfers to colleges in the earliest years of the non-collegiate institution, and in the 1890s, has been noted already (see pp. 68, 72, 104); and in their Report to the Senate of 12 March 1894 the Board had shown which were the favourite colleges, or the most receptive, of the migrants of the previous three years:[2]

To			To		
	St Catharine's	21 Students		Ayerst's	5 Students
	St John's	11		Sidney	4
	Downing	11		Trinity Hall	3
	Emmanuel	10		Queens'	2
	Christ's	8		Jesus	2
	Peterhouse	7		Clare	1
	Gonv. and Caius	5		Corpus	1
	King's	5			

A comparison of these figures, particularly for St Catharine's and Downing Colleges, with their figures for matriculation over the same period (St Catharine's 41, Downing 30), emphasizes the extent of their dependence on the non-collegiate body as a source of additional undergraduates. That Ayerst Hostel[3] should have been a receiving institution at all is significant, for it suggests that one of the motives for transfer was that 'college' rooms of almost any kind were preferred to the isolation of widely scattered lodgings.

In these circumstances it is not surprising that only rarely did a non-collegiate undergraduate win high academic distinction. The winner of the Porson Prize (twice), and the only two first class men among those admitted by Mr Somerset have already been mentioned (pp. 52, 75n.) and under the next two Censors there were no more than twelve over a period of twenty-five years. Notable among them were two lawyers, of whom one, W. J. Whittaker, a Clothworkers' Exhibitioner in 1886, was at the top of Part I of the Tripos in 1888, and was a Chancellor's medallist.[4] The other, N. J. de Wet, was unusual in that, after being placed in the second class in Part I of the Tripos in 1894 – a year in

---

[1] Mr Venn's percentages of honours graduates to matriculations for the years 1851–1906, although doubtless arithmetically correct, are similarly misleading, for the numbers of honours men in the colleges include non-collegiate migrants, and the corresponding figures for the non-collegiate body exclude them.
[2] *University Reporter*, 1893–94, p. 649.
[3] See p. 14 and footnote.
[4] See also p. 543.

which his countryman J. C. Smuts, of Christ's College, was in the first class in both parts – he became a non-collegiate student, with a *bene discessit*[1] from Downing College, and a year later was in the first class in Part II, when he also won a Chancellor's Medal. He must have been the most successful of the comparatively few migrants to the non-collegiate institution, and Censor Huddleston, when he informed his Board of de Wet's achievement, did not lay undue emphasis on his collegiate origins. Although he did not, in his Cambridge career, match the exceptional excellence of Smuts, de Wet was not to lack distinction in later years, for he was Minister of Justice of the Union of South Africa from 1913 to 1934, and became Chief Justice in 1939. Another academically successful non-collegiate student, who also was to spend some years in South Africa, and was something of a traveller before that, was H. H. W. Pearson. Coming into residence in 1893, he was in the first class in Part I of the Natural Sciences Tripos in 1896, and proceeded B.A. He then moved, first to Christ's College where he

---

[1]   In their Report of 1852 the Oxford Royal Commissioners refer to 'two kinds of removal short of expulsion'. 'These are known', they continue, 'by the names of "Liceat migrare" and "Bene discessit", which are the first words of the Latin forms, in which members of the Society received permission to transfer themselves to another. The "Liceat migrare" is given in cases sufficiently serious to warrant the delinquent's exclusion from his College, but not from the University. A student so removed can migrate either to another University or (after the expiration of one year) to any Society in Oxford which may be willing to admit him. The "Bene discessit" is granted in less grave cases; usually when the student has failed to pass his public examinations within a given time. He may in that case be immediately admitted elsewhere.'

The term *bene discessit* appears not infrequently in the minutes of the Non-Collegiate Students Board, but it seems that the distinction between it and the *liceat migrare* was not observed, for on the only occasion when the latter was granted it was associated with a minor failure of the kind that, in Oxford, would have earned a *bene discessit*.

The issue of a *bene discessit* did not necessarily imply unsatisfactory progress or misconduct, but had long been part of the arrangements for transfers from one college to another, whether on the initiative of an undergraduate who wanted a change, of his college if he was less than satisfactory, or of any college desirous of securing his admission; and the term came to be used for the certificate of fitness without which (by University regulation) no member of a college could be admitted as a non-collegiate student – a rule which ensured that college authorities would not be left unaware of intended moves – and, much more frequently, for certificates supplied to non-collegiate students seeking acceptance by a college.

These arrangements gave rise to considerable difficulty, and to occasional embarrassment, as, for example, when successive Censors discovered by chance the admission of their students to colleges; or when a *bene discessit*, duly supplied, was lost and a duplicate urgently needed. See also p. 156n.

In 1827 there were published two light-hearted little volumes – *Alma Mater* by a Trinity-Man in which (vol. 1, pp. 167n.) the author supplies his own definition of the term *bene discessit*: 'This is a paper stating, in Latin, that you're a decent sort of fellow, but can be spared.' Taken as referring to exchanges between colleges, this does not seem far removed from the heart of the matter.

obtained another first class in Part II, and then to Caius, taking his M.A. degree in 1900. After a spell at Kew, he was Professor of Botany at the South African College in Cape Town from 1903 until his death in 1916, at the early age of forty-six. Just before he died, he had been made Fellow of the Royal Society.

One other name may perhaps be mentioned here – that of H. E. J. Curzon, a member of the Cambridge Day Training College for School-masters, who was among the earliest of those members of Training Colleges in Cambridge to enrol as non-collegiate students in order to qualify for admission to Tripos examinations. In later years the class-lists of Fitzwilliam Hall or House were to include in this way the names of a large number of able men, particularly from Westminster College and Wesley House; and in 1903 Curzon was the first non-collegiate Wrangler (21st). After his graduation in that year he was Lecturer in Mathematics for a short while at St Luke's College in Exeter, and then for thirty years was at the Goldsmiths' College in London (see also p. 156n.).

These men brought distinction to themselves, and credit to the insti-tution to which they belonged, but to a community which, in spite of all its handicaps, was growing more and more conscious of its corpo-rate existence, their successes must have been a galling reminder of what might have been if, in the terminology of another age, there had been no brain drain to carry their best men away.

One further episode also deserves a passing mention, even if it tells little of academic distinction; unless, indeed, in those days the mere fact of entry for honours, irrespective of result, counted for righteous-ness. In 1876, when Wodhams appeared among the *Senior Optimes*, the name 'Williams'[1] was also, by the narrowest of margins, included in the list of mathematical honours. The *Cambridge Chronicle* of 6 February 1876, tells the story:

Degree Day

The first Congregation of the Lent Term was held on the morning of Saturday last when most of the successful candidates in the Mathematical,

---

[1] And nothing else, for in those days names and colleges were given in the class-lists, but (except for women candidates when in 1881 they were admitted to University examina-tions) initials were given only to distinguish between men of the same surname in the same Tripos. As the *non ascripti*, by definition, had no college, their names appeared unaccom-panied until 1893, when most of the examiners (but not the Theologians or the Historians) adopted the abbreviation *Non Coll.*

Williams (Charles) came from the village of Sharow, near Ripon, and was followed by Alfred Wynne Williams, probably his brother, who migrated to Peterhouse in the Lent term 1881, after entering as a non-collegiate student in the Michaelmas term 1879.

Moral Sciences, Natural Sciences, Law, History and Theological Triposes were admitted to the Bachelor's degree by the Vice-Chancellor, the Master of Emmanuel College.

The doors of the Senate House were opened at half-past nine o'clock, and the hall was soon filled – the floor by ladies and friends of the candidates and the galleries by undergraduates. Admission was obtainable only by ticket, which passports were eagerly sought after, so that the house was densely crowded. The students soon manifested a care for what they considered the dignity of the house, by raising cries of 'Cap! Cap!' when anyone appeared covered on the floor of the house; and in one case showers of coppers fell around a well-known senior who gave no heed to their cries. A good deal of fun was provoked by accompanying gentlemen with shouts of 'Right' and 'Left', as they paced the floor in quest of a seat. Presently Professor Fawcett, accompanied by his friends, came in by the doctors' entrance, and was loudly cheered. In the course of the subsequent proceedings pointed allusions were made to personages who were prominently connected with the circumstances which agitated the town in November last, and cheers were given for the Recorder, 'who did justice to Wheeler'. The Senior Proctor, Mr Hardy, also came in for a cordial reception. Mr Ward, the senior wrangler, and Mr Mottram, the second wrangler, were vociferously cheered on being presented to the Vice-Chancellor; and the exploits of students noted on the river or running path were recognized in the same way. Meanwhile, from what was taking place in the galleries, it at first seemed not unlikely that the practice of presenting 'the last of the Apostles' with the traditional wooden spoon would be frustrated; but the students packed themselves into two impenetrable masses on the north and south galleries, and retained possession of the cord by means of which the 'trophy' was to be lowered to the recipient. In due course, the turn of the last one came, and a pair of large wooden spoons, lavishly decorated with non-collegiate colours, were dangled in his face as he turned from the chair. With commendable promptitude he cut the string, and bore off the spoons in triumph, the audience lustily cheering him.

Cheers were afterwards given for the Queen, the Prince of Wales, Mr Disraeli, Captain Webb, the ladies (especially those in blue) &c.; and the proceedings lasted until eleven o'clock.[1]

---

[1] Henry Fawcett (Trinity Hall) was Professor of Political Economy from 1863 to 1884. He was, at the time, Liberal Member of Parliament for Hackney, and later (1880) became Postmaster General.

William Campbell Wheeler, a freshman of King's College, had been convicted on 10 November of assaulting a police constable at a concert held two days previously at the (then) new Corn Exchange. On 12 January the Recorder quashed the conviction, on appeal.

The reference to the 'last of the Apostles' is mistaken. They were the last twelve of the candidates approved for the poll degree.

Captain Webb had swum the Channel in August 1875.

In their social habits some, at least, of the non-collegiate students began to draw together as soon as their circumstances made this at all possible; and in a pamphlet entitled *Non-Collegiate Memoranda*, printed in 1874,[1] they give some account of the use they made of one of the rooms which Mr Somerset had then recently secured for his Board's purposes. After an introductory statement under the heading 'Non-Collegiate Students of the University', in which they give the membership of the Board and the names of the ninety-eight students then on the books, they announce that the Censor has assigned a room for their use at certain hours, and that he appoints at the beginning of every term a committee of resident students to have the entire management of it. The first Chairman of the committee was W. L. Brereton (the second non-collegiate graduate, and son of the Rev. J. L. Brereton, Chairman of the Trustees and Directors of Cavendish College); and the room was to be normally available as a common room on weekdays from eleven to six o'clock, and on Sunday afternoons from three to four. The committee then set forth rules for its management, which, they say, may be altered only with the Censor's approval. Then follow Rules for four clubs or societies – a Newspaper and Magazine Club, a Debating Society, a Boat Club and a Cricket Club. These were not amalgamated, but were separate institutions; amalgamation came later. The Newspaper Club, with a terminal subscription of one shilling and sixpence, contrived to take in fourteen daily or weekly publications. The Debating Society held its first meeting on Saturday, 10 May 1874. There was a terminal subscription of one shilling, meetings were to be held every Saturday evening during that part of the term when most men were likely to be in residence, and began at seven o'clock in the Michaelmas and Lent terms, and in the Easter term at eight, the room always being closed at ten. The Boat Club, of which the Censor was President, was to consist exclusively of non-collegiate students, and depended for its income on a terminal subscription of fifteen shillings. It appears that the boat went down in the afternoon or the evening, and members of the crew who arrived later than 2.30 or 5.45, as the case might be, were fined one shilling, or two shillings for absence. Every member of a crew was required to appear in the costume of the club, but this is not described. Nothing is said about the use of a boat or of a club house. The Cricket Club was open to any non-collegiate student on payment of an annual subscription of five shillings, due on 1 May. Its officers were to be elected by ballot early in the Easter term. In the absence of any notice to the contrary, Monday, Wednesday and Friday

1   J. W. Clark Collection, University Library.

in each week were to be field-days with play beginning at 2.30. A member bowling at practice was held responsible for the ball he used, and if it was lost he was required to pay three shillings to the Treasurer (who, appropriately enough, was Mr Wodhams, the future *Senior Optime*). 'Bats and other articles' were furnished by the club.

As a matter of history, it is recorded that

The Non-collegiate Cricket Club played their first match on the 19th May (1874), on the Trinity Ground, against an eleven of Trinity College. The score was as follows

Non-coll.	1st Innings	124
	2nd Innings	78 (with 6 wickets to fall)
Trinity	1st Innings	132

The three clubs, and one society, already established in 1874 were all in being at the turn of the century, although from a report by Mr Somerset it seems that the Debating Society had soon been temporarily dissolved through lack of interest. Rather surprisingly, Mr Somerset adds 'This I do not regret.'[1]

Much information about undergraduate activities is to be found in the *Cambridge Review*, first issued in 1879, which under the heading of *College Correspondence* published each week in full term items of news about undergraduate affairs. The contributions vary greatly in volume and quality, but in all they present an illuminating picture of many aspects of student life, all the more interesting because it is drawn by the undergraduates themselves.

It was not long before one or other of the non-collegiate clubs found themselves in financial difficulties. In this they were by no means alone, and among the Cambridge colleges Christ's, in 1881, was the first to experiment with a central committee, charged with the duty of calling for estimates of the needs of the individual clubs, and apportioning centrally such funds as might be available.[2] The immediate success of the plan soon led to its adoption by some of the colleges, and in the Michaelmas term 1883 the non-collegiate correspondent of the *Review* clearly has the possibility in mind. 'If all the clubs', he says, 'were amalgamated, it is possible that they might be kept out of debt, but it is so uncertain whether everyone would join, that we have great hesitation in adopting the system. It is certain that some of the clubs must be given up, or that a general arrangement must be made between them'.[3]

---

[1] Censor's Reports to the Board, 1869–81; Report of 7 December 1876.
[2] *Cambridge Review*, 1883–84, p. 198.
[3] *Ibid.*, p. 72.

After further consideration, it was decided to take the plunge, and in January 1884 the Amalgamation Club, as it was for some time called, was formed, with the Boat, Cricket, Football, Lawn Tennis, and Newspaper Clubs, and the Debating Society as constituent members. It seems that the decision was justified, for at the end of the term the General Secretary was able to announce a small surplus.[1]

In the following October a General Meeting of the Amalgamation Club requested its standing committee to report at the beginning of the Lent term 1885 on the question of giving the Club a name (or, rather, of changing its existing name of 'Non-Collegiate Students' Amalgamation Club'); but at the next General Meeting, on the advice of Mr Cooke, for reasons which are not explained, but which are doubtless along the lines of those given by the Non-Collegiate Students Board in the following year, the matter was dropped.[2] Early in March 1886 it was raised again, this time by the Debating Club, when a largely attended meeting approved unanimously a motion (proposed by F. G. Rowcroft, Boat Captain) 'that it is highly desirable that a name be adopted by the Non-collegiate Body or, failing the feasibility of that, by the Amalgamation Club',[3] and appointed a committee to draw up and present a memorial to the Board. They lost no time, for on 13 March the Board received a petition, signed by about a hundred residents, which ran as follows:

> We the undersigned non-collegiate students in residence, beg to call the attention of the Board to the disadvantages under which we labour, both individually and collectively, from the fact of our bearing no positive and distinctive name. At the present time a very large proportion of the non-collegiate students migrate to Colleges before taking their degrees; and it is evident that they do so chiefly because our body has no distinctive name, since they usually delay doing so to as late a period as possible of their University course. The effect of these continual migrations is seriously to lessen that "*esprit de corps*" which it is so desirable to develop. They are also the main causes of our inferiority in athletics to the specially designated bodies, and this inferiority, we firmly believe, is the prime factor in producing that lack of cohesion which we lament. We therefore earnestly request the Board to change our present negative designation and to bestow on us some distinctive appellation such as is borne by the remaining bodies of which the University is composed; and, if that is beyond their power, to urge the Senate of the University to do so.

---

1   A.C. Minutes, 24 April 1884.
2   *Ibid.*, 15 October 1884, 26 January 1885.
3   *Cambridge Review*, 1885–86, p. 265.

That the Board received the undergraduates' representations with sympathy and understanding is evident from the reply which the Deputy Censor was at once asked to send:

> The Board have carefully considered the Petition presented to them. With regard to any change in the official title of the Students, no suggestion has been made, either now or on any previous occasion, which seems appropriate, or that meets all the requirements of the case. The Board are therefore unable to approach the Senate in the matter, as yet. With regard to the very different question, namely, the name for the Students' Clubs, the Board heartily sympathise with the wish. But they feel that the matter may very well be settled by the Students independently of the Board, with the consent of the Censor and the Assistant Censor. Should the Students desire the approval of the Board for any name they may select, they may rely on securing that approval, provided the name agreed upon be generally appropriate and free from objection. But they feel that the Students should know that the question of buildings, which has long been, and still is, under the consideration of the Board, has a close connection with this question of a name, both for the Clubs and for the body as a whole. It is quite possible that the buildings, when a site is obtained, may bring with them, either by association or position, a name which it would be natural for the Students to assume both for themselves and for their Clubs. It seems therefore that the best policy would be not to run any risk of hastily assuming a name which might soon have to be exchanged for one obviously more desirable and appropriate.[1]

There the matter rested, but not for long; for at a General Meeting of the Club held early in the Lent term 1887, a special committee was appointed 'to give the Club a name', and at the next General Meeting 'Bloom, as secretary of the committee appointed to give the Club a name, gave an outline of what had been done, and after an interesting discussion it was resolved that all non-colls should be asked to vote in favour of either Somerset, Fitzwilliam, Devonshire, or St Mary's, and of Buildings, House or Hall.'[2] The result of the vote is not known, but on 15 February a member of the Board proposed that the name Fitzwilliam Hall should be given to their premises. After the proposal had been approved on 26 April,[3] a General Meeting of the Amalgamation Club accepted unanimously a motion of the General Secretary that 'in consequence of the name "Fitzwilliam Hall" having been given by the

1 Minutes, 13 March 1886.
2 A.C. Minutes, 19 January and 7 March 1887. A colourful character, James Harvey Bloom (B.A. 1887) rowed five (at 14st. 4) in the 1887 Lent boat, and was Boat Club Secretary in his last term (Michs 1887). Father of Miss Ursula Bloom, he figures largely in her *Parson Extraordinary*.
3 Minutes, 15 February, 26 April 1887.

Board to the present buildings the Non-Collegiate Students Amalgamation Club be called the Fitzwilliam Hall Amalgamation Club, and that
the text of the rules be altered accordingly'. At the same meeting the
Club approved proposals that 'the present armorial bearings be altered'
and 'the present colours be altered', and appointed committees to
consider both these matters. They also asked Mr Cooke to express
their appreciation of the Board's action, presumably in deciding to call
their premises Fitzwilliam Hall, and at their next meeting the Board,
having received a letter from Mr Cooke to this effect, also gave permission for the use by the students for their boat flag, provided that sanction was obtained from Earl Fitzwilliam, of 'the Fitzwilliam arms with
the University arms in chief'.[1]

Of the activities of what may be described as the 'crest' and
'colours' committees, the Club's minutes say very little of the former
(which was concerned with armorial bearings in general). They merely
record 'a cordial vote of thanks to Bloom for his care and attention to
the matter of a crest for the Club', asking him to continue his good
offices, and in due course to present a design suitable for note paper
and similar purposes. There is no further mention of armorial bearings
until the beginning of the Lent term of 1888, when, we are told, 'the
final design for the crest was sanctioned', and the General Secretary
was asked to arrange for club badges, shields and the like, to be made
available. The Amalgamation Club minutes nowhere describe this final
design, but there is no doubt that it was the same as that of the composite device approved by the Board in May 1887 for use on the Boat Club
flag. Of any application to the University authorities for leave to make
use of its coat of arms there is no trace; and although it is believed that
sanction was obtained from Earl Fitzwilliam, the propriety of the adoption of the composite device was to be challenged some sixty years
later by the College of Heralds.[2]

If information about armorial bearings is scanty, there is no lack of it
about colours. From their minutes it is clear that the question was
raised by the Amalgamation Club in May 1887, when it was resolved

---

[1] A.C. Minutes, 2 May, and Board Minutes, 26 May 1887. The proposal for a change in the
armorial bearings suggests that others may have been used previously. There appears to be
no specific reference to an earlier usage, but it must be possible that some form of the University's own shield which appears, for example, in a letter heading used by Censor
Huddleston (see Censor's Reports 1882–98), was appropriated by one or other of the clubs.
[2] On 21 January 1911, a General Meeting of the Amalgamated Clubs referred to a special
committee a motion 'to delete the University arms from the coat of arms, and to restore the
Norman lozenges to their original size; and to substitute the crest (coronet and feathers) for
the shield on the Amalgamated Clubs blazer'; but nothing came of it.
For intervention by the College of Heralds, see p. 481.

that 'the present colours' be altered; and, from subsequent discussions on the merits of various suggestions then put forward, it also emerges that these present colours were 'blue and buff. Blue and buff, however, were not the earliest choice of all, for in a record of the results of the Lent Races of 1875 the uniform of the Boat Club is described as 'a grey blazer trimmed with ruby, white straw hat with grey and ruby striped ribbon'. A year later this had become 'a white jersey and white straw hat trimmed with orange and blue, blue blazer, with orange facings'.[1] When, therefore, on 2 June 1887, the Amalgamation Club, after considering a number of alternatives, settled for 'red and grey', they were returning to an earlier design, used by the Boat Club, at least, before the separate clubs were amalgamated in 1884. Details of the arrangements of the new colours were decided shortly afterwards, and the General Secretary was asked to invite tenders from tailors in the town, and choose which seemed best. At the beginning of the Michaelmas term he reported that of four tenders received he had accepted that submitted by Messrs Charles Dixon, of Downing Street, 'which is', he says, 'as follows':

	Cash	Credit
Boating		
Blazer, grey with grey and red		
diagonal ribbon	16/-	18/-
Cap, eight quarters red and grey	2/6	3/-
Socks, red and grey	2/-	2/6
Vests, trimmed red and grey	3/6	4/-
Ribbon for Straw Hat	2/6	2/8
Football		
Blazer (as Cricket and Boating)		
Cap, half red and grey	2/6	3/-
Shirt, red and grey in halves,		
slieves [sic] altern.	9/6	10/6
Silk sash, red and grey	4/-	4/6
Stockings, red and grey	2/6	3/-
Tennis and Cricket		
Blazer, red with grey stripes	16/-	18/-
Cap (as Boating)		
Tie, red and grey	2/-	2/6

Whites, Sweaters, Mufflers, Straws &c.&c. at ordinary prices, according to quality.[2]

---

[1] *The Cambridge University General Almanack and Register* 1876, p. 315, and 1877, p. 300.
[2] A.C. Minutes, 2 and 8 June, 13 October 1887. Messrs Dixon conducted their business at no. 6 Downing Street, now occupied, after rebuilding, by the Royal Insurance Company, together with numbers 3, 4, 5.

Having, in the Easter term of 1887, selected new colours, and deter- mined how they should be used by the several clubs, and having made, in the Easter term of 1888, their final choice of armorial bearings, the Amalgamation Club drafted consequential amendments to their Rules; which, embellished with the composite shield and crest, and under their new title of 'Fitzwilliam Hall Amalgamation Club', were examined in proof at a meeting held at the beginning of the Easter term of 1888, when the secretary was instructed to circulate them as soon as a list of Vice-Presidents could be completed.

The Rules of 1888 provide the earliest remaining evidence of the use of the new armorial bearings, and the first example of the use of the new title 'Fitzwilliam Hall Amalgamation Club';[1] and if they are there- fore of more than usual interest, they are also unusual in that, from the Club's point of view at least, they were issued only just in time, and in disregard – whether by design or inadvertence – of a further ruling by the Board some months previously in November 1887. At the beginning of that Michaelmas term, after a move by certain Board members to replace the word 'Hall' in the title by another, it was decided that the word should be retained, but that its use should be restricted; and the Censor was instructed to inform the men 'that the name "Fitzwilliam Hall" is simply the designation of the buildings in Trumpington Street in the occupation of the Board; that the title should not be used as an official or collective designation of the Non-Collegiate Students; and that the title "Fitzwilliam" may appropriately be given to any Club consisting of Non-Collegiate Students'.[2] Formal notice of this ruling, however, does not appear to have been taken until the end of the Easter term 1888, when an Amalgamation Club minute reads 'By the request

---

[1]   A.C. Minutes, 23 April 1888, and College Archives.

[2]   Minutes, 14 October, 11 November 1887. On 14 October letters were received from Mr J. A. Robinson, of Christ's College, and Mr G. F. Browne, of St Catharine's, who had ceased to be a member of the Board in 1877, 'with regard to the name "Fitzwilliam Hall"'; and Mr Robinson gave notice that at the next Board meeting he would propose that it be changed. This he did on 11 November, by a motion seconded by Mr J. T. Ward, of St John's. That Mr Browne, no longer a Board member, should seek to intervene suggests some strength of feeling of the point. He was a Fellow of Catharine Hall, a name which he preferred to 'St Catharine's College', and may have disapproved of the application of the word 'Hall' to a non-collegiate institution. The point was to be made again, some forty years later (see p. 202).

   In day-to-day speech this careful distinction, between buildings and clubs on the one· hand and the body of non-collegiate students on the other, was not observed, and 'Fitzwil- liam Hall', like the later 'Fitzwilliam House', was increasingly used as the 'collective desig- nation of Non-Collegiate Students' – a usage much encouraged by successive Censors, par- ticularly W. F. Reddaway, who made no secret of their dislike of the 'negative appellation'. Censors also were known by the shorter and more acceptable title.

of the Non-Collegiate Students Board the word "Hall" is to be struck out from the official designation of our Clubs. Thus the "Fitzwilliam Hall Cricket Club" is to stand [*sic*] the "Fitzwilliam Cricket Club" and so on.'[1] In the meantime, however, in consequence of the Board's earlier decision, the Amalgamation Club, and doubtless also its individual clubs, had begun to use the new title, and although in the light of the Board's ruling they dropped the word 'Hall', it had crept back into their minutes and, it may be assumed, into more general use by the Michaelmas term 1892. Thereafter, whether by accident or design, the minutes usually contrive to do without a name, the description 'Fitzwilliam Amalgamation Club' rarely occurs, and when the Rules were next revised in 1897, the new code was entitled *Rules of the Fitzwilliam Hall Amalgamated Clubs*.[2] This not only confirmed the use of the former title, applied to the clubs as well as to the building, but also discarded the earlier description 'Amalgamation Club' in favour of 'Amalgamated Clubs', which was to persist until 1969, when the whole system was changed.

The Rules of 1888, in giving effect to decisions then recently taken, had announced the new colours; but it seems that their draftsman left matters unclear, for Rule 13 for the Club, which declares that its members may wear 'an Amalgamation blazer and cap', does not specify colours for them; and from subsequent editions of the Rules it appears that the final clause of this regulation, declaring the club colours to be red and grey, was not intended to apply to the blazer and cap. The matter was put right in the 1897 Rules, in which the corresponding regulation confirms red and grey as the club colours, but describes the uniform which all members may wear as 'a dark blue blazer with gilt buttons, and with the crest on the pocket, and a dark blue cap with the letters F.H.A.C. in old English'. It seems very likely that this was intended, but by oversight not provided, in 1888, and this choice of dark blue for their blazer was retained for all members of the Clubs, with various alternatives, until 1969.

In 1890, no more than two years after this considerable debate about colours and their permutations, it is at first surprising to find a resolution, carried unanimously but without comment, for a change from grey to red as the background colour of the boating blazer. The *Review* correspondent is more explicit, and emphatically monosyllabic: 'The new one [blazer] is a red ground bound with grey silk. It was found necessary to do this, as the grey ground of the old one went pea

[1]   A.C. Minutes, 8 June 1888.
[2]   *Ibid.*, 16 October 1897.

green.'[1] By the Easter term of 1892 the rowing journalists had opted for 'cardinal and French grey', and, in revised Rules of the Clubs approved in 1908, the official description had become 'maroon and grey'.

One problem which confronted all the players of ball games was the question where they should play their 'home' matches. There was always Parker's Piece, and the non-collegiate undergraduates were not the only ones to use it. The Board did not see their way to buy, or even hire, a ground, and the men were left almost entirely to their own resources. In the Easter term 1880, 'our new ground', we read, 'seems to give general satisfaction. There is ample room for cricket practice, and three tennis courts are in full swing.'[2] In the Michaelmas term 1880, again 'This is the first season we have had an organized Football Club. It is hoped to have three practice days a week, on our ground at the top of Hills Road.'[3] An expression of regret at Mr Somerset's retirement in October 1881 mentions the Club's indebtedness to him for what he had done to find a field for lawn tennis and cricket.[4] In the Michaelmas term 1883 the clubs, 'having secured a ground of their own, hope for better things';[5] and in the Lent term 1884 the Amalgamation Club decided 'to retain the cricket field',[6] but this seems to have been found impracticable, for in the Board's Accounts for the year 1883/84 is a sum of £9 which they received from the sale of hurdles bought to enclose a cricket ground which was disposed of for financial reasons before the hurdling was done.[7]

No further attempt to secure a field seems to have been made until 1896, when there was a flurry of activity in what was a better year than usual for clubs as a whole. In the Easter term a proposal was made at a General Meeting of the Club for the hire of a ground. Mr W. G. Bell, recently elected President, was apprehensive about cost, but it was agreed to make enquiries, and in the Michaelmas term the Finance Committee of the Club was given authority, if it should be thought feasible, to hire a field for football, cricket and tennis in conjunction with the Perse School. The committee asked the President and others to

---

1   *Ibid.*, 23 April 1890; and *Cambridge Review*, 1890–91, p. 36.
2   *Cambridge Review*, 1879–80 (C), p. 24.
3   *Ibid.*, 1880–81, p. 25.
4   *Ibid.*, 1881–82, p. 9.
5   *Ibid.*, 1883–34, p. 22.
6   A.C. Minutes, 20 February 1884.
7   College Archives. Presumably it was the cricket pitch, and not the whole ground, that was to have been enclosed.

inspect various fields, including one of about eight acres on the Hills Road near Cavendish College, which could be had on a yearly tenure only, as the land was being advertised for building, and another of five acres on the Madingley Road. The Hills Road field was found to be unfit for cricket and tennis without relaying of turf, and two members of the committee were authorized to look for a small football field for the Michaelmas term 1896 (at a cost of less than £10), and also to investigate the possibility of coming to an arrangement with Downing College for sharing a ground for the term. No temporary arrangement, however, proved possible, and the question of a permanent field was shelved.[1] It cropped up again in 1900, when it was said that there were hopes of finding a field, but again with no result until the Lent term 1904, when a General Meeting of the Clubs 'unanimously agreed to hire a field from Caius College for cricket and three tennis courts in the May term, and for three days a week in the winter terms for football and hockey, at £50 a year.'[2] An agreement with the College was approved on 22 November. This field, described as 'commodious and prettily situated', is referred to by the Non-Collegiate Students Board in a Report to the Senate, when they mention a field adjoining the Coton footpath as having been hired for cricket, football and the like.[3] Before long, however, the College needed the field for its own purposes, and in the Easter term 1906 the University football ground was hired for tennis and for cricket practice. The Finance Committee of the Clubs also asked that enquiries should be made about a ground, somewhere, which all players of ball games might share, and voted a sum of ten shillings for an advertisement in the local papers; but not much progress seems to have been made, for the next development, in the Easter term 1907, was an offer from Cheshunt College for the joint use of their ground.[4] Whether the offer was accepted is not recorded; possibly the matter was overtaken by events at the coming of the new Censor.

　　An anonymous contributor to the newly founded *Fitzwilliam Magazine* has left his own account, written in the Michaelmas term 1909 when this particular problem had been solved, of the circumstances in which the non-collegiate games players – except for the rowing men, who had trials enough of their own – found themselves at the turn of

[1]　A.C. Minutes, 9,14,16,19 October, also 5 December 1896.
[2]　*Ibid.*, 26 February, 22 November 1904.
[3]　*University Reporter*, 1904–05, p. 768. This will have been a Caius College ground, adjoining what is now the Emmanuel ground on Wilberforce Road.
[4]　A.C. Minutes, 24 February, 25 April, 17 October 1906; also 29 January, 24 April 1907.

the century. What he says applied not only to three University generations, but to the clubs since their first beginnings:

> We were very hungry for land. Less than two years ago we coveted any patch of Cambridge clay that might be called 'a ground of our own'. For three (University) generations or more we had been wandering in the desert, driven from every oasis by inexorable landlords. In earlier days we, like many other University clubs, frequented for both cricket and football Parker's Piece, where the batsman strains his eyes to disentangle the ball from the background of a passing omnibus, only to be run out by a fielder skilfully ambushed behind a crowd of lookers-on. After that we found a welcome refuge for a season or two in a field off the Coton footpath, newly laid down by Caius, but when it came to maturity we were compelled to move on. 1907 found our cricketers reduced to a practice net on the 'Varsity' Rugger ground, and in 1908 even this could not be had. With great difficulty we made a temporary arrangement with the Perse School for one match per week and a few practices.
>
> Meanwhile our Tennis Six occupied, first a quaking bog by the Granta, which shook beneath their feet, then a new ground laid down – and laid down very badly – near West Road, then the new ground of Caius aforesaid, finally another new ground in Grange Road, which became a very good one and has now been taken by the C.U.L.T.C. For winter play an ash court (rather expensive and very dirty) near Parker's Piece was engaged.
>
> At the beginning of last year, therefore, we had the prospect of playing in summer occasional cricket at two miles' distance from our grass courts, and in winter occasional football and hockey on the incurably slimy ground to which we had migrated when banished by Caius – at two miles' distance from the ash court – and in each case on sufferance.[1]

The early uncertainty about the willingness of the undergraduates to join the Amalgamation Club was understandable in a community as heterogeneous as the non-collegiate body, of which it might be said that if there was one thing in which its members would be likely to resemble one another, it would be in the need to save their money. When the Club began in the Lent term 1884, it had 62 undergraduate members out of 117 in residence. By the Michaelmas term 1888 there were 40 out of 106, and in the next term there were 31 members, of whom 5 were officers or members of the Board, and 8 paid a reduced subscription for membership of a Literary Society only. In the Michaelmas term 1890, when there was a particularly popular and vigorous General Secretary, there had been 56 full members of the clubs, and 13

---

[1] *Magazine*, December 1909, p. 131.

of the Literary Society, out of a total of 120 resident undergraduates.[1] In 1895 the numbers were about the same, but in the Michaelmas term 1898 there were 15 active members – 'pulling members' they were called in one college – of the Boat Club, 8 of the Football Club, and 9, of whom 4 were described as occasional, of the Lawn Tennis Club.[2] These figures reflect the composition of the student body, and suggest that whether by force of circumstances or from personal preference, a very substantial proportion of the men had only a limited interest in the clubs' affairs.

In consequence, there was the greatest difficulty in running them, and in keeping out of debt; and the cost of any considerable item of capital expenditure, such as an eight, could be met by private subscription only. At the beginning of each academical year it became customary for the President of the Clubs to appeal for an increased membership, and in especially bad times there was anxious consideration whether this or that club could continue. As the most expensive of the clubs, and often the least successful, the future of the Boat Club came up for periodic review. The pamphlet *Non-collegiate Memoranda*[3] lists it as being in existence in 1874, but the club was twice suspended, once for three years and once, on financial grounds, for two,[4] during the remaining years of the century, and even when it was in existence a boat was not always put on, particularly in the May Races.

The Lawn Tennis Club was suspended in 1889; in 1892 it was considered doubtful whether the Cricket Club could continue, and although it was kept going this was possible only by a decision that if the Amalgamation Club met the cost of practice on Parker's Piece the expenses of any matches that might be arranged must be borne by the members of the side themselves.[5] In the Lent term 1899 the Clubs determined that as there seemed to be so little interest in the game no football should be played, and suggested that such footballers as there were should turn their attention to rowing; and then, again, there was a debate, this time inconclusive, on the advisability of closing down the Boat Club. The most depressing moment of all must surely have been in the Michaelmas term of 1888 when 'it was resolved', says a minute of the standing committee of the Amalgamation Club, 'that in view of the unsatisfactory financial position of the Club – the annual accounts shewing a deficiency of £40 – a General Meeting be held at an early

---

[1] Censor's Reports; Report dated March 1892.
[2] A.C. Minutes, 15 October 1898.
[3] See p. 121.
[4] *Cambridge Review*, 1879–80, p. 42; also A.C. Minutes, 17 January 1889.
[5] A.C. Minutes, 9 March 1892.

date in the Lent term to consider the question of the continuance or dissolution of the Club'.[1] But, although individual clubs might be put in abeyance from time to time, the organization of the Club as a whole did, somehow, survive.

Subscriptions for membership varied periodically. The full terminal subscription was never higher than the sum of one guinea with which it appears to have begun in 1884, and in the Lent term 1889, when the Club's fortunes were at their lowest ebb, it was halved, presumably in the hope of attracting more members. The hope was not realized, and after only one term it was put back to a guinea, to be dropped again to 10s.6d, and, after a short spell at 15s and then 16s, it became £1 in the Lent term 1893, with an entrance fee of 5s, first introduced two years previously. From the early days there had been a disposition to admit at a reduced subscription members who did not make full use of the Club's facilities – there is also an allusion to 'non-active members', but no definition of the term – and in the Michaelmas term 1888, after the issue of new Rules of that year, a list of members shews that there were three rates of subscription, at £1, 10s.6d, and 5s. These rates may well have applied to full members of the Club, to honorary members, and to members of the Literary Club or Society, as the former Debating Club and Newspaper Club had jointly come to be called. In 1896 it was agreed that 'men engaged in schools' should be permitted to pay an entrance fee of 2s.6d, and a terminal subscription of 10s, and that all users of the Reading Room should be liable to pay the 5s. subscription to the Literary Society; and in 1897, on the occasion of another altera- tion of the Rules, the rates were fixed at 5s for entrance, £1 for full membership, and 5s. for membership of the Literary Society only. In 1903 there was a new departure in a decision to make compulsory the hitherto voluntary subscription of 5s to the Reading Room and Literary Society, but neither the precise intention nor the effect of this decision is clear. Shortly afterwards, a new subscription of 15s was introduced for membership of a single games club, and the extension of this arrangement to the Literary Society in 1907 meant that the subscription to that society, at one time as low as 2s.6d, was then trebled.[2] There is here an anticipation of the friction between the games players and those whose interests lay elsewhere which was to spring into promi- nence in years to come, at a time of unprecedented success in all games, when the predominantly athletic character of the Amalgamated Clubs was to be called in question.

[1] *Ibid.*, 6 December 1888.
[2] *Ibid.*, 1884–1904, 1904–13.

The Accounts of the Non-collegiate Students Board do not refer to the finances of the Amalgamated Clubs, except when in times of particular adversity the Board might decide to help with a special grant from funds at their disposal. The Clubs' minutes commonly allude in the most general fashion to the terminal estimates and statements of accounts which were presented at General Meetings, and only occasionally do the minutes give information about membership. The 1897 Rules prescribe that the General Secretary shall print and circulate a balance sheet of the Accounts for the preceding academical year at the beginning of each Michaelmas term, and it is reasonable to suppose that this was in continuation of established practice. Copies of three of these balance sheets, in the period with which this chapter is concerned, are still in the records, the first, for the year 1895/6, being in the book of Censor's Reports to the Board (1882–98), and the other two, for the years 1897/98 and 1898/99, in the Minute Book of the Amalgamated Clubs for those years. All provide evidence of the way in which the Clubs managed their affairs, and the statement which is reproduced below is unusual in being prefaced by a letter from the General Secretary who, as was becoming customary at the time, describes himself as Captain of the Clubs. Except for the boats, the clubs had prospered more than usual during the year, although this was one of the periods when they had no ground; and it had been a real achievement to clear off an inherited debt of £80 or so, which in those times and to those men was a formidable sum. Mr Ross was a good officer (although he does not seem to have excelled as a correspondent to the *Cambridge Review*), and the clubs must have very much regretted his loss when in January 1897, after his second term as General Secretary and at the beginning of his fifth term of residence, he was admitted as pensioner to Jesus College.

Fitzwilliam Hall
Amalgamated Clubs and Literary Society.

DEAR SIR,

I beg leave to present to you the Balance Sheet of the Amalgamated Clubs and Literary Society for the past year, together with a short summary of the doings of the various Clubs. From the Balance Sheet it will at once be seen that the Clubs prospered financially; they not only paid their own way but contributed about £30 to clear off debt.

The Football Club had a very good Season, three or four matches being played every week, with the result of giving the Team some very good games. The Boat worked hard, and if not quite so successful in the races as was expected, some allowance must be made for the loss of two good men a week or so before the races commenced. Cricket went on well in the May Term, many most enjoyable matches being played, including one at St. Edmund's Coll., Ware, some great victories falling to our share. The handsome Average Bat improved the scoring. The greatest success of the year was our Lawn Tennis Six, an unbroken record of victory being their contribution to the year's achievements. Then too, we must not forget the Literary and Debating Society, whose efforts in the way of getting up Concerts, Debates, &c., afforded many of us who were unable to take an active part in athletics great recreation and pleasure.

Now, what is needed to ensure the continuance of this success is that each member of Fitzwilliam Hall, more especially each Freshman among us, should loyally do his best to support all the Clubs, either by taking part in one or other of the games himself, or by paying his subscription and becoming a Member.

In conclusion I wish on behalf of the Clubs to thank those Members who so generously came forward with their donations and helped materially to wipe off the outstanding debt. I give the names of those who contributed last year. The previous year's contributions were acknowledged in last year's report.

I am,

Yours faithfully,

NEVILLE W. ROSS,

Capt. F.H.A.C.

DONATION LIST

	£	s.	d.
B. C. Dorrell, Esq.	0	5	0
A. F. Heald, Esq.	0	5	0
G. Goode, Esq.	0	10	0
Rev. J. H. B. Masterman	1	1	0
E. W. Harrison, Esq.	2	7	0
C. S. Thomas, Esq.	0	10	0
J. H. H. Goodwin, Esq.	1	1	0
H. F. Carling, Esq., 2nd donation...	0	5	0
	£6	4	0

FITZWILLIAM HALL AMALGAMATED CLUBS.

Receipts

	£	s.	d.	£	s.	d.
Balance, October 1, 1895				1	4	2
SUBSCRIPTIONS.						
Oct. Term, 1895	46	9	0			
Lent Term, 1896	38	18	6			
May Term, 1896	37	17	6			
Unpaid Subscriptions	7	0	0			
				130	5	0
				£131	**9**	**2**

Expenditure

	£	s.	d.	£	s.	d.
BOAT CLUB.						
Logan, Oct. Term, 1895	6	2	4			
Logan, Lent Term 1896	8	19	10			
Logan, May Term 1896	4	12	6			
Logan, Long Vac. 1896	7	0	0			
Training Dinners	3	0	6			
Set of Oars	3	10	0			
Hire of Bicycle	1	1	0			
Race Expenses	1	16	0			
C.U.B.C. Tax	6	10	3			
Small Payments	3	13	0			
				46	5	5
LAWN TENNIS CLUB.						
Ayres, Oct. Term, 1895	4	0	0			
Ayres, Lent Term, 1896	4	0	0			
Ayres, May Term, 1896	15	18	9			
Small Payments	1	0	4			
				24	19	1
CRICKET CLUB.						
Hayward, May Term, 1896	15	12	6			
Small Payments	0	14	3			
				16	6	9
ASSOCIATION FOOTBALL CLUB.						
Hayward, Oct. Term, 1895	5	6	0			
Hayward, Lent Term 1896	1	15	0			
Brake to West Wratting	0	19	6			
C.U.A.F.C. Tax	1	1	0			
Small Payments	1	12	3			
				10	13	9
GENERAL EXPENSES.						
Clerk	4	10	0			
Printing, &c.	2	9	0			
Small Payments	2	13	7			
				9	12	7
Carried to Debt Account				23	10	0
Balance, September 30, 1896				0	1	7
				£131	**9**	**2**

FITZWILLIAM HALL LITERARY SOCIETY.

Receipts

	£	s.	d.	£	s.	d.
Balance, October 1, 1895				3	1	8
SUBSCRIPTIONS.						
Oct. Term, 1895	5	10	0			
Lent Term, 1896	6	5	0			
May Term, 1896	6	0	0			
Unpaid Subscriptions	1	5	0			
				19	0	0
SALE OF PAPERS.						
Oct. Term, 1895	1	17	6			
Lent Term, 1896	2	15	8			
May Term, 1896	1	6	7			
				5	19	9
				£28	**1**	**5**

Expenditure

	£	s.	d.	£	s.	d.
Periodicals—						
Oct. Term, 1895	5	1	10			
Lent Term, 1896	6	1	7			
May Term, 1896	5	3	7			
				16	7	0
Writing Paper and Envelopes				2	9	2
Printing, &c.				1	3	0
Small Payments				0	6	9
Organ at Popular Concert				1	1	0
Carried to Debt Account				6	4	6
Balance, Sept. 30, 1896				0	10	0
				£28	**1**	**5**

DEBT ACCOUNT.

	£	s.	d.		£	s.	d.
Donations (94-95)	17	8	6	Original Debt, Oct. 1894	77	10	0
Donations (95-96)................	6	4	0				
*From Literary Society (94-95)	5	0	0				
From Literary Society (95-96)	6	4	6				
From Amalg. Clubs (95-96)	23	10	0				
Balance of Debt still due	24	3	0				
* [Apparently, included in error]	£77	10	0				

	£	s.	d.
By Board	20	0	0
Per Censor.....................	4	3	0
Extinguished	£24	3	0

Mr Ross did not date his letter or the balance sheet, but they were issued early in the Michaelmas term 1896, and relate to the previous academical year. The title may be found misleading, for it could be read as implying that the Amalgamated Clubs and the Literary Society were separate organizations; but although there is evidence of earlier disagreement about the voting rights of those who were members of one club only, and although the separate presentation of the accounts might similarly suggest a distinction between them, the 1897 Rules state specifically that the Literary Society is a constituent member of the Clubs.[1] The statement shews clearly how dependent the Clubs were on their income from subscriptions, which in the year 1895–6 was about the average of the figures now known, the highest terminal amount being £68 in the Lent term 1884 (the first term of all), and the lowest £28 in the Lent term 1899. The larger total in the Michaelmas term 1895, probably reflects the numbers in residence, which tended to decrease in the course of the year; and it may also be that some freshmen, persuaded to join the Clubs on coming into residence, did not keep up their membership. Three years later the discrepancy was much greater, for the Lent term figure of £28 had been £51 the term before; but whatever the reasons may have been, they do not seem to have affected the Literary Society, which maintained its numbers throughout the year. But neither the Games Clubs nor the Society were free from trouble over unpaid subscriptions, for in one year when the paid up subscriptions came to £114 there was an amount of £22 in arrears.

On the expenditure side, Logan was a boat builder, to whom payments were made for the hire and housing of boats and, on occasion, for their purchase, and for repairs. In those days oars were cheap, but

[1] A.C. Minutes, 16 October 1907.

the University Boat Club levy was a constant burden, and on one occasion a weighty argument in favour of taking the boat off the river was the fact that if this were done the Boat Club would be free from tax until a boat was put on again. The hiring of a bicycle was presumably for a coach; the corresponding estimate had been for a horse, at seven times the price. Ayres was in charge of the lawn tennis courts at Fenner's, where the club preferred to play its games if courts were available, and payments would be made to him for the hire of courts (three in the Easter term), and the purchase of tennis balls, which it was found necessary to control with some care. There is also an occasional reference to the hire of ball-boys for an important match. Hayward was a member of the famous Cambridge cricketing family, probably the Daniel Hayward who was groundsman at Fenner's and at the University football ground on Grange Road, and brother of the senior partner in one of the most famous pairs of opening batsmen in the history of cricket. Payments by the Cricket Club would be for the preparation of wickets on Parker's Piece, for the erection of a tent in the days when there was no pavilion – this was mentioned as an expense which would be saved if the Hall had a field of its own – for the purchase of equipment and the hiring of umpires, each at 5s a game. Payments were no doubt made, privately, at The Prince Regent, a tavern in Regent Street, kept by members of the Hayward family and handily placed at the close of play on 'The Piece', or in later years at Fenner's. The Football Club would be charged for the use of pitches on Parker's Piece, and it does not seem fanciful to suppose that the smaller expenditure in the Lent term was due to the calls of the Boat Club, which in 1895–96 had a boat in the Lent Races. The West Wratting fixture was a regular event, and supporters were allowed a seat in the brake for a shilling. A principal feature of the year's accounts was, however, the wiping out of the Clubs' accumulated debt, with the help of a grant of £20 from the Board, and a donation of the remainder (£4.3.0) from the Censor.

Of the individual clubs, the Boat Club held pride of place, but it is nevertheless the Boat Club that supplies the most striking evidence of the tribulations – hardly too strong a word – of the undergraduates in their outdoor pursuits. For a body wishing to improve its status there was every incentive to seek distinction on the river, but everything was against the non-collegiate boats, for good rowing men came from the big rowing schools, which were not likely to advise them to go to the University as non-collegiate students. The club suffered from a persistent shortage of men, and from a constant difficulty in assembling at the same time and place nine men living in lodgings all over the town. The Previous Examination cast its shadow over freshmen, and not over freshmen alone, and rather more demanding tests might stand in the way of the May Boats. Migration was a nightmare, for it might break up a crew at short notice, and a consequential scarcity of senior men made it hard to find coaches.

In 1875, when the non-collegiate boat made its first appearance on the river, the boats were arranged in three divisions, of which the first and second rowed in the May Races, and the second and third in the Lents. In the Lent Races of their first year, the non-collegiate boat, starting as the last of twelve in Division III, rowed over on four days, although from one account they gained so considerably on Christ's II as to make the race 'a very hot one'. The same correspondent also understood that they called themselves 'The Herons'.

Being in Division III of the Lents, the boat was not eligible to enter the May Races in 1875; but in 1876 there followed (in the light of subsequent events) a most surprising year; for, starting again at the bottom of the river, the boat made four bumps, and, presumably on this account, was promoted to Division II, thus becoming eligible for entry in the Mays, where they made four bumps again. It is, perhaps, unfortunate that the club's first bump in the May Races was made at the expense of a boat (Downing) which fouled the bank at the start, but the successive overhauling of St Peter's and Magdalene suggests that the luck of the first night may not have been altogether undeserved, and the tally was completed by a bump on St John's. As claims were to be made for up to forty years that Fitzwilliam had then, for the first time, caught a representative boat, it is to be noted that these bumps in the Mays of 1876 were all made on first boats, although in St John's College there were already three crews of the Lady Margaret Boat Club.

For the next three years the boat remained in Division II, their highest point being tenth and their lowest, at the end of the May Races of 1879, sixteenth at the bottom. In the following Michaelmas term the non-collegiate correspondent of the *Cambridge Review* writes 'Our Boat Club is to be wound up. The almost insuperable difficulties we have to meet with, both in the constant migration of our men to the Colleges, and in the disunion which must prevail among men separated from each other as Non-Colls are, have been regarded as sufficient reason for giving up a club which cannot be successfully carried on.'[1] And so, for

[1]   From the Michaelmas term 1879, the *Cambridge Review* is a principal source of information. Of the races between 1875 and 1879 there are records in the *Cambridge University*

three years there was no boat in Lents or Mays. In 1883 the Lent boat appeared again, with scant encouragement from the rowing press, who judged it to be 'about the worst crew that ever rowed in the Lent Races'; but Emmanuel II seem to have escaped notice, for they were caught on the last night. Thereafter for many years there was little to cheer about. From 1884 until 1888, when the races were abandoned on the third day after a fatal accident in the Clare boat, the boat rowed over at the bottom of the river. (In 1888, also, they were first described as of Fitzwilliam Hall). As a consequence of their absence again in 1889 and 1890, permission was given to Ayerst Hostel to fill the vacancy, on the understanding that if Fitzwilliam were to be revived Ayerst Hostel would forfeit its place. In 1891 Fitzwilliam made two of its total of three bumps gained in the last twenty years of the century, but the gain was speedily lost in the following year when, on the first night, they were overbumped by 1st Trinity V, and for the rest rowed over at the bottom. 'Number 7 failing us on the last two days made matters worse' was the rueful observation made by a supporter, who seems to imply that the defaulter saw no sufficient reason to take his place in a boat which, if it had little prospect of going up, was at least not in a position to go further down. If the observation was justified, it supplies evidence enough of dispirited indifference born of repeated failure. In 1893 and 1894 there was again no boat, and in 1895 the Lent Races were cancelled because of an epidemic of influenza, doubtless to the mortification of those colleges which had escaped it. On its resumption the boat remained at the bottom, or near it, of the lower division, until 1899 when it began at fourth place in a newly created Division III, and straightway lost four places. Its absence in 1900 meant a resumption at the bottom of that division also, and with occasional gains wiped out in recurring bad years the boat was never for any length of time safely away from the bottom. The Lents of 1905 were exceptional, with bumps on Queens' II, Jesus III, and Christ's II, and oars were awarded; but the whole of that gain was lost in the next year; and in 1907 there began a pattern, followed with some frequency, whereby Fitzwilliam Hall would begin one place away from the bottom, and end in the lowest place of all, after being caught by the year's getting-on boat, usually on the first night.

General Almanack and Register (1876–80). The reference to Christ's College was made in the *Evening Standard*; but a *Cambridge Chronicle* reporter had other views: 'Christ's College rowed clean away from the Non-Colls.' (13 March 1875). They may have been at different parts of the course; or have referred to different days, for the non-collegiate boat followed Christ's on the third and fourth day of the races. For a further note on the first boat of all (Lent 1875), see *Journal*, 1979, p. 21.

After the winding up of the club in 1879 Fitzwilliam did not compete in the May Races until 1886, when a boat was put on for two years (and rowed over at the bottom on all eight nights), only to be taken off again from 1888 to 1890. Between 1891 and 1894, when the boat never finished more than one place above the bottom, there were a number of encounters with Magdalene College, of which one was fortunately unusual,[1] and in 1892 there were bumps not only by Magdalene, but also by Ayerst Hostel, which, in spite of the return of Fitzwilliam to the river, had been allowed to retain a place in the Mays. Another gap of two years was followed by a single unsuccessful appearance in 1897; after which there was to be no Fitzwilliam May boat for fifteen years.

There is no reason for surprise in the scanty success of the non-collegiate boats in their early years; but what does remain surprising is the prosperity of the club at its very beginning, with four early bumps in the Lent races of its second year, and in the Mays four on the first boats of other clubs. The first appearance of Cavendish College in 1879, and its continued success, suggests a possibility that the College may have previously helped to man the non-collegiate crews; but there was no Cavendish man in the non-collegiate boats of 1877 or 1878, and there seems no reason to suppose that during the time of its non-collegiate status Cavendish College ever joined forces with the main non-collegiate body on the playing field or on the river.

The successes of Cavendish College, and of Ayerst Hostel even, support the frequent contention of non-collegiate undergraduates that one of their principal difficulties arose from their wide separation in scattered lodgings, which hindered the emergence of a student community, and made more difficult, even among such as might be that way disposed, any effective participation in corporate activities of the usual college kind. This had been the burden of the *Review* correspondent of 1879; and in 1885, after the Lent races in which the boat had rowed over every day at the bottom of the lower division, a supporter had given vent to his feelings with the comment 'Considering the encouragement we get from our own men, we wonder, not that the boat is last, but that there is a boat at all.'

Outside comment was no more encouraging. In the previous year an observer had written just before the Lent races 'Jesus IV, Clare III, and the Non-Collegiates raced for the last three places, coming in so named … Non-Collegiates were quite outclassed, and it seems a pity that so poor a crew should be allowed to keep a position which they cannot

---

[1]   In the Races of 1891. For the circumstances in which a bump by Magdalene, on the third night, was disallowed, see *Cambridge Review*, 1890–91, p. 398.

hope to improve, especially when Non-Collegiate students are already represented by Cavendish and Selwyn boats.'[1] He was wrong about the status of the two institutions, which had by then become public hostels, but his attitude to those who remained non-collegiate had already been expressed when Cavendish College and Ayerst Hostel, with better boats, were pressing their claims for admission to the Mays. Even less restrained was another comment: 'Non-colls will probably end as they start, and have started for years – bottom. Why don't they amalgamate with Ayerst's Hostel, and try to make a fair combined boat?'[2] And yet, the refusal to give up altogether, and the readiness of the undergraduates, by definition men of straitened circumstances, to help, when by hook or by crook a new boat just had to be bought, command respect and admiration. In a Boat Club minute book, which has somehow been preserved, of the Easter term 1896 there is a laconic statement: 'This term Fitzwilliam Hall was again unrepresented on the river.'[3] What would this generation of '96 have said if they could have been told where their first Lent boat, and then their first May boat, would be in '69?

Of the other games, it is known that in the Lent term 1880 there had been a move to form a Lawn Tennis Club, and in the following Michaelmas term it was established and did well. Simultaneously, there was for the first time an organized (Association) Football Club, and in the Michaelmas term 1881 there was also a Rugby Football Club, but it seems to have met with very little success – on one occasion its auditor could not remember how many tries the opposition (Leys School) *had* scored – and the club was disbanded in 1883, though there are sporadic references to the game from time to time. In the Lent term 1888 the standing committee of the Amalgamation Club approved a proposal that there should be an Athletic Sports section of the Club, and at the next election of officers Lawn Tennis and Athletic Sports were treated as a single club, having as its secretary the originator of the proposal that Athletic Sports should be recognized. Nowhere, however, is there an estimate for Athletic Sports, and at the end of the academical year the name drops out of the picture.[4] In this same term the Newspaper Club and Debating Society were replaced by a Literary Club (more

1   *Cambridge Review*, 1884–85, p. 247; 1883–84, p. 231.
2   *Ibid.*, 1886–87, p. 224.
3   College Archives, F.H.B.C.1890–97.
4   Although they had no Athletics Club, there was in these early days one non-collegiate undergraduate who ran for the University against Oxford: W. P. Phillips, of Cavendish College, who was fourth in the Mile in 1881. See also p. 344.

usually referred to as the Literary Society) one of whose responsibilities, as these were set forth in a Code of Rules drawn up in 1897, was the maintenance of a Chess Club; but chess is little mentioned thereafter until it was declared to be 'revived' at a General Meeting of the Amalgamated Clubs held on 11 October 1902. Just previously, on 23 April, the possibility was raised of forming a Swimming Club, to be affiliated to the University Swimming Club, but nothing came of it, because there were not, it was thought, enough members in prospect to keep a club going. This too was to be the subject of a 'revival' in later years. On 23 January 1904, another General Meeting agreed that a Hockey Club should be started; and a match against Westminster College was probably the club's first fixture. By 1907 there had been no further accessions to the Amalgamated Clubs, which therefore then comprised the Boat, Cricket, Football, Lawn Tennis, and Hockey Clubs, with the Literary Society.[1]

In the colleges there were many other opportunities for undergraduates to associate with others whose interests they shared, and of these two were afforded by their chapels and by dinner in hall, both being part of the established, and at that time the required, Cambridge pattern. With its non-collegiate students the University had been cautious about chapel, and had made a particular point that although as far as possible provision was to be made for due attendance, there was to be no requirement imposed upon those who were not members of the Anglican Church. About dinner little could be done at first, for there was no place where it could be held, or prepared. The men did not, however, wait until they had premises of their own, for the first mention of a communal dinner is by Mr Somerset in his Report to the Board of 7 December 1876: 'The common Reading Room and the Boat Club are the means of bringing many of the younger students into habitual association with each other. This term a number of them (15 or 16, often) have dined together daily. With this experiment I have not interfered; I have only watched it, as I had the opportunity, so as to suggest cautions against increasing expenses or management by unsuitable persons.' There is here an echo of the arguments advanced in favour of admitting to the University men who, not being members of a college, would be free to practise the most rigid economies without exciting unfavourable comment which might well be made by others in more fortunate circumstances, if they were all college men. The same point had been put against the formation of halls or hostels for poor men, on the grounds that at any common table there would be some individuals

[1]   A.C. Minutes, 1884–1904, 1904–13.

who would be unwilling to accept extremes of economy which others, if left to themselves, would prefer.

In the Lent term 1882, Mr Howard told the Board that the men had asked for permission to sign their names, for residence purposes, at the Bird Bolt Inn, where they had arranged to dine.[1] On the question of signatures, the Board decided to take no action for the time being, but Mr Howard gives more information about the dinner in his Annual Report in the Easter term. 'A Hall dinner has been organized by the students', he tells the Board, 'at the Bird Bolt Inn, with the permission of the Senior Proctor, and under regulations sanctioned by myself. The hour for dinner during the winter months was 5.30, and the number of those who attended was about 25. This term there have been two dinners daily at 1.30 and 7, and it is proposed to try a similar arrangement next term.'[2] Except for a passing reference, some years later, to the possibility of holding a weekly dinner there, there is no further mention of dining at the Bird Bolt Hotel (as it seems to have called itself), but there was a new departure in 1888, when, 'on Saturday, 3 March, the first of what is hoped will be a terminal non-collegiate dinner took place in the Bath Hotel. Fifty-seven men were present, and a most enjoyable evening was spent. Dinner was served at 6.30, and was followed by toasts, speeches and songs. A very cordial letter was received from the Censor, and the toasts of the various non-collegiate clubs and institutions were warmly received and ably responded to. Altogether the evening was a pronounced success.' In the following term, probably on Saturday, 19 May, the dinner, to which it was decided to invite former non-collegiate students who had migrated, was repeated, this time at the Lion Hotel, and was attended by the Assistant Censor (A. H. Cooke). In the Michaelmas term it was held again, on 10 November, and the *Review* correspondent makes a point of the satisfaction afforded by the attendance of 'old non-collegiate students whose interest in our proceedings seems in no way abated'.

There were no further developments of the kind until 1892, when an inaugural dinner was held on 29 October in the dining hall which the Board had provided in the building purchased for them by the University in 1887. Of this the liveliest remaining account is given by an undergraduate:

> The great event of the week, if not of the term, was the dinner to inaugurate the new buildings, which took place last Saturday evening at Fitz-

---

[1]   Minutes, 7 February 1882.
[2]   Censor's Reports 1882–98, Report dated June 1882.

The Bird Bolt Hotel, 30 St Andrew's Street

William Hall, and which was an unqualified success. The Censor, the Lecturers (Mr E. S. Shuckburgh, Mr C. Geldard), the Architect (Mr W. M. Fawcett), the Rev. H. P. Stokes, Vicar of St Paul's, Dr Ingle, Mr Skinner (Christ's), several old Non-collegiate Students, including Mr W. J. Whittaker (Trinity), Mr Willis (Caius), and J. H. B. Masterman, and a large number of present students, in all more than eighty, were present. '*Non nobis Domine*' having been sung, the Censor, who took the chair, proposed the toast of 'Prosperity to Fitzwilliam Hall', coupled with the name of the Architect, who in his reply detailed the difficulties connected with the transformation of the building into its present condition. Mr Shuckburgh proposed the health of the old members, coupled with the names of Whittaker and Masterman. All present then joined in singing 'Auld Lang Syne'. Mr Whittaker in replying described the building as he first knew it, and the exploits of the boat in his day, and assured us of his continued interest in our welfare. Masterman replied for a later generation of old members and proposed the Present Members, coupled with the name of the Amalgamation Club Secretary. R. H. Davis responded, and Salmon, the clerk, was then uproariously summoned to make a speech, which he did. Steggall proposed the healths of the Presidents of the Amalgamation Club and Debating Society, appropriately dividing his subject into Parts I and II.

Mr Geldart and Mr Shuckburgh replied. Keelan then proposed the Censor, a toast which was drunk with great enthusiasm.

The Speeches were interspersed with songs by P. C. W. Hague Ingram, W. A. C. Sadler, H. H. Heap and E. J. Stream. It is to be hoped that this is only the first of a series of similar pleasant reunions. Possibly a terminal dinner might be arranged in connection with the general meeting of the Amalgamation Club.[1]

Many of the names mentioned in this account have already become familiar. Mr Fawcett had done work for a number of colleges. Dr Ingle (B.A. 1884) was the first, and at the time the only, non-collegiate Doctor of Medicine of the University. Mr Skinner, of Christ's College, was Assistant Lecturer in Natural Sciences at Clare and, it may be surmised, helped with the teaching of the non-collegiate undergraduates. The presence of Mr Stokes is a reminder that it was he who allowed his church to be used for week-day morning services; and the brevity of the reference to the speech delivered by Mr R. A. Davis (not R. H. Davis) suggests that he, as General Secretary, supplied the notice to the *Cambridge Review*. Steggall (General Secretary 1891–92) had migrated to St Catharine's in the previous March; and of the singers Sadler had gone to Peterhouse in September, and Heap had come from Ayerst Hostel in the Easter term.

The possession of a hall had made it possible for the non-collegiate undergraduates to dine together in their own building; but there is little evidence of regular communal dining. Censor Huddleston gave figures from time to time, and his highest average number of diners had been fifteen, in the Lent term 1899, out of a resident population of 102.[2] More came to occasional special functions, like the terminal dinners later recalled by Reddaway, and made much of in his time. Smoking Concerts also seem to have prospered, and once, at least, in the Lent term 1907, to have been combined with a 'Boat Supper' – with greater success, it may be supposed, than could reasonably have been anticipated from such a combination in more recent times.

Among the undergraduates' non-athletic organizations, in addition to the Non-Collegiate Debating Society and the Newspaper Club, already active in 1874, came the gradual formation of a Literary Society first mentioned in the academical year 1883–84, when there was a meeting of the Literary and Debating Society on 14 January, at which there was a three hour discussion of the 'Deceased Wife's Sister Bill'. On 27 November 1884 'the Debating Society took a holiday, giving the night

[1] *Cambridge Review*, 1887–88, pp. 251, 328; 1888–89, p. 88; 1892–93, p. 60.
[2] Censor's Report dated 25 February 1899.

to readings and recitations'; and there were other occasions when, instead of conducting a debate, the society listened to the reading of papers. By the Amalgamation Club Rules of 1888, the Club consisted of five sections, of which the last was the 'Literary Debating and Musical Society', whose object was to be 'the promotion of Debates, reading of Essays and other literary Exercises, and musical Entertainments'. At the same time the society took over the functions of the earlier Newspaper Club, and was required each term to hold a meeting for the selection and sale of periodicals. Musical doings came to notice with the first (and very successful) Smoking Concert on 21 October 1886, when 'tea and coffee were provided, the cost being defrayed by subscription'; and the musical side of what came to be known simply as the Literary Society was sufficiently important to justify the appointment, in the Michaelmas term 1889, of an Assistant Secretary with responsibility for the society's musical activities. Inevitably, this officer became known as the 'Musical Secretary', but the duties of a 'Musical President', with the curious exception of two years in the 1890s, continued to be undertaken by the President of the Literary Society, which included the musical folk among its members.[1]

Musical activity at this time was largely directed to the presentation of the Smoking Concerts, usually held fortnightly in the Michaelmas and Lent terms, or of musical supplements to periodic dinners, particularly the terminal dinners, themselves also arranged to follow General Meetings of the Amalgamated Clubs. Orchestral music could not be attempted; and programmes were usually made up of solo instrumental performances, of songs, recitations, and readings. The most ambitious concerts were given when the Fitzwilliam Hall Musical Society (boldly announcing itself as such) took its turn in sponsoring one of the series of Popular Concerts given in the Guildhall; as in 1893, when the Chairman for the evening was Mr Sedley Taylor of Trinity College, himself no mean musician, then also Chairman of the Non-Collegiate Students Board.[2]

[1] For this paragraph, except where otherwise stated, see *Cambridge Review*. The exceptions occurred with the appointment, without explanation, of a President of the Musical Society (F. D. Vaughan) for the Michaelmas term 1890, and of Mr Huddleston (then Censor) for the Michaelmas term 1891, and the Lent term 1892.

[2] The programme has been kept in the book of the Censor's Reports (1882–98). Given on the evening of Saturday, 18 February, this was the 127th concert of a series presented by the University Penny Popular Concert Association. Known as 'Penny Pops', they drew their audiences not from the town alone, but, often on bicycles, from considerable distances in the surrounding countryside.

For a fleeting impression of Sedley Taylor (as a 'runner' from the Senate House, with Tripos papers for women candidates sitting the examination in Bateman Street) see Mary Paley Marshall *What I Remember* (C.U.P., 1947), p. 17.

The musicians will have been particularly encouraged in 1890, when they acquired a new Broadwood piano, the joint gift of William Braginton, Henry Frew-Simson, and Augustus Austen Leigh.[1] Frew-Simson and Braginton (who was later the founder, and the Headmaster, of The Strand School) matriculated in 1888, while Austen Leigh, Provost of King's College from 1889 to 1905, was at the time also Chairman of the Non-Collegiate Students Board and President of the Cambridge University Musical Society.

Three other groups figure in the story of the Hall in the latter half of the nineteenth century. There is a fleeting mention of the founding of a Dramatic Society 'of which we shall hope to hear more',[2] but of which for some time, surprisingly in view of its conspicuous success in later years, no more is heard. Then follow two of the most successful ventures of the kind. 'The first meeting of the Fitzwilliam Historical Society', says the correspondent, 'was held on Wednesday evening, November 14th [1900] at King's College, when Mr Reddaway read a paper on Economic History. The paper was followed by a general discussion, and at the end of the meeting a division was taken upon the question "Are economic considerations the chief cause of political events?" Ayes, 6; Noes,4.'[3] This notice is typical of the accounts of the meetings of the society, for they usually took place in Mr Reddaway's rooms in King's College; they usually ended with a vote on some topic relevant to the subject of the paper; and they were regularly held.

On 13 May 1902 the Fitzwilliam Hall Theological Society first met, under the presidency of Mr Crafer, Lecturer in Classics and Theology to the non-collegiate students, and from 1902 to 1917 Vicar of All Saints'. The society, which also made a promising beginning, met in the library, in Mr Crafer's rooms in Downing College, and, on occasion, was entertained by Mr Crafer and his lady at their vicarage. As President, Mr Crafer seems to have been particularly fortunate, or judicious, in his list of speakers at the society's meetings.[4]

The non-collegiate scheme had been brought into being not merely to enable more students to come to the University, but also to admit a class of applicant who had hitherto been deterred from seeking admission by the cost of life in a college. There can have been little difficulty in finding candidates for admission, for within five years the number of *Non Ascripti* in residence was seventy-one, already larger than in eight of the colleges. It could therefore fairly be held that the scheme was mak-

[1] *Cambridge Review*, 1890–91, p. 82.   [3] *Ibid.*, 1900–01, p. 96.
[2] *Ibid.*, 1901–02, p. 178.   [4] *Ibid.*, 1901–02, pp. 306, 339.

ing a substantial contribution to the extension of the University; and it was also providing the means whereby the more successful of the new men were enabled to become members of a college.

Of the phenomenon of migration we shall form, at this distance of time, a better balanced judgement if we remember that in the University as a whole it was commoner than it has since become, even if not on the scale which it reached among the non-collegiate students. In no way was the practice of migration in conflict with the intentions of those who had brought the scheme into being: it might be counted a gain that not only were more students coming to Cambridge but also that the best of them were securing for themselves, while they were at the University, the advantages of college membership, and after graduation the prestige of a college name. That those responsible should lose their best pupils was in no way at variance with the purposes for which they had been appointed. That colleges should find in the non-collegiate undergraduates a promising field of recruitment (as some undoubtedly did) was no bad thing; and it might even be held that it was convenient that a college should be spared the unpleasantness of sending out of residence men whose only misdemeanour was a persistent unreadiness to present themselves for the not unduly rigorous examinations which, it was hoped, would qualify them for their poll degrees, if there was a half-way house where they might seek refuge, and after a spell of comparative industry again be deemed worthy of admission to a college, or of re-admission to their own.

It was not to be wondered at that such ideas should find distinguished expression – though the time and place may appear surprising – when, in 1896, Mr Gladstone, thirty years previously member for Oxford University, wrote a letter, in his own hand, for the first number of its *Non-Collegiate Students' Magazine:*

> I look upon the Non-collegiate Body as a standing reserve established in favour of the Colleges which I must presume by their attractions establish on their own behalf a perpetual drain upon its best ingredients. But then I also hope that the knowledge that this system opens an honourable road to incorporation in the Colleges may act upon the country at large by drawing in more and more largely fresh infusions of vigorous blood.

The editor of the *Magazine* will have been gratified at being privileged to count so eminent a public figure among his first contributors, but he would have been better pleased – and said so – if Mr Gladstone had preached more acceptable doctrine.[1]

---

[1] *The* (Oxford) *Non-Collegiate Students' Magazine*, No. 1, October 1896. (Censor's Reports 1882–98).

The Cambridge Commissioners of 1852 had been unwilling to propose the admission to the University of men who should not belong to any college, because they believed that colleges and 'non-colleges' (like Fellows and 'non-Fellows' a century later) would not go well together; and when, under pressure of public opinion, the experiment was tried, they were soon found to be right. In so collegiate a University no anonymous assembly of young men was likely to be content to remain an anonymous assembly for long. If the non-collegiate students had all been older men, married men, or had all been in employment in the town or neighbourhood, they might not have felt the need for a society of their own to further their common interests; but a sufficient proportion of them were of the usual undergraduate age and outlook for it to seem right that, within the strict financial limits imposed upon them, they should conduct themselves like their more fortunate neighbours. This feeling may not have been prevalent in the beginning, but already their first Censor, in reporting to his Board on the effects of migration, was falling into the way of thinking of his non-collegiate undergraduates as a body, and was becoming increasingly aware of the manifold disadvantages which they suffered by reason of the loss of many of their best and most senior men. This corporate spirit was to reach new heights under W. F. Reddaway, but under Somerset, Howard, and Huddleston efforts had been made to improve the conditions under which the men worked and lived, and improvements naturally took the form which had stood the test of time in the colleges. Here were the makings of disagreement, and of conflict, for although the non-collegiate students and their masters might do all they could to raise their status and better their conditions, there were many in the University who held, not unreasonably, that it had been no part of the University's intention that the admission of non-collegiate students should lead to the creation of another collegiate institution. Even the Oxford Commissioners, who had shown the way, had declined to recommend the foundation of a college for poor men.

As the non-collegiate institution enters into a new and vigorous phase, in which the corporate spirit of the men was more and more prominent, and as transfers to colleges, very frequent in the past, came to be looked upon almost in the light of desertions, there is one circumstance of these early years that should not pass without notice. The authorities, and the players of competitive games, abhorred migration and all its works; but there is little evidence of resentment against individual migrants. At a General Meeting of the Amalgamation Club in the Easter term 1890, the chairman, supported by the Censor, proposed an enthusiastic vote of thanks to an outstanding General Secretary, and of congratulation 'on his success at St Catharine's',[1] where, having been accepted for admission in that term, he continued as a scholar of the College his reading for a pass degree, and in the fullness of time was placed in the third class in the Special Examination in Theology.

If it be said that this is an isolated incident, it is nevertheless of a kind with the account of the 1892 Inauguration Ceremony,[2] furnished, as will be remembered, by an undergraduate, where among those invited not only to be present but to play a leading part in the celebrations were a number of former non-collegiate students who had gone off to the colleges. And so, although in games reports, and over the class-lists, there may have been frequent lamentations at the loss of many prominent men, and one solitary passing reference to 'renegades',[3] the impression remains that, at least until the turn of the century, the men who had transferred their allegiance kept up their interest in the affairs of the Hall, and returned to its meetings and its merrymakings in a fashion that would not have been possible if there had been hard feelings or embarrassment on either side.

[1] A.C. Minutes, 30 April 1890.
[2] See p. 144.
[3] *Cambridge Review*, 1891–92, p. 157.

CHAPTER V

William Fiddian Reddaway
and Fitzwilliam Hall

Thatcher on Reddaway – incompleteness of records – value of Censor's Reports to
his Board. Exhibitions tenable at Cambridge Day Training College – teaching for
honours – 'migration and disabilities' – Information Circular (1908) – Board membership – expansion of teaching staff – undergraduate expenses – Orders of the
Board. Censor's Report 1911–12 – increase in corporate activities – diminishing
migration and improvement in class-lists – 1912 Exhibition Fund. The war years –
appointment of resident Chaplain (1914) – the *Fitzwilliam Magazine*.

Playing Field purchased by Reddaway (1908) – leased to Amalgamated Clubs (1910) –
Red Cottage built (1910) – prolonged work on the playing field. Shortage of student
accommodation – 25 Fitzwilliam Street (The Hostel) – other Fitzwilliam Street
houses – establishment of Fitzwilliam Hall Trust – its indebtedness to Reddaway –
Chaplaincy Endowment Fund, 1912 Exhibition Fund, Hirst Player Bursary Fund. War
Memorial (playing field) Fund – purchase of field (and Red Cottage) by Trust – perplexities of Trustees.

Report of Royal Commission on Oxford and Cambridge Universities. Fall in numbers
and consequent financial difficulties. Syndicate 'on the position of the Non-Collegiate
Students Board' (1924) – recognition of value of communal life of the non-collegiate
institution – its title, but not its status, changed – annual grant – Censor's Gift Fund
– anomalous position of Fitzwilliam Hall Trust – inconclusive discussions over its
future. Varied reception of Syndicate's recommendations – their eventually beneficial
effects – resignation of Censor – appointment of his successor.

The Michaelmas term 1907 marked a dividing line between the old and
the new Fitzwilliam. For in that term Mr W. F. Reddaway came into office
as Censor, and with him a new outlook and policy. Previous Censors had
done much to promote the welfare of their students as is witnessed by
their reports, and latterly by the acquisition and opening of Fitzwilliam
House. But though minor rebels they had accepted the *status quo* and had
only pressed gently for the few amenities which existed.[1]

So, in 1965, wrote Mr W. S. Thatcher. He had known Reddaway,
had seen him at work, and his opinion must be respected; but there
may be here some danger that Reddaway's predecessors have received a
little less than their due, for Reddaway was wise enough to build on

[1] *Journal*, December 1965, p. 21.

what was already there, and what he did, at least at first, was made possible by the achievements of those who had gone before. For seventeen years Reddaway's great gifts were devoted unsparingly to the service of the non-collegiate students, but it is no injustice to him to remember that in one respect he enjoyed a purely accidental advantage over earlier Censors, for he was helped by the passage of time. Taking office as he did some forty years after the inception of the non-collegiate scheme, he began his work when the origins of the scheme were less clearly remembered, when not everybody recalled that its sole purpose was to bring a university education within the reach of men whose circumstances were too narrow to permit them to become members of colleges, with no thought that they might come to belong to a college of their own. The blurring of these memories must have been a help to Reddaway, and his claim for equality of status was strengthened by the fact that the University had already allowed, *de facto* if not *de jure*, a measure of collegiate life to his men, so that there was some basis for his contention that their status, being already in many respects similar to that of members of colleges, could not fairly be kept at a lower level.

Reddaway had another advantage – his retention of his fellowship, his lectureship, and his rooms in King's College; and ready access to the College at all times will have been an encouragement for him, and a relaxation, when as Censor of the non-collegiate students he encountered indifference, misunderstanding, or open hostility. Furthermore, he did not continue in the censorship in old age; he retired when he was fifty-one, with nearly twenty-five years of life before him, many of them productive years, as a list of his writings will show.

In the Michaelmas term 1924 the Non-Collegiate Students Board authorized the Censor (W. S. Thatcher) to purchase 'a filing cabinet, and other necessary furniture';[1] and it was Thatcher, many years later, who said that Reddaway was 'essentially the don of the pre-war generation, with an active dislike of, and even contempt for, office organization'.[2] This being so, material for the domestic history of the non-collegiate body is not to be found in the personal records of the men who made it, for they do not appear to have been kept. Reddaway knew about them, but, as Thatcher also said; 'I found he had taken all the archives with him – as indeed he had to, for they were in his head'.[3] Material is not, however, entirely lacking; and as before it is to be found principally in the Censor's Reports to his Board, in the Board's

[1]   Minutes, 13 November 1924.
[2]   *Journal*, December 1949, p. 13.
[3]   *Ibid.*

minutes, and – a new source of information – in the *Fitzwilliam Hall Magazine*,[1] first published in 1908, though this, like the minutes of the Amalgamated Clubs, is more closely concerned with exclusively undergraduate activities than with the institutional history of Fitzwilliam Hall. One previous source of information – the Board's own Reports to the Senate – had almost entirely dried up. Although they were not required to do so, the Board had reported to the Senate at the end of the first year of the non-collegiate scheme,[2] and again in 1873, recommending its renewal.[3] In 1874 they decided that they ought to report annually, but did not. There were, nevertheless, seventeen Reports to the Senate in the first forty years, and although some were about particular topics most of them contained important information about the general progress of the scheme. From 1907 to 1924, on the other hand, there are two Board Reports only, of which one merely communicates to the University at large a Report by the Censor to the Board for the year 1911–12, and the other is exclusively about fees.

But although the Board were under no obligation to report to the Senate, it was, at the very beginning, part of the Censor's duty to report to the Board term by term; and this Mr Somerset did, in much detail, for his first few years. This must have proved irksome, or have been regarded as unnecessary, for the Reports became less frequent, and by June 1876 they were being made twice a year, a practice, formally sanctioned in March 1877,[4] which continued until June 1886, when Mr Howard began to report annually, although there is no Board resolution to that effect. Thereafter, until the end of Mr Huddleston's tenure, Reports continued to be made once a year except, it seems, when the Board themselves had occasion to report to the Senate. Thus, there appears to have been no Censor's Report in 1891, 1894, 1901, or 1905. Reddaway made no change in these arrangements, except that from 1911 onwards he reported in November instead of May, and so was able to give an account, each time, of the doings of a whole academical year. He seems to have submitted Annual Reports throughout his time as Censor, even during the war of 1914–1918, and all have been preserved except the Report for the year 1912–13 which, although it now appears to be lost, was presented to the Board at the proper time.[5]

Of the Board's minutes it may be said that while, at times, they

1   See pp.174–5.
2   Camb. Univ. Reg. 60,16, University Archives. See also p. 60.
3   *University Reporter*, Easter Term 1873, p. 23.
4   Minutes, 26 March 1877.
5   *Ibid.*, 20 October 1913.

record trivialities in most punctilious detail, at other times they are provokingly reticent on matters which now seem to have been of greater moment. 'The Censor's Report dated April 27, 1909, was read by the Chairman and discussed by the Board'[1] does little more than suggest that members of the Board had not seen the Report before their meeting, and is not, particularly in the absence of supporting papers, of much assistance to the historian. The minutes do, nevertheless, afford glimpses of the policies of the new Censor, and of the methods he adopted in his efforts to improve the status of his non-collegiate students, and the conditions in which they lived, worked, and played. At Reddaway's first Board meeting, the first minute, after the minute confirming the minutes of the meeting before, records the Board's approval of the action of the Chairman and Censor in letting rooms in the House to Mr Alston, of Christ's College, in return for assistance given to students in Economics.[2] Reddaway is continuing the practice of his predecessor who, it will be remembered, had similarly provided rooms for the earlier lecturers in History and Classics, and had also let rooms 'free of rent, rates and taxes, and charges for coal and gas' in return for an undertaking by the tenants to be accessible for at least two hours a week to direct and assist students in their several subjects.

There is a new departure at the next meeting, when the Board gratefully accepted the Censor's offer to provide annually an exhibition of £15, usually tenable for three years by non-collegiate students who were members of the Cambridge Day Training College for Schoolmasters (of which Mr Oscar Browning, of King's College, who had been a candidate for the Censorship in 1881 and 1890, was Principal). A further step which, though not an innovation, became a more frequent practice, was the making of a grant of £25 to the students' Clubs. Again, Reddaway does not allow his Board to overlook their agreement in the previous Lent term to require a payment of £3.3.0, on migration, from any non-collegiate student admitted after May 1907. A committee was appointed to consider the provision of teaching in honours subjects, and an Honorary Director of Studies in Music is appointed (E. J. Dent, of King's, later to be Professor in the University). Another matter that was not allowed to rest was 'the proper title of non-collegiate students', although on this occasion, after a discussion initiated by the Master of Magdalene, no decision was reached. All these questions were raised by Reddaway in his first term as Censor.[3] In the following

---

[1]   *Ibid.*, 28 April 1909.
[2]   *Ibid.*, 15 October 1907.
[3]   *Ibid.*, 3 December 1907.

Easter term, when the Board received the report of a committee on honours teaching, they resolved that all men reading honours ought to receive direction if they wished, as far as possible at the Board's expense;[1] and by August 1908 Reddaway was able to announce the names of two lecturers and one assistant lecturer, and of eleven Directors, or Honorary Directors, of Studies.[2] Still in his first year, a committee was appointed, consisting of the Chairman of the Board, Monsignor Nolan (Head of St Edmund's House), and the Censor to 'make enquiry into the alleged disabilities of non-collegiate graduates in competing for educational appointments, and to recommend action to remove the possibility of students, who have been in reality non-collegiate during the whole of their residence, graduating as members of a College'.[3] This body, which became known as the 'Committee on Migration and Disabilities', reported at the end of the Michaelmas term 1908, and on its advice the Board resolved 'not to oppose migrations at any period when the student has obtained a scholarship or exhibition at a College, but to impose in such cases the ordinary migration tax at any part of their undergraduate career; and to limit the standing for migration to six terms from matriculation in other cases'. The Board also instructed the Censor to inform the tutor of St Catharine's College that they would not grant any *bene discessit* or any certificate of terms unless they were applied for before the undergraduate concerned was admitted as a member of his College.[4]

Reddaway had not been slow to demonstrate the combativeness that he had observed in his predecessor; and already in his attitude to the problems caused by the prevalence of migration was displaying a tenacity that was to be characteristic of his conduct of affairs for much of his period of office. Mr Somerset had bewailed the effects of migration; in Huddleston's day the Non-Collegiate Students Board, by a series of arrangements for the payment of fees, made migration more

---

1 Minutes, 25 May 1908.
2 See p. 161.
3 Minutes, 25 May 1908.
4 *Ibid.*, 3 December 1908. The attitude of the Board was not unreasonable, for there had been a conspicuous failure by receiving colleges to observe even the most elementary courtesies. In an envelope bearing, in Reddaway's hand, the legend *St Catharine's Coll. 'Bene discessits' July 1907 and other curiosities* is a letter written by Huddleston to A. W. Spratt, Tutor and Praelector of St Catharine's, about an especially regrettable example of the trouble caused by frequent last-minute requests for duplicates (which had to be sealed by the Chairman of the Board) of lost *bene discessits*, without which their subjects would not be entitled to proceed to their B.A. degree. In 1907, also, another college, without notifying the Censor, presented for his M.A. degree a non-collegiate Bachelor of Arts (H. E. J. Curzon, see also p. 119).

expensive for the undergraduate and financially less damaging to the institution; and Huddleston himself had been at pains to expose irregularities of procedure when his men were taken by colleges; but under Reddaway the Board very soon resolved that, except for scholars and exhibitioners, migration should not be allowed at all beyond a certain point in a man's career, even though this might mean some falling off in the number of applications for admission. It is noticeable, too, that having got his rule accepted in principle, Reddaway was not unwilling to waive it in practice in what might appear to him to be deserving cases.

At the end of this same Michaelmas term, Reddaway also reported on the progress made by the Migrations and Disabilities Committee in ascertaining the opinions of non-collegiate graduates about their educational disadvantages; but we are not told what he said, either then or at the Board's next meeting, when he is described as reporting further progress.[1] The newly founded *Fitzwilliam Hall Magazine* gives the text of a circular letter sent to a number of 'our graduates who hold professorships, inspectorships of schools, masterships, and other similar posts':

> The Non-Collegiate Students Board invite your kind assistance in dealing with a matter which seriously affects a number of students and the status and well-being of our body as a whole. A widespread impression exists that, in competition for educational appointments, members of the University who are not members of a college are placed at a disadvantage, and that posts, which might have fallen to them, are likely to be assigned to men of inferior qualifications, whose names have been on the boards of a college at the moment of taking a degree. In seeking to discover to what extent this impression is justified, the Board turn first to those graduates who, like yourself, hold such appointments. They will further welcome any expression of opinion that you may think fit to make with regard to the best remedy.
>
> Our graduates must, from the nature of the case, be men of independence and vigour, while, as the *Information Paper* and *Magazine* indicate, we have every opportunity of enjoying a full measure of corporate life in the University. The Board cannot be satisfied until these facts obtain due recognition.[2]

In the next issue of the *Magazine* the Censor (presumably it is he) gives some account of the answers received, and in passing mentions what was to become a familiar source of difficulty encountered in

[1] *Ibid.*, 3 December 1908, 25 February 1909.
[2] *Magazine*, November 1908, p. 56.

attempts to get in touch with old members – the lack of an Old Students' Register. A number of the replies have been kept, and it is curious that, whereas most of them confirm the existence of a widespread preference among employers for members of colleges, Reddaway's summary presents a more favourable picture, for in the letters which he quotes there is certainly no unanimous view that non-collegiate graduates as such are handicapped in their search for jobs. It is almost as though Reddaway, torn between a desire for confirmation of the prejudice in order that he may set about getting rid of it, and a deep-seated reluctance to allow that it was at all widespread, laid unwitting emphasis on the more favourable replies. The reader is led to expect further reference to the subject, but there is no later mention of it, either in the *Magazine* or in the minutes of the Board.[1]

From the beginning of the non-collegiate scheme a circular had been prepared for the information of applicants for admission, and the first of Reddaway's circulars, in 1908, summarizes the main features of the arrangements made for undergraduates at the beginning of his time as Censor. Entitled 'Information relating to Non-Collegiate Students in the University of Cambridge', it continues:[2]

> NON-COLLEGIATE Students are members of the University without being members of any College or Hostel. They are governed by the Chancellor and other Officers of the University, and by a Board of nine members appointed by the Senate. They are supervised by a Censor. They keep Terms by residing in Cambridge in lodgings duly licensed, or with their parents, or, in special cases sanctioned by the University authorities, under the care of other persons, or in their own or in hired houses. They are matriculated, examined, and admitted to Degrees in the same manner and possess the same status and privileges as Collegiate Students. Thus they may use the University Library, Museums and Laboratories, attend the Professors' and all Intercollegiate Lectures, and compete for Scholarships and Prizes open to the whole University, under the same conditions as other Students.

---

[1] *Magazine*, February 1909, p. 69; also College Archives. For a very definite opinion, see remarks made by the Rev. T. C. Fitzpatrick, President of Queens' College and Chairman of the Non-Collegiate Students Board at the time, at the discussion of the Report of the Council of the Senate on the Constitution and Government of the University. 'Only a proportion of them [the non-collegiate students]', he said, '...remained for the whole of their time members of the Non-Collegiate body. The fact was that the outside world demanded that they should be members of a College...' *University Reporter*, 1909–10, p. 927.

[2] Information Papers, College Archives.

Fitzwilliam
Hall.
The centre of their corporate life is Fitzwilliam Hall, a house built in 1727 and situate opposite the Fitzwilliam Museum in Trumpington Street. It contains Reading and Writing Rooms, a Library, a Dining Room, Censor's and Lecturers' Rooms, Clerk's Office, etc. At present the Director of Students in Economics, L. ALSTON, M.A., the Censor's Secretary, J. E. STALEY, B.A., and the Clerk to the Board, F. W. SALMON, reside in the building.

The annual subscription of £1.15s. to the Fitzwilliam Hall Amalgamated Clubs confers membership of the Debating, Boating, Cricket, Football, Hockey, and Lawn-Tennis Clubs, and admits to the use of the Reading Room.

The Fitzwilliam Hall Magazine is issued terminally by the Clubs to their members without charge. Old Students may become Honorary Members of the Clubs on payment of 5s. a year or of a life composition of £3.3s.0d. During the Michaelmas and Lent Terms Debates and Concerts are held, and the Fitzwilliam Historical Society and the Fitzwilliam Hall Theological Society meet for papers and discussions.

Some or all of the junior members of the following institutions are Non-Collegiate Students. Applications for admission or for further information with regard to them should be made to the respective Principals.

The Cambridge University Day Training College. Principal: OSCAR BROWNING, M.A., King's College.

S. Matthew's House, Abbey Walk, Cambridge. A community of lay workers in the parish of S. Matthew. Warden: Rev. H. PAIN, M.A.

S. Edmund's House. Only Roman Catholic Students who, if not already ordained, intend to receive Holy Orders are admitted. Principal: The Very Rev. Mgr. NOLAN.

Cheshunt College. Founded in 1768 by the Countess of Huntingdon. For Students in Theology. Resident Tutor: E. W. JOHNSON, M.A.

The Board.
Members of the Board have been appointed as follows:–
The PRESIDENT OF QUEENS' COLLEGE (until 1910), *Chairman.*
Rev. V. H. STANTON, D.D. (until 1908), *Vice-Chairman.*
The MASTER OF MAGDALENE COLLEGE (until 1908).
The Very Rev. Mgr. NOLAN (until 1908).
Rev. F. J. FOAKES-JACKSON, D.D. (until 1909).
W. DURNFORD, M.A. (until 1909).
J. H. FLATHER, M.A. (until 1909).
J. R. ROXBURGH, M.A. (until 1910).
Rev. H. F. STEWART, B.D. (until 1910).

The Censor. All applications for admission and other communications are to be addressed to the Censor, W. F. REDDAWAY, M.A., Fitzwilliam Hall, Cambridge.

Admission. Each applicant for admission must produce a Testimonial to character, with a reference to two respectable persons, and also, if not 21 years of age, a statement from his Parent or Guardian that the applicant has his permission to reside at the University. An applicant who has at any time resided as a member of any College or Hostel in the University must produce a certificate, as prescribed by the Senate, from the Head of his College or the Principal of his Hostel. No Graduate of the University can be admitted.

Residence. There are three Terms in the year, viz. the Michaelmas Term, beginning October 1st and ending December 19th; the Lent Term, beginning January 8th and ending shortly before Easter; and the Easter Term, beginning shortly after Easter and ending June 24th. Full Term begins later and ends earlier than Term. In the Michaelmas Term 1908, Full Term begins on October 13 and ends on December 11.

Nine Terms' residence is required for each of the Degrees, B.A., LL.B., and M.B. It is necessary to reside three-fourths of every Term, that it may count for a Degree. In each Term Students are expected to return into residence on or before the first day of Full Term. They call on the Censor without special summons on their arrival in Cambridge, and towards the end of each Term's residence. They should not engage lodgings without his consent, nor for more than one Term in advance.

Hall. Dinner in Hall is served at 7 p.m. at a charge of one shilling. Breakfast, Lunch and Dinner in Hall are provided at an inclusive charge of 17s.6d. a week.

Chapel. A short Service is conducted by Mr Crafer in the Brassie Side-Chapel, King's College, on Mondays, Wednesdays and Fridays at 1.5 P.M. Students may also attend the daily Services in King's College Chapel, where special seats are allotted them.

Signing in. Students who do not dine in Hall or attend Chapel are required to sign on five days of the week at Fitzwilliam Hall during the following hours:—Sundays 3–4 P.M. Weekdays 10 A.M.—1 P.M.; 4.30—6.30 P.M.

Studies. Lectures for the Previous and General Examinations are delivered at Fitzwilliam Hall and Direction in the various Studies of the University is provided by the Board without charge. Students who desire to receive regular weekly supervision of study by the Directors pay a fee of £1.11s.6d. per Term.

Staff. LECTURERS. *Classics:* W. W. WALKER, M.A.; *Mathematics:* W. G. BELL, M.A.; *Assistant Lecturer:* R. W. B. GARRETT, B.A.

DIRECTORS OF STUDIES. *Poll Degree:* W. G. BELL, M.A.; *Classics:* W. W. WALKER, M.A.; *Economics:* L. ALSTON, M.A.; *History:* H. M. V. TEMPERLEY, M.A.; *Law:* C. J. B. GASKOIN, M.A.; *Mathematics:* W. G. BELL, M.A.; *Medieval and Modern Languages:* A. J. WYATT, M.A.; *Moral Sciences:* C. FOX, M.A.; *Natural Sciences:* The PRESIDENT OF QUEENS'; *Music:* E. J. DENT, M.A., Mus.B.; *Theology:* Rev. T. W. CRAFER, M.A., B.D.

Expenses. It is estimated that the cost of living as a Non-Collegiate Student is in ordinary cases from £80 to £90 a year. Part of this sum consists of fees and dues paid to the University and to the Board respectively.

Fees and dues to the University are the same as for Collegiate Students. The (Matriculation) fee to the University on Admission is Five Pounds, and a quarterly Capitation Tax of Ten Shillings must be paid.

Every Undergraduate Student pays to the Board Six Guineas on Admission, Three Guineas for each of the first three terms, and One Guinea for the fourth, fifth, and sixth terms. For the seventh, eighth, and ninth terms and for admission to the first Degree no fee is charged by the Board, but after nine Terms the fee for each term of residence payable to the Board by an Undergraduate Student is £1. No Caution Money is required. All fees must be paid in advance; and no Student whose payments shall be in arrear will be considered as resident in the University. No fee is paid to the Board for presentation to the first Degree, but Three Guineas is paid on admission to every Degree after the first. A fee of £3.3s. is charged in certain cases on migration to a College.

In ordinary cases the fees payable as above are the following:

	£.	s.	d.
To the Board, Admission Fee	6	6	0
To the Board, for nine terms	12	12	0
Capitation Tax, for eleven quarters	5	10	0
Matriculation Fee	5	0	0
Previous Examination	2	10	0

and further, for Candidates for the Ordinary B.A. Degree,

	£.	s.	d.
General Examination	2	0	0
Special Examination	3	0	0

or, for Candidates for Honours,

	£.	s.	d.
Additional Subjects in the Previous Examination	1	5	0
Tripos Examination	3	0	0

All these fees are to be paid through the Censor. Cheques should be made payable to the "Non-Collegiate Censor's Account" with Messrs Barclay and Co., Cambridge.

The Fees payable to the University for Degrees are:—

	£.	s.	d.
for B.A. or LL.B. taken at the ordinary times	7	0	0
for B.A. or LL.B. taken at other times	10	10	0
for M.B. (except when B.A. has been taken previously)	8	0	0
for M.A.	12	0	0

Exhibitions, etc.

The Clothworkers' Company give six Exhibitions of £30 a year (with an addition of £10 on admission to a degree) to Non-Collegiate Students at Cambridge, who are Candidates for a Degree in Honours and intend to take Holy Orders; two of these are awarded annually in November to Students nominated by the Censor.

Four Exhibitions also of £25 a year, limited to Non-Collegiate Students of at least two terms' standing, are given by the Leathersellers' Company after due examination and enquiry.

Three Exhibitions of £15 a year, tenable by members of the University Day Training College who are Non-Collegiate Students, are given by the Censor. These Exhibitions are awarded in December and may be prolonged.

A Student, usually in his third year of residence, is appointed Librarian at a stipend of £15.

Grants may be made by the Board to Candidates for Honours in their third year.

The fees for admission to Intercollegiate Examinations in Honours are paid by the Board.

The Gibson Prize of Seven Guineas in Books is awarded annually for proficiency in the Greek Testament.

FITZWILLIAM HALL, CAMBRIDGE,
August, 1908.

NOTE.

The attention of Candidates for admission is directed to the following Orders made by the Board:—

(I) ORDERED by the BOARD that if any Student have failed, except for some cause to be approved by the Board,

(1) at the end of five terms from the commencement of his residence, to pass one part of the Previous Examination;

(2) at the end of seven terms from the commencement of his residence, to pass both parts of the Previous Examination; or

(3) at the end of nine terms from the commencement of his residence, to pass the General Examination for the Ordinary B.A. Degree or the Examination in the Additional Subjects required from Candidates for Honours, he shall forthwith cease to reside in the University; and that he shall not be allowed to continue a Non-Collegiate Student unless within twelve months he pass the Examination necessary under the foregoing order to entitle him to resume his residence.

Ordered also that, except for some cause to be approved by the Board, no Student who is not *bonâ fide* a Candidate for Honours be allowed to reside in the University beyond the end of the tenth term from the commencement of his residence, or be allowed to remain a Non-Collegiate Student unless he have passed the Examinations necessary for his Degree within twelve months from the end of the said tenth term.

II. ORDERED by the BOARD that every Student who wishes to reside in Cambridge during any term which he is not keeping as a term of residence for a degree must obtain leave to do so from the Board through the Censor, whether his ordinary home be in Cambridge or elsewhere.

III. ORDERED by the BOARD, that any Student who shall continue out of residence more than two Terms at once without having obtained leave from the Board shall be removed from the list of Non-Collegiate Students.

Reddaway's opening paragraphs are typical of the way in which, in a public document, he makes the very best of his non-collegiate institution; and, by drawing attention to its resident staff, does what he can to emphasize its collegiate character. Of the institutions of whose members some or all were also non-collegiate students, St Matthew's House was taken over by the Church Pastoral Aid Society in 1912, and when it was closed in 1915 it had for some thirty years been the means of providing a university education, and practical training in parish work, to more than sixty men. Cheshunt College, founded when six Anglican students were expelled from St Edmund Hall in Oxford because of their suspected Methodist leanings, had come to Cambridge in 1905 from Cheshunt in Hertfordshire, and occupied two houses in Cintra House in Hills Road, until the completion in 1914 of its new buildings at the corner of Bateman Street and Brookside. It was notable among the theological colleges in Cambridge in not being restricted to members of a single denomination. Other institutions, notably Westminster College and Wesley House, which trained candidates for the Presbyterian and Wesleyan ministries, were to be added in later years.

Reddaway's Non-Collegiate Students Board was a distinguished body. Mr T. C. Fitzpatrick, who had been in the first class in the Natural Sciences Tripos in 1883, and again in 1885, first became a member of the Board, as Fellow of Christ's College, in 1893, and served for three years. He was re-appointed in 1899, and was made Chairman in 1904. Having been elected President of Queens' in 1906, he served as Vice-Chancellor for two years from 1915 (and again in 1928), but he continued to preside over the Board until 1922, and was throughout a most admirable Chairman. He was notable, too, for his sustained interest in the affairs of the Workers' Educational Association. Dr Stanton, a Wrangler in 1870 who had also been in the second class of the Classical Tripos in the same year, had served as Senior Dean and then Tutor of Trinity College, and was Ely Professor of Divinity. The Master of Magdalene (Stuart Alexander Donaldson) was also an undergraduate at Trinity, was in the first class in the Classical Tripos in 1877, and until his appointment as Master had been an assistant master at Eton. He too in due course became Vice-Chancellor. Monsignor Nolan entered Trinity as an advanced student in 1897, at the age of forty, and from 1896 until 1902 was Chaplain to the Roman Catholic undergraduates of the University, and was Master of St Edmund's House from 1904 till 1909. Dr Foakes-Jackson graduated from Trinity in 1879 with first class honours in theology, was Lightfoot Scholar a year later, and had become Assistant Tutor and Dean of Jesus College. Walter Durnford, fourth classic and Fellow of King's in 1869, was at Eton from 1870 till 1899, when he returned to King's, was Mayor of Cambridge in 1905, and Provost in 1918. J. H. Flather, of Emmanuel, in 1876 another first class classic, and Lightfoot Scholar in 1877, was Master of Cavendish College from 1888 until its closure in 1891, and thereafter was Assistant Secretary and then Secretary for Examinations at the Local Examinations and Lectures Syndicate. J. R. Roxburgh graduated from Trinity Hall, in 1886, as *Junior Optime* (and so brought some variety into the Board's membership), took the LL.B. degree a year later, and coxed the University Boat in 1888. He was a prominent Freemason, and was Bursar of Westminster College from 1902 to 1911. Dr Stewart, another Trinity classic, was Chaplain of the College from 1900 to 1902, when he went to St John's as Fellow and Dean, returning to Trinity in 1918 to a fellowship which he held until his death in 1948. He was University Reader in French from 1922 until 1944, and won international recognition for his work on Pascal.

Of the Lecturers and Directors of Studies not previously mentioned, Mr Walker, of Christ's College, had been second classic in 1872, and was a Fellow of the College for some years. He was College Lecturer at Clare and Caius, and was well known in the University as a coach. Mr A. J. Wyatt came into residence as a non-collegiate student in 1888, being already a graduate of London and Birmingham. He migrated to Christ's in 1889, took his degree two years later with first class honours in modern languages, and in 1892 won the Winchester Reading Prize. He was never elected to a fellowship, but became a coach, and was for nearly fifty years associated with the University Correspondence College at Burlington House. He lived at number 6 Queen Anne Terrace, in close proximity to, and then briefly surrounded by, Ayerst Hostel before its move to Mount Pleasant.[1] Charles Fox also matriculated as a non-collegiate student, in 1897, having been at school in London and New York. In 1898 he too migrated to Christ's, where he graduated with first class honours in natural sciences in 1900, and was also in the first class in the Moral Sciences Tripos in the next year. After lecturing at the Westminster Hospital Medical School he became Lecturer in Education at the Cambridge Day Training College, and was later (1919–38) Director of the University Training College for Schoolmasters in Brookside. Like Wyatt, he was never a Fellow.

In 1909 Reddaway prepared a statement of the expenses incurred by non-collegiate students, and found no reason to change his general estimate of £80 to £90 a year, which, he is careful to add, was the average expenditure, including money spent on books and stationery but not on clothes or travel, incurred in Cambridge by his men of all classes. His minimum figure was £165 for a course of three years. 'By a somewhat larger expenditure, however', he adds, 'the course can be made more pleasant and profitable. Additions may be made for...

    (d) recreation, clubs and small social expenses;

    (e) longer residence;

    (f) additional fees (as after failure in examinations);

    (g) more books (especially for candidates for honours);

    (h) special kinds of instruction.'

By 'special kinds of instruction' Reddaway clearly has private tuition in mind, and this he believes to be necessary for a small minority only. A backward student, he says, may need it for a term or two, or possibly

[1] See p. 14.

more; while those who seek high honours in mathematics will require it almost continually. Its usual cost was then £9 a term, and ten guineas for the months of July and August.[1]

The Orders made by the Board dated from 1875, and remained substantially unaltered for thirty years or more, but in 1911 the first was amended so as to reduce the period of residence allowed before the completion of the Previous Examination;[2] and Order III was changed in 1909 so as to require the removal from the books of the name of any student who failed, without leave, to keep a term by residence (instead of two terms).[3] These amendments were incorporated in the Information Sheet for July 1911, which also included two new regulations which reflected the Board's stiffer policy on migration, imposing a limit of standing and a fee. Curiously, these last two Orders were omitted from the next Information Sheet (December 1911); it almost seems that, having made his point, Reddaway was reluctant to draw attention to so undesirable a possibility.

If the Board's minutes record decisions approved and action taken, it is the Censor's own Reports which draw attention to those matters that in his view were of the most urgent importance. From the start of his censorship all Reddaway's actions were governed by one single concept: that the non-collegiate body should be raised from its inferior position in the University, and should be accorded the same kind of recognition as a college. All he said and did was in conformity with this principle, and throughout his censorship he never for one moment wavered in his endeavours to put it into practice. There is no reference by Reddaway to the origins of the non-collegiate scheme, and if he had been reminded of them he would have declared that, in a University otherwise composed of colleges, they were no longer relevant to an institution which had already been permitted to behave like a college, to the extent that its woefully slender resources might allow. To Reddaway the place had long since ceased to be non-collegiate, and he regarded its continued official description as such as an affront, a damaging misrepresentation which was also a grievous hindrance to further progress and to a wider acceptance of what it already was.

In Reddaway's first Report to the Board, dated 21 May 1908, there are the customary statistics about numbers in residence, examination results and the composition of the student body, but there is a fresh note of urgency in its final section:[4]

---

1   Information Papers, College Archives.   3   *Ibid.* 25 February 1909.
2   Minutes, 11 May 1911.   4   Censors' Reports.

I. The number of Undergraduate Students in residence has been: Mich. Term 116, Lent Term 107, Easter Term 104.

II. The number of admissions was 66, of migrations to Colleges 24, of migrations from Colleges 3.

Students migrated to Colleges: 1 during his first Term, 6 after 1 Term, 2 after 2 Terms, 8 after 3 Terms, 1 after 4 Terms, 2 after 5 Terms (Cath. Sidney), 2 after 6 Terms (Cath. & Down.), 1 after 7 Terms (Down.), and 1 after 8 Terms (Down.)

King's, St John's, Peterhouse, Clare, Pembroke, Caius, Trinity Hall, Queens' & Sidney received 1 Student; St. Cath., Christ's & Downing received 5.

III. Of the 104 Undergraduates now in residence 47 are in their first, 28 in their second, and 27 in their third or fourth year, and 2 Advanced Students. Ten are married, 8 live with parents or guardians, 16 are assistants in schools, 4 members of the Day Training College, 2 curates, 2 Nonconformist ministers, 8 at St Matthew's' House, 5 at St Edmund House, 16 at Cheshunt House (of whom 8 are in lodgings), 12 natives of India, 1 German, 1 Greek, and 1 Egyptian.

IV. Summary of results in University Examinations.

15 Students have taken the B.A. degree of whom 3 have taken Honours.

Previous Examination	Cl I	Cl II	Cl III	Cl IV	Failed
Part I	4	8	5	14	15
Part II	8	4	6	16	11
Additional subjects	1	14	–	–	12

General Examination	Cl I	Cl II	Cl III	Cl IV	Failed
Part I	2	2	9	4	5
Part II	7	3	4	2	2
Honour Examinations	–	2	3	–	2
Special Examinations	6	4	11	–	2
2nd M.B.					1
3rd M.B.		Approved 1, Failed 1			
Intercollegiate Examinations	2	6	9,	partly examined 2	
		not classed 3			

Exhibitions have been awarded as follows:

Leathersellers' Exhibitions to T. C. Witney (Cl I Theol.), J. F. McNulty (Cl II Hist.), A. O. N. Lee (Cl II Theol.).

Clothworkers' Exhibitions to W. Harvey (Theol.) and R. L. Hussey (Hist.).

A Censor's Exhibition to J. R. Swallow (Hist.).

V. Fuller information with regard to the events of the year will be given by the Fitzwilliam Hall Magazine of which the first number is now in the press.

I record with pleasure a greatly increased use of the Building particularly at dinner in Hall. The various societies have shown great activity, and the result of systematic efforts to increase the membership of the Amalgamated Clubs encourages the hope that next year no student will fail to become a member.

VI. Receipts and payments for the year ended Midsummer 1907.

	£	s.	d.		£	s.	d.
Degree				Rents & Interest	72	16	10
fees	28	7	0	Total receipts			
Admission				(ordinary)	1095	5	4
fees	382	4	0	Expenses			
Term fees	550	12	0	(ordinary)	1074	10	5
Lecture				Surplus	20	14	11
fees	61	5	6				

VII. Presents.

The following presents have been received during the year:– From Dr. Oliver:– books for the Library; from Mrs. Reddaway:– embroidered panel for fire-screen; given anonymously:– wooden pavilion; from the Censor:– furniture of the writing-room.

VIII. Needs of Students.

The welfare of the students would, in my opinion, be best promoted by attention to the following needs:–

(1) The establishment of a number of exhibitions open to students in their first year of residence.

(2) The acquisition of funds for defraying the cost of lectures in Honour subjects.

(3) Official enquiry into the alleged disabilities of Non-collegiate Graduates in competing for educational appointments.

(4) Effective action to remove the possibility of Students, who have been in reality noncollegiate during the whole of their residence, graduating as members of a College.

In the year before Reddaway's appointment as Censor there had been thirty migrations to colleges or hostels, and the loss of as many as twenty-four men in his first year will have been especially vexatious to him, for he knew that little improvement could be expected in the reputation of his institution if it continued to be known as a place from which many men felt obliged, in their future interest, to remove themselves if they could; and although his Board had already imposed a limit of standing on migration, Reddaway returned to the charge in his second Report: 'The corporate life lived at Fitzwilliam Hall has been described in its various aspects in the Magazine. I believe that our students may – and for the most part do – enjoy in a high degree the benefits commonly expected from residence in the University, that their life is pleasant, that they may receive at the smallest possible expense expert advice in their studies, and opportunities of social life, athletic exercise and assistance in developing any talent that they possess. But it is clear to me that, at present, in very many cases, these advantages are regarded by them as inferior to the anticipated advantage of the "College name".'[1] Reddaway then repeats his suggestion that migration should be made more difficult, that money should be found for the assistance of needy honours men, and that exhibitions should be established for men in their first year. In this last, he had himself shewn the way.[2]

By 23 May 1910, when he made his third Report, after submitting the usual facts and figures Reddaway felt able to write: 'I have pleasure in reporting a marked improvement in the status of our students and in the collegiate character of their life. This is due to many causes, among which may be mentioned: the kindness of members of the Board in entertaining us and in becoming members of our Clubs; the interest shewn by members of the staff in all our activities; the acquisition of a fixed and suitable place in which to play; the increase in attendance at Hall; the circulation of a Students' Magazine; the presence in our building of two residents; the great and self-sacrificing energy of the officers, almost without exception, of the Amalgamated Clubs, to which practically all the students belong.'

Then follows a revealing short passage: 'The improvement in status appears to have affected the stream of migrations to colleges, which is much less perceptible than last year. It should further be remarked that during the past three years the great majority of those who have quitted our ranks in this way have been missed but little, while in a few cases their continued presence in a society which lives a close corporate life would have caused embarrassment.' The Report closes with a request for authority to refuse admission to professional men (he has schoolmasters in mind) who propose to migrate to colleges, and with an invitation to members of the Board to promote as far as possible the use of the name 'Fitzwilliam Hall' in Cambridge.[3]

---

[1]   Report dated 27 April 1909. Cf. p. 69 for a similar expression of opinion by Mr Somerset. Many years later, Dr G. G. Coulton, who took his B.A. degree from St Catharine's in 1881, was to write '... the College had in my time only from 50 to 52 undergraduates. A notable proportion had begun as non-collegiates, whom our Tutors had admitted for their third year to jump off from the College.' *Fourscore Years* (C.U.P., 1943), p. 111.

[2]   See p. 155.   [3]   Censors' Reports.

If Reddaway proved to have been a little over-optimistic about the migrants in 1909/10 – for, although when he wrote his Report there had been no more than five, the year's total came to 21 – he was doing no more than ancicipate events, and the Report is of interest for a quite different reason, for Reddaway showed it to J. E. Staley, who had been his Secretary for the academical years 1907–09. There must have been a great deal of correspondence between Reddaway and his young men, and it is much to be regretted that more of it was not kept. Staley was delighted with a proposal to be cautious about intending schoolmaster migrants, and mentions some by name who, he thought, took unfair advantage of the place; and there is an illuminating reference in his letter to the great and encouraging improvement in the affairs of the Hall since 'our first uphill year 1907–08'. Reddaway's hopeful forecast proved to be justified in the following years, for in his own account of the year 1911/12, which the Board published as a Report of its own, he mentions three migrations, with one further possibility, and thereafter there is almost no allusion to this hitherto constantly recurring problem until, curiously enough, the last Report of his censorship, written by his successor for the year 1923/24, when there were seven.

The Report for the year 1911/12 is the happiest of all. It has much to say about almost all the matters that Reddaway regarded as significant; and opens with an account of the typically collegiate doings of the undergraduates, which to him were all-important. There follows the inevitable reference to the iniquity of their official designation. Numbers are up; and there have been applications from members of colleges for admission as non-collegiate students – an occurrence which will have afforded Reddaway a satisfaction almost as complete as the satisfaction to be derived from the necessity of rejecting as unworthy all but one of them. The year's class lists, with sixteen honours men out of thirty-five graduates, are in marked contrast with those of his first year, when there were three out of fifteen. He is at some pains to express his approval of the work of his student secretaries, but here his comments may be thought to read a little oddly, for there must have been occasions when confidential consultation would have proved more convenient in their absence.

Some years later Reddaway, recalling his early years as Censor, wrote 'We had at that time several notable friends – the President of Queens', Dr Foakes-Jackson, Monsignor Nolan, Dr Crafer, and others – but the supreme good fortune was the accession in 1907 of an unsurpassed band of freshmen. With all sections working together, we enjoyed seven years of unchecked progress until 1914. The most incandescent moment, I think, came in 1912, when the Exhibition Fund was inaugurated at a terminal dinner, and men living on £80 a year contrived to make handsome contributions.'[1] This is what the last paragraph of the 1911/12 Report is about. That it should be referred to in such terms after eighteen years – years that had seen the First World War come and go – is testimony enough to the impression made upon Reddaway at the time.

I have pleasure in reporting to the Board [says Reddaway] that, so far as I can judge, the hopes with which the past year began have been realised or even surpassed. Our vitality has been shewn not merely, nor chiefly, by the successes in examinations which are recorded below, but by the vigour of our old organisations and the formation of new. Thus, choosing results almost at haphazard, (i) "Halls" have increased by more than one thousand, and it is now difficult to indicate any Undergraduate who absents himself without good cause; (ii) Beside the Historical and Theological Societies, which have continued their valuable career, a Science Society has been founded; (iii) The Lent Boat has escaped from the bottom of the river, and a May Boat has been put on; (iv) The Football XI. has far surpassed its previous excellent record; an Athletic Club has begun its career with victory, and a substantial contingent has served in the Officers Training Corps.

It is natural, but none the less gratifying, that such achievements have visibly enhanced our prestige among both the junior and senior members of the University, and in the wider world. One of the most welcome proofs of this progress has been the increased use, by custom or deliberate courtesy, of our corporate title, in place of an official style which becomes every year more misleading.

I. The number of resident Undergraduates was during the Michaelmas Term, 127; Lent, 123; and Easter, 125, – as against 122, 117 and 111 in the corresponding Terms of the year 1910–1911. The increase was due, not to more numerous matriculations, (59 in each year), but in part to the exceptional number of by-termists in April, and in part to an increase in the average period of residence. The matriculations were in the Michaelmas Term 47; Lent, 6; and Easter, 6.

Bachelors of Arts in residence numbered about 25 throughout the year.

Several applications for admission were made by Undergraduates, but only one, a student who had left St. John's some years earlier, was accepted. The others failed to comply with the preliminary conditions that such applicants should have reached at least as high a standard as is prescribed for our own Students, and that cordial goodwill towards the proposal should be expressed by the College concerned.

Two Students migrated from us after their first term (St John's, St.

[1] *Journal*, April 1930, p. 20.

Catharine's); two after their second (St John's, Corpus); one after his third (Christ's), and another application has been received. So far as any common motive was assigned, it consisted in the belief that a "Non-Collegiate" Student would be supposed, by persons outside the University, to have lived in isolation.

II. Thirty-one Students graduated B.A. during the year: eighteen on the results of Triposes. One (T. A. Sullivan) gained a First Class in History, and one Advanced Student (P. Dunsheath) attained the standard of a First Class in Mechanical Sciences. One was placed in the Second Class (Upper Division), 2 in the Second Class (Lower Division), 4 in the Second Class (undivided), 7 in the Third Class, and 2 were allowed the Ordinary Degree.

In the final Special Examinations, 4 were placed in the First Class; 4 in the Second; and 5 in the Third.

Of these 31 Graduates, one (F. Thatcher) is assisting me, 9 remain in Cambridge for further study, 4 are reading elsewhere for Ordination, 2 are already Clergymen, 3 Presbyterian or Congregationalist Ministers, 6 or 7 are teaching; 2 are in Government Service in England and one in the Indian Police.

Two other Students (one an Advanced Student) qualified for graduation in Honours so soon as they shall have kept the necessary terms. Including these, further Tripos results were as follows: three Students were placed in the Second Class, six in the Third Class, and one was excused the Special Examination.

In Inter-Collegiate Examinations in Honours, one Student (G. H. Harris) was placed in the 1st Class, two in the 2nd Class, three in the 3rd Class, and three failed. M. J. Le Goc B.A. gained the Frank Smart Prize in Botany; G. H. Harris, the only "First" in the Inter-Collegiate Examination in Theology (2nd year), and Y. A. Godbole was placed 70th in competition for the Civil Service.

III. The year has been notable in the history of the three Hostels with which the Board are especially connected. St Matthew's House has passed from the control of its founder, Canon Hargrove, to that of the Church Pastoral Aid Society. St Edmund House, under the Mastership of Fr. Williams, has gained the most distinguished academic successes that it has ever yet achieved. In Cheshunt College, which will be removed to Brookside in 1914, the vacant post of Principal has been filled by Dr Campbell Morgan, Mr Johnson continuing to act as Resident Tutor.

IV. After five years' experience, I have pleasure in expressing to the Board my indebtedness to the Students who have acted as Censor's Secretary, and my belief that the office merits permanence. While not neglectful of their post-graduate studies, they have performed their many duties with unfailing zeal and not a little skill. I am not aware of any grave mistake that they have made, or of any case in which their presence has embarrassed a fellow-student in his relations with myself.

V. The arrangements made by the Board for the reception of a considerable number of Indian Students appear to be working well. No one who lives at Fitzwilliam Hall for a single day can suppose that our Indian visitors are "segregated, isolated or rudely treated."

During the year European Students have been appointed Principal of the Zamorin's College, Calicut, Professor of Economics in the University of Agra and Classical teacher in St Joseph's College, Colombo; while seven Indian Students, including four Advanced Students, have returned to professorial or administrative posts in India.

VI. I record with regret that for the first time extraordinary expenditure has fallen upon the reserve fund, which has been reduced below £200. This has been due in part to the reduction by the Board of the Admission Fee in special cases. Although every Student who desires it can now obtain direction in study without payment, the total sum paid by the Board to the Teaching Staff and the Censor did not greatly exceed £600. In view of the extent to which economy in expenditure has been carried, and of the necessity of providing Exhibitions to replace some at least of those which the Leathersellers' Company can no longer afford, it may be difficult to avoid a further reduction of the reserve.

In this connection I may mention the effort initiated within Fitzwilliam Hall to provide a new endowment. At the Terminal Dinner of January, 1912, I mentioned our loss, and suggested that those present might perhaps consider the possibility of doing something to make it good. After due consideration, a remarkably large number of Students privately assured me of their support. They appointed a representative Committee, resolved that the contributions should accumulate for some five years, and invited the Chairman of the Board and Censor to act as Treasurers. For the present, the promises and payments of Residents remain secret; but sums paid by Non-residents may be announced in the *Fitzwilliam Hall Magazine.* All our Residents have now been informed of the scheme, and some Non-residents, chiefly old Exhibitioners, have been invited to subscribe. Of the latter, not a few have generously responded. But the most striking feature of the movement has been the enthusiasm and munificence of the Residents, including the members of Cheshunt and Westminster Colleges, whose allegiance is naturally dual. It cannot be doubted that the sums already paid and promised will suffice for the endowment of at least one Exhibition.

Fitzwilliam Hall,   W. F. Reddaway.
10th October, 1912.

This Report of 1911/12 marks the end of an era; for, with the loss of the Censor's Report for the following year, there is now no other until November 1914.

During the war numbers fell. In 1914 there were 50 matriculations compared with 75 the year before, and by the Easter term 1918 the number of residents was 43 as against 156 in the last pre-war term. Continuity, however, was maintained, and two qualities become more and more noticeable in Reddaway as the time passes: his astonishing imperturbability, and his determination to keep things going so that when peace returns the Hall may be ready to take its proper place as a collegiate institution in a collegiate University. That he was unruffled by the accidents of war was certainly in no way due to a lack of interest in the fortunes of his men, for of that the *Magazine* supplies abundant evidence; and his forward-looking attitude is well illustrated by a brief paragraph written at the end of 1915, when , he says, 'The outstanding fact of the year is that by the aid of the Resident Chaplain (A. O. N. Lee) continuity has been preserved in the life of the Hall. The Board may now feel some confidence that whether we emerge from the War as a large body or a small, we shall not impair the traditions of a Collegiate University.'[1]

In his first *Information Sheet* Reddaway had referred to arrangements made for non-collegiate students in the chapel of King's College, and in his first Report to the Board had mentioned the issue of the first *Fitzwilliam Hall Magazine*.[2] Of a chapel – a chapel of their own – more will be heard in a separate note on its part in the life of the hall and House.[3] The *Magazine* was first mentioned in an unsatisfactory minute of a General Meeting of the Amalgamated Clubs, held on 22 January 1898, which refers to the approval of a 'motion re magazine', but there is no indication of the nature of the motion, and the Finance Committee of the Clubs, to which it was referred, merely asked for further particulars. At the next General Meeting, however, the proposer (C. W. Cunnington) reported that 'owing to lack of support the projected term [sic] magazine would be dropped'.[4]

After this false start, the Censor, at a Finance Committee Meeting held on 29 February 1908, proposed that a General Meeting of the Clubs be called with a view to introducing a 'Fitzwilliam Hall Magazine', and also proposed that it should be issued by the Clubs, and distributed free of charge to their members. At a General Meeting on 11 March the Censor again spoke to the proposal, which was unanimously approved; and a committee was appointed under Mr Alston, who had recently succeeded Reddaway as President of the Literary and Musical Society, 'for the working of the *Magazine*'. From a subsequent com-

[1]   Censor's Reports.   [3]   See pp. 441–56.
[2]   See pp. 160, 168.   [4]   A.C. Minutes, 26 March, 1898.

munication by the Censor, it is apparent that the editor of the first four numbers was Mr Alston himself,[1] and when he resigned at the end of the Easter term 1909 the editorship was taken over by an undergraduate (T. F. Scott).

Reddaway's conception of the function of the *Magazine* is made clear in a Censor's letter in its first number:

> I gratefully accept your invitation to contribute to the first number of the *Magazine* a letter to our Old Students. Permit me at the same time to offer the *Magazine* my most cordial good wishes, and to express my strong hope and expectation that, by providing an unfettered means of communication between our resident and non-resident Members, it will render most valuable service to our cause. During the short time that has passed since our Board conferred upon me the honour of the Censorship, nothing has impressed me more than the evidences of sustained enthusiasm on the part of men who have long since left Cambridge, but at the same time the lack of any apparatus for continuing or restoring a connection from which both we and they should profit. The coming extension of our Amalgamated Clubs and the establishment of the *Magazine* will, I believe, do much to remedy the malady of decentralization from which we suffer.[2]

The editor adds that the *Magazine* has come into existence largely for the benefit of the old students, that it will be issued terminally as the organ of the Amalgamated Clubs, and that men who have gone out of residence may become honorary members of the Clubs, and receive it on payment of 5s a year. As a responsibility of the Clubs, the *Magazine* received an annual subvention, which in the year 1907–08 amounted, for one issue, to £7.5.6,[3] to which the Board added a grant of £5.[4] Thereafter for some years its annual cost was of the order of £20. There is no doubt that in the early years it reached a high standard; it certainly fulfilled the Censor's intentions in starting it; it is a mine of information about undergraduate activities; but nobody could foresee how very valuable it was to become, with Reddaway – perforce – as its editor and principal contributor, in time of war.

In an unsigned article entitled 'The Playing Field', published in the *Fitzwilliam Magazine* for December 1909 and written quite possibly by T. F. Scott, the author recalls the circumstances in which the acquisition of the field became publicly known: 'It was', he says, 'not surprising that the Junior Dean purred audibly through the rest of the evening

---

[1] Speech made at a terminal dinner on 16 October 1909 (*Magazine*, December 1909, p. 114).
[2] *Magazine*, May 1908, p. 6.
[3] A.C. Minutes, 15 October 1908 – Statement of Accounts for the year ending 30 September 1908.
[4] Minutes, 9 March 1908.

when the Doctor invaded a concert, bringing in triumph a contract for the purchase of six acres or more of meadow. From that day (March 14, 1908) to this, the manufacture of a playing field has never paused.'[1]

The conveyance of the field from John Piddock, described as a retired printer 'of 7 Benson Street, Huntingdon Road, near Cambridge', to Reddaway, then living at 2 Huntingdon Road (a little nearer to Cambridge), is dated 1 April 1908, and shews that the field of just over six and a half acres, together with two entrances from Oxford Road each measuring 40' by 100', was bought for £650.[2] Of the two entrances, one still gives access to the ground; of the other, at the south-east corner of the field, a piece 34' wide had been sold by March 1910 to a Mr F. J. Chapman, the owner of what was then 31 Oxford Road, adjoining.[3] The remainder (6' by 100') was also to be sold to him in 1924 for £25.[4]

The field, roughly oblong in shape, has its long side parallel to Oxford Road, running approximately S.S.W. to N.N.E., and is about twice as long as it is broad. From north to south the level rose, over all, by about three feet, and there were 'hills and hollows' along its length, attributed to excavations for the building of roads in the neighbourhood. By November 1908 Reddaway was able to give this progress report in the *Magazine*:

> Since the beginning of April, steady progress has been made with the task of turning a meadow, originally self-sown and for twenty-five years uncared for, into a ground of the class which Cambridge now expects. The tiny practice pitch, laid under a scorching sun, was soon tested by snowstorms, and passed through this two-fold ordeal as well as could be hoped. All through the summer we viewed with longing eyes the hills and hollows which our surveyor had condemned to removal, but which could not be

---

[1] The 'Doctor' must be Reddaway. The identity of the 'Junior Dean' is not know. Neither is it known how the field first came to Reddaway's notice. On 28 February 1911 the Finance Committee of the Amalgamated Clubs approved unanimously a proposal, made by Mr A. O. N. Lee at the Censor's suggestion, that L. J. Lock should be made an honorary life member of the clubs 'for valuable work done in connection with the Playing Field'; and many years later the *Journal* (April 1934, p. 22) referred to Lock as 'the discoverer of our playing fields'. Lock (B.A. 1909) was captain of the unbeaten tennis VI of that year. He lived at 12 Huntingdon Road, in temporary medical practice, it seems, while reading for orders. He died on 21 April 1937 (see also *Journal*, May 1937, p. 6).

[2] College Bursary.

[3] The College Bursary has no record of this transaction. That it had been concluded by 8 March 1910 is evident from an agreement of that date between Reddaway and Chapman on access to the remaining six foot strip. On 25 March 1910, W. G. Bell appears to value the thirty-four foot frontage at £69.16.6 (A.C. Finance Committee Minutes, 25 April 1910).

[4] Trust Minutes, 5 November 1924. See also p. 190–1.

disturbed before the rains of autumn. Meanwhile the hedges, fences and ditches were set in order, a new approach from Oxford Road constructed, plans and estimates procured, our small pavilion removed from the old football field, and, above all, the cleansing of the turf begun. This last seems to have succeeded beyond all expectation. In April every kind of weed luxuriated, and we took 250 plantains from seven square yards of soil. Before the end of September the field showed as pure a surface as some which have received many years of treatment.

At Michaelmas, although the soil was still hard, the constructive stage began in earnest. Five weeks of labour by one gang of men, and some two hundred loads of brick, stone, ash and lime, have given us two admirable courts for lawn tennis. At the same time the buttresses of King Henry VI's Chapel at Eton were once more reproduced in brick and plaster in order to provide the form of corporal punishment known as Eton fives. A hockey pitch, let for two seasons to Emmanuel, was prepared, a place for our own hockey practices provided, the pavilion equipped, and nearly half of the great central hollow filled and returfed. At the southern end of the field the levelling necessary for six or seven grass courts was begun and is still proceeding. The hardest task of all, however, was the creation in four weeks of the football pitch adjoining our northern boundary. This demanded an amount of toil and minute care which cannot easily be realized by those who see only the results.

We have now in the near future to create a cricket pitch, to abolish the central hollow, to complete the grass courts, the football pitch and the roadway, to extend the accommodation for bicycles, and to provide a shelter for football players and spectators. The way will then be clear for making a second hockey or football pitch in the western portion of the ground.[1]

Reddaway may possibly have overestimated the extent to which others shared his longing to begin removing the hills and hollows; but there is no doubt that his enthusiasm inspired, or shamed, an astonishing number of his undergraduates (and colleagues) into presenting themselves for duty at the ground. He lost no time over the Eton fives court, for there is an agreement dated 7 September 1908 whereby the owner of the house immediately to the south of the entrance grants the use of part of its north wall 'to serve as the masonry of a fives court'. For his part Reddaway undertakes 'to cover this part of the wall with cement and the remainder with oil before the end of October 1908'.[2] Of recent years the game has been less popular, and the court was sadly encumbered with miscellaneous equipment. It is now roofed over to

[1]   *Magazine*, November 1908, p. 45.
[2]   College Bursary.

serve as a shed, and King Henry's buttresses have been removed, but traces of Reddaway's cement are still visible above the roofing, as evidence of more spacious days. The letting of a hockey pitch is a reminder of the difficulties that Emmanuel had, at first, with their now splendid field at the end of Adam's Road (Wilberforce Road did not then exist), next door to the 'commodious and prettily situated' ground hired by the Fitzwilliam Hall Amalgamated Clubs from Caius College for a season or two in 1904. The ash courts were first used in the Michaelmas term, and the football pitch was inaugurated on Monday 2 November with a friendly game against King's II, in which the first recorded goal was scored by H. Morrisey (of St Edmund's House), and the game won by three goals to two.[1]

The story is taken up again in the *Magazine* for February 1909, and there can be little doubt that Reddaway is the teller:

> The nett result of the levelling operations is as follows. – At the southern end a dead level, amply large enough for five grass courts, has been excavated, built up, turfed, and kept under careful supervision during many weeks. It promises to be firm and true enough to satisfy all requirements in the coming term, and to enable us to sub-let match-courts to our Westminster allies as in former years. If summer – as a cynic once said – "sets in with its usual severity," enthusiasts may have recourse to the ash-courts close at hand.
>
> Digging has nowhere been carried deeper than two feet, and archaeological 'finds,' therefore, have not been numerous. A mass of red bricks and brick dust was unexpectedly discovered on the site of the grass courts, as were traces of an old gravelled roadway towards the northern end of the hockey pitch. A Roman coin, fragments of pottery, pronounced (probably correctly) by the finder to be Roman, and a number of quaint clay tobacco pipes (also confidently attributed to the Romans), an old seal, and numerous relics of the farm to which the field formerly belonged, have also come to light.
>
> From the northern edge of the tennis plateau, the field, whose former hills and hollows were in great part due to excavations for the making of the neighbouring roads, begins a descent of some three feet to the lower edge of the football pitch, 190 yards away. This descent is not uniform, as, in the interests of cricket, a dead level, eighteen inches lower than the tennis courts, is being made across the middle of the field. The hockey pitch along the eastern boundary has been much improved by filling up most of the hollow along its length – one of the hollows which a labourer remembered as skating places in wet seasons of his boyhood. The surface of the southern part of this level, of which the flatness appears perfect to every

---

[1] *Magazine*, November 1908, pp. 52, 54.

eye, was prepared by a skilled workman without the use of spirit level and pegs; whereas the northern part, which obviously slopes upward into the hill, is in fact a most carefully surveyed dead level.

Before the hockey pitch was interfered with, some experience had been gained by the partial filling-up of two considerable hollows extending across the football pitch. ...

The last piece of work accomplished on the field was of a rather unusual kind. It had become necessary to move our pavilion rather more than a hundred yards, and the conventional resource of rollers was impossible, for structural reasons. On February 18, [1909,] therefore, some fifty of our number, aided by a few friends from Westminster and other colleges and by several labourers, essayed to carry it bodily to the new site. Eight long timbers, borne by two or three men at each end, were placed athwart the building, and men grasped every foot of the floor at the front and back. With a few halts, but practically no damage done, the unwieldy ark reached its destination.

And so the work went on. The cricket pitch and the lawn tennis courts were in use by the Easter term 1909, and another grass court was being prepared for the men of St Matthew's House, which was reported as being in play by the Easter term 1910. In the Christmas vacation of 1909 more than sixty loads of material ('ashes, ground lime, bricks, stones, gas lime and clinkers'), most of it given by A. C. Davis, an undergraduate,[1] was put down for an extension of the ash courts from 96' by 90' to 120' by 100', thus providing a third court and a longer 'run back'; and preparations were also made for more grass courts along the eastern side of the field (by Oxford Road). By March 1910 there had begun the first preparation of a screen along the eastern and northern boundaries against the building of unsightly houses, and twelve Canadian poplars were planted 'along part of the north-eastern boundary'. In April 1910 some attention was given to the precise determination of part of the southern boundary which, by what Reddaway describes as 'a friendly action at law', was set back by some eight feet in the neighbourhood of the ash tennis courts, and troublesome trees removed; and friendly though the action may have been Reddaway was awarded damages and costs.

---

[1] Matriculated in the Easter term of 1900, his name was on the books until 25 March 1902, but during that time he kept no term, and offered himself for no examination. Re-admitted on 8 January 1909, he resided for four terms, and was entered as reading for Part II of the Previous Examination, which he did not take. His name was again removed at Michaelmas 1922. In 1924 he published *One Hundred Years of Portland Cement (1824–1924)*; and in 1909 he had given to the Fitzwilliam Hall Library a copy of an earlier volume, *Portland Cement*, of which a second edition had been published in that year. As Sir Charles Davis (Kt 1944), he was Lord Mayor of London in 1945–46. (*Who was Who*, 1941–50).

By December 1910, under the direction of R. J. Tollit, another Fitz-william undergraduate, who at the same time was an architect and sur-veyor practising in the town, Reddaway had built a house for a groundsman (Red Cottage) so designed that two ground floor rooms facing the field, by the removal of partitions, could be turned into a pavilion, surmounted by a balcony of the same size for onlookers at cricket matches. In the Michaelmas term 1910 there was further level-ling of the football ground, after a survey by Walter Harvey (B.A. 1910) who, having trained as an architect,[1] had come to join a Cam-bridge firm but had then decided on ordination; and drainage was also undertaken with the help of Mr K. J. J. Mackenzie, Director of Studies and University Lecturer in Agriculture. By June 1911 there were sixty trees, many of them given by past or present Fitzwilliam men, and a privet hedge had been planted along the whole of the northern, and part of the eastern, boundary. In the summer of 1911, a year of drought still remembered, 'the field has taken little hurt', says the *Magazine* correspondent, 'but the grass courts will need special care for some time to come. Of the newly planted trees, the poplars are all thriving, as is the privet, but the thujas have not done well. We hope that past and present students will send in liberal contributions for planting, as many more are wanted to make a satisfactory screen on the eastern side, and where more white-brick cottages will be built in the near future. In this connexion, we are glad to report a recent stroke of good fortune, for though the orchard, which runs for fifty yards along our boundary, has been lately sold, by auction, at a price of over £1100 per acre, thus frustrating a plan which had been formed for keeping it in friendly hands, the purchaser, we learn, intends to develop it, for the present, on existing lines, and it is to be hoped that when the inevitable buildings arise our tree-planting scheme will have made them harm-less.' It seems not unlikely that Reddaway himself had designs on the orchard, renounced when it realized, in pounds per acre, ten times as much as the field he had bought three years earlier.

By the end of 1911 iron gates had been put up at the entrance, and during the ensuing Lent term the last remaining hills and valleys to the south of the cricket pitch were evened out, with so much voluntary labour that the net cost to the Clubs of levelling some nine hundred square yards came to thirty shillings. During this term also the drought

[1]   Harvey's training as an architect was to be put to further use in 1927, when the old wooden shed (still in use for other purposes) was replaced by a pavilion built to his design. An artist's impression appears in the *Magazine* for June 1927, and the *Magazine* for December 1928 contains a statement of accounts for the completed building, with a photograph showing the Fitzwilliam coat of arms (Harvey's personal gift) on its southern wall.

of the previous year proved an uncovenanted source of revenue, for a hockey pitch was let to Magdalene College, whose new ground had not recovered from it. In March 1913 extensive further planting is reported on the north-eastern boundary, much of it a gift from the Censor; and a new privet hedge was begun between the groundsman's house and the ash courts to the south. In July 1913 the grass tennis courts are ceasing to shew the effects of the drought two years before (they must have been severe), and there is rejoicing that the large field to the north-east is to be turned over to allotments and not made into new streets. Finally, at the end of the year the *Magazine* correspondent (again, almost certainly Reddaway) is able to record that after five years of successive improvements the condition of the playing field was such that further developments were not to be expected until a need should arise to find a ground for rugby football.[1]

All this activity by Reddaway and, following his example, by many willing helpers, was only a part of his plan. Having bought the ground himself in April 1908, he did not intend to leave matters there. One curiosity in the Clubs' minutes is that there is no formal reference to their acquisition of the ground. In April 1907 they were given 'the first chance of the joint use of the Cheshunt football ground for next season'. On 7 February 1908, it was agreed 'to lend our field [wherever that was] to The Authentics Football Club on Saturday 8 February for 5/-'. The Clubs were then much taken up with starting the *Magazine*, and with the re-drafting of their Rules, and the first definite allusion to a ground of their own is to be found in the minutes of a Finance Committee held on 8 December 1908, when J. E. Staley, as Censor's secretary, gave an account of the expenses incurred by the Censor for work on the field, and informed the committee that, as their landlord, he was prepared to give a practice pitch for hockey for use during the Lent term 1909, on condition that the Clubs provided netting on its southern boundary to protect the tennis courts. Similarly, he would provide five grass tennis courts at a rent of £2 each for the Easter term 1909, and would let a cricket pitch for the same term at a rent of £5, if the Clubs would be responsible for labour and expenses. He would also give a practice cricket pitch rent free if the Clubs would see to its levelling, but would pay half the cost of the levelling himself if the pitch were not used in the Long Vacation. Naturally, these offers were accepted, and for two years there follows a whole series of measures for the improvement of the ground, including the engage-

---

[1]   This summary of work done on the playing field between 1909 and 1913 is based on articles published in virtually every number of the *Magazine* at the time.

ment of a groundsman (Cullop), Reddaway undertaking to employ him during the Long Vacation. And so the record continues, with Redda-way helping the Clubs along, and encouraging them to assume such re-sponsibilities as he thought they could accept, and as often as not sub-sequently modifying in their favour conditions previously agreed.

In November 1909 the President of the Clubs (W. G. Bell) told their Finance Committee that he had received a letter from the Censor offering to lease the ground to them for seven years at an annual rent of three and a half per cent of the capital expenditure he had incurred, with an additional rent of £7 for the ash tennis courts; other conditions being that the Clubs should look after hedges and fences, that they should have the right to terminate the lease at the end of three or five years if they desired, and that the Censor should have the right of veto on sub-letting. After due consideration, the committee agreed, on 22 November 1909, to recommend to a General Meeting that the Clubs should take a lease on the conditions proposed by the Censor at an annual rent of three and a half per cent of a capital expenditure of about £1,000, together with £7 for the ash courts. This recommenda-tion was approved at a General Meeting held on 4 December, and after discussions between the President, the General Secretary and the Cen-sor it was resolved that the capital expenditure already incurred should be reckoned at £954.10.6, and that there should be added to it a sum of £45.9.6 for work to be done forthwith on the football ground.[1] The Clubs would therefore be able to hire their playing field, with two ash courts, for an annual rent of £42. On 30 April 1910 they appointed as their Trustees Messrs Huddleston, Flather, Peck, Wyatt, Lee, and Bell; and a lease was drawn up (seemingly free of charge) by Mr Ernest Vin-ter, who was elected a life member of the Clubs, and on 4 June 1910 became their honorary solicitor.

Within weeks of Reddaway's statement that no further development of the ground was to be expected until it became necessary to provide for rugby football, a Rugby Football Club was founded, but there is no mention of special provision for it, and within a year all normal activity in the Clubs was overtaken by the declaration of war in August 1914. In June 1915 it is reported that an opportunity, afforded by the virtual cessation of games, had been taken to make various improvements in the field, including further levelling of the football pitch, and top dres-sing the match tennis courts, which had been left fallow for the season. The screen of trees along Oxford Road had been completed by planting more poplars, and a line of Douglas firs had been put in behind the ash

[1]   A.C. Minutes, 25 April 1910.

tennis courts. Throughout the academic year 1915/16 more levelling was done on the football and cricket grounds, largely in order to provide employment for the groundsman, who was awaiting his call-up; potatoes were grown, and the Clubs' donkey, having been bought by the Censor and the Chaplain, was presented to the Red Cross, and sold for £3.6.0. By July 1916 it had been recognized that there would be no more games for the time being, and the field had been given over to hay. Apart from an announcement in June 1918 that the annual subscription to the Clubs would be reduced to one guinea, there is no further mention of the field until after the war, when in December 1918 Reddaway proclaims that football will be resumed in the Lent term 1919, and that, except for one acre which he will retain 'for agricultural purposes', the Clubs may expect to be in full possession by Lady Day. It was likely to take a couple of years to reestablish the tennis courts and the various pitches, but with the passage of time the screens of trees had grown up so as to add considerably to the privacy of the field. In the Michaelmas term 1919 the foundation of a Rugby Football Club was formally approved, although it was to be without a ground for the whole of that season.[1]

In the years immediately before the war of 1914 Reddaway became acutely aware of the need, particularly in the interests of the corporate activities of his men, of more living accommodation in the neighbourhood of Fitzwilliam Hall itself; and in the early war years he also foresaw that such accommodation would be in very great demand, if, when the war was over, there should be a large, and sudden, increase in student numbers in the University. Reddaway's acquisition of these additional premises, and his arrangements for their administration, lead on to the story of one of his most imaginative and most successful ventures – the formation of a body known as The Fitzwilliam Hall Trust.

In 1913, as a first step, the Board appointed their Chairman, their Auditors (internal), and the Censor as a committee 'to investigate the conditions on which the house, no. 25 Fitzwilliam Street, could be secured and, if desirable, to hire it'.[2] Reddaway lost no time (possibly the ground had been prepared), for at the Board's next meeting he reported that he had been offered a ten-year lease of the house by Mr E. S. Peck, except for that part of it which was used as a chemist's shop, and added that he was prepared to sub-let to the Board for one year, on the same terms as those of the offer made to him; and there

[1]   *Ibid.*, 11 October 1919.
[2]   Minutes, 1 December 1913.

and then outlined a scheme for the provision of rooms for six students, and for their superintendence. Whether the Board, or their nominated representatives, were competent to hold property appears not to have been debated, for their minutes merely record general approval of the scheme, with an instruction to the Censor to apply to the Lodging-Houses Syndicate for authority to house the students in their premises.[1] There is an account of this transaction, over Reddaway's signature, in the *Magazine*. Entitled 'The Hostel', it reads:

> What may prove to be an important step forward will be taken at Midsummer, when we may, if we choose, enter upon a ten years' tenancy of Mr. Peck's house, situated between Fitzwilliam Hall and Fitzwilliam Street. The portion now occupied by Messrs. G. Peck and Son for business purposes is, of course, excluded; but the remainder is sufficiently large to give ample accommodation for our Library, as well as to house half-a-dozen men. As the new residents would naturally include such officials as the Librarian, the Censor's Secretary and the Organist, an immense gain in convenience must follow, while it is not unreasonable to hope that the benefit which has resulted from the presence within our walls of several hospitable Seniors may be extended.[2]

There is little information about the terms of Reddaway's lease, except that it was for ten years. In the Board's Summary of Accounts for the year 1914–15 there first appears a payment of £96 for rent, which almost certainly refers to this property, sub-let to the Board on an annual basis.

It appears to have been in the Michaelmas term 1913 that the Non-Collegiate Students Board first discussed the 'suggested appointment of Fitzwilliam Hall Trustees for the furtherance and custody of future endowments', and directed the Censor to take legal advice.[3] To legal advice there is no subsequent reference, but in the following term the Board resolved unanimously that they were willing 'to sanction the appointment of the Chairman and Censor for the time being as the Trustees of property which the donors may desire to place in their custody for the benefit of members of Fitzwilliam Hall'.[4] This resolution also, described as highly significant, was published, doubtless at

[1]   Minutes, 23 January 1914.
[2]   *Magazine*, March 1914, p. 39. The 'Hostel', leased from the Peck family from 1914 until 1963, is variously, and confusingly, described as of 25 Fitzwilliam Street, and 30 Trumpington Street. It consisted of those parts of both houses not used by the owners for their chemist's business.
[3]   Minutes, 20 October 1913.
[4]   *Ibid.*, 23 January 1914.

Reddaway's instigation, in the next issue of the *Magazine*.[1] During the war no further progress was made in the appointment of trustees to hold such property as the non-collegiate body might acquire, but the question was raised again in the Easter term 1919, when a General Meeting of the Amalgamated Clubs discussed the advisability of appointing a body of Fitzwilliam Hall trustees 'to take over the various houses', and approved a motion 'that a body of Trustees and a Committee of Management be appointed to take over such houses as they may deem expedient, and the endowment funds'.[2] At the next General Meeting of the Clubs, in the following Michaelmas term, the President, doubtless again at Reddaway's instigation, asked the Censor for a statement on the houses, and Reddaway is recorded as saying that the scheme was satisfactory, and that five freehold properties in Fitzwilliam Street (numbers 3,9,10,19, and 21) had been taken over, and four leasehold (17 and 22 Fitzwilliam Street; 28 and 29 Trumpington Street). Of the nine, six had been bought and three rented (28 and 29 Trumpington Street, and 17 Fitzwilliam Street, also bought in March 1920)[3]. In his Annual Report for 1918–19, dated 18 November 1919, Reddaway informed his Board of the Clubs' agreement to the appointment of a permanent body of trustees, and added, possibly a little mysteriously, that he had reason to believe that they might soon have additional responsibilities – an oblique reference, no doubt, to his plans for the Oxford Road ground which he had acquired in 1908. The Board's minute is brief – it is in Reddaway's hand – for it merely says 'The Censor's Report was received. The Board resolved that the present understanding with regard to the Hostel be continued, and endorsed the proposed appointment of trustees to hold the extraneous houses.'[4] In agreeing to continue 'the present understanding' the Board were presumably referring to nothing more than the payment year by year to Reddaway for rent. The hostel never became a responsibility of the Fitzwilliam Hall Trust, for Reddaway continued to sub-let it directly to the Board until 1924, when a new lease was negotiated with Mr E. S. Peck by the University, on the Board's behalf.[5]

Reddaway lost no time in taking steps to incorporate, under the Companies Acts 1908 to 1917, a company to hold property and administer funds on behalf of the body of non-collegiate members of the University, referred to as 'Fitzwilliam Hall', who had no legal corporate

[1] *Magazine*, March 1914, p. 39.
[2] A.C. Minutes, 10 June 1919.
[3] *Ibid.*, 11 October 1919.
[4] Minutes, 21 November 1919. See also Censor's Reports.
[5] Minutes, 17 June 1924.

existence of their own. The first members of the Company, in their several capacities, were Frank Thatcher (Chaplain), W. F. Reddaway (Censor), W. S. Thatcher (Director in Economics), E. H. Ezard (Director in Medicine), C. J. B. Gaskoin (Lecturer in History), Metford Watkins (Student), and C. G. Joseph (Director in Geography). The certificate of incorporation is dated 7 June 1921, and on 6 June, one day ahead, Reddaway reported to the Board that the Fitzwilliam Hall Trust had been duly established. This, we are told, 'was noted, but no motion was made'.[1] To the certificate of incorporation there was added, on 25 June, a licence to hold lands not exceeding fifty acres in all.

In the *Fitzwilliam Journal* for April 1929 there is an account of the activities of the Trust which mentions the various houses as its principal assets, and among its liabilities 'chiefly money borrowed from a friend of Fitzwilliam Hall, and an occasional overdraft at the Bank'. There is no reason to doubt that the allusion is to Reddaway.[2] Among the records of the Trust is a *Register of Land and Schedule of Documents*, compiled in 1922,[3] which shews that, between 31 January 1919 and 22 April 1922, twelve houses in all were purchased or rented; and when the Trust had been formally established, Reddaway either transferred properties to it, if he had acquired them before its incorporation, or, if he obtained them subsequently, caused them to be conveyed directly to the Trust by the vendors. By either method the Trust assumed responsibility for the administration of the properties, and became indebted to Reddaway for their purchase price.

The financial indebtedness of the Trust to Reddaway was great, but it would have been heavier had it not been for support from independent sources, inspired indeed by Reddaway, but made possible by a quite astonishing spirit of generosity among the members, many of them junior members, of Fitzwilliam Hall. In May 1923 the trustees of a Chaplaincy Endowment Fund transferred to the Trust a sum of £500 – the proceeds of an appeal addressed by Reddaway, mainly to the men of 1913–16, for the endowment of a resident chaplaincy – in return for an undertaking by the Governors to administer the house at 10 Fitzwilliam Street, and to apply the income derived from it in furtherance of

[1]   Minutes, 6 June 1921.
[2]   *Journal*, April 1929, p. 8. The account was written by Walter Harvey, then recently appointed Assistant Censor and Bursar of Fitzwilliam House. There are other similar references. See, for example, p. 180, where the *Magazine* correspondent (probably Reddaway himself) mentions a plan, frustrated by the price, for keeping in 'friendly hands' an orchard on the boundary of the playing field. Similarly, when in June 1915 Reddaway took a seven year lease of 24 Fitzwilliam Street, he informed the Board in his Annual Report that the house had 'passed into friendly hands for a long term'.
[3]   College Bursary.

the purpose of the Fund.[1] In February 1925, subject to the consent of the Non-Collegiate Students Board, which appears not to have been effectively withheld, and in consideration of the transfer to the Trust of the sum of £1,095 and a small amount in Stock, the Governors made a similar arrangement for no. 19 with the trustees of the 1912 Exhibition Fund.[2] The extent of the Trust's dependence on Reddaway himself is sufficiently illustrated by a resolution of the Governors, taken under his chairmanship on 20 February 1924. Mr Frank Thatcher's minute, signed in due course by his brother as a correct record, also illustrates the attraction for Reddaway of the complex, almost, as it sometimes appeared, for its own sake. 'The sole trustee [Mr Reddaway] of the Eric Noel Player and Hirst Bursary', says the minute, 'offered to pay the sum of £407 ... for the freehold of 4 Fitzwilliam Street – Dr Ezard proposed and R. S. Ball seconded that 4 Fitzwilliam Street be allocated to the Eric Noel Player and Hirst Bursary, and the trustees hereby declare that from 25 March 1924 they hold the house in trust for the said Eric Noel Player and Hirst Bursary. It was agreed that the purchase price be paid by handing over to Mr Reddaway £300 5% War Bonds due 1928, who agrees to take them at middle price on Lady Day 1924, and to pay the sum due by drawing upon his credit balance with the Trust. The balance of the purchase price is to be satisfied by drawing upon the credit balance of the Eric Noel Player Bursary's account with the Trustees.'[3]

Such assistance notwithstanding, by 30 June 1924 the Trust's debt to Reddaway (and to Mrs Reddaway) amounted, with interest, to some £4,500.[4] This loan was allowed to run on for some years after Reddaway's retirement from the censorship; but by 30 June 1933 it had been reduced to £850, and in October 1933, at his request, it was repaid.[5]

The Trust was soon to run into heavy weather, but before an account is given of these difficulties, which involved the non-collegiate institution as a whole, and also ran over into the time of Reddaway's successor as Censor, there should be mentioned two further aspects of the Trust's affairs. Some months after its formal constitution Reddaway presented to the Non-Collegiate Students Board a Memorandum

[1]   Trust Minutes, 23 May 1923.
[2]   *Ibid.*, 28 February 1925.
[3]   *Ibid.*, 24 February 1924. For a rather more emphatic expression of the same opinion, see W. S. Thatcher, 'Fitzwilliam House under Mr W. F. Reddaway' *Journal*, December 1965, p. 27): 'In finance he could be so obscure and roundabout as to drive me almost mad. Fortunately ... he had my brother as his steward and accountant, and he had the patience of Job.'
[4]   Trust Minutes (Annual General Meeting), 23 January 1925. The indebtedness had at one time probably approached £8,000.
[5]   Trust Minutes, 16 October 1933.

on the Fitzwilliam Hall Trust, in which he recited the circumstances
leading to its establishment, and put down for the record his opinion of
the importance of what it had already been able to do: 'I have several
times mentioned to the Board', he writes, 'my belief that the work of
the trustees has been one of the greatest factors in the success of their
own efforts to cope with the post-war situation. If the fifty men from
our new houses had been dispersed in distant suburbs the strain upon
the staff would have been intolerable. The Board have at their command two means of helping the new body. Individual members may
enter it, and a collective investigation may be undertaken with its
natural outcome in a formal resolution.' It does not appear that any
Board member took Reddaway's hint about individual membership of
the Trust, and there is no evidence of 'collective investigation'; but
Reddaway got his motion, in general terms, for the Board 'having considered the Censor's *Memorandum* ... resolved *nem. con.* that they welcomed the incorporation of the Trust'. It must be supposed that the
words '*nem. con.*' were used advisedly, and it may be noted that two
members were absent; but this expression of opinion was not without
value, for it stood as evidence that in setting up the Trust the Censor
had not proceeded against the wishes of his Board, or without their
knowledge.[1]

Of Reddaway's provision for the future, however distant that future
might be, and however improbable the contingency which he had in
mind, the Trust's Memorandum of Association supplies one splendid
instance, in prescribing that, in the event of the dissolution of the
Association, such assets as might remain after the satisfaction of its
liabilities should be transferred to any corporation constituted by Royal
Charter (or by Letters Patent) in which might be vested the functions
then vested in the Non-Collegiate Students Board. And so it was that in
the fulness of time the way was found to be open for the transfer to
Fitzwilliam College of the, by then, considerable property of Reddaway's Trust. It should, perhaps, be added that in interpreting the text
of Reddaway's dispositions the officers of the College were in some
temporary perplexity, for it appeared that at a material point a negative
had been omitted; but with the assistance of Counsel the difficulty was
removed, and the clause still stands as a memorial to Reddaway's
vision, and to his steadfast faith in the future of the institution for
which he did so much.[2]

[1] Minutes, 2 March 1922. See also p. 206.
[2] Fitzwilliam Hall Trust. Memorandum and Articles of Association, Clause 9. College Bursary. See also p. 488.

In 1919 Reddaway had suggested that the Fitzwilliam Hall Trust might shortly be asked to assume fresh responsibilities;[1] and he had not awaited the Trust's formal constitution before he set his plans in motion. In his Censor's letter to the *Fitzwilliam Magazine* of March 1920 he makes the first public reference to a project which, until its realization some years later, was to remain one of his most urgent concerns. 'Our domestic efforts', he writes, 'have lately been concentrated on the purchase of the playing field by the Clubs as a permanent memorial to their members fallen in the war. All their contemporaries here feel that this is what they most would have rejoiced in had they survived, and a steady accession of subscriptions from older benefactors gives great encouragement to the plan.'[2] Reddaway is following his habitual practice of doing good by stealth, and the gaps need filling in. He had come to think that it would be very much better for the Clubs to own their field than to rent it; and he was willing to sell it to their trustees for £1,000, the figure which had been accepted as his capital outlay over its purchase and improvement when he had leased it to the Clubs in June 1910, since when its value must have doubled, at the very least. The target for the War Memorial Fund was, therefore, £1,000, and by November 1920 more than half had been raised. By March 1923 Reddaway is able to proclaim that the whole sum had been subscribed. 'The completion', he writes, '– except for a few outstanding promises – of the Fund for the purchase of the Playing Field will afford great satisfaction to the men of 1919, who started it, and to all other Fitzwilliam men, past and present. The trustees, who become the legal owners of the field, have seized the opportunity to purchase also the Red Cottage and Fives Court, hoping that at a later date the Clubs may invest in this valuable and convenient property. For the present they have raised a loan, the interest on which is more than covered by the rental of the premises.'[3] Again the gaps need to be filled in, for it was Reddaway who provided the loan of £700 which enabled the Fitzwilliam Hall Trust to make the purchase, and he it was, also, who paid the rent; for as soon as the purchase was completed he took out a seven year lease of the Cottage and fives court. Here, too, he adds a little to the history of the Cottage which, it may be remembered, had been so designed as to be capable of providing a pavilion on the ground floor, and a grandstand on the roof. At the outbreak of the war, however, this idea was given up, and with the addition of a small flat Red Cottage assumed its present form.

---

[1] See p. 185.   [2] *Magazine*, March 1920, p. 5.
[3] *Ibid.*, March 1923, p. 36. The conveyance is dated 12 February 1923.

Reddaway, however, had not quite finished with Oxford Road. Among the projects which he had initiated was the raising of a Fund, begun in 1918, in memory of Fitzwilliam men who had fallen in the war, which should provide a suitable memorial in the chapel, and exhibitions for needy undergraduates; and by 1924 over £500 had been subscribed. In the Michaelmas term of this year, however, he conceived the idea of using the money for another purpose, in consequence of what he described as 'recent legislative changes' which appeared to him to have made possible a somewhat more liberal provision for the assistance of poor men, but which also, he thought, would impose a serious handicap on the corporate efficiency of the Clubs. Reddaway must be referring to the recommendations of a Syndicate appointed in the previous Lent term, to consider the position of the Non-Collegiate Students Board, then in financial difficulty owing to a decline in student numbers. The Syndicate, by securing an annual grant of £1,000 for the Board, had created opportunities for the financial support of non-collegiate undergraduates most in need of it; but, by also making specific provision for men who might not wish to join in corporate activities, they had, in Reddaway's view, made it likely that fewer men would join the Clubs, which would therefore be in need of assistance for years to come.[1]

In these circumstances Reddaway proposed that the capital of the War Memorial (Exhibitions) Fund should be used not for the award of exhibitions, but as a means of helping the Amalgamated Clubs to acquire Red Cottage which, he thought, could with advantage be in the same hands as the playing field, and with the field would constitute a War Memorial worthy of the name.[2] In the minutes of a meeting of the Governors of the Fitzwilliam Hall Trust held on 13 September 1924, there is a passing reference, but nothing more, to the possibility that Red Cottage might become the property of the Clubs, and by December Reddaway had obtained the consent of the subscribers to the Fund to his proposed change of use. On their part, the Clubs had agreed that if the Fund were used for that purpose they would make up from their own reserves the difference between its capital value and the purchase price of £700. They also requested the Governors of the Trust to sell what was left in their possession of the entrance from Oxford Road to the south-eastern corner of the field by the ash courts.[3] This passage, for now it was little more than a passage, was duly sold for £25 to

---

[1]   See p. 202.
[2]   *Magazine*, December 1924, p. 18. For the Memorial in the Chapel, see p. 347–9, 451.
[3]   A.C. Minutes, 23 October, 1924. See also p. 176.

Mr F. J. Chapman, of 36 Huntingdon Road, who had bought the greater part of the entrance from Reddaway in 1910, the conveyance being signed, according to the minutes of the Trust, on 5 November 1924.[1]

There follows a period of indecision on the part of the Trust Governors, for, having declared on 15 October 1924 that 'from today the nett proceeds of the Red Cottage, now leased to Mr Reddaway, be held in trust for the Amalgamated Clubs', and having resolved on 5 November that 'the War Memorial Fund Trustee and the Amalgamated Clubs be requested to have the consideration for Red Cottage ready for Lady Day 1925', they appear to have been in some doubt whether they were legally entitled, or would be allowed, to hold it in trust for the Clubs.[2] The reason for this uncertainty may be better understood in the light of unfavourable opinions expressed about the Trust by the Syndicate in its Report published in the previous Easter term (see p. 206). In October 1925 the Censor (by then, W. S. Thatcher) again 'raised the question of the legal position of the Trust as regards the Red Cottage', but the Governors resolved 'to await developments, and deal with the matter in a few months' time.'[3]

In the meantime, Reddaway who had all along intended that the Trust should hold both the field and the Cottage on the Clubs' behalf, had written to the Governors on 27 June 1925:

> In pursuance of instructions given by the Subscribers of the Fitzwilliam Hall Memorial Fund, I, acting as the sole Trustee of the Fund having handed to you the sum of £535.13.10 (five hundred and thirty-five pounds thirteen shillings and ten pence) the capital subscribed for the said Fund now in the name and by the authority of the said subscribers or the majority of them request that you will receive the said invoices and in consideration thereof will administer the Estate known as the Red Cottage and playing fields situate in Oxford Road in the Borough of Cambridge the freehold of which was conveyed to you by an Indenture dated February 12th 1923 as Trustees for and on behalf of the Amalgamated Clubs connected with Fitzwilliam House. You are hereby authorized to invest any or all of the monies aforesaid in the purchase of real estate.[4]

The conditions under which Red Cottage was held by the Trust had been left unclear on a previous occasion, for in December 1922, when the transfer to the Trust of the field and the Cottage was first being contemplated, with the intention at that time that the Governors

---

[1] The copy of the conveyance in the College Bursary is undated.
[2] Trust Minutes, 6 May 1925.
[3] *Ibid.*, 28 October 1925.
[4] College Bursary.

should hold the field in trust for the Clubs and acquire the cottage for themselves, their solicitor advised that whereas the conveyance should be in the form of a simple transfer of both properties from Reddaway to the Trust, the minutes of the Trust should show which was to be held for the Clubs, and which was to become its general property.[1] The conveyance was therefore drafted in the form of a sale by Reddaway of both properties, but, just as then no formal decision appears to have been recorded that Red Cottage was to be a part of the Trust's general property, so now there is no recorded resolution of the doubts expressed by the Censor, as Chairman of the Trust, in October 1925; and, although the Governors appear to have complied with the request contained in Reddaway's letter of 27 June 1925, their minutes do not refer to that letter at all.

The difficulties of the post-war years overshadowed a little the con-clusion of Reddaway's campaign, begun in 1908, on behalf of the undergraduate clubs; but by the end of his censorship his men, no longer in occupation 'on sufferance' of hired property, had a ground to call their own, eminently fit to be compared with the grounds of such colleges as had them, and were well on the way to the ownership of adjacent premises which Reddaway had built, which they were to pur-chase from him with funds which he, largely, had collected, and were then to lease to him for seven years. W. S. Thatcher, a freshman in 1907, retained a lasting impression of Reddaway's activity at this time. 'When I came up', he wrote in 1965, 'we had no playing field, which was a grave disadvantage, as we never knew where we should play. This was made good in my second year by Reddaway's generosity. He bought the present field and rented it to us at a very modest rent. When he acquired it, it was a meadow with the old pattern of ridge and furrow which was ill adapted to games. I can remember seeing it one very bleak day and being invited to spud up plantains. By the time I went down it was already taking good shape. The survey was made by Walter Harvey who became Bursar later with me. The levelling was done by squads of students and took some three years. After the war Reddaway sold the field to the Clubs for the same price as he gave for it, and also made a handsome contribution.'[2]

It was wholly in keeping with Reddaway's devotion to the institution over which he presided that what was above all his own creation should be commemorated in two inscriptions placed on a wall of Red Cottage at the entrance to the field:

[1] Trust Minutes, 10 December 1922.
[2] See *Magazine*, June 1923, p. 75; and, for a photograph of the first part of the inscription, p. 90.

TO THE FORTY THREE FROM
FITZWILLIAM HALL WHO
FELL IN THE GREAT WAR THIS
PLAYING FIELD IS DEDICATED
BY THEIR SUCCESSORS. 1923

ALSO THIS HOUSE BY
THEIR PARENTS FRIENDS
AND SUCCESSORS. 1925

In following Reddaway's Oxford Road manoeuvres to their virtual conclusion, this summary has not only continued into the time of his successor, but has left almost without mention the outcome, so far as concerned Fitzwilliam Hall, of the findings of two bodies appointed shortly after the Great War – the Royal Commission of 1919 on the Universities of Oxford and Cambridge, and, within the University, the Syndicate commissioned to consider the position, particularly the financial position, of the Non-Collegiate Students Board. Both were to have a substantial influence on the fortunes of the non-collegiate institution, and in particular, as it now seems, both may have raised in Reddaway's mind the most insistent doubts about his willingness, or even his ability, to remain in office as Censor.

The Royal Commission, appointed on 21 May 1919 in connexion with applications for State assistance received from the Universities of Oxford and Cambridge, was instructed to enquire into the government of the two Universities, into their financial resources, and into the financial resources of their colleges.[1] The Commission, which reported early in 1922, was mentioned, infrequently, at meetings of the Non-Collegiate Students Board; first, on 5 November 1920, when a minute says: 'The question of a communication to the Council regarding the description of students in the unofficial part of the *Reporter* was deferred. It was understood that a corporate title had been suggested to the Royal Commission, and their report was expected.'[2] A minute of a

---

[1] *Report of the Royal Commission on Oxford and Cambridge Universities, 1922.* Cmd 1588.
[2] At the end of the previous term Reddaway had taken exception to the description of certain of his men (but not all) as 'Non-Coll.' in the lists of the Inter-Collegiate examination results, then published in the unofficial part of the *University Reporter*. In 1919 the abbrevia-

meeting held on 21 January 1921 is more explicit: 'A resolution unanimously adopted[1] by twenty-four members of the staff meeting "that the University should be approached with a view to the recognition of the collegiate character of the students, by a positive title in place of the present negative" was discussed. It was pointed out that a similar resolution had been passed by the Board just before the outbreak of war, and that the course proposed had been advocated before the Royal Commission on the Universities which is still sitting. The Board was of the opinion that no action could usefully be taken until the Commission had reported.' The only other mention of the Commission at a Board meeting was on 13 March 1923, when the Censor, in a discussion of its financial difficulties, is recorded as asking how far the Commission's recommendations, and the University's guarantee of a sum of up to £100 in any year in which the Board might incur a deficit, might affect the Board's policy; and his Chairman suggested that these questions might be raised at the discussion in the Senate of a Board Report then in preparation on the need for increases in fees. This Report, dated 17 May 1923, came before the Senate on 24 May,[2] but there was no reference to Reddaway's questions in a discussion largely taken up with criticism of its proposal by the Rev. E. W. Johnson, tutor of Cheshunt Training College, on the grounds that an increase of six guineas in the Board's fees for the three years of the undergraduate course, which had been fixed at £18.18.0 in 1896, and had remained unchanged, would fall hardly on men in severely straitened circumstances, among whom were members of the theological training colleges who stood in no need of the 'kindly and efficient shepherding' provided by the Board. Their requirements would be better and more economically met by 'direct access' to the University through the Registrary. The Board's Report was approved by Grace 9 of 16 June.

On 23 December 1919 the Commission had sought information on a number of matters concerning non-collegiate membership of the University. Their enquiries, under the heading 'Preliminary List of Ques-

tion 'Fitzw. Hall' had been used in at least one list, very possibly by oversight. The Registrary, after consulting the Vice-Chancellor and without prejudice to the future, authorized the adoption of the courtesy title in any list for which the previous year had provided a precedent; but in the Michaelmas term he put the point to the Council of the Senate, who appear to have asked for a statement of the Board's views. From a draft letter to the Registrary prepared by Reddaway for the Board's consideration on 6 November, it seems that the scope of the matter had become somewhat wider, and that Reddaway was seeking authority to ask that the title 'Fitzw. Hall' should be used 'wherever it is not expressly precluded by the Ordinances'.

[1]   This is a little misleading. See p. 198.
[2]   *University Reporter*, 1922–23, p. 1010. For the Discussion, see p. 1088.

tions addressed to the Censor of Non-Collegiate Students', read as follows:

A. Finance.

1. The Commission will be glad to receive a copy of the accounts and balance-sheet of the Non-Collegiate Delegacy or Syndicate for 1912–13 and 1918–19.

2. Please state what pecuniary aid was given by the University or Colleges, or by the Local Authorities, City Companies, or Charitable Funds, so far as is known, towards (*a*) the expenses of Non-Collegiate Students generally, (*b*) the cost of teaching them, and (*c*) the cost of their central accommodation, in each of the five years ending 1912–13 inclusive, and in 1918–19. What Research Studentships, Scholarships, or Exhibitions for proficiency in work were specially reserved for them, as Non-Collegiate Students, during the same periods?

B. Teaching Staff and Students.

1. Of whom was the Non-Collegiate tutorial and teaching staff composed in 1912–13, and what were the several emoluments of that staff from Non-Collegiate funds? The names, qualifications, and emoluments of the existing staff should also be given. It should be stated in which cases the work of the tutor or teacher is devoted (*a*) entirely, (*b*) mainly, or (*c*) partly to the Non-Collegiate Students.

2. What percentage of matriculated Non-Collegiate Students who went down from the University as Non-Collegiate Students in each of the five years ending 1912–13 inclusive obtained a degree (*a*) in Honour or partly Honour Schools (stating class or classes) or by research, or (*b*) in Pass Schools, or (*c*) a diploma (with or without distinction)? How many of them obtained no degree?

3. What was the total number of Non-Collegiate Students in residence in 1870–1, 1880–1, 1900–1, and 1912–13, and what is their present number?

4. How many of the present students are (*a*) graduates of other Universities, (*b*) married men who have presumably joined the Non-Collegiate organisation on that account only, (*c*) members of a Theological College, (*d*) probationers for the Indian Forest Service or other such services, and (*e*) students not falling into any of the above categories? From what schools did the present members of class (*e*) come? How many Non-Collegiate Students came directly from artisan or clerical, &c., work?

5. What are the conditions of entrance with which applicants must normally comply before becoming Non-Collegiate Students?

C. Expenses of Undergraduate Life.

What are (*a*) the minimum and (*b*) the average total expenses (including board and lodging, but excluding clothes, books, and other items of varying personal expenditure, travelling, and vacation expenses), classified under separate heads, of a Non-Collegiate Student at the present time, including all subscriptions, entrance fees, &c.? Please state what courses, if any, necessitate the payment of extra fees, and what those fees are?

D. *Poor Students, and Grants for their Assistance.*

What assistance, apart from Research Studentships, Scholarships, and Exhibitions for proficiency in work, was granted to poor Non-Collegiate Students during the five years ending 1912–13 inclusive, and in 1918–19?

E. *Students from Abroad.*

What provision is made for students from (a) the Dominions, (b) Colonies and Protectorates, (c) India, and (d) Foreign Countries?[1]

On '*Finance*' Reddaway 'has the honour to enclose a copy of the desired documents, and to state that the answer to *Question 2 a, b,* and *c* is, in each case, None'. In an extract from his Information Sheet he adds, however, particulars of the annual award of two Clothworkers' Company Exhibitions, and mentions the possibility of a small number of awards by the Non-Collegiate Students Board, or from a fund established by the men of 1912, and of a War Memorial Exhibition and an E. N. Player Bursary 'in the course of endowment'. To fill in his list, he mentions the Gibson Prize, and a Harvey Prize for History. The tentative nature of Reddaway's statement, and its scanty content, make only too plain the slender resources at his Board's disposal.

Under Section *B* Reddaway gives. details of nineteen members of staff in 1912/13, and of twenty-one in 1919/20. Their academic qualifications are impressive. Of the latter, three devoted themselves mainly to the instruction of non-collegiate students; the others partly so. Between 1908 and 1913, 69 men had taken honours (five in the first class), 77 a pass degree, and 54 no degree at all. Numbers of residents in the years named were 18, 254, 153, 163, and 252; and of the 252, 28 'appear to be graduates of other Universities'. Reddaway is at his most typical in his reply about 'married men who have presumably joined the Non-Collegiate organization on that account only'. There may be two or three, he says, (out of a total of fifty-six), but he will not allow the Commissioners to overlook those 'who are known to have entered here on account of their personal preference or family connection with Fitzwilliam Hall'. He seems to have had difficulty in arriving at a figure for the residual class (*e*), which could 'only be determined approximately as not exceeding 217', of whom three were Church of England clergymen, two non-conformist ministers, and one an artisan. The list of schools for 169 of the maximum of 217 is unremarkable; twenty of the

[1] *Royal Commission on Oxford and Cambridge Universities. Appendices to the Report of the Commissioners* (H.M.S.O., 1922, Appendix 3, p. 98.

men were from schools in Cambridge. In his statement about undergraduate expenses Reddaway is cautious. 'The Censor and Assistant Censor of Fitzwilliam Hall', he writes, 'hesitate to offer a precise estimate of either the minimum or the average total expenses of a student at the present time, since such expenses vary considerably according to the course of study pursued, e.g. Arts or Natural Sciences, and the standard of living adopted in different cases. They have, however, consulted with a student occupying in-college rooms, whose habits of careful economy are well known to them, and compiled the following estimate.

> Owing to various corporate economies the expenses of those students who occupy in-college rooms are somewhat lower than is possible elsewhere.

> *Estimate of Average Expenditure of an Arts Student.*

		£.	s.	d.
1.	Lectures and Tuition	19	13	0
2.	Other college fees	5	11	0
3.	Rooms	27	0	0
4.	Coal and light	3	18	0
5.	Meals in hall	32	5	3
6.	Lunches and teas in rooms	8	8	0
7.	Subscriptions to clubs	2	7	0
		99	2	3

Finally, Reddaway's answer to both Sections *D* and *E* is 'None', 'except that the number of Indian Students is limited in pursuance of an inter-College arrangement to normally not more than five admissions per year, exclusive of Research Students'.[1]

In addition to this information supplied on request, two other documents were submitted to the Royal Commission. The members of the Fitzwilliam Hall tutorial and administrative staff, when they resolved at their meeting on 13 November to urge the Non-Collegiate Students Board to take up again with the central authorities of the University the desirability of replacing by a more positive title the negative official description of the non-collegiate body, appear also to have appointed a committee to take the question further if the Board should decline (as they did on 21 January) to pursue it; for among the submissions to the Commission which were not subsequently published, but were copied and made available for consultation, is a paper by Mr W. G. Bell, Mr C. J. B. Gaskoin and Dr E. H. Ezard (Director of Studies in Medicine)

[1]   *Ibid.*, pp. 214–16.

in which, as members of this committee, they again advance the arguments for a clear recognition of the collegiate character of their student body. After informing the Commission of the virtually unanimous adoption of the resolution of 13 November by the twenty-five members of the staff (the President of Queens', as a member of the Council of the Senate, had refrained from voting), they continue 'Our desire is that the merely negative title of "non-collegiate students", which connotes a congeries of isolated units [surely Gaskoin's phrase] with no common or associated action, be replaced by a style free from misleading implications'; and after a recital of the habitual corporate activities of the men, they remind the Commission that by virtue of their long and intimate association with Fitzwilliam Hall, they speak with personal feelings and a knowledge unlikely to be found in any other body, however great its interest and goodwill.

The second unsolicited memorandum addressed to the Commission was from Mr E. W. Johnson, who as Resident Tutor of Cheshunt College since 1905, put forward, on behalf of the Governors of his College, the objections to the existing arrangements for members of the theological training colleges which he was to repeat at the discussion of the Non-Collegiate Students Board's Report of 17 May 1923.[1]

The Commission also took oral evidence from various witnesses, including on one occasion (9 August 1920) the President of Queens' College, as Chairman of the Non-Collegiate Students Board, the Censor, and the Rev. G. H. Harris, Assistant Censor. In view of later comments it is desirable to put on record the President's support of 'the desire of the students for a corporate name', and also the part taken by Reddaway in the discussion. 'Mr Reddaway', says the summary, 'believed very strongly that the idea of unattached students – students attached to an abstraction like the "University" – had really no vitality. He therefore was much in favour of making Fitzwilliam Hall into something like a College but with greater flexibility and less compulsion. It was most important to keep down the cost. They were able to do so by reason of their very small establishment, staff and machinery. He considered that the staff was adequately paid. The lecture fees of students differed little from those of other students as the men paid for lectures in the ordinary way. Only two of the teachers were subsidised by the Hall. In addition to the fees which constituted the main income, the Hall also received the Board of Education Grants and were treated for that purpose as a Collegiate body.'[2]

[1] Memoranda with regard to Reforms at Cambridge, U.L. Cam. a.922, 5. Papers nos. 1, 16.
[2] Summaries of Evidence of Various Witnesses, U.L. Cam. a.922.9(5), p. 30.

The opinion of the members of the Royal Commission on the non-collegiate system is sufficiently evident in their recommendations for its future. These recommendations, numbered 92 to 98 in their Report, are as follows:

92. That suitable steps be taken by both Universities to make known to the public in future the advantages of the Non-Collegiate bodies from the point of view of economy.

93. That the Non-Collegiate bodies study the needs of, and provide all possible facilities for, students who come up from other Universities as Research Students or for short courses.

94. That steps be taken by the Non-Collegiate bodies to raise the intellectual standard of the Non-Collegiate students generally.

95. That part of the grant recommended for the Universities be expended by them on subsidies to the Non-Collegiate bodies, so as to enable them to provide a sufficient number of highly qualified teachers and to give further support to poor students, and so as to secure such improvements as may be required in the central rooms to which Non-Collegiate students resort for work and recreation.

96. That the responsible authorities bear in mind the supreme importance of avoiding, as far as possible, changes calculated to increase the average expenditure of Non-Collegiate students.

97. That the above recommendations apply, generally speaking, not only to the Non-Collegiate organisations for men at Oxford and Cambridge, but also to the Society of Oxford Home Students (women).

98. That in future the stipends of all the Principals of the Non-Collegiate bodies be fixed at a definite sum not depending on the number of students in residence.

Effect was given to the last of these recommendations when Reddaway's successor was appointed in 1924, and the Syndicate of 1924 had the Commission's Report in their minds when they recommended an annual payment of £1,000 to the Non-Collegiate Students Board, of which £200 was to constitute a Gift Fund administered by the Censor for the assistance of particularly needy students.

The Commissioners attached little weight either to the representations of the witnesses who appeared before them, or to the submissions of Mr Gaskoin and his colleagues, on behalf of the non-collegiate teaching staff; and they were at some pains to explain why. They referred to the revival of non-collegiate residence in the nineteenth century with its declared intention of providing a more economical form of residence than life in college, in order that poorer men might be enabled to come to the University. They considered that this objective had 'to some extent been achieved', and stressed the importance of resisting as far as possible all proposals which would tend to add unnecessarily to the cost of non-collegiate life. 'For this reason', they continued, 'we do not recommend, in spite of some arguments which we have heard, either the taking of further steps to alter the character of the Non-Collegiate bodies or the adoption of a Collegiate title in lieu of the title "Non-Collegiate". The probable result of such a change would be a demand for the re-establishment of a Non-Collegiate body on fresh lines afterwards, in order once more to secure the full advantages of Non-Collegiate residence.'[1]

After many years W. S. Thatcher, upon whom the Commission's Report had made a lasting impression, had little that was good to say about its recommendations concerning the non-collegiate institutions in the two Universities. 'The Royal Commission', he wrote, 'in due course made its Report, but paid little attention to the Non-Collegiate system which it thought should go on as before. The paragraphs in the Report show no constructive thought, only indifference or ignorance. Maybe Reddaway was slightly to blame, for he was too Victorian to put his case. Always he emphasised what had been achieved, however slight, and spoke of this as if some great material and financial progress had been made. The very senior members of the University, whose attitudes the war had not touched, were only too ready to take him at his word, as did the Commissioners.'[2] Mr Thatcher thought that an opportunity had been lost of inducing the Commission to do more for Fitzwilliam Hall; and his reference to Reddaway's habit of stressing what had been done was well founded; but, given the unwillingness of his Board to make any move, it is difficult to see how Reddaway could have taken further effective steps to influence the Commissioners, or, in particular, have caused them to alter their views on collegiate status, especially disappointing though these were to many in the non-collegiate institution at Cambridge.

After the war the number of undergraduates in residence, which in the Easter term 1918 had fallen to 43, rose to 314 in the Michaelmas term 1920, and although these numbers created the severest administrative problems for Reddaway and his small staff they greatly benefited the

---

[1] Report p. 158. This is exactly the view expressed by Dr H P. Stokes (Vicar of St Paul's Church in Cambridge) in a letter to Reddaway on 25 April 1912, after he had been sent a document setting forth Reddaway's aspirations (probably his Report to the Board for the year 1910–11, in which he refers to 'the galling title "Non-Collegiate"').

[2] *Journal*, 1967, p. 28.

finances of the Hall, and tended to thrust into the background difficulties that would be certain to arise when the abnormal post-war population began to diminish. At the end of the Michaelmas term 1922 the Board received a report from their internal auditors on their income and expenditure account for the previous year, when the average student population was about 290, which shewed a deficit of some £600.[1] As it was plain that the Board's financial troubles were due, in the main, to increased costs not matched by higher fees – their fees had not changed since 1896 – they felt obliged to report to the Senate recommending that their fees should be raised, for three years' residence, from £18.18.0 to £25.4.0, the increase of £6.6.0 to be met by a terminal payment of one guinea during the students' second and third years. The Board added that even with the proposed increase they feared that they would be unable to avoid a deficit until the new charges became fully effective. The recommendation contained in their Report was approved, though not without an expression of considerable misgiving by the Tutor of Cheshunt College at its discussion.[2]

Under the new arrangements it was estimated that a minimum of 200 resident students would be needed if the Board's accounts were to balance, but by the Michaelmas term 1923 undergraduates and research students together numbered no more than 164, and the Board, having incurred a second consecutive deficit, of £284, in the year 1922/23, faced the probability of yet another, reckoned at £500, in 1923/24. With their capital fund reduced by successive losses to £348, they saw no possibility of meeting their liabilities, and no likelihood of any improvement in their position. In November 1923, therefore, they sought the advice of the Council of the Senate on the policy they should follow, particularly in the immediate future until their higher charges should become more fully effective; and at the beginning of the following term, on the Council's recommendation, a Grace was approved by the Senate for the appointment of a Syndicate to consider the Board's position, and to report by the end of the Easter term.[3] The members of the Syndicate were the Vice-Chancellor (Dr Pearce, Master of Corpus), Dr Fitzpatrick, Mr W. W. Rouse Ball, Mr F. H. Colson, Mr J. R. Roxburgh, Mr F. J. Dykes and Mr Will Spens. Four were members of the Council of the Senate, and four of the Financial Board. Besides the Vice-Chancellor, Mr Colson and Mr Roxburgh were on the Non-Collegiate Students Board, and Dr Fitzpatrick might

[1] Minutes, 7 December 1922.
[2] See p. 194.
[3] Grace 1 of 18 January 1924.

very properly be regarded as the Board's fourth representative, for he had only recently resigned its chairmanship after serving for eighteen years.

The Syndicate conceived that their first duty was to decide, as a matter of principle, whether the non-collegiate organization should revert to its original arrangements, whereby almost no facilities were provided for the social life of the students, or whether provision should continue to be made for certain communal privileges which, like members of the colleges, the students had come to enjoy. They recognized that among the non-collegiate undergraduates there were some to whom these privileges did not appeal, and that others belonged to institutions with a social life of their own, but they considered that for the rest these privileges were of value, and that there should be an organization capable of providing them. Having thus early in their deliberations, and without apparent dissent, reached this conclusion, the Syndicate then addressed themselves to the consideration of ways and means, and their principal recommendations, which took account of certain relatively minor observations made at the Senate's discussion of their Report, were as follows:

1) that no pressure should be put on such non-collegiate students as might not wish to participate in a communal life, and that those who did should be required to pay an additional terminal fee, but not such as might act as a discouragement. Payment of the communal fee would give the right to dine in Hall, and to use the common room, the reading room, and the library;

2) that the Board's practice of collecting a large proportion of the students' fees at an early stage in their period of residence should cease, and that migration should be forbidden after the end of a student's first year, save in exceptional circumstances approved by the Board;

3) that the institution responsible for the organization of the communal life of the students, and its building, should be known as *Fitzwilliam House* 'to avoid any confusion with older foundations'; and that the communal side of the scheme should be in the hands of a Committee of Management comprising the Censor, and other members partly appointed by the Board and partly by resident members of the Senate on the books of Fitzwilliam House;

4) that from the grant recommended for the University by the Royal Commission (of 1919) an annual sum of £1,000 be paid to the Board for the expenses of the non-collegiate scheme, and that of this sum £200 be set aside as a Censor's Gift Fund, for the assistance of poor students unable to meet their full educational expenses, or to pay the extra fee which would entitle them to the benefits of communal life.

Fitzwilliam House 1934–63 (comprising, from the left, 32 and 31 Trumpington Street and, except for most of the ground floor, 30 Trumpington Street and 25 Fitzwilliam Street). On the right of the picture, 24 Fitzwilliam Street, owned by the Fitzwilliam Hall Trust, was occupied by Fitzwilliam House for some forty years.

The Syndicate considered that it would be unsafe to assume a student population of more than 120, of whom 80, they thought, might be expected to pay the communal fee. They believed that for this number of students there should be a staff consisting of a Censor, an Assistant Censor (who would also act as Bursar), and a Clerk, with necessary domestic staff. On this basis they put the annual cost of the scheme at £2,000, of which, if their proposals for an annual payment and a gift fund were approved, an amount of £1,200 would have to come from fees. They recommended an entrance fee of £3.3.0, and a terminal fee of £2.2.0, for all students, with an additional terminal fee of £1.5.0 for those who wished to avail themselves of communal privileges. The total of the fees paid in three years by those who took no part in communal life would thus be £22.1.0, and £33.6.0 by those who did, compared with the existing total of £25.4.0 for all students. The Syndicate added that as their figures were based on estimated student numbers it might be necessary for them to be adjusted in the light of events, and recommended that the Board should propose this, if necessary, in an

Annual Report to the Senate – an oddly indirect way of requiring an annual report from the Board, for which, however, more definite provision was made in draft regulations giving effect to the recommendations appended to the Syndicate's Report.

The Syndicate also mentioned one step which, on their initiative, had already been taken with regard to the Board's finances. They had been informed that an amount of over £1,600 was owing from students, of which the Bursar expected to recover about half, the recovery of the remainder being doubtful or unlikely. On the Syndicate's recommendation, the University had set aside a sum of £1,000 for the writing off of debts as far as this might be necessary, and they also recommended, in order to prevent the recurrence of similar debts, the adoption of a system of prepayment, at the beginning of each term, of an amount calculated to cover such fees as were likely to be incurred.

The Syndicate reported on 30 May 1924, and their recommendations were approved by the Senate, with effect from the beginning of the following Michaelmas term, on 21 June.[1]

In retrospect it is not difficult to perceive that this Report marks a clear step forward in the non-collegiate institution's progress towards collegiate status. That too much had been required of it for too long is not to be denied; and in particular the weight of the burden thrown upon its officers in the years immediately following the war invited a complete breakdown. From this the Syndicate rescued the whole system. Financially the non-collegiate body was set on its feet again; it was authorized to write off the worst of its debts, and was given, as of right, an annual grant which, if meagre in comparison with the aid which Oxford continued to provide for the sister institution, was to prove of critical importance in the lean years that followed. Of no less importance, the benefits of the 'collegiate' activities of the place and the desirability of their continuance had been openly avowed by high authority; and, for the first time, the institution, as well as the building in Trumpington Street, was given a name, published in the University Ordinances and, in 1926, included in the University Statutes. All this, when the dust had settled, was clear gain; but in 1924 to many past and present Fitzwilliam men the Report came as a heavy disappointment. Already discouraged by the Royal Commission's frosty reception of their hopes for a change, they found it only too easy to allow their attention to wander from the potentially substantial advantages of the

---

[1]   *University Reporter*, 1923–24, p. 1122. The Report was discussed in the Senate on 10 June, and on the same day the Syndicate signed an amended Report taking account of points made in discussion. (*University Reporter*, 1923–24, pp. 1209, 1272).

Syndicate's proposals, and only too difficult to accept the recommendation that, for the avoidance of confusion with older foundations – the Syndicate's use of the plural misled nobody – their courtesy title of Fitzwilliam Hall, whose gradually more general use in Reddaway's time had become a touchstone of their wider recognition, should be exchanged for a name which, though official, had not even the merit of novelty, but came to them at second hand, – for was it not already borne by a substantial private residence in the vicinity of the Railway Station?

To the broader question whether there could be some modification in the official style of the non-collegiate body the Syndicate did not, in the preamble of their Report, refer at all. It was said that members of the Syndicate were not averse to making a change, if they could find sufficient justification for it, and could think of a suitable alternative;[1] but the difficulty was that statutorily the place was not a college, and in the statutes, therefore, it could not be wrong to describe it as non-collegiate. Furthermore, the contention that a closer resemblance in status between the non-collegiate body and the colleges would be likely to be accompanied, or at least quickly followed, by a corresponding rise in the cost of non-collegiate education – as it then was – could not, without trial, be proved wrong; and twenty years were to come and go, and another war, before it was accepted that there was no longer a need for a place in the University for the education of those who could not afford to be members of colleges, and that very few men indeed preferred not to avail themselves of communal facilities if they were offered. To all this there is no allusion in the body of the Syndicate's Report, but their conclusion is set out plainly enough in the last regulation of their draft Ordinance:

> 16. In all cases in which the name of his College is placed after the name of a member of a College, the contraction 'Non-Coll.' shall be placed after the name of a Non-Collegiate Student.

It is unlikely that the order in which these regulations were framed was intended to be of especial significance, but as the Syndicate's last word – literally their last words – the regulation assumes a finality which had the air not so much of closing the door, as of slamming the door, upon the hopes of those for whom their official title, in the strictest sense correct, had come to seem harmfully misleading.

On another matter the Syndicate, while they put forward no recommendation for Senate approval, did not hesitate to express an emphatic

---

[1] See remarks at the Discussion made by Mr Dykes, Secretary to the Syndicate.

opinion – the place in the non-collegiate arrangements of the Fitzwilliam Hall Trust:

> The Athletics Clubs should, as at present, be entirely unofficial, and it is here necessary to draw attention to an organization known as the Fitzwilliam Hall Trust, which holds various property, including the playing field. This Trust was formed in 1919 with the knowledge of the Board,[1] one of its objects being to secure lodging houses, near Fitzwilliam House, in which Non-collegiate Students could be accommodated at practically cost price, the houses being run by caretakers; but this scheme has broken down and most of these houses are now let to lodging-house keepers. The playing field, which is also held by the Trust, was bought largely by subscriptions from Non-Collegiate Students in residence since the war. The Trust also holds funds to provide for certain prizes open to Non-Collegiate Students. Under its memorandum of association power is taken to perform a number of functions which, under the Ordinances, are assigned to the Non-Collegiate Students Board.
>
> The Syndicate think that in any scheme of reorganization it is essential that the University, either directly or through the Board, should control the whole system, and that all property should be held in the name of the Chancellor, Masters and Scholars of the University. They are of opinion that this is not consistent with the continuance of the present independent Trust, although they would see no objection to independent trustees for the playing field.

On 12 May 1924, before the Syndicate signed their Report, their Secretary (Mr Dykes) wrote to Mr Frank Thatcher, the Secretary of the Trust, informing him of the general sense of the second of these paragraphs and inviting the comments of the Trustees. The Governors' minutes (of 14 May) are obscure, but seem to suggest an inclination to emphasize those of the Trust's activities to which the Syndicate offered less objection, to ignore the remainder, and to ask for 'a more precise proposal' by the Syndicate.[2] The minutes of their next meeting, held on 4 June just after the Syndicate had published their Report, record a number of resolutions which have all the appearance of having been hurriedly taken, for after hearing that arrangements had been made to sell no. 3 Fitzwilliam Street the Governors decided 1) to transfer nos. 4 and 10 to the University 'when desired', 2) to divest themselves of all responsibility for the management of the 1912 Exhibition Fund, and of the War Memorial Fund, 3) to sell nos. 9 and 17 Fitzwilliam Street, and 4) to repay certain small loans which they held. They also asked a method should be devised 'of shortening the time of payment of inter-

---

[1]   The date of the incorporation of the Trust was 7 June 1921.
[2]   Trust Minutes, 14 May 1924.

est to K.W.R. and W.F.R.'[1] It would be tedious and, in the absence of a sufficiently precise record, unprofitable, to try to unravel here the complications of the consequential decisions taken by the Governors of the Trust; it may be enough to say that they were not all carried out, possibly owing to the more favourable attitude towards the Trust eventually adopted by the Non-Collegiate Students Board.

On 12 May Mr Dykes had sent a similar letter to the Secretary of the Non-Collegiate Students Board (W. S. Thatcher, acting for Reddaway who was on leave of absence), and on 19 May a meeting of five of the Board's nine members passed *nemine contradicente* a motion by Messrs Colson and Roxburgh, both members of the Syndicate, 'that the Board having heard the resolution of the Syndicate desire to express their entire agreement and order the Acting Censor to communicate this minute to the Secretary of the Syndicate'.[2]

Mr Dykes's letter also informed the Board of his Syndicate's views on the regulation of the communal activities of the non-collegiate students. 'The Syndicate as at present advised', he writes, 'are however of opinion that the communal life should be under the control of a committee of the Board, consisting of the Censor, three members of the Board, and three M.A.s elected by resident M.A.s who are members of Fitzwilliam Hall.' The Board's minute does not make it clear that their approval extended, whether unanimously, *nemine contradicente*, or not at all, to this second expression of the Syndicate's views, but the committee, which came to be known as the House Committee, was brought into being, although it was seldom asked to consider matters of importance.[3]

The Board were then much occupied with other business, but they resumed their consideration of the Trust's proper functions in the Michaelmas term, and instructed the Censor (by then W. S. Thatcher) to inform the Secretary of the Trust that they saw no objection to the Trust's continuance provided that its activities were limited to the holding of houses and other properties. They also asked that the University might be informed if the Trust had in mind the sale of no. 24 Fitzwilliam Street.[4] On 23 January 1925 the Censor, as Chairman of the Trust, was able to report to the Governors that the attitude of the

---

[1] *Ibid.*, 4 June 1924.
[2] Minutes, 19 May 1924.
[3] There is a minute book of the Committee (College Archives), which appears to have been singularly ineffective. After a meeting held in January 1932, the Censor wrote, some years later, that it had 'lapsed through sheer lack of work to do'. It was reconstituted in May 1938 (Grace 2 of 13 May), and met again once on 22 April 1939.
[4] Minutes, 13 November 1924.

Board towards the Trustees had changed considerably; and that subject to some curtailment of the powers of the Trust the Board was favourable to its continuance. When the Censor, at the request of the Governors, asked the Board which of the Trust's objects, as defined in its Memorandum of Association, they found unacceptable, the Board, having again discussed the relationship of the two bodies, sought legal advice, particularly, on the proffered transfer of nos. 4 and 10 Fitzwilliam Street ot the University, and received their solicitor's letter at their meeting on 12 May. This letter is no longer among the Board's papers, but their conclusions on the delimitation of the functions of the two bodies may be gathered from their minute and from the statement of the Trust's objects, as set forth in its Memorandum of Association to which the minute refers.

The objects of the Association were...

3. (a) The organization assistance and encouragement of the non-collegiate students and members of the University of Cambridge (hereinafter referred to collectively as "Fitzwilliam Hall" and individually as "Members of Fitzwilliam Hall") as a society for the promotion of learning education and religion by all or any of the following means or any other means that the Association may from time to time think proper that is to say

  (1) by the provision of instruction.
  (2) by making provision for religious worship.
  (3) by the provision and care of educational books and apparatus.
  (4) by the provision equipment and maintenance of lecture rooms reading rooms and other accommodation for instruction or study.
  (5) by the provision of dwelling accommodation with all auxiliary services.
  (6) by the provision of scholarships and exhibitions to be held either during residence at Cambridge or during courses of supplementary study at hospitals or other centres of instruction or research.
  (7) by the provision of funds for research including travelling and research fellowships.
  (8) by the provision of special or occasional assistance for members of Fitzwilliam Hall in aid of their education at the University of Cambridge by grants of money for payment of fees and other necessary purposes.
  (9) by the provision of land buildings and apparatus for cricket football rowing lawn tennis gymnastics boxing and other athletic sports and exercises or for military training and
  (10) by the provision of rooms and equipment for recreation and social intercourse.

   (b) To hold and administer property and funds of all kinds on behalf of clubs and societies constituted wholly or mainly of members of Fitzwilliam Hall.

(c) To undertake and administer any trusts for the furtherance of any of the objects of the Association or any like objects and hold and administer any property or funds subject to any such trusts.

(d) To purchase take on lease or in exchange hire or otherwise acquire any real or personal property and to construct maintain alter furnish and equip any buildings necessary or convenient for the purposes of the Association.

(e) To borrow or raise or secure the payment of money in such manner as the Association may think fit and in particular by the issue of Debentures charged upon all or any of the property of the Association or by mortgage or charge of any such property.

(f) To sell any real or personal property of the Association and to grant leases or tenancies of any property and to accept surrenders of leases and tenancies and to make allowances to and arrangements with tenants.

(g) To employ and pay a Secretary and any other professional or other servants or agents.

(h) To invest any moneys not immediately required for the purposes of the Association in any manner that the Association may think proper with power to vary the investment thereof but so that any money subject to the jurisdiction of the Charity Commissioners for England and Wales shall be invested only in or upon investments authorised by law with regards to trust funds.

(i) To do all such other lawful things as are incidental or conducive to the attainment of the above objects.[1]

The Board's minute reads:

Mr Francis' reply to the Board *re* the relationship of the Board to the Trust was read and the whole matter discussed. It was decided with reference to the objects of the Association set out under Section 3(a) of the Memorandum of Association that in the case of clauses 2,6, and 8 the Board were willing to receive donations towards the purposes mentioned under the respective clauses and that the sums be applied by the Board in accordance with these clauses.

That the activities mentioned in clauses 1,3,4,7 and 10 should not be exercised by the Trust.

That the activities mentioned in clauses 5 and 9 may still be exercised by the Trust.

That further the Board require from the Trust with reference to clauses 3(b)–(i) inclusive an undertaking that in future the Trust will undertake no further obligations without the consent of the Board.[2]

The Governors of the Trust had already undertaken not to act without the consent of the Board, although it is doubtful whether they

[1] Memorandum and Articles of Association, p. 1.
[2] Minutes, 12 May 1925.

intended the undertaking to apply to the whole of their future activities. Their minute on the subject of the Board's latest communication is not illuminating, for it runs as follows:

> The Chairman having reported that Dr Ezard had suggested the tenor of a reply to the minute of the Non-Collegiate Students Board as to the position of the Trust and that such reply needed verbal manipulation before being presented to the Board, it was proposed by Dr Barker and seconded by Mr Ball that the Censor be requested to bring before the Board the sense of the Governors with reference to the minute as a whole.[1]

There is no mention in the Board's minutes of anything that Mr Thatcher may have said, but this summary of the foundation and the early adventures of the Fitzwilliam Hall Trust under Reddaway may be regarded as being brought to an end when Thatcher, as Reddaway's successor and the Trust's Chairman, informed the Governors a year later that the Financial Board 'was disposed to allow the Trust to continue indefinitely.'[2]

The Syndicate's Report, signed on 30 May 1924, was published in the *University Reporter* of 3 June,[3] and at the opening of the Discussion on 10 June the Master of Emmanuel, who presided in the Vice-Chancellor's absence, read a letter from him, in which he said,

> I think perhaps that it would be well if you would inform the Senate, before the discussion begins, that the Censor has decided to give up his work for the Non-Collegiate Students Board. It is desirable, therefore, that the Board should be able to start the new system in October under a new Censor. This will, of course, only be possible if the Syndicate are able to meet such criticism of the Report as is made at the discussion.[4]

The Censor's resignation was not referred to by any of the speakers. The Vice-Chancellor, as Chairman, communicated it to the Board at their next meeting, on 17 June, when they approved the following minute, and requested the Vice-Chancellor to send the Censor a copy:

> The Board desire to express to Mr Reddaway their great appreciation of the work which he has done during the past 17 years for the Board and for the non-collegiate students, both in the normal work of the Censorship and in fostering the social life of the students; they are confident that Mr Reddaway will be rewarded by knowing that his work will, under the new regulations recommended by the Special Syndicate, be carried on as part of the official work of the Board.[5]

[1] Trust Minutes, 3 June 1925.
[2] *Ibid.*, 28 April 1926.
[3] *University Reporter*, 1923–24, p. 1122.
[4] *Ibid.*, p. 1209.
[5] Minutes, 17 June 1924.

Even though the Vice-Chancellor, in his letter of 19 June in which he informed Reddaway of the Board's resolution, told him that they had received the news with 'a very natural and proper regret', the omission from the minute of any expression of their regret seems strange.

W. S. Thatcher, writing many years afterwards, suggests that Reddaway had some time earlier made up his mind that he would retire, but had 'disguised it by asking for a year's leave of absence'.[1] There is now no further information in the non-collegiate records about Reddaway's decision, and no copy of any communication from him to the Vice-Chancellor, but it seems very reasonable to associate the resignation with the Syndicate's Report, published a week or so before the news of the resignation became public. It is not clear when it took effect, but a statement in the notice 'Vacancy in the Office of Censor', published by the Vice-Chancellor in the *University Reporter* of 21 June,[2] that Reddaway 'has resigned the office' suggests that he wished to go there and then, which would be less difficult than it might have been had not an acting Censor already been appointed for the academical year, when Reddaway was on leave of absence.

That Reddaway should have disapproved of the Syndicate's recommendations is not remarkable. Throughout the whole of his term of office he had strenuously objected to the 'negative appellation' of his institution and of his men, and with considerable success had encouraged the use of the title 'Fitzwilliam Hall', applied not only to his building (sanctioned by the Board in 1887) but to the non-collegiate institution, although he had not been able to secure the consent of those in authority for its use in the Tripos lists. This question of name so completely preoccupied Reddaway that it is no exaggeration to say that it became an obsession with him; and the increasingly frequent appearance of the courtesy title he regarded as evidence of growing respect and higher prestige. The Syndicate, as they said, for the avoidance of confusion with older foundations – W. S. Thatcher was persuaded that nowhere had there been any collective expression of opinion in the matter – had recommended the substituion of 'Fitzwilliam House' for the familiar 'Fitzwilliam Hall'; and had insisted on the retention of the contraction 'Non-Coll.' after the name of a non-col-

---

[1] *Journal*, 1967, p. 30.
[2] *University Reporter*, 1923–24, p. 1214. The sense of urgency imparted by Reddaway's resignation to the closing deliberations of the Syndicate, first apparent in the Vice-Chancellor's letter to the Master of Emmanuel, and very evident in the speed with which the Syndicate seem to have drafted their amended Report, appears to have communicated itself to the Registrary, who published on 21 June the Vice-Chancellor's notice dated June 23rd.

legiate student in all cases in which the name of a college would be placed after the name of one of its members. To Reddaway this would have seemed a reminder, after thirty years, of sentiments expressed in a fly-sheet which referred to the University as a place 'in which not to be a member of one of the Colleges is universally recognized to give inferiority of status to a man, both while in Cambridge and throughout his after life'.[1]

The Syndicate had been equally severe in their judgement of the proper (or improper) place in the non-collegiate system of the Fitzwilliam Hall Trust. Reddaway had brought it into being, and his opinion of its very great value has been quoted; but the Syndicate declared its existence to be incompatible with their conception of the non-collegiate instituion as a body administered, as it should be, solely by the University.

Yet again, the Syndicate's special provision for a class of men disinclined to take any part in the communal activities of Fitzwilliam House – men non-collegiate in the completest sense – was likely, Reddaway thought, to increase their numbers, and render more difficult the work of officers of clubs and societies, whom he regarded as the natural leaders of the community. Time was to prove him wrong in this last respect, but when the Syndicate reported the matter was still one of opinion, and Reddaway's opinion is not difficult to understand. All in all, from such information as is now available, it would appear that Reddaway, already upset by the findings of the Royal Commission, and profoundly disturbed by these fresh proposals which he rightly believed would be passed by the Senate, and which he did not feel able to put into practice, resolved to return to his College and his scholarly work, and leave in other hands the execution of plans that he could not bring himself to adopt.[2]

If this is a correct assessment of the events of the Easter term of 1924, they make up a sad closing chapter in the story of a fine censorship; and it is a matter of lasting regret that Reddaway, who had brought such distinction to the office, should have felt compelled by differences of opinion to lay it down so long before his time.

On 5 August 1924 the Board, at a meeting held exceptionally at the

---

[1]   Fly-sheet, dated 4 March 1891, by Alfred Caldecott, Junior Dean of St John's College, in opposition to the proposed establishment of the Cambridge Day Training College. Camb. Papers FM 251, University Library.

[2]   After his retirement, Reddaway was to remain in Cambridge, for nearly twenty-five years. After his death on 31 January 1949, the *Cambridge Review* published (on 26 February) a memorial notice by C. J. B. Gaskoin. This also appeared, with notices by Walter Harvey and W. S. Thatcher, in the *Fitzwilliam Journal* of the following December.

University Offices (St Andrew's Street), and attended by six of their nine members, received eight applications for appointment to the censorship. On the motion of the Provost of King's College (Sir Walter Durnford) they appointed William Sutherland Thatcher, then recently made Assistant Censor in succession to Mr G. H. Harris, who had resigned his office at the end of 1922. The Board agreed that as Censor Mr Thatcher might continue his work as Secretary of the Inter-Collegiate Indian Students' Committee, and that he might lecture in Economics, but not supervise. It had been decided previously that a new Censor should receive a stipend of £600, with no capitation payment, and that appointment should be for five years.[1]

[1]   Minutes, 17 June, and 5 August, 1924. Mr Thatcher had been appointed Lecturer in Economics on 1 March, and Mr Harris, who was also Vice-Principal of Ridley Hall, Assistant Censor from Lady Day, 1920.

CHAPTER VI

The House between the Wars.
The Long Haul Begins

Small student body – its unusual composition – Oriental students. Renewed protest over 'negative title' – its removal from the class-lists. Obligations of Fitzwilliam House with regard to research students – continued decline in undergraduate numbers.

World War 1939–1945 – virtual closure – future plans. Heavy pressure of immediate post-war years – need for larger premises – possible sites – alternative plans for extension of existing building. Recommendations of Special Committee on the future of Fitzwilliam House (1954) – their rejection by the Council of the Senate. First allusion to possible independence of Fitzwilliam House – the Memorialists – conditional agreement of Regent House to the termination of the non-collegiate system.

Building needs and further possible sites – appeal to 'Friends of Fitzwilliam House' – wider public appeal abandoned – disagreement over draft constitution, and collapse of negotiations for change of status.

The year during which W. S. Thatcher became Censor was an anxious and depressing one for Fitzwilliam House. The most serious of the Board's anxieties arose from the smallness of the student body, and from its composition. The number of undergraduates, which at a total of 314 had reached its peak in the Michaelmas term 1920, was less than half that figure by the Easter term 1924; and this rapid fall had been the cause of the appointment of the 1924 Syndicate to rescue the non-collegiate scheme from complete disaster. The lowest total of all in the post-war period (139) was reached in the Easter term 1925; but thereafter the numbers show a fairly steady upward trend until October 1931, when there was a sudden check. Thatcher himself tells the story:

> Numbers went up until they reached 271 in the Michaelmas term 1930, and would have been even greater in 1931 but for the great world economic depression which hit Great Britain about this time. Admissions had always been a chancy business as the great majority of our men had little money. Father was, only too often, looking round for the last ten pounds, and so financial decisions and applications tended to be made in the late summer months. We never completed our admissions much before the end of October, and quite a high percentage came in late September or early October, when the family finally gambled and plunged. But in the summer of 1930 I had closed my admissions for the coming Michaelmas term, and had settled the lodgings. For the first time I could go on holiday feeling

that all was well. Then came the blizzard. Nearly forty of my freshmen withdrew. The letters were all of the same melancholy nature. The family income had dropped or, worse still, father was now unemployed, and so the lad could not come and would have to try to get a job himself. After that there was a steady fall until the Easter term 1939, when there were only 175 in residence.[1]

In Thatcher's view, however, the size, simply, of the student population was not the end of the matter, for problems arose not only from the smallness of the student body, but also from its make-up.

Of the total 160 (in the Michaelmas term 1925) only some 105 [he writes] were from the United Kingdom. Of the rest, 21 were Indians; 10 came from various Asian countries; 2 were African – the Africans were not yet on the move. The rest were Europeans or from the Dominions or the U.S.A. The theological colleges supplied some 35 of the 105, and these lived very much apart. Quite a few were professionally employed in the day-time, and several were older men running up to middle age...[2]

Elsewhere Thatcher gave his opinion that in these circumstances a total of 200 was necessary if Fitzwilliam House was to be free from financial worry, and to hold its own among the colleges of the University.[3] Already, before the end of his first year of office, he drew his Board's attention to one aspect of his problem, for in his Report for the year 1923–24 he had presented them with an analysis of the men in residence, according to their nationality, and had remarked on the high proportion of those of non-European parentage. No comment by the Board is recorded, but in 1926 Thatcher tried again, suggesting that there should be no more than one fifth of these students, and the Board went so far (but no further) as to leave the decision to the Censor's discretion.[4] Thatcher's difficulty was not imaginary. As Adviser to Indian students in the University he had experienced no little difficulty in securing places for them in the colleges, which, he believed, would be equally unwilling to admit other candidates from Asia, and from Africa. As Censor it was his duty to arrange for the admission of suitable applicants to Fitzwilliam House, and the hesitation of the colleges in admitting non-Europeans need not necessarily have caused him any lasting difficulties had not this question become entangled with the

---

[1] *Fitzwilliam House from 1924 to 1955* (manuscript), p. 19 (College Archives). For 'in the summer of 1930', read 'in the summer of 1931'.
[2] Ibid., p. 20.
[3] Censor's Report for 1924–25.
[4] Minutes, 26 April 1926.

need to find colleges for students accepted by the University to under-take courses of research, of whom a not inconsiderable, and increasing, number were of Asiatic or African origin. This led to differences of opinion, which fortunately remained friendly differences, between R. E. Priestley, Secretary of the University Board of Research Studies, who was embarrassed when students approved by his Board as suitable to follow a course of research could not gain admission to a college, and Thatcher who foresaw that, if the colleges did not find room for these men, his Board would be strongly urged to take them. He held that it was not in the best interests of the men themselves that they should be gathered together in a single institution, and that the reputa-tion of his House would suffer if it became known that its student body consisted so largely of men who could not gain admission elsewhere. Furthermore, as a class, research students from wherever they might come took a less active part in the communal activities of the House. In these circumstances some disagreement was unavoidable, as when, in the Michaelmas term 1927, Thatcher refused to accept two Egyptian research students on the grounds that 'the ten per cent quota of Orien-tal students had already been completed'. On the Vice-Chancellor's advice the men were admitted 'without prejudice to the 10% policy' – here the records are confusing, for there is no reference in Thatcher's time to any previous request for a limit below the 20% for which he had asked a year or so earlier – and again, after a discussion on policy, the Board made no motion.[1] In 1928 they were a little more venture-some, for after being persuaded to admit an individual research student rejected by the Censor they did not challenge his draft minute record-ing their endorsement of his imposition of the ten per cent limitation. This conflict of interest arising from the University's wish, on the one hand, to admit increasing numbers of students to courses of research, with its accompanying requirement of membership of a college or of Fitzwilliam House, and on the other Thatcher's determination to build up a community collegiate by inclination if not by statute, was not to be resolved for many years, but at the end of the 1920s the growing number, and the improved quality, of the men accepted for a three year course leading to the B.A. degree made the problem less acute, and both parties might well have agreed to allow it to be worked out in practice had not the economic crisis of 1931 caused a sharp decline in applications from those whom Thatcher would have described as 'ordi-nary' (and more desirable) candidates for admission, with a consequen-

---

[1]   See Minutes of 14 October 1927 for Thatcher's presentation of his case to R. E. Priestley; and Policy File 1927–42 (College Archives) for correspondence.

tial increase, to a level which he regarded as unacceptable, in the proportion of overseas members of the student body. So, again, in the
Michaelmas term 1933 he is asking his Board for authority 'to reduce
the Oriental admissions so as to maintain the 10% ratio'. The Board, as
before, took refuge behind their Censor's discretion;[1] and by the Easter
term 1938 'ordinary' applications had dwindled to such an extent that
the percentage had risen to twenty-two per cent, which in Thatcher's
time had been exceeded only in his earliest years, before he had come
to grips with what in his view was a problem so crucial that upon its
satisfactory solution might depend the success or the failure, as he saw
the matter, of the institution committed to his charge.

On 10 January 1933 Thatcher wrote to his Chairman (the Rev. G. A.
Weekes, Master of Sidney Sussex) expressing concern at his diminishing numbers, showing their effect on the House's finances, and how
small were such economies as could even be contemplated. This
brought him back to what to him, as to Reddaway before him, had
been a main cause of difficulty to the non-collegiate scheme – its non-
collegiate name.

> Actually the paucity of applicants [he writes] is not due to the expense,
> for, while a certain flow may be cut off for this reason, one would expect,
> if other things were equal, that a new source would appear in those fami-
> lies who now find the College charges too high. But one finds that candi-
> dates who cannot afford to go to a College very rarely apply to Fitzwilliam
> House and, at the moment, such applicants are almost nil.
>
> This unwillingness on the part of parents to send their sons, or of the
> schools to recommend their pupils, is based either upon ignorance as to
> what Fitzwilliam House is or upon prejudice. There is no doubt that both
> factors are important but the latter is by far the more so, as owing to preju-
> dice the schools are unwilling to inquire and find out whether any changes
> have taken place in the past years.
>
> There is no doubt that a major factor encouraging this prejudice is our
> title of Non-collegiate. So long as this title persists so long will the schools
> and the outside world discriminate against us. They will believe that there
> must be some fundamental difference between us and the Colleges: that
> the type of education and control is different and inferior: that only an
> inferior degree can be obtained: that the student will suffer in his after life.
>
> I would urge, therefore, that the Board consider very seriously whether
> the time has not come when this title, which is completely obsolete,
> should not be done away with and Fitzwilliam House be the sole name in
> future. I believe such a change would make a great difference to our future
> progress. It can only be opposed on the grounds that somehow or other

---

[1]   Minutes, 5 December 1933.

such a change must increase the cost of living for our students. Such would not be the case.[1]

The Chairman brought the Censor's letter to the Board at their first meeting of the Lent term, and, after considering it at a special meeting held for the purpose on 8 February, a memorandum addressed to the Council of the Senate drafted by the Chairman and giving reasons why the Board desired the abolition of the non-collegiate title was approved on 7 March.

The Board have come to the conclusion [says the memorandum] that the students under their regulation are placed at a serious disadvantage by the use of the term "Non-Collegiate" in the class-lists and the notices of awards of Scholarships, Studentships, and Prizes issued by the University.

Statute H, II, 3 provides that "there shall be an institution ... called Fitzwilliam House, affording opportunities for corporate life to those Non-Collegiate Students who desire to become members of it, and to such graduates as are admitted to membership." This Statute has been of great benefit to Non-Collegiate Students, and experience has shown that only in very rare instances do students desire to remain outside the corporate life of Fitzwilliam House ...

The Board are assured that no sort of pressure is put upon entrants to join Fitzwilliam House. Naturally the advantages of the institution are explained to them, and the fact that in recent years so few have remained outside it, together with the very small additional expense involved in joining it, must influence any who are inclined to hesitate, but the Board can find no evidence of the existence of a class of students who either desire the independence and freedom from social obligations which they might secure by remaining literally non-collegiate, or cannot afford the expenses of membership of Fitzwilliam House. (The "communal fee" is 25/- a term, the subscription to the Amalgamated Clubs 30/6 a term, and the charge for dinner 2/- a night. The Censor has discretion to reduce or remit the subscription to the Clubs, so that no member of Fitzwilliam House is debarred by poverty from joining them. He also uses his discretion in excusing members from dinner in Hall.)

It has been a great advantage to the Non-Collegiate Body that by the institution of Fitzwilliam House the University has given it 'a local habitation and a name', but there remains a real disadvantage in the fact that the name is not used for the academic purposes mentioned above. The use of the title 'Non-Coll.' emphasizes the disadvantages rather than the advantages of non-collegiate status.

The Board sympathizes with the dissatisfaction which is felt by the Non-Collegiate Body, and consider that it is based on practical as well as sentimental grounds.

[1] Policy File 1927–42.

I. There is no doubt that the official use of the term 'Non-Collegiate' is misunderstood outside Cambridge, and is often taken to mean what 'external' means in London University; and for this reason our Non-Collegiate Graduates are handicapped in getting posts. But, apart from this, the Non-Collegiate Body suffers, because, partly owing to its name, it does not get those for whom it is intended. Certain County Councils and other bodies refuse to award their most important Scholarships to Non-Collegiate Students, though they can be held at the local non-collegiate Universities. Masters of public schools and Directors of Education sometimes discourage poor men from becoming Non-Collegiate Students because of the drawbacks attaching to the title in later life.

Perhaps the strongest evidence of the practical disadvantages of the title is the present dearth of applicants for admission. If there were not a widespread notion that Non-Collegiate status at Cambridge is hardly better than not coming to the University at all, it would have been expected that at the present time Fitzwilliam House would have attracted some of those who for financial reasons cannot join a College, as the expenses of education are still very considerably less than in the Colleges. But on the contrary it appears that Fitzwilliam House is suffering very much more than the Colleges from the financial stringency.

II. There is a sentimental objection to the use of the negative title. It is clear to the Board that a strong corporate loyalty has grown up among the members of Fitzwilliam House, and they attach real importance to this sentiment, and desire to encourage it. They consider that participation in the athletic and social activities of a House is a valuable element in the training of undergraduates, whether they are members of a College or not, and that the use of a positive title would do much to foster corporate loyalty.

The Board desire to make it clear that they do not suggest anything involving a change of Statute. All they ask is that in future those Non-Collegiate Students who choose to join Fitzwilliam House may be so described in official lists. They presume that any who elect to remain outside the institution would still be described officially as 'Non-Collegiate'.

In conclusion, they desire to point out that the University of Oxford has recently decided to give its Non-Collegiate Body the title of 'St Catherine's Society'. The use of the title 'Fitzwilliam House' would put the Cambridge Non-Collegiate Students on a level with their fellows at Oxford.[1]

This memorandum was signed by the Chairman of the Board, and by the six of its other eight members who were at the meeting. On receiving it the Council appointed a committee to advise them, and in June the Chairman of the Board reported that the Council's committee did not approve the Board's proposed change of name to 'Fitzwilliam

---

[1] *Ibid.*, and Minutes, 8 February and 7 March 1933.

House', and that it had considered a number of other possibilities, in particular 'Fitzwilliam Society', but had reached no conclusion. In December the Chairman informed the Board that the Council had refused their request that their representatives might meet the Council's committee for further discussion, but had suggested that a Syndicate might be appointed 'to inquire into the present status of the present Houses of Residence'.[1] To this, 'after considerable discussion', the Board agreed.

There has been preserved a memorandum to the Chairman and members of the Board, written, it appears, during the Long Vacation of 1933 by Mr C. J. B. Gaskoin, Director of Studies in History,[2] which throws some light on the unwillingness of the Council's committee to support the adoption of the name 'Fitzwilliam House' as the official title of the non-collegiate body, and on the consideration given to the alternative of 'Fitzwilliam Society'. Mr Gaskoin, who was strongly opposed to the alternative, even if only because it was already the name of an association of old Fitzwilliam men of the kind familiar to many of the colleges, understood that the Council's reluctance to accept the name desired by the Board arose, in part, from their feeling that if they did accede to the Board's request they would be proposing for the Board just the kind of concession which they had recently refused to propose for the houses of residence,[3] and partly also from a fear that if the members of Fitzwilliam House who shared in the communal activities of the place were given the statutory title which the Board proposed, a completely non-collegiate membership of the University would become correspondingly less attractive. On the first point Mr Gaskoin, who was a man of spirit, maintained that Fitzwilliam House, which was a constituent part of the University, was in a different posi-

---

[1] Minutes, 5 December 1933.
[2] Policy File 1927–42.
[3] See *Ordinances* 1933, p. 611. Westminster College, Cheshunt College, St Edmund's House, and Wesley House had been recognized as Houses of Residence under this regulation by Grace 10 of 19 February, 1926. Fitzwilliam House had been similarly recognized in 1924 on the recommendation of the Syndicate on the position of the Non-Collegiate Students Board.

In March 1931 the Registrary had asked the Board for their opinion on an enquiry received by the Council of the Senate whether a non-collegiate student, being also a member of one of the theological training colleges, who won a University prize or was classed in a Tripos, might have the name of his training college appended to his own in a class list or a notice of award. The Board could hardly be expected to welcome an arrangement whereby the names of their particular training colleges would accompany the names of those non-collegiate students who belonged to them, whereas other Fitzwilliam House men would be described as 'Non-Coll.'. They were unanimous in rejecting the idea, and the Council did not pursue it.

tion from the theological colleges, which were not; and, on the second, proposed 'that the boon we ask should be granted alike to men who choose to live the full corporate life and to the most confirmed misanthropic hermit that ever comes to our body, as well as to those whose aloofness is excusable or right'.

With little further delay the Council recommended the appointment of a Syndicate 'to consider and report upon the Houses of Residence and their relation to the University and to membership of Fitzwilliam House'.[1] The Vice-Chancellor (Mr Cameron) was the Syndicate's Chairman, and of its seven other members five were, or had been, members of the Board. The Report, dated 25 May 1934, passed the Regent House on 3 November, and consequential alterations of statute were approved by the King in Council on 4 May 1935.[2] It is an interesting, and, at first sight, a somewhat surprising document. The Syndicate stated that they did not wish to propose any alteration in the relationship to the University of the four theological training colleges, but added that, since their members often received direction of studies and much of their instruction in their training colleges, it was reasonable that when any such member won a University award the name of his training college should appear in an announcement. They did not, however, 'owing to practical difficulties' propose that this should be done in the class-lists.

The Report continues:

> The Syndicate have given careful consideration to strong representations which have been made to them that the work of the Non-Collegiate Students Board is greatly hindered and its usefulness much impaired, particularly outside Cambridge, by the purely negative title 'Non-Coll.' which is used in all University lists to describe their students. This is often interpreted as meaning that the students are not full members of the University and that little or nothing is done for them either in the way of direction of studies or in the provision of any communal life. This of course is by no means the case. The students are matriculated members of the University, and the regulations governing Non-Collegiate Students make provision for direction of studies and for opportunities for corporate life by means of the institution known as Fitzwilliam House; the Syndicate are informed that almost all Non-Collegiate Students do in fact become members of this institution. The Syndicate have been convinced that the negative title is a real disadvantage to the students and to the Board, and they wish to propose that a positive title should be substituted in all University lists. They do not see that any useful purpose is served by giving a distinguishing title

---

[1] *University Reporter*, 1933–34, p. 595; Grace 3 of 26 January 1934.
[2] *University Reporter* 1933–34, p. 1067; *ibid.*, 1934–35, pp. 325, 914.

to the institution at present known as Fitzwilliam House. They therefore propose that the Non-Collegiate body as a whole should be called Fitzwilliam House, and that in all cases in which the name of his College is placed after the name of a member of a College the contraction Fitzw. should be placed after the name of a Non-Collegiate Student. Those Non-Collegiate Students who wish to avail themselves of the opportunities for corporate life will be able to do so if they give notice to the Censor and pay the appointed fee.

Mr Gaskoin's paper had been well timed, for the Syndicate accepted his suggestion, or reached the same conclusion on their own account, about the abolition of the distinction between the very few out and out non-collegiate members of the place, and the men who took part in its corporate activities. Their ready acceptance also of the Board's view of the disadvantages of the 'negative appellation' which, in the opinion of successive Censors, had played havoc with the corporate aspirations of the non-collegiate body from its earliest days, may appear surprising, but while this may have been due in part to the Board's dignified and persuasive presentation of their case, some explanation of the Syndicate's attitude may also be found in the last paragraph, and particularly in the last sentence, of their Report:

> The Syndicate have discussed with the Censor the policy and practice which he has followed in the matter of the admission of Non-Collegiate Students to the University. They wish to express the opinion that the practice of the Censor in dealing with applications for admission, including those of Research Students, has proved satisfactory. In regard to Research Students they consider the right principle to be that no application for the admission of a Research Student, who has been accepted by the Board of Research Studies, should be refused except on grounds of moral character, and they are of the opinion that the Non-Collegiate Students Board should confirm this principle as a rule for the future.

The minutes of the Board confirm nothing. They do not mention the Syndicate's Report again; and in this absence of comment by the Board the 'right principle' enunciated by the Syndicate, but prudently not made the subject of a regulation, assumed the force of a virtual commitment which enabled the University to enrol, over a period of some thirty years, a substantially larger number of research students than the colleges were prepared to admit. Thatcher had won his campaign for a 'positive name', at the cost of a partial loss of control over his admissions. In retrospect, it seems right that Fitzwilliam House, as a University institution, should have performed this service for the University, though the presence of a very considerable number of research students, some of whose affairs demanded a disproportionate expenditure of tutorial time, over and above the large numbers of men reading for the B.A. degree in the post-war years, imposed a heavy strain on its staff and its quite inadequate premises, until in the 1960s the pressure was relieved by a greater willingness among the colleges to accept research students, and by the establishment of new foundations for the encouragement of postgraduate study.

When, in October 1934, the Censor, taking as a favourable omen the absence of remarks on the Syndicate's Report at its discussion by the Senate on 16 October, informed his Board that the Report had given immense pleasure to past and present members of Fitzwilliam House, and that he believed that it would be of the greatest assistance to the House in future years, he was thinking of the change of name;[1] but it is not difficult to suppose that the Syndicate's Chairman, at least, foresaw that the moral obligation which the Board were being asked to assume might well prove a valuable return for the removal from the class-lists of the label 'non-collegiate', attached to the names of members of an institution already entitled by University regulation Fitzwilliam House, which had been permitted to become so little non-collegiate in character that its continued description as such was an anachronism.

When the Censor expressed his satisfaction at the disappearance of the title 'Non-collegiate' from the class lists, he also said that he did not anticipate any immediate benefit to Fitzwilliam House from the change, and as far as numbers were concerned this forecast appeared to be well founded, for applications for admission continued to fall. Numbers in residence declined from 193 in the Michaelmas term 1933 to 175 in the last pre-war year, and Thatcher reverts to his earlier preoccupation with regard to the unusual composition of his student body. 'Students in residence', he says in one of his Annual Reports to the Board, 'may be divided into (1) the normal three year undergraduate attached directly to Fitzwilliam House, (2) undergraduates attached through membership of the attached Houses, (3) miscellaneous students including research students, one year students, students professionally employed during the daytime, (4) Oriental students. The serious fall has taken place in (1), who form the solid core round which the others group themselves. These men supply the real drive in the active life of Fitzwilliam House. The rest are largely passive.'[2]

This is a recurring theme with Thatcher at this time, and his prefer-

---

[1] Censor's Report for 1933–34.
[2] *Ibid.*

ence for undergraduates who followed the usual three year course for the B.A. degree will have been due to a variety reasons, chief among which, maybe, was the fact that they, more than any others, would contribute to the development of the non-collegiate institution along collegiate lines, and bring about its readier, and more complete, acceptance among the colleges at large; and that their admission was under his own control, and did not depend on their approval by University authority for a University course.

It will be remembered that in their statement to the Council of the Senate in 1933 the Non-Collegiate Students Board had attributed the lack of applications for admission to Fitzwilliam House to emphasis laid on its non-collegiate status by its description in the class-lists; but in 1939, with numbers still declining, the Censor, in a forthright Report to his Board, suggested that potential candidates for admission were being deterred by high costs, and went on to develop the thesis that Fitzwilliam, and by implication the University, was failing in its primary duty of providing a university education for poor men. As he also maintained that costs at the House could not be significantly reduced, he was clearly putting in a plea for further subvention by the University; but before this possibility could be pursued the outbreak of war removed it from the sphere of practical politics.

Financially, the fortunes of the House during the period between Thatcher's appointment in 1924 and the outbreak of war in 1939 reflected the rise and fall in student numbers. Thus it was that, after deficits in his first two years, in 1926/27 the Board's Accounts shewed a surplus of some £250, followed by surpluses, which in one year exceeded £1,000, until 1933/34 when the full effect was felt of the fall in numbers which began in the Michaelmas term 1931; and, except for one year, there were deficits, sometimes very small and never disastrous, until September 1939. Over the period as a whole, surpluses exceeded deficits by about £2,500, and there was no immediate fear of bankruptcy, though this appeared much more likely when war broke out, and special measures were again necessary.

It was fortunate that the need to incur what for the Board was then a considerable expenditure on the reconditioning and alteration of their premises made itself felt at a time when their finances had begun to improve; for over a period of some five years the whole of their building (including that part of nos. 30 Trumpington Street and 25 Fitzwilliam Street in their occupation after its lease had been renewed for fifteen years in 1928) was redecorated and largely refurnished, and the kitchens reconstructed so as to be capable of providing for a hundred men. The cost of this work was about £6,000, to which the Council of the Senate made a grant of £1,000, and either approved or obtained approval for three further grants, each of £500, from the funds of the Local Examinations Syndicate. The cost of the remainder was met from the Board's own funds, without, it seems, recourse to a loan of £1,250 authorized by the Financial Board, at 4½% interest, and repayable by equal instalments over twenty-five years.

As Fitzwilliam House usually completed its lists of undergraduate admissions later than the colleges, the outbreak of war had a more immediate effect on its numbers than in the University as a whole, for many who might have applied in September 1939 for admission in October did not do so; and, according to Mr Thatcher, the freshman entry fell to 35, and the total of those in residence to 134, compared with 180 in the previous year.[1] Already in August the students' common room and the reading room had been let as offices to Addenbrooke's Hospital, the Parlour being handed over as a common room for the men, while the members of the staff met in the Censor's room on the first floor. In the latter part of September the authorities of St Bartholomew's Hospital and of the London School of Economics each enquired whether some of their students could be catered for in the House, but in the event the medical students went elsewhere and the School of Economics, based on Peterhouse, agreed to send a score or so, only, of its men and women for lunch and dinner, at a charge of twenty shillings weekly; but even this number had dwindled to a half dozen by the following Easter term.

When all was over, Mr Thatcher resumed in the *Fitzwilliam Journal* his habitual contribution to what he called the 'Administrative History' of the House, and tells the story of the war years in an account compiled at the close of the Long Vacation of 1946.[2]

> It is so long [he writes] since any record of the administration of Fitzwilliam House was published that it will probably be as well to take up the story from the Lent Term 1940. It is until 1945 a history of disintegration, of falling numbers and of the efforts to keep alive some little spark.
>
> Numbers had been falling even before the War but the Michaelmas Term 1939 saw only 134 in residence though this number was maintained throughout the year. After that when the national machine had really got to work numbers fell rapidly until we touched bottom in the Michaelmas/Lent Terms of 1943/4 with 19. By V.E. Day we had already reached 26 after which the tide began to flow. The Michaelmas Term 1945 opened

---

[1] Censor's Report for 1939–40. In *The Historical Register*, Supplement 1931–40, the total of matriculations for the year 1939–40 is given as fifty-two.

[2] *Journal*, December 1946, p. 4.

with 86 and the Easter Term 1946 ended with 137. This coming Michaelmas Term will see us over 280.

As numbers fell so did the teaching and administrative staffs. Mr. Gaskoin went early to the Postal Censorship in which he had served during the first war. Mr. Harvey joined Leys School as history master and went with them to Scotland when they moved. Dr Evans joined a Government Research Department though he would suddenly appear and disappear again from time to time. Miss Parsons, the House-keeper, remained until Bedford College for Woman [*sic*] came into temporary possession but went, shortly afterwards, on sick leave. Albert was in due course called up, while Holmes was transferred to the Mill Lane Lecture Rooms. Even Miss Barrett, my secretary, went to the Extra Mural Board so that eventually only Mr Barrett and myself were left lodgers in our own building now occupied by Bedford College. As time went on other smaller bodies crept in such as the Polish Club, which occupied the Parlour: and the British Council which took over Mr Gaskoin's rooms. All this coming and going meant much work and much moving of furniture; dreary and depressing for destruction is never pleasant.

As a result of all this and also in consequence of the demands made by the S.T.C. and other organisations there were no organised games. Most of the men found life busy enough without. The S.T.C. demanded two half days weekly with additional time when conducting field days and night operations which were not infrequent. Fire watching after the second winter became more and more nominal and no doubt because of their excessive toil during the day the fire watchers slept well at night.

On one celebrated occasion the N.F.S. had staged a full rehearsal at the Fitzwilliam Street corner with torrents of water from furlongs of hoses playing on the roofs and the windows of the buildings, but the fire watchers did not mind, and knew nothing of it until told the following day by the Censor who does not sleep so soundly.

Dinners gave place to lunches and the Dining Hall became also the Common Room, a pleasant combination for the small numbers. Even lunches ceased when Bedford College took over. Though the High Table kept its continuity in the form of coffee and spam sandwiches eaten by a few of the faithful in the Censor's room once a week. It was a horrible meal but eaten with grim determination that if 'London could take it' so could we. They were particularly bad sandwiches and the coffee was always cold.

In spite of these drastic reductions the balance sheet was generally on the debit side though not too much. The Playing Field too ticked over with King as a full time paid Warden but doing odd jobs in his spare time.

Bedford College moved back to London in the summer of 1944 and we began to expand slowly again. Dinner in hall began again in the Michaelmas Term with about 16 dining of whom two were natives of the British Isles ...

The others came from the whole earth. It was a most pleasant and happy table and a shining example of what things might be if only we humans could forget our nationality, colour, and race, and remember only we are men.

With the prospects of peace came demands for plans for the better world. The University Authorities have been asking all departments for blue prints of future development as well as for the immediate peace. We have produced our print but as it is still confidential we can say no more. For the immediate peace the Board agreed to take up to a maximum of 300, but for this demanded a Junior Tutor in addition to a Bursar.

Appointments had now to be made as Mr Gaskoin would not return having passed the age of 70, and Mr Harvey had accepted a living near Hitchen [*sic*] and it was necessary to fill their places. As Junior Tutor Mr N. J. G. Pounds, an old Fitzwilliam student, was appointed and came into residence in the Michaelmas Term 1944. Mr T. F. Reddaway, the eldest son of Mr W. F. Reddaway, former Censor of Fitzwilliam House, was appointed Bursar and Assistant Censor and was to take office in the Lent Term 1946. Unfortunately Mr Reddaway resigned before he could take up his office though we were fortunate to get Mr W. W. Williams, another old Fitzwilliam man, recently out of the Army.[1] In the office Mr Dorban came after demobilisation as an understudy to Mr Barrett [Chief Clerk, first appointed in 1924]; and Miss Barrett returned as Censor's Secretary. On the domestic side Mrs Metten who came as cook in the Michaelmas Term 1945 was appointed Housekeeper in the Lent Term 1946. Mr Holmes also came back and later Albert from his travels in Africa.

It has been a very busy time since September 1945, not so much because of the numbers for as will be seen they were not very great but because of the difficulty in obtaining supplies, labour and accommodation: and in the great shortage of university teachers.

Accommodation has been and is something of a nightmare, and has been the major activity of Mr Pounds. Up to date he has visited personally more than 4,000 houses and has secured 200 sets of rooms. If anyone thinks this is an easy task let him try it for a month. This term we have a special clerk to look after landladies and rooms. Labour at first was an acute problem and twice the kitchen staff left with about an hour's notice. Only the Housekeeper's great determination made it possible for dinners to be served. Now, happily, we have a good staff though we still lack waiters, the men taking it in turns to wait ...

The food problem is now the really acute and insoluble one. This coming year we have so many men that in spite of double halls we can only feed men four times a week on the average. As a 'catering establishment' we are allowed 1d worth of meat per man and it is hard to feed warriors on that. Even flour is now rationed so the Housekeeper is worried.

---

[1] See also p. 230.

On the academic side the lack of teachers and supervisors is very grave. The University in peace days allowed appointed lecturers to teach for eight hours a week. This was to safeguard their learning and encourage research. Last year one was more than doubling the number, while this year it will mean three or four at supervision. The laboratories are overcrowded and the colleges are rationed as to engineers, doctors, physicists and chemists.

The applications have been very heavy. At Fitzwilliam we have had more than 1,200 since last October. This has meant a large and often complicated correspondence as men who have been in the Forces for many years very naturally need a good deal of guidance. Further, as most of these men are coming on Government Grants there is a considerable flutter of paper to keep the Civil Servants busy. ...

Certainly the Michaelmas Term will be a busy and congested one with its 180 Freshmen who will outnumber the Seniors. In order to get the interviewing done in time the Freshmen are being brought up early and staggered alphabetically. Then the Seniors. By the time all these interviews are over the tutors will be ready for a rest cure. But in spite of everything it is an exhilarating sight to see the place alive again. Better to die of over-work than fade out with anaemia.[1]

Such were Thatcher's memories of war-time as it affected, particularly, the fortunes of members of his staff, and the domestic life of his community. It also disrupted his non-collegiate institution as a department of the University. Financially, the effect of the war was to continue, and increase, the deficits caused by falling numbers in the 1930s. The Board's accounts for the last pre-war year shewed a loss of £266.19.8, which in 1939/40 became £822.17.0 and rose to £1,146.10.0 two years later. From October 1942 almost the whole of the Board's

[1] Among those especially mentioned by Thatcher, Walter Harvey, Assistant Censor, Bursar, and Chaplain since 1925 (and also Vicar of Horningsea from 1934 to 1936) joined the Leys School staff in the Michaelmas term 1939, and went with the School to Pitlochry in the summer of 1940. As an officer of the House, he retired finally on 30 September 1943, on his appointment to the living of St Paul's Walden, near Hitchin. For a most appreciative, and well deserved, tribute to his work by Thatcher, see *Journal*, December 1946, pp. 14–17. Dr R. C. Evans, then of Clare College, had succeeded Mr F. I. G. Rawlins in the Michaelmas term 1934 as Director of Studies in Natural Sciences, and became Honorary Treasurer of the Amalgamated Clubs in the Lent term 1937. 'Albert' was Albert Holmes, under-porter to his father A. J. Holmes. E. P. King had been groundsman since March 1919, and in 1944 received from the House, the Clubs and the Fitzwilliam Society a silver tea service in recognition of devoted performance of his duties for twenty-five years. He retired in 1957.

Relations between Thatcher and the Polish Club appear to have been cordial. In his Report for 1944–45, when he informed the Board that the Club were to vacate the Parlour at the end of the year, he added that they had been 'exceedingly considerate and pleasant tenants', and that he was sorry to see them go. Two years later, after his retirement, Thatcher was made Knight Commander of the Order of Polonia Restituta, and in his acknowledgement at the presentation ceremony, spoke of his pride at having the reputation of being 'the only man in Cambridge able to understand a Pole when he got excited' (*Journal*, 1956, p. 9).

premises (with some houses in Fitzwilliam Street) was let to Addenbrooke's Hospital and Bedford College for Women, and in 1943/44 the amount received in rents was £785.7.6, compared with an annual prewar figure for room rents from students of about £225. This, with savings on salaries and wages of members of academic and assistant staff who had left, reduced the deficit in that year to £110.17.10. Bedford College returned to London at the end of July 1944, and, the British Council and the Poles in the Parlour notwithstanding, the consequent loss of rents and the engagement of staff in anticipation of post-war needs, without at that time a compensating increase in the number of residents, resulted in a deficit for the year 1944/45 of £231.17.11, even though in that year the Non-collegiate Students Board had received an additional grant of £1,000 from the University Chest.

The total deficit from 1 August 1939 to 31 July 1945 was £3,719.7.6 – a sum which would then have provided the stipend of a Professor of the University for three years – and, although changes in the value of money may obscure the significance of figures relating to different periods, it may be thought that the University was fortunate in not incurring a heavier loss on behalf of one of its departments which through no fault of its own had been disrupted for so long.

Although in 1928 the University had obtained from Mr E. S. Peck a fifteen year lease of those parts of his premises previously occupied by the Non-Collegiate Students Board, it was not long before Thatcher began to refer to the limitations of the accommodation at his disposal. 'We have continued', he says in 1930, 'the policy of improvements, but these are now rather minor matters. The outstanding problem is that of more accommodation. Some day Fitzwilliam House must be extended, and it is with this end in view that one welcomes the increased annual surpluses which in time ought to grow to a very useful sum.' Nothing more was said for some years, when owing to the economic depression numbers had fallen steeply, but in 1934 Thatcher again complained about the inadequacy of the premises, and renewed his complaints in 1939 in his outspoken Report on the need for reduced costs and improved amenities.[1] During the war the matter was naturally dropped, but the great increase in numbers in the post-war years and continuing pressure thereafter, except for one year when in 1950 there was a fall in admissions, led to great difficulty, and to a growing dissatisfaction

[1] Censor's Reports, 1929–30, 1933–34, 1938–39. See also a memorandum addressed to the 1934 Syndicate, whose secretary (the Rev. G. A. Chase, then Tutor of Trinity Hall) wrote acknowledging its receipt on 5 March, saying 'I am sending round your memorandum as it stands. It is a bit strong, but you clearly feel strongly, and you might as well show it, as it seems to me.' (Policy File 1927–42).

that the non-collegiate institution should, apparently, be expected to assume responsibilities altogether out of proportion to its resources, whether in premises or in staff.

Although the thirty years of Mr Thatcher's censorship fall conveniently into three separate periods – from his appointment in 1924 to the outbreak of the war of 1939, the war years, and from the Michaelmas term 1945 to his final retirement in 1955 – they are not sharply divided; and as early as the Easter term 1942 his Board were discussing how they should replace Mr Harvey and Mr Gaskoin; who were then on leave of absence and would not return when the war was over. In the following Michaelmas term the Censor, who anticipated in the immediate post-war years an increase in applications for admission comparable with that which had followed the war of 1914–18, told the Board that he wished to appoint an Assistant Censor and Bursar, and a Junior Tutor, 'of about 34 and 26, respectively'; and he did not omit to remind the Board of his earlier plea for a less costly education for his non-collegiate students.[1] In due course, after authority had been obtained from the Council of the Senate, the posts were approved, and, as we have seen, Mr W. W. Williams (Fitzwilliam House, B.A. 1925) was appointed Assistant Censor and Bursar from 1 January 1946, and Mr N. J. G. Pounds, who had also been an undergraduate at the House (B.A. 1934), became Junior Tutor on 1 October 1944.[2]

At this time the Board did not lack opportunities of making their views known to the University authorities about their policy for the future. Their first statement of the kind was compiled in reply to an enquiry addressed to colleges in December 1943 by the Council of the Senate, asking how many students they would be prepared to admit during an anticipated temporary period of exceptional pressure in the immediate post-war years, and thereafter when conditions had become more normal. The Board replied that during the first period, if they could have a fourth member of staff (additional, that is, to the Censor, the Assistant Censor and Bursar, and the Junior Tutor) they would be willing to have 300 men in residence then, and thereafter not more than 250, unless there could be considerable changes, both in their staffing arrangements and in their buildings.[3] Shortly afterwards, in common with other University departments and institutions, the Board received a request for an account of their immediate post-war needs,

[1]   Minutes, 7 December 1942.
[2]   Minutes, 8 January 1944, also 21 December 1945. See also letter dated 13 January 1944 from the Censor to the University Registrary (Policy File 1943–50). Mr T. F. Reddaway had been appointed to a Readership in the University of London.
[3]   Minutes, 8 January 1944.

and of proposals in the longer term for the development of their work, as far as this could be foreseen. They replied quickly (on 26 March 1944) with an important statement which was to represent their policy for some years; they had nothing to add to their list of immediate requirements, but they thought that the time had come when better provision should be made for their students than was possible in their existing premises. A new and larger building was needed, preferably on an extension of their existing site or, if that was impracticable, on a different site altogether. At pre-war prices, the cost of this building, which should contain rooms for the Censor and the Tutors, rooms for supervision, and the usual communal accommodation found in colleges, would be about £60,000, and for its maintenance their annual grant from the Chest would need to be raised from £1,000 to £3,000. Finally, the Board expressed their opinion that they ought to have at their disposal not fewer than six exhibitions to attract able candidates for admission, which at an annual value of £50 and with a tenure of three years would need an annual subvention of £900.[1] Shortly afterwards, in answer to a further enquiry from the Council, they said that their most urgent need was an increase in their grant from the Chest to £2,000, then a new building, and lastly the six exhibitions.[2]

In January 1946 the Board again discussed their policy as it had been set forth in their letter of 26 March 1944, but with no fresh conclusions;[3] and at the end of July the Censor, who some months earlier had thought that the University might do something for Fitzwilliam House, was coming to fear that other needs were being regarded as more urgent, and that a new building for the House was not likely to be provided for some years.[4] Nevertheless, in the following Michaelmas term the Board did not hesitate to press for it, in correspondence with the University Treasurer about their estimated expenditure for the quinquennium 1947/52, or to ask for authority to appoint the fourth member of staff for whom they had asked more than two years previously, or to apply for funds to permit the appointment of Directors of Studies at acceptable stipends.[5]

On 24 November 1947 the Board returned to the charge, and enquired of the Council of the Senate whether they might be autho-

[1] Minutes, 24 March 1944.
[2] *Ibid.*, 30 May 1944.
[3] *Ibid.*, 21 January 1946. See also Policy File 1943–50.
[4] Policy File 1943–50, letter dated 31 July 1946 to F. I. G. Rawlins.
[5] Minutes, 1 October 1946. See also Policy File 1943–50, for reply of 17 October to a letter dated 19 August 1946 from the University Treasurer requesting a statement of the needs of the Non-Collegiate Students Board for the quinquennium 1957–62.

rized to prepare detailed plans for a new building. To this the Council did not feel able to agree;[1] but they were not entirely unmindful of their non-collegiate students' needs, for in the Easter term 1948 they appointed a committee 'to consider Fitzwilliam House with regard to its central accommodation, its amenities and its arrangements for staff and teaching'.[2] The committee informed the Council that they had based their consideration of the matters within their terms of reference on an assumption that provision was needed for a student population of the order of 300, of whom about 200 would be undergraduates and not more than 100 research students. They also assumed that these figures would not include members of attached houses of residence who were also members of Fitzwilliam House. They were satisfied that the accommodation then available could not be made to provide adequately for 300 men, and they did not believe that the existing site could be enlarged to permit of a proper reconstruction of the buildings. They therefore recommended that there should be a new building on a site within easy reach of the centre of the town, and they recommended also that it should include dining accommodation for 120 persons.

The Council of the Senate referred their committee's Report to the Non-collegiate Students Board, whose reception of it, at least as it is recorded in their minutes of their meeting held on 3 June 1948, seems a little lacking in appreciation of the importance in their affairs of the committee's clear recognition of the need for a new building. The Board, possibly through a misunderstanding of what was required, limited their comments to a unanimous resolution that the proposed dining accommodation for 120 persons should also allow for the needs of a High Table, and – a new requirement – to an expression of opinion that their building should provide 'a certain amount' of living accommodation. The minute adds that discussion of this and other points was deferred to a more appropriate time; but of any such discussion there is no further mention, for at their next meeting, held on 27 July, the only reference to the subject is contained in a statement, very welcome to the Board, from Dr Whitehorn, that the Council's committee had proposed that the new building should be on the site of a former Fellows' Garden of Corpus Christi College in Sidgwick Avenue.[3]

[1] Policy File 1943–50, letter dated 20 January 1948 from the University Registrary.
[2] Ibid., letter dated 29 April 1948 from the First Assistant Registrary to the Rev. R. D. Whitehorn, Principal of Westminster College, Acting Chairman of the Board.
[3] Minutes, 27 July 1948. The Board owed much to the forceful advocacy of Mr P. C. Vellacott, as the Vice-Chancellor's deputy their Chairman, who urged most strongly, both as a member of the committee and of the Council, that immediate attention should be given to their needs.

There followed a considerable period of indecision and of frustrating delays, for the site of the new Fitzwilliam buildings was not chosen finally for another ten years. On 31 January 1949 the Council of the Senate, in a Report to the University recommending the appointment of a Syndicate on the development of the Sidgwick Avenue Site, said that they accepted the view of their committee appointed to consider the needs of Fitzwilliam House, and that they had also approved their Sites Committee's proposal that the former Fellows' Garden of Corpus Christi College should be assigned for a new building.[1] On learning from the Syndicate, however, of the Non-collegiate Students Board's wish that Fitzwilliam House should ultimately be able to offer residence to its members to the same extent as the colleges, the Council, who were of the opinion that the site was not suitable for residential accommodation on this scale, asked the Board whether they preferred to remain in their existing premises, with lodging houses near at hand, or to move to Sidgwick Avenue where there would be ample room for headquarters accommodation but no provision for residence. The Board received this enquiry at their meeting on 25 November 1949 and resolved that they

firmly adhered to their view that Fitzwilliam House should develop upon a residential basis and that provision should be made not solely for the headquarters accommodation (with the addition of a chapel) already discussed with and agreed by the Council's committee, but also for residential accommodation for the staff and for 100 junior members; that, from the point of view of situation, room on the Sidgwick Avenue site would be desirable but that, if on grounds of general planning policy for the University the site already allotted there, namely the Corpus Christi Fellows' Garden, cannot be made available to provide residential accommodation, it is preferred that Fitzwilliam House should remain for the time being in its present building because of the importance attached by the Board and the Censor to the residential accommodation provided by the houses in Fitzwilliam Street belonging to the Fitzwilliam Hall Trust; but at the same time it is urgently begged of the Council that provision should be made for another suitable site e.g. the Huntingdon Road/Oxford Road site near the playing fields of Fitzwilliam House which can give the full accommodation deemed necessary by the Board.[2]

[1]   *University Reporter*, 1948–49, p. 764.
[2]   Minutes, 25 November 1949. In a letter dated 11 March 1948 the University Treasurer had informed the Censor that the Council of the Senate had decided that no satisfactory recommendation could be made about the purchase of this site, then occupied by Welch's Nurseries, until the University had come to a decision about its future policy for Fitzwilliam House. (Policy File 1943–50).

Nothing further appears to have been heard, at that time at least, of the proposal to build on the Huntingdon Road; but in January 1950 the Board were asked whether, subject to the concurrence of St John's College, a site of some seven or eight acres to the north of Clarkson Road would be acceptable. This suggestion they welcomed warmly, but by June they were told that the College wished to conduct a survey of the Clarkson Road area before deciding on the use of the site proposed, and had offered instead land on Herschel Road (Thorneycreek), which the Council's committee thought inadequate. In March 1951 the Board were informed that there was little likelihood that they would get the Clarkson Road site, but that a much smaller site of about three acres, belonging to the University, had been suggested at Bredon House, between Selwyn Gardens and Barton Road; and in April they resolved to inform the Council that, while they found Bredon House less attractive than Clarkson Road, they considered that it would be suitable for their purposes, and hoped that the Council would publish a Report to the University on their whole scheme for the accommodation of the non-collegiate students, and would recommend that the site should be assigned to them.[1]

At their Long Vacation meeting in 1951 the Council approved a Report on the Future of Fitzwilliam House, which they referred to the Non-Collegiate Students Board for their comments before its intended publication in the Michaelmas term. The Report gave an account of the Council's deliberations up to the point at which they had abandoned their proposal to provide for the House on the Sidgwick Avenue site, and went on to say that after considering a number of possible alternatives they and the Board were agreed in thinking that the grounds of Bredon House would be suitable.

The Report continues:

> 4. In a statement of their needs for the quinquennium 1952–57 the Non-Collegiate Students Board have submitted to the Council a proposal for new premises for Fitzwilliam House to provide for 200 undergraduates and not more than 100 research students; it is the Board's aim to provide residential accommodation for at least 100 of these students. The Board's proposal is to accomplish this in two stages:
>
> Stage I, the administrative headquarters, with accommodation for 30 resident students; these buildings would replace the existing administrative headquarters and adjacent houses in which a number of students now reside.
>
> Stage II, the addition of accommodation for a further 70 resident stu-

[1]   Minutes, 20 January, and 23 June, 1950; also 8 March, and 21 April, 1951.

dents, with a proportionate number of sets for teaching and administrative officers.

5. The new administrative headquarters for the Board would be provided by Bredon House itself. The remainder of the accommodation for which they ask amounts in all to about 60,000 square feet, but the Board have emphasized that this total should not be regarded as final. While it is impossible to offer anything but the roughest estimate of costs, some indication of them may be given by the statement that a building of the required size and of three floors with an average width of 30 feet would, at five shillings a cubic foot, cost in round figures about £230,000 (Stage I about £135,000 and Stage II about £95,000). To these estimates must be added provision for furniture and equipment and for professional fees, making a total approaching £300,000. These figures might need substantial amendment in the light of detailed plans when they became available, and of the level of costs when the work came to be undertaken.

6. It is no less difficult to offer a reliable estimate of the recurrent costs of the Board's proposals, but the Council think that, on the assumption that the students concerned would have to pay room-rents and establishment charges reasonably related to running costs, but not to pay interest on the capital costs involved, the annual grant from the Chest to the Non-Collegiate Students Board would need to be increased by not more than £4000 on the completion of Stage II. It is more difficult to determine how much of this increase would be attributable to each stage separately, and the Council do not think that reliable estimates can at present be prepared with sufficient precision to enable them to publish separate figures for the two stages.

7. The Council concur in the proposals of the Non-Collegiate Students Board. They are satisfied that the inadequacy of the present buildings of Fitzwilliam House is an obstacle to the development of its corporate life. The Council wish to make it clear that if these proposals are accepted Fitzwilliam House will remain an institution controlled and administered by the University and not an autonomous College; but they think that it should be enabled to offer to its students a greater share than is at present possible of the amenities that a College provides for its members. The provision of new administrative headquarters, with residential accommodation for about 30 students, is therefore in the Council's view necessary, and is represented by Stage I of the Board's proposals. The Council are satisfied also that the next step to be taken in the development of the corporate life of Fitzwilliam House is the provision of residential accommodation for about 70 students: this represents Stage II of the Board's proposals. The Council accordingly seek the general approval of the University for these proposals. It is clear, however, that no steps can be taken toward their implementation until the financial position of the University permits. The Council accordingly propose that the date from which Bredon House should be assigned to the Non-Collegiate Students Board be

determined by Grace on the recommendation of the Council with the con-currence of the Financial Board.

8. The Council accordingly recommend

I. That the general approval of the University be given to the policy for the future development of Fitzwilliam House outlined in this Report.

II. That, if Recommendation I is approved, Bredon House and the land surrounding it be assigned to the Non-Collegiate Students Board, from a date to be determined later by Grace on the recom-mendation of the Council with the concurrence of the Financial Board, for development in accordance with the policy outlined in this Report.[1]

This is what the Council had in mind to say in July 1951; the Board, save for one small amendment, had no wish to suggest anything different, and the Council obtained permission from the Planning Authority to use Bredon House in the way they proposed, but the Council's Report did not appear in the Michaelmas term, and at the end of February the Board heard from them again:

> At more than one meeting this term the Council have felt obliged to give their proposals further consideration, and they have now instructed me, with great regret, to inform your Board that, in view of the heavy cost of implementing the policy outlined in the Report and of the uncertainties of University finance as a whole, they do not feel justified in putting proposals before the University at the present time. [Letter of 26 February, from Registrary to Censor][2]

The Board took their time over their reply to the Registrary's letter, and they replied to some effect. In a letter dated 18 April, largely the work of their Chairman (Mr S. C. Roberts, Master of Pembroke, who had succeeded Mr Vellacott as deputy to the Vice-Chancellor a few months previously), they expressed their keen disappointment at the Council's decision not to proceed with the publication of their Report drafted six months before, embodying as it did the results of discus-sions almost continuously in progress since 1944. The Board reminded the Council that in January 1949, in their 'Report on the appointment of a Syndicate to consider the development of the Sidgwick Avenue Site' they had affirmed the importance of encouraging the corporate life of Fitzwilliam House, and that at the discussion of that Report this view had not been challenged. The Censor's letter concluded:

[1] Policy File 1951–
[2] *Ibid.*

My Board wishes to emphasise that it fully appreciates the financial obstacles which stand in the way of the immediate implementation of the Council's policy and that it recognises that it would be impracticable to press forward building schemes at the present time; but it does not understand why, with the necessary reservations as to finance, the Council should now hesitate to disclose its policy and its future plans to the University.[1]

The Board's representations were not without effect, for on 26 May the Council agreed to publish their Report, although in a modified form, on which the Board were not, this time, invited to submit their observations; for the Registrary contented himself with enclosing a copy of the revised Report with his letter to the Censor notifying him of the Council's decision to publish.[2]

The revised Council Report of 26 May 1952 differs not a little from the draft which they declined to publish three months before. Its recommendations are less definite; they are no longer necessarily linked with Bredon House; and the realization of Stage II of the project is regarded as so remote that it is thought unwise to mention even an approximate estimate of its cost. The Council no longer concur in the Board's proposals; the provision of new administrative headquarters is no longer declared to be necessary, and the Council do not commit themselves, or seek to commit their successors, to the assignment of a site against the day when it might be possible to build. The two recommendations of the earlier draft Report are replaced by a single, and far more cautious, recommendation in its final version:

> That the general approval of the University be given to the policy of encouraging the corporate life of Fitzwilliam House by the provision of new administrative headquarters and residential accommodation, but that such provision be dependent upon the approval by the Regent House of a Grace proposed by the Council of the Senate after receiving an assurance from the Financial Board that the financial circumstances of the University allow it.[3]

The Council's Report was approved on 17 June,[4] after two speakers had expressed regret, at a Discussion held a fortnight earlier, that the Council had not made any specific proposals in support of their policy of encouraging the corporate life of the House; and in August, after the

---

[1]   *Ibid.*
[2]   *Ibid.*
[3]   *University Reporter*, 1951–52, p. 1336.
[4]   *Ibid.*, p. 1527 (Grace 2). The speakers at the discussion were Dr R. C. Evans (St Catharine's), and Professor Bruce Dickins (Corpus).

Cambridge Reunion of the Fitzwilliam Society, its president had written to the Censor, also welcoming the Council's declaration of general policy, but expressing concern at the prospect of delay in its implementation.

In the following term the Non-Collegiate Students Board held only one meeting, at which there was apparently no reference to the discouraging outcome of the long discussions upon which during the previous academical year so many hopes had been built; but matters were not to be allowed to rest at the point at which the Council of the Senate, for whatever variety of reasons, had sought to leave them in their Report, in which, as a condition of further progress they had insisted on an assurance that the Financial Board were most unlikely to give for a considerable time. On 15 January 1953 the Censor, the Assistant Censor, and the Tutor (R. N. Walters, appointed in 1950 as successor to N. J. G. Pounds) presented a memorandum to the Board, with a request that it should be forwarded to the Council. This memorandum supplies ample evidence of the strain imposed upon the staff by the conditions in which they had been required to work, and the despair to which they had been reduced by the probability that these conditions were to be permitted to continue indefinitely.

By way of background, the memorandum summarizes the course of discussions between the University authorities and the Board during the previous ten years, and proceeds to a statement of the needs of the House, both as regards accommodation and staff. Some members of the Board, even, will have found it a revealing document; and as a matter of history it remains an important source of information about the limited amenities available to the large number of the University's non-collegiate students of the post-war years. In the Board's minute book it is entitled *Memorandum presented by the Staff to the Board with the request that it be forwarded to the Council.*[1]

In December 1943 [it reads] the Registrary asked for an estimate of the maximum number of persons in statu pupillari whom we could accept for 'a relatively short period of exceptional pressure' and also for an estimate of numbers 'after the period of exceptional pressure is over'. In their reply the Board informed the Registrary that they 'would be prepared to accept 300 men provided an additional fourth member were appointed to the Staff during that period.' That after the 'period of exceptional pressure' was over the maximum number should not exceed 250 unless the Authorities decide upon considerable changes in the matter of building accommodation and staff.

[1]   Minutes, 15 January 1953.

At the present moment the numbers in residence exceed 400 while the staff consists still of only three.

It is now turned seven years since this 'period of exceptional pressure' began. During these years the Censor and his two colleagues have endeavoured to carry out the wishes of the University and their Board. What they have achieved has demanded not only unremitting effort, but the complete sacrifice of any claim to scholarship. In this they do not claim any particular merit, but they now venture to point out to the Board that the 'period of exceptional pressure' may fairly be said to have ended when the great influx of ex-service men had ceased and that we have now passed into the second phase mentioned in the Registrary's letter of 23 December 1943.

During these past seven years there has been a considerable correspondence between the Board and the Council of the Senate about the future of Fitzwilliam House and we venture to think that the Council, as well as the Board, have altered considerably their attitude towards Fitzwilliam House and its functions. This has shown itself in the recently published Report of the Council which recognised the necessity for new buildings if Fitzwilliam House is adequately to fulfil its purpose. It was, therefore, with profound regret and discouragement that we learned that any steps to carry out these recommendations had been shelved *sine die*.

In a letter dated 25 February 1944, last paragraph, the Registrary summarises the views of the Colleges on the matter of numbers and brings out their insistence that the residential character of the University must be maintained. There can be no doubt that the feeling in this matter has very definitely grown and not diminished. If this be so for the Colleges, can it be less for Fitzwilliam House whose problems are much more difficult and complex than those of any College?

Yet we are required to make bricks not only without straw, but with very little clay. Fitzwilliam House is now the fifth largest body in this University and yet this great body of men have only three seniors to care for them. That in itself is an excessive demand. It is impossible to give the students that individual care which they need now even more than before the war. Nor is this all. In every way the building is completely inadequate. The dining hall will accommodate only 65 men and so necessitates three halls each evening, as well as equally excessive crowding for lunch. What ever may have been argued against dining in the past can no longer be urged in times when landladies very often refuse to prepare meals or to cater in any way for their men. The only alternative is for them to feed in restaurants, with the concomitant waste of time and money.

The Kitchens which supply these meals are wholly inadequate in layout and militate in every way against any further economies in service.

The Common Room will hold thirty students with comfort and fifty with active discomfort, yet somehow at least twice that number must be in the building at meal times. The result is that the men are normally com-

31 Trumpington Street, the dining hall

pelled to stand in the stair-way and landings and even in the street. The so called cloak room for all these men consists of a narrow passage 12ft. by 5ft. On wet days the congestion and discomfort are beyond description.

There is no place or room where the students can be assembled when required by their seniors. At the beginning of the academic year, freshmen have to be taken to the Mill Lane Lecture Rooms when we wish to talk to them. For general Congregations and Matriculations there is no place where they can be assembled except in a back garden in Fitzwilliam Street, when they are at the mercy of the weather.

All this is demoralising for the men and especially the freshmen. Nor can it be argued as it could be forty years ago, that even if there were these discomforts and lacks, the costs were well below that of the Colleges. Fitzwilliam House to-day is a very little cheaper than the Colleges, though in no way can it be called cheap.

It has been suggested that these discomforts and lacks can be diminished and mitigated by reducing present numbers to a suggested 250, of whom 100 would be research students. To this suggestion several objections can be made. (1) We feel strongly that it is our duty to make Cambridge a place of education to as many as possible. (2) As already pointed out in a

Memorandum to the Board dated 8 March 1951, the suggested figure of 250 is not viable if one has in mind a full community life and the particular problems of Fitzwilliam House. (3) To so reduce numbers would involve the University in much financial loss, both directly and indirectly, and also in much embarrassment, as Fitzwilliam House takes in all those post-graduate students refused by the Colleges.

We would venture, at this point, to remind the Board but particularly the University Authorities, that Fitzwilliam House though by regulation a department of the University is, by its very nature *sui generis*. While not a college *de jure*, it is so *de facto*. The whole history of its development, from its very inception, is that of a body of men who in spite of the old title "Non Collegiate" and the old attitudes, have passionately desired a corporate life and standing. This can be seen in the early petitions to the Censor that students be allowed to dine together and in the attitudes developed by all the Seniors who have attached themselves to this body; and it has at last been admitted by the University itself in the recent Report. Fitzwilliam House has a very real life and pride, though these are constantly frustrated by the inadequacy of its buildings and the unhelpful attitude of the University Authorities. This last statement is made with reluctance, but one is compelled to make it. Too little is known of Fitzwilliam House and its problems by those in Authority and too often decisions are made by those who have never put foot inside the building and who know nothing of its working, its life and its hopes.

We would ask that those in control, whether immediate or removed, should take the trouble to see Fitzwilliam House as a working institution. And this cannot be done in an odd half hour. We would ask them to see the congestion and the adverse conditions under which we are required to work – conditions which would not be tolerated for a moment by anyone in a College. It is this continued ignorance by those who control us through the Council and the Registry, which so actively discourages those of us who have the welfare of Fitzwilliam House at heart and who are also proud of being Cambridge men.

Some of the old hostilities to the development of Fitzwilliam House were based upon two objections (1) that no development in Fitzwilliam House should be to the detriment of the Colleges (2) that Fitzwilliam House could not expect the Colleges to tax themselves for her benefit. Whatever validity there was in such arguments, they are no longer valid now. If Fitzwilliam House were to shut down tomorrow the College numbers would not go up, while it is no longer true that any expenditure on Fitzwilliam House comes out of College taxation.

We, the Staff, venture, therefore, to ask the Board to consider whether, in spite of what has been decided, something could not be done to reopen the whole matter and that should this not be possible, the Board will consider what can be done to ameliorate the present intolerable conditions. We wish to represent this position to the Authorities with as much emphasis as possible. The situation is unsatisfactory for those *in statu pupillari*; it is discreditable to the University which is responsible for it while we, the three University officers most concerned, find it so discouraging as to be almost intolerable.

For these reasons we have decided to ask the Board to treat the items enumerated below as matters requiring immediate attention.

(A) ACCOMMODATION

(1) *The provision of a dining hall to seat 150 men.*

(2) *The provision of proper kitchens to serve the dining hall.*

(3) *The provision of a common room in which 150 men can meet on official or social occasions.*

(4) *A cloak room for the coats etc. of 200 men, and lavatory accommodation on the same scale.*

and on a slightly lower priority

(5) *A chapel to seat 100 men*

(6) *An adequate library*

(7) *Baths for men living in lodgings where no bathroom exists*

All of these facilities would be best supplied in a new building on another site, but some relief would be afforded, the Memorandum continues, if the existing site could be extended by the purchase of adjacent property or, if that were not possible, by the acquisition of a house and garden at the eastern end of Fitzwilliam Street; but these alternatives are mentioned only because of the apparently indefinite postponement of the new building which the Council had earlier been disposed to provide.

The need for new accommodation looms large in the Memorandum, both in its preamble and in its specific requests; but there is also a request for authority to appoint an additional tutor, for the establishment of a post of chaplain, and for a review of the remuneration of the Assistant Censor and the Tutor, including the payment to them of allowances for entertainment, and of the wages and conditions of service of some members of the assistant staff. The introduction of an establishment charge is also suggested, as a means of raising revenue, but there is no attempt to disguise to fact that most of these proposals would mean an increased charge on University funds.

The Board, who must have realized that their officers were near to breaking point, took a very careful look at their Memorandum; and, while they preferred not to forward it to the Council as it stood, they decided to write a Report of their own. This differed very little in substance from the Memorandum, repeated its statement of immediate needs (except the last), amplified considerably its financial proposals,

32 Trumpington Street, the main staircase

and – previous misadventures notwithstanding[1] – made bold to ask the Council to agree to the making of a public appeal for funds. They requested

I. That the Council consider the future of Fitzwilliam House as a matter of urgency.

II. That the Council authorize the appointment of a Joint Committee of the Buildings Syndicate and the Board to consider the possible development and expansion of the present site of Fitzwilliam House, with leave to consult an architect.

III. That the Council agree in principle to the financial proposals contained in paragraphs 15 to 19 of this Report.*

IV. That the Council authorize the appointment of an additional Tutor of Fitzwilliam House, to act also, if suitably qualified, as Chaplain.

V. That the Council review the stipends of the officers of the Board and consider whether entertainment allowances might be granted to the Assistant Censor and the Tutor.

VI. That the Council agree in principle to the making of a public appeal for funds for the development and endowment of Fitzwilliam House.

*These paragraphs read as follows:

15. The Board have considered the question how the developments that they have in mind should be paid for. With regard to the capital cost of building the Board have reason to believe that University Grants Committee might be prepared to make a contribution to that part of the expenditure that might be for the benefit of Research Students. They hope that the University will recognize the urgent need for some provision from other sources towards expenditure for the benefit of undergraduates.

16. The Board would also hope in due course, if their proposals contained in paragraphs 18 and 19 below are approved, to contribute some part of the cost from savings out of income, or preferably to obtain a loan from the Chest to be repaid out of such savings. They would wish to add, however, that they might well be able to raise a substantial sum for capital development and perhaps endowment by making a public appeal.

17. At present the annual income of the Board consists of
(a) the fees prescribed by Ordinance (Regulation 5, p. 588), and
(b) the annual grant from the Chest (applied for each year under Regulation (4(b), p. 582, approved under Regulation 5, *ibid.*); this grant, which includes £200 for the Gift Fund (Regulation 11, p. 590), has been at the following rates

	£
1925–1945, each year,	1000
1946	3000
1947–1949, each year,	2500
1950	200
1951	1200
1952	1249 (= £1000 + £249 for increases of Assistants' wages)

[1] For an account of an earlier attempt to secure Council consent for the making of a limited appeal, see pp. 430–2.

18. The Board would welcome an opportunity of making savings from their annual income which might be used as a contribution to capital expenditure, or for repayment of a loan obtained from such expenditure. Such an opportunity would be provided if the size of the grant from the Chest were fixed in advance and, as before the war, could be depended upon over a period of years. Since the war this has not been so: the grant has varied widely and has been calculated closely in relation to expenditure, and the Board must suppose that any saving in one year would, under present arrangements, be followed by a reduction in the grant for the following year. The Board could look forward to the future with greater hope if

(*a*) the Council could determine quinquennially what grant they would propose for payment from the Chest to the Board; it would then be possible for the Boad to make savings out of revenue and to use them for capital expenditure, without thereby incurring any reduction in their annual grant; and

(*b*) the annual grant could be raised to such a level that its purchasing power would be closer to that of the pre-war £1000.

19. The present level of tuition fees charged at Fitzwilliam House is well below the level of fees charged by the Colleges generally. If the proposals contained in the previous paragraph were approved the Board would be prepared at a suitable point, in virtue of actual or projected improvements in the amenities offered to non-collegiate students, to propose increases in the fee for direction of studies (10s. 6d. a term) to a rate not exceeding five guineas a term (to cover a substantial part of the cost of tutorial services) and to propose that non-collegiate Research Students be charged a tuition fee of, say, two and a half guineas a year if they are graduates of this University, and a little more if they are not. This course of action would enable the Board to make further provision for additional expenditure.

The Board approved their Report on 5 March; and in view of their second request the Council referred the Report to the Financial Board. On 5 May the Registrary told the Censor that the Council had agreed to appoint a committee on which the Council, the Financial Board and the Non-Collegiate Students Board would be represented, whose terms of reference would be 'to consider in the light of Grace 2 of 17 June 1952 the present and future position of Fitzwilliam House and its finances as a whole, and to consider also the possible development and expansion of the present site of Fitzwilliam House with leave to consult an architect'.[1] The committee was constituted by the end of the Easter term 1953, and presented two Reports. The first, dated 24 December 1953, was before the Council at their first meeting of the following term, and was concerned with two matters in need of immediate attention, on which the Council had sought the committee's advice: the appointment of a successor to the Censor, who was due to retire under the age-limit on 30 September 1954, and the question of student numbers at Fitzwilliam House. The committee took the view that no appointment should

---

[1] Policy File 1951–   . Letter dated 5 May 1953 from the Registrary to the Censor.

  Its members were the Rt Hon. H. U. Willink (Vice-Chancellor), Sir Lionel Whitby, and Mr L. P. Wilkinson (Council of the Senate); the Rev. J. S. Boys Smith, Mr E. P. Weller, and Mr A. E. L. Parnis (Financial Board); Mr S. C. Roberts, Professor F. G. Young, and Dr R. C. Evans (Non-Collegiate Students Board).

be made to the censorship until the University's policy on the future of Fitzwilliam House had been determined, and recommended that, on his retirement, Mr Thatcher should be asked to perform for one year the duties appertaining to the censorship. On the question of numbers, the members of the committee were all agreed that some reduction was necessary, at least for so long as the facilities at Fitzwilliam House remained as they were, and they recommended that the Non-Collegiate Students Board should be asked to reduce their admissions from October 1954, especially the admission of those described as 'ordinary undergraduates', to a figure that would be appropriate to a student body of 300, excluding members of the attached houses of residence. (The committee recognized that an eventual reduction to a total of 300 must take some time.) The Council accepted these recommendations, and gave effect to them.[1]

The Committee's second Report, dated 22 February 1954 and laid before the Council on 1 March, was a more substantial, and, as they had anticipated, a much more controversial document. It opens with a summary of the Council's Report of 26 May 1952 on the future of Fitzwilliam House, with its very guarded recommendation that the University should approve the policy of encouraging the corporate life of the House by providing new administrative headquarters and residential accommodation – a recommendation which did indeed secure approval for the policy, but, as the committee observed, made its implementation dependent on a condition difficult of fulfilment. The committee then referred to the Non-Collegiate Students Board's Report to the Council of March 1953, with its protest that matters could no longer be allowed to remain as they were, and its request that the Council should arrange for their urgent consideration – a request that had led to their own appointment. 'The Special Committee' [they said] 'have taken their terms of reference as a direction to review as a whole, and in the light of all relevant considerations, the University's policy with regard to Fitzwilliam House, with a view to an early and conclusive definition of a practicable policy.'

The Special Committee were satisfied that the buildings of Fitzwilliam House were quite inadequate for a student population of 400 (as it then was); and they believed that the development of the site to provide adequately for one of 300 would cost some £40,000, in addition to the heavy cost of further land that would be needed. But it was not primarily on grounds of expense that the committee based their recom-

---

[1]   Council of the Senate papers for 18 January 1954; also Minutes of the Non-Collegiate Students Board of 25 February 1954.

mendations on the subject of the size, and the nature, of the non-collegiate student body. They acknowledged the claims of members of the attached houses of residence for admission, and were agreed that they should not be counted in any total that might be fixed. They reminded the Council of the view, expressed in 1934 by the Syndicate on houses of residence, that Fitzwilliam House should in general be required to accept applications for admission from research students approved by the Board of Research Studies, and in re-affirming this as a principle to be followed they recommended that the non-collegiate student body should contain up to eighty research students in residence. The committee also recommended that the House should be required to admit some forty-five candidates for diplomas and other post-graduate courses, because the introduction of these new types of study might otherwise be hampered by what they described as a reasonable hesitation on the part of colleges to adjust their admissions policy to take account of them. It was, however, on the policy that should govern the admission of undergraduates that the committee made their most significant pronouncement:

> 20. The University is essentially collegiate in character, and special reasons are necessary to justify it in continuing to maintain a non-collegiate student body similar in composition to those of the Colleges. Such reasons, as the Special Committee have indicated above, are available to justify the maintenance of a non-collegiate body of Research Students and candidates for Diplomas and the like; for the maintenance of an undergraduate non-collegiate body cogent reasons have existed in the past, but it is less clear that they continue to exist. Such a reason has been the desirability of making provision for poor students – perhaps the fundamental *raison d'être* of the non-collegiate body in the past. Such provision, however, is now freely made in other ways, by the grant by central and local government authorities of awards of sufficient value to maintain their holders at the Colleges. The cost of living has risen more than have fees for instruction and the like, and cannot now be much less for members of Fitzwilliam House than for members of a College; and it is, indeed, possible that a poor man who is state-aided will fare better financially at certain of the Colleges than he would at Fitzwilliam House.

> 21. Another reason for maintaining a non-collegiate undergraduate body has in the past been the existence of a substantial number of candidates of the necessary quality who, if not admitted as non-collegiate students, would not have been able to go to a University. The strength of this argument has been much reduced by the increase in the number of undergraduates accepted by the Colleges and by the development of the civic Universities. It is true that the experience of the Colleges themselves suggests that a number of candidates are refused admission who could be

admitted without any lowering of standards. It does not, however, necessarily follow that any obligation rests on this University to make it possible for them to be admitted without regard to vacancies available at other Universities, especially if, as some believe, this University has for the present at least grown in numbers as much as it safely can without the loss of the characteristics that make it what it is.

On these grounds the committee recommended that, with certain limited exceptions, the University should cease to provide for a noncollegiate undergraduate body. The exceptions, about seventy-five in number, might include, if they had special reasons for pursuing their studies in Cambridge, men above the normal undergraduate age to whom collegiate life might not be attractive; men employed in Cambridge wishing to read for a degree in their spare time; married men; and students from other countries residing for one academical year or less. The committee made it plain that in their proposed student body of 200 they assigned their highest priority to the research students, and that they attached least importance to the undergraduates. They were fully aware that they were proposing that Fitzwilliam House should become a predominantly graduate society, which would not need the residential accommodation approved in principle in 1952, and for which they proposed by way of new administrative headquarters no more than a modification of the existing buildings at a cost of about £10,000. They would be glad, they said, to shew the Non-Collegiate Students Board drawings which their architect had supplied, and to formulate with the Board proposals for the work.[1]

The committee were not wide of the mark in describing their proposals as controversial, and they did not manage to submit an agreed Report to the Council. Two of the three representatives of the Non-Collegiate Students Board (Mr S. C. Roberts and Dr R. C. Evans) appended to the majority Report a forthright comment of their own, in which they stated that their principal reason for not signing the Report was that its recommendations sought not to modify, but to reverse, on grounds other than those of finance, a policy proposed by the Council and approved by the University nearly two years previously, without criticism or opposition, subject to its financial viability. 'We find it difficult to understand' [they said] 'how the policy of encouraging the corporate life of Fitzwilliam House can be interpreted to apply only to activities and amenities of graduate students; and the proposed elimination of the "normal" undergraduates who have been largely responsible for the corporate life which at present exists appears to us to be a

[1] Council of the Senate papers for 1 March 1954.

flat denial of the undertaking given by the Council and endorsed by the University.'

The Special Committee's recommendations about the size and composition of the non-collegiate body appear to have met with a frosty reception in the Council, for, having received the Report on 1 March and adjourned its discussion at two meetings, they gave their unanimous approval on 15 March to a motion by Mr S. C. Roberts, seconded by Sir Henry Thirkill, that the committee's proposal to confine undergraduate members of Fitzwilliam House to the classes specified be rejected; and authorized Mr Roberts, as Chairman of the Non-Collegiate Students' Board, to inform Mr Thatcher, in confidence, of their decision.[1] On 3 May the Council also concluded, without prejudice to wider issues still under examination, that it was desirable that improvements should be made in the Fitzwilliam House buildings, even if only to make them more useful to a new occupier if the House were to move.[2] Accordingly, the architect's sketch plans were submitted to the Non-Collegiate Students Board with a request that they would inform the Council whether they were willing for them to be put before the University. On 27 May the Board asked their Chairman to draft a reply to the effect that they observed that the architect had confined his recommendations to the House itself, and had not considered adjacent property mentioned in their Report to the Council, and that while they were prepared to admit that he had made the most of this restricted opportunity, more fundamental changes were needed.[3]

In the meantime, with the Council's consideration of the Board's Report and of the Second Report of their own committee still incomplete, events had taken a new turn. When they resolved that there should be no immediate appointment of a successor to the Censor, the Council published, on 3 March 1954, a notice to that effect in which they also said that, with the Financial Board and the Non-Collegiate Students Board, they had under consideration certain important questions relating to the future of Fitzwilliam House.[4] From another notice published in the *Cambridge Review* three days later, it would seem that there was in the University at large no little speculation – not far wide of the mark – about the deliberations of the Council and their committee.

1   Minutes of the Council of the Senate, 15 March 1954.
2   *Ibid.*, 3 May 1954.
3   Minutes, 27 May 1954, and, for the Board's letter of 1 June, Policy File 1951– .
4   *University Reporter*, 1953–54, p. 882.

Alarm over the future of Fitzwilliam House [said the *Review*] is premature. The many Fitzwilliam supporters whose voices have recently been heard raised in indignant anticipation of impending disaster would do well to await the publication of the Council's report. It is unlikely that even the Council could be so foolish or so out of touch with University opinion as to put forward any proposals for liquidating an institution which for many years has played such a useful part in the University. Fears might, however, be justifiably entertained if there were any truth in the rumour that the Censor himself is being excluded from the present deliberations of the Council's Committee. What is, and has been for some time apparent, is that the authorities at Fitzwilliam House are in general kept too much in the dark over their own affairs. The University awaits the Council's report with lively expectation.[1]

The fears of the writer will not have been allayed by a letter, of the same date, addressed to him by the Censor, who wrote:

Sir,

Your paragraph in 'News and Notes'. Apart from being with the Special Committee for half an hour at the very beginning of their enquiry months ago, neither myself nor my colleagues have been present at any of the deliberations. Nothing has been mentioned throughout these deliberations to the Board, although three members of the Board are on the Special Committee. I know as much about what is going on in all this long enquiry as you do or as the undergraduate member of Fitzwilliam House knows.[2]

The Council's decision to authorize Mr Roberts to inform the Censor in confidence of their rejection of their committee's recommendations about the composition of his student body was doubtless inspired, at least in part, by the prevalence of rumours that the Special Committee was likely to be unfavourable to the continued existence of Fitzwilliam House as an undergraduate institution, and these same rumours may also have influenced a group of teachers of the non-collegiate students to write to the Censor on March 17th:

We are distressed at the reports about the future of Fitzwilliam House, reports extremely damaging to the morale of the House. We are sure that you will share our anxiety, and can promise you whole-hearted support in any move to counter attacks on the House.

There is a very great measure of goodwill towards Fitzwilliam House in this matter, and we all believe that a move towards full collegiate status would receive wide backing in the University. We are therefore writing to ask if we might meet yourself and your staff on, say, Tuesday or Wed-

1   *Cambridge Review*, 1953–54, p. 358.
2   Independence File.

nesday next, March 23rd or 24th, so that we may make a concerted effort to ensure the future well-being of Fitzwilliam House.

If you should feel able to discuss this with us, could you kindly let Mr Rupp know what time would be convenient to yourself and your staff?[1]

This letter is noteworthy in that it contains what appears to be the first recorded reference to full collegiate status as an objective for the non-collegiate institution; and it is reasonable to suppose that it was written after informal consultation with the officers of Fitzwilliam House, who may have hesitated, at this stage, to play any leading part in advocating so pronounced a change of policy, particularly as this had not been put forward by their Non-Collegiate Students Board. However this may have been, Thatcher welcomed the initiative taken by his colleagues, and at a meeting held on 24 March (also attended by the Assistant Censor), having told them that the Council's committee were believed not to have reached agreement, he invited their views.[2] The idea was then developed that whereas proposals for the advancement of the non-collegiate institution had previously been on the basis that it should remain a responsibility of the University, which would mean that it would always be likely to be in competition with other departments for the insufficient funds at the University's disposal, it might be better to seek independent status for the House, which would then be responsible for its own finances. Its beginnings would be modest; but of the benefits of independence there could be no doubt, and an autonomous body might well prove more attractive to potential benefactors than a University department.

At this meeting it was agreed that a short historical account should be prepared of the development of Fitzwilliam House, and of the part it had played in the University; and, subject to advice from the Master of Pembroke, it was resolved to hold a further meeting on 7 April, to be attended by the Heads of the attached houses of residence, by representatives of the Fitzwilliam Society, by Directors of Studies and Fitzwilliam graduates in University office, with the idea of constituting a committee to support the officers in such representations as they might make to the Non-Collegiate Students Board. At this further meeting, which invited members of the Fitzwilliam Society were unable to attend, suggestions were put forward for the submission of a memorial to the Council of the Senate on the future of Fitzwilliam House, and a

---

1   *Ibid.* This letter bore the following signatures: Gordon Rupp, C. L. Wayper, R. W. Haywood, A. Hyde, D. J. P. Wood, B. M. Herbertson, and R. Kelly. All were Directors of Studies save Dr Wood (University Demonstrator in Geography).
2   See Minute Book of a 'Negotiating Committee'. (College Archives).

committee of six, known as the Acting Committee (all Directors of Studies), was appointed under the chairmanship of Mr R. W. Haywood, University Lecturer in Engineering, and President of the Fitzwilliam Society in 1954–55.[1] The committee lost no time, for Mr Haywood, in company with the Censor and the Assistant Censor, presented the Memorial to the Vice-Chancellor at his Lodge on 30 April. The Council of the Senate received it on 3 May, with copies of a letter from Mr Roberts, as Chairman of the Non-Collegiate Students Board, and of a memorandum on the history of the non-collegiate institution. Through the good offices of Mr F. J. Stratton (B.A. 1932), a past President of the Fitzwilliam Society, sufficient copies were printed of this memorandum for immediate circulation to the Regent House, and to Fitzwilliam undergraduates, and for eventual dispatch to all past members of the House. Mr Robert's letter, written by agreement of the Non-Collegiate Students Board after they had received copies of the Memorial, informed the Vice-Chancellor that the Board, recognizing that the suggestions made in the Memorial were different from those contained in the Board's Report of 5 March 1953, were very willing for the consideration of that Report to be put into abeyance, and would welcome a conference between members of the Council and representatives of senior members of the House and of the Fitzwilliam Society.[2]

The decisive rejection by the Council of the recommendations contained in the majority Report of their Special Committee marks the end of a critical period in the history of Fitzwilliam House, and the beginning of a chain of events culminating in the approval by the Queen in Council in 1966 of a Charter and Statutes for Fitzwilliam College as an autonomous foundation.

When, in March 1954, the Council decided, against the advice of their committee, to re-affirm their earlier policy of encouraging the corporate life of Fitzwilliam House, they acted without delay, and to such purpose that whereas in the Lent term some of their number, at least, had contemplated the suppression of the University's non-collegiate institution as a place of undergraduate education, in the following June the Council were seeking advice about possible ways in which the University might lawfully assist the House, if it became an indepen-

---

[1] In a note, written in 1959, on the history of the Negotiating Committee, Mr R. N. Walters stated that the Acting Committee was set up to deal with the whole matter of the possible development of Fitzwilliam House. The minutes of this meeting of 7 April make no mention of the terms of reference of the Acting Committee, all of whose members had signed the letter of 17 March.

[2] Minutes, 29 April 1954.

dent foundation, from University funds. In this climate of opinion, the initiative of Mr Thatcher and his colleagues had been well timed, for the Council might reasonably be expected to receive with favour a document which, with its new approach to the problem of the future of Fitzwilliam House, might suggest a way round the financial difficulties of a policy already approved in principle.

The subscribers to the address presented to the Vice-Chancellor, thenceforth known as 'The Memorialists', took as their card of entry into the University's discussion of a policy for the future of Fitzwilliam House the Council's notice published on 3 March.

Having only recently become aware, [they said] as the result of the announcement in the Reporter of 3 March, 1954, that the Council of the Senate is considering the future of Fitzwilliam House, we beg leave to request that, in the present deliberations on the development of the House, consideration may be given to the views presented in this memorial.

We have given exhaustive consideration to the problem of the development of Fitzwilliam House in the light of the Report of the Council of the Senate of 26 May, 1952. Whilst the University found it necessary, in 1869, to set up a body for the administration of Non-Collegiate Students, the change in social conditions since that time has resulted in the virtual disappearance of that class of undergraduate for whom the scheme originally catered. Parallel with this development, Fitzwilliam House has evolved over the years, gradually establishing a distinctive tradition which the University has recognized, particularly in the Grace of 17 June, 1952, when approval was given to the policy of encouraging the corporate life of the House.

It is our considered conclusion that, with the fuller provision of public money, lack of means no longer prevents men from taking a full part in University life, so that it is more than ever necessary that Fitzwilliam House must offer to its members all the advantages of a college if it is to continue to play a worthy role within the University. We believe that the time is opportune for a decisive step to be taken towards self-government for the House. Without this, no provision of material amenities, on however lavish a scale, would enable the House to retain the academic and administrative services of its more distinguished graduates. Furthermore if, under present conditions, the House is to attract able men in the numbers which it has in the past, it will be vital to endow open awards, and ultimately, offer residence to the same extent as the Colleges. As the result of enquiry we find that identical views are held by the officers of substantial local education authorities throughout the country.

In order that both the University and the House should be enabled to make the best possible contribution to the fulfilment of these aims, we suggest that, within the very much larger body which enjoys the corporate life of Fitzwilliam House, administrative provision could be made for undergraduates and research students desiring purely non-collegiate facilities in accordance with the provisions of the original Statute of 1869. This would enable the former[1] group, and the members of the Attached Houses, to be *administered* by the House on behalf of the Non-Collegiate Students Board, whilst Fitzwilliam House itself could then develop as a completely autonomous body.

We are of the opinion that if there were a firm declaration that it was the policy of the University to recognise the House in the near future as an Approved Foundation, enjoying self-government and financial independence, then funds for the provision of open awards and for buildings would be forthcoming, not only from the former members of the House, but also, given University support for a public appeal, from other benefactors. We further believe that the initiation of such a policy would be greatly facilitated if there could be consultation between the Council of the Senate and senior members of the House and of the Fitzwilliam Society.

We submit these proposals for the consideration of the Council of the Senate with the greater confidence in that they would, if implemented, relieve the University of a financial responsibility at a time when there are very heavy calls upon its resources. Moreover, the collegiate system is, in our view, one of the most effective remedies for the excessive departmentalism of unrelated specialists which has to some extent characterised recent University development. The corporate solidarity necessary for the successful establishment and growth of a new collegiate body cannot, however, be fostered artificially. On the other hand Fitzwilliam House has arrived at that stage in its development at which the grant of self-government would give recognition of its maturity, since, in face of the greatest obstacles, it has developed a vigorous corporate life and a loyalty to its traditions equal to that of any Society in the University. In developing along collegiate lines, the House could therefore make a most valuable contribution to the life of the University.

In concluding, we wish to make clear that an independent Fitzwilliam House, while offering to the great majority of its members amenities in return for increased fees, could also admit to membership, at a lower fee than at present and without entitlement to more than administrative services, members of the Attached Houses and any other undergraduates or research students who do not desire the full collegiate life.

We appreciate that it may not be possible for the Council of the Senate to present a matter of this moment to the University as a statement of declared policy. In that event, we request that the substance of this prayer may be included in a Report presented to the University for discussion in

---

[1] For 'former' read 'latter'.

the Regent House, so that the feeling of the University on this question may be ascertained prior to any decision on the future of Fitzwilliam House.

LIST OF SIGNATORIES

Fitzwilliam House

W. S. Thatcher, M.C., M.A. (Fitzw.), Censor.

W. W. Williams, M.A. (Fitzw.), Bursar.

R. N. Walters, M.A. (Jes. and Fitzw.), Tutor.

Attached Houses

W. A. L. Elmslie, D.D. (Chr.), Principal, Westminster College.

W. F. Flemington, B.D. (Jes. and Fitzw.), Acting Principal, Wesley House.

A. Victor Murray, B.D. (Joh.), President, Cheshunt College.

E. Gordon Rupp, B.D. (Fitzw.), Wesley House, and Director of Studies in Theology, Fitzw. H.

The Fitzwilliam Society

E. Saville Peck, D.L., M.A., President.

J. R. W. Alexander, C.B.E., M.A., LL.B., Vice-President.

G. Granville Sharp, Q.C., B.A., LL.B., Vice-President.

F. J. Stratton, C.B.E., M.A., Past-President.

P. Dunsheath, C.B.E., M.A., Trustee.

J. W. Whitlock, J.P., M.A., LL.B., Trustee.

G. Milner Walton, M.A., Secretary.

E. J. Saunders, M.A., Cambridge Secretary.

Resident Members and Directors of Studies of Fitzwilliam House

John Wisdom, M.A. (Trin. & Fitzw.) Professor of Philosophy.

L. C. Harmer, M.A., Ph.D. (Trin. & Fitzw.), Draper's Professor of French.

H. R. Mallett, M.A. (Fitzw.), Mayor Designate of Cambridge and County Councillor.

A. C. Taylor, T.D., M.A. (Fitzw.), City Alderman of Cambridge and County Councillor.

W. G. Points, M.A. (Fitzw.), City Councillor of Cambridge.

C. L. Wayper, M.A., Ph.D. (Cath.), Director in History.

J. B. Whitworth, Ph.D. (Sid.), Director in Natural Sciences.

R. Kelly, M.A. (Tr.H.), Director in Modern Languages.

A. Hyde, M.A. (Fitzw.), Director in Geography.

R. A. Lyttleton, M.A., Ph.D. (Joh.), Director in Mathematics.

S. Dickinson, M.A. (Emm.), Director in Agriculture.

R. W. Haywood, M.A. (Fitzw.), Director in Mechanical Sciences.

B. M. Herbertson, M.A. (Magd.), Director in Medicine.

J. W. Cecil Turner, M.A., LL.B. (Tr.H.), Director in Law.

Margaret M. Braithwaite, M.A. (Newn.), Director in Moral Science.

P. A. Tranchell, M.A., Mus.B. (King's), Director in Music.

D. P. J. Wood, M.A., Ph.D. (Fitzw.), University Demonstrator in Geography.

Members of the Senate

R. Corboy, M.A. (Chr.), Rector, St Edmund's House.

Cecil B. Hurry, M.A. (Trin., Sid. & Fitzw.).

F. W. R. Cowles, M.A. (Fitzw.).

H. Humm, M.A. (Fitzw.).

G. E. R. Brownson, M.A. (Fitzw.).

E. R. Cro, M.A. (Fitzw.).

W. F. Grant, M.A. (Fitzw.).

L. J. M. Coleby, M.A. (Fitzw.).

D. F. Osborne Doyle, M.A. (Fitzw.).

Eric E. Douglas-Smith, M.A. (Fitzw.).

Norman St John Stevas, M.A. (Fitzw.).

R. Zdanowich, M.A. (Fitzw.).

W. J. M. Dennis, M.A. (Fitzw.).

C. J. B. Gaskoin, M.A. (Jes. & Fitzw.).

D. G. Crane, M.A. (Fitzw.).

W. P. M. Katz, Ph.D. (Fitzw.).

T. C. Walters, M.A. (Fitzw.).

F. C. D. Swann, M.A. (Fitzw.).

J. A. Horvat, M.A., Ph.D. (Fitzw.).

R. P. Thorne, M.A. (Fitzw.).

F. I. G. Rawlins, M.Sc. (Trin.).

L. J. Gamlin, M.A. (Fitzw.).

J. A. W. Sainsbury, M.A., LL.B. (Fitzw.).

R. Openshaw, M.A. (Fitzw.).

W. H. Palmer, M.A. (Fitzw.).

H. A. Schlossmann, M.Sc. (Fitzw.).

Members of Fitzwilliam House not Members of the Senate

T. H. Martin, B.A. (Fitzw.).

Ingram J. Lindner, Q.C., B.A., LL.B. (Fitzw.).

Robert S. Ball, M.A. Honoris Causa (Fitzw.).

ADDITIONAL SIGNATURES RECEIVED ON SEPARATE COPIES OF THE MEMORIAL

Members of the Senate

W. B. Reddaway, M.A. (Cla.).

T. F. Reddaway, M.A., F.S.A., F.R.Hist.S. (King's & Fitzw.).

K. W. Reddaway, M.A. (Girton).

J. Lough, M.A., Ph.D. (Joh.), Professor of French in the University of Durham.

Robt. J. Cobb, M.A. (Fitzw.), Past-President, The Fitzwilliam Soc.

H. T. England, M.A. (Fitzw.), Past-President, The Fitzwilliam Soc.

C. H. Watson, M.A. (Fitzw.), Past-President, The Fitzwilliam Soc.

S. J. Bach, Ph.D. (Fitzw.).

Alan Hadfield, M.A. (Fitzw.).

A. L. Ireson, M.A. (Fitzw.).

D. W. Markwick, M.A., LL.B. (Fitzw.).

E. F. R. Stearn, M.A. (Fitzw.).

Members of Fitzwilliam House not Members of the Senate

J. C. C. Slater, B.A. (Fitzw.), Past-President, The Fitzwilliam Soc.

Brian M. Jones, B.A. (Fitzw.).

Graham Montague Jones, B.A. Fitzw.).

A. E. Silvester, B.A. (Fitzw.).

Received late

H. H. Weil, M.A., Ph.D. (Fitzw.).

G. W. Barman, M.A. (Fitzw.).[1]

The Council at once agreed that there might be discussions with the senior members of the House and representatives of the Fitzwilliam Society, and a meeting was arranged for 24 May, at which no important new issues were raised, except that the Memorialists expressed their

[1] See *Journal* for December 1954, pp. 15–18.

hopes that if a new college came into being the University might find it possible to treat it generously, either by the grant of a loan, or by the gift or sale at a nominal price of the buildings in Trumpington Street in its ownership. Also, in reply to a suggestion that there might be an intermediate stage at which the House, though still a department of the University, might be afforded a greater measure of autonomy, they made it clear that they attached so much importance to the immediate acceptance of full independence as an objective that they could not see that any half measures would serve a useful purpose.[1] Shortly after this meeting the Council authorized the Vice-Chancellor to inform the Memorialists that they were considering their proposals with great sympathy; and on 3 August Mr Haywood received a letter from the Registry setting forth the principal conclusions reached by the Council:

(1) that it would be reasonable to seek the opinion of the University on the general proposition that steps should be taken to abolish the non-collegiate status provided that there could be established a new autonomous Recognized Institution which would be limited in size and would be bound to take over certain functions now performed by Fitzwilliam House;

(2) that consideration of the question whether and to what extent the Council might recommend the University to contribute to the endowment of a new autonomous institution must be deferred until the University's agreement has been obtained to the general proposition. Before recommending the University to approve any gift of money, land, or buildings that it might be possible for it to make, the Council would need to be satisfied that sufficient endowment had been or would be received from other sources to ensure the long-term financial stability of the institution.

The Registry added that if action on the lines of these conclusions was agreeable to the Memorialists, and if the general proposition were accepted by the University, the Council would await the submission of a detailed scheme for the conversion of Fitzwilliam House to an autonomous institution, but would be prepared to appoint a committee to confer with the Memorialists and to act as a channel of communication between them and the Council.[2]

One feature of the negotiations conducted in the Easter term 1954 had been the active part played in them by certain members of the Fitzwilliam Society, to whom, at a time when the future of the House was

[1]   See Independence File for a note of this meeting presented to the Council of the Senate on 31 May. The Council were represented by the Vice-Chancellor, the Master of Pembroke (Mr S. C. Roberts), the Master of St John's (the Rev. J. S. Boys Smith), Mr H. C. Whalley-Tooker, and Mr C. L. G. Pratt; and the Memorialists by Messrs F. J. Stratton, J. R. W. Alexander, R. W. Haywood, I. J. Lindner, and J. W. Whitlock, with the Censor and the Assistant Censor.   [2]   *Ibid.*

still very uncertain, Mr Thatcher had turned for advice and help. Thatcher himself, writing for the *Fitzwilliam Journal* (December 1954) drew particular attention to the leadership of Mr Stratton, as Chairman of the joint group of Cambridge and London representatives, and its spokesman in discussions with representatives of the Council of the Senate.[1]

The Registrary's letter of 3 August was evidence enough both of what had been achieved, in a surprisingly short time, and, not less, of what remained to be done; and on receiving it Mr Haywood's Acting Committee resolved, at a meeting held on 16 September, that the value of the services rendered by the 'London members' (as they came to be called) in the discussions with the Council representatives should be more formally acknowledged, and future business expedited, by their appointment to the committee, together with Mr F. I. G. Rawlins and the officers of the House.[2] This larger body, thenceforth known as the Negotiating Committee, had Mr Stratton as its Chairman, and as its secretary Mr Haywood, until his resignation in February 1955, when he was succeeded by Mr R. N. Walters.

On 25 September the Negotiating Committee were able to send the Registrary their reply, from which it appears that they found no difficulty in accepting the conditions under which the Council were prepared to seek the University's approval of the termination of the non-collegiate system, their only reservation being that they hoped that the Council would be willing to recommend the approval of Fitzwilliam House not as a Recognized Institution, but as an Approved Foundation. By University statute the terms under which a Recognized Institution received recognition could be varied without its consent, and this, the committee felt, might make it much less attractive to possible benefactors. They also thought that in virtue of its history and its traditions the House merited Approved Foundation status.[3] Mr Roberts made the same point, quite independently, in a letter written to the Registrary some weeks later, when he was given the opportunity of commenting on a draft Second Report of the Council of the Senate on the future of Fitzwilliam House. 'I feel in general', he wrote (from America), 'that "Approved Foundation" is more suitable. After all,

---

[1] *Journal*, December 1954, p. 24.
[2] Negotiating Committee minutes. The reconstituted Committee thereupon consisted of the five 'London members' (Alexander, Lindner, Rawlins, Stratton, and Whitlock), and, from Cambridge, of Thatcher, Williams, and Walters, with eight Directors of Studies: Dickinson, Haywood, Hyde, Kelly, Lyttleton, Rupp, Wayper, and Whitworth; and Wood (University Demonstrator in Geography).
[3] *Ibid.*

Fitzwilliam House has been an institution, not merely recognised by, but belonging to, the University for many years, and to "recognise" it now strikes me as slightly absurd. "Foundation" seems to me to emphasise the proposed change of status much more clearly.'[1] By the time Mr Roberts's letter was received, the Council had conceded the point. Their Report of 25 October summarizes the history of the Council's deliberations on the subject since May 1952, and sets out fully the reasons which had led them to propose the ending of the non-collegiate system, and the conditions attached to their proposals.[2] At the Discussion held on 16 November there was no criticism of the Report, which was welcomed by Mr Thatcher; and by Dr R. C. Evans, in a graceful tribute to Thatcher's unwavering pursuit, throughout the thirty long years of his censorship, of an objective brought encouragingly nearer by the Council's proposals. The Report, approved by Grace 5 of 27 November 1954, is a landmark in the history of the non-collegiate institution of the University:

1. The Council have for some years been much concerned about the future of Fitzwilliam House. On the one hand, they believe that it is important to encourage the corporate life of the House by the provision of new administrative headquarters and, if possible, some residential accommodation. On the other hand, they have been unable to recommend or to form any idea of when they will be able to recommend the allocation from University funds of the considerable sum of money that would be needed for the implementation of such a policy.

2. By Grace 2 of 17 June 1952 the Regent House approved the following recommendation made by the Council in their Report, dated 26 May 1952, on the future of Fitzwilliam House (*Reporter*, 1951–52, p. 1336):

> That the general approval of the University be given to the policy of encouraging the corporate life of Fitzwilliam House by the provision of new administrative headquarters and residential accommodation, but that such provision be dependent upon the approval by the Regent House of a Grace proposed by the Council of the Senate after receiving an assurance from the Financial Board that the financial circumstances of the University allow it.

In March 1953 the Council received from the Non-Collegiate Students Board a Report which referred to the fact that the Council clearly envisaged a substantial interval before the University's policy could be implemented, and indeed had said that they could not long be allowed to remain as they were and requested the Council to consider the future of

---

[1] Letter dated 27 October 1954.
[2] *University Reporter*, 1954–55, p. 281. For Discussion see p. 435, and for approval p. 449.

Fitzwilliam House as a matter of urgency. The Council accordingly appointed a Committee with the following terms of reference: 'to consider in the light of Grace 2 of 17 June 1952 the present and future position of Fitzwilliam House and its finances as a whole, and to consider also the possible development and expansion of the present site of Fitzwilliam House with leave to consult an architect.' The Committee, after a full survey of the position, reported to the Council making certain recommendations, which were not unanimous, for an adaptation of the present buildings of Fitzwilliam House which would make them reasonably convenient, but only provided that the student population of Fitzwilliam House was substantially reduced.

3. While the Committee's Report was under consideration the Council received a 'Memorial in regard to the development of Fitzwilliam House' signed by many past and present members of Fitzwilliam House and other members of the Senate. The purpose of the Memorial was to ask the Council to bring before the University for discussion, if not for immediate decision, a proposal that the future development of Fitzwilliam House should be on the basis of an autonomous institution recognized by the University, not on the basis of an institution for non-collegiate students administered by the University. The proposal was made on three main grounds. First the original purpose for which arrangements were made for admitting to membership of the University persons who were not members of Colleges no longer exists; changes in social conditions and the availability of assistance to students from public funds have removed the class of undergraduates who, though unable to meet the expense of membership of a College, could afford to come to Cambridge as Non-Collegiate Students. Secondly, there are and will continue to be students in excess of the number that can be provided for by the existing Colleges but equally well qualified for admission to Cambridge. For such students in a collegiate University non-collegiate status is neither adequate nor justifiable; if they are held to be worthy of admission to the University they should have the same status, and, as far as possible, the same advantages as other members of the University. Thirdly, Fitzwilliam House, in the face of the greatest obstacles, has developed a vigorous corporate life and a loyalty to its tradition equal to that of any society in the University. It has arrived at that stage in its development at which the grant of self-government would give recognition of its maturity. Even the availability of more adequate accommodation would not enable it to overcome the handicap that is imposed by apparently lower status, but if it could in future develop as an autonomous institution on collegiate lines it could more effectively than ever further the interests of the University and contribute to its life.

4. The Council's consideration of the problem had previously been on the assumption, clearly stated in their Report of May 1952, that Fitzwilliam House would remain an institution controlled and administered by the University. The Council thought that the University should maintain an

institution through which provision could be made for certain classes of students for whom membership of the University was desirable but could not be attained by admission to Colleges. Examination of the Memorial has, however, convinced them that the aims of the Memorialists are not inconsistent with the Council's purpose, and that the functions which have been performed by a Non-Collegiate institution could, in so far as they are still required, be performed with greater success by an autonomous institution which was prepared to accept certain special obligations.

5. In so far as candidates for the B.A. Degree are concerned, the Council are satisfied that there is no longer any need to maintain an institution under the control of the University to provide for students for whom it would be impracticable to apply for admission to Colleges, and they agree that the establishment of an autonomous institution for the accommodation of a number of such students not exceeding the number now admitted as Non-Collegiate Students, would be to the advantage, not only of the men concerned, but also of the University. The Council would not, however, be willing to recommend the recognition of a new autonomous institution for men unless it were so constituted as to make it possible to dispense altogether with Non-Collegiate status. A considerable proportion of the body of Non-Collegiate Students consists of Research Students approved by the Board of Research Studies but in excess of the capacity of the Colleges, and of members of certain Houses of Residence recognized by Grace. The Council are agreed that it would not be in the interests of the University to sponsor any development of Fitzwilliam House which would have an adverse effect on the interests of these classes of student, but they recognize that an autonomous institution could not be required to admit them unless such obligation were laid upon it by the terms of its own Instrument of Foundation. The Memorialists were well aware of this problem. They indicated that, in their view, an independent institution could make the necessary provision, and the Council have ascertained in discussion with their representatives that the propsed institution would accept as one of the terms of its Instrument of Foundation an obligation to admit or place on its books Research Students recommended by the Board of Research Studies and such members of Houses of Residence recognized by Grace as wished and were qualified to matriculate.

6. The Council are aware that the conversion of Fitzwilliam House from an institution under the control of the University to an independent body would not in itself solve the problems which are raised by lack of suitable accommodation. They agree, however, with the Memorialists in thinking that it might make those problems easier of solution. The essential difficulty is financial. The University, with many strong claims on its own limited resources, would not be in a position to find the large sums that would be needed for the building and equipment of adequate premises for Non-Collegiate Students, unless they were to a large extent derived from outside. An appeal for money by the University for this purpose

might well be unsuccessful, since there is a strong feeling among those who are most interested in Fitzwilliam House that the status of the institution should be advanced, and that such advance might be hindered rather than furthered if its present status as a Non-Collegiate institution were, as it were, confirmed by the expenditure of a large sum of money. Furthermore, even if the money were forthcoming, it might be very difficult, if not impossible, for the University to give to buildings for Fitzwilliam House priority over other urgent University building claims, for instance, the development of the Sidgwick Avenue Site and new buildings for the University Library. The amount of money that would be needed by an autonomous institution would, it is true, be even greater, for such an institution would ultimately, if not immediately, need endowment for the provision of Fellowships and Scholarships as well as money for buildings, and the Memorialists do not imagine that all that would be needed would be forthcoming at once. But they are convinced that an appeal for funds issued by or on behalf of an institution which had or was promised independence and had every prospect at no distant date of becoming a College in the University would be much more successful than an appeal for funds to re-equip Fitzwilliam House as an institution for Non-Collegiate Students. There is the further point that any building scheme that might be financially possible would not, if it were promoted by an autonomous institution, be in direct competition with University building schemes.

7. The present policy of the University is to improve, as financial circumstances may permit, the conditions in which Fitzwilliam House is administered as an institution for Non-Collegiate Students under the control of the University. This policy, as has been indicated, raises great difficulties and offers no prospect of meeting urgent needs except at the cost of measures which the Council believe would be unacceptable to the staff and the members, past and present, of Fitzwilliam House itself. The Council therefore welcome a new approach to the problem, and in view of what is said in the preceding paragraphs they think that the Regent House may wish to substitute for the policy which they approved in 1952 a policy, which, if it proved to be practicable, might achieve better objectives and achieve them not only with less difficulty and delay but also with the full support of those who are most intimately concerned with the fortunes of Fitzwilliam House. The Council are not at this stage asking the University to agree to recognize a particular autonomous institution. Recognition must clearly await detailed information about the constitution, objectives, and finances of the institution which seeks it. Responsibility for formulating detailed proposals and for securing the necessary financial support will fall on the sponsors, but the Council think that it would be unreasonable to expect them to embark on these tasks until they can be assured that the University would be willing to seek power to terminate the Non-Collegiate system and to recognize in place of an institution under its own control an autonomous institution which would be bound to the acceptance of certain obligations.

8. The Non-Collegiate system could not be brought to an end until the necessary changes of Statute had been approved by Her Majesty in Council, and the Council of the Senate would not make proposals for such amendments until they were satisfied that if they were sanctioned by Her Majesty in Council suitable provision would concurrently be made for the students affected; but if the Regent House approved the recommendations of this Report, the sponsors of the proposed autonomous institution would have a sufficient indication of the University's intentions to enable them to proceed with their plans. The Council would await submission of proposals for the constitution and government of Fitzwilliam House as an autonomous institution which would ensure that the interests of those whose membership of the University is at present dependent on admission as Non-Collegiate Students would be adequately protected, and when such an institution had been approved for the receipt of an Instrument of Incorporation they would recommend the University to recognize it as an Approved Foundation under Chapter I of Statute H from such date as the University's obligation to maintain an institution for Non-Collegiate Students was removed by the repeal of Chapter II of that Statute. The view of the Council is that the new institution, if granted the necessary Charter, should in due course become a constituent College in the University, and they are of the opinion that, provided that the necessary endowment and adequate buildings were forthcoming, there should not be long delay in the achievement of this end. They think, however, that the immediate purpose of their proposal, namely the substitution of an autonomous institution for an institution for Non-Collegiate Students under the control of the University, would be achieved more quickly and more satisfactorily by way of an Approved Foundation.

The Council accordingly recommend:

That approval be given to the general proposition that steps shall be taken to terminate the present Non-Collegiate system, provided that Fitzwilliam House can be recognized as an Approved Foundation bound to limitation of the number of its undergraduate members and to the performance of certain functions now performed by it as an institution for Non-Collegiate Students.

HENRY WILLINK,	A. J. ARBERRY	H. C. WHALLEY-TOOKER
Vice-Chancellor	W. K. C. GUTHRIE	L. P. WILKINSON
LIONEL WHITBY	DAVID THOMSON	R. Y. JENNINGS
BRIAN W. DOWNS	G. F. HICKSON	C. L. G. PRATT
J. M. WORDIE		

The University had approved what the Council called their general proposition that the non-collegiate system should be brought to an end, subject to their being satisfied that the constitution and the finances of Fitzwilliam House were such that it could properly be proposed for recognition as an Approved Foundation; and the Council had also made it quite clear that it would be for the sponsors of the new institution to provide detailed information which would enable the Council to recommend its recognition as an independent body.

Before the approval of the Council's Report the sponsors of Fitzwilliam House had already given thought to the steps that would need to be taken in the event of approval, and we have seen how the Acting Committee, by which the moves for autonomy had been given form and substance, had in September 1954 given way to a larger body, known as the Negotiating Committee, consisting of former members of the House resident in London, and of those in Cambridge who were responsible for its administration and for the teaching of its undergraduates. The Censor had made earlier contacts with the 'London members', for a minute of a meeting of the Non-Collegiate Students Board held on 23 April 1953 records that he told the Board that there was to be an informal meeting of certain members of the Fitzwilliam Society in order to discuss possibilities of raising funds for new Fitzwilliam buildings. The meeting was to be in Fitzwilliam House on 9 May, and the Chairman of the Board had agreed to˙attend it. It will be remembered that this was shortly after the Board had addressed to the Council their request that the future of the House should be urgently considered, a request which led to the appointment of the Council's Special Committee. In January 1954 Mr Stratton was writing to the Censor to find out what funds the House possessed which might be used for building purposes; and this, again, was at the time when speculation was widespread in the University that the committee was likely to report unfavourably on the future of Fitzwilliam House as a place of undergraduate education.

It seems, therefore, that after the publication of the Council's Report in 1952 the Censor began to turn to his old members in the hope that they might be able to find a way forward which had eluded the Non-Collegiate Students Board. Former resident members of the House had subscribed to the Memorial, which had brought about a speedy, and impressive, improvement in the House's prospects, and the readiness of the Council to join with them in discussing the House's future suggests that, initially at least, the Council hoped that their opinions on its government and eventual development would be of value.

The Negotiating Committee had undertaken a threefold task. They had resolved to seek afresh for a site for a new building, to obtain money for it, and for the building itself; and they had to frame a constitution suitable for an Approved Foundation.

Of the sites that had been considered the last had been at Bredon House, specifically linked with the provision of a new administrative building (and residential accommodation) in the Council's draft Report of 1951, but omitted from the revised version of 1952.[1] Thereafter the Board, discouraged by the wariness of the Council and faced with indefinite delay, abandoned their search for a new site, and turned their attention, as we have seen, to the possibility of improving the Trumpington Street building, although they rejected Mr D. W. Roberts's plans for this in May 1954. In that year, however, under the stimulus of the movement for independence, the search was renewed, and in July Mr Haywood, as Chairman of the Acting Committee, received notice that The Grove, in Huntingdon Road, was likely to come on to the market. It was described as of roughly nine acres, with a main house, a lodge, a gardener's cottage, and two houses in Storey's Way, from which it could also be approached.[2] After a preliminary inspection the sponsors had not decided on any further action when, in October, they were informed that the Council of New Hall hoped that they would not seek to secure the property because New Hall wished to acquire it as an extension, in whole or in part, of an adjoining property already in their possession which was not by itself sufficiently large for a collegiate building. The Council of New Hall was not then, it seems, willing to consider a sharing of the Grove site. In this situation, satisfactory to none but the house agent and his client, the Negotiating Committee, as it had then become, looked for other sites, and from an informal discussion with the Senior Bursar of St John's College (the Rev. J. S. Boys Smith) Mr Haywood learned that whereas the College had previously been unwilling to part with any site to the University for use by the Non-collegiate body, there was not likely to be the same objection to its use by a college; and sites in Herschel Road (Thorneycreek), to the north of Clarkson Road, and to the west of the southern section of Storey's Way at its junction with Madingley Road, were considered.

This informal consultation was followed on 10 December 1954 by a letter from Mr Haywood to Mr Boys Smith asking whether his College would be willing to offer the Negotiating Committee an option to purchase either the Clarkson Road or the Madingley Road site, with a slight preference for the former. On 10 January Mr Boys Smith replied

[1] See pp. 234–7.

[2] The Grove was first brought to the notice of the Bursar (W. W. Williams) in a letter of 2 July 1954 from Messrs Hockey and Son. Mr Haywood was given an order to view for 12 July. In various quarters, and at various times, there seems to have been some uncertainty about the area of the Grove estate, which was 10.8 acres (College Archives – Independent Status, Correspondence, 1).

to the effect that the College would be willing to consider the sale of an appropriate area of land on Madingley Road as a site for Fitzwilliam House (as an independent foundation), and, as a first step, to consider granting an option to purchase if Fitzwilliam House were not in a position to purchase at once. The possibility of an option was said to be still under discussion when the Negotiating Committee submitted their draft constitution to the Council of the Senate in September 1955, but at some point thereafter it appears to have been allowed to lapse.[1]

In 1954 the Council of the Senate had acknowledged that lack of money was a principal obstacle to the provision of suitable accommodation for Fitzwilliam House, in competition with other urgent needs of the University. Moreover, a reason for the Council's approval in principle of the termination of the non-collegiate system was their belief that an appeal for funds might be more successful if it were made for a body which had a prospect of independence at no distant date, than if it were made for a University department. At the same time the Council had laid squarely on the shoulders of the sponsors of the new institution the responsibility of submitting detailed proposals for its constitution, and of securing necessary financial support.

Against this background the Negotiating Committee began their search for funds, on the assumption that if buildings were to be put up and endowment obtained this would have to be without help from the University or, through the University, from Government funds. On 6 December 1954 the Committee agreed that the cost of a new administrative building would be of the order of £180,000, including a sum of £25,000 for a site, with room, presumably, for residential buildings if money could be found for them. They also agreed that it would be prudent to raise a sum of £200,000 before embarking on a building programme, and approved an overall target of £500,000.[2]

On the same day, the Governors of the Fitzwilliam Hall Trust discussed 'the question of raising funds for the purpose of the Trust by

---

[1] The course of the negotiations for the grant of an option to purchase is far from clear, particularly in the light of a note, prepared for the Financial Board, of a meeting held on 8 November 1956 to discuss the question of a site. This note refers to an option obtained by the sponsors, whereby St John's College had agreed to sell to an independent Fitzwilliam House part of a site of thirty-seven acres on Madingley Road. No trace, however, can now be found of any such option. The College file on the subject has, it seems, been destroyed; there are gaps in the Fitzwilliam papers of the time, and on the occasion of a search, in 1974, by the late Sir John Stratton it appeared that a whole file was 'absent without leave' from his London office. Without further evidence, it can now only be supposed that the increasing improbability that Fitzwilliam House would achieve independence within a measurable distance of time prevented the completion of negotiations for the option on terms provisionally agreed in the course of 1955.

[2] Negotiating Committee Minutes, 6 December 1954.

means of an appeal to past and present members of the House, and to other possible sources of financial help'; and agreed to make available up to £150 for appeal expenses, to receive subscriptions, and to appoint as members of an Executive Committee for the appeal those Governors who were members of the Negotiating Committee.[1] In accordance with an earlier decision that any appeal within the University or to members of the House should be organized in Cambridge (whereas efforts to secure more widespread and, it was hoped, more substantial support would need to be directed from London) a Friends of Fitzwilliam House Appeal was launched in Cambridge in the New Year, to all Fitzwilliam men, by Mr Stratton, as Chairman of the Fitzwilliam Hall Trust, Mr Thatcher, on behalf of the House, and Mr Haywood, President of the Fitzwilliam Society for the year 1954-55.[2] By the time that covenants made under this appeal had been completed, it had realized about £30,000.

Meanwhile, as part of a more general effort to engage public attention in Fitzwilliam House affairs, attempts were made to enlist the interest of the Press and of influential individuals; and tentative approaches were made to selected foundations, with little success; and when in June 1955 the Council of the Senate declined to support a general appeal for funds until the University had approved a constitution for Fitzwilliam House as an Approved Foundation, it became only too evident that there could be no further progress without an acceptable Instrument of Government; and the Negotiating Committee resolved to go no further, for the time being, with the public appeal, but to devote themselves to the necessary preliminary work of framing a constitution, without which there could be no change of status.[3]

On 27 October 1954, the day of the publication of the Council's Second Report on the future of Fitzwilliam House, Mr Haywood, then recently elected Secretary of the Negotiating Committee appointed to act for the Memorialists in all matters relating to the conversion of the House into an autonomous collegiate body, had called a meeting of officers and Directors of Studies, known as the House Committee, to discuss what should be done, and who should do it, if the University were to approve the Council's recommendation. At an early stage, it had been accepted that while Fitzwilliam House, by whatever name, would hope eventually to petition for a Royal Charter as an independent college, as an Approved Foundation it would need to apply to the

[1]   Trust Minutes, 6 December 1954.
[2]   Independence file.
[3]   Negotiating Committee Minutes, 13 June 1955.

Board of Trade for a certificate of incorporation under such conditions as the Board, in accordance with the provisions of the Companies Act (1948), might see fit to impose.

This House Committee arranged for the preparation, in Cambridge, with a view to its approval by the London and Cambridge members of the Negotiating Committee, of a draft Instrument of Government for Fitzwilliam House as an Approved Foundation, setting forth its constitution and objectives, with an accompanying paper, addressed to the Registrary, supplying information required by the Council about building policy and financial management, together with suggested ways and means of obtaining support sufficient to ensure the lasting financial stability of the new institution. That this task was found more difficult, and much more time-consuming, than had at first been anticipated, there is now no reason to doubt. In December 1954 there was still talk of the possibility of presenting an agreed constitution, with its accompanying paper, to the Council by the beginning of the next Lent term, and of achieving the new status by the beginning of the next academical year, but in the event the first drafts were not in the Registrary's hands until the end of September 1955.

The draft constitution, as submitted to the Council of the Senate in September 1955, was set forth in a Memorandum and Articles of Association of a Company incorporated under the name of Fitzwilliam Hall, and referred to throughout as 'The Foundation'.[1] The Memorandum of Association declared that the objects of the Foundation were
(a) To found and carry on a self-governing Approved Foundation in the University of Cambridge ... for the higher education of men, and to promote its development into and to carry it on as a college of the University ...
(b) To advance education, learning and research in the University.

In pursuit of these main objects the Memorandum provided particularly that in taking over from the University the organization and administration of those students who had previously been members of Fitzwilliam House the Foundation should comply with the requirements of the Council of the Senate with regard to Research Students, to members of the houses of residence recognized by Grace, and to those classes of persons whose membership of the University had been dependent on their admission as non-collegiate students. It also gave notice of the Foundation's intention to petition, in due course, for a Royal Charter.

But it was the drafting of the Articles that caused the greatest

[1] Independence file.

difficulty. Rules were prescribed for membership of the Foundation; and its control was to be vested in two committees – a Governing Body (Court), with overriding powers except where otherwise laid down, and a Council, consisting of the teaching and administrative officers of the Hall, which should be responsible for its academic policy and day-to-day administration. On enquiry, the Council of the Senate advised that a majority of the Governing Body should be resident University or college officers, and that it would be appropriate if up to half of its members were paid teaching or administrative officers of the Hall. With this guidance the Negotiating Committee, on 13 June 1955, agreed to propose a Court of twenty-one members, of whom three should be *ex-officio* members of the Council of Fitzwilliam Hall, and seven appointed by the Council from among their own number; five should be appointed by the Foundation in General Meeting; and five should be University or college officers appointed by the Court; with, in addition, one representative of the Council of the Senate. Under these arrangements, ten of the twenty-one members of the Court would be paid officers of the Hall, and sixteen would be likely to be resident members of the University. Three months later, when the draft constitution was submitted to the Council of the Senate, the total membership of the Court had been raised to twenty-three, with a relative decrease in the proportion of salaried officers of the Hall, and of those members who might be expected to reside in Cambridge.

The Council of the Senate appointed representatives to report to them on the draft Memorandum and Articles of Association, and at a meeting, on 5 December, with Mr Stratton, Chairman of the Negotiating Committee, Mr Walters, its Secretary, and the Acting Censor (Mr Williams), they made a number of observations, which are recorded in a note of the meeting agreed with the Registry.[1] These observations, except for some which were no more than suggestions for drafting improvements, would be of greater interest now if the proposed constitution had not eventually been abandoned altogether in favour of other arrangements; but some are of interest still because of their apparent effect on the course of events. On the Memorandum there was little comment of substance, except for a suggestion that the advancement of religion might be included among the Foundation's objects; but the Council representatives were critical of some of the Articles as being unsuitable for a institution expected to become a college of the University, and likely to cause embarrassment at such time as application might be made for full collegiate status. An arrangement whereby the

[1] *Ibid.*

Master of the institution would not preside over his own Governing Body was alien to Cambridge tradition; also undesirable, they thought, was the limitation of a particular category of members of the Court to non-residents; and the procedure proposed for the appointment of officers implied a lack of continuity between the existing non-collegiate body and the projected Approved Foundation.

On 14 December the Negotiating Committee appointed a sub-committee of members from London and Cambridge to report on amendments to the Constitution,[1] and in January the Cambridge members of the sub-committee prepared a report for discussion in London, and, when approved, for submission to the full Negotiating Committee. The Report, which never reached the committee, recommended a revision of the September draft in the light of advice given by the representatives of the Council of the Senate, which would have diminished somewhat the powers of the Court, and its effective control over the Council, and would have provided a Constitution rather more in keeping with Cambridge custom. A particular recommendation, and source of disagreement, was that the Court should revert to the total membership of twenty-one, with its higher proportion of Council members, and of resident members of the University. The recommendations proved unacceptable to the London members of the sub-committee, and on 1 June Mr Stratton, in a letter to Mr Walters, gave notice of their resignation.[2] On the question of the composition of the Court, which had been an immediate occasion of the final breakdown, Mr Stratton stated his opinion that if money was to be raised for educational purposes 'in this day and age' potential benefactors might wish not only to be informed about the objects of an institution they were being asked to support, but also for an opportunity of continuing their interest in the conduct of its affairs.[3] The London resignations were followed by those of Mr Thatcher and Mr Haywood.

Some months later Mr S. C. Roberts, in correspondence with the Acting Censor, after saying that the activities of the Negotiating Committee were not his affair (and that he had no wish to become involved in them), compiled what he described as a statement of his own position, and declared his willingness for it to be shown to the Negotiating Committee. The statement is of interest as the comment of an uncommitted observer on the situation in which the sponsors of a new Fitz-

---

[1]   Negotiating Committee Minutes, 14 December 1955.
[2]   Independent Status, Correspondence, II.
[3]   *Ibid.* When, in 1962, the University issued its appeal on behalf of Fitzwilliam House, no subscriber expressed any such desire. Cf. p. 303.

william House then found themselves, and for its references to other, more successful, efforts to assist its development.

1. The main difference of opinion on the Negotiating Committee [said Mr Roberts] is, as far as I understand it, as follows:

    (a) For the period during which Fitzwilliam House would be an Approved Foundation, the London members envisaged a constitution under which non-residents would form a powerful element in the governing body.

    (b) The Cambridge members opposed this on principle and particularly in the interests of the present members of the staff.

2. This controversy does not directly concern me as Chairman of the present Board, but it has some relevance to the Appointments Committee of which I am an *ex officio* member.[1]

3. About the Appointments Committee it would obviously be improper for me to say anything except that it has felt obliged to delay any action in view of the uncertainties of the present position.

4. As Chairman of the Board I have concentrated my efforts on securing new buildings for Fitzwilliam House, as it exists today, without prejudice to any plans for independent status in the future.

5. Whether these efforts will be successful must largely depend upon the response of the University Grants Committee to the representations of the University.

6. In the event of this response being favourable, I conjecture that the University will proceed to consider the whole situation afresh and that it may then seek to enlist the help of old Fitzwilliam men.

The Negotiating Committee decided that this statement called for no reply, save for its paragraph 1(b). On this, they did not accept Mr Roberts's opinion that their views on a constitution for Fitzwilliam House as an Approved Foundation had been influenced by considera-

---

[1] On 11 May 1955 the Council of the Senate published a notice (*University Reporter* p. 1345) referring to their decision in March 1954 not to proceed to the appointment of a successor to Mr Thatcher, who would reach the retiring age on 30 September; and to invite Mr Thatcher.to perform during 1954–5, as Senior Tutor, the functions appertaining to the Censor. The Council remained of the opinion, they continued, in view of the possibility of the termination of the non-collegiate system, that it was still inappropriate to consider the appointment of a new Censor, and they had asked the Assistant Censor (Mr W. W. Williams) to act 'from 1 October 1955 until such time as may be determined in the light of further developments'.

This was the Council's official intimation to the University. In the light of subsequent events it should perhaps be noted that Mr Roberts, when he informed the Non-Collegiate Students Board of the Council's decision, said that Mr Williams had been asked to act 'during 1955–56, and possibly for a little longer'. In accepting the Council's invitation, Mr Williams will have been well aware that he would be assuming a most onerous task.

For Mr Roberts's statement, of 27 March 1957, and the draft of a reply by Mr Williams, appointed Chairman of the Negotiating Committee on 8 June 1956, see Independent Status, Correspondence, II.

tion for the interests of existing members of staff. From other correspondence it appears that the predominantly Cambridge view of the proper composition of a Governing Body for the new foundation was based on a belief in the need to ensure continuity between the non-collegiate body as it then was and the Approved Foundation that it was hoped it would become – a point touched on by the representatives of the Council of the Senate in discussion – and that this belief was held as a matter of principle, and not, primarily, in the interests of individuals.

In this brief conspectus of the main events of the mid-1950s there has been no attempt to pronounce on the rightness of the views held in what had unhappily – and with unfortunate future effect – become two separate camps. Such as may read will form their own views on the information before them; to which is now added a letter addressed to the Vice-Chancellor by – to use his own kindly word – one of Fitzwilliam's most eminent sons, closely associated with the House during the four years immediately preceding his translation to Manchester University as Professor of Ecclesiastical History.

I hope it may not be impertinent [said Professor Rupp] for me to write about the affairs of Fitzwilliam House, but my four years there as Director of Theological Studies, 1952–6, have deepened my concern for its affairs, and my respect and gratitude towards its officers. Since the integrity of its officers and of its Directors of Studies seems to have recently been called in question, may I say for them something which they cannot say for themselves, but which might reasonably come from somebody removed from the scene?

While we all regret the division of opinion which developed between the two parts of the committee concerned with the move to turn Fitzwilliam House into an Approved Foundation, I am bound to say that in my opinion the Cambridge rather than the London end of it had in mind the kind of college best suited to the traditions and future of the University. It is always invidious to make comparisons and question motives, and all I will say is that I have great confidence in the present officers of Fitzwilliam House and their personal integrity.

It has always seemed to me that if Fitzwilliam House is to play a useful part in the future of the University, its growth will involve real continuity with its past. The case for allowing Fitzwilliam House the new status rests surely on the fact that it has since its origin developed a real corporate life. The present Fitzwilliam House, going concern as it is, must be the basis of the new foundation. It may be that in the future, scholars of even greater eminence will be found among its Directors of Studies than at present. But at this critical stage, the all important thing is that they should be a happy

and united team, supporting loyally officers whom they like, trust and respect. If the Cambridge committee has stressed this, and thought less of a
prospectus with names which might attract outside donors, it is for the
reasons I have mentioned. It is entirely unnecessary and indeed rather
bogus to import into the situation motives of self seeking which have not
operated, and which I do not believe to exist.

At my last meeting with the committee in Cambridge I was happy to
move the resolution of confidence in the present officers, and this represents my considered judgment, and my honest gratitude for much kindness
received at their hands. It is in the hope that an expression of friendly
opinion may not come amiss that I write this letter.[1]

In the Michaelmas term of 1956 the Non-Collegiate Students Board
and the Council of the Senate were informed of the circumstances
which had led to the resignation of the London members of the Negotiating Committee, and were also told that the committee, reconstituted and determined to go forward with its plans, hoped to submit a
further draft Constitution by the end of the term.[2] This draft, sent to
the Registrary on 17 November 1956, incorporated the modifications
suggested by the Council's representatives in the previous December,
and increased somewhat the powers of the Council of Fitzwilliam Hall,
and the number of resident members of its Governing Body (the name
'Court' disappears).[3] In April 1957 the Registrary was also informed
that, as a consequence of the London resignations, the first Governors
under the revised Constitution as it had been submitted would all be
resident Fitzwilliam men; and he was asked to embody a provision
whereby, in addition to resident members of Fitzwilliam Hall, the first
Governors would include members of the Non-Collegiate Students
Board, the Head of a house of residence recognized by Grace, former
members of Fitzwilliam House, and members of the Council of the
Senate.[4]

In May 1957 the Council resolved, on the advice of their committee
appointed to examine the earlier draft, that, as they saw no early prospect of the establishment of Fitzwilliam House as an independent foundation, and as a different approach might commend itself to those who
might at some future time be authorized to formulate proposals, it

---

[1] Independent Status, Correspondence, II.
[2] Minutes, 18 October 1956. B. M. Herbertson, Assistant Tutor and Director of Studies in
Medicine, A. D. I. Nicol, Assistant Secretary of the University Appointments Board, and
P. A. Tranchell, Director of Studies in Music, were elected members of the Committee
on 17 October, and P. R. Ackroyd, Director of Studies in Theology, on 29 March, 1957.
[3] Independent Status, Correspondence, II.
[4] *Ibid.*

would be premature for them either to approve the amended draft in principle, or to make any comments on it.[1] This was the Council's last word on the proposed application to the Board of Trade under the Companies Act 1948; and there the matter rested for some years, until, as the Council had surmised, a different approach to the subject did commend itself to the Non-Collegiate Students Board, with the concurrence of a newly constituted body of Fellows of Fitzwilliam House.

For a brief period, both before and after the publication of the Council's Report in 1954, the limelight had fallen on the Memorialists and the advocates of the new institution which, they hoped, would soon receive Approved Foundation status; while the Non-Collegiate Students Board, charged with the superintendence of the non-collegiate body, had remained in the background. The Memorialists, with their combined London and Cambridge membership, had been largely instrumental in obtaining the University's acceptance, under certain conditions, of the proposition that the non-collegiate system should be terminated. In Mr Thatcher's words, they had led Fitzwilliam House up to its new start-line; but the fulfilment of the conditions attached to the acceptance of the principle proved to be beyond their powers. They were unsuccessful in preparing the ground for a general appeal for funds, and – more important, possibly, since the Council of the Senate made this a *sine qua non* of their own further assistance – they were disastrously divided in their conception of the instrument of government which they should submit as suitable for the Approved Foundation which they hoped to bring into being. As, therefore, it began to appear less likely that the movement for constitutional and financial independence would achieve any measure of success in the foreseeable future, the initiative in Fitzwilliam House affairs passed from the Negotiating Committee back to the Non-Collegiate Students Board and the central authorities of the University.

---

[1]   Independent Status, Correspondence, II. Letter, dated 3 May 1957, from the University Registrary.

CHAPTER VII

New Buildings and New Status

Possibility of new buildings for the non-collegiate institution – sites (45 Hills Road, Herschel Road (Thorneycreek), Madingley Road). The Grove acquired (1958) – appointment of architect. New Censor appointed. The Fitzwilliam Hall Trust and its continuing activities.

Building plans and building procedures. Architect's proposed college for Fitzwilliam – start of Stage I (Michaelmas term 1961) – its unexpected continuation. Completion of present College buildings (Michaelmas term 1967).

Renewal of negotiations for status of Approved Foundation – financial proposals of Non-Collegiate Students Board – public appeal for funds (1962). Election of first Fellows of Fitzwilliam House (1963). Admissions policy. Draft statutes (1964) – charter and statutes for independent College approved (1966).

In the meantime, neither the Non-Collegiate Students Board – or, at least, its Chairman – nor the Council of the Senate had been idle. In his statement of 27 March 1957, Mr Roberts tells how he endeavoured to secure new buildings for Fitzwilliam House, as it then existed, without prejudice to any plans for its independent status in the future; and, as early as the Michaelmas term 1955, before the Council had expressed their opinion on the first draft constitution submitted by the Negotiating Committee, they were considering the possibility that a high priority might be assigned to an administrative building for Fitzwilliam House in the University's Statement of Needs for the quinquennium 1957–62.[1] The matter was not free from complication, because the University Grants Committee, even if they were willing to help, could only provide funds for a University institution, and the Council were disposed to seek the committee's advice on the propriety of including in the University's Statement of Needs for the next quinquennium an application on behalf of a body which, before the quinquennium was over, might have become independent. Furthermore, there was no certainty about the attitude of the Negotiating Committee, whose Cambridge members appeared to assume, more readily than their London counterparts, both that the acceptance of a government grant would mean delay in the gaining of independence, and that delay should be accepted if thereby it would be possible to obtain the new building for which the Non-Collegiate Students Board had been pressing for so

[1]   Minutes of the Council of the Senate, 28 November 1955.

long. On the other hand, it was acknowledged by both parties that the possession of the new building, as evidence of the University's continued practical interest in Fitzwilliam House, might be of considerable assistance in a public appeal for funds for the new Foundation.

In order that all doubts and ambiguities might be removed, the Council arranged a meeting on 26 March 1956 with representatives of the Negotiating Committee at which, according to a letter written shortly afterwards by the Vice-Chancellor (Professor B. W. Downs) to Mr Stratton, it was suggested that, although a grant from the University Grants Committee could be made only to the University, it should not necessarily be assumed that the University would not be permitted to use it for a building for Fitzwilliam House, even though, by the time it was completed, the House might be expected to become autonomous.[1] In view of this the Negotiating Committee representatives agreed that an application might be made, although it seems likely that its London members had also in mind the possibility that an offer of a grant might be declined if its acceptance should after all prove an obstacle to independence. At this meeting the question was also asked, but not answered, whether the University would be prepared to assist the new Foundation by the payment of a capital sum equivalent to the current value of the Trumpington Street premises, and of a subvention of £3,000 a year, this being the estimated amount of its annual deficit.

In the result, the Secretary of the Negotiating Committee informed the Registrary on 25 April that the committee wished the University to apply for a grant 'in the strongest possible terms', adding that although they hoped that the acceptance of a grant would not delay autonomy for Fitzwilliam House, this was not made a condition of the application.[2] At their meeting on 30 April the Council resolved to discuss with the officers of the University Grants Committee (on the committee's quinquennial visitation to the University) what would be their proper action in relation to an application for a grant for the coming quinquennium in view of the possibility that Fitzwilliam House might cease to be a University institution before its end.[3] On 28 May the Registrary reported that this would cause no difficulty if the University was satisfied that the autonomous institution was suitably organized and sufficiently stable;[4] and in a statement of the University's needs for the quinquennium 1957–62, submitted by the Vice-Chancellor on 30 July

[1] Independent Status, Correspondence, II.
[2] *Ibid.*
[3] Minutes of the Council of the Senate, 30 April 1956.
[4] *Ibid.* 28 May 1956.

1956, after informing the committee that there was little prospect that an independent institution would be inaugurated in the near future, and emphasizing the need for new premises quite apart from any possible change of status, the Council included, among a number of projects to which no priority was assigned but which were likely to be given high priority when sites became available, the erection of an administrative building for Fitzwilliam House, to provide for between 350 and 400 students at an estimated cost, on the basis of figures supplied by the Non-Collegiate Students Board, of about £200,000. At this stage the Council did not include in their plans for the new administrative building any provision at all for undergraduate residence; nor is there yet any suggestion that on the site of the administrative building there should also be space for undergraduate rooms. The Council added, however, that they had a promising site under consideration, and that they hoped to be in a position to submit proposals to the University Grants Committee during the quinquennium, if not before.[1]

---

[1] *Needs for 1957–62*, pp. 79–80, and Table 12, Council of the Senate papers, 15 October 1956.

In the Lent term 1944, when the Non-Collegiate Students Board had first informed the Council of the Senate that provision could no longer be made for the men in their existing building, they had put the cost of a new building at approximately £60,000, at pre-war prices. Their first published notice of their requirements appeared in 1952 in *Needs of the Faculties, Departments, and other Institutions in the University*. This statement, dated 30 June 1950, which also formed the basis of later calculations, proposed new premises to provide for 300 men (200 undergraduates and 100 research students), of whom 100 would be resident. Building would be in two stages, of which the first would comprise an administrative building, a chapel, and living accommodation for 30 men, and the second stage living quarters for a further 70 men, with proportionate provision for staff. On architect's advice, the cost was reckoned at £120,000 for Stage I, and £80,000 for Stage II.

In May 1952, when the Council of the Senate were still considering Bredon House as a possible, though rather less probable, site for Fitzwilliam House, they put the cost of Stage I at £200,000, but this figure appears to have included the cost of some residential accommodation, and also, exceptionally, to have taken into account professional fees and furnishings. As a round figure, it was also adopted by the Bursar in a draft statement of needs for the quinquennium 1957–62, which was not, however, submitted to the Council, as the Board preferred simply to declare that their needs, still unsatisfied, remained as they had been five years previously.

In the Lent term 1956, when it seemed that the Council might be willing to consult the University Grants Committee on the possibility of a building grant, even though Fitzwilliam House might become an independent institution before the quinquennium was over, estimates were prepared which, on the advice of the Chairman of the Board, were based on Stage I of the 1950 programme, with the omission of the chapel, and of all undergraduate living accommodation. The cost of this modified scheme was put at £126,500, in the belief that its restrictions would be balanced by higher building costs. The larger figure of 'about £200,000' for a building for 350 to 400 students contained in the Council's statement *Needs for 1957–62* may be accounted for by the assumption that prices would rise, by the larger numbers contemplated, or by a simple change of opinion.

When, in February 1957, the Council finally resolved that a site ought to be obtained and

Which site the Council had in mind is not entirely clear, but it is very likely that it was an area of three acres at 45 Hills Road, now known as Highsett. The Council knew that the Non-Collegiate Students Board did not wish to go to Bredon House;[1] and when at their Long Vacation meeting they learned that the Treasurer had informed the Registry on 14 July that Jesus College had offered to make the Hills Road site available to the University, they agreed that the Board (and the Fitzwilliam House officers) should be given the opportunity of inspecting the property, with a view to its purchase by the University for allocation to the Board.[2] On 15 October, having heard from the Board's Chairman that he and his colleagues were favourably impressed by the site, the Council asked the Financial Board to consider the matter further. Nothing came of the idea, however, for the Financial Board declared themselves unwilling to proceed on the grounds that planning consent was unlikely to be obtained, because the proposed use of the site would contravene the general principle of the Cambridge Plan, whereby University and college development was limited to the north and west of the city. The Financial Board also professed themselves uneasy lest an application might prejudice the success of future applications that the University might wish to make.[3] They did, however, arrange for a discussion of available sites by their own representatives and representatives of the Non-Collegiate.Students Board; and after considering a number of possibilities the representatives agreed, on 8 November 1956, that the two most promising were Thorneycreek, on Herschel Road, and the Madingley Road site, on part of which the

a building provided for Fitzwilliam House, they took into account, not the most recent estimates of the Lent term 1956 but another document entitled 'New Buildings' drafted by the Bursar in 1955, but not then used. For this adoption of the earlier figures 'as a general guide' no reason appears to have been given. The areas allowed for in the two sets of estimates are similar, but the Council may have regarded the 1955 figures as more suitable than those of 1956, in that they were based on a student population of between 350 and 400 (as against 300), they included temporary provision for a chapel, and allowed for some undergraduate accommodation, which the Council had come to regard as desirable.

These 1955 estimates of the cost of an administrative building for 350 men, with living accommodation for 30 undergraduates at £1,500 a set, and an allowance for passages and staircases, suggest, at a figure of £4.10.0 per square foot, a total cost of about £165,000; and in 1958 they were adopted as a basis for discussion with the University Grants Committee (Financial Board paper F.H.58.1.).

[1] The Registry, in answer to his enquiry, was so informed in a letter dated 10 February (see Council of the Senate papers for 13 February). From correspondence two years later (see Independent Status, Correspondence, II) it appears that it was not realized in 1956 that the Bredon House site included a field to the west of the house. Without this field the site had been thought undesirably narrow.

[2] Minutes of the Council of the Senate, 30 July 1956.

[3] *Ibid.*, 22 October 1956.

Negotiating Committee had sought an option to purchase. The Grove was mentioned again, apparently as something of an afterthought. The Non-Collegiate Students Board were unanimous in putting the Madingley Road site at the head of their list, and they expressed to the Council their hope that negotiations might be opened with St John's College for the purchase of part of it (some five acres). At the meeting on 26 November the Council agreed to ask the Financial Board to negotiate with the College.[1]

On 15 February 1957 the Treasurer informed the Registrary that negotiations had begun, but that the College anticipated some little delay before a reply could be given. He added that his Board could not escape the feeling that the College might be reluctant to sell unless they were satisfied that the land sold would be developed for a purpose of which they approved; that it could not be in the best interests of the non-collegiate students to provide them with an administrative block, and a dining hall, so far away from their lodgings, and without adequate transport; and that, therefore, if The Grove could be obtained there might be much to be said for its development jointly for Fitzwilliam House and New Hall, since The Orchard and The Grove together would provide some eleven acres, and this could be sufficient for both institutions. The Treasurer also said that a decision on the matter might well be of considerable assistance to the Board in negotiations with the University Grants Committee for the acquisition of The Grove, for whereas New Hall needed only two of its eight acres the committee could be expected to receive much more favourably an application from the University if it were known that the rest of the site would meet a second urgent need.

The Treasurer went on to make a significant enquiry of a more general kind about the situation of the non-collegiate body as it had developed:

> The first and most fundamental question is what is the present official policy of the University in regard to Fitzwilliam House. The Financial Board noted that the latest Report to the University was that dated 25th October 1954, and that this Report, which was subsequently approved by Grace, recommended the termination of the non-collegiate system, subject to certain conditions, and the development of an autonomous institution with the responsibility for formulating detailed proposals, and for securing the necessary financial support, falling upon the sponsors ... But the Financial Board have gathered, from discussions with the representatives of the Non-Collegiate Students Board ... that for various reasons the policy

[1]   *Ibid.*, 26 November 1956.

approved by the University in 1954 is not at present making much progress, and that in those circumstances the Non-Collegiate Students Board regard the policy as having reverted to that which was recommended in the Report dated 26th May 1952, and subsequently approved by Grace, namely the encouragement of the corporate life of Fitzwilliam House by the provision of new administrative headquarters and residential accommodation.

The Treasurer concluded by enquiring whether the Council's recommendation of 1954 or that of 1952 was to be regarded as the approved policy for Fitzwilliam House, and if it was the latter whether it still included the provision of residential accommodation. He also asked what body would be associated with the Financial Board in acquiring a site and in planning the buildings. Should it be the Non-Collegiate Students Board or the sponsors of the new Foundation?[1]

On 18 February the Council agreed that the Financial Board should be told

(a) that the long-term policy with regard to Fitzwilliam House was the replacement of the Non-Collegiate Institution by an independent College, but that the immediate policy was as stated in *Needs for 1957–62*;

(b) that the body with which the Financial Board would be associated in the acquisition of a site and the planning of the buildings would be the Non-Collegiate Students Board;

(c) that planning should be on the assumption that Fitzwilliam House would become an independent College with 350 to 400 members, and that residential accommodation for 200 persons in addition to Fellows would ultimately be needed;

(d) that, subject to the concurrence of the Non-Collegiate Students Board, The Grove should, if possible, be obtained and be developed jointly for Fitzwilliam House and New Hall;

(e) that negotiations with St. John's College for the Madingley Road site should be continued in case it were not possible to obtain The Grove.

The Council also directed that the Non-Collegiate Students Board should be informed that they were inclined to prefer The Grove to the Madingley Road site which had been suggested to the Board; and, having accepted as a general guide figures supplied by the Acting Censor in a memorandum on building needs, they agreed that from twenty to thirty undergraduate rooms should be provided at an early stage.[2]

In this statement of their policy the Council had gone a long way towards meeting the wishes of the Non-Collegiate Students Board: they had selected the site which was finally secured; they had stipulated that

[1] For the Treasurer's letter see Council of the Senate papers for 18 February 1957.
[2] Minutes of the Council of the Senate, 18 February 1957.

it must be capable of providing, eventually, residential accommodation for 200 men, and they had virtually agreed that there should be some undergraduate rooms in the new building from the beginning. On their part, the Non-Collegiate Students Board expressed some surprise that it was now proposed to consider The Grove in place of the Madingley Road site which, at the invitation of the Financial Board, they had chosen; but, in saying that their chief anxiety was that new buildings should be put up during the coming quinquennium, they appeared to wish to raise no objection to the proposed change.[1]

A month later, the Council took the final step; and, by assigning to the new Fitzwilliam House building the second place in the University's list of applications for capital grants from the University Grants Committee in respect of major building works to be undertaken from 1960 onwards, they ensured, beyond reasonable doubt, that it would be begun, if not completed, during the quinquennium 1957–62.[2]

The Non-Collegiate Students Board were not, however, yet out of the wood. No further progress appears to have been made in acquiring any part of the Madingley Road land, and certainly none had been made public. Negotiations for the purchase of The Grove were protracted, and in November 1957, long before their completion, the publication by the Council of proposals for a club for senior members of the University appeared to the non-collegiate body as yet another obstacle to their plans, especially in the light of the Council's cautionary reference to the likelihood that the establishment of a club would mean delay in other University developments.[3] It is hardly surprising that, at the discussion of the Council's Report in the following February, two members of Fitzwilliam House were moved to emphasize the importance of a proper regard for priorities.[4] And then, before the Council had brought themselves to the point of replying to the remarks made at that discussion, there appeared an impressive treatise on the foundation of a new college, addressed to a startled Regent House (for, in Cambridge, the secret had been well kept) by its Trustees, and introduced with a welcoming preface by the Council.[5] Non-collegiate fears that this might prove another lion in the path were not allayed by the Trustees' reference to the availability of land for their new college, which to all appearances encompassed the site which the Negotiating Committee

[1]   Minutes, 28 February 1957.
[2]   Minutes of the Council of the Senate, 18 March 1957.
[3]   *University Reporter*, 1957–58, p. 455.
[4]   *Ibid.*, p. 835.
[5]   *Ibid.*, p. 1398.

had considered, and the Council had sought to acquire for Fitzwilliam House. The Council were constrained to issue, in consecutive numbers of the *Reporter*, two notices. The first, dated 19 May, assured the University that the erection of a building for Fitzwilliam House would not be delayed by the establishment of a University Club;[1] and in the second the Council reminded the University of their general policy for the well-being of the House, as it had been affirmed in their Reports in 1952 and 1954, and went on to express the hope that the acquisition of a site for its new building would not be long delayed, and to say that as the University Grants Committee had agreed to include the building among those for which grants would be made in the period 1960–63, and to place it in their programme for 1961 if the University was ready to start then, the bulk of the money needed could be regarded as assured. 'The Council understand', the notice concluded, 'that their recent announcement ... in which they undertook to report in due course recommending the University to promise the proposed Churchill College recognition as an approved foundation has led some members of the Regent House to suppose that the policy approved by the University for the future of Fitzwilliam House has been prejudiced. The Council feel it necessary to state categorically that this is not the case.'[2]

On this occasion, the Council appear not to have been unduly optimistic. The Financial Board, conscious, perhaps, that in the past they might have protested too much in the matter of Fitzwilliam House, discovered no impediment to compliance with the Council's instructions, and on 29 July 1958, at a meeting summoned for the purpose, the Non-Collegiate Students Board were told by the University Treasurer of the almost certainly successful outcome of the University's negotiations for the purchase of the Grove estate, and of its application for a building grant.

> The Treasurer explained [says the Board's minute] that negotiations for a site for Fitzwilliam House and for the funds required to build a new administrative block were now almost completed. It seemed certain that an agreement would be reached between the University and Mrs W. J. Armstrong for the purchase of 10.8 acres of land on the Huntingdon Road, known as The Grove. The transaction was subject to certain conditions: Mrs Armstrong would be permitted to retain the house and part of the grounds during her lifetime, and various safeguards would be made in respect of the gardener's cottage, the tenant in one of the houses on the south side of the property, maintenance of the drive and maintenance of the

---

[1] *University Reporter*, 1957–58, p. 1478.
[2] *Ibid.*, p. 1511.

house. The Treasurer explained that part of the site was earmarked for New Hall, to supplement their adjoining site, The Orchard (Byron House School).[1] It was expected that the site would cost approximately £50,000. The University Grants Committee would provide funds for the greater part of it, but the University would purchase, at a probable figure of £20,000, that part of the site which Mrs Armstrong is to retain during her lifetime. The University did not intend to charge rent to Fitzwilliam House.

The Treasurer then referred to two matters of immediate importance, the Site Committee and the Building Committee.

Site Committee. The Financial Board, he said, had appointed a committee for the management of the site as a whole. This committee consists of Sir Leslie Martin, Professor of Architecture, the Rev. J. S. Boys Smith, Senior Bursar of St John's College, and Mr B. Cooper, Bursar of Clare College.

Building Committee. The Board was informed that the University Grants Committee had undertaken to provide £220,000 and had included this building in their final programme for 1961. It was made clear that this sum is for building alone, and that it does not include professional fees, furniture and the cost of the site, for which separate provision will be made.

The Treasurer pointed out that if building is to begin in 1961, as the University Grants Committee stipulate, the final design should be agreed by the autumn of 1959, complete plans should be ready for submission to the University Grants Committee early in 1960, and tenders should be in by November 1960. This means that the Building Committee should be formed without delay and that they should meet before the next Michaelmas term. The Financial Board had already nominated Mr J. Grantham, Bursar of Downing College (as Chairman) and Mr R. E. Macpherson, First Bursar of King's College, and they had invited Mr H. L. Roy Matthews to be an outside member. The Board was asked to nominate two members to complete this committee, and it was agreed that they should be the Chairman (*ex officio*), and Dr R. C. Evans. Mr C. K. Phillips, Assistant Treasurer, would act as secretary to this committee.

The terms of reference of the committee included the planning and supervision of buildings within an approved Statement of Needs, and in terms of the £220,000 available for building from the University Grants Committee, or a larger figure should any benefactions be made in the meantime. Their first duty would be to choose an architect. This appointment should be made by 31 December 1958.[2]

The Fitzwilliam House Building Committee, whose membership was completed forthwith by the Non-Collegiate Students Board, lost no time in addressing themselves to the business of choosing an architect, for on 6 August, on the advice of Professor Leslie Martin and Mr Noël

[1]   See p. 284n.
[2]   Minutes, 29 July 1958.

Dean (University Director in Estate Management), they resolved to invite four firms to give their preliminary ideas on the planning of a new college on the site available, in accordance with the policy laid down by the Council of the Senate, with particular reference to the satisfaction of its immediate needs, within the financial limits imposed by the University Grants Committee's grant of £220,000. The firms selected were Denys Lasdun, Chamberlin Powell, and Bon, Eric Lyons, and Architects' Co-Partnership.[1] On 29 October, having previously interviewed Messrs Lasdun, Chamberlin, and Capon of Architects' Co-Partnership, and also Mr A. C. Crook of the University Department of Estate Management, the committee, after rejecting the idea of promoting a limited competition between the first three – largely on the grounds that the time taken in briefing architects for it would be better spent in a detailed study by one of them – agreed to recommend the appointment of Mr Denys Lasdun, in the terms of their minute, 'to prepare an overall development plan for Fitzwilliam House on the Grove site, and to design and supervise the erection of the buildings comprising Stage I of the development, i.e. those included in the Statement of Needs'.[2] This recommendation was accepted by the Financial

---

[1] Fitzwilliam House Building Committee minutes, 6 August 1958.

[2] *Ibid.*, 29 October 1958. The apportionment of the site between the two institutions was found to be not entirely free from difficulty. In 1957, when possible sites for New Hall were being discussed, an area of about five acres in all had been declared sufficient, and Mr Lasdun, having been told that it was expected that two or three acres of the Grove site would be needed for New Hall, had designed the Fitzwilliam buildings with this in mind. The Site Committee were, however, informed by the New Hall architect that his plans had been prepared on the assumption that it would be possible to extend the Orchard site to the south and east. However this assumption came to be made, it was without foundation; but Mr Chamberlin maintained that a satisfactory development plan for New Hall was possible only if Mr Lasdun's building were moved westwards at least beyond The Grove. Understandably, the Fitzwilliam House Building Committee were unwilling to accept so drastic a revision of their plans, particularly as their architect had kept within his instructions from the beginning; and after considering briefly an approach to Trinity Hall with a view to the possible purchase of their property at Wychfield, the Site Committee reached a compromise which enabled Mr Lasdun to preserve the essentials of his plan by moving his buildings twenty feet nearer the Trinity Hall boundary, with the consequential loss, only, of a small number of rooms. This division of the site left Fitzwilliam House with an area of 7.3 acres; and in order to improve the access from Storey's Way, which had suffered from the change of plan, the University purchased from Trinity Hall an area of half an acre in the north-western corner of the site, leaving Fitzwilliam House with 7.8 acres in all, and New Hall with 3.5 acres, to add to their original site of 2.8 acres at The Orchard.

This agreement was reached in February 1960, but it did not settle the boundary, for within a few weeks, when Mr Chamberlin presented fresh proposals designed to bring the two sets of buildings into a more harmonious relationship, it was found that a chapel, with a Porters' Lodge beneath it, had been placed within a seventy foot strip between the buildings of the two institutions, which was to be kept free of building. At a special meeting of the committee held on 29 July, after considerable discussion during which it was made plain

Board of the University, who published a notice of Mr Lasdun's appointment on 19 November.[1]

At this time too, the appointment was announced of a successor to Mr Thatcher, and the Council of the Senate also agreed that any discussions on the future of Fitzwilliam House should no longer be with the Negotiating Committee, but with the Fitzwilliam Hall Trust. Of these steps the first was taken after prolonged deliberation.

It was in the Michaelmas term of 1957 that the Council of the Senate had been persuaded that they ought to terminate the interregnum in the censorship. When the events of 1954 had made it seem possible, or even likely, that Fitzwilliam House might become independent, it was understandable that the Council should think it best to defer the appointment of a successor to Mr Thatcher, who was due to retire at the end of the academical year, even if only because the appointment might devolve not upon the Appointments Committee of the Non-Collegiate Students Board but upon whatever might become the governing body of the new foundation. As time passed, and the prospect of independence became more distant, the senior members of the House, and its undergraduates, came to feel that it was increasingly undesirable to prolong an interregnum which by reason of its uncertainties was irksome to those who were temporarily in charge, and unsatisfactory to all who were concerned with the non-collegiate body, about whose future the University appeared unwilling, or unable, to make up its mind. At the beginning of the Michaelmas term 1956, the Registrary advised the Council, 'in the light of the virtual certainty that the status of Fitzwilliam House will remain unchanged for a number of years', that they ought to reconsider their earlier decision. For good measure, he added that, although this decision might have seemed reasonable at the time, there was no statutory provision for the postponement of an appointment when a vacancy occurred.[2] The Council, therefore, invited the Non-Collegiate Students Board to choose their representatives on the Appointments Committee, with effect from 1 January 1957, so that a meeting of the committee might be held soon after-

---

that the placing of a Porter's Lodge, particularly, so close to the Fitzwilliam buildings was undesirable, and subject to prescribed limits as to height and exact location, the Site Committee, in consideration of renewed representations from New Hall on the need for more space, approved the placing of a chapel block within the prohibited area.

The minutes of the same meeting also record an agreement that neither institution would permit the use as a throughway for motor vehicles of the thirty-five foot strip on either side of their common boundary.

[1] *University Reporter*, 1958–59, p. 428.
[2] Council of the Senate papers, 22 October 1956.

wards.[1] In March the committee, having been asked to report on the
duties and stipend of a Censor, informed the Council that they had
postponed their consideration of an appointment pending further information from the University Grants Committee concerning new buildings for Fitzwilliam House.[2] On this the Registrary's note is discreet,
but uninformative, for he added that Vice-Chancellor would report
verbally the Appointments Committee's reasons for this decision.

There followed another period during which it seems that little was
done; and then at the beginning of the next Michaelmas term there was
laid before the Council a letter, written a couple of months previously
to Mr Roberts, as Chairman of the Non-Collegiate Students Board, and
signed by ten Directors of Studies of Fitzwilliam House:

> We have for some time been concerned about the absence of a Censor.
> The reasons for not appointing an immediate successor to Mr Thatcher
> were well appreciated, but it was in all our minds that this state of affairs
> could only be temporary, and we hoped that it would not last more than a
> year or so. If one includes Mr Thatcher's year as Senior Tutor, the House
> has been without a Head for three years, a generation of undergraduates
> has come and gone, and there is no doubt that the young men at the House
> are increasingly puzzled and made anxious by the apparently provisional
> nature of the institution to which they belong.
>
> For our part, we feel that Mr Williams's position has become an almost
> impossible one. To be the Acting Head of Fitzwilliam House in times like
> these has been a most difficult task. Whilst it was reasonable to expect him
> to act as Censor for one or two years, we believe that to allow him to con-
> tinue for an indefinite period in an acting capacity would be most unfair to
> a man who has done so much for Fitzwilliam House and the University,
> and for the men under his care.[3]

In forwarding this letter to the Registrary, Mr Roberts expressed his
personal opinion that an appointment should be made for a limited
term, and also said that he hoped that the committee would be summoned without much delay. The Council resolved that if they were
asked to waive the customary probationary period of three years they
would direct that the appointment should be for a term not exceeding
five years.[4] By the beginning of December the committee had decided
to offer the censorship to Dr W. W. Grave, Fellow of Emmanuel College, Principal of the University College of the West Indies, and for-

[1]　Minutes of the Council of the Senate, 22 October 1956.
[2]　Council of the Senate papers, 11 March 1957.
[3]　*Ibid.*, 14 October 1957.
[4]　Minutes of the Council of the Senate, 14 October 1957.

merly Registrary;[1] and the Council agreed, their previous resolution notwithstanding, that his appointment should be until the retiring age, or until Fitzwilliam House had ceased to be an institution controlled by the University, whichever might be the earlier. The appointment was announced in February 1958, with effect from 1 January 1959.[2]

The Council's willingness to treat with the Fitzwilliam Hall Trust over the future of Fitzwilliam House is evidence enough of a change of attitude on the part of the University authorities towards the Trust since 1924 when the Syndicate of that year had recommended a severe limitation of the Trust's activities. In the light of the opinion expressed by the Non-Collegiate Students Board,[3] then also deep in the Syndicate's shadow, the Governors of the Fitzwilliam Hall Trust spent much of their time in looking after the properties acquired by Reddaway in the Fitzwilliam Street area; and in the exercise of their effective trusteeship of the Amalgamated Clubs. Mindful also, no doubt, of the Board's willingness, conveyed to them rather with the air of conferring a favour, to 'receive donations' for the assistance of needy undergraduates, and for the provision of religious worship, they supplied, from rents of houses allocated for the purpose, the 1912 Exhibitions and the Hirst Player Bursary, to which they were the formal electors; and, as administrators of Reddaway's Chaplaincy Endowment Fund, they helped greatly with payments, small at first but considerable as their means increased, to successive Chaplains, whom, on occasion, they also appointed.

At one time or another the Trust owned the houses numbered 3,4,8,9,10,17,19,21,22, and 24 in Fitzwilliam Street, and rented 28 and 29 Trumpington Street. Some were let to landladies who took in undergraduate lodgers in the usual way; in others caretakers might rent basement rooms, and look after the houses on the Trust's behalf. By 1926 nos. 3,8,9, and 10 had been sold, and the leases of 28 and 29 Trumpington Street were not renewed in 1939. The rest continued in Trust ownership until 1958, when the Governors sold no. 4 with the prospect of a higher return from capital investment than could be obtained from rents; and in 1963 the remaining five houses, no longer needed with the move to Huntingdon Road impending, were put up for sale at the Lion Hotel on 20 March. Bought in the 1920s at prices between £700 and £1,300, they were all sold to Peterhouse for £34,200.[4]

1   *Ibid.*, 1 December 1958.
2   *University Reporter*, 1957—58, p. 847.
3   See p. 207.
4   The five houses were those numbered 17,19,21,22,24, and they were sold for £6,300,

As they disposed of these houses in Fitzwilliam Street, the Governors took such opportunities as offered of acquiring property in the Huntingdon Road neighbourhood, with a view to obtaining accommodation for undergraduates or assistant staff. Already in 1930 they had bought from Reddaway the groundsman's cottage (no. 93) in Oxford Road, made over to the Amalgamated Clubs in 1935, and the deeds of two other houses were to pass to the College in 1971, when the Trust was wound up, one of them made available on very favourable terms by a former Fitzwilliam man.[1]

Some account has been given of the part played by the Trust in assisting the Amalgamated Clubs to purchase the playing field, formerly leased from Reddaway, and Red Cottage built by him in 1910 to house two fourth year men, and to provide accommodation for the groundsman; and in spite of doubts, apparently unresolved, about their legal standing in the matter,[2] the Governors of the Trust continued to hold the Cottage on behalf of the Clubs, and, as it was not later used for the groundsman, busied themselves in looking after it – obtaining tenancies and, when funds allowed, in paying annual subventions, of £60 more often than not, to the Clubs' general funds.

The Trust continued to concern itself with major items of business affecting the playing field or the Clubs in general, or with any which might involve a question of principle, as when, by a somewhat surprising resolution, the Governors agreed in November 1939 – an Emergency decision, no doubt – that the purchase of a much needed motor mower should be assisted by a grant from the Groundsman's Pension Fund. They were called in again twenty years or so later, when in the Michaelmas term of 1958, after complaints had been received about the dangerous condition of the poplars on the field's north eastern boundary – planted soon after its purchase in 1908, and not, as was thought by some, as a war memorial – they arranged, with the consent of the planners, for them to be felled early in 1959. In 1958 also, on behalf of

---

£8,500, £5,500, £5,600, and £8,300 respectively. In one particular the auction was unusual. Having acquired the first three, Peterhouse also tried for no. 22, but at £8,100 were outbidden by an agent acting for Pembroke College, who thereupon informed the auctioneer (Mr P. C. Gray) that he had made a mistake, and asked to be released from his bid. Mr Gray agreed, and at a second attempt the house went for £5,600 to Peterhouse, who also acquired no. 24, in spite of bids, this time correct, on behalf of Pembroke. The sale had been a good one, and, on enquiry, the Governors of the Fitzwilliam Hall Trust advised the auctioneer that they did not wish him to take any action in respect of the difference between the prices of the two sales of no. 22.

[1] 92 Huntingdon Road, and 120 Oxford Road, the latter owned by Mr F. E. E. Harvey (B.A. 1905).

[2] See p. 191–2.

the Boat Club, and with generous assistance from the Fitzwilliam Society, they carried through, with effect from 15 December, the purchase of a boathouse from Messrs Banham for £5,250;[1] and agreed that their trusteeship should be put on a more formal basis by accepting responsibilities which the Clubs sought to lay upon them in a new code of Laws of that year, to the effect that as trustees they should appoint, from their own number, the Clubs' senior officers, should carry out all major financial transactions, provide grounds and other premises, hold all deeds, and negotiate contracts respecting property or servants. Many of these functions they had already performed, but this was the first occasion on which they had been spelled out.

The Trust had also become involved in events following on the approval given by the Regent House, under certain conditions, of the termination of the non-collegiate system. On 7 May 1954, shortly after the presentation of the Memorial to the Vice-Chancellor,[2] a meeting of the Council of the Governors was summoned 'to discuss the relationship of the Fitzwilliam Hall Trust to the movement for collegiate status'; and immediately afterwards the Governors raised their authorized number to fifteen,[3] and made five new elections, to which a sixth was added in the following December, four of these being of persons not habitually resident in Cambridge. It seems inconceivable that the clearly stated requirement of Cambridge residence was overlooked, and it can only be surmised that the Governors were persuaded to make these elections as they did, on the basis of a shaky interpretation of one of their Articles of Association, with which in another respect they plainly failed to comply. Two years later, with perceptions possibly sharpened by intervening differences of opinion, the tenure of the four non-resident Governors was terminated on the grounds that by reason of their non-residence they were not qualified to serve, the resulting vacancies being filled, and the chairmanship assumed by Mr W. W. Williams, then Acting Censor.[4]

Like the breakdown of the Negotiating Committee,[5] this unhappy sequel, in the Fitzwilliam Hall Trust, to the high hopes of 1954 when

---

[1] See p. 435.
[2] See p. 253.
[3] Trust minutes, 7 May 1954. The Council of Governors had powers to determine the number of Governors, and had raised the original four to five on 23 May 1923. Between 1923 and 1954 there is no record of any decision to raise the number again, but more than five attendances are frequently mentioned. In May 1954 the number appears to have been eight.
[4] The part played by the Trust in the Friends of Fitzwilliam House Appeal has been described (see p. 266–7).
[5] See p. 270.

Fitzwilliam men in Cambridge had sought to join with earlier generations in united attempts to advance the House's fortunes, did little to
encourage a belief in the University that the non-collegiate institution
was ready for self-government; and although in view of the invalid elections of 1954 it is difficult to see what else the Governors could have
done when their mistake was brought to light, the dismissal of the non-
residential Governors left a legacy of resentment which threatened to
become an obstacle to the success of alternative approaches to autonomy made in later years.

In 1957, it will be remembered, the Council of the Senate saw no
early prospect of the establishment of Fitzwilliam House as an independent foundation, and declined to comment on an amended draft
constitution submitted to them by the Negotiating Committee of the
Memorialists in the preceding Michaelmas term.[1] The initiative of 1954
was spent; and in December 1958 the committee resolved 'that in
future negotiations with the University for the welfare and ultimate
autonomy of Fitzwilliam House, which have since September 1954 been
carried out by the Negotiating Committee on behalf of the Memorialists, should be carried out by the Fitzwilliam Hall Trust, if the Trust
is willing to act.'[2] The Governors of the Trust agreed, and, the Council
of the Senate having raised no objection, the Negotiating Committee was
dissolved. In the event the Trust played no prominent part in subsequent discussions, for two reasons: the Memorialists no longer exercised any appreciable influence on the course of affairs; and it was not
to be supposed that the Governors of the Trust would wish to encroach
upon the business of the Non-Collegiate Students Board, particularly as
their Chairman, Sir Sydney Roberts (as he had then become), had made
impressive progress over one of the essentials for independence – the
acquisition of adequate premises. This the Governors were quick to
realize, and they agreed that the Censor, as their Chairman, should act
in concert with the Chairman of the Board, and report back to them as
seemed desirable from time to time. The Governors were kept
informed of events, and were consulted over matters that were their
particular concern, but it was the Board whom the Council of the
Senate were to consult over the 1962 Appeal, and the preparation of a
charter, and statutes, for an independent college.

Planning for the new buildings proceeded apace; but it quickly
became apparent that there was likely to be difficulty in reconciling

---

[1] See p. 273–4.
[2] Minutes of the Negotiating Committee meeting held on 4 December 1958, and Trust
     minutes of 11 December.

what were felt to be the reasonable requirements of a Cambridge college with the building standards adopted by the University Grants Committee. Expenditure on University residential accommodation between 1960 and 1963 amounted to some £15,000,000, and this alone would probably have caused the committee to review their procedures for the assessment of building grants; but they also believed that the cost of recent halls of residence had been high in comparison with similar buildings put up by the Ministry of Education. It had been usual to assess proposals for new halls at a rate of about £1,500 'per student place' for comprehensive halls, and of £1,000 for study–bedroom blocks. This method suffered from certain disadvantages: it led to an undesirable inequality of standards as between Universities; it was not sufficiently flexible to take account of varying needs; and it had been found difficult to determine whether the cost of a particular project was reasonable until it had reached a stage at which major changes would seriously disrupt a building time-table.

The committee had therefore abandoned the 'student place' method of assessing building costs, and had decided to adopt a procedure designed to leave the Universities free to plan their buildings in such a way as to meet their individual requirements. Under this system the basis of calculation would be a 'study–bedroom unit' representing the value of one study–bedroom, with its share of ancillary accommodation – bathrooms, passages, storage space and the like – necessarily associated with it. All other kinds of accommodation, such as common rooms, space for dining, offices and housing for staff, would be calculated in terms of this study–bedroom unit, with due regard to the relative cost, and the desirable areas, of accommodation of different types. The area assigned to a study–bedroom unit would be 225 square feet, and its cost, exclusive of furniture, would be fixed at £840.

The officers of the committee were at pains to emphasize the flexibility of the new procedure, and to shew that when once the total expenditure of a given project had been approved, a University would be at liberty to apportion, according to its peculiar needs, the areas to be devoted to accommodation of different kinds. In practice, however, the extent of this flexibility was restricted by a proviso that a 'reasonable amount' of any class of accommodation assessed for grant must be provided, and by the difficulty, under the terms of a scheme in which areas and costs had been so carefully determined, of making adjustments without adopting standards which might be undesirably low, and incurring high costs of maintenance by saving on capital expenditure.

This new procedure was made known to Universities by the Chairman of the University Grants Committee in the Lent term 1959;[1] but preliminary notice had been given to those who were responsible for the Fitzwilliam building at a meeting held at the committee's offices on 9 December, attended by the University Treasurer, the architect and the Assistant Censor, at which the application of the new formula to the Fitzwilliam project was discussed. The Cambridge representatives were doubtful about its suitability for a Cambridge college, with needs substantially different from those of a hall of residence of the usual kind – for example, the library of a Cambridge college was the principal working tool of many of its undergraduates, and bore little resemblance to what was needed, and was usually found, in a hall of residence; and the Cambridge system of supervision required more space for academic staff. It appears to have been accepted that it was in some respects unfortunate that the scheme for Fitzwilliam House, with its special problems, should be the first to be administered under the new arrangements, and the meeting agreed that the architect should proceed with the planning of communal buildings of a size to meet the needs of the full scheme (for 400 students, of whom 200 would be resident), so that the grant for which the buildings would qualify under the formula might be compared with the estimated cost of the buildings as planned. Finally, at this meeting, the question was asked whether it would be open to Fitzwilliam House to supplement a Treasury grant from other sources. On this, the officers of the committee did not give a definite ruling; and the question was to be raised again, and not only in Cambridge.

The Fitzwilliam House Building Committee, when they were informed of this meeting with the officers of the University Grants Committee, noted that recent college buildings in Cambridge had cost between £1,800 and £2,500 for each undergraduate place (not including a due proportion of the cost of communal areas); and that, whereas areas of recently built bed-sitting rooms had been as much as 195 square feet, the new formula would allow for a room of not more than 120. They agreed that it would be undesirable for the University to be committed to rooms of that size for a whole college. They also agreed that since the number of men at Fitzwilliam House already stood at about 450, and was not likely to be reduced, communal accommodation could not be planned for less than 400; and they thought that it was essential to remove all doubts about the use, in a Grants Committee building, of funds from other sources. The committee accordingly

---

[1] In a letter to Vice-Chancellors dated 19 February (Financial Board papers F.H.59.2).

resolved, at a meeting held on 20 January 1959, that their architect should be authorized to prepare an initial scheme for the College as a whole, as economically as possible but without necessarily adhering to the Grants Committee formula at that stage.[1]

In October 1959, after a series of meetings with the officers of Fitzwilliam House, which resulted in certain modifications and additions to the Statement of Needs approved by the Council of the Senate in February 1957, the architect presented his 'Proposed College for Fitzwilliam', in which he prepared two estimates known as Cost Plan I and Cost Plan II, of which the first was for a building at a minimum standard, recommended neither by the architect nor by the Department of Estate Management of the University, and the second for a building in no way extravagant but more suitable for a college, and designed so as to avoid the heavy costs of maintenance likely to be incurred if building were undertaken at the standard of Cost Plan I. Each plan gave estimates for communal accommodation (library, dining hall, common rooms, and the like) with 201 undergraduate rooms, and also with 61 undergraduate rooms, this being the smallest number of residents which the architect felt able to regard as satisfactory for the nucleus of a college. The estimates were as follows:

	Central accommodation and	
	201 rooms	61 rooms
Cost Plan I	£343,450	£231,305
Cost Plan I	£461,990	£335,490 [2]

These proposals were examined by the officers of the University Grants Committee, and at a meeting held in London on 8 January 1960 the committee's Chairman announced that it had been accepted that the complete scheme for Fitzwilliam House justified an expenditure of £394,500, an amount £51,000 greater than the estimated cost of Mr Lasdun's first plan. For Stage I of the scheme (the communal areas and 22 undergraduate rooms) the committee were prepared to raise their earlier grant of £220,000 to £242,000. At this meeting, also, further light was shed on some questions which had exercised the minds of the Building Committee, for Sir Keith Murray said that it was recognized that in Stage I of the scheme the undergraduate accommodation might be provided by the temporary adaptation of areas intended for other

[1] Fitzwilliam House Building Committee minutes, 20 January 1959.
[2] College Archives.

purposes; and there would be no insistence on the exact number of 22 rooms. It was also explained that in arriving at a total authorized cost of £394,500 the committee had regarded the residential part of the scheme as comparable with a hall of residence of the ordinary kind, but had costed the remainder at the higher rate, usually applied to a new Arts building in a University, of ninety shillings per square foot.[1] On the question of the use of private funds, Sir Keith Murray said that his committee would not be embarrassed if they were used for a particular identifiable purpose, especially if this could be related to the needs of a college, as distinct from those of a hall of residence of the usual kind, but that they would be embarrassed if private funds were used for the general and substantial improvement of an agreed standard of building. If, for example, a benefaction were received for the building of a dining hall or a library, of a standard higher than would be permitted under the committee's rules, the committee would deduct from their total grant the amount that would have been allowed for the particular building, and would then not wish to prescribe its quality. The Cambridge representatives at the meeting formed the impression that if such a deduction were made from the Fitzwilliam grant, and if also the full number of undergraduate rooms had not been built, there would be a strong case for an application for authority to use the sum deducted for more undergraduate rooms. Finally, Sir Keith Murray said that if the University saw fit to include Stage II of the Fitzwilliam scheme in a later building programme, he had no doubt that his committee would be willing to receive an application for a grant to enable it to be undertaken.[2]

On being informed of the outcome of these discussions, the Building Committee, on 28 January 1960, agreed to invite tenders for a building to cost £245,000, to provide a central collegiate building, and, by a temporary modification of an earlier design, 22 undergraduate study–bedrooms. On 16 June plans and elevations were received, and on 15 July after further consideration of these, and of models of the building, a draft report was approved for submission to the Financial Board and the Council of the Senate, with a view to its publication before the end of the Long Vacation, and its discussion early in the following Michaelmas term.[3] The architect's exposition of his plans was favourably

---

[1] This represented an increase of about 20% on the approved cost of residential accommodation.

[2] Fitzwilliam House Building Committee papers, 28 January 1960.

[3] For the Report of the Council of the Senate on new buildings for Fitzwilliam House, see *University Reporter*, 1959–60, p. 1896; and for its discussion *ibid.*, 1960–61, p. 337.

received at a meeting of Directors of Studies of Fitzwilliam House, and at a meeting of the Non-Collegiate Students Board, with members of the Fitzwilliam Hall Trust, and, with no adverse criticism at the Discussion held on 18 October, the Council's recommendation that the architect's plans be approved, and the Financial Board be authorized to accept a tender, passed the Regent House at a Congregation held on 29 October.[1] By May 1961 six tenders had been received; four of them from Cambridge firms. The lowest fixed price tender, from Messrs Johnson and Bailey, was for £270,984 which, when allowance had been made, on the one hand, for the cost of built-in furniture included in the contract, and on the other for the additional cost of preliminary site works, was £20,055 more than the building grant. After further negotiation, the University Grants Committee raised their grant by £12,500, and on 15 June 1961 the Building Committee accepted the tender on this basis, with a contract time of twenty months for completion in March 1963; and also agreed that such savings as were still necessary should be made on external works, and not on the college kitchens, which on the advice of consultants[2] had been designed on a scale more generous than was at first intended.

The first stage of the building programme was completed with reasonable expedition. The dining hall was first used for a Degree Day lunch on Saturday 22 June, and Midsummer Day was regarded as the day of general occupation. Meanwhile the Bursar, much preoccupied with builders and buildings, was unobtrusively seeking relaxation in negotiations of a different kind; and through the good offices of Rear-Admiral C. R. Darlington, Director of the Naval Education Service, a suggestion that a ship's bell would be a welcome feature of the new building was conveyed to the Board of Admiralty. Not only did the Board agree, but the First Sea Lord, Admiral Sir Caspar John, expressed a wish that the bell of his last ship, the aircraft carrier H. M. S. *Ocean*, should be presented to the College. The sequel is recorded in a plaque, also the gift of the Royal Navy, at the entrance to the dining hall.

> On the 21st January 1964 this Bell, the gift of the Royal Navy, was presented to the Censor and Fellows of Fitzwilliam House by Admiral of the Fleet Sir Caspar John, G.C.B., Captain of H.M.S. *Ocean* 1945–1946, First Sea Lord and Chief of Naval Staff, 1960–1963.

[1] *Ibid.*, p. 361 (Grace 3).
[2] Messrs Joseph Lyons.

The Bell was formally handed over [says the *Fitzwilliam Magazine* for 1964] to the Censor and Fellows by Admiral Sir Caspar John, who brought with him Admiral Sir Nigel Henderson, formerly Commander of *Ocean*, and now Commander-in-Chief, Plymouth, and Rear-Admiral Darlington, Director of the Naval Education Service. During the course of what was, for us, a delightful evening we had further evidence, if indeed evidence was needed, of the thoroughness and thoughtfulness of the Royal Navy; for as we made our way to the Combination Room after dinner Admiral Henderson was observed to be measuring the bell's clapper with his handkerchief. Apparently it was not quite right; at all events, there came with the plaque a bigger and better clapper, and a splendid and colourful tassel for ceremonial use.

This refreshing escape from ordinary routine remains a most pleasurable recollection for the Fellows who were there, and the gift itself – entirely impervious to cracks – with its daily summons to succeeding generations is a constant reminder of the courtesy and generosity of the donors.

Meanwhile events had taken an unexpected turn. There had been few members of the Regent House who were not prepared to concede that the University's most urgent building need was the renewal, or the replacement, of the science buildings on the New Museums site (to the north of Downing Street, between Corn Exchange Street and Free School Lane); and in January 1960 Mr Denys Lasdun had been appointed architect with the task of preparing a comprehensive scheme for its redevelopment. This is not the place to tell of the difficulties encountered over this project, which began to impinge on the proceedings of the Fitzwilliam House Building Committee in February 1962, when it seemed doubtful whether any building at all could be begun on the New Museums site before the end of 1964; and the University Financial Board recommended that, in order that building allocations for 1963 and 1964 should not be forfeited, a priority should be determined for alternative schemes to be begun in those years. Already in May 1960 the Council of the Senate had included Stage II of the Fitzwilliam scheme, at a possible cost of £150,000, in a list of buildings proposed for the years 1964 to 1968, without placing it in any order of priority; and in November 1961 they invited Fitzwilliam House and New Hall to plan new buildings, against the possibility or, as some might then have said, the necessity, of putting them up.[1] Fitzwilliam was well placed, for from the beginning its new building had been

---

[1] Minutes of the Council of the Senate, 8 February, 16 May 1960, 27 November 1961.

planned as a whole, and its second stage consisted largely of a repetition of study–bedrooms designed for the first.

By March 1962 the Building Committee had approved plans for what came to be called Stage II(a) of the scheme. They provided for 162 undergraduate rooms, with a number of Fellows' sets, and also for certain other desirable accommodation not included in the original Statement of Needs submitted to the University Grants Committee in 1959, consisting principally of nine larger single rooms for non-resident Fellows, useful for teaching, a recreation room for undergraduates, and a board room for Governing Body meetings. While the inclusion of this new accommodation meant the loss of 26 study–bedrooms, this was made good by adding a third storey to the south-west and north-west wings of the building; but a small number of rooms had also been lost by a modification of the site for the convenience of New Hall, and 36 rooms, in what became known as Stage II(b) of the scheme, could not be built so long as the Grove boundary remained unchanged. Nevertheless, it could be confidently expected that when in due course Stage II(b) could be undertaken all but three of the 201 rooms which had been planned in 1959 would be provided.

When in March 1962 the Building Committee first approved Stage II of the 1959 development scheme they were advised that its cost would be of the order of £300,000, a figure which had to be reconciled with the £171,000 building grant approved by the University Grants Committee (this being what, with an adjustment for higher building costs, was left of their original grant of £394,500 for the whole project after the deduction of £242,500 for its first stage). For Stage II(a), the limit of building then possible, the corresponding figures were £263,600 and £137,000, but the latter sum was raised to £222,000 when account had been taken of the additional accommodation provided in the modified plans, leaving £41,600 to be found. A variety of ways of closing the gap were under discussion, and were in principle accepted by the Building Committee, although they knew that this would mean higher maintenance costs, when the building plans were altered again, and again by events outside their terms of reference.[1]

In October 1963, following the publication of the Report of Lord Robbins's Committee on Higher Education,[2] colleges were asked what additional numbers of students they could accept for an emergency period of four years, beginning, probably, in 1965; and the Non-Col-

[1] Fitzwilliam House Building Committee, papers and minutes, 19 March 1962, 30 October 1963.
[2] H.M.S.O. (Cmnd. 2154).

legiate Students Board informed the Vice-Chancellor that they did not wish to decrease the proportion of their men living in College, but that if thirty additional rooms could be provided they were willing to accept an increase of fifteen per cent, say sixty, and that if certain essential conditions were fulfilled this increase could be permanent.[1] At first the architect took the view that it was not possible to put more rooms on land immediately available without departing from his development plan – which he was unwilling to do – but after further persuasion he put forward suggestions for a free-standing study–bed-room block, possibly of six storeys each with eight rooms; and the Building Committee agreed to examine the possibility of placing this block near the western corner of the site, but not so as to prevent the eventual construction there of a Master's Lodge. Before this possibility had been looked at more closely, the architect made an alternative pro-posal that the additional rooms should be provided by increasing the width of the south-east and north-west wings of the building (those adjacent to New Hall and Wychfield).[2] This proposal was adopted by the Building Committee and approved also by the University Grants Committee, who in May 1963 agreed to raise the grant by £28,350 to a total of £250,350. After more negotiation they added another £8,500 for the nine additional larger rooms, in return for an agreement by Fitz-william House to accept a corresponding number of students. To the resulting sum of £258,850 a four and a half per cent increase was allowed for higher costs since October 1963, and by September 1964 the final building grant was fixed at £270,498. At the same time the University was authorized to accept a fixed price tender negotiated with Messrs Johnson and Bailey for a building contract of £286,985, with authority also to make up the difference from its own resources. In order to avoid delay the Chairman of the Non-Collegiate Board and the Censor of Fitzwilliam House agreed that the prospective difference between the building grant and the contract price should be made up, if necessary, from sources available to the Board and the House respec-tively; but in the event the Financial Board recommended that the

---

[1] Minutes, 28 November 1963.
[2] With the growth of the building the orientation of its various parts has at times been given loosely, and confusingly, by reference to a single point of the compass. The Huntingdon Road building line does not run north and south, but rather from north-west to south-east, and the proper descriptions are those adopted here (as in the 'Second Report of the Council of the Senate on New Buildings for Fitzwilliam House', of 27 April 1964). Where descrip-tions are found to be by single compass points, it is to be understood that the North Front faces Huntingdon Road; the East Wing New Hall, the South Wing Churchill College, and the West Wing the Trinity Hall building at Wychfield.

deficiency of about £16,500 should be charged to the University Sites and Buildings Fund (Grace 3 of 21 October 1964) – a typical instance of the benevolence of the University authorities towards the non-collegiate institution in its closing years.

There is here evidence enough of the vigilance of the University Grants Committee in their superintendence of authorized building projects; and the Fitzwilliam House Building Committee, in their turn, not only kept their contractors reasonably up to time in the first stage of building but also contrived to show a saving of £4,300 on the building grant, which, exceptionally it seems, they were permitted to carry forward. Over Stage II(a) there was more trouble, for in 1965 a shortage of facing bricks compelled a virtual cessation of work on the north-west wing, in order that the south-east wing, at least, might be ready for the Michaelmas term 1966; and it was not until a year later that the whole building was occupied, whereas the date for completion had been set at the end of June 1966, and occupation itself was to be far from trouble-free.

This account of the progress of the University's building programme for Fitzwilliam House – with, or without, change of status – has left far behind the story of the steps taken to comply with the two remaining conditions imposed by the Council of the Senate for the acquisition of independent status; namely, the possession of funds sufficient to ensure stability, and the submission for University approval of a suitable instrument of government. Both had previously seemed unattainable; but in 1959, with a site acquired, and buildings in part at least assured, the Non-Collegiate Students Board took up the running.

In taking up where their predecessors had left off, the Non-Collegiate Students Board addressed themselves first to the question of finance, and on 22 December 1959 Mr Arthur Armitage, President of Queens' College and successor to Sir Sydney Roberts as Vice-Chancellor's deputy in the chairmanship of the Board, informed the Registrary that his Board believed that the time had come for an attempt to be made to raise funds, from sources outside the University, in order to complete the Council's approved building programme for accommodation for a College of four hundred men, of whom two hundred would be resident, and also to provide an endowment income suitable for an independent institution. At this point the Board put their target figure at some £700,000, of which they thought that £250,000 would be needed for building. They added that they were persuaded that an appeal for funds from outside sources would have far greater prospects of success, whether it were made publicly or by private approach, if it were made by the University. The Board, with the agreement of the Fitzwilliam Hall Trust, therefore asked whether the Council would agree that an attempt should be made to obtain funds for the purposes they had described, and whether they would feel it proper for the name of the University to be associated with such an attempt, either by public appeal or by an approach to particular bodies. They thought that both might be necessary.[1]

On 14 March 1960 the Council agreed that they would sponsor on the University's behalf an appeal for funds for Fitzwilliam House. They would not themselves organize the appeal, but would leave this to the Non-Collegiate Students Board. They wished, nevertheless, to be informed of the procedure which the Board proposed to adopt, and to have the opportunity of commenting on the text of any appeal document. They were in some doubt about the inclusion of buildings among the appeal's objects, but might have more to say about this when building programmes had been discussed with the University Grants Committee in the near future.[2] In June the Censor was informed that as there was likely to be heavy pressure on such monies as the Committee might allocate for major building schemes as far ahead as 1968, the Council were disposed to think that an effort should be made to raise by public appeal funds which would cover the cost of Stage II of the buildings, as well as provide the necessary endowment. They still, however, wished to have the opportunity of considering the matter again when they saw the draft of the appeal. The Registrary added one important point: the Council did not think that the date by which they would be prepared to recommend the University to recognize Fitzwilliam House as an Approved Foundation would be affected by the fortunes of Stage II of its building, for they were agreed that the recommendation might properly be made when Stage I had been completed, or virtually completed, provided that Fitzwilliam House then had sufficient funds to maintain itself.[3]

The draft of an appeal, which assumed the Council's agreement to the inclusion of money for building as one of its purposes, was sent to the Registrary on 9 June; and within a matter days the Censor was informed of the Council's approval, subject to one or two verbal changes.[4]

There followed a considerable period during which the Board sought

[1]   For this letter, see Minutes 4 December 1959.
[2]   Minutes of the Council of the Senate, 14 March 1960.
[3]   *Ibid.*, 6 June 1960.
[4]   *Ibid.*, 13 June 1960.

advice on their appeal policy, and for help in making preliminary arrangements for the appeal itself. There was general agreement that it was of the greatest importance that there should be no room for doubt that it was being made by the University, and it was decided that, in due course, in a brochure printed by Cambridge University Press, the appeal should be introduced by a brief letter signed by the Chancellor and other representatives of the University, by the Chairman or Sponsor of the appeal when he was appointed, by a number of persons prominent in industry and commerce, and by members of the Fitzwilliam Society, including some who had served on the Negotiating Committee when the move for an autonomous institution was first made. It had been intended to leave the field clear for the sponsor of the appeal, but in the course of preliminary discussions it began to seem that certain charitable foundations might be willing to entertain a request for assistance,[1] and two applications were submitted towards the end of 1960; but by the middle of the next year it was clear that they had failed. The year 1961 was regarded as unpropitious for fund raising, but in December, through the good offices of the Chancellor, a sponsor was found who was prepared to approach possible benefactors as soon as arrangements could be completed – the Honourable Maurice Bridgeman, of Trinity College, Managing Director and Chairman of the British Petroleum Company, who was willing not only to put his very considerable influence at the disposal of the University, but also to make personal approaches to a large number of concerns whose record suggested that they might be sympathetic to the University's and Fitzwilliam's needs. The appeal was launched publicly in *The Times* on 12 July 1962, in a letter signed by Lord Tedder as Chancellor, Professor Sir Ivor Jennings (Vice-Chancellor), Mr R. A. Butler (High Steward), and Mr Bridgeman; and on 18 July there appeared a turnover article, with an account of the history, the needs, and the plans of Fitzwilliam House, whose achievement and aspirations were summarized in its last paragraph:

> In order to end the non-collegiate system and establish a new college a general appeal has been launched (as announced in *The Times* last Thursday) for £900,000 for the completion of buildings already begun and for the provision of endowment income. The University itself is thus seeking the means of founding a college on the basis of an institution which has served it well for nearly a century. The existing community has, on the one hand, shown its ability to encourage those whose interests lie principally in original research; on the other, in circumstances of great difficulty, it has won

[1] The Ford Foundation, and the Wolfson Foundation.

the loyalty of many generations of undergraduates. As an independent college it will stand side by side with Churchill College, with the Trinity Hall hostel at Wychfield, and with New Hall, as part of an extensive twentieth-century development of the University west of the Cam.

At the same time the Vice-Chancellor invited contributions from the colleges of the University, and from livery companies in the City. The Censor wrote to all old members of Fitzwilliam whose addresses were known.

These efforts brought in a sum of £200,000; much less than had at first been hoped; and there is little doubt that the very large sums raised for Churchill College, and to a smaller but still substantial degree for St Catherine's College in Oxford, were an important reason why more money was not raised by the Fitzwilliam appeal; for the opinion was frequently expressed that much had recently been done for Oxford and Cambridge, and that if there were to be further calls on the liberality of private benefactors, these should rather be for the benefit of the newer universities. Herein lies a principal reason for regret over the disagreements of the 1950s, which had frustrated earlier plans to put Fitzwilliam House on the way to collegiate status.[1] To a lesser extent it was also unfortunate, and in this respect unavoidable, that the proposed development of the House held out no prospect, at that time, of an increase in the number of undergraduates who could be admitted; for what was to be provided was not more undergraduate places, but (as might not unreasonably have been said) more comfortable places for those who could, somehow, already be taken. At a time when quantity was being represented as highly desirable in the Universities of the United Kingdom, this was a disadvantage.

In one respect, however, the University's appeal was fortunate, for the unexpected diversion of funds originally intended for the re-development of the Cavendish site,[2] to an extent which in the end almost matched the cost of such further building as the limitations of the Fitzwilliam site then permitted, meant that the proceeds of the appeal, with the exception of one or two contributions for specific purposes, could be put to endowment; and in 1964 the Council of the Senate declared that their stipulation that, before becoming independent, Fitzwilliam House should have some income of its own could be regarded as satisfied.[3] The appeal, therefore, though less successful

[1] See p. 270.
[2] See p. 296.
[3] 'Report of the Council of the Senate on amendments of the statutory provisions for colleges and other collegiate institutions'. *University Reporter*, 1963–64, p. 1174.

than had been hoped, had played an essential part in making independence possible; and, as no contributor had expressed a desire to be associated with the government of the new autonomous institution, its Governing Body would be free, subject to the University Statutes and their own, to manage its affairs as they saw fit, after the manner of any of the established Cambridge colleges.

By the end of the Easter term of 1962 the Non-Collegiate Students Board had done all they could about the Fitzwilliam House buildings, and had made arrangements whereby they hoped to secure an income sufficient to enhance its claims for independent status. They were doubtless encouraged to learn of the Vice-Chancellor's opinion, communicated to the Council of the Senate in a paper on appeals,[1] that although the sum of £500,000, which the Board had fixed as their target for endowment purposes, should certainly be obtained if possible, the proposal to convert Fitzwilliam House into a college was not contingent on the whole, or even the greater part, of that sum being found, because a college with what he described as a full array of buildings could very largely support itself from its Internal Revenue Account. Even so, the Board might well have awaited the outcome of their appeal before approaching the Council of the Senate again had it not been for another circumstance which, they thought, made it imperative to press on with preparations for an independence which they were coming to feel might not now be long delayed. In the previous March Lord Bridges's Syndicate had published its 'Report on the Relationship between the University and the Colleges';[2] and among the Syndicate's recommendations was a scheme for increasing considerably the number of college fellowships held by University teaching officers. Although the colleges showed little inclination to adopt the Syndicate's recommendation in the form in which it was made – this applied to most of the Report's proposals – the number of elections to fellowships during the months that followed publication was sufficient to be of some concern to the Non-Collegiate Students Board, who were not then in a position to elect fellows, and foresaw that by the time Fitzwilliam became independent the supply of college teachers in the more popular subjects might be greatly diminished by their election elsewhere.

For these reasons, at the beginning of the following Michaelmas term, the Board enquired whether the Council would agree that, with immediate effect and until Fitzwilliam House should be recognized as

[1] Council of the Senate papers, 4 June 1962.
[2] *University Reporter*, 1961–62, p. 1073.

an Approved Foundation, there might be attached to the House twenty-four non-stipendiary fellowships, to which the Board would be the electors; that on the completion of the move to the new buildings Fellows should be granted privileges similar to those enjoyed by Fellows of colleges; and that the Board should be authorized to delegate to the Censor and Fellows powers relating to internal government and discipline, retaining for themselves the responsibility of supervising the funds and property of the House while they remained in the ownership of the University. The Board added that as they hoped that it might soon be possible to set Fitzwilliam House on the way to collegiate status they would propose forthwith to undertake the preparation of a Charter of Incorporation for the House, and the drafting of its first statutes as an Approved Foundation under the Statutes of the University.[1] The Council welcomed the Board's proposals, of which they informed the University in their 'Third Report on the Future of Fitzwilliam House', dated 19 November 1962.[2] They said that they thought it very desirable that the House should be enabled to receive into its society a number of University officers who had no close college associations, and that appointments to fellowships would be appropriate in a body already largely collegiate in character. They had invited the Non-Collegiate Students Board to prepare forthwith a draft charter and statutes for Fitzwilliam House, in order that it might be recognized as an Approved Foundation at the earliest possible moment. Although no change of University statute was necessary to give effect to the proposals, the Council thought that the University *Ordinances* should be amended so as to give the Board the specific power of appointing to fellowships; and by reporting to the University they gave notice of the Board's intentions, and for their approval, at least by implication, by the Regent House. A Grace for the amendment of the *Ordinances* as recommended by the Council passed the Regent House on 15 December.[3]

The Board lost little time. At their first meeting of the Lent term 1963 (twice adjourned) they agreed on certain general principles. Fellowships would be reserved for holders of the offices of Tutor, Assistant Tutor, Bursar, Domestic Bursar, Praelector, Librarian, or Director of Studies of Fitzwilliam House; and, with the exception of a Professor in the University, for University administrative or teaching officers as defined in the University Statutes. No Fellow would hold his

[1] Minutes, 18 October 1962.
[2] *University Reporter*, 1962–63, p. 512.
[3] *Ibid.*, p. 622 (Discussion); p. 659 (Grace 4 of 15 December).

fellowship after the end of the academical year in which he reached the age appointed by the University for the retirement of University teaching officers.

First, as a recognition of his services to the House, the Board elected Mr W. W. Williams, and invited him to attend the remainder of their discussions.

By 20 February they were able to announce the election of seventeen Fellows, of whom eleven were University teaching officers, and three held other posts in the University. Three had been Fitzwilliam undergraduates. By the end of the academical year the total reached twenty-three, leaving unfilled only one of the fellowships for which authority had been given the previous December. On 7 March they had also, with acclamation, elected to an honorary fellowship Mr W. S. Thatcher, Censor *emeritus*.[1]

From the inception of the new arrangements the Non-Collegiate Students Board, under the guidance of their Chairman, had shewn themselves not only willing, but anxious, to involve the Fellows in every possible way in the management of Fitzwilliam House's affairs, against the time when they would become the governing body of an independent institution, collegiate in nearly everything but name. In May 1963, on learning of the impending departure from Cambridge of two of their members, the Board agreed to suggest to the Council that they might nominate the Censor and the Senior Fellow to succeed them; and again, although they were not unmindful of their special responsibilities for certain aspects of the House's business, they resolved that in all matters they would welcome proposals from the Fellows, and, in particular, that after they had approved a first draft of statutes for Fitzwilliam House they would wish to submit them to the Fellows for their comment.

In the meantime, with the need to prepare a constitution for an independent body very much in the minds of the Board and of the Fellows, there were other matters, over and above the day-to-day running of the House, which demanded their attention – Stage II was being planned, having unexpectedly become a practicable possibility; the appeal was not yet over; and the publication of the Report of Lord Robbins's Committee had raised urgently the question of student numbers. It was this last problem, accompanied by the complexities of a new procedure for admissions, that particularly engaged the attention

---

[1] Minutes of 17 January to 17 October 1963. When, in 1966, Fitzwilliam House became Fitzwilliam College, Mr Thatcher, without further election, became the College's first Honorary Fellow. See also pp. 523–531. below, and *University Reporter*, 1963–64, p. 559.

of the Board, and of the Fellows and officers of the House.

In the belief that the quality of the entry might thereby be improved, the Acting Censor had obtained leave from the Board to hold an Entrance Examination in the Lent term of 1956. The arrangements for it were almost entirely made by Mr R. N. Walters and his staff, with the help of Directors of Studies and Supervisors as examiners. For this first examination there were some 250 candidates, and the list of admissions was completed on its results.[1] In 1957 the number of candidates was nearly 300, and four Entrance Exhibitions were awarded (the two Clothworkers' Exhibitions, with two from a bequest by Mr R. H. Clough).[2] By 1958 the candidates numbered nearly 500, for 32 places, and five awards were made.[3] A year later there were seven awards, and the examination had established itself. Its date proved to have been well chosen, for, although there were occasional clashes with similar examinations at Oxford, and consequential withdrawals in favour of an offer by a college there, the examination in February provided another opportunity for good applicants who had not obtained an award or a place in the Open Scholarship Examination in the previous December, and also attracted some younger boys who had not been ready for the December examination, but had subsequently shown promise.

After the Entrance Examination of February 1963, however, these very satisfactory arrangements had to be abandoned, as the result of an agreement by the Oxford and Cambridge colleges, under pressure from other Universities, to complete by 31 January in any year their lists of admissions for the following Michaelmas term. As there was no other season of the year in which a separate examination could be conducted, it was decided, in order that Fitzwilliam House might have as many opportunities as possible of securing award holders, and also pensioners, to apply for membership of the Queens' group of colleges for the purpose of open awards, and to the Trinity group, which held a separate examination for candidates for entrance only, for the admission of pensioners.[4]

With so much good will from all parties, the new arrangements were as favourable as they could well be, but the discontinuance of a

[1] Minutes, 1 March; 26 April 1956.
[2] Ibid., 28 February 1957. Mr Clough graduated B.A., LL.B. from Fitzwilliam Hall in 1922. His bequest was announced by the Vice-Chancellor on 3 May 1954; and regulations for the annual award of two Entrance Exhibitions of £40, tenable for three years, were approved by Grace 3 of May 1956 (University Reporter, 1955–56, pp. 1323, 1423).
[3] Minutes, 27 February 1958.
[4] Minutes, 7 March 1963.

successful scheme for admissions, with its wide choice of applicants, was a source of concern to the Fellows, who began to feel that they might perhaps be wise not to assume full responsibility, particularly financial responsibility, for the House until they could see their way more clearly. Some hesitation was understandable, especially in an institution which would be almost entirely dependent on its numbers for solvency. There was a world of difference between the competition for admission in the 1958 Entrance Examination and in the Open Scholarship Examination of 1963, in which no more than twenty candidates, out of a total of 1100, had expressed a first preference, and very few more a second preference, for Fitzwilliam House; and whereas the Tutor for Admissions will have been gratified at being in a position to recommend awards to eleven candidates in the Open Scholarship Examination (three scholarships and eight exhibitions), one of these candidates, only, had put Fitzwilliam at the head of his list of preferences.[1]

The Non-Collegiate Students Board, from the time when they had sought the Council's authority for the election of Fellows of Fitzwilliam House, had consistently believed that progress towards independence should be as rapid as possible; although they had never failed to listen to what the Fellows had to say, even though this might not fall in with their own wishes. But, in March 1964, it was the Council of the Senate who provoked a further move, in their 'Report on Amendments of the Statutory Provisions for Colleges and other Collegiate Institutions'. The purpose of this Report, which was an outcome of the recommendations of Lord Bridges's Syndicate and of the discussions they provoked, is briefly summarized in one of its paragraphs:

> The Council do not think that the present and future need for collegiate provision can possibly be met on the basis of existing collegiate institutions alone or on the basis of those institutions augmented by such new institutions as could be established and recognized under existing Statutes. They believe that the conditions which an institution is required to satisfy in order to qualify for recognition by the University should be made more flexible. In particular, they think that it would be desirable not to exclude from the possibility of recognition an institution of which membership is open to both men and women, or an institution which does not admit students.[2]

This is not the place for further description of the measures recommended by the Council to give effect to their intentions, but it is

[1] *Journal* 1969, p. 15.
[2] *University Reporter*, 1963–64, p. 1174.

worthy of note that, although they did not propose any change in Statute H,II, which regulated the affairs of the non-collegiate body, they went out of their way to express their hope that this statute would soon no longer be needed. They recalled that 'as long ago as November 1954' the University had approved the general proposition that, subject to certain conditions, steps should be taken to terminate the non-collegiate system, and said that they had already invited the Non-Collegiate Students Board to prepare a charter and statutes for Fitzwilliam House, in order that it might be recognized as an Approved Foundation at the earliest possible moment. They added that they were satisfied that Fitzwilliam House had complied with the conditions which had been declared necessary for recognition; and, this time, they went further, declaring that for these reasons, and also because it had for so long been collegiate in character, they thought that Fitzwilliam House should not be required to seek recognition in the first instance as an Approved Foundation, but that it would be more appropriate if it were included in the statutory list of colleges as soon as arrangements could be made.[1]

The feelings of those who were to be the first to benefit from this fortunate display of the 'flexibility' desired by the Council in the University's arrangements for collegiate institutions were happily expressed by a former Chairman of the Board for Non-Collegiate Students, lured from his retirement to attend the Discussion at which the Council's Report (and also another Report by the Council on Stage II of the Fitzwilliam buildings) was brought before the Senate.

> The sole justification, [said Sir Sydney Roberts on 12 May, 1964] for my very brief re-emergence in this scene lies in the opening words of paragraph 11 of this Report. Those words are 'As long ago as November 1954'. For some years before, and for some years after, that date I had the responsibility of the chairmanship of the Non-Collegiate Students Board and, as you will remember, Mr Vice-Chancellor, there was a series of very considerable obstacles, financial and other, to the full implementation of what was then the declared policy of the University in relation to the non-collegiate problem. Happily for me, before my retirement the first of those financial hurdles was surmounted, and since then I have been delighted, as others have, to see the emergence of the first part of the building scheme and the announcement, in another Report that is to come before us for discussion to-day, of the conception of the second part of the scheme. But, as I take it from this Report, the Council has realized that it is faced with a hurdle other than financial – the constitutional one, in the form of the

[1] *University Reporter*, 1963–64, p. 1177.

statutory necessity of the intermediate status of Approved Foundation. And I am delighted to see that the Council has taken, if I may so express it without disrespect, a flying leap over this statutory provision in order to facilitate the final implementation of the policy of 1954.[1]

The first draft of statutes for Fitzwilliam House as an independent College of the University was prepared during the Long Vacation of 1964, and submitted to the Non-Collegiate Students Board at their first meeting of the ensuing Michaelmas term. The Board took the view that they were not concerned to ensure that the statutes were correct in every detail, but that it would suffice if they could be satisfied that they would form a workable instrument of government for the College; and without more ado they sent them to the Fellows for their comment. They also asked that every effort should be made to get the Statutes to the Council of the Senate early in the following term.[2] That this time-table proved impracticable was not, in the event, of much importance. The Board were aware that their Chairman had been through the draft with considerable care, but even so this delegation to the Fellows of the task of ensuring that the statutes should contain no serious error of policy or procedure – work that had to be done even though the Board preferred not to do it – was a striking expression of the Board's confidence in the judgement, and the industry, of the body of Fellows whom they had chosen. And, be it now said, that confidence was not misplaced.

The Fellows remitted the draft statutes to a small committee, whose Report they received at the beginning of the Lent term 1965; and thereupon devoted eight consecutive meetings to a detailed scrutiny of the statutes, taking also into consideration such amendments as their committee had suggested. At the last of these meetings they agreed on a draft for submission to the Board,[3] who received it at their first meeting of the Easter term, accepted it almost without alteration, and directed that it should be submitted to the Council of the Senate.[4]

Of the Censor and Fellows of Fitzwilliam House the Censor alone had been a Fellow of a college, a circumstance which was not without influence upon their collective attitude towards the first draft of the

---

[1] *Ibid.*, p. 1848. The Council's recommendations were approved on 30 May 1964 (Grace 2 of 20 May).
[2] Minutes, 15 October 1964.
[3] Minutes of meetings of Fellows of Fitzwilliam House held between 10 February and 10 March 1965 (Archives).
[4] Minutes, 29 April 1965.

statutes for a college of which they were shortly to become the Governing Body. Their draftsman had drawn extensively upon the statutes of the colleges, particularly of Gonville and Caius, Queens', St Catharine's, St John's, and Emmanuel, with the result that from the beginning the Fitzwilliam Statutes were of a kind which had stood the test of time, but were, nevertheless, in some danger of being thought – to their detriment – conventional, or even outmoded. The debate, conducted throughout with the completest urbanity, was not long in getting under way, for there were differences of opinion on the first sentence of the first clause of the first statute, which affirmed that the College was called Fitzwilliam College in the University of Cambridge. There was no marked inclination to press for the retention of the name 'Fitzwilliam House', but there were some who would have preferred 'Fitzwilliam Hall', which was known to be attractive to former non-collegiate students, and in retrospect appealed to them all the more strongly, perhaps, as an accepted courtesy title of which they regarded themselves as having been deprived in 1924 by the Syndicate appointed to rescue their institution from bankruptcy. The advocates of the name 'College' were persuaded of the need to make known as widely as possible the change of status achieved by a body which had suffered great disadvantages from the ambiguity of its title, and although the old name was beyond doubt to be preferred on grounds of euphony – a point not made in discussion – as well as of sentiment, a large majority of the Fellows resolved that the new start ought to be matched by a new name.

The second clause of this statute, prescribing that the College should be for men only, was also challenged, but after the defeat, by fifteen votes to twelve, of a motion that this question be left for decision, at any time, by a two-thirds majority of the Governing Body, the draft Statute was approved as it stood. (This was rather more than a year before the first of the men's colleges (King's) resolved to delete from its statutes the provision that no woman should be a member of the College).

Of all the amendments to the original draft proposed by the Fellows' committee, that which had, possibly, provoked their liveliest concern related to the statute first entitled *Of Divine Service: and of the Dean and Chaplain*. The committee recommended that this statute should provide for the appointment of a Chaplain only, effectively a Dean of Chapel, with no disciplinary responsibility, and that the field of his appointment should be widened so as to include not only those in Holy Orders in the Church of England, but ordained ministers of any church in full membership of the World Council of Churches. These recommendations were accepted *nemine contradicente* by the Fellows, and in due course passed into the body of the statutes of the college.

Among the matters of greater moment on which the Fellows made their opinions known, an observer would have found much of interest in the occasional comments made by the members of this newly constituted collegiate body – in the rigour with which they scrutinized the statutes governing the appointment, conditions of tenure, and the retirement of the Master, willing for him to be *primus inter pares*, but determined that there were limits beyond which even a college should not go; in their considerate desire to lighten the penalties customarily imposed upon wayward Fellows who might not attend Governing Body meetings with proper regularity; in the degree of sensitivity which found unsuitable a statute entitled *Of the College Servants*, and substituted for it the heading *Of the College Assistant Staff*; and in the alphabetical designation of the several classes of fellowship, adopted because the more usual classification would have included the description 'Supernumerary Fellows', which to those not familiar with its origin appeared unflattering.

The changes made by the Non-Collegiate Students Board related to Statutes V (*Of an Executive Council*) and XLV (*Of Persons in Statu Pupillari*). In the former they widened slightly the scope of the business which the Executive Council was empowered to conduct, and in the latter they made amendments defining more closely the disciplinary penalties which might be imposed, on the one hand, by the Master and Tutors collectively, and, on the other, by the Governing Body as a whole.[1]

With the assistance of the body of Fellows, the Board had completed their principal task of framing a body of statutes for the new College, but there remained still to be prepared the draft of a Charter of Incorporation setting forth the objects of the proposed College with a statement of the measures designed to assist in its establishment. In the draft submitted to the Council these included

(a) the advancement of education, religion, learning, and research in the University;

(b) the provision of a place wherein men who were members of the University should be enabled to work for its degrees, or follow postgraduate or other special studies;

(c) the acquisition of such property as the University might transfer to the college;

[1] Minutes of Fellows' meeting of 19 May 1965.

(d) the acquisition of the assets of the Fitzwilliam Hall Trust (as was provided in the Trust's Memorandum of Association);

There was also provision for the appointment of a Visitor to the College, and of its first Master; and for vesting its government entirely in the hands of the Governing Body as defined in the statutes.

This draft Charter, with a Petition praying that Her Majesty might be pleased to grant it as submitted, or on such other terms as might seem proper to Her, was sent to the Registry on 24 August 1965 (the statutes having been sent to him previously), and was remitted by the Council to a committee appointed to advise them on submissions of the kind.[1]

With independence round the corner, and conscious, perhaps, of their own approaching demise, the Board thought it opportune to raise with the central authorities of the University the question of the financial arrangements that should be made for Fitzwilliam House in its new status; and in a letter to the University Treasurer the Censor, as the Board's Chairman, sought a ruling on four matters. He supposed that the University would wish to determine what should be done about the ownership of the Trumpington Street premises, but added that his Board did not wish to ask for an immediate decision. He asked that the University should transfer to the College the balance in the Non-Collegiate Board's Reserve Fund, then standing at £35,000, and likely by the end of the financial year to amount to about £40,000. The Board hoped that the University would be willing also to transfer balances of £9,000 in a Repairs and Decorations Fund, and a Furniture Fund which had been built up with a view to the move to the new buildings, and similarly a number of smaller balances in other funds amounting in all to about £1,500. Lastly, the Chairman was instructed to enquire whether the University would be able to assist the College, at a time of unavoidable financial uncertainty, and in mitigation of the full impact of the ending of the Board's grant from the Chest of £16,500, by bearing the cost, for one tenure, of the stipend and allowances attached to the mastership, if the Censor of Fitzwilliam House should be appointed to it.[2]

---

[1]   As chairman of this committee, the Censor of Fitzwilliam House was conveniently able, in one capacity, to assist in advising the Council on questions which he had addressed to them in another.

[2]   Minutes, 14 October 1965. In 1956 the Negotiating Committee had enquired whether the University would be prepared to pay to Fitzwilliam House, as an Approved Foundation, a sum equivalent to the current value of 31 and 32 Trumpington Street. In 1892 the purchase price and the cost of renovations had together amounted to £4,639, of which £973 had

On 1 November the Council of the Senate were advised by their committee that, with very little alteration, the draft charter and statutes which they had received from the Non-Collegiate Students Board would constitute a suitable instrument of government for an independent college; and the Council approved forthwith a Report to the University recommending the submission of the Petition, with the charter and statutes, for the approval of Her Majesty in Council, and, subject to that approval, the submission also of consequential alterations of the statutes of the University, of which the most completely satisfying, and comprehensive, was the brief amendment of Statute K 'by adding Fitzwilliam College to the list of Colleges in Section 3(a)'.[1]

If the Council's recommendations were welcome, the preamble to their Report was no less so. It recited the story of the University's deliberations on the non-collegiate question since 1954, and drew attention to a difficulty created by the Council's own conclusion (in 1964) that Fitzwilliam House should proceed, not to the intermediate status of an Approved Foundation, but without delay to the status of a college. The Council nevertheless reaffirmed that conclusion, and, in a paragraph of their Report surely drafted by the Registrary, resolved the difficulty:

> 5. When the Council recommended and the University agreed in 1954 that steps should be taken to terminate the non-collegiate system, provided that Fitzwilliam House could be recognized as an Approved Foundation under the provisions of Statute H, I, it was contemplated that such recognition would be subject to a condition prescribed by Ordinance (and therefore variable or withdrawable by Grace) that the autonomous institution would continue to perform its existing functions with regard to the admission of Research Students approved by the Board of Research Studies in excess of the capacity of the Colleges, and for the presentation for matriculation of members of certain Houses of Residence recognized by Grace. In concluding in 1964 that it would be more appropriate for Fitzwilliam House to receive independence as a College in the University than as an Approved Foundation, the Council were aware that the imposition upon it of formal obligations of this kind would be much more difficult. The University cannot impose conditions on a College by Ordinance. If it wished to require a College to perform particular functions it would have to refuse consent to the College's Statutes unless those Statutes bound the College

---

been raised privately, and might have formed the basis of a claim for compensation when the premises were relinquished. The Board did not revert to the matter; nor did the body of Fellows or the governing body of the College wish to pursue it.

[1] Minutes of the Council of the Senate, 1 November 1965. For the Council's Report, see *University Reporter*, 1965–66, p. 399.

to perform the functions. But, in the Council's opinion, there is now no
case for imposing on Fitzwilliam House any formal obligations in connexion with the admission of students. The position with regard to
Research Students has been transformed since 1954 by the willingness of
existing Colleges to admit larger numbers and by the establishment of new
collegiate societies for graduates, and the recent amendments of Statute H
have made it easier for an institution which receives students but has no
power to present them for matriculation to apply for recognition as an
institution which has such power. Furthermore, the Censor and Fellows of
Fitzwilliam House who, if the recommendations contained in this Report
are approved by the University and the draft Charter and Statutes are
approved by the Queen in Council, will become the nucleus of the
Governing Body of Fitzwilliam College, have assured the Council that the
College will, for so long as there is a need, admit students in the special
circumstances in which they are now admitted to Fitzwilliam House. The
Council regard this as a sufficient guarantee that the incorporation of Fitzwilliam House as a College would not prejudice the interests of candidates
for admission to the University.

So was finally removed the obligation laid on the Censor of Fitzwilliam House in 1934 by the Syndicate, presided over by the Master of
Caius College, on the houses of residence, and on the policy and practice of the admission of non-collegiate students to the University.[1]

The next paragraph of the Report shews how smoothly the arrangements were completed, and how favourably the Council, with the concurrence of the Financial Board, responded to the hopes expressed by
the Non-Collegiate Students Board in their Chairman's letter about the
financial steps that might be taken when the time came for Fitzwilliam
House to go off on its own:

6. The Council have now received from the Non-Collegiate Students
Board a draft Charter and draft Statutes for Fitzwilliam House as a College
of the University, together with a Petition that they be approved by Her
Majesty in Council. The Council have examined the draft Charter and
Statutes and they are satisfied that the aims of the proposed College as set
forth in the draft Charter are appropriate, and that a College founded
under it would be eligible for inclusion among the Colleges listed in University Statute K, 3(*a*). The draft Charter and Statutes are available for
inspection in the University Registry. The Petition recites the circumstances in which the University is making application for the grant of a
Charter to Fitzwilliam College, states the willingness of the Chancellor of
the University to become Visitor of the College, and declares the University's intention, subject to the approval of the draft Charter and Statutes by

[1]　See p. 222.

Her Majesty in Council, to transfer to Fitzwilliam College the site and buildings of Fitzwilliam House, together with the proceeds of an appeal issued in 1962, and to appoint the present Censor of the House to be the first Master of the new College. The Council have approved the terms of the Petition and submit it for the approval of the University. The Council intend to transfer to the new College the various balances at present held in the Non-Collegiate Students Board accounts, and to make an allocation from the Chest to meet the payment to Dr Grave, during his tenure of the Mastership of Fitzwilliam College, of the stipend appropriate to a Professorship, which he has been receiving as Censor of Fitzwilliam House.[1]

The Report came up for discussion by the Senate on 23 November, when it was welcomed by all the speakers – with reservations by one about the statutory title of the College and of its Head – and was approved by the Regent House on 11 December (Grace 22 of 1 December). The Common Seal of the University was affixed to the Petition for the grant of a Charter and to the Amendments of Statutes on 17 December 1965.[2]

On 4 May 1966 the Registrary received comments from the Privy Council Office on the draft statutes, most of which concerned matters of phrasing or terminology and were readily accepted.[3] There were, however, a small number of observations of greater substance, of which the first related to Statute XLV (*Of Persons in Statu Pupillari.*). Students and their rights, if not their obligations, were becoming a matter of increasingly strident concern, and in the previous January the Member of Parliament for Watford (Mr Rafael Tuck) had enquired in the House whether the Secretary of State for Education and Science would initiate legislation for the establishment of a tribunal to hear appeals from university students against decisions of their college to send them down. Mr Crosland refused; on the grounds that it was for the universities to make their own arrangements for student discipline, and, on being asked further to accept the desirability of a right of appeal, he refused again; but added that when he was asked to approve

---

[1] At this time the Council of the Senate were also considering far-reaching proposals whereby, through the gradual cessation of college contributions for University purposes, the University and the well endowed colleges might be enabled to assist collegiate foundations in greater need. See 'Report of the Council of the Senate on Amendments of the Statutory Provisions Governing the Financial Relations between the University and the Colleges, and the Establishment of a Colleges Fund' (*University Reporter,* 1965–66, p. 1363). These proposals, approved by Grace 1 of 4 May 1966, made provision for the receipt by Fitzwilliam College, by the end of 1981, of grants of the order of £400,000.

[2] *University Reporter,* 1965–66, pp. 539, 683, 905.

[3] For these comments, and subsequent correspondence, see 'Petition, Charter, and Statutes for Fitzwilliam College' (Archives).

new University charters he tried to ensure that they contained some provision for a formal hearing 'by the senate, or a committee of the senate', before a final decision was taken to suspend or expel a student. It was doubtless by analogy with this policy that the Clerk of the Privy Council advised the Registrary that it was considered that the Fitzwilliam Statutes should provide for the right to such a formal hearing, and asked that similar provision should be made for officers of the College (Statute XXXIX). The Council of the Senate, and the Fellows of Fitzwilliam College agreed, and the two statutes were amended; and when all was settled the Registrary wrote to the Heads of Colleges to tell them that provision for giving a student the right to be heard in his own defence had been included at the request of the Privy Council.

Of the statutes as they were submitted to the Privy Council one only gave rise to any appreciable difficulty – Statute LIII (*Of the Application of Capital Moneys and Management of Land*). In drafting this Statute conferring upon the Governing Body of Fitzwilliam College the customary powers of colleges in the purchase and sale of property and management of estates, the opportunity had been taken of including a section, modelled upon a recently approved amendment of the Statutes of Gonville and Caius College, providing for the application of the Statute to 'any specific trust for purposes connected with the College of which the College is trustee', excluding only trusts which might be constituted after 1 October 1966. The Registrary, however, had been informed that it was considered very doubtful whether the statute could be so applied.

As it appeared to the Council of the Senate that the proposed statute differed in no material respect from the Caius Statute to which Privy Council approval had recently been given, arrangements were made for the point to be examined with the Clerk of the Council by the Bursar of Caius College (Mr E. P. Weller) and the Censor, and it was only after a somewhat perplexed discussion that the point was clarified. The Clerk maintained that the powers which the section sought to confer in relation to trusts could not be so conferred because the charter and statutes for Fitzwilliam College would be granted under Royal Prerogative, and the Queen in the exercise of her prerogative could not override the law of the land, under which trust investments must be in accordance with the Trustee Acts of 1925 and 1961, except as might be provided by any Trust Instrument. In the light of this opinion, the Council of the Senate agreed to delete all reference to trusts from the statute. They also agreed, at the suggestion of the Privy Council, to provide for the establishment of an investment advisory committee to formulate the general investment policy of the College.

The Clerk of the Privy Council also expressed the opinion that once the charter and statutes had been approved it would be open to the College to submit an amending statute like the Caius Statute, and that there appeared to be no reason why this should not be approved, because such approval would be given under the Universities of Oxford and Cambridge Act, 1923, by the exercise of statutory powers, as distinct from prerogative powers. The amending statute would thus have the force of an Act of Parliament, and override the Trustee Acts. It was on these grounds, presumably, that it had been possible for the Privy Council to approve the Caius Statute, whereas it could not make similar provision for Fitzwilliam, which was not, until its charter and statutes had been approved, a college to which the Universities of Oxford and Cambridge Act could be applied.

By 2 June 1966 the Privy Council had accepted the amendments or additions submitted by the Council of the Senate, and on 28 July Her Majesty in Council approved the grant of a charter to Fitzwilliam House under the name and style of 'The Master, Fellows and Scholars of Fitzwilliam College in the University of Cambridge'. On the same day an Order in Council was issued to the Home Office ordering the preparation of a warrant for sealing. The charter passed under the Great Seal on 9 September, and the statutes came into effect on the following day.[1] The Non-Collegiate Students Board had ceased to exist; its last meeting, on 2 June 1966, was by chance held on the same date as its first in 1869.[2] The Governing Body of the College first met on 12 October.

[1] The Charter and Statutes, with Her Majesty's Order in Council, were printed for the College at the University Printing House in Cambridge in 1973, and entitled *Charter and Statutes of Fitzwilliam College in the University of Cambridge.*

[2] The *Journal* for 1967 (p. 18) has a note on the membership of the Board during its last year. 'As the old order changes', says the *Journal,* 'it seems fitting to place on record the names of the Non-Collegiate Students Board as it was last constituted. The list provides striking evidence of the willingness of busy members of the University to give their time to the affairs of the House, and to the advancement of its interests. The names were last published in the *University Reporter* of April 13, 1966. They are: Sir Joseph Hutchinson, of St John's College, Drapers' Professor of Agriculture; Dr C. M. P. Johnson, Bursar of Selwyn College; Dr R. C. Evans, Tutor and Financial Tutor of St Catharine's College, University Lecturer in the Department of Mineralogy and Petrology; Dr B. C. Saunders, of Magdalene College, University Lecturer in the Department of Organic and Inorganic Chemistry; Mr Brian Cooper, Bursar of Clare College, University Lecturer in the Department of Engineering; Mr R. E. Macpherson, of King's College, University Treasurer; and Dr Frank Wild, Senior Tutor of Downing College, Research Chemist in the Faculty of Medicine. There were also three members of the House: Mr Williams, Bursar; Mr Walters, Tutor; and the Censor, by custom Secretary of the Board, and during this last year its Chairman as deputy for the Vice-Chancellor.'

'Officers of the Board'

1. Ralph Benjamin Somerset, M.A., Censor of Non-Collegiate Students 1869–1881;   2. Francis George Howard, M.A., Censor of Non-Collegiate Students 1881–1889;   3. Tristram Frederick Croft Huddleston, M.A., Censor of Non-Collegiate Students 1890–1907;   4. William Fiddian Reddaway, M.A., Censor of Non-Collegiate Students 1907–1924;   5. William Sutherland Thatcher, M.C., M.A., Censor of Non-Collegiate Students 1924–35, Censor of Fitzwilliam House 1935–54;   6. Walter Wyatt Grave, C.M.G., M.A., Hon.LL.D., Censor of Fitzwilliam House, 1959–66, Master of Fitzwilliam College, 1966–

1   2

3

4

5

6

CHAPTER VIII

Status Pupillaris 1907–69

(a) Reddaway and the Clubs
(b) Societies and Clubs 1924–69
(c) The Class-lists 1907–69

(a) Reddaway and the Clubs

'Of the Clubs, which contribute so much to our prestige and to our daily enjoyment, it may suffice to say that they now constitute Fitzwilliam Hall in its widest sense.'[1] So Reddaway was to write within three years of assuming the censorship; and, as he had never thought otherwise, it is not surprising that very soon after his first appearance in the non-collegiate institution as its Lecturer in History he became comprehensively involved in the Clubs' affairs. In the Easter term of his first year he was made a member of a committee 'to draw up rules for the Clubs', when the lack of a proper code of rules, or disregard of them, had caused no little trouble. In that same term he was busy raising a cricket side for a game against the Hall; and to this annual fixture he added, in 1901, a match against the Tennis VI. He had audited the Clubs' Accounts for the year 1897/98, and in 1901 was made a member of their Finance Committee. From 1902 he was President of the Literary Society until, upon his appointment as Censor five years later, he retired in favour of Mr Leonard Alston (of Christ's College), then lately appointed the first Director of Studies in Economics to the non-collegiate students.

It would be wrong to regard Reddaway's attitude to the Clubs simply as another example of a widespread partiality for the successful athlete. Reddaway himself was no mean gamesman – he had played lacrosse for the University for seven years (and was captain of the side in 1895/96), and at lawn tennis he was a player to be reckoned with for a considerable time – but while he was by disposition on easy terms with the athletes and other leaders of his community, he believed that their success was likely not only to win the respect of the colleges, but also to enhance the reputation of Fitzwilliam Hall in the outside world, and help to make a rule rather than an exception the 'unsurpassed band of freshmen' of 1907, of whom he retained a vivid memory after many

[1] *Magazine*, December 1910, p. 2.

years.[1] Reddaway found the leaders of his community congenial, and believed them to be men of real worth. His concern for their welfare, which he regarded as a necessary accompaniment to the prosperity of Fitzwilliam Hall, he never lost; for if it was a preoccupation with him when he first came it was still this same concern, at the end of his period of office, which prompted the last minute change in the form of the memorial to his men who had fallen in the war of 1914. It will be remembered that Reddaway's fear that the measures proposed by the Syndicate of 1924 might lead to decreasing support for corporate activities within the House was responsible for his proposal that the monies collected originally for the foundation of Exhibitions should be put towards the purchase, on behalf of the Amalgamated Clubs, of Red Cottage on the playing field.[2]

In 1929, five years after his retirement, Reddaway was a contributor to the *Fitzwilliam Journal*, which was celebrating the diamond jubilee of the foundation of the non-collegiate institution, by then styled Fitzwilliam House. Entitled '*A Retrospect*', it is reasonable to suppose that Reddaway's contribution recalls those features of the place which made the liveliest impression on him at the time:[3]

My own Fitzwilliam memories extend over rather more than half of the sixty years. They owe their origin to the influenza which seized on the present Bishop of Plymouth in the spring of 1895. Himself an old alumnus, he held the post of Lecturer in History, which imposed the duty of giving two lectures each week to poll men, for the General Examination, now extinct. As his deputy, therefore, I, the most junior of graduates, found myself expounding the Protectorate to a class of unknown men, two of whom wore beards. And next year, when presented to a Plymouth living, he turned to me again, thus giving me an advantage which secured my ultimate election to the post of Lecturer in the face of otherwise overwhelming competition.

Thirty-five years stands for little in the lifetime of a University, but those days seem almost incredibly remote. A cyclist had not long ceased to be "a cad on castors," nor was it many years since a Master had endorsed an application from Newnham to attend Mathematical lectures in his College "No modest female would prefer such a request." The quiet of Trumpington Street was broken chiefly by the jingling harness of an occasional hansom, a curiously alluring sound, and, six times in every week-day hour, by the clank of the horse-drawn tram. Early-closing day was a voluntary innovation, but on Sunday all external life, save that of

---

[1] See p. 322.
[2] See p. 190.
[3] *Journal*, April 1930, p. 19.

church-goers and bedecked pedestrians, seemed to cease. The University, as compared with to-day, might be said to have the numbers, half the subjects of study, and twice the prejudice against change.[1]

In such a soil new saplings, like the Women's Colleges and ourselves, found it by no means easy to strike root. Towards the end of the last century the rejection of a proposal to give degrees to women was followed by serious damage to the gates of Newnham, and the son of a Colonel of Regulars was debarred from entering the University Rifle Volunteers.[2] In some ways, however, enthusiasm could win reward more easily than to-day. Two or three keen men might create a team which could defeat many of the smaller Colleges in those less overwhelming times, and the Ordinands of St Matthew's House, eight in number, have been known to form a vigorous skeleton crew. The Lawn Tennis VI sometimes ranked among the best in the University. The terminal dinners, when the Censor spoke and a concert followed, rallied a large body of men, and were much enjoyed; while the Debating Society and the Historical Society held regular and not undistinguished meetings.

In 1907, when Mr Huddleston closed the longest reign in our history, I hoped that Mr W. G. Bell or the present Dean of Norwich[3] would succeed, but they urged me to stand, and I was elected. We had at that time several notable friends – the President of Queens', Dr Foakes-Jackson, Monsignor Nolan, Dr Crafer, and others – but the supreme good fortune was the accession, in 1907, of an unsurpassed band of freshmen. With all sections working together, we enjoyed seven years of unchecked progress until 1914. The most incandescent moment, I think, came in 1912, when the Exhibition Fund was inaugurated at a terminal dinner, and men living on £80 a year contrived to make handsome contributions. No. 19 Fitzwilliam Street, a house once occupied and enlarged by Bishop G. F. Browne, was eventually purchased as the result.[4]

The War took toll of our best men, and threatened to break the continuity of our development. At one time we were reduced to a motley forty, and after the Armistice inflated to a dangerously homogeneous three hundred – dangerous because as ex-servicemen they could leave no successors, while our old clientele the Ordinands had shrunk ominously, and some other valuable constituents had disappeared. On the other hand, in new times a new body found life easier, and "blues" and other under-

---

[1] There is an omission here. In the academic year 1869–70 there were 2,019 undergraduate members of the University (*University Calendar* 1870); in 1929–30 there were about 5,000, including 181 advanced students (*Cambridge Review*, 18 October 1929, p. 29).

[2] Reddaway's reference must be to C. V. Sherlock, son of Colonel W. W. Sherlock, University Lecturer in Hindustani. See also p. 107.

[3] The Rev. D. H. S. Cranage (King's College). Secretary of Cambridge University Local Lectures 1902–24; Secretary of the Board of Extra-mural Studies 1924–28; Dean of Norwich 1928–45. He was a member of the Non-Collegiate Students Board for just over three years from 1 January 1905.

[4] See p. 187.

graduate distinctions came with refreshing frequency. A share in the State subsidy to the University next became ours by right, and the practice by which each generation contributes something permanent to the common weal has gone on unbroken, as the new pavilion shows. The O. F. Society and its devoted officers form a priceless asset, organising as they do intercourse for men who have left Cambridge, and moral backing for those who remain there. In about five years' time, when the effect of the reduced birth-rate during the War reaches the University, a new testing time must come, but with the present administration, I, for one, have no fear of the result.

Communal Dining

Of the non-athletic activities of the non-collegiate undergraduates none seemed more important to Reddaway than their dining together in hall. Indeed, he mentions it so frequently that it almost has the air of a yardstick by which he measured the health of his community. He presents his information, as is not unusual, with a flourish. After saying in 1908 that the number of diners had 'greatly increased',[1] in his Report to the Board for the year 1910/11 he adduces as evidence of the energy and skill of the first resident graduate Steward (A. O. N. Lee) the circumstance that during that year a total of 5,881 hall dinners were served, which on the basis of, say, twenty-six weeks residence suggests a daily figure of thirty or so, out of an undergraduate population of about one hundred and twenty. This substantial growth in the practice of communal dining was maintained, and was further increased until in the Michaelmas term of 1913 Reddaway, again varying his method of presentation, announces a total of more than eleven hundred in three weeks, as against a thousand a month three years earlier[2] – a daily attendance, that is, of about fifty undergraduates, out of the one hundred and fifty then in residence at the various institutions which made up the non-collegiate student body.

The terminal dinners 'when the Censor spoke and a concert followed' had their beginnings before there was a kitchen to provide them, or a hall in which they could be served; and when, like so much else, they were given a new impetus under Reddaway, the *Fitzwilliam Magazine* was quick to take notice, for an early number contains a reference to a Terminal Dinner held on 15 October 1908, attended by a company of sixty-two.[3] The Censor made his customary speech, and the dinner, which had been preceded by a General Meeting of the

---

[1] Huddleston had given figures from time to time. His highest average number of diners had been fifteen, in the Lent term 1899, out of a resident population of 102. See p. 146.

[2] *Magazine*, December 1913, p. 1.

[3] *Ibid.*, November 1908, p. 26.

Amalgamated Clubs, was followed by a concert. This pattern was followed in the Lent term, and in the Easter term the date was put forward so that the occasion might mark more suitably, for men in their third year, the end of their time at the University. The change appears to have been a success, in so far as for the first time it was found necessary to turn away at the door customers who had omitted to book their seats. In the following Michaelmas term there was a record attendance of eighty-four, and in his speech Reddaway took the opportunity of announcing the resignation of Mr Alston from the editorship of the *Magazine*, and the choice of an undergraduate as his successor.

The established pattern – a General Meeting of the Clubs before the dinner, and a concert after it – was maintained, and recorded with fair regularity, until the Lent term 1912, afterwards remembered for the Censor's announcement of the termination of the Exhibitions given since 1894 by the Leathersellers' Company, and for his appeal to the undergraduates there present for help in making good the loss.[1] Their response, supported by old members to whom Reddaway also addressed his appeal, led to the establishment of two 1912 Exhibitions, primarily intended for the assistance of men in residence who had rendered good service to the Hall.

In June 1914, at the last pre-war dinner, the attendance of one hundred and three was higher than ever before. The Censor spoke, and was often to speak again; but of three other speakers two were to lay down their lives in France, W. B. Hirst within a year, and H. E. Martin in 1916.

The dinners were kept up with surprising success throughout the war years. In October 1914 the company of a hundred included a number of Belgian guests; in the Lent term 1916 the seventy diners exceeded the total number of undergraduates in residence; in the Easter term Reddaway refers to a 'welcome infusion of khaki'; and so until the Lent term of 1919, when the gathering included a substantial number who, having laid their khaki aside, had returned, or come into residence and set about the business of obtaining a degree. This occasion also differed from its predecessors in that, we are told, 'sudden demobilization'[2] deprived the company of its waiters, whose places were supplied by volunteers among the guests. Six months later a confident reference to the 'inevitable Terminal Dinner' of Michaelmas

---

[1] The response to this appeal made for Reddaway the 'incandescent moment' to which he referred a quarter of a century later. See p. 322. For a note on the Leathersellers' awards, see pp. 546–8.

[2] 'Industrial action', presumably.

1919 seems to have flown in the face of Providence, for shortly after-wards Reddaway himself announced its demise, not indeed from inade-quate support, but from lack of space. 'The old "Terminals" are now no more', he writes, 'for even with two Halls in the day we are liable to an overflow dinner in the Lecture Room.'[1]

The long continuance of these special occasions, often in circum-stances of considerable difficulty, is a notable example of Reddaway's determination to promote any activity which would bring his men together, and encourage them in their corporate pursuits. At these dinners they met in good fellowship, and in relatively large numbers, and Reddaway seized the opportunities they presented of bolstering the morale of his community – underprivileged they might be, but if he could prevent it they should never for long be dispirited.

The Debating Society

Of the societies specifically mentioned by Reddaway as in being at the turn of the century, the Debating Society[2] was still under the wing of the Literary, Debating, and Musical Society, and, according to such copies of the Rules as have been preserved, it was not until 1923, when the Literary Society drops out of the official list, that the Debating Society again appears as an individual constituent member of the Clubs. Nevertheless in common usage its earlier title died hard; and with the coming of the *Magazine* there are frequent references to the Debating Society, and to its President and other officers; and Reddaway himself appears to subscribe to a general uncertainty when he refers to 'our traditional organisations for Music and for Debate, for Theological and Historical study'.[3] Debates and Smoking Concerts are often recorded by way of editorial comment, and not in individual reports such as were usually supplied to the editor of the *Magazine* by secretaries of other clubs. Whether for this reason, or because debates are matter for speeches, the written accounts of Debating Society activities seem not to excite such lively interest as those of some other societies or clubs.

The Society was not disbanded during the war of 1914–1918, and at least at its beginning the usual number of debates were held – three or four in the Michaelmas and Lent terms, with fewer in the Easter term. In the Michaelmas term of 1916, at a debate which took place in the library because there were no fires in the reading room, the House decided, by a small majority, that the United States of America ought to enter the war on the side of the allies. A year later there are sugges-

---

[1] *Magazine*, November 1920, p. 6.
[2] See p. 146.
[3] *Magazine*, December 1910, p. 2.

tions of an attempt to revive flagging interest; in the Michaelmas term 1918 three meetings were held, and in March 1919, with an average attendance of twenty-six, the society thought itself well on the way to a resumption of its pre-war routine. In the immediate post-war years the society appears to have been unusually active, for its correspondent declares that in the year 1921/22 it had been regarded as the most vigorous of College Debating Societies. 'We have', he adds, 'received and visited Girton, and have also entertained many of the Union Society's officers, together with two local lady magistrates and labour candidates.' And in G. G. Sharp it had provided, in the Easter term of 1921, the Union Society's first Fitzwilliam Hall President.

The Musical Society

At the time of Reddaway's election as Censor, musical occasions, like debates, were still the responsibility of the Literary, Debating, and Musical Society; but in 1910 the 'Musical Secretary', since 1889 an official of the composite society, became an officer of the Amalgamated Clubs, and the music makers came to be regarded more and more generally, if unofficially, as a society of their own, although their estimates of expenditure were not, as such, included among those of the Clubs before the Michaelmas term 1920; and it was not until 1923, when the Rules were revised, that the Musical Society also became a member of the Amalgamated Clubs in its own right.

The Society continued to organize concerts with programmes similar to those of earlier years; and in the Easter term of 1908 an experiment was tried of having both concerts and debates every week, but after one term this arrangement was abandoned in favour of the former practice of holding them on alternate Saturday evenings. Programmes changed little, but opportunities were devised of offering them more frequently. In the Easter term of 1908 the Musical Society announced itself 'At Home' to all comers (from Fitzwilliam Hall), and for the first time ladies were invited as guests. On this occasion, conjuring was added to the list of attractions, and this experiment was repeated. At the end of the following Michaelmas term the first Freshmen's Concert was held; and on 20 February 1909 the Non-Collegiate Students Board lent a hand as hosts to members of Fitzwilliam Hall, when, we are told, nearly one hundred guests enjoyed their hospitality and musical items of the kind that had become customary on these social occasions. This function was followed on 18 March by the Lent Terminal Dinner, with the Censor's usual speech (in which he did not miss the opportunity of proposing a toast to a successful football team), and, again, with the

usual songs, recitations, and instrumental solos. In the Michaelmas
term of 1909 a Fitzwilliam Quartette (vocal) made its appearance (after
a false alarm or two, it seems), thereby establishing a precedent for the
name of a string quartet of real distinction, but not consisting exclusively of Fitzwilliam men, some sixty years later. And so, until 1914,
the pattern was repeated – Freshmen's Concerts, Board' Receptions,
Musical Society 'At Homes', Terminal Dinners – advantage being taken
of almost any suitable chance to make music or provide entertainment,
either as an accompaniment to other functions, or, failing that, at
Smoking Concerts arranged independently two, three, or even four
times in each of the Michaelmas and Lent terms. And to these were
added, in 1913, two new departures, when there was a May Week Concert on 7 June, and a reception by the Censor and Mrs Reddaway on
June 20th.

The Musical Society of these years, only partially recognized as an
independent group, was beyond doubt among the most active and,
within its self-imposed limits, the most successful, of all the non-collegiate clubs and societies. Reasons are not far to seek: quite apart from
its special attraction for the musically gifted, music was an interest that
could be cultivated in the evenings, when nearly all the men could
arrange to be free; and, within its prescribed range, the society could
make do with comparatively very little equipment – a piano, and such
instruments as their fortunate possessors might be capable of playing. It
is impossible not to admire the resourcefulness of these early undergraduates, their readiness to make their own amusement, and, it seems,
their ability to afford a great deal of pleasure to their fellows.

In the Michaelmas term of 1914 the proceedings of the Musical
Society (like the Debating Society) were, we are told, almost as usual,
though audiences were small; and a year later the two societies still
held their meetings on alternate Saturday evenings in the Michaelmas
term; and concerts still followed Terminal Dinners, as, indeed, they
did throughout the War, even if on one occasion performances were
impromptu. In the Lent term of 1918 the Censor himself organized a
concert, and repeated the venture a year later with a cast which drew
lots for the order of its appearances, and included guests from Trinity,
Peterhouse, and Caius. In the following Michaelmas term there was a
return to normal with a Freshmen's Concert, but there was one other,
only, during that term; and thereafter musical activity is not mentioned
again for more than two years. In the Lent term of 1922 the musical
correspondent of the *Magazine*, after hinting that the University Musical Club was absorbing a relatively large share of the interest of the

members of his society, mentions one Smoking Concert, implies that the 'distinguished efforts' of guest performers had somewhat outshone home-grown products, and ends by suggesting that concerts might be better if they were better attended. After an apparently uneventful Easter term, there were three concerts in the following Michaelmas term, of which the first was given by the freshmen, and the last – apparently very successful – received only a passing mention some months afterwards in a report to the *Magazine* devoted largely to an 'O.T.C. Smoker', presumably organized in support of the University Officers Training Corps, of which W. S. Thatcher was an enthusiastic advocate. There is also an appreciation of the kindness and hospitality of Mr R. S. Ball,[1] the first President of the society after its elevation to the ranks of the Amalgamated Clubs.

Something of the busy spontaneity of earlier days seems to have departed; and it is probably no coincidence that in his review of the happenings of the year 1922/23 the editor of the *Magazine* makes no reference to the Musical Society; and certainly from such accounts as continued to appear during the rest of Reddaway's time its activities were greatly diminished, and were not held in anything like the same esteem as they had once been. In the post-war years there were many more students, and in this larger and more heterogeneous body corporate pursuits may have found themselves in greater difficulties than in the smaller well-knit community of previous years.

The Historical Society

The Historical Society[2] lost its President soon after his election as Censor, for in the Lent term 1908 Reddaway resigned in favour of H. W. V. Temperley, another Kingsman, who had been elected Fellow of Peterhouse in 1904. The society then met in Mr Temperley's rooms (once occupied by the poet Gray); but not for long, for by the end of that same academical year Mr Temperley had given up his presidency and directorship of studies, and was succeeded by Mr Alston, in whose rooms the meetings were held – rooms with a brief association with another Professor of History, for they had been let to Lord Acton at the time of his election as Regius Professor, although there is no evidence that he ever lived in them.[3]

---

[1]   Robert Steele Ball. A graduate of the Massachusetts Institute of Technology, and an Honorary Master of Arts of the University (1914), he appears in the *University Calendar* as a supervisor in Mechanical Sciences for Fitzwilliam House from 1929 to 1945. He was also for three years (1922–25) President of the Amalgamated Clubs, and was a Governor of the Fitzwilliam Hall Trust from 23 May 1923 until 23 October 1945. See also p. 488n.

[2]   For brief earlier references to the Historical and the Theological Societies, see p. 148.

[3]   See p. 113.

No minutes of the society have survived; and, by this Society of all societies, none are now kept. That this was not always so is evident from the *Magazine* for June 1911, which refers to the (nearly completed) 'Record Book, which contains the minutes for our 158 meetings', and also mentions a suggestion that it should be bound (out of the society's surplus of ten shillings), and placed in the archives of the Hall. Apparently nothing was done. From 1908 the *Magazine* was supplied, with fair regularity, with accounts of the society's doings. Papers were usually read by junior members; but on 30 November 1910 the 150th meeting was addressed by the Head of St Edmund's House (the Rev. T. C. L. Williams), who as a non-collegiate undergraduate had served as Secretary for the year 1901/02 (and had been a mainstay of non-collegiate cricket). In 1911, when Mr Alston gave up his directorship, he was followed, jointly, by Mr Williams and Mr Gaskoin, but remained as president for another year, and was succeeded by Mr Gaskoin in the Michaelmas term of 1912. At some point during the year 1915/16, the war notwithstanding, the society celebrated its 210th meeting, when the Censor appears to have spoken on the history of early Cambridge. By the Lent term 1916 the President was at the War Office, and the Secretary (C. B. B. Clee) at the war, but unlike the lawyers and the scientists the historians were against a total suspension of their activities. By 3 November 1921 forty more meetings had been held, for on that day the 250th was commemorated at a gathering addressed by the Orator (T. R Glover, of St John's College, then recently Senior Proctor) on the early history of the University. In the Michaelmas term of 1922 a joint meeting with the Dramatic Society was the occasion of a play reading (*Richard II*) – a departure possibly inspired, and undoubtedly supported, by the President of the two societies. In the Censor's last active year (1922/23) a seemingly casual observation by the editor of the *Magazine* to the effect that 'even the Chess Club and the Historical Society met regularly and happily' suggests some loss of vigour. Whether this led to a more frequent recourse to outside help is uncertain, but it is noticeable that at this time the society counted among its guest speakers Dr J. H. Clapham of King's ('Witchcraft and some Historians'), Mr Bernard Manning of Jesus College, and the Rev. R. G. Laffan, of Queens'.

The Theological Society

Games Clubs apart, one other undergraduate group had come into being before the beginning of Reddaway's censorship – the Theological Society, established in the Easter term 1902 as a common meeting ground for non-collegiate ordinands, of whom by 1907 there were more than forty. From 1908 onwards the society's doings were regularly reported, and well reported, in the *Fitzwilliam Magazine*, and the Secretary for the year 1908/09 (Walter Harvey) takes pains to emphasize that although ordinands as such are members without election, membership is not limited to them. At that time meetings were held weekly in term, alternating between formal occasions when papers were read, usually by junior members of the society but also by senior guests, and less formal discussions. Each term, generally at the end, corporate communion was celebrated in All Saints' Church by the President, who then with Mrs Crafer entertained the company to breakfast; and at the year's end a society photograph was taken, after the Service and before breakfast, at what one Secretary described as the 'gothic' hour of 8.15.

The Michaelmas term of 1909 was especially remembered for an address, on 19 November, by Dr Montagu Butler, Master of Trinity, on 'William Wilberforce'. In March 1910 there is another reminder that visitors were welcome at all meetings of the society, and that services at the Brassie Chapel in King's College[1] were open to all members of Fitzwilliam Hall. In the following Michaelmas term there were expressions of indebtedness to the authorities for permission to hold daily services in the library at 1.05 o'clock, an arrangement shortly afterwards changed to three weekday services at 7.45 a.m. Among the speakers in the Lent term of that year was the Rev. B. T. D. Smith, Vice-Principal of Westcott House, who as a non-collegiate undergraduate was awarded a Lady Kay scholarship in 1906, and migrated to Jesus College. In the Easter term of 1913, for the first time, the Secretary's regular report does not appear in the *Magazine*; but material about the chapel was not lacking, for the editor published a valuable note on its history by an anonymous contributor, together with G. H. Hewitt's illustration of his proposals for its furnishing, when the library was handed over for its exclusive use.[2]

The provision of a chapel in Fitzwilliam Hall, modest though it was, quickly brought about a major change in the arrangements of the Theological Society, a change which is recorded in the words of G. H. Hewitt, who had become its Secretary. 'The Theological Society', he says, 'has started out under a new rule. The Society had been formed by the President many years ago, to fill a distinctly spiritual need: no

---

[1] The third chapel from the west on the south side. The College Council had made it available in the Michaelmas term 1905. Board minutes of 21 November 1905.

[2] *Magazine*, June 1913, pp. 221–5.

Constitution had ever been drawn up; every ordinand was *ipso facto* a member of the Society. It was felt that the need for such a Society had passed. The Chapel took over the fulfilment of the first function; and lest it should be thought that the Theological Society, as such, had anything to do with the Chapel, the Committee asked to be allowed to draw up a new Constitution.'[1] The committee's draft was accepted, and the society became 'simply a Society for theological discussion'. As such it appears to have prospered, for during the academical year 1913/14 there were more than sixty members. With the coming of the war, its activities were restricted, but were not abandoned altogether. Two meetings were held in the first war year, of which the second, addressed by Charles Raven, then Dean of Emmanuel, appears to have aroused a lively interest, and there were occasional meetings until the Easter term of 1917, when the last of customary notices of the society also records the departure to a living in London of Dr Crafer, its founder, and its President since 1902. Thereafter, during Reddaway's censorship, with the single exception of a passing reference to a meeting held on 29 January 1919, at which the speaker was the Rev. J. K. Mozley, Dean of Pembroke College, the Theological Society, like the chapel, no longer figures in the *Magazine*, and the only reference to any topic associated with either is an occasional honourable mention of the progress of a fund for the endowment of the stipend of a Chaplain, started by Reddaway in 1916, and inspired by his sense of the value of the work of A. O. N. Lee. He announces its completion in 1923, when £500 had been subscribed and handed over to the Fitzwilliam Hall Trust for the purchase of no. 10 Fitzwilliam Street.[2]

The seeming indifference of post-war undergraduates to organized religion was matched by the relatively very small number among them who read for Holy Orders. Reddaway's reference to this in 1930 confirms his regret, even though, apparently, he made no public reference to it at the time. Other consequences were not lacking, as in the growing difficulty of finding suitable academically qualified ordinands to hold the Clothworkers' Exhibitions, in spite of concessions in their favour; and, possibly most strikingly of all, in the affairs of the Amalgamated Clubs themselves. If, as Reddaway declared, the Clubs played a prominent part in the fortunes of Fitzwilliam Hall, they in their turn leant heavily on their principal officers, the General Secretaries; and a casual speculation on the nature of the office and the selection of its holders (by the Clubs' representatives) has proved to be not without

[1]   *Ibid.*, December 1913, p. 14.
[2]   See p. 186–7.

interest. From the Lent term 1884, when amalgamation was introduced, to the Easter term 1969 there were eighty-one General Secretaries; from 1884 to 1918 there were thirty-eight, of whom twenty-one
had followed a course of some kind in Theology; from 1918 to 1969
there were forty-three, and of theologians, two.[1]

The roll of General Secretaries also bears testimony to the improving
quality of Reddaway's applicants for admission, and to his success in
keeping them, for of the twenty-eight General Secretaries who held
office between the Lent term 1884 and the Easter term 1907, nine
became members of colleges. Of the remainder, four did not graduate,
six graduated with honours, and nine with a pass degree. In the
academical years 1907–69 there were fifty-three; none joined a college;
and all graduated, forty-one with honours (including those who were
classed in an honours examination and received allowances for
approved national service).

The Science Society

The inaugural meeting of the Science Society was held on 27 January
1912, and the first paper was read on 13 February by Dr Marett Timms,
Director of Studies in Medicine. From a subsequent report of his
replacement on going out of residence, it appears that the society's first
Treasurer was Percy Dunsheath (B.A. 1912), one of the oldest living
members of Fitzwilliam Hall.

The society seems to have met fairly regularly, three or four times a
term, until the outbreak of the war, when its activities were suspended.
It was revived, with weekly meetings, in the Lent term 1920, and began
with a flourish, for on 1 March its guest speaker was Sir Ernest Ruther-
ford. At that time regarded, at least by itself, as the largest of the Fitzwilliam societies, numbers began to fall, for there is more than one
appeal for more members, particularly of the first and second years.
Ladies were invited to a meeting in the Lent term of 1923, an innovation which appears to have met with approval.

The Law Society

On 22 November 1913, at a meeting held in the Censor's rooms of men
reading Law at Fitzwilliam Hall, it was resolved that a society should be
formed 'for the purpose of hearing papers read on some legal subject,
and discussing the same'. Mr N. G. Scorgie, of Trinity College and

[1] Of the eighty-one General Secretaries, three were placed in the first class in a Tripos examination: Metford Watkins (Maths. II, 1921); H. M. Burton (English, 1923); and T. H. B.
Hollins (Mod. and Med. Langs. (French) 1934).

Director of Studies in Law, was elected President, and the Censor and Mr Gaskoin Vice-Presidents. The society's first meeting was held just two months later, when the President read a paper entitled 'Some Early Law Societies'. In his article 'In War Time', Reddaway speaks of the suspension of all activities of the Science and Law Societies, and of the latter there is no information, from Fitzwilliam sources, until the Easter term of 1918, when the society is said to have 'vindicated its renaissance', doubtless after having been responsible for the conduct of a breach of promise case also mentioned by the *Magazine* correspondent.

There is then silence for more than four years, followed by a most notable burst of activity during the academical year 1922/23; when – it can be no coincidence – the Secretary was J. R. W. Alexander, who, a year or so later, was to be a moving spirit, or rather the moving spirit, in the foundation of the Fitzwilliam Society. The Law Society's reappearance is announced with a proclamation of its 'particularly flourishing' condition; Reddaway is elected President; and it may still be of interest to some that Dr P. H. Winfield, of St John's College, became Mr Gaskoin's fellow Vice-President. Four meetings were arranged for that Michaelmas term; at the second a paper was read by A. J. Knight, then a Fitzwilliam undergraduate, and later Archbishop of the West Indies in Georgetown; the last meeting was to be the occasion of an Annual Dinner, to be held at the Union Society on 6 December; and, for good measure, Alexander promises papers in the coming Lent term by Mr A. D. McNair (Lord McNair) of Caius College, and by Mr Gaskoin.

The Secretary's report of the Lent term 1923 is excellent: lively, substantial, and interesting. Again there were four meetings. At one Mr Gaskoin duly read a paper on 'The Postal Censorship in War-time'; at another Mr McNair presided over a Moot; and the last was given over to preparations for Mock Trial to be held, in collaboration with the Dramatic Society, before Judge Farrant on 2 May. This proved a most successful venture, and an account of it pays eloquent tribute to the organizing ability of the Secretary. The part of the leading lady in the case was taken by G. M. Walton. When all was over, the Secretary, in a postscript, informed all and sundry of various publications (including the *Cambridge Law Journal*) in which further particulars might be found; and expressed what was no doubt general satisfaction that among members of the public in Court had been a Harvard professor and Mr H. A. Hollond of Trinity College, Dr Oliver of Trinity Hall, Mr A. L. Goodhart of Corpus Christi, and the Chief Constable.

And then, of the Law Society, by common consent so successful in 1922/23, no more is heard in Reddaway's time. Whether from reaction, exhaustion, or, as is more likely, from the lack of a really keen and capable successor to an officer in these respects outstanding, some years were to pass before its next appearance in the records.[1]

The Dramatic Society

In the Lent term 1921 Reddaway, in his Censor's letter to the *Fitzwilliam Magazine*, salutes (with respect) two new societies – the Economics Society and the Dramatic Society, of which the second, on its merits, doubtless assisted by a flair for publicity not surprising in a group whose business it was to catch the public eye, won widespread recognition by town and gown alike, and brought no little credit to its non-collegiate parent body. The earliest account of the foundation of the new society is contained in a *Magazine* notice, which proclaims the formation, under the guidance of J. L. Van Hoylandt, of the Fitzwilliam Hall Amateur Dramatic Society (FHADS in embryo), and declares the society's intention of producing *The Younger Generation* (Stanley Houghton) 'as soon as a Theatre is available in the Easter term'.[2] Fifty years later, two of its founder members compiled an informative account of the society's doings, with a list of its productions.[3] *The Younger Generation*, described as a bold adventure, was duly performed at the A.D.C. Theatre, and the presence at the play of Professor Sir Arthur Quiller-Couch may not unreasonably be attributed to prompting by Julius Herman,[4] who, as one of the players, and his research student pupil, no doubt suggested to Sir Arthur where his duty lay. The *Cambridge Review* was most encouraging in its account of this 'maiden production' of the society, with especial praise for the performance of G. M. Walton. Among others named, Herman was said to have 'made the utmost of the smallest part in the play'.

In the following year there was a three nights production of *Cupid and the Styx* (Sackville Martin), in which G. M. Walton confirmed his reputation as an unusually competent actor in women's rôles. The society had hoped to play again at the A.D.C. Theatre, but at the last moment this proved impossible, and they had to make do with very

---

[1] See *Magazine*, March and December 1914, June 1918, December 1922, March and June 1923, June 1929. In addition, the *Cambridge Law Journal* (1921.1) refers to the revival of the society in January 1918.

[2] *Magazine*, March 1921, p. 25.

[3] 'Fitzwilliam Hall Dramatic Society and Fitzwilliam Theatre, 1921–1971', by G. M. Walton and H. M. Burton (*Journal*, 1972, p. 20).

[4] See pp. 476–8.

severely limited facilities at the Alexandra Hall. Although the performance met with approval, the society seems to have been discouraged
('affronted' may be the better word) at the lack of support from Fitzwilliam Hall itself, for of more than three hundred residents not more
than sixty put in an appearance. The *Review*'s correspondent did not
think much of the play but spoke highly of the players. 'If the
F.H.A.D.S.', he concludes, 'choose their third play more carefully and
act as keenly, their performances should be sold out.'

The lack of suitable premises was a serious handicap, for the cost of
hiring a hall in the town was burdensome, and the Trumpington Street
building, in other ways preferable, was too small; and, when two light-
hearted sketches were presented in the Lent term of 1923, there was
also some anxiety about the safety of the common room floor.

For the remainder of the academical year 1922/23 the activities of
the society, if not of some of its individual members, were limited to
sharing with the Law Society in the organization of a Mock Trial, but in
the Lent term of 1924 a notable production seems to have put the
society firmly on its feet, when a single performance in Fitzwilliam Hall
of A. A. Milne's *The Dover Road* was so well received that, by request,
four additional performances were put on in May Week in the Liberal
Club in Downing Street, when, says the notice, 'on one night alone,
the Vice-Chancellor, some Masters of Colleges, leading dons and much
of Cambridge Society came to see us.'[1] The *Review*, in its account of
the earlier showing in Fitzwilliam Hall, had this time picked out for
particular encomium the performance of C. J. B. Gaskoin, by then
elected to the presidency of the society,[2] which he was to occupy for
many years.

At the beginning, the society's choice of plays was much hampered
by its acceptance of the custom, prevalent among similar Cambridge
groups, whereby women's rôles were played by men. With considerable help from Gaskoin as President, this arrangement was shortly to be
changed, to the society's benefit, and the greatly increased enjoyment
of its audiences.

The Boat Club

In the year 1906/07, a few weeks before the announcement of
Reddaway's appointment as Censor, the Fitzwilliam Lent boat – there
was, of course, only one – found itself, on the last night of the Races,

---

[1]   *Journal*, January 1972, p. 21.
[2]   He is first described as President on a menu card of a society dinner held on 11 June 1923
      (see an album *F.H.A.D.S. 1921–1934*, in the College Archives, presented to the Society by
      G. Milner Walton).

at the bottom of the river, having lost one place to the getting-on boat (Queens' II); and this programme was repeated in 1908, with Magdalene II as the getting-on boat. There had been no May Boat for some years; the freshmen of 1908 had little taste for rowing; and this, combined with repeated lack of success in the Lent Races, brought about a decision that the Boat Club, which absorbed a disproportionate share of scanty available funds, and added little to the Clubs' prestige, should be disbanded altogether. The boat, if possible, should be sold; and the proceeds, with an annual sum of £5, should be put to a special Boat Club Fund, against the day when the club might be revived. Two years later, we are told, there was a genuine desire for a re-start, backed by voluntary subscriptions of £20. An Acting Secretary (but no Captain) was appointed, and a sum of £10 allowed by the Amalgamated Clubs for expenses for the Michaelmas term, and at the end of that term it was agreed that the club should be re-established, in the first instance for the remainder of the academical year.[1]

The results of the Lent Races in 1911 did not quite conform to the usual pattern of one adverse bump and three rowings over. As before, the boat went down on the first night; and, again as before, rowed over on the second; but on the third they caught Christ's III; and then, in one of the river's not infrequent tangles, were re-bumped in the last race. A. O. N. Lee's account of the affair was well done, and is very revealing. He could not disguise the loss, over all, of one place; but his readers are almost, if not quite, persuaded that he is right in claiming success for the venture of 're-establishing the Boat Club'. After all, as he also says, 'we *had* made a bump'.[2] In 1912, with bumps on Clare III and Caius IV, the boat rose to forty-fourth place out of forty-six. The year was in general a comparatively good one for Fitzwilliam Hall, and, in a rare burst of confidence engendered by an escape from the bottom place of all, the question was raised whether, after fifteen years,[3] the Hall might again appear in the May Races. Reddaway's advice was sought, and on 4 March he wrote to W. G. Bell, then President of the Amalgamated Clubs. 'To my mind', he says, 'it is chiefly a question of how keen the rowing men are. If there are twelve men who are or will be up to the necessary standard of efficiency and who wish to put a boat on, it would be hard to convince me that we ought not to do so. They ought to realize that in all likelihood they will be bumped on the first night and row over the next three. But I feel sure that if the men who

1   A.C. Minutes, 19 November 1908, 21 October and 8 December 1910.
2   *Magazine*, March 1911, p. 52.
3   From time to time it has been said that there was no May Boat from 1894 to 1912. There

have rowed in the Lents are again available, they will do us no discredit and that the skill acquired will tell next year. Short of twelve good men to choose from, I should think it very doubtful.'[1] On the same day the Finance Committee of the Clubs resolved that the Boat Club might be carried on in the Easter term, and voted a sum of £10 'for the purpose of converting the Lent into a May Boat'. The boat was, presumably, converted. At all events it appeared, having been coached by C. M. Fiddian of King's, a cousin of Reddaway, and later Master over the choristers, and Headmaster of King's Choir School. Reddaway's prophecy was fulfilled: the Boat was bumped by Caius III, and rowed over at the bottom on the other three days. When the war came, the Lent boat had risen five places from the bottom of the river; but the May boat was still there.

After the war, the club, stimulated by one of its members who had stroked the boats in 1914, had hopes of beginning again in the restricted Lent Races of 1919; but war wounds and lack of men compelled them to wait for the Mays, in which they resumed their pre-war place at the bottom of the second division, and at once caught Peterhouse.[2] With two more bumps, they stood ready for the following year at twenty-eighth out of thirty-one, when the scene changed spectacularly with the creation of a third division, leaving Fitzwilliam much further from the bottom, if no nearer to the top. They dropped one place to the bottom of Division II, and stayed thereabouts until Reddaway's last year, when in June 1924 they lost two more places, and finished fourth in Division III (thirty-fourth out of forty-six).

In the Lents the club fared rather better. In 1920 they resumed their pre-war place (forty-first out of forty-six), but like the May boat found themselves in a relatively exalted position with the addition of a fourth division, and made four bumps (Caius III, Lady Margaret IV, King's II, and Queens' II), all, for good measure, before First Post Corner. In the next year (1920/21) a second boat got on, and went up three places. In 1924 the first boat finished fifth in Division III, after being third in 1923, and the second was three places from the bottom of the river, at thirteenth in Division IV. Their respective placings over all were thirty-fifth and fifty-eighth.

During the censorship of Reddaway the club had returned its May

was a boat in 1897, put on so late that it was omitted from the *Cambridge Review* list of crews expected to row, but included in the table of race results (see also *Review*, 1896–97, p. 435).

[1] Reddaway's letter of 4 March 1912, in his own hand, has been kept in the minutes of a meeting of the Finance Committee of the Amalgamated Clubs, of the same date.

[2] Not, as has been claimed, the first bump made on a representative boat. See pp. 139, 494.

boat to the river, even if its less vulnerable position was due to the creation of a third division. The Lent boat – apart from similar additions lower down – had escaped from its former place at the foot of the third division, and a second Lent boat had got on. Also, in 1924, the club must have come very near to celebrating the award of its first trial cap, for the Boat Captain (F. B. Priest) was superseded as stroke of 'B' Crew only after the eights had gone to Ely for their final week's practice.

Although the club's material gains, if modest, were beyond dispute, Reddaway's most telling influence on its fortunes was his gift of self-respecting enthusiasm in the face of apparently hopeless odds. Even after fifty years, this remained a lively memory in the mind of Mr George Litchfield, stroke in 1914, and in 1919 'non-playing' Captain of the Boats (his war wounds were still troublesome). 'By May 1919', he wrote, 'we had nine boys who upheld 1914 keenness, and when we bumped Peterhouse Mr Reddaway hugged me and danced on the towpath … Always, all winds and weathers, there was "Redders" on the towpath.'[1]

The Cricket Club

'We cannot help wondering', says the cricket Secretary in the summer of 1910, 'why Cricket and Cheshunt do not seem to go together.'[2] In these early years this was true of non-collegiate undergraduates in general, and it is not a matter for wonder, among men apt to be too heavily engaged in the less exciting business of obtaining a degree – if possible, with honours – to devote whole days to the game in an Easter term: whole days they might well be, with the morning of a match only too liable to be spent in speculation on the probability of rain, the long afternoon (if fine) on the game itself, when the value of book reading by the lower orders in the batting side was fictional, even if the book was not, and the evening given over to recapitulation of triumphs or to scrutiny of disaster. All this was not for the non-collegiate undergraduate, whose cricket, moreover, had suffered from further inconveniences. In the Lent term of 1908 the Secretary had been unable to draw up a list of fixtures; he did not know where matches could be played, or even whether practice would be possible. Only two games were arranged, eventually, with college sides (Queens' II and Selwyn II), but there were other engagements with the County School, the

---

[1] *Journal*, 1969, p. 21.
[2] The notes in the remainder of this chapter are largely taken from information contained in the *Magazine*, and the Amalgamated Clubs minutes.

Perse, and the Friends' School at Saffron Walden, and with the Censor's XI. An annual match at West Wratting Park and a game at Madingley had to be cancelled, probably because a side could not be raised. In all, of eight games actually played, four were lost and two won. Home games were played on the Perse School ground 'some distance along the Hills Road'; and the season, which began on 6 May, ended in early June, when, after a brief life at the most awkward time of the year, cricket lapsed into oblivion for ten months. In the meantime, the club hoped for good freshmen, who would 'help Fitzwilliam Hall to be as respected on the Cricket as on the Soccer field'; and a reference to 'better arrangements' to be made with the Tennis Club seems to reflect inevitable rivalry between the two clubs for the services of a scanty supply of eligible recruits.

The conveyance of the new ground to Reddaway is dated 1 April 1908, and very few weeks had passed before a net was provided for cricket, and some kind of practice pitch contrived, but it appears that the 1909 season was the first on the Oxford Road ground, and that the first home match, against Selwyn II, was played (and lost) on 4 May of that year. By June it was being said that the wicket was 'proving fast and true', though much remained to be done by way of levelling out the hollows running from north to south in parts of the outfield. At all events, by 1909 the club had been relieved of the embarrassment of having to seek accommodation, wherever it might be found, for home games.

In immediately succeeding years, matters improved very little. 'A study of last year's Cricket group', says the Secretary for 1910, 'shows our numerical loss. Five only remain, and of these one, perhaps considering it "about the limit", has abandoned the game altogether; another only deigns to think of it as a pick-me-up after Tennis; and a third – last year's Captain in fact – now considers cricket balls too hard. Only the Captain and the Secretary are left to welcome the new comers.' A year later there is a second XI, which would give the previous season's first side a very close game – but only because that side had been so very undistinguished. One revealing comment is that the fixture list of 1910 contained only one side (Saffron Walden School) in the list of the previous year. In 1911 poor fielding let the side down, as it so often did, and the only redeeming feature of the season was the selection of H. A. Dubois for the Freshmen's Match; but he scored no runs, and took one wicket, only, in two innings. (He had, however, won the high jump against Oxford a few weeks before.) In 1912 the Tennis Club and the Boat Club 'each took a former Captain'. The picture is a little brighter in the two seasons which immediately preceded the war of 1914–1918, for in 1913 five matches out of twelve were won, and only once was it necessary to scratch because a side could not be raised; while in 1914, of five games won three were against college first elevens – Trinity Hall, Corpus, and Magdalene – but if the story is to be complete, it has to be added that the return match against the Hall was lost by nine wickets.

With little or no cricket in prospect for an unknown future, it was decided in the Michaelmas term of 1914 to re-lay part of the wicket, in the hope that its southern end would thereby be made less fiery; and additional levelling made room for more net practice. Thereafter, the game is not mentioned until 1919, when the first post-war Captain was G. G. Sharp.[1] The side quickly resumed its pre-war habit of dropping catches and giving away boundaries, in games with St Catharine's, Trinity Hall, Peterhouse, Downing, and Selwyn, with gains and losses, nevertheless, about equally divided. For the rest of Reddaway's time, there is little of note to be found in the Cricket Reports of the *Magazine*, and of the 1921 season there is no mention at all. In 1922 J. W. Knight (Captain in the previous year) who had played for Wiltshire, appeared in two University trial matches, but nothing came of it. The 1924 season was spoilt by rain, and was otherwise unremarkable, save that the fielding of the side was said to be good, and the captain (N. A. Lesser) was some forty years later to be Primate and Archbishop of New Zealand.

Between 1907 and 1924 it appears that nine of the colleges figured in the Fitzw'lliam fixture-lists, whether as second elevens, 'A' sides, or occasionally as representative teams; but the Fitzwilliam list continued to depend appreciably on other clubs, for as late as 1923, when games were played with Peterhouse (twice), St Catharine's College, and Downing College, there were matches with North Essex Wanderers, the old boys of Newport School, the Cambridgeshire Wanderers, St Giles's Club, and the New Chesterton Institute. The three colleges, for whatever reason, were those which appeared most frequently among the Fitzwilliam fixtures; they were also those whose examination lists at the beginning of the century had been shown by Dr J. A. Venn to have benefited most perceptibly from their absorption of non-collegiate students in mid-course.

The Association Football Club

The Association Football Club had a disastrous season in Reddaway's first year as Censor, for they did not win a match. Even so, they con-

[1] See also p. 326.

gratulated themselves, in the light of their scanty resources, for never failing to field a side for any game, and for managing to stay in Division III (the lowest) of the League. In 1908/09, the first year at Oxford Road, they rose to second place in their division; and there was even some mention of a second XI. At this time there were annual fixtures with the Friends' School at Saffron Walden, and in February 1909 they beat the School for the first time. In 1909/10 cycling was, apparently, a rival attraction; and the Censor was in the winning side in a 'Football Sixes' tournament, for which for a number of years entrance fees were charged, and put to the fund for the purchase of the playing field. The first XI were at the head of Division III in 1910/11, and in that year a first visit was paid to St Catherine's in Oxford. After the side had been runners up in Division II in 1913/14, all organized football was abandoned until 1919/20, when W. A. Woods returned from active service to the captaincy to which he had been elected five years earlier, and the side were at the top of Division II, with sixty-six goals for, and nine against. In 1920/21 the second XI were in Division III, and went to the head of that division a year later, when there was also talk of a third XI, with the result that in 1922/23, the club's best year in its history until that time, the first XI were fourth in Division I, the second were the only second XI in Division II, and the Hall had its first blue in A. R. Chalk. But in Reddaway's last year the fortunes of the club were as disappointing as they had been in his first; inevitable falling numbers had their almost inevitable effect; the first XI sank to Division II, and the second disappeared from view.

The Lawn Tennis Club

In the summer games, it is refreshing to turn from the comparative sameness of the Cricket Reports to the optimism of the first *Magazine* account of the Lawn Tennis Club, with its opening announcement that a good deal more tennis is being played than formerly, and that the club has been able to put out two 'sixes' on the day of a first XI cricket match. The first pair, consisting of the Captain (L. J. Lock, the 'discoverer' of the playing field) and C. W. Janvrin (Captain of the Boat Club, Secretary of Tennis in 1908/09, and General Secretary in the following year), won nearly all their matches. In those days the Censor played, and not only in friendly games. In the first match on the ash courts (in the Michaelmas term 1908) he and L. L. Whiteway, who had both been in the VI in 1897, defeated the first pair. The next season was the club's best for many years, for it was unbeaten, and won twelve matches out of fourteen. Reddaway was moved to arrange, and pay for, a group photograph in which he himself appears, then in his thirty-seventh year, with Whiteway, whose return was warmly welcomed when, some years after his eventual graduation, he came back into residence at Ridley Hall. During this academical year the ash courts were turned round, so as reduce the extent to which the players had to face the sun, and they were thereby much improved.

By 1910 a third ash court had been put down, together with two new grass courts, the latter principally for the use of a recently formed Seniors' Club, and for the men at St Matthew's House. For the first VI this was not so good a year; and for the second, who lost everything, it was worse; and there was little improvement in the club's fortunes in the succeeding years. Members were often urged to make greater use of the opportunities for out-of-season practice afforded by the ash courts; and it was not infrequently found difficult to finish, in the Lent term, a singles competition for a racquet given each year by Mr Philip Whiteway, though entries were not lacking. By 1913 the club had still failed to get away from Division III of the League, but even so it comes as something of a surprise to discover, in April 1914, a decision by the Finance Committee of the Amalgamated Clubs, that, on account of the Clubs' financial situation, the Lawn Tennis Club should withdraw from the League in order to save expense. Fixtures were to be limited to 'friendly' games, and the lawn tennis estimates of £8.2.6 were reduced to eighteen shillings. Other clubs fared better, and the decision to economise on tennis will have been due to its disappointing record, and its relatively limited appeal to the undergraduates.

As with other games, little tennis was played after the Easter term of 1914, and the match courts were top-dressed, and left fallow for the 1915 season. There is then no mention of tennis in the *Magazine* until June 1919, when it was, apparently, thought undesirable to arrange for many matches; and two, only, were played – both against Peterhouse, and both lost. Thereafter references to the game are spasmodic: in 1922 there were two sixes, and the club's record was by no means discreditable; but hopes of rising to Division II were not realized. The only event of note was the winning of a blue for doubles by O. G. Miller, Captain in 1921. An article entitled '1922–23: An Interesting Year' does not refer to tennis, and, more surprising, there is no allusion to it in Reddaway's regular Censor's letters. A Secretary's Report does appear in June 1923, but it is brief, and contains little to satisfy the reader, or to capture his attention.

The Hockey Club

Admitted to Division III of the Inter-Collegiate League in 1905/06, the

Hockey Club's hold on membership was precarious from the start. In the Lent term 1908 five games were cancelled through inability to raise a side, and 'on this account', says the Secretary, 'we complied with the wishes of the Hockey League Committee, and withdrew from the League'. A year later, the club's application for re-admission was turned down because of its lateness; and there is the familiar complaint that players are few, and prevented from necessary practice in the Michaelmas term by their commitments to other games. In 1910 the side returned to the League, but 'fared badly', with no particulars given. In 1911 the report is limited to five lines of print (but the team was photographed), and at the time of writing three League games out of four had been lost, no doubt in part owing to the impossibility of counting on the same side twice running. In 1912 hockey is 'our one and only sport which has not flourished', and again there is the plea for practice in the Michaelmas term. A year later, unexpectedly, the side is half-way up Division III, and there is praise for the pitches, which, in a wet season, had stood up well to hard wear from three separate college sides 'to say nothing of occasional Lacrosse matches'. In the next season, three League games had been won by March 1914 – and then came the war.

With more men about after the war the fortunes of the club improved considerably. In November 1919 few fixtures were arranged 'because of other claims', but two men (R. E. Nation, and O. G. Miller) were in University trials, and the side finished the season as runners-up in Division III. In 1920/21 A. H. V. Welch was given a freshman's trial; and the club was again second in the League, and was also unfortunate in forfeiting a point for failure on one occasion to appoint a referee. Promotion to Division II came at length in 1922, and in the two follow-ing seasons in higher company the side's record was not unsatisfactory. In 1922/23 Welch was in a seniors' trial, and O. G. Miller, on occasion selected to play for the University, was capped for Scotland.

The Athletics Club

The Athletics Club was another which, after a false start some twenty-five years previously, came again into being in Reddaway's early years. The question of its formation was discussed at a General Meeting of the Amalgamated Clubs on 14 October 1911, when the Censor's view was that time was not ripe, but that there was a favourable opportunity to take initial steps by entering the Inter-Collegiate Competition for a challenge cup then recently presented by Mr W. W. Rouse Ball, of Trinity College. A committee was appointed to look into this possi-bility, with power to make whatever arrangements might be needed, provided they did not spend more than £5. At a General Meeting three months later a motion that the club be started was carried *nemine contradicente*, and E. G. Semple was elected the club's first President. Shortly afterwards the Finance Committee of the Clubs authorized the use for prizes of such part of the £5 grant as had not been spent. The club duly entered for the Inter-Collegiate Competition, and easily defeated St Catharine's College in the first round of Division II, but just lost to Peterhouse in the second, semi-final, round. For the St Catharine's contest all the prizes were given by Reddaway, except those for the Hurdles and the Weight, which came from Mrs Reddaway. In 1912/13 Semple was again President, and in the Michaelmas term the club figures for the first time in the list of approved estimates, with a modest grant of £5.9.0, and authority also to spend, on prizes, a sum of £5. In the Inter-Collegiate Competition Selwyn and Peterhouse were beaten, but in the final Fitzwilliam lost heavily to Queens', by eighty points to twenty. All this was as promising a beginning as had been achieved by any Fitzwilliam club; and it was a matter for real regret that in the next season, the last before the war, the club, in no uncertain fashion, ran into the familiar Fitzwilliam difficulty of making up a side. In the Michaelmas term 1913 they survived the first round, again against Peterhouse, but could not compete at all in Round II, because of the whole non-collegiate student body seven, only, had taken out membership of Fenner's, and of sixty-six freshmen no more than two, said the Secretary, had shown 'any enthusiasm for Athletics'.

Just before the formation of a Fitzwilliam Hall Athletics Club there had been one other non-collegiate undergraduate in a University team against Oxford – H. A. Dubois.[1] He won the High Jump in the Freshmen's Sports of 1910, and was chosen as second string against Oxford in the following March; and in conditions of extreme cold won outright with, at that time, a highly meritorious jump of 5'8¾". In consequence he was awarded a full blue, and was picked to represent Oxford and Cambridge against Harvard and Yale Universities in the following Long Vacation.[2] His Cambridge career, even for those days, was unusual. Apparently taking time off from his duties in the Indian Police, he was admitted as a non-collegiate student in the Michaelmas term 1910, but kept no term by residence. His academic horizon was bounded by Part II of the Previous Examination, which he passed in the fourth class in

[1]　See p. 142.

[2]　The Finance Committee of the Amalgamated Clubs, at a meeting held on 22 February 1911, agreed that the Clubs should give Dubois his light blue cap and blazer 'as an appreciation of his prowess in the Sports'.

the Easter term of 1911. He took his name off the books in the following August, and might well have done so even sooner had he not wished to remain eligible to compete in America. As an athlete he went from strength to strength, for in 1913 he jumped 6'2" at Poona, and was said to have had hopes of competing in the Olympic Games of 1916, in the event not held because of the war.

When the war was over, the Athletics Club first came to notice in the 1920/21 season, when, in the first round of the Rouse Ball Competition, they lost to Magdalene College; a result which set the pattern for succeeding years, for between 1921 and 1924 they won only once – against Trinity Hall in the Michaelmas term of 1922. Two *Magazine* accounts, in successive years, seem to suggest a general apathy towards athletic sports among Fitzwilliam undergraduates of that time. In June 1922 there appears a dismal, and not altogether accurate, recital of recurring difficulties, in which the writer deplores the lack of support which, all question of competence apart, could at times prevent the club from fielding a team which was, even numerically, complete; and in 1923 the editor of the *Magazine*, in a review of what had for the clubs in general been a good year, is nothing if not critical. 'Even the Athletics Club', he writes, 'got to the second round of the Intercollegiate Sports'; and in 1923/24 the only matters for congratulation arose not from any achievement of the club as a whole, but from the winning of half-blues by two of its members – A. E. F. Young (cross country), and R. E. Nelson (quarter-mile). Nelson also ran against Oxford in the Relay Races.

The Rugby Union Football Club

Those representatives of the Amalgamated Clubs who, on 29 November 1913, attended a Special General Meeting convened to consider the formation of a Rugby Union Football Club either were unaware of the disasters of thirty years earlier or took fresh courage, for, after one adjournment, they agreed by twenty votes to five, on the motion of W. B. Hirst, that a club should be founded; and at a meeting held on the same day the rugby football players elected E. N. Player to be their Captain. The club's formation thus came to be linked with two men whose brief association with Fitzwilliam Hall was to be lastingly commemorated by a Bursary which still bears their names. The *Magazine* notice, over the initials 'E.N.P.', mentions some concern lest the creation of the new club might be harmful to those already in being – another reminder of the perennial difficulty of finding players – but hopes for the best; and adds that it has been possible to put out two fifteens for practice games. The club's first match, against the Perse School, was lost by twenty-five points to fourteen, and the second, against the County School, won by eleven points to six. W. A. Woods scored the first try, and W. B. Hirst kicked the first goal.

After the gap of the war years it was apparently thought desirable to authorize afresh the formation of the club, and this was done at a General Meeting of the Amalgamated Clubs held on 11 October 1919. There were, it seems, some twenty people from whom fifteen might be selected, and appeals were made for recruits, even those who had never played before. The club's officers evidently felt themselves at a disadvantage in lacking a field of their own, for both 'home' games and practices were out of the question. Their finances also were, at first obscure, for there is no reference to estimates before the Michaelmas term of 1920, when an unspecified sum was approved to meet the cost of 'seven balls and fixture cards'. Even at this time of abnormally large undergraduate numbers, it is clear that rugby football was not a Fitzwilliam game. In the Michaelmas term 1920, the club's first match against Downing College was lost by forty-three points to three, and in eight further games they scored no more than fifteen points; and although there was some improvement in the following term, one game, only, was won. The 1920/21 season opened auspiciously with three men in the Freshmen's Trial, but that was the most noteworthy feature of that season, or of the next, save that in the Lent term of 1922 the side was playing in a College League, and finished 'joint seventh' in their division. In the Michaelmas term 1922 J. B. C. Grundy, Captain of the side, was in the Seniors' Trial, and in the following term there occurs the first mention of the Colleges Knock-out Competition, in which, with the help of a bye in the first round, and a win over Queens' College, the club reached Round III, but then lost to Clare by thirty-five points to none. There was, however, some encouragement in that year, for besides beating Queens' they won against Downing for the first time, but when the Secretary compiled his report for the Michaelmas term 1923 – Reddaway's last Michaelmas term, although he was on leave of absence – there was little to be cheerful about. 'The first XV', he says, 'has to date lost nine matches, and drawn one. The second XV has lost every match.'

The Chess Club

In the Michaelmas term of 1922 the players of chess (apparently regarded by the editor of the *Magazine* as a 'Sport') announced their intention of reviving the Chess Club 'lost in oblivion for some time past'. The club had been similarly revived some twenty years earlier, with little effect;[1] but its affiliation to the Amalgamated Clubs in the Michaelmas term of 1923 held out for it some hope of a less fitful existence.

By the end of Reddaway's time the Amalgamated Clubs consisted of ten clubs and societies, of which eight were organizations for games of one sort or another, the two exceptions being the Debating Society, which dated from 1874 as a non-collegiate undergraduate association and was a founder member of the Amalgamation Clubs ten years later, and the Musical Society. The heavy bias towards athletics had already become evident, for there were five other societies, two of long standing, which existed independently of Amalgamation, and had little or no voice in its management.

1914–1918

When, in the Easter term of 1918, Reddaway first announced his appeal for a memorial to those members of Fitzwilliam Hall who had died on active service, he had thought that the memorial might take the form of some permanent commemoration in the chapel and of exhibitions for needy undergraduates. We have seen, however, that the monies so collected were in the event put towards the purchase of Red Cottage, so that with the purchase also of the playing field, made possible by a separate appeal, it might, in Reddaway's own words, 'constitute a memorial worthy of the name'.[2]

Over the memorial in the chapel there was considerable delay. In December 1924 Reddaway refers to an illuminated Roll of Honour by W. R. Smith (a graduate of 1922), placed by the altar in anticipation of some more permanent commemoration,[3] but nearly three years were to elapse before this was finished, its cost being met not from the War Memorial Fund but from the tiny resources of the chapel – a remarkable achievement by an institution whose annual income rarely exceeded the £7 or so of its voluntary collections. In December 1927, in one of the *Magazine*'s infrequent references to the chapel, the editor hoped that the Roll would be ready within two or three months, and when at last it was nearly completed Walter Harvey, writing in the *Fitzwilliam Journal*,[4] gave his readers some idea of what they might expect: an illuminated triptych bearing the names of those who had given their

---

[1] See p. 143; and A.C. Minutes of 11 October 1902.
[2] See p. 190.
[3] *Magazine*, December 1924, p. 18.
[4] April 1928, p. 9.

The War Memorial of 1914–1918

lives, done by Albert Cousins,[1] an artist then working in the Fitzwilliam Museum, in whom Harvey had a justifiable confidence. Mr Gaskoin, in an account of the first Cambridge Reunion of the Fitzwilliam Society in the Long Vacation of 1928, alludes to the exquisite workmanship of the triptych, then in the chapel, and to the good offices of the Bursar in obtaining it for the House.[2] In a later note Mr Harvey speaks of the general approval with which the memorial has been received, and looks forward to a time when it might be moved from its place in the upper room in Trumpington Street, and find an ampler home in new Fitzwilliam buildings.

The triptych, in natural oak, has on its side panels, inscribed in vellum, forty-four names:

Alan C. G. Alford	Arthur E. Morris
Cyril H. Allison	Donald Munro
Victor H. A. Barraud	William H. Norman
Cyril W. Bartlett	Fred^c W. L. G. Norton-Fagge
Charles B. H. Beck	Eric N. Player
Alec E. Boucher	Philip Rolfe
Sydney Bowler	Harold E. Rose
Robert S. Brand	Frederic Scott
William H. S. Carter	Harold Serginson
Cyril A. E. Davis	William Shaw
Bernard V. R. Downman	Charles E. Skinner
Oswald C. F. Elliott	Francis E. Smith
Percival J. Flory	William H. Stokes
William H. Flory	George F. Stout
Reginald Foster	Trevor W. Stuart-Harris
George F. Glaister	John R. Swallow
William Haslam	James C. F. Tunstall
William G. Haynes	Arthur G. Tyndall
Frank A. Heath	Russell M. Wheeler
Wilfred B. Hirst	Horace A. White
Frank S. Long	Eric F. Wilkinson
Horace E. Martin	Alfred M. Woods

[1] Mr Cousins (born 28 June 1879) taught calligraphy and illumination at St John's College Choir School, and was appointed in 1928 to the staff of the Fitzwilliam Museum, where, in the 1930s, he was put in charge of the collection of armoury. He retired on 30 September 1946, and died on 3 March 1964. (See *Cambridge Evening News*, 5 March 1964)

[2] *Journal*, April 1929, p. 7.

(b) Societies and clubs 1924–69

The Debating Society

In W. F. Reddaway's last Lent term the society held three debates, which, we are told, were successful and well attended; and, in passing, it may be noted that in the following term the society elected as president W. W. Williams, who was to graduate a year later, and return to Cambridge in 1946, to render yeoman service to the House for twenty years.

Three was not an unusual number for debates held in each of the Michaelmas and Lent terms, with none in the Easter term, save for an occasional jamboree in a post-war May Week, in the garden of Fitzwilliam House, with beer supplied. The subjects of debate were not remarkable – occasionally of political or educational interest, and often light-hearted; sometimes with nation-wide implications, and sometimes of more local concern, as when in the year 1958/59, we are told, one of the more serious debates was on the motion 'That this House would reject Collegiate Status'. The motion was defeated, but, says the *Magazine* report, 'it was clear that there was some disagreement about the welcome that should be given to Fitzwilliam College'.[1] Those who compiled the records were not always able to declare that debates were both successful and well attended. Good debates, no doubt, there often were, but there were also constant complaints about the thinness of the house, and on one occasion in the Lent term of 1948 poor attendance caused a debate to be cancelled altogether. All kinds of devices were tried in the hope of stimulating public interest; and among the most effective was the holding of joint debates with the women's colleges, first on the initiative of Girton College in 1922; and from 1933, when there was a joint debate with the College's Psyche Society, these fixtures, with Girton and Newnham Colleges and then with Homerton, became more frequent, and rarely failed to bring in more people. In the Lent term of 1936, for example, a visit from Homerton attracted an audience of fifty or so – twice the usual number – to a debate on a motion deploring the segregation of the sexes in education. These arrangements were renewed after the war, when Hughes Hall was added to the list, and may be said to have reached their culmination in the year 1965/66 in what was described as a marriage with New Hall Debating Society (doubtless inspired by the example of the chapel communities of the time), when Canon Montefiore, then of Caius College, was among the speakers to an audience of seventy.

[1] *Magazine*, Easter term 1959, p. 26.

Occasionally the help of senior members was enlisted, as in the Lent term of 1926, when W. F. Reddaway and C. J. B. Gaskoin were the principal speakers on a historical motion, and again in 1932 when there was a full-dress Dons' Debate, with fifty present, addressed among others by Bernard Manning of Jesus College, W. T. Whalley-Tooker of Downing, and P. W. Duff, later Professor of Civil Law, from Trinity. This particular experiment, successful though it was, seems not to have been repeated; but visiting speakers were often invited, whether in their own right – Union committee members were much sought after – or as members of a college team.

In 1952, in a Michaelmas term of unusual activity, the society resolved, probably in another attempt to widen its appeal, that it should not devote itself to debates alone, but should seek to fill a need for a Literary Society. The idea, even, of putting on a revue was canvassed, but abandoned; and in a burst of energy six meetings were held during the term, three for debates, and three for talks given by Lionel Gamlin, Fred Hoyle and, in a Mill Lane lecture room, by Nikolaus Pevsner, then Slade Professor of Fine Art in the University. A further touch of novelty was added to the term, when a recent graduate presented the society with a presidential bell, in the interests of good order, and an economical expenditure of speakers' time.

This improvement, however, was not maintained; for within a year there are renewed pleas for better support, and a secretary dwells on his embarrassment when a scholar from the Victoria and Albert Museum, invited to address the society at a meeting thrown open to other societies, is received by an audience of barely twenty. Soon afterwards a decision is taken not to invite distinguished guest speakers until larger audiences can be assured; but this assurance was not forthcoming, for, although there might occasionally be a better evening, numbers fluctuated, as in 1963, from three to thirty-five (at a debate with Queen Mary College, London). The new Fitzwilliam building brought no improvement; in 1965 'audiences have not been high this year, with the exception of the "Newnham Nights", and interest has been limited'; and even after the marriage with New Hall, there is still a plea for the presence at debates of more of the inhabitants of the new college rooms; while for 1968 and 1969, most unusually for this society, there is no *Magazine* report at all.

The debaters were not unusual in experiencing this decline in their affairs, particularly among the non-athletic groups in the House; and it is by no means unlikely that with matriculations running at twice the level of thirty years earlier – when everybody knew everybody else –

enthusiasms were more difficult to kindle in the rather differently constituted, and less coherent, student body of the fifties and sixties.

In June 1951, the society, originally The Non-Collegiate Debating Society, whose title had always indicated that debating was at least part of its business, appeared under a new name: The Somerset Society. The advocates of the change, conscious that some explanation was due to their public, had desired some departure from the custom whereby the non-collegiate clubs and societies were known as Fitzwilliam this or Fitzwilliam that, and decided to adopt the name 'of our first Censor, whose portrait may be seen in Hall'.[1] Very soon, however, another change was made, seemingly in deference to the wishes of members, not up from Somerset, who deprecated the possibilities of confusion allowed by the new style; and by the addition of the first Censor's first name the society became The Ralph Somerset Society.[2] Whether the alteration, in either form, would have found favour had its proposers known of Mr Somerset's observation to his Board in 1876, that he did not regret the dissolution of the society when it had collapsed (temporarily) owing to lack of interest, can now be no more than a matter for speculation.[3]

The presidency of the University Union Society held by G. G. Sharp (Easter term 1921), and Lionel Gamlin (Michaelmas term 1930) has already been noticed. Three other Fitzwilliam undergraduates were also President: Norman St John Stevas (Easter term 1950), N. H. S. Lamont (Lent term 1964), and J. V. Cable (Easter term 1965). It is curious that these elections appear nowhere in Debating Society reports in the *Magazine*.

The Musical Society

In the Easter term of 1935, after a silence of some years, the Secretary of the Musical Society ventures on a modest prophecy of a revival to be attempted at the beginning of the next academical year. With some show of diffidence, he supposes that it should be possible to form a small male voice choir (chiefly for its own entertainment) and ultimately to get together a small orchestra. This sort of thing had been

---

[1] *Magazine*, June 1951, p. 33. The only portrait, as distinct from the medallion portrait, of Mr Somerset now in the College's possession is the photograph, of unknown origin, reproduced on p. 318. A *Fitzwilliam News Letter* of February 1943 mentions the receipt of a painting of Mr Somerset from the estate of Mrs Pattrick, widow of Mr F. G. Howard, who died in October 1942, but of this there is no trace. The medallion portraits of Mr Somerset and Mr Howard are at Huntingdon Road.

[2] *Ibid.*, January 1954, p. 48.

[3] See p. 122.

said before, but this time it seemed not to be without justification, for in the next issue of the *Fitzwilliam Magazine* there appears a notice written by Dr R. C. Evans, of Clare College, President of the Musical Society, who was then beginning his tale of invaluable service to Fitzwilliam House (not least in rescuing the Amalgamated Clubs from financial disaster) in which he records, without detail but also without doubt, the triumphant success of a concert given in the combined common room and lecture room on 27 February 1936, to an enthusiastic audience of well over a hundred. A year later, Dr Evans, still the society's President and still assisting its Secretary in the performance of his duties, is able to report continued success in a Lent term concert, to which members of colleges (Corpus, Sidney, and King's) had contributed in no small degree. In December 1937 the society presented an ambitious programme, again in the Common Room, and again with much help from outside the House, some of it professional; and throughout the year informal concerts were arranged on Sunday evenings, and there were to be concerts also at the end of the Lent and Easter terms.

It is apparent that in the late thirties the music makers had bestirred themselves, and had restored music to its place among the corporate pursuits of the House; but it is also noticeable that in his account of the December 1937 concert – an event of considerable musical importance – the Secretary of the society feels bound to deplore the small number of Fitzwilliam undergraduates in the audience. If he felt this to be a bad omen, he may have been right, for there is no record of any music making during the academical year 1937/38; and of the last pre-war year all that now survives is a reference in a report for the year 1946/47, to its last meeting, held 'during May Week of 1939'.

Within a couple of years of its revival the society had evolved a routine to which it kept for ten years or so. Of two or three musical occasions in each term, the last would be a formal concert: in the Michaelmas term it came to be regarded, and described, as the society's Christmas Concert, with a programme chosen accordingly; while special efforts were made for May Week, as in 1948 when, in what was thought to be a more than usually ambitious venture, performances were announced for 13 and 14 June of Mozart's operetta *Bastien and Bastienne*, followed by the first Scene of Humperdinck's *Hansel and Gretel*. In 1952 the choice was *Acis and Galatea*; and in 1954 the society took to Gilbert and Sullivan with *Trial by Jury*, and with *The Sorcerer* in 1958. In between the main functions of the year, there were various less formal entertainments. The year often began with a freshmen's concert, in the hope that it might reveal talent to take the place of what had been lost the previous June. There were sessions of recorded music; or occasional lectures by distinguished musicologists – very notably when in the Lent term of 1953 the society and its guests filled the concert hall of the University Music School to hear Mr Thurston Dart, then Lecturer, and subsequently Professor, of Music in the University, on 'English Keyboard Instruments', and to see displayed his superbly built harpsichord and clavichord. The Fitzwilliam Singers made their first appearance, in madrigals and part-songs, in 1947, when it was hoped that they would replace the choir of pre-war days, and reappeared from time to time, either by themselves or, as in the Michaelmas term of 1949, in a 'choral ensemble' of ten voices drawn from the Singers, from members of the Cambridge Philharmonic Society, and 'other sources'.

Borrowing was frequent enough to give rise to announcements of 'all-Fitzwilliam' performances on the comparatively rare occasions when they occurred; and, indeed, it was not uncommon among the colleges. The society's indebtedness in the Lent term of 1952 to the Cambridge Civil Servants Orchestra for most of the string players, and to the Dominie Society of Hughes Hall for madrigals, or in its Christmas Concert of 1953 to the Dominie Society again, and to the Raleigh Society of Newnham College, was not untypical. External assistance was not limited to groups or societies, for there are many references to individual performers, of whom some were professional musicians. From the colleges they most frequently came from King's – very naturally, in view of its resources, and the associations of Kingsmen over the years with the House – and from St John's. Residents in the town came too; indeed, an impression grows upon the reader that, like the Fitzwilliam Amateur Dramatic Society, if not quite to the same degree, the Musical Society was a means of bringing town and gown together, and also of bringing Fitzwilliam House to the favourable notice of a considerable public, who came to feel a more than passing interest in its fortunes. Already in 1947 the society opened to the general public a recital in the Music School by a particularly welcome guest, when on 28 January Madame Jelly d'Aranyi performed works by Bach (unaccompanied), and by Schumann and Beethoven, accompanied by the Secretary of the society for the year, Mr J. N. Hind.[1]

As they had no larger room, the society's performances were usually given in the Parlour at 31 Trumpington Street, where space was even

---

[1] *Magazine*, July 1947, p. 28.

more limited than it had been when, as the Lecture Room, by the removal of a screen it could be thrown into a single room with the Common Room facing the Fitzwilliam Museum across the road. In spite of its limitations, however, the Parlour was found very acceptable for the more intimate of the society's performances, and, on occasion, its capacity was more than adequate, for audiences were very uneven: fifty was regarded as a record (in spite of bad weather) in March 1949, and it is to be hoped that five at a mid-term concert in 1952 still stands as a record too.

All in all, the musicians usually appear as a small enthusiastic group, with, at any given time, a quite unpredictable number of adherents. On one occasion the secretary celebrates the presence in a male voice choir of the Captains and 'most of the secretaries' of the four major field games – rather after the fashion of the Dramatic Society rehearsing for one of its plays – while on another he is full of surprise, and regret, that so large an undergraduate population should supply no more than four or five Fitzwilliam Singers. And so it was with instrumentalists; when they came they were welcomed with open arms, and made much of; when they did not, the society would lean more heavily on outside help. One invariable feature of the story, however, was the help and inspiration derived from successive Presidents. Mr N. J. G. Pounds had presided over the revival of the society's activities after the war, and was a constant source of encouragement, and of material help, until his departure for the United States of America in 1950; and to Mr P. A. Tranchell, of King's College, the society was especially beholden for his services as producer or pianist, and, on occasion, as composer.[1]

In this brief synopsis it is hardly practicable to enter into particulars of the society's programmes; and it is not necessary, for much information is given by successsive Secretaries in their reports to the *Fitzwilliam Magazine* – reports which, for these years, are as well done as any reports of clubs and societies, at any time. There is, however, preserved for posterity the story of one most enterprising, and most successful, venture, which deserves to be included here. Entitled 'Fitzwilliam House Musical Society's May Week Concert, June 8th, 1950', and written by D. A. Appleby (B.A. 1950), Assistant Secretary to the society for the year 1949/50, himself a much appreciated pianoforte player, it reads:

The concert had its beginning in a discussion over lunch at the Garden

---

[1] Mr Tranchell composed an operetta, *Daisy Simpkins*, for presentation by members of the Society in the Michaelmas term 1957.

House Hotel, Cambridge, towards the end of the Lent term. Mr. W. J. Smith, who was resident at Fitzwilliam House in 1909, was responsible for the original idea. A rare catalogue of the works of Vivaldi had come into his possession, from which it was apparent that a wealth of unpublished music by this prolific composer lay in the University Library at Turin. It was therefore decided to attempt to arrange a concert for May Week, the programme consisting entirely of the works of Antonio Vivaldi.

The difficulties were legion. The music had to be obtained from Turin; it was by no means certain that permission to copy the manuscripts would be given; it would be necessary to enlist outside help to form a suitable orchestra, there being too few instrumentalists in Fitzwilliam House; and, as the Parlour would be much too small for the type of concert envisaged, some other hall would have to be found.

However, Mr. Smith, who was returning to his residence in the south of France after Easter, offered to visit Turin and seek music appropriate to the musicians in Fitzwilliam House: a violin concerto for Ronald Wilkinson, a bassoon concerto for Peter Speak, bass and tenor arias, and overtures for the orchestra which the Secretary undertook to raise in Cambridge.

An unsuccessful attempt was made to secure the use of the Italian Room of the Fitzwilliam Museum for the concert; but eventually we were lucky to be afforded the use of the Music School's excellent Concert Hall.

Early in the Easter Term word reached us from Italy that suitable scores had been found, and that Mr. Smith and John Lanchbery were hard at work in Turin copying out orchestral parts from the original Vivaldi manuscripts. Immediately, posters and invitation tickets were designed and printed. An orchestra had to be recruited, and there was only four weeks in which to do so. It was known that orchestras were being formed for six other college concerts and were already rehearsing; but a circular letter was sent out to a large number of instrumentalists in the hope that perhaps some fourteen or fifteen would accept the invitation to play. By persistent effort, and a careful arrangement of rehearsal times, a body of capable players was collected. They were all playing in other May Week concerts, and it was only through their keenness and willing co-operation that the performance was possible.

Most of the music arrived in Cambridge with Mr. Smith on Whit Monday, a week before the concert rehearsals began, under the direction of John Lanchbery, formerly conductor of the Metropolitan Ballet. Soloists and orchestra responded eagerly to his expert guidance and fine interpretation. The fifth and final rehearsal took place the night before the concert, when the addition of two oboes and a double-bass greatly improved the balance of the orchestra.

The concert, which had aroused considerable interest among music-lovers in Cambridge, was a great occasion, and, in every way, a great success. The large and enthusiastic audience which assembled in the Music

School enjoyed a performance of an exceptionally high standard. One could justly continue to write in superlatives of the contributions of all the artists concerned; but we hope we shall not be accused of petty partisanship if we mention only the fine solo performances in the concertos of two Fitzwilliam men – Peter Speak, and Ronald Wilkinson, whose accomplished musicianship is only equalled (and, alas, sometimes obscured) by their personal modesty.[1]

By the late 1950s something of the zest which had characterized the Musical Society in the immediate post-war years had been lost; or, at the very least, there was less concern for musical things in the House at large. Already in 1955 a Secretary, while proclaiming the society's high standard – fit, he says, to stand comparison with most of the colleges – also claims that it deserved more support nearer home than it was getting. The general pattern of activities did not alter greatly, save that there were fewer functions than before. All but the most ambitious concerts were given in the Parlour; but, exceptionally, on 4 December 1962 the society went to the Round Church for its Christmas Concert, where it presented a French eighteenth-century Midnight Mass, and a selection of Mozart *Kirchensonaten*. That Michaelmas term was notable for the best freshmen entry, musically, for some time, and while the secretary 'for fear of omissions' refrains from mentioning any performer's name, it should not go unrecorded that among the freshmen of 1962 was David Atherton, who in 1968 was to be the youngest conductor ever to conduct at a Promenade Concert in the Albert Hall, and, also in 1968, was to become Resident Conductor at the Royal Opera House in Covent Garden.

In 1963/64 the music makers must have felt that at last they had entered into their heritage, with *three* concert rooms in the new building: the Minstrels' Gallery, high up in the dining hall (but not the hall itself), the Music Room behind, and the Reddaway Room, large enough for any likely concert audience. The first concert in the Reddaway Room was given in the Michaelmas term 1963, when two concerts for chamber music were also given in the Music Room, which was found to be very suitable for the purpose. The main Lent term concert, also in the Reddaway Room, was for the most part in the highest degree experimental, but regained equilibrium at the close with works by Mozart and Haydn. The successful use of the Minstrels' Gallery for

---

[1] *Magazine*, June 1951, p. 18. Mr Smith, who lectured in Music for the Department of Education for many years, was not at Fitzwilliam Hall in 1909. He kept the academical year 1906/07 at Sidney Sussex College, resided as a non-collegiate student for the Lent and Easter terms of 1921, and took his degree on 18 June.

madrigals on the last Tuesdays of the Michaelmas and Lent terms of the year 1965/66, largely for the entertainment of the Fellows at High Table, revealed an unsuspected fact; for whereas the acoustical properties of the Dining Hall, from any position even remotely tenable by an after-dinner speaker, left much to be desired, the Gallery, for words and music alike, proved entirely satisfactory.

The following year saw a development which was a natural outcome of the almost simultaneous establishment of three colleges side by side on the left bank of the Cam, when the Musical Societies of New Hall and Churchill and Fitzwilliam Colleges combined to hold two concerts on a scale larger than any of them could have managed from its own resources. For the first, in the Michaelmas term of 1966, a programme of choral and instrumental music from the seventeenth to the twentieth centuries was arranged and conducted by the Secretary of the Fitzwilliam Society, and was probably given in Fitzwilliam College. The second, arranged by Churchill College, included choral works, the first Horn Concerto by Strauss, and Mozart's *Coronation Mass*, and for both concerts it was still found necessary to seek help outside the walls. There was, however, no doubt that the experiment had been very favourably received; and in the Lent term of 1968 it was repeated, in the Wolfson Hall, with works from Hindemith, Haydn and Mozart. For the Haydn (*Passion Oratorio*) the large choir was almost wholly drawn from the three colleges.

Meanwhile, in Fitzwilliam, there seems to have been an increase of activity at the less formal, but more frequent, concerts held in the Reddaway Room; or in the smaller, and very congenial, Music Room hard by; and the closing years of the decade were notable for the success of a larger madrigal group, for the participation of two, at least, of the Fellows of the College (Dr A. M. Brown and Dr D. A. T. New), and for the distinction achieved by members of the society – notably by R. K. Garland as leader of the C.U.M.S. orchestra for two years, and by two of its members in what came to be known as the 'Fitzwilliam Quartet'. The story of this group is told in the *Fitzwilliam Journal* for 1972; and by its inclusion here forms a most gratifying coda to this tale of Fitzwilliam music in its first hundred years:

> Nicholas Dowding and John Phillips came into residence in the Michaelmas Term, 1968, Dowding from Katharine Lady Berkeley's Grammar School, Wotton-Under-Edge, and Phillips from High Storrs Grammar School for Boys in Sheffield. In their first term they conceived the idea of forming a regular string quartet, and sought out two other freshmen – Alan George of King's (viola), and Ioan Davies of St John's (violoncello). The

quartet took the name of the College; its members kept together throughout their three Cambridge years, and achieved unusually high standards for
an undergraduate group of musicians. They helped in college concerts, and
on March 1, 1970, they gave a first performance, in the Reddaway Room,
of Sebastian Forbes's Quartet No. 2, commissioned by the Governing Body
of the College in commemoration of its centenary year. They were all
members of the University Musical Club, and last year Phillips and Dowd-
ing were, respectively, the Club's President and Secretary. Also during last
year, having acquired a substantial repertoire, the quartet gave a highly
successful series of lunch-time recitals in the Fitzwilliam Museum.

Here the story might well have ended, but after their three years of residence in Cambridge the members of the quartet resolved that they would
like to keep together, and applied for appointment as Quartet in Residence
at York University. At the end of April they heard that in the face of considerable competition they had been selected. This first appointment of a
resident quartet, which is for three years, has been made possible by the
Yorkshire Arts Association, and it is intended that it shall be followed by
similar appointments at other universities in the county. The members of
the quartet have been provided with living accommodation in the University, and have also received grants which will relieve them of financial
anxiety. They are expected to give 26 recitals a year in Yorkshire, and two
each term in the University itself. They will be required to teach, and will
themselves receive tuition with the help of a further substantial grant from
the Association.

Readers of the *Journal* will share with those of us who were in residence
at the time a feeling of delight that an opportunity of this kind should
nowadays be available at all, and of most lively satisfaction that two undergraduates of the College should have shared such enviable distinction.
They will also be glad to learn that the members of the quartet wish to
continue under the Fitzwilliam name.

The Historical Society

In the 1920s the Historical Society went on its way very much as
before, with three meetings in each of the Michaelmas and Lent terms,
and none thereafter. The first meeting of the academical year was commonly devoted to the election of officers and members, until in 1947
the election of members was abandoned. At this time, too, the society
gave up the practice, instituted by Reddaway in the beginning, of
expressing a formal opinion on some question connected with the topic
of the evening. One meeting in the Michaelmas term was commonly
given up to play reading with the Dramatic Society, with Mr Bernard
Shaw, decidedly, as the favourite playwright. The earlier preference for
visiting speakers persisted, and was particularly manifest in the year

1946/47, when Mr N. J. G. Pounds, who had succeeded Mr Gaskoin as President, was making strenuous efforts to revive the society after the war. In that year, of six speakers one was W. F. Reddaway, then in retirement, followed by five others of whom three became Professors in the University, one a Reader, and the last Professor in the University College of the West Indies, before ending up in Harvard.[1]

In the meantime, the society was much given to dwelling on its senior standing among the Fitzwilliam societies and clubs: its two hundred and seventy-fifth meeting was commemorated on 19 November 1924, at a dinner at the Union Society, attended by the President, the Vice-Presidents, and ten members, but not, it seems, by the guest of the evening, whose health was proposed *in absentia*. In the same vein, the three hundredth meeting on 25 January 1928 was made the occasion of a dinner in Fitzwilliam House, with George Macaulay Trevelyan, then recently elected Regius Professor of Modern History, as the guest of honour, and this was followed by similar celebrations at the proper intervals at the three hundred and twenty-fifth and three hundred and fiftieth meetings, when the presence of Professor Adcock and Professor J. H. Clapham, respectively, spoke for Reddaway's gift for encouraging, and maintaining, an interest in Fitzwilliam affairs among members of his own College. At the time of the latter of these celebrations, to which twenty-three members came, there were thirty or more members in all. This was in the Michaelmas term of 1934, which appears to have been a good term for the society; but before it there had been gaps in the records supplied to the *Magazine*, and after it nothing at all appears until July 1947.

The disproportionate interest taken by the society in its relatively venerable status died hard, for it survived the Second World War, and figures again in three successive reports contributed to the *Fitzwilliam Magazine*. In the Easter term of 1949 the Secretary's proclamation that 'this the oldest Fitzwilliam Society' had met three hundred and eighty-three times is of greater interest in that it called forth a gentle protest from a former resident (A. O. N. Lee), and roused the society to make some effort to substantiate its claim. With Mr Gaskoin's help 1900 was established as the foundation year, but this did nothing to dispose of Mr Lee's contention that the Debating Society was perhaps older. It was – much older, for as we know the Debating Society was in being in 1874. The fact also emerges that in the Easter term of 1950 the

---

[1] The five speakers were Messrs Butterfield, already a Professor, Grierson, Rich, Kitson Clark, and Parry.

society's then current minute book (the second) went back to 1912, and that the first had been lost.[1]

In his account of the society for the year 1946/47, the Secretary alludes to its renewal 'after a lapse of almost eight years'. If this is correct, it takes the story back to, say, the end of the Michaelmas term of 1938; and from what is known of the society between its three hundred and fiftieth meeting in November 1934 and its three hundred and eighty-third in June 1949, it is clear that, although successive Secretaries may not have thought it worth their while to supply annual reports for the benefit of posterity, the activities of the society did not cease after November 1934, and that meetings were held during the next four calendar years, if less frequently than had been usual.

The first post-war year had seen the society, to all appearances, firmly re-established; and for a brief space the impetus imparted by a forceful President, and a competent Secretary, carried its members forward through a number of successful sessions, fortunate in their choice of speakers. In the Michaelmas term of 1947, after an address by Henry Steele Commager, second Visiting Professor of American and Institutions in the University, on 'The Frontier in American History', the society seems to have embarked on a policy of extracting papers from successive holders of that Chair, partly, no doubt, as an agreeable means of relieving pressure on other speakers, and on its own members. Another favourite guest was Dr V. W. Purcell, of Trinity College, who on a number of occasions spoke from his own experience on aspects of life in the Far East.

By the year 1951/52, however, there were clouds on the horizon: in the Lent term, after the second meeting had been poorly attended, the third was cancelled through lack of support; and there was speculation whether the society should be disbanded altogether. A year later one speaker, who deserved better of his hosts, was rewarded with an audience of seven, and it seemed prudent to assure members of other faculties that their presence would be welcomed at the society's meetings. At the end of the Lent term of 1954 the score of meetings crops up again – as four hundred and five, the four hundredth having apparently been overlooked; and after a gap of two years another Secretary, seemingly with perfect seriousness, wonders whether improved attendances in 1956/57 are attributable, at all, to a free provision of coffee and cigarettes.

And so, with no information for 1957/58, it comes as no surprise

[1] Like the second, which disappeared in the 1950s.

that after a single meeting in 1958/59, and two in 1959/60, the shortest of all reports is followed by a total silence, brought to an end after eight years, in a special centenary issue of the college *Magazine*, by the writer of a brief essay on his conception of the objects of any historical society, and on the way – the different ways – in which, by this particular society, those objects had been achieved.

The Law Society

It was not until the Lent term of 1929 that eleven members of the House, at a meeting presided over by Mr Gaskoin and held in his rooms, resolved 'to awaken the Fitzwilliam House Law Society, which had been allowed to fall asleep in 1923'.[1] It seems not unlikely that H. H. Meyer, a popular and unusually energetic individual, as the Dramatic Society had also found, had a hand in this revival. At all events he was elected Secretary and Treasurer, and Gaskoin became President in succession to Mr N. G. Scorgie, of Trinity College, the society's first President in 1913. There was no further activity until the beginning of the next academical year.

Between the revival of the society and the centenary year of the College, its records as supplied to the *Magazine* are irregular and often perfunctory. One of the most frequently reported items in the annual programme was its Annual Dinner (to which in the Lent term of 1935 there came Professor Buckland), and which in later years was supplemented by a sherry party, or a garden party in May Week; and Moots were a favourite pastime, generally with St John's College, doubtless because Professor P. H. Winfield, who was a good friend to Fitzwilliam lawyers, was for many years a Fellow there. For such papers as were read to them the society, like the historians, leaned heavily on senior members of the University, and occasionally on visitors from London. The smallness of the society's membership was a preoccupation, and in the Michaelmas term of 1933 the possibility was considered of an amalgamation with the Law Society of Sidney Sussex College, or of the formation of a joint Fitzwilliam Society of Law and Economics; and while nothing came of these ideas their discussion was so time-consuming that the first meeting of the year was not held until 22 November, and then in conjunction with the Historical Society on a topic of common interest. There then follows a gap in the records, which included the war years, and was not closed until 1950, and then only for a single year.

In this somewhat lonely report the President, a graduate of the pre-

[1] *Magazine*, June 1929, p. 94.

vious year, contends that although little has been heard of the society this is no reason for assuming that it has not enjoyed a healthy and active existence. Nevertheless, he goes on to give reasons for what he calls its apparent nonentity: the handicap of not being a member of the Amalgamated Clubs – he has grounds for believing that this will soon be remedied – the small number of Fitzwilliam lawyers (seldom more than twenty), and the superior attractions of the University Law Society. After one meeting had been postponed at the beginning of the Lent term, the year's only activity had been the holding of a successful Moot on 9 February, and the account ends with nothing more substantial than an expression of hopes for the future; and for another four years that is all, until a brief report on the year 1954/55, headed with a full complement of officers, of whom the President is Mr I. J. Lindner, Queen's Counsel (B.A. 1934), also prominent as one of the 'London members' who had been called upon to support moves then being made to obtain what, it was hoped, would be early independence for Fitzwilliam House. There was a recent Fitzwilliam graduate as Chairman of the society, with a Secretary and a Treasurer. Reasons are given why a full programme for the year could not be arranged, one meeting only is recorded, held jointly with the Debating Society, and there was the usual Annual Dinner. In the following year three meetings out of four were thrown open to members of other colleges, one being a Moot held jointly with Caius College; and then, after a gap, the year 1958/59 showed some improvement, with a fuller and better supported set of proceedings, to be completed, surprisingly, with a May Week garden party at which legal topics were to be among those to be discussed.

With more men reading Law, it seems that the year 1959/60 brought better support for the society's activities, but the Secretary's account tells of little that is new, beyond the prospect of a visit in the Easter term of an officer of the Law Society to talk about the solicitors' profession, and of a cricket match with a Borstal institution after the examinations. The improvement, if such it was, proved to be temporary, for only twice between 1960 and 1969 did successive Secretaries find anything they thought worthy of comment in the *Magazine*. The year 1964/65, with few but well supported activities, was noteworthy for the election as President of C. M. D. Byron, a West Indian who had come into residence from St Kitt's very shortly after his father had spent a year at Fitzwilliam House following the University's Overseas Services Course. From the report for 1967/68, a brief disquisition on the benefits of what the writer describes as 'mooting', it does not appear whether anything happened at all, except a sherry party in the Lent term.

F.H.A.D.S.

Whereas for many clubs and societies the Second World War marks a great divide, the history of the Fitzwilliam House Amateur Dramatic Society, although there was a gap of ten years between its last pre-war performance and its successor in 1949, falls more naturally into different periods – its time under C. J. B. Gaskoin as President from 1923 (at the latest) until his death in 1955, and the years from 1963 onwards when, by the provision of the Reddaway Room in the new buildings, the University did for the indoor pursuits of Fitzwilliam House and College what Reddaway himself had done for the Amalgamated Clubs when he found them a playing field in 1908.

As might be expected, the earlier period was much the more difficult; and without Gaskoin's encouragement and active help the Dramatic Society could hardly have survived. His friends and acquaintances swelled its audiences; the women among them, from a performance of *Three Wise Fools* in 1925, joined the cast, as he often did himself; and most of all the society was in debt for his absorbing interest in 'the fun and games' of acting; and for the knowledge and wisdom which made him so valuable a member of the company. 'He did not need', said a founder-member many years later, 'to be playing an important part; he enjoyed just *being* there while others were planning, discussing, rehearsing, and talking theatre.'[1]

There are a lot of marks to be gained – and, did they but know it, lost – by participants in a corporate activity who do, or do not, attend to the less exciting matter of clearing up when all is over; and Gaskoin in this respect was beyond reproach, for his regular notices of successive performances, even if they sometimes seem a little indulgent, form a most valuable contribution to the history of the society. He wrote well – that he liked writing is neither here nor there – and the society, as well as posterity, is much in his debt.

Attached to this note is a list of plays put on, with, as far as can now be ascertained, the dates and places of their presentation. From Gaskoin's review it is clear that he regarded the performance of Noël Coward's *Hay Fever,* in January 1928, as the society's best until then; equalled, if not surpassed, three years later by *The Young Idea,* also at the A.D.C. Theatre, and the first to be repeated, publicly, since

---

[1] H. M. B(urton) in the *Journal*, December 1955, p. 18.

The Dover Road, when in the following term there were four performances which raised a very respectable sum of money for an Addenbrooke's Hospital Fund. The play was notable for the presence in the
cast of representatives of Newnham College (and also in the Easter
term from Girton), and of two college ladies from Peterhouse, soon
to be joined by two with King's connexions, of whom one, as W. F.
Reddaway's daughter, was especially welcome.

That these early productions of the society attracted favourable
attention outside Fitzwilliam House is evident from Press notices. In
1928 a *Cambridge Review* account of the performance of *Hay Fever* was
complimentary to players and producer alike; and in 1929 the enthusiasm of the members is held up as an example for others to follow. By
1930 the *Review* is referring to the long run of successes the society has
enjoyed; and after four more years its dramatic critic, eight years or so
behind the times, is surprised, and pleased, to find women in the cast.
How considerable an innovation that had been is revealed in 1935 (also
in the *Cambridge Review*) when an accredited representative of the Amateur Dramatic Club asks the editor to give publicity to his committee's
decision to invite members of Newnham and Girton Colleges to act in
public club productions (but only when 'necessary', and subject to the
safeguard that in any four productions one shall be reserved to an
exclusively male cast). 'Such members of Newnham and Girton', furthermore, are not to be deemed members of the club, or to be allowed
the use of its common room at any time.[1]

Except when prevented by circumstances outside their control – the
death of King George V in 1936, and illness in 1937 – the members of
the society continued to appear each year until January 1939, when
their last pre-war production (*Painted Sparrows*) was declared by Gaskoin, in his usual prompt report, to have been a 'surprising success'.
The list attached to this brief historical summary includes only those
invitation performances given in Cambridge, and does not represent
the whole of the society's activities, for there was much reading of
plays, often with a view to subsequent performance, and from February
1930 frequent entries, with considerable success, in Competitions for
the Eastern Area, organized by the British Drama League. On occasion,
the society also took its productions to places in the Cambridge neighbourhood; and performed works written by Miss Catherine Gaskoin,
sister of its President.

[1] *Cambridge Review*, 27 January 1928, p. 205; 1 February 1929, p. 240; 21 January 1930,
p. 227; 2 February 1934, p. 217; 1 March 1935, p. 293.

It is not surprising that the society should also have figured in the larger world of the University Amateur Dramatic Club – as in 1930/31, when L. J. Gamlin was President, and five other members of the society belonged to it. Of the six, three had appeared in a production of *The Magistrate* in the previous Easter term, and the selection of H. H. Meyer, an undergraduate in residence at the age of fifty-eight, to play the lead must have been without precedent.

By this time however, the society was more than a source of talent for associations of longer, and higher, standing, gratifying though that will have been. Firmly established through its own efforts, for there were then no grants in aid, it was already attracting the favourable attention of both town and gown to the institution whose name it bore; and for this its casting will have been at least partially responsible. The 1930s, relatively good years for Fitzwilliam House as a whole, were not less so for its Dramatic Society.

From its beginnings the society had been handicapped by the lack of adequate premises. Fortunately the A.D.C. Theatre was often available, but its cost was higher than could be contemplated with equanimity, especially in the earliest years when audiences were small. The Alexandra Hall (Y.M.C.A.) was tried once, and found unsuitable, and the Lecture Room in Fitzwilliam House, even when thrown into the Common Room by the removal of an intervening screen, was far too small. There were bookings of the Liberal Club in Downing Street for *The Dover Road*, but that can only have been in anticipation of larger audiences for request performances in May Week. The Central Hall in Market Passage, with accommodation for three hundred, and a suitable stage, was satisfactory, but after its use in 1925 it was damaged by fire a week before the next performance was due, thereby causing a hasty flight to the Central School, off Parkside, where, says one report, five hundred guests were entertained.[1] Thereafter, for some years the society played at the A.D.C., until in November 1930 it too caught fire, and, with the Central Hall by then a cinema, the society was obliged to take to what in those days will have been regarded as the southern outskirts of the town, and play in the St John's Parish Hall in Blinco Grove. And then for two at least of the remaining pre-war years there was a return to the A.D.C.

Uncertainty about a theatre was to affect the society's fortunes for some time, until at length in 1963 it found a permanent home in the new buildings in Huntingdon Road. On its revival in 1949, with

---

[1] *Magazine*, June 1927, p. 47.

Gaskoin still its President, the society was fortunate in being able to hire a room in Houghton Hall, in Lensfield Road, and in the Lent term *The Master Builder* was put on, followed in March 1950, in accordance with a declared intention of performing one major work each year, by *The Doctor's Dilemma* chosen at least in part because of its predominantly male cast. Both appear to have been successful, and productions continued annually until, in the Michaelmas term of 1953, the society was thrown off course by the news that after 31 December Houghton Hall would be no longer available. The play for 1953/54 was therefore brought forward to the end of that term; and there followed a period of less regular activity in which the society missed, one suspects, not only its theatre but the guidance and enthusiasm of its President, no longer in residence in Fitzwilliam House. Play reading lost its point, said one correspondent, if there was no knowledge whether a full production would ever be possible; and there was no play at all between 1955 and 1959, when the society experimented with the less exacting requirements of intimate revue within the confines of the Fitzwilliam House Parlour.

In 1960 the members of the society contrived a brief escape from the limitations of their own environment by combining in an ambitious programme with the Shirley Society in St Catharine's; and after a completely blank year in 1961 made a determined attempt to revive past enthusiasms with the production, without décor, of Jean Anouilh's *Antigone* in the Parlour. This excited sufficient interest to encourage two similar performances in the following Michaelmas term, when casting was made much easier by an accession of competent freshmen, and by the discovery that Homerton College was not only willing, but able. By this time the players had their eyes on the future, and in February 1963 they essayed their first full-scale production for some time with *The Fire Raisers*, which the critics found acceptable in spite of the limitations of the Carpenter Hall in Victoria Street.

On Thursday 21 November 1963 the society, henceforth to be known as Fitzwilliam Theatre, performed its first play (Cocteau's *Orpheus*) in the new building; and the editor of the *Fitzwilliam Magazine* for 1964 was most fortunate in being able to call upon the Chairman of a newly constituted Theatre Committee (Mr T. R. Smith) for an admirable account of the committee's endeavours, its immediate plans, and its future policy.[1]

As a multi-purpose room the theatre, as such, suffered from certain

---

[1] *Ibid.*, May 1964, p. 5.

limitations; but there was a general disposition, nevertheless, to recognize that it provided the House with advantages not commonly enjoyed by the colleges of the University. It had met very adequately the demands of the first production, before audiences which, said Mr Smith, had caused the members of the cast to wish that they had played not two nights, but three, with, furthermore, a charge for admission. For the future the committee intended, in general, to use their modern theatre for the production of modern plays, with freedom to experiment, before audiences drawn not only from the House but also from knowledgeable theatre-goers elsewhere. Among the productions of the following years attention was particularly attracted in the Lent term of 1965 to first performances in this country by an all-African cast of two African plays, followed a year later with *The Lion and the Jewel* (Solinka), put on by Fitzwilliam Theatre in conjunction with the Cambridge African Students' Society. In February 1967 there was another joint venture in association with the University Spanish Society in a production of Alejandro Casona's *La tercera palabra*; while as evidence of the committee's eagerness to cast its net as far as was reasonably possible its correspondent recalls how in preparation for the presentation of Brecht's *The Caucasion Chalk Circle* 'this must be the first college production in which the General Secretary, the Captain of Boats, and the Captain of Rugger were all auditioned for the same part'.[1]

There follows the list, mentioned above, of the performances given by the society between 1921 and 1969.

19,20,21 May 1921   *The Younger Generation* (Stanley Houghton)   A.D.C.

19,20,21 January 1922   *Cupid and the Styx* (Sackville Martin)   Alexandra Hall

1 December 1922   *French as he is spoke* (Tristan Bernard), *Browne with an E* (Leopold Montague)   Fitzwilliam Hall

26 February 1924 *The Dover Road* (A. A. Milne) Fitzwilliam Hall; 7,8,9, and 10 June 1924   The Liberal Club

7 February 1925   *Three Wise Fools* (Austin Strong)   Fitzwilliam House

7 December 1925   *Thread o' Scarlet* (J. J. Bell), *How he lied to her Husband* (G. B. Shaw), *The Stepmother* (Arnold Bennett)   Central Hall (Conservative Club)

4 December 1926   *The Autocrat of the Coffee Stall* (H. Chapin), *The Great Broxopp* (A. A. Milne)   Central School

---

[1]   *Magazine,* May 1965, p. 22.

20,21 January 1928   *A Traveller returns* (Clemence Dane), *Hay Fever* (Noël Coward)   A.D.C.

(?) January 1929   *A Night at an Inn* (Lord Dunsany), *The Torchbearers* (George Kelly)   A.D.C.

24,25 January 1930   *The Charity that began at Home* (St John Hankin), *Two Gentlemen of Soho* (A. P. Herbert)   A.D.C.

23,24 January 1931; 30 April, 1,2 May 1931   *The Young Idea* (Noël Coward) A.D.C.

22,23 January 1932   *Mary, Mary, quite Contrary* (St John Irvine)   A.D.C.

3,4 February 1933   *Well Caught!* (Anthony Armstrong)   A.D.C.

26,27 January 1934   *The Wrong Number* (Harvey O'Higgins & Marriett Ford) St John's Parish Hall, Blinco Grove

22,23 February 1935   *The Lady of Alfaqueque* (Quintero brothers), *The Confutation of Wisdom* (F. Sladen Smith)   A.D.C.

28,29 January 1938   *The Bear* (A. Chekhov), *Mr Faithful* (Lord Dunsany) probably A.D.C.

27,28 January 1939   *Painted Sparrows* (Paxton & Hoile), *A Short Way with Authors* (Gilbert Cannan)   A.D.C.

Lent 1949   *The Master Builder* (H. J. Ibsen)   Houghton Hall

8,9,10 March 1950   *The Doctor's Dilemma* (G. B. Shaw)   Houghton Hall

Lent 1951   *The Drunkard* ('W. H. Smith and a Gentleman')

Lent 1953   *You can't take it with You* (Hart & Kaufman)

Michs 1953   *The Male Animal* (J. Thurber)   Houghton Hall

Lent 1955   *The Parlour Game* (Intimate Revue)   The Parlour (F.Ho.)

Lent 1959   *Backcloth and Ashes* (Revue)   The Parlour (F.Ho.)

Lent 1960   *The Future is in Eggs* (E. Ionesco), *The Exception and the Rule* (B. Brecht)   (With the Shirley Society, St Catharine's)

8 March 1962   *Antigone* (Jean Anouilh)   The Parlour (F.Ho.)

15 November 1962   *The Lady's not for Burning* (Christopher Fry)   The Parlour (F.Ho.)

5 December 1962   *Marching Song* (John Whiting)   The Parlour (F.Ho.)

22 February 1963   *The Fire Raisers* (Max Frisch)   Carpenter Hall

6,7 June 1963   *On with the Feet* (Revue)   The Parlour (F.Ho.)

November 1963   *Orpheus* (J. Cocteau)   Reddaway Room

20 February 1964   *Four Minute Warning* (David Campton) (Trilogy: *Soldier from the Wars Returning; Mutatis Mutandis; Little Brother, Little Sister*) Reddaway Room

Easter term 1964   *St Joan* (G. B. Shaw)   Reddaway Room

23–27 November 1964   *The Causasian Chalk Circle* (B. Brecht)   Reddaway Room

3–6 February 1965   *The Happy Haven* (John Arden)   Reddaway Room

1–5 March 1965   Two African Plays: *The Masquerade* (J. P. Clark); *The Trials of Brother Jero* (Wole Soyinka)   Reddaway Room

Easter term 1965   *If it Fitz* (Revue)   Reddaway Room

22–26 November 1965   *Everyman; The Death of Bessie Smith* (Edward Albée); *Temptation Sordid or Virtue Rewarded* (Winifred Phelps)   Reddaway Room

28 February – 4 March 1966   *The Lion and the Jewel* (W. Soyinka)   Reddaway Room

8,9,10 June 1966   *Missfitz* (Revue)   Reddaway Room

15–18 November 1966   *The Trojan War will not Take Place* (Jean Giraudoux) Reddaway Room

9,10 February 1967   *La tercera palabra* (Alejandro Casona)   Reddaway Room

Easter term 1967   *Fitz the Bill* (Revue)   Reddaway Room

Michs term 1967   *A Scent of Flowers* (James Saunders)   Reddaway Room

28 November 1968   *Poor Bitos* (Jean Anouilh)   Reddaway Room

3–5 March 1969   *The Dumb Waiter* (Harold Pinter); *The Old Tune* (Robert Pinget); *A Slight Ache* (Harold Pinter)   Reddaway Room

10–12 March 1969   *The Fitzette Gripola* (Centenary Revue)   Reddaway Room

Michs term 1969   *Adventures in the Skin Trade* (Dylan Thomas)   Reddaway Room

The Boat Club[1]

Between the wars there were, for most of the time, two Lent boats.

---

[1] The remaining notes on this chapter have been taken from various sources, of which the most reliable are the minutes of the Amalgamated Clubs themselves. From the beginning of the Michaelmas term 1939, however, until the end of the Michaelmas term 1957, these minutes are missing, a loss only partially remedied by the Bursar's copies of the Clubs' audited accounts from 1935/36 onwards, with the exception of the year 1953/54. The *Cambridge Review*, until 1939, is a principal source, especially for the Boat Club, but also for much else. The *Magazine*, with occasional lapses, may usually be relied upon until 1969, when, for nearly every useful purpose, it comes to an end. The *Journal* provides additional material. The *Light Blue*, an undergraduate publication, issued terminally (except for Michaelmas 1965) from the Michaelmas term 1950 to the Lent term 1966, has also been of use on occasion; while for rowing matters the Press, both national and local, has had items of interest, mainly, as the years go round, in February and June.

From 1926 to 1928 the second disappeared, having reached the bottom of Division IV in 1925. For a brief space there was a third boat, but after its 'getting-on' year it did not prosper; and the other two finished the inter-war period much as they had begun it. A decision of some significance appears to have been taken in the Michaelmas term of 1927, when the Boat Club secretary hinted at the possibility that, 'in the hope of making more bumps', the club might adopt the 'Jesus style'. Once taken, the decision seems to have had immediate effect, for in the next Lent Races, under a Jesus College coach, the first boat won its oars, at the expense of Trinity Hall IV, Emmanuel II, First Trinity IV, and Selwyn II; and in the following year (1929), with a second boat again on the river, the two between them went up eleven places, the first boat entering Division II, for the first time since the formation of a third division in 1899. In 1933 the first boat, at twenty-fifth on the river, and half-way up the second division, stood higher than ever before, the second made three bumps, and the third made the only two of a brief career. Then there was something of a decline. In 1936 the third boat lost four places, and went off the river; and the first and second boats, having each lost three places in 1938 and four in 1939, were then placed, respectively, half-way down Division III at thirty-eighth, and bottom at sixty-fifth.

In the May Races the record is not dissimilar. The first boat rose four places in 1933, entered Division II, and at twenty-eighth on the river was at its highest between the wars. Competition at that level, however, was too severe; and in 1935 it was back in Division III; and, even with the help of four bumps in 1938, ended the period just about as far from the top of the river as it had been at its beginning (but not so close to the bottom). A second May boat got on in 1932, but never rose far above the bottom of Division IV, and in 1936, after falling to first Trinity V on the first night, rowed over at the bottom on the other three, and vanished.

In the early days the Boat Club was too closely concerned with attempts to improve its lowly position on the river to contemplate commitments elsewhere, but with increasing confidence the club began to look for opportunities of establishing a reputation beyond the limits of the Lent and May Races. Already in the Easter term of 1913 a 'cordial invitation' had been received from the Mayor of St Ives to compete in his local regatta, which the Boat Captain of the time clearly regarded as an important step in the club's development; and a Clinker Four was to be sent in – with what result is not known. 'It is a long way from St Ives to Henley', the Captain wrote, 'but we have our little ambitions.!' It was indeed to be a long way. Henley is mentioned again in 1922, though only as gossip by the editor of the *Magazine*, who had heard that there was a possibility of entering a boat in that year. Nothing came of it (the May boat's performance proved disappointing), and it was nearly thirty more years before a Fitzwilliam boat appeared there, in an eliminating race for the Thames Cup, and forty before a Fitzwilliam boat competed in the Regatta proper. In the meantime, the Lent boat made in 1928 what seems to have been a first excursion to the tideway, and was third in the Head of the River race (Clinker Division) at Putney; and the May boat lost by half a length to Thames Rowing Club III in a final round of the Putney Amateur Regatta. On the Cam, the club was competing in 1930 in the Fairbairn Races, established in 1929, and in 1931 entered three crews of which the first and second substantially improved on their finishing positions of the previous year. This became almost an annual event for the club, with ups and downs, the 1934 race being unusual, in that the second crew rowed a man short for virtually the whole of the course, but nevertheless improved on their previous time, and moved up one place. In 1934 – a new departure – two boats were entered for the Clinker Fours.

It has been obvious that if the Fitzwilliam games clubs had anything in common it was their dissatisfaction with the numbers of men at their disposal. This is a constant complaint, and to this fact one club after another attributed its lack of success. It seems, therefore, worth while to note that the Boat Club's best results between the wars were obtained during that period in the early 1930s when the economic depression of 1931 had brought down the non-collegiate entry with startling suddenness. The colleges were not much affected, but the Fitzwilliam admissions did not again reach their 1930 level until after the Second World War. And it was not only the fortunes of the Boat Club that improved, for, in what might not at first blush be considered a closely related field, the Tripos results of those years were to stand comparison with those of any similar period in non-collegiate history.[1]

Non-collegiate matriculations for the year 1938/39 numbered eighty; from 1939 to 1945 there were one hundred and thirty-three all told, of which fifty-two were for the first of those years. In consequence, although there were spasmodic attempts to arrange occasional fixtures by some of the clubs, all organized rowing in Fitzwilliam House was abandoned for the duration of the war; and it was not until 1946 that a single Lent boat appeared again (considerably penalized to take account

[1]   See p. 411.

of absence in the intervening years), and just managed to maintain its new position at fifty-sixth on the river, in the middle of Division IV. In 1947 the authorities relented, and although to the uninitiated their calculations may seem obscure, clearly made some attempt at reparation, so that the first Lent boat, starting some eight places higher than it had finished in the previous year, and making three bumps, was able to enter Division III. The second boat won its oars, but the third dropped three places to the bottom of the river. There was still a long way to go; and the story of the next twenty years or so is of the sustained determination of successive Boat Captains and their crews, well illustrated by the record of the first Lent boat, admittedly the best, but not widely different from that of the others. In twenty-two years only twice (in 1955 and 1958) did the boat lose a place overall; it won its oars on six occasions, was not always content with four bumps, and finished with a remorselessly consistent rise of two places a year between 1965 and 1969, which in 1969 was perforce limited to two, because there were no boats left to overtake. Nor were particular excitements lacking at different stages of this steady progress. The first boat entered the second division in 1953, and in 1955 the second was no longer the lowest of all second boats – modest triumphs, these, but in those days a reason for much rejoicing. In the Michaelmas term 1955 the level of the river was so ruthlessly lowered that a Clinker Four trained at Clayhithe, and there was tubbing on the Backs; in 1963 the weather drove the boats off the Cam (after one Fitzwilliam boat had been holed by ice); conditions at Earith were no better, and training was continued at St Neot's – all to little immediate purpose because ice still on the Cam caused the races to be cancelled. In 1961 the first Lent boat climbed into the first division, with five bumps all made within two minutes, following on what the Boat Secretary of those days described as 'interval and repetition training' introduced by his Boat Captain. This will doubtless be readily comprehended by all oarsmen; its effects, moreover, seem to have been more than momentary, for in 1964 the first and second Lent boats, in winning their oars, made all their eight bumps before Grassy Corner. In the following year the third boat rather more than made its point, when, on the first day, it was found to be a man short, but was not thereby prevented from making an overbump. At the same races the fourth boat went up nine places; but even so it was possibly a little unfortunate in its timing, for there still remained within recent memory the most remarkable episode of all:

> The rowing achievement of Fitzwilliam House III [said *The Times* on 1 March 1962] overshadowed everything on the first day of the Lent races at

Cambridge yesterday. First they overbumped their way from fourth in the fifth division to head of it, then, half an hour later as sandwich boat at the bottom of the fourth division, they bumped Lady Margaret VI passing on the way six boats each pair of which had been involved in a bump. This was a net gain of 10 places in one afternoon's racing, which is unique in the history of rowing.[1]

The third Lent boat of 1962 was fortunate – even if only in being given a clear run by six boats in line ahead, when any small mishap could have stopped it in its tracks; but its persistence and, no less, the unswerving optimism of its cox, whose quarry must have been out of sight for much of the course, brought the club a record which can hardly fail to stand for many years. Not surprisingly, the boat made a bump on each of the remaining nights, and finished with a total of thirteen.

The year 1946 had also seen the return of Fitzwilliam House to the May Races. There were two boats: the first, which had forfeited more than twenty places by reason of its absence from the river since 1939, started ninth in the fourth division, caught Emmanuel III, and rose one place; the second lost a place, and at sixty-second finished bottom of all. In the May Races of 1947 the effect of the University's change of heart in the matter of penalties for the lost years was startling, for the first boat, on the eve of the races, found itself promoted by twenty-three places to be sandwich boat in Division III, and, not surprisingly, could not stay with such company, and was bumped on three nights out of four. Then followed two indifferent years for the club; until, in 1950, its fortunes changed. Oars were won by three of the four boats then racing, with the first finishing near the top of Division III, and the second, with five bumps, entering Division IV. During the rest of the 1950s the first boat made some progress, getting into the second division in 1955; and then the final rise began, for only twice (in 1958 and 1959) did the first boat fail to go up in any year. Winning its oars on four occasions between 1960 and 1967, at fourth on the river it seemed poised, as the phrase goes, for the kill; but then came a check. 'Unfor-

---

[1] News of this escapade was received, first, with incredulity, and then with mounting astonishment. The Boat Captain was not ill pleased to receive this enquiry: 'I am not a rowing man', said Lord Brabazon of Tara, 'and consequently am not very well up in bump races but I saw in *The Times* that Fitzwilliam House went up ten places in a day and that this had never been done before and probably would never be performed again. I have several times in conversation remarked upon this wonderful feat, only to be told that it was impossible and I was not telling the truth and how could I explain it. Well, frankly, I never could. I wonder if, out of the kindness of your heart, you would tell me how it happened... I shall then be able to face the world with confidence.'

tunately', says the *Fitzwilliam Journal*, 'the first boat had a disastrous start in the May Races, for on the first night sickness led to an untrained man having to be included at the very last moment, and it was bumped.'[1] The full crew speedily made such amends as were then possible; and, in the end, disappointment in 1968 enhanced the final triumph of 1969 – the centenary year – resulting as it did in the simultaneous attainment of the headship of both Lents and Mays; and the general satisfaction was not significantly marred by the observation of a local journalist to the effect that Fitzwilliam had achieved not one double but two, for, with its first May Boat at the top of Division I, its seventh was at the bottom of Division VII.[2]

May Races: First Division 1964–1969

Starting Order for 1964	1964	1965	1966	1967	1968	1969	Starting Order for 1970
1. Queens'							1. Fitzwilliam
2. 1st & 3rd Trinity							2. Queens'
3. Jesus							3. Jesus
4. Pembroke							4. Lady Margaret
5. Clare							5. 1st & 3rd Trinit
6. Emmanuel							6. Clare
7. Lady Margaret							7. Pembroke
8. Magdalene							8. St. Catharine's
9. St. Catharine's							9. Christ's
10. Christ's							10. Magdalene
11. Trinity Hall							11. Caius
12. Downing							12. Downing
13. Selwyn							13. Selwyn
14. St. Catharine's 2							14. Corpus Christi 1
15. Lady Margaret 2							15. Lady Margaret 2
16. Peterhouse							16. St. Catharine's 2
S.B. Fitzwilliam							S.B.

Corpus Christi 1   Caius   Selwyn

For the club as a whole, the 1969 May Races were far more successful than the Lents had been: in the Mays, of seven boats the seventh, alone, went down; in the Lents the first, alone, had gone up; and, among the lower boats taken together, in the Lents ten places had been lost; in the Mays, thirteen won.

[1] At the time this had seemed a major disaster, for it was not until the second boat had gone out that it became known that five in the first boat would not row, and an untrained substitute had to be brought in. They were caught by Lady Margaret at the end of the course, having been within feet of Pembroke. The substitute, eminently worthy of mention, was P. D. Matthewman, five in the second boat in the previous year.

[2] *Cambridge News*, 9 June 1969.

The club was not slow to resume its pre-war practice of seeking experience outside the limits of the Lent and May Races, for, in 1947, possibly encouraged by the performance of the Lent boats, and by the (involuntary) advancement of its first May boat, two crews entered in a regatta to be held in Amsterdam on 28 and 29 June – with results not now known. In 1949 there were hopes that a crew might be sent to the Marlow Regatta, or even to Henley; and, says the *Magazine*, 'an invitation to a continental regatta is eagerly awaited'. A year later a boat did go to Marlow, and was narrowly defeated in the Junior Eights. In 1951 they were at Marlow again, and beat Peterhouse, Downing and Oriel Colleges, and Thames Rowing Club II before losing by a length to Pembroke College (Cambridge) the eventual winners, and winners also, in that year, of the Ladies' Plate. It was in 1951, too, that Fitzwilliam made a first appearance at Henley, where they lost to King's College in an eliminating heat for the Thames Cup. Some idea of the expansion of the club's out of Cambridge programmes may be gathered from a list of its undertakings in the academical year 1955/56, in which a four rowed against King's School, Ely; an eight was entered in the Thames Rowing Club Invitation Regatta; two eights competed in each of the Head of the River races at Reading and Putney; in the Easter term the first May boat narrowly defeated St Catherine's College, Oxford, and took part in the Putney Amateur Regatta; and after the May Races the club was represented by eight of its members at a regatta at Stratford-on-Avon, where one of them carried off the sculling event – a success which he repeated shortly afterwards at Huntingdon.

As time passed, growing success in the bumping races was matched not only by more frequent participation but by more and more notable performance in these outside events. In the year 1961/62 after the Lent races, the first VIII retained the Clinker trophy in the Head of the River race at Bedford, and the Coronation Cup for the Clinker Division at Reading. Down the river, the Boat Secretary writes, not without a touch of arrogance, 'As a new entry in the Tideway Head, they started very low down in the order of boats and in consequence finished fiftieth out of three hundred, owing to loss of tide and the congestion of inferior boats.'[1] And, at length, for the first time in the Regatta proper – not being required to compete in any eliminating heat – Fitzwilliam entered for the Ladies' Plate. The luck of the draw was against them, for they were beaten in the first round by first and third Trinity, who went on to the final; but they had made their mark, and had gained

[1]   *Magazine*, May 1963, p. 14.

The First VIII (1969). Head of the River
Back Row: S.N.S. Robertson 2, C.R. Benyon bow, C.M. Lowe 5, F.W. Edmonds 4; Front Row: K.J. Lowe stroke, G.M.A. Proffitt 6, A.J. Price 7, C.G.S. Wallis 3; with R.A. Sanders, cox

gained experience which was to be of value, as in the following year when they scored their first Henley win against Downing College in the first round of the Visitors' Cup, and in 1965, again in the Visitors' Cup, when they reached the final round, and lost by two lengths, suitably enough, if they had to lose, to St Edmund Hall, then head of the river at Oxford.[1]

On the Cam, the other events in which Fitzwilliam most frequently appeared were the Fairbairn Cup races for eights, and the Clinker Fours. In July 1947 the *Fitzwilliam Magazine* makes no mention of either, but from a Boat Secretary's subsequent statement that in the Michaelmas term of 1947 the first boat had gained thirteen places, and the second lost six, the club must have resumed its participation in the Fairbairn Cup competition by the Michaelmas term of 1946. There appears to have been no entry for the Clinker Fours until the Michaelmas term 1950, when the first IV reached the final; and, in the same

---

[1] In 1966 St Edmund Hall and Fitzwilliam College were to enter into their 'sisterly' relationship.

term, with the three eights all improving their position in the Fairbairn Cup, the first VIII rose to fifth. By the mid-1950s the races for the Fairbairn Cup had become so much part of the Cambridge scene that the first term of the year was known as the Fairbairn term; and the Fitzwilliam boats entered regularly, with varying success, until 1962 when the first VIII, at fourth on the river, reached its highest point; to rise to second place in 1965, with the second VIII at thirteenth, ahead of nine college first boats. And so the club continued, usually with two crews, until, as with so much else, a climax – in this case an unusual climax – was reached in the year 1968/9.[1]

For some years after the success of 1950 the results of the Clinker Fours were not distinguished. In 1960 one Fitzwilliam four knocked out the other, and got as far as the semi-final before losing to St Catharine's. In 1964 the second IV won the pennant for the fastest college second crew, but in general the club's performance in the Clinker Fours was below its standard in other races. In these later years new events appear in the Fitzwilliam calendar – two crews were entered in a Head of the Cam race in the Easter term of 1966, in which they were placed, respectively, seventh and twenty-sixth; and in 1967 the first rose to fourth. In the Michaelmas term 1967 the College, as it had by then become, tied with first and third Trinity in the final heat of the Light Fours.

The year 1967 was also notable for the appearance of the first Fitzwilliam blue – R. N. Winckless, who rowed in three successive years, and in 1968/69 was President of the University Boat Club. Another noteworthy personal distinction was that of J. H. Reddaway, grandson of W. F., who was in the winning Cambridge crew in 1968.

The tale of the College's centenary year, the last in the life of its Amalgamated Clubs, and by common consent the best, was summarized by their Senior Treasurer, Mr G. F. Hickson, who in a like capacity was shortly to be especially helpful to an infant Junior Members' Association. None, indeed, was better qualified to appreciate, and extol, the achievements of the Fitzwilliam Boat Club in 1968/69, for Hickson, well nigh half a century earlier, had rowed at five in the Clare first May boat throughout his undergraduate career. He wrote,

> Pride of place must be given to the Boat Club, with its victory in the Light Fours and Headship of both Lent and May races. The College VIII was also timed to be the fastest crew in the Fairbairn Eights race, but incurred a

---

[1] See *Journal*, 1969, p. 5: 'The first boat recorded the fastest time in the Fairbairn Cup, but, after having been penalised 3 s. for an over-enthusiastic start, were eventually placed second to Jesus by 1 s.'

penalty of three seconds for a false start and eventually came second. Three Fitzwilliam men gained Blues and two rowed in the Goldie boat, which also beat its Oxford counterpart. The achievement of the 1st May boat in going Head was even more remarkable in that it was deprived of three Blues, the Varsity boat for the first time having been kept together throughout the summer. It also won the "Head of the Cam" (timed) race and the Senior VIII in Peterborough Regatta, and rowed as the Varsity 2nd boat in the Pangbourne National Universities Regatta. The Boat Club also won the Junior Fours and Eights in the Cambridge Regatta in the summer. All these achievements represent the culmination of sustained enthusiasm, combined with hard training and hard rowing over recent years, and they also reflect the hard work put in during this period both by coaches and by successive Captains and other officers of the Boat Club.

From this brief synopsis of the more prominent features of the story of the Fitzwilliam Boat Club, much has been omitted, whether by design or, not improbably, by inadvertence; but there is one small further episode which may be thought worthy of mention.

Members of the College will find no difficulty in following, in the chart of the first division of the May Races from 1964 to 1969, (*see* p. 375), the progress of their boat from the foot of the ladder to its topmost rung. With a little more attention, they may observe that in 1967 Jesus College I was the third of four Fitzwilliam victims; and in the following November the Master was sent a copy of the Annual Report for 1967 of the Jesus College (Cambridge) Society, with a note from its editor (Dr Frederick Brittain) calling his attention to a particular passage. After observing that the Jesus boat had not been lower in the May Races at any time since 1904, Dr Brittain continues:

> We cannot share the feelings of those who think there is something shameful in our having been bumped by Fitzwilliam. Such critics are living in the remote past, when Fitzwilliam, with the poorest resources, with almost every man's hand against them (and not merely in sporting matters), and with no supply of oarsmen from rowing schools, were understandably bottom of the river. Their steady rise from that position to the fourth place in the first division, in spite of their lack of funds and their never having possessed a boat-house of their own, reflects the greatest credit on the dogged determination and enthusiasm of Fitzwilliam men. Since Jesus cannot possibly go head of the river next year, the writer of these lines very much hopes that Fitzwilliam will do so.

When, on 7 June 1969, the Fitzwilliam boats were told of these sentiments, addressed by a devoted Jesus man to Jesus men, they received them with a proper appreciation; and those who are now for the first time made aware of them may feel that, as a postscript to this tale of Fitzwilliam rowing, they deserve rather more durable currency than was afforded by a passing reference in a Bump Supper speech.

The Cricket Club

In cricket the pattern evolved with Reddaway's help persisted without much change throughout the time of his successor, for it still seemed that cricket and Fitzwilliam House did not go together. For some thirty years there was little of distinction in the doings of the Cricket Club, and many of the old features, and faults, remained. For a variety of reasons, many of the games were not played; in 1926 the General Strike disrupted programmes, and that, at least, could not be helped; in 1930 six matches out of sixteen were scratched because of weather, or examinations; in 1932, again, six were abandoned; the club's fielding standards are a continuing source of disquiet, and are frequently blamed for its lack of success – a welcome relief in the teadium of reading about them is afforded by a livelier correspondent than usual who, in an account of the 1952 season, compliments his fast bowlers on an aggressiveness which brought them eighteen wickets apiece (no bad total in a Cambridge season of six weeks), 'not to mention', he adds, 'at least a dozen possible slip catches they neglected to hold, off each other's bowling'. Other reports in the *Magazine* are at times perfunctory, inaccurate, or, occasionally, are missing altogether.

Fixture lists were still made up only in part of games with colleges; probably because of an unwillingness in both parties to arrange encounters between sides of widely differing capacity. In 1947 the club had twenty-seven members in all. In 1948, when there were more men about, the list was longer than usual (sixteen first XI games in an examination term), and particular pleasure is expressed at recurring matches with Ely City and the Camden Club, and new fixtures are recorded with Broxbourne, and, wrongly, with the St Giles' Club. There follows a somewhat unusual comment: 'The policy of increasing the number of Club matches has been pursued because we feel the experience we gain is broader in these than in College matches.' About this time, too, there were games with Luton Town, and, surprisingly, with the Northamptonshire second XI. In the early 1950s matters mended a little. The 1951 season was perhaps the best, with eight wins in fourteen games; and 1953 was not far behind in the club's performances, and was unusual in the quality of the account furnished by the Secretary. In these years, also, there were three Crusaders.

For a game in the Summer term, with eleven-a-side, a league programme was impracticable: it would have remained incomplete in poor
weather, and even if the weather was fine would have been unacceptable to many men preoccupied with examinations, beginning, some of
them, within five weeks of the start of Full Term. The compilers of
reports contented themselves with a brief selection of such happenings
of particular interest as there might be from year to year, and usually,
but not always, supplied statistics of results, which would mean more if
the names of the opponents had also been given. And so, in 1960, we
are told how the captain took forty-six wickets, forty of which
required no help from the fieldsmen, which, says the Secretary, was
just as well. That season's list of fixtures was widely spread, for it
included St Peter's Hall and St Catherine's Society in Oxford, Selwyn,
Queens' and Christ's Colleges, Leicester University, Rydal School, and
Felixstowe. In all, sixteen games were played, eight were won and four
drawn; and after ninety years Fitzwilliam House had its first cricket
blue.[1] This was a good year, and one of its minor benefits was the publication of a photograph of the side in the *Magazine*, with which, even
more helpfully, were also given the names of the players.

This improvement was maintained; for Fitzwilliam names began to
appear more frequently at Fenner's; in 1962 the opening pair scored
eighteen hundred runs between them; and in the following year two
hundred and fifty-six runs were taken off an unfortunate Jesus College
in an hour and fifty minutes. In 1964, when there were five Crusaders,
Fitzwilliam was beaten by Corpus Christi in the first round of a new
Inter-Collegiate Knock-out Competition; and thereafter interest centres more and more in the 'Cup', and in the end of term tours, often in
Sussex, and always successful. The Cup was first won in 1967, retained
in 1968, and lost to Emmanuel in the final round in 1969 – a result possibly affected, for some members of the side, by their attendance at the
annual dinner of a prominent social club the evening before the match.
During these years there were blues aplenty: one in 1966, 1967, and
1968, and two (the University Captain and Secretary, respectively) in
1969. Two others had caused a light-hearted satisfaction in the House,
when in 1963 a far-sighted Captain of Association Football sought
admission to the University of Oxford's course for the Diploma in
Education, and in one and the same year also obtained (effortlessly, for
the purposes of the story) the blues in football and cricket that had
eluded him for three years in Cambridge.[2]

[1]   J. B. Brodie.
[2]   C. J. Saunders.

The Association Football Club

Whereas in some games a prudent selection of opponents might do much to ensure a better table of results at a season's end, the existence of a College League in association football, and the later introduction of a Knock-out Competition in the Lent term, provided more reliable tests of real, as distinct from comparative, merit. While, therefore, it appears from the Secretaries' reports – or their absence – that the footballers enjoyed a very limited success in the middle 1920s, this impression is confirmed by the earliest reference to the Knock-out Competition in the Lent term of 1926, in which Fitzwilliam House lost to Magdalene College by three goals to one, in the first round; and receives even more emphatic confirmation from a report of the only two games played in the Lent term of 1927, in which, after beating March Grammar School by three goals to two, the side lost to Pembroke College in the first round of the Knock-out Competition by nine goals to nothing.

By the same token, the fortunes of the club recovered in 1928/29, when for the first time they reached the second round of the Knockout Competition by beating Magdalene College by three goals to none (but lost narrowly to Jesus in the next round), and as winners of the League in their division were promoted to Division II in the following Michaelmas term, only to find life there too difficult, and suffer relegation after a single season. Thereafter for some years the side continued in Division III, with a good season in 1935/36 (under A. G. MacLeod of Westminster College)[1] when of fourteen games played they had won eight. Twice, but only twice, they won their matches in the first round of the Cup Competition (against Corpus Christi in 1933, and Sidney Sussex in 1938); and in 1939 they appear somewhat surprisingly in Division II of the League, and were also represented by J. A. Stone in the Oxford and Cambridge match, which in that year was played in spite of the war, although no blues were awarded.

The immediate post-war years showed, in reverse, how constantly in more normal times Fitzwilliam sides had suffered from their lack of numbers; for yet again in the late 1940s a very greatly increased resident population – drawn, furthermore, from men whose football was of the association rather than the rugby kind – brought startlingly better results. On its performance in the experimental season of 1946/47, the club was placed in Division I of a newly constituted League in the following year, and after a Michaelmas term of mixed

[1]   The Rev. A. G. Macleod, since 1963 Principal of Westminster College.

success won its greatest triumphs in the following term, by disposing of Corpus Christi, Jesus, Clare and, finally, of St Catharine's College in the Knock-out Competition – all this under a Captain of considerable seniority,[1] who by a skilful use of what was left of his time found his way into the first class in all three examinations in Engineering Studies. In this season, too, the second team was at the top of what was known as the Second Eleven League.

After a comparative relapse in 1948/49, post-war numbers and post-war confidence achieved in 1949/50 the best season the club had ever had. Head of Division I with the loss of a single point, they were beaten in the second round of the Cup Competition by St John's College, the eventual winners, whom they had trounced the term before by nine goals to two. T. S. Davies won his blue as goal-keeper, and four members of the side were elected Falcons. The second XI also did well, with so much assistance from Wesley House that there was said to have been some speculation whether there was in Cambridge any Methodist who did *not* play association football. The impetus acquired after the war still drove the club forward, and in 1950/51 they were runners up in the College League, and when in the Michaelmas term of 1951 they won it outright with two matches still to play, the side had had an unbeaten run of twenty-five games in the first division, spread over three seasons, and at length brought to an end by Emmanuel. In the Lent term 1952 Fitzwilliam performed creditably in the Cup Competition, but in the semi-final round were again beaten by Emmanuel, who knocked them out on three occasions between 1951 and 1955. For some years the XI stayed in Division I, with safety but without distinction (except for the winning of a blue in 1956),[2] until the season of 1959/60 when they were again at the top of the League, and also reached a Cup semi-final. Two seasons later, winning only one League match, they were relegated, after fourteen years; and, for good measure, lost to Magdalene at the earliest possible moment in the Cup Competition. The next time round, however, as runners up in Division II they came back, and so continued until 1967/68, a year of contrasting fortunes, when in the Michaelmas term, without their three blues, they went down again, and with them won the knock-out. The see-saw persisted, this time fortunately, when the side completed its share of the celebration of the College centenary year by winning, in the Michaelmas term of 1969, a return passage to the first division. In the meantime

---

[1] Alexander Urquhart.
[2] K. S. Pellow (see p. 518).

the second XI, promoted from Division IV in 1960, stayed in Division III with comparative comfort, and distinguished themselves as finalists, but not as winners, of the Second Eleven Cup Competition of 1968.

These last years were notable for the numbers of Fitzwilliam men who played in the Oxford and Cambridge match: one in 1963, 1964, and 1965; three in 1966 and 1967; five in 1968; and two, including the University Captain, in 1969.

The Rugby Union Football Club

The inter-war years were depressing for rugby footballers in Fitzwilliam House, and it was not until after the Second World War, with greatly increased numbers in residence, that the club began to count in college rugby. Constant defeat brought disenchantment, and there were even complaints, admittedly rare but significant, about the failure of players to put in an appearance at college matches. Inevitably it is in the Cup Competition that weaknesses were most obvious – in 1929 Fitzwilliam lost by a margin of thirty points to Christ's College, but that seemed almost a matter for congratulation in comparison with a gap three times as large two years previously. It comes as no surprise to find a suggestion that games should be arranged, if possible, with less overwhelming opposition; and some small improvement by the middle thirties may have been due to a more discriminating fixture list; but, even so, in 1934 a match with Ridley Hall, lost by thirteen points to ten, is described as the season's best display; and in the knock-out games of 1937, in a preliminary round, the score against Jesus College was five points to forty-four. In the Michaelmas term 1939 the club found itself in a newly constituted College League, and won no single game; and, on this last occasion before the interruption caused by the remaining years of the war, after the luck of the draw had given them a bye, the side achieved a rare success in beating Corpus by eleven points to eight, only to lose to Queens' College in the third round by forty-three points to three.

In the 1946/47 season the club found itself in the third division of the League, with unsatisfactory, and in some respects curious, results. They won almost nothing; but relegation to Division IV appears to have been due to their failure to complete their programme, a failure for which they blamed the weather (reasonably enough, it will seem, to any who can remember the temperatures of that Lent term). They did not stay down for long, however, as after one season they qualified for promotion; but oddity persists, for having earned their promotion from Division IV in 1947 they are found in Division II in 1948, and so far prospered that, after a single season, they very nearly went higher still. Thereabouts, also, blues began to appear, and it was no longer to be taken for granted, by members of the side or by anyone else, that Fitzwilliam would leave the Knock-out Competition after the first round. In 1951, for example, having beaten Sidney Sussex, they lost to Caius College by no more than six points, a margin very different from the monster overdrafts of pre-war years. It remains true, however, that in the next year, after beating Trinity Hall, they again came up against Caius, and lost by thirty-seven points to nil.

While all this was going on, the second XV, now a regular part of the establishment, as runners up in Division V in 1947/48, went up to Division IV in the following year, but went down again as soon as possible, and stayed down for a considerable time. A third XV appeared in 1951, and for some years provided light-hearted entertainment, not only for themselves.

It was in the Michaelmas term of 1958 that the club, for the first time, found themselves in the top division of the League; but briefly, only, for they were down again three years later, and had to wait until the season of 1964/65 for more lasting, and more comprehensive, distinction. For some years their Cup performances had been creditable, and in 1962 they reached the third round of the competition, losing to Christ's College by six points to none. In 1963 the competition was frozen out; in 1964 they got into the final, losing, again to Christ's, by twenty-nine points to eight; but in the season of 1964/65, at length, everything came right. Winning the League in the Michaelmas term, in the following term's Cup competition they beat Magdalene, Trinity Hall, and Christ's (a great triumph), and in the final Jesus College, by eight points to nil. Fifteen resident Fitzwilliam men played in some University side during the season; two were blues, and another was Captain of the LX Club in its match with Oxford. The 'double' had not been achieved by any college for over thirty years.

It was not to be expected that such success would continue, but in 1965/66 the side was in the final of the Cup for the third consecutive year, losing to Queens' College – or, as might not unreasonably have been said, to C. M. H. Gibson and others, of that College – by thirteen points to eight. In 1967/68 they won the League again; and, finally, although the following season was unremarkable for the side as a whole, for they only just managed to stay in Division I, and were beaten, again by Queens', in the semi-final round of the Cup, it brought distinction to two individuals, A. M. Jorden and I. R. Shackleton, both of whom, after playing against Oxford, were to be capped for England.

The second XV, too, had prospered: in the Michaelmas term of 1960 they had come up to Division III; but soon found the pace too hot. They recovered, however, and in 1967/68, in Division II, were the most highly placed second XV in the University.

The Lawn Tennis Club

The apparent lack of enthusiasm among the tennis players, and the indifference of the rest of the House (if the *Magazine* is to be taken as typical), continued for some time. The club's programme consisted of matches in the Inter-Collegiate League, and in the Knock-out Competition, with some friendly games, including an occasional fixture outside Cambridge. Such information as is now available is to be found in the *Magazine*, but it comes irregularly; and in the inter-war period there is frequently nothing at all. After an indifferent account of the 1925 season, the most arresting feature in 1926 is a reference to the effects of 'industrial unrest'; and it is not until 1929 that a better season produced a better account, with the first VI winning six of its seven matches in Division IV. At the time of writing, a second VI resuscitated in that year had lost all its matches, but there had been unusual success in the doubles of the Cup competition when, with the help of a bye, the team reached the semi-final before losing to Jesus College.

That tennis, like other games if not more than most, suffered from lack of players is made startlingly plain, in 1931, by a statement that at the beginning of the season the club consisted of three members – its Captain, its Secretary, and the President (the Censor), but even so a VI was made up somehow, and the full complement of seven League matches duly played (all against college second sixes), and three of them won. It was, perhaps, no bad thing that the weather was poor; as it seems also to have been in 1932, when ten out of eighteen matches were scratched, and of eight League fixtures the last, against Emmanuel, four times postponed. And then, except for the season of 1934, when only two League matches were lost, tennis all but disappears from the scene until after the war.

The first post-war season seems to have been that of 1947, when the club had a large membership, but entered one VI only in the League competition; and made a promising start by winning Division III in its first season. The Secretary is full of confidence for the future, but regrets the lack of a hard court for practice when the grass courts are unplayable – a deficiency which was shortly afterwards remedied. There were two teams in 1948: the first were runners up in their first year in Division II; the second did well in their first year in the League

(Division VI), a performance they improved upon a year later when they won their division, and entered Division V in 1950, when they again earned promotion, this time to Division IV. The first VI, however, speedily found the opposition too strong in Division I, and after a single season started on a disastrous course which led them to Division IV in 1956; and, unpredictable as always, wavered between the second and the fifth division until 1967, as did the second VI two divisions lower down. In 1967 both teams won all their League matches, and rose in 1968 to Divisions I and II respectively, the second team's ascent being even more spectacular than the descent of the first some years earlier, for they went from Division VI to Division II in four years. Both teams could now look forward to playing against nothing less than a college first VI in either division.

For twenty years or so after the war comparatively little attention is paid to the inter-college Knock-out competition, which is frequently not mentioned at all in reports to the *Magazine*. In 1949 Fitzwilliam reached the semi-final round of the singles and lost to Queens' College, and in the doubles were beaten by Clare. In 1957 the correspondent limits himself to an observation that the House could hardly do worse in that year than it had done the year before. In 1962 and 1963 the singles were lost to Caius, and in 1964 and 1965 to Downing, in both years the eventual winners. No blue was won between 1947 and 1969; but there were two Grasshoppers (the brothers D. J. and G. R. Bone) in the Oxford match in 1963, and one (P. A. Lucas) in 1967.

The Hockey Club

Having somewhat precariously contrived to stay in the second division in 1924 and 1925, the XI, with five wins in six matches, qualified for promotion in 1926, but, as not infrequently occurred with Fitzwilliam sides, could not stay the pace, and was back in Division II in 1927/28, after a single season, although the final result was a close-run thing, arrived at in a play-off against Caius College, after two periods of extra time. In 1927/28, also, new arrangements were devised by which each college played six friendly matches in a season, thus making it possible, but not, it appears, necessary, for every college to play against every other college within three years. An unusual feature of the scheme was a divisional Knock-out competition in which the final winner qualified for promotion, and the worst loser, presumably, for relegation. There was a similar competition for second elevens. These changes brought little benefit to Fitzwilliam, for in the second year of the scheme the side was in Division III, where it stayed until the war. During the thirties enthusiasm for the game seems to have fallen off, membership of the club varied between twenty and thirty, and little of note is recorded, save that in 1931 there was a Fitzwilliam blue (C. A. Lane), and again in 1932, when, as the oldest man in the side, he saved the game with the hundredth Cambridge goal in the series. He was also capped on a number of occasions for Scotland. At this time knock-out games are not always mentioned, and when they are the scores are not always given; but it was not unusual for the side to go out in the first round, if not invariably as decisively as in 1939, when Jesus College won by thirteen goals to none.

Surprisingly, nothing is recorded about the first post-war season of 1946/47; but abnormally large numbers appear in hockey to have had the same effect – briefly, at least – as in other games, for in 1947/48 the XI reached the final round of the Knock-out competition (and then lost to Trinity Hall). In the League, which seems to have become again the avenue for promotion and relegation, they did little more than keep their place in Division II, with reasonable comfort, but without distinction save by occasional flash in the pan performances, to the general surprise, and no less to their own, as when in 1954/55 they were the only side to defeat Pembroke College in the League competition; and, in the Knock-out competition three years later, when they overcame St Catharine's, winners of Division I, but themselves finished the season very near the bottom of Division II. The root of their trouble lay no longer in a small number of residents, but with the scarcity of those interested in playing hockey – in 1954 the club Secretary had complained that no more than twenty out of four hundred were willing to turn out twice a week, particularly for a second XI game.

Towards the end of the 1950s there were, however, signs of rather more permanent improvement in the fortunes of the club, for in 1958/59 they again beat St Catharine's in the Knock-out competition (though they lost to Clare College in the next round); and there were, in one and the same year, two blues in the side, of whom one, P. D. Fishwick, was later to be capped for England. There was also some disposition to branch out in other directions. In 1957 the club appeared in the Easter vacation Hockey Festival at Lowestoft; and in 1960, in addition to fixtures in Oxford, London, and Edgbaston, there was an Easter vacation tour in Holland; and in the next year they were at the Folkestone Hockey Festival. The club's form, however, remained unpredictable, for having at length reached the top division of the League in the season of 1960/61, they went down again at once, and almost spent alternate years in Divisions I and II, until in 1968 they again earned promotion, and, for good measure and with a timing rivalled only by the Boat Club, celebrated the college's centenary year by winning the Knock-out competition for the first time. These years were notable, too, for individual honours: in 1965 and 1966 there was a Fitzwilliam blue; in 1967 and 1968 there were three, and three again in 1969, when P. J. T. Svehlik, playing in his third consecutive year, was University Captain.

The Athletics Club

It has frequently been evident that the Fitzwilliam undergraduate clubs suffered from lack of recruits; and this is a recurring theme among the athletes, who in this respect appear to have been handicapped more than most. There are even lamentations at the loss of a single performer, as in 1924, when a 'fifth year fresher' who had kept three terms at Caius College four years previously,[1] was debarred by authority from competing in inter-collegiate events, when he eventually came into residence as a non-collegiate student. In 1926 Fitzwilliam House was not represented at all in five events in College Trials against Downing and Corpus Christi, and in 1930 the Michaelmas term brought the club no more than a half dozen new members. Twenty years later there was little change, for in the competition for the Rouse Ball Cup in the Lent term of 1952 the Fitzwilliam team consisted of seven competitors. But numerical shortages were not the whole trouble; unless, indeed, they were at the root of others. At times there was a listlessness about the Athletics Club, as when in 1950 failure in a three-mile Relay Race was due to the non-appearance of the third of the four runners to take the baton; and even in 1964, when the Fitzwilliam clubs as a whole were making their mark in the University, the club's prospects of promotion to Division I of the Relay Races competition were ruined by the failure of the high hurdlers to appear in time for their event.

A *Magazine* correspondent of 1950 reveals an attitude which persisted for many years:

> Athletics is something of a Cinderella of sports at Fitzwilliam House. Our present position near the bottom of the second division may be a tribute to our complete indifference to public opinion, but it is a sad reflection on our numerical strength as a College. From among four hundred or so members of the House we ought to be able to raise a team for every event in the College Athletic programme.

[1] F. H. J. Trayes, who may have wondered a little on learning, in the following term, that a half-blue of 1914 (A. G. de L. Willis, of Emmanuel) was being allowed, on his return from the Services, to compete against Oxford in 1925.

He ends with the hope that, at no distant date, the Athletics Club Report will be a chronicle of achievement, 'instead of the usual apologia for things not attempted'.

From time to time reasons are advanced to explain the general lack of enthusiasm for running and jumping – the Fenner's membership fee is mentioned as a deterrent – and there is little doubt that a principal impediment to success was the dependence of the club on the services of casual recruits whose abilities and whose main interests lay elsewhere. A wing-threequarter or an outside-left with a hitherto unsuspected turn of speed might be persuaded to run a hundred yards, or a quarter-mile – even though it might prove uncommonly hard to convince him that hurdles, especially high hurdles, were anything but unsuitable obstacles to a smooth progress much more comfortably achieved without them – and a full-back, or one of the larger members of the scrum, might be willing to put the weight or throw the discus, and there may well have been among the professional athletes a somewhat rueful admission that the performances of these 'part-timers' were apt to be at least as successful as those of the athletes proper, who had trained the season long. Be all this as it may, the club's first entry in 1955 into Division I of the Inter-collegiate Field Events Competition was a landmark in its history, even though it was followed a year later by relegation. Their return to the upper division in 1963, at the beginning of a period of unprecedented prosperity for the Amalgamated Clubs as a whole, was matched in 1964 by promotion to Division I of the Competition for the Rouse Ball Cup, also followed by a return to Division II after a single year – a result possibly influenced by a clash of dates with an important rugby football match, for the Athletics Club was still dependent on help from others. In 1965, however, the Relay Team went up, and stayed up; and in 1968, by again winning the second division of the Rouse Ball Cup, the club made sure that in the College's centenary year all three of its teams were in their respective top divisions.

The club did not lack individual performers who achieved high distinction, and brought reflected glory, its members felt, to the institution to which they all belonged. Four stand out as worthy of particular mention, three of them in Field Events. The success of H. A. Dubois has already been mentioned.[1] The next, in point of time, was Ali Irfan, a Turk who came into residence in 1933; and, having broken the record for the Weight in the Freshmen's Sports in his first term, won the event

[1] See p. 344.

four times against Oxford, setting a new record on three of these occasions, and finishing in 1937 with a putt of 49′3¾″. It was not unusual for the heights achieved by distinguished athletes to be offset by academic depths, but Irfan, although he did not raise his sights above the Ordinary B.A. degree, was placed in the first class in all three of his examinations for it, a feat by no means negligible in a foreigner whose chosen course included the Special Examination in English Literature. The holding of a farewell lunch in Irfan's honour, attended by seniors and juniors alike, is additional evidence of his popularity among members of the House.

Two of the four of these pre-eminent Fitzwilliam athletes were also Presidents of the University Club. Ivar Emil Vind came into residence (for two years only) in the Michaelmas term of 1946, and in his first Oxford Athletics match he won the high jump and the pole vault, and was second in the discus. In the following Michaelmas term he ran the anchor leg in the high hurdles Relay Race, and in the 1948 Oxford match he set a new record in the high jump (6′3″), and also won the pole vault and the discus. In the same year he was a gold medallist at the World Student Games in Paris, and on four occasions was national High Jump champion of Denmark, setting a record (6′3″) in 1947 which stood for fifteen years.[1]

The second Fitzwilliam president of the Cambridge University Athletics Club was M. J. Winbolt Lewis. In all three of his years at Cambridge he ran against Oxford in the Relay Races, and in all three he also won the quarter-mile. In 1966/67 and 1967/68 he was second in the hundred yards and the two hundred and twenty yards, but in his last year, when he was President, he stood down from these, and to his quarter-mile added only the half-mile, which he won. Meanwhile, in the Autumn of 1968, he had run for Great Britain in the 400 metres, and in the 1,600 metres Relay Race at the Olympic Games in Mexico.

Before embarking on any account of the fortunes of the more recently established clubs or societies, there can hardly be omitted some reference, at least, to the most unfortunate incident in the whole history of

[1] See also p. 515. Vind's early career and his sustained interest in Athletics led him to take a prominent part in their administration; and from 1959, when he became a member of the International Olympic Committee, he was active in many aspects of the organization of the Olympic Games. He died, at the early age of fifty-seven, on 11 February 1977.

Amalgamation.[1] That something was wrong first became apparent (outside the Fitzwilliam House office) at a meeting of the Finance Committee of the Clubs held on 27 January 1937, at which the Treasurer (Mr C. G. Joseph) was to have presented his balance sheet for the previous year, but could not do so, says the minute, 'owing to several complications'. Mr Gaskoin, from the Chair, seems to have let fall a hint that the Treasurer was likely to resign. On 18 February the Censor informed another meeting of the committee that the audited accounts of the Clubs, up to 31 January 1937, showed that a sum of rather more than £600 was missing, and that it was probable that a larger sum had been lost, with little possibility of recovery. The matter had been reported to the Non-Collegiate Students Board, who had laid it before the Council of the Senate. In June the Board were informed that a report submitted to the Vice-Chancellor by a firm of accountants had revealed that a sum of just under £2,750 had been unaccounted for. In making this statement the Board's Chairman appears to refer exclusively to the affairs of the Amalgamated Clubs, but conflicting accounts make it hard to determine whether this round sum of £2,750 included misappropriations from funds administered by the University's Adviser to Indian Students, or whether, as alleged by Counsel for the prosecution at the Hertfordshire Assizes on 13 May 1938, the latter amounted to an additional £1,300. When all was over Dr R. C. Evans, of Clare College, the new Treasurer of the Clubs, informed his committee, in a perfectly clear statement, that more than £2,000 had been missing from the Clubs' accounts between 1924 and 1936. Dr Evans also told the committee that the auditors and bankers had accepted responsibility for the losses, and had agreed to refund a sum which, after the deduction of the auditors' fees, amounted to £2,100. Dr Evans's appointment as Treasurer was made formally on 11 March 1937, but he had been prominent before that in an immediate enquiry into the Clubs' affairs, set up in order to prevent a repetition of recent disasters. On his proposal the Laws were amended so as to provide for an internal audit, for the appointment *ex officio* of the Bursar as one of three internal auditors, and for improved procedures for banking and keeping accounts. The Laws were also modified for the appointment *ex officio* of the Bursar as a member of the committee, and for the attendance of the Censor, at his discretion, at committee meetings in an advisory capacity. Dr Evans had then only recently entered the Fitzwil-

---

[1] For the whole of this episode, see minutes for the year 1937, A.C. Minutes (in particular) of 27 January and 18 February 1937, and, for the Court case, the *Cambridge Daily News* of 18 June 1937.

liam scene, first as supervisor in Mineralogy and then, after a brief interval, as Director of Studies in Natural Sciences, an office which he held until his election as Fellow of St Catharine's in 1947. For ten years Dr Evans continued as Treasurer of the Amalgamated Clubs; he was also a Governor of the Fitzwilliam Hall Trust from 1939 until its winding up in 1971, and a member of the Non-Collegiate Students Board from January 1953 during the last thirteen years of its life. It is appropriate to place on record here the College's appreciation of the value of all that he did, and not only in these various capacities, but also for his long continued interest in all non-collegiate doings, and his help whenever help was urgently needed. Mr Thatcher, after his retirement, in an unfinished essay 'Fitzwilliam House from 1924 to 1955',[1] clearly regarded as not the least of the benefactions of F. I. G. Rawlins, who had himself been Director of Studies in Natural Sciences for three years, that he should, on leaving Cambridge for the National Gallery, have brought Dr Evans to the notice of those in authority.

The Council of the Senate had conducted their own enquiry into the defalcations, and on 11 November 1937 a brief report of their committee on the matter, which appears to have been part, only, of their findings submitted to the Council, was the subject of a discussion between the Non-Collegiate Students Board and the Masters of Clare and Caius Colleges, members of the Council's committee. An undated copy of the report makes no reference to the payment of compensation by the auditors and bankers, of which the Board had been told on 15 October, and is not free from criticism of the Censor, who might, it suggests, have brought about an earlier disclosure of what was going on. After further deliberation, the Board instructed their Chairman to draft a reply to the Council, which was sent on 3 December. It rejects criticisms of Mr Thatcher's part in the affair, and affirms the Board's views that his responsibilities had been properly discharged.

Thatcher himself, thirty years later, in observations on the whole of this unhappy episode, does not conceal his conviction that among those in high authority in the University there were some who were hostile to him personally, and unsympathetic to his non-collegiate institution.[2] It may be no coincidence that at this same time there were difficulties and long delays after an approach to the Council of the Senate for their approval of an appeal for money for buildings to be launched at the instigation of the Fitzwilliam Society;[3] and Thatcher's feelings in the

[1] See p. 46 (College Archives).
[2] *Ibid.*, pp. 36–8.
[3] See pp. 430–2.

1930s were not unlike the exasperations of Mr S. C. Roberts twenty years later, when on behalf of the Non-Collegiate Students Board he seemed to encounter from the Financial Board repeated, and, as it appeared to him, unjustified hesitations over the selection of a building site for Fitzwilliam House, whether as a University institution or as a body on the road to independence.[1] As they reflect on the history of the University in the last half-century, there may well be some who have become conscious of possible links in a chain of responsibility for this persisting attitude towards the non-collegiate institution. They may also detect a similar unfriendliness in the Report of the Joint Committee on the present and future position of Fitzwilliam House – or, rather, in the majority Report of that committee – whose recommendations were rejected by the Council of the Senate early in 1954.

Other Clubs and Societies

Of the more recently established of the clubs and societies, as distinct from the veterans of Reddaway's time and earlier, two were first included among the Amalgamated Clubs in a code of Rules promulgated in 1934 – Swimming, admitted to membership on 19 January 1929, and Squash Rackets (31 March 1933). The first appearance of Badminton, in the Laws of 1936, is something of a curiosity, for it was not admitted until 11 November 1937. Table Tennis was also recognized at the same time. Of these clubs, Swimming had a University Captain (M. C. Anderson) in 1958/59, but Badminton and Table Tennis, with Lacrosse, Boxing and Basket Ball, seem to have been the most consistently active or successful, if success be measured by frequency of appearance in University sides; and on the score of longevity, the Chess Club, 'revived' in Reddaway's last year as Censor, but unusually prominent in the earliest days of all, still deserves an honourable mention.

In Badminton Fitzwilliam House supplied a University Captain in 1948/49, and another in 1953/54, at a time when the Fitzwilliam game owed much to the Heah brothers, from Malaya. There was a Fitzwilliam Captain (M. S. Allwood) in Table Tennis in 1936/37, which seems to have encouraged the club's recognition as one of the Amalgamated Clubs in the following year, and there were three University Captains in the 1960s – B. G. Jones, T. P. Nicholson, and J. C. Tulloch. In Lacrosse the first Fitzwilliam names occur as early as 1920/21, long

---

[1]   Independent Status – Correspondence II. Notes made by Mr Roberts for a speech to the Council of the Senate on 18 February 1957. They leave no doubt about his feelings.

before the formation of a club or its admission to amalgamated status (it first appears in the Accounts in 1946/47), and after the Second World War there were blues at intervals, and a University Captain (A. F. Thomas) in 1965/66. The club is unusual in that only once, over a period of more than twenty years, did its officers contrive to furnish the *Fitzwilliam Magazine* with some account of its activities. In Boxing and Fencing, as it then was, G. A. Wootten (1897/98) was among the first non-collegiate students to represent the University against Oxford in a sporting contest; but he remained in isolation as a boxer for more than fifty years, for it was not until the 1950s that Fitzwilliam boxing came into its own, with one or more blues in every year from 1955/56 until 1968/69, and a University Captain (R. F. Bannister) in 1959/60. Golf, included in the Amalgamated Clubs grant list in 1950, had its first blue in 1963, and a Rugby Fives Club, started in 1952, was divided into separate clubs for Rugby and Eton fives by a decision of the Clubs taken in the Easter term of 1964.

The Basket Ball Club, first supported with a modest grant of seven shillings and sixpence in 1953, celebrated its official recognition in 1955/56 with an unbeaten season. In 1957 the Secretary's description of the team as consisting of 'one Lebanese, one Chineseman, two Canadians, one Southern United Statesman, one New Yorker, one Cockney, and one Welshman' suggests some reliance on outside help (as in Badminton), and to some purpose, for in 1958 Fitzwilliam provided a University Captain (N. A. Es-Said, from Beirut), and in 1959, for the fourth consecutive year won the Cup Competition, and the League.

There were many other clubs and societies at some time or other between 1924 and 1969, particularly during the latter half of the period. At the outbreak of war in 1939 there were eleven clubs and two societies under the Amalgamation Rules, with at least two independent societies of considerable seniority (the Historical and the Amateur Dramatic Societies). During the last three years of Amalgamation (1966–69), under the constitution of 1958, there were thirty-five in receipt of grant in one or more of those years. With fluctuations throughout the period, caused by the brief appearance of ephemeral groups, the number of those who had figured in the accounts of the Amalgamated Clubs between 1936 and 1969 approached fifty.

Not all short-lived clubs or societies will have gone unlamented. In 1956 the Secretary and Treasurer of a Modern Languages Club tells how it had been brought into being two years previously, with the intention of seeking money to form at least the nucleus of a Modern

Languages section of the Fitzwilliam Library, very obviously starting from scratch. The venture clearly had the blessing of the authorities, and for three years the club received some assistance from Amalgamated Clubs funds, and was instrumental in providing the library with some two hundred and fifty books, mainly in French and German. After this promising beginning, however, the club disappeared.

The list of grant-aided clubs and societies is not free from surprises. Polo, for example, and Racquets, or Ski-ing, can have had few followers in the House, even if the inclusion of Ice Hockey may be attributed to the persuasiveness of research students from North America for whom no college had found room. Also unusual is a grant in 1957/58 to a Catholic Society, discontinued in the following year when a new constitution excluded all religious clubs or societies from membership. The occurrence of some pursuits is curious, on grounds of sheer triviality: it is hard to suppose that Ten-pin Bowling, or, with due allowance for the misfortune of its name, Tiddly-winks, can have been taken seriously by any but the merest few. Among these groups which came and quickly went, were others of longer life which nevertheless left only spasmodic records of their doings, save when their members found their way into University sides. There were Cambridge captains against Oxford in Billiards (P. H. C. Constable, as far back as 1926/27); Cross Country (R. S. Ellis, 1950/51); Ice Hockey (D. C. F. Leigh, (1953/54); Shooting (G. T. Martel, 1957/58); and Polo (V. Lukshumeyah, 1958/59). Fencing came into prominence in 1962, when P. J. Kirby, a half-blue in that and the previous year, won the National Foil Championship.

The Research Club

With eighty-two research students in residence, and with every likelihood of an increase in this already large number, the Michaelmas term 1950 saw the formation of a Research Club, with the object of providing a meeting place for men of all faculties, and of bringing them into closer touch with the corporate activities of the House. It seems not unlikely that R. N. Walters, then recently appointed Tutor, and J. A. Leonard, a research student originally of German nationality who had come into residence as an undergraduate in the Lent term of 1947 to read for the Moral Sciences Tripos, were responsible for the new venture; and at all events it was Leonard who invited the Censor to perform the official opening of two club rooms on the first floor of number 19 Fitzwilliam Street on 24 April 1952. Newspapers and periodicals, playing cards, chess-men, and wireless were provided in the rooms, which were to stay open throughout the year, and the kitchen was handily placed for supplies. According to Leonard, writing as Secretary in the *Magazine*, Fitzwilliam House was first in the University in supplying such special facilities for research students, and he very evidently appreciated their being made available at a time when the resources of the House were strained to the limit.

The club soon settled on a programme of weekly meetings in full term – at first on Thursday evenings, and then on Wednesdays – and increasingly seems to have invited senior members of the University to read papers or to lead their discussions. Various groups branched out into social or sporting pursuits – squash rackets and (in summertime) lawn tennis were played, and in 1954 a Research Students Eight first appeared, and after negotiating the 'getting-on' races rowed in the Mays. In 1954, also, a change in the club's title to Fitzwilliam House Research Students and Graduates Club betokened eligibility for membership of all Fitzwilliam residents with graduate status; and in 1961 there was a membership of eighty-six research students, and forty-eight graduates reading for diplomas or other special courses.

The well-being of the club has always tended to depend on the enthusiasm of one or two individuals. With an energetic secretary, the club would flourish; without, it flagged; but over the years there has been a growing closer association with senior members, fostered by special dining arrangements, or other social gatherings. In 1963 the club was given a handsome room in the new buildings, and, according to the club Secretary of the time, became in 1964/65 'a fully-fledged and active member of the Amalgamated Clubs' – a puzzling statement, for there is no record in the minutes of the Clubs of any such change. Financially, the Research Club had been supported from its beginnings, with a modest grant of £2.2.4 in the first year, and thereafter with an average annual subvention of about £60, until this was doubled in 1963/64, when the Finance Committee of the Clubs, on the grounds that the members of the Research Club were paying far more in subscriptions to the Amalgamated Clubs' funds than they were receiving by way of amenities, resolved that the grant to the Research Club should be on the basis of a terminal rate of 10s. for each member. On 1 January 1968 came the appointment of a Tutor for Research Students[1] (Dr David Kerridge) – a most successful innovation; and in 1969 the body of graduate students, designated the Middle Common Room in

[1] By an amendment of University Statutes the Board of Research Studies had become the Board of Graduate Studies on 31 January 1966, but the use of the familiar name died hard.

the constitution of a new Junior Members Association, emerged as something akin to a Third Estate in the college.

'The Billygoats'[1]

In the *Fitzwilliam Magazine* for June 1948 there appeared a preliminary notice under the heading 'Billygoats Society': .

> Oarsmen, past and present, who have raced for Fitzwilliam House are invited to join a new dining society now being formed to support and give continuity to the traditions of the Boat Club.
>
> The social functions of the Society will be two dinners annually, one in London on Boat Race night, and the other in Cambridge on the night of the Fairbairn Cup race.
>
> Further details may be had of the Joint Organizers, J. Hunter and F. J. Willett, at Fitzwilliam House.

The 'organizers', then at the end of their second year, had rowed four and five, respectively, in the first boat of the previous Lent term. This notice was followed by a further announcement in the next issue of the *Magazine* to the effect that the society had been duly founded, with the object of 'fostering a spirit of continuity between past and present members of the Boat Club'. Rules had been approved and the first officers elected at a General Meeting held in Fitzwilliam House on 15 June 1948. Among the officers Major F. J. Stratton was elected President, Mr C. L. Wayper Secretary, and the Bursar of the House (Mr W. W. Williams) Treasurer. This meeting was followed by lunch, at which, says the *Magazine* 'the Censor gave the Society his benediction'. The Rules, published in the *Fitzwilliam Journal* for December 1949, declared that the society's name was to be 'The Billygoats'. In addition to its already proclaimed purposes, it was to provide moral and financial support for the Boat Club; and its membership was to be open to all past and present members of the Boat Club who had raced for Fitzwilliam in a race organized by the Cambridge University Boat Club, or by any other properly constituted rowing authority. The provisionally announced arrangements for annual dinners were confirmed. There would be an annual subscription of half a guinea (but of five shillings for undergraduates); and, finally, the society was to have 'a red tie with embroidered goat's head and crossed oars, together with the last two digits of the last year in which the member rowed for F.H.B.C.'

---

[1]   This account owes much to the minutes of the society, which have been regularly kept since 1 December 1951.

It seems that the society treated its Rules with a cheerful disregard, for at its first meeting, in appointing Mr Wayper to be its Secretary, it did not remember that candidates for the secretaryship had to be members of the Fitzwilliam House Boat Club; and when a similar difficulty, this time not overlooked, arose shortly afterwards over the appointment of Mr R. N. Walters as Treasurer the offending rule was changed.

There are now no minutes of meetings of the society during its first three years, and it is not clear that there ever were. At first, there are some accounts of its doings in the *Magazine* and *Journal*, the latter on occasion being an unaltered repetition of the former, and so by a simple lapse of time out of date and misleading. The society's first dinner was held on 27 November 1948, presumably in Cambridge, and was attended by the Fairbairn crews and a 'sprinkling' of older members, about forty in all; and there was also a dinner on the Boat Race night of 1949, in the Connaught Rooms. On both occasions the President entertained the company beforehand. Owing to lack of support no dinner, after the first, was held on Boat Race night, and the society soon settled into a routine Annual General Meeting, and Annual Dinner, in Cambridge on the night of the Fairbairn Cup race. Instead of holding a London dinner members were encouraged to come to Bump Suppers in Cambridge. After two years, at the Annual General Meeting of 1950, the society elected as its second President in succession to Major Stratton, F. B. Priest, who had come so close to a Trial Cap in 1924. Efforts to expand had resulted in a membership of seventy-eight (including, says the secretary, a number of honorary members who paid no subscription), and an appeal had been made for the support of crews at Henley, Marlow, and on the Tideway.

After June 1951 the *Magazine* makes no further reference to the society, and there are sporadic references, only, in the *Journal*. It is doubly fortunate, therefore, that on 1 December 1951, at a meeting of the society's committee, the President and the Treasurer insisted on the need for minutes of all meetings, and for properly audited accounts.

Rarely absent from the minds of those who guided the society's affairs was the hope that one day they might be faced with the need, and supplied with the means, to assist the Boat Club to compete in the Henley Royal Regatta, and in other competitions in which it might enhance its reputation outside Cambridge. At first, the society could offer only modest help, and its earliest recorded benefaction is the gift in November 1952 of £4 for books for the club's Rowing library. A year later the society's membership was said to be sixty-seven, and its assets £89.9.7; and it appears that at an Extraordinary Committee Meeting held in May 1954, on the proposal of the President, supported by his Treasurer, a grant of £1 was made to members of the crews who had rowed in the Reading Head of the River race in the previous March; and this monetary support for the club was followed at the next General Meeting by another grant of £25 for its general expenses – a decision rather out of line with the society's preference for saving its money for outside events. Previously assets had for the first time just exceeded a hundred pounds (£100.16.6), and membership stood at seventy-two, of whom forty-six were ex-members, and twenty-six present members, of the Boat Club.

The General Meeting of 1955 was much taken up with the consideration and approval of changes in the society's Rules, chiefly for the more convenient tenure of its officers and committee members, to come into effect in 1956, when postal voting also was to be allowed. Membership is differently recorded: there were forty-seven subscribing members, and thirty-seven 'in statu pupillari', and it is possible that this latter category was erroneously regarded as the equivalent of those previously described as 'present members of the Boat Club'. At this meeting mention is also first made of funds on deposit, with assets consisting of £79.12.5 on deposit, and £34.13.5 in the society's current account. A pleasant last minute of the meeting tells of the presentation of a 'prow' to K. C. A. Smith, the retiring Secretary, by way of appreciation of his coaching, and other activities on the society's behalf. At its Annual General Meeting of November 1958, on the recommendation of the Treasurer (R. W. Haywood), the society, anxious to be associated in some small way with a most important acquisition by the Boat Club, resolved to present the club with a College Crest to be suitably placed in the boathouse then recently purchased from St Catharine's College with generous help from the Fitzwilliam Society; and the presentation was duly made on the last night of the May Races of 1959.

With the passage of time, and as a natural consequence of the continued success of the boats, the society became increasingly preoccupied with one of its principal long-term aims – the problem of ensuring that no sufficiently competent Fitzwilliam boat should be prevented by lack of money from entering for Henley in any year – and correspondingly less disposed to permit its exiguous resources to be frittered away on comparative trivialities. In the minutes of the late 1950s there are references to a 'usual annual grant of £10 to the Boat Club', and also to the society's share, at first as much as a half, in the cost of crock pots, on occasion presented at the Annual Dinner, but in 1959, on receiving its committee's recommendation for expenditure on these items, the Annual General Meeting expressed the hope that the Boat Club would in future do without the annual grant, so that a larger balance might accumulate for Henley, and imposed further restrictions on the society's payments for crock pots. The sums involved were small, but the point had been made, and there are thenceforth few years in which the feasibility of entering at Henley is not considered.

Even the most cursory perusal of the records reveals that the events of the year 1962 mark a significant step forward in the society's life. In November 1961 the Secretary (F. J. Willett, who as an undergraduate had helped to bring it into being) had reported total assets of £206.5.5, and a membership of eighty-two of whom twenty-one were life members, and fifteen up to two years in arrears in the payment of their subscriptions. There were also forty-five whose membership had lapsed. All this notwithstanding, in 1961 it was agreed that there should be an Appeal Fund to send an eight to Henley in the following year, and a further agreement to support the appeal to the extent of £50. In the Regatta the boat, exempt for the first time from eliminating heats, did itself credit, even if it was beaten in the first round of the Ladies' Plate by First and Third Trinity, eventual finalists. At all events, at the next Annual General Meeting of the society there was general agreement that it was 'a good thing to send a boat every year', although it was recognized that financing it presented something of a problem. The year was noteworthy in at least two other respects: for the election of J. V. Adams as Secretary (he was to render invaluable service for many years) on the departure of Willett for Australia; and for the first hint that the society might seek charitable status. After protracted negotiations, during which at one point the new Secretary reported that the Ministry of Education was 'still considering in silence' the society's application for registration, the matter was finally resolved in 1966, after modifications in the definition of its declared objects (in no way detracting from its original purpose of supporting the Boat Club) agreeable to the Income Tax authorities, and to the society itself. This final outcome, important though it was and generally regarded as highly satisfactory, nevertheless left with the Secretary the not inconsiderable burden of attempting to ensure that subscriptions should in future be by covenant, and of collecting each year from covenanters the declarations necessary for the recovery of tax.

In 1962 also, at the Annual General Meeting in December, it was decided that the Rules of the society, thought in particular to impose inconvenient restrictions on its choice of officers, should be revised;

and a new constitution was approved in 1963, and further amended in 1966, when the definition of the society's objects was modified for the purpose of its registration as a charity, and while the holding of an annual dinner was no longer to be compulsory its committee was required to hold a second meeting each year on the last night of the Lent Races.

Henceforward the society, either in General Meeting or in its committee, was very largely concerned – once its charitable status had been confirmed, and apart, also, from such temporary diversions as the choosing of a new tie – with Henley, and with the Boat Club's recurring need for new boats. In 1963 a sum of £30 was made available from a balance of monies collected for 1962, and it was also agreed to ask members of the society to make up an amount of £40 or so still required. In 1964, out of total assets of £370 a sum of £330 was set aside as a nucleus of a permanent Henley fund, and, having accepted as a general rule that the interest of this fund, only, should be used, the society voted £15 for a four. At this time it appears to have been assumed that the members of a Henley crew would themselves each contribute £20 towards expenses, but it soon became an object of the society to raise sufficient capital to ensure that this undergraduate contribution would never need to be more than £10. In the meantime, the amount of the society's annual interest had risen from £15 to £20; and in 1968, on learning that the expenses of an eight would be increased by £100 owing to an exceptional gap between the end of the Easter term and the beginning of the regatta, the society, with the encouragement of its Treasurer (P. J. Nott), agreed to meet half the additional cost, if necessary by an overdraft.

At first, the society had perforce not concerned itself with the purchase of boats, and as late as 1964 what seems to have been an exploratory approach was firmly discouraged by the President, and a minute records its committee's opinion that the society's funds should not be used for the purpose. Nevertheless, the possibility appears to have persisted in some quarters, for a committee minute of 27 November 1965 refers briefly to 'a New Boats Fund which had been started in the Summer'; and early in 1966 R. W. Haywood who, says the minute, had acted on behalf of the society and the Boat Club, reported an offer from Major Stratton to purchase a Light Four, it being understood that the offer was being made to the Boat Club through the society. This was not the first of Major Stratton's benefactions, for in 1963 he had undertaken to subscribe £50 annually for seven years to the society's general funds. The four, made by Sims, and at the request of the society named 'John Stratton', was launched by the donor at the boat-house on 26 November 1966. Finding itself in the boat business after all, on the same day the society agreed, through its committee, that the next objective for the New Boats Fund should be the purchase of a fine sculling boat, with a rider to the effect that the fund should not in general be used to buy Clinker Eights.

Two years later, greatly assisted by a promise of up to £150 from Mr Stanley Gittins (father of a member of the College first VIII) the society bought the fine sculling boat out of the New Boats Fund, and was also able to buy a fibreglass sculling boat at a cost of £85, agreeing for the second time to incur an overdraft if necessary. Both boats were in hand by the Lent term 1969, but there was to be trouble over the first: returned to the makers as unsatisfactory, its replacement was 'also no use' (November 1969), and a fine sculling boat was still to be on the list of requirements in November 1970. On hearing, also in the Lent term 1969, that the next requirement of the Boat Club would be a 'Restricted Four', costing about £400, with no suggestion that the Amalgamated Clubs (or their successors) would pay for it, the Treasurer of the society was moved to remind his committee that the New Boats Fund was overdrawn by £50.

Here we must leave The Billygoats, in the year of their coming of age, of the centenary of their College, and of the remarkable successes of the Boat Club in whose interest they had been brought into being. Neither numerous nor wealthy – by 1969 there were about one hundred members, and capital assets of £1,000 or so, over and above the payments made on the Boat Club's behalf – the society remains a striking instance, and an example, of what can be done by a small group of former residents with an affection for the College, and a sustained interest in the fortunes of their own particular undergraduate successors.

Lastly, in the *Fitzwilliam Magazine* of January 1953, another group announced itself, by name not unsuitable for inclusion in this long list, as a kind of footnote. Probably formed in the Michaelmas term 1951, it appears only once, and once also in the accounts of the Amalgamated Clubs, with a grant of nine shillings for the year 1951/52.

THE ASTERISKS

Some 12 months ago it was decided to form a club consisting of the three senior members of staff and a maximum of seventeen others who should represent the best interests of Fitzwilliam House as a community and should thus provide a nucleus of students to meet regularly and informally with the senior members of staff. After considerable discussion it was decided to call this club "The Asterisks."

CLUB FUNCTIONS

The club meets for dinner just prior to the beginning of each term and also holds informal coffee meetings during the term. New members are elected by existing members of the club who are in residence. It should be clearly understood that the Asterisks is a society bound to the loyal service and furtherance of the prosperity of Fitzwilliam House, and that in this spirit its meetings and deliberations are held.

The following is a list of student members at present in residence:– D. L. Curtis, T. Dewhurst, D. Gibbin, M. G. Hall, R. F. G. Holmes, D. G. Honey, P. Liversedge, J. E. Noble, D. R. Reid, W. O. Rice, B. A. Skinner, K. C. A. Smith, W. R. Stirling, W. V. Tidswell, I. M. Webster.

The three senior members of staff will have been the Censor, the Assistant Censor, and the Tutor. The fifteen junior members of the club were, with one exception, academically respectable, some highly so. They included men prominent in the corporate activities of the House, and, not unlike other fifteens on occasion, a high proportion of geographers. Their interest lies, mainly, in the way in which they set about getting what they wanted. They felt the need of closer contact with their seniors, so that they might help in the search for ways of removing the disabilities suffered by their non-collegiate body; and they devised this agreeable means of strengthening their lines of communication, with no hint of the strident demands of a later decade.

The editor of the *Fitzwilliam Journal*, always on the look-out for copy, was prompted to write for his next issue an account of a similar club in his own time, known as 'The Prodigals'.[1] They had a short life too, and ran into trouble with their contemporaries, who thought them presumptuous in supposing that they, more than any others, were likely to influence the future of Fitzwilliam Hall.

There remain for comment two matters which were the concern of the Amalgamated Clubs as a whole, rather than of their constituent members individually: the commemoration of those Fitzwilliam men who

[1] See *Journal*, 1953, p. 49, for the editor's note; and for a photograph, with names, of the members of the Prodigals Club in 1922. For an earlier account of their activities, see also *Journal* for 1930.

died on active service in the Second World War; and the transformation of the whole machinery of amalgamation by a new Constitution, with effect from 1 July 1969, towards the close of the College's centenary year.

The War Memorial of 1939–1945

On the War Memorial our information is incomplete, owing to the disappearance of the Clubs' minutes of the period. It is first mentioned in the *Fitzwilliam Magazine* of July 1947, where the Bursar reports strong support at three General Meetings of the Clubs for a 1939–1945 War Memorial Fund, with a possible appeal target of £2,000. Among subsequent announcements is a further report by the Bursar in 1949 of a resolution by the Clubs that the proceeds of the appeal should be divided between two hard tennis courts, and table silver for which the sum of £100 was to be set aside. By 1952 it had been agreed that the silver should be in the form of a replica of the Warwick Vase, bearing the Fitzwilliam coat of arms, the inscription

Quique sui memores aliquos fecere merendo
1939–1945

and, round its base, the names of the twenty-six members of the House who had lost their lives:

G. C. Bond	G. T. Lowry
A. B. Bryan	J. N. Maas
J. L. Cohen	G. F. Measures
S. B. Dearing	H. T. Measures
D. Donahue	C. W. Oliver
N. S. Embiricos	J. E. Oliver
I. P. L. Fleming	M. H. Parry
C. R. Frenkiel	D. L. Petrie
F. W. M. Greaves	L. E. Pill
R. C. Horton	A. L. Sadd
E. T. Humphreys	J. J. E. Schmitz
D. G. Image	G. L. Stewart
E. V. Knowles	P. C. Wheeler[1]

The Junior Members' Association

At the end of the Easter term of 1968 the attention of the Governing Body of the College was called to a possibility that, in matters of particular concern to persons *in statu pupillari*, consultation between its senior and junior members ought to be more regularly, and perhaps more formally, arranged. There had not been wanting signs of an undergraduate desire for a larger say in such matters, and in the Long Vacation the General Secretary of the Amalgamated Clubs, and the President of the Graduate Club, were invited to arrange for the appointment of representatives to serve on a committee of senior and junior members of the College, to consider the setting up of formal machinery for consultation. Much water was to flow under the bridges before any tangible results were forthcoming, and a great deal of time was spent (and, as some thought, wasted) in these discussions, as when

---

[1]   The name of Johannes Schmitz, who served in the German Army, was by general agreement included in the list.

    Towards the total cost of £799.5.0 (tennis courts £689.5.0, vase £110), private subscriptions provided £603.15.4, the remainder being made up from Amalgamated Clubs funds.

open meetings were advertised, only to be postponed in the interests of other matters which the undergraduates, possibly quite rightly, conceived to be of greater urgency; or to be so poorly attended as to suggest that a large part of the undergraduate body were less concerned with the government of the College than the more vociferous few were apt to claim. At this time, however, conditions were not unfavourable to change – there had been unrest in the student world at large, and in Cambridge a body which took the title of Student Representative Council was doing what it could to arouse among the junior members of the University some enthusiasm for what it conceived to be their corporate responsibilities; and although the situation was more manageable in a University made up of a large number of independent colleges, there was in Fitzwilliam College an understandable feeling that in a new institution new procedures were not inappropriate, and might prove more readily acceptable than in long established foundations with firmly rooted traditions.

Although in the broader field of 'participation' change was slow and insignificant, the junior members of the College, by its hundredth year, could point to one important achievement in a wide-ranging re-organization of its Amalgamated Clubs. Since the formation of the Amalgamation Club in 1884, Rules had been modified from time to time, but the constitution of the Clubs had remained essentially unaltered up to, and including, their last codification in 1958; and there were two principal reasons for the changes advocated in the 1960s: a growing desire among undergraduates to be seen to be managing their affairs, with an extension of their scope where possible; and a generally diminishing interest in college games, especially noticeable, perhaps, among those who did not play games in a College where the players were enjoying a period of quite unusual success.

These attitudes found expression in the course of the year 1968/69 in proposals for the replacement of the Amalgamated Clubs by a Junior Members' Association so constituted as to lay more emphasis on the corporate pursuits of a Junior Common Room, and less on the activities of the games players; and also to reduce, somewhat, the importance of the rôle of the senior officers. As before, Trustees would conduct all major financial transactions, would provide grounds and premises, and would hold all deeds, and negotiate contracts respecting property and employees. They would also appoint the Senior Officers of the Association.

Proposals along these lines were first brought before a special meeting of the Amalgamated Clubs on 17 February 1969 at which, though approved, they did not secure the majority required by the constitution of the Clubs for the amendment of Laws[1] – a result which unsettled the meeting a little, and, in an atmosphere incompatible with reasoned argument, served only to produce a clamour for an immediate second vote on the original motion. This the Chairman refused; and the meeting was closed in the hope that a respite might allow time enough for heels, and heads, to cool. A fortnight later amended proposals were put before the Clubs, and duly approved with a request that they be sent to the Governors of the Fitzwilliam Hall Trust, as the Clubs' existing Trustees, for ratification. The Trustees, who received them sympathetically, held out every prospect of ratification if certain further alterations could be accepted, made largely for purposes of clarification, but also to strengthen their own financial authority. They also proposed, in view of the impending demise of the Trust itself, that the College, through its Governing Body, should assume the trusteeship of the Association. These further alterations were accepted by the Clubs on 3 June, and formal ratification, with effect from 1 July, followed on 8 August, when the Trustees asked that the operation of the new arrangements should be reviewed not later than 31 December 1970.

Under the Constitution in its final form, the business of the Association was to be conducted by five committees:

1. A Junior Common Room Committee, consisting of a Junior President (elected by all members of the Association), seven ordinary members, being undergraduates elected by undergraduates, and not more than three representatives elected by the Student Representative Council; all with general responsibility for affairs affecting undergraduates only, and particular responsibility for the maintenance, in co-operation with the Governing Body, of facilities provided by a Junior Common Room, and for general social intercourse.

2. A Middle Common Room Committee, being a similar body, similarly constituted, for graduate members of the Association.

3. An Amalgamated (Athletics) Clubs Committee, consisting of a representative of each member Club, to co-ordinate the interests of the Clubs, and act as a budgetary committee of the Junior Members Council (see below).

4. An Amalgamated Societies Committee, being a similar body for non-athletic organizations.

5. A Junior Members' Council of 14 members, being the Senior Officers of the Association (3), its Junior President, the seven elected ordinary

[1] A.C. Minutes, where the votes for the approval of the proposals are given as 'For 172 (167); against 101'. The tellers disagreed, and the Chairman accepted the larger number of votes in favour.

members of the Junior Common Room Committee, a Junior Treasurer (an undergraduate elected by all the members of the Association), and two representatives of the Middle Common Room Committee. In this Junior Council would be vested the ultimate responsibility for the financial affairs of the Association, save only for those powers reserved to the Trustees, and to the Middle Common Room Committee in the expenditure of its prescribed grant.

The creation of this Junior Members' Council, and its powers, were the most significant features of the new Constitution. The former committee of the Amalgamated Clubs had largely consisted *ex officio* of Captains (or similar officers) of the clubs or societies, among whom, simply by virtue of larger numbers, the games men had preponderated (although it was not suggested that this had led to any unfairness in the allocation of the funds available). Of the Junior Members' Council, on the other hand, no principal officer of a club or society was as such entitled to be a member; and to point the moral was the subsidiary position assigned to the Amalgamated Clubs and Amalgamated Societies Committees, composed as they were of persons who had previously as of right been members of the controlling body.[1]

---

[1] Particulars of these transactions may be found in the papers of the Fitzwilliam Hall Trust, and in the minutes of the Governing Body. After revision, the Constitution was printed in 1971.

(c) The class-lists 1907–69

During the first forty years of the life of the non-collegiate institution, academic distinction had been achieved, if at all, by the remnant of its members who had no wish to migrate, or were unable to gain admission to a college; and it had been clear, both from the successes of those who did make a move and from the comparative lack of success of those who did not, that the practice of migration had a most damaging effect on non-collegiate academic performance.

From 1907 onwards Reddaway set himself to improve the academic reputation of his society by doing what he could to keep his men for the whole of their time of residence, and by raising the standard, and increasing the amount, of the teaching provided for them. What he did must have needed time to take effect, and the immediate improvement which followed his appointment as Censor will have owed something to measures taken by his predecessor. Improvement there certainly was, for although numbers were small the general tendency is plain. In 1907, of fifteen graduates three went out in honours; in the next year the corresponding figures were twenty-one and nine, and the proportion of honours men to the total number of graduates in the years immediately preceding the First World War rose to more than half, compared with 72 out of 262 during the period from 1891 to 1907, and this in spite of continuing migrations on an appreciable scale.

Of the years at this time for which figures are readily available, the best was 1911, with eighteen honours men out of twenty-five. The results of the following years were also good; and the discerning reader will find in Reddaway's account of them a notable example of his seemingly incurable, but none the less engaging, habit of making the very utmost of any circumstance creditable to his men. 'Thirty-one students', he told his Board, 'graduated B.A. during the year: eighteen on the results of Triposes'.[1] This is very true, but not before the end of the paragraph does it appear that two of the eighteen, on their Tripos performance, were allowed the Ordinary B.A. Degree.

The extreme pressure of applications for admission immediately after the war was in due course reflected in the numbers of graduates –66 in 1921, compared with 39 in 1914, followed by 93 and 72, respectively, in 1922 and 1923. The proportion of pass degree candidates was again substantial, but after 1923, when just over half the graduates were pass men, the entry became more normal, and the number of men reading for the Ordinary B.A. degree declined to about one tenth in the last

[1] See p. 172.

year before the Second World War. In the late 1940s the pattern of twenty-five years earlier was repeated, and for a time the pass degree men made up about a quarter of the total. By 1952 the number had dropped to a sixth, of whom the majority were in subjects for which there was then no honours course, and the Censor, in his reports to the Non-Collegiate Students Board, was careful to distinguish between, for example, those who were reading Agriculture or Architecture and the men who were completing an Ordinary degree course because of their failure in Tripos examinations, or because they had found it more prudent not to read for honours at all. Thereafter the Fitzwilliam lists contained progressively fewer pass men, and their disappearance was virtually complete by 1967, when of just over four hundred candidates one, only, was seeking the Ordinary B.A. degree.

Such was the improvement, by a somewhat irregular progression, in the general academic standard of Fitzwilliam graduates as measured by their distribution between honours and pass degrees; but this advance, though within these limits appreciable, left much room for improvement in the more detailed examination results; and for Reddaway the reason was not far to seek. In his Report for 1920/21 to the Board he compliments C. J. B. Gaskoin on the results achieved by his honours candidates in history – all thirty-nine had passed, with nineteen in the second class – but goes on to say that without Entrance Scholarships first classes could hardly be hoped for. The absence of entrance awards was doubtless one reason why the level of academic performance fell below that of the colleges as a whole, even when migration had virtually become a thing of the past; and it is in the first class that this inequality is most evident. Before the war of 1914, in any year the number of non-collegiate Tripos candidates had not exceeded thirty-four (in 1911), and two had been the highest number of 'firsts'. In 1921 the ex-service men brought the total of candidates up to eighty-nine, and with ten in the first class the number was far higher than it had ever been, and the proportion (11.2%) was within a fraction of what it had been with the small number (17) of candidates in 1914. The percentage of 17.6 (in 1923), with nine first classes out of fifty-one, was exceeded only once, in 1941, an abnormally small war-time year. In the 1930s, though the number of admissions was affected by the economic crisis of 1931, quality was maintained; but the results in this decade, as again in the 1950s, owed much to the consistent successes of the theological students of Wesley House, who appeared in the class-lists under the Fitzwilliam name.[1]

[1] See pp. 502–6.

Just as in the distribution of Fitzwilliam men between honours and pass degrees, so in the proportion of first classes in the Tripos the pattern of the early 1920s was repeated twenty-five years later; and with greatly increased numbers the examination results of 1947 and 1948 were comparatively good, with 8.1 and 10.7 per cent in the first class. In the next decade, however, although there was no lack of applicants for admission, the level of ability, in terms of first class honours, was not maintained; and while it is true that there had been an appreciable falling off in the University as a whole, for in 1954 10 per cent of all the candidates were in the first class, compared with 17 per cent twenty years earlier, this decline was particularly noticeable in the Fitzwilliam results, where the 1934 figure of 12.5 per cent fell to 2.4 in 1954, and had been as low as 1.6 in 1953. Furthermore, although there was some improvement in the years immediately following the introduction of an entrance examination in 1956, the proportion of 'firsts' never again rose, in the first hundred years, above 6.2 per cent, which in 1968 was approximately half the corresponding figure for the University at large.

At the other end of the lists the results also tell their own tale. In the years before the First World War it was common, among the non-collegiate students, for the third class to be the largest, and not unknown for it to be larger than the other two combined; and when the war was over numbers in the class remained high, until in 1926, after two unusually lean years, the proportion dropped dramatically in one year, from 48 to 27 per cent, and thenceforward, with some variation, stood at about one third of the total results, with some rather more consistent improvement in the 1960s. In 1934, 34 per cent of the Fitzwilliam results were third class, in comparison with 30 per cent in the University as a whole; in 1954 the corresponding proportions were 26 and 31 per cent and in 1968 28 and 18 per cent.

The second class results are more difficult to compare over the years, because of differing practices whereby that class was divided by some examiners and not by others, but a comparison based on all candidates in that class, whether divided or not, shows that the Fitzwilliam results have kept close to the average for the University. The general picture, in the period embraced by this summary (1907–69) shows that among the non-collegiate students there have been relatively few of the highest ability, and where there has been improvement in their academic performance this has been apparent in larger numbers in the second class, and fewer in the third. The relatively small numbers in the first class in times of great expansion – except when, as after the two wars, age groups overlapped – also suggests that the number of really able men was limited, or that men of real ability who failed to gain admission to a college in Cambridge preferred to go to another university.

Guy Milner Walton

CHAPTER IX

The Fitzwilliam Society

Association of old members of Fitzwilliam Hall proposed 13 June 1924. Formation of Fitzwilliam Society, open to all matriculated members of Fitzwilliam House, 9 December 1924. Objects of the Society – its first officers. Its concern with events in Cambridge. The Society's first Annual Dinner. Its small initial membership and precarious finances. The *Fitzwilliam Journal* (1926). The first Cambridge Reunion. Change of Secretary/Treasurer. Membership of undergraduates. The *Journal* (1928) – its continuing publication and growing historical significance.

Fall in numbers in the early 1950s – preponderance of undergraduate members – its consequences. Financial policy of the Society – efforts to accumulate capital. The *Journal*'s mounting cost. The Society and fund raising. Gifts to Fitzwilliam House and recognition of services rendered. The events of 1954 – the Cambridge Reunion of that year – the Memorialists.

Officers of the Society – their election and tenure.

'It is true to say that when the Society was founded in 1924 it began its career without money, without influence, and without aid.'[1] So wrote the Fitzwilliam Society's Honorary Secretary and Treasurer, already twenty years in office, in December 1947, when the officers were girding their loins for a resumption of normal activities laid aside at the beginning of the Second World War.

Appended to the minutes of a General Meeting of the Amalgamated Clubs held on 13 June 1924 is a letter, dated 11 June, addressed to the General Secretary (G. M. Walton) by J. R. W. Alexander, then an undergraduate in his last term of residence, giving notice of his intention to submit to the meeting a recommendation that the members of the Clubs and such old Fitzwilliam Hall men as might be present should 'consider the advisability of forming in the immediate future an Association of old members of Fitzwilliam Hall, and the desirability of circularising such members with a view to calling a Meeting in London, or elsewhere, with the object of bringing such an Association into being'. Those present at the meeting (there is no list of names) were unanimously in favour of Mr Alexander's proposals, and he was asked to take such steps as he might think fit to give effect to them. As he expressed a wish that others should join him in the preliminary organization of an Association, Mr Gaskoin was appointed to help in Cam-

---

[1] *Journal*, December 1947, p. 5.

bridge and Mr H. M. Burton in London, where it was hoped that its headquarters would eventually be.

On 28 November a letter was sent to some thirteen hundred former Fitzwilliam residents:

THE FITZWILLIAM SOCIETY.

19 STRATFORD PLACE,
LONDON, W.1.
28th November, 1924.

Dear Sir,

At a General Meeting of the Amalgamated Clubs held in Fitzwilliam Hall (now Fitzwilliam House) on June 13th, 1924, it was unanimously decided to support in every possible way the efforts which former and present Members of Fitzwilliam Hall contemplated making to form a FITZWILLIAM SOCIETY. Mr. C. J. B. Gaskoin, Mr. H. M. Burton and the Writer were requested to arrange a Meeting and a Dinner in London, at a convenient date, to form such a Society, for election to which all matriculated Members, former and present, of Fitzwilliam Hall would be eligible.

The objects of the Society would be:—

(a) To promote closer relationship among old Fitzwilliam Hall men, and between them and the Hall.

(b) To publish and circulate among the Society's Members an Annual Report, a List of Members with their addresses, and news of interest about the Hall and its former and present members, and to send without charge to each Member of the Society one or more copies annually of the Fitzwilliam Hall Magazine.

(c) To ensure the permanence and success of the Society's Dinner held annually at the Holborn Restaurant, Kingsway, London, W.C.1, on the day of the Inter-University Rugby Union Football Match.

(d) To collect material for a Fitzwilliam Hall Register.

(e) To further the interests of Fitzwilliam Hall.

The only liability would be a Life (not a yearly) Subscription, which could be fixed at ONE GUINEA if a reasonable membership is obtained, and a satisfactory arrangement is made as to the cost of printing and circulating the information and publications referred to in paragraph (b) above.

The arrangements which have been made are as follows:—
The Meeting and the Dinner, at both of which all former and present Members of Fitzwilliam Hall are invited to be present, will be held at

THE HOLBORN RESTAURANT, Kingsway, London, W.C.1,
On Tuesday, DECEMBER 9th, 1924 ("RUGGER NIGHT").
The MEETING at 5.30 p.m.

Agenda:— 1. To form the Society.
2. To elect Officers and a Committee of
Management.
3. To elect a Committee to draw up Rules
for submission to the next
General Meeting.
4. Other business.

The DINNER at 6.30 p.m. for 7 p.m.
Price 10/-, exclusive of Wines and Gratuities.
Dinner Jacket or Morning Dress.
The Dinner Subscription may be paid now, or, together with
the Life Subscription, at the Dinner.

NOTA BENE.
(1) Whatever your views and intentions may be as to the proposed
Society, and whether this communication reaches you in time for the
gathering or not, YOU ARE EARNESTLY REQUESTED TO RETURN,
for purposes of record, THE ENCLOSED POSTCARD, which is self-
explanatory. Such replies must be received not later than first post on
December 8th, 1924. Suggestions and/or criticisms will be welcomed,
especially if sent before the Meeting.
(2) You are particularly requested to attend the gathering if you
can possibly make it convenient to do so. It is desired to make the Meeting
and the Dinner as large and as representative as possible. Your presence
does not necessarily involve your joining the Society. Many promises to
attend have been received already, and Mr. W. F. Reddaway has consented
to occupy the Chair.
(3) You are asked to be so kind as to persuade at least one former
Member of Fitzwilliam Hall to attend the gathering, and/or to join the
Society. Particulars will be sent to any address you care to forward to the
writer. Notices will appear in the Daily Press.
(4) All communications regarding the proposed Society should be
addressed to the writer at the above address.
The Writer desires to add that the arrangements which have
been made, and the suggestions, and they are no more, which have been
put forward in this letter, meet with the entire approval of his collabo-
rators, Mr. C. J. B. Gaskoin and Mr. H. M. Burton.
Yours faithfully,
J. R. W. ALEXANDER.[1]

[1] *Journal,* April 1933, p. 9.

The meeting to which Mr Alexander's letter refers was duly held under the chairmanship of Mr C. J. B. Gaskoin, and, says the minute,

> about thirty-five old Fitzwilliam men were present, including Messrs I. K. C. Bell, S. N. Chauduri, W. R. J. Copplestone, the Rev. T. W. Crafer, E. E. Douglas Smith, T. R. G. Fendick, R. Fontaine, J. B. C. Grundy, W. S. Hale, the Rev. B. Hardwick, I. V. Hoskins, F. B. Macrae, F. Martin, J. B. Seymour, the Rev. J. W. Shipley, W. Spooner, A. J. Trayhurn, L. Watkins, G. M. Walton, C. H. Watson, and C. L. Webb.

The minute continues,

> Mr Alexander, at the request of the Chairman, stated that the meeting had been called to consider the desirability of forming, and if necessary to form, a Society of old Fitzwilliam men. He said that the formation of such an Association had been discussed on many occasions, but that the idea did not take any definite form until it was unanimously resolved, at a meeting of the Amalgamated Clubs held in Fitzwilliam House (then Fitzwilliam Hall) on June 13th 1924, to support in every way possible the efforts which it was proposed former and present members of the House should make to form such a Society.

Mr Alexander added that replies had been received to 188 of the 1350 letters which had been sent out, and that of these 177 favoured the formation of a Society. The meeting then proceeded to a discussion of the whole matter, during which it was agreed, on grounds of cost, not to undertake to send copies of the *Fitzwilliam Magazine* to members of the proposed Society, and some doubts were voiced about the suggested date of its Annual Dinner. As being of future interest, it may be noted that there was general agreement that when the Society had become properly established it might wish to hold a long vacation or terminal dinner in Cambridge; and that the opinion was expressed that 'appeals for funds for any purpose should not, as a rule, be made through the Society'.

At the end of the discussion the meeting approved Mr Alexander's definition of the objects of the Society, save for Clause (b) in so far as it related to the issue of the *Fitzwilliam Magazine,* and resolved 'that the Society, for election to which all matriculated members, former and present, of Fitzwilliam House shall be eligible, shall be, and hereby is, duly formed'. By other resolutions the life subscription was fixed at £1.1.0; Mr W. F. Reddaway was elected the first President, Mr Thatcher and Mr Gaskoin Vice-Presidents, Mr Alexander Honorary Secretary and Treasurer, and Mr Metford Watkins Assistant Honorary Secretary. The newly elected officers were constituted a committee, with the General Secretary of the Amalgamated Clubs (Mr E. E. Douglas-Smith), to manage the affairs of the Society until the next Annual General Meeting, to which they were also asked to submit draft Rules. It should perhaps be recorded that by a last resolution the meeting was formally deemed to be the First Annual General (Inaugural) Meeting of the Society, and the dinner which followed its First Annual (Inaugural) Dinner.

Although it was not made the subject of a resolution, there was one other topic brought before the first meeting which, as a matter of history, merits more than a passing mention. It is unlikely that the founders of the Society would have dissented from the view that its first four aims were ancillary to the last, and that their one comprehensive purpose was the furtherance of the interests of the body of which they were all still members, even if no longer resident in Cambridge. Of the *Journal* there will be occasion to make mention later, but it may be observed here that in April 1928 the editor suggests that the Society came into being when it did at least in part because of a belief among Fitzwilliam men at large that the loss of the old name might have been avoided if the Cambridge residents had had the organized support of those who had gone down.[1] A minute of the meeting held on 9 December 1924 certainly testifies to the concern with which they had heard of events in Cambridge. It tells how a number of letters were read, expressing alarm at the recent changes, at what was called 'the refusal to recognize Fitzwilliam Hall', at the change of its name, and the decline in status caused by greater emphasis on its non-collegiate character. These complaints were accompanied by suggestions that the Society should endeavour to bring about a restoration of the former title, and recognition of the Hall (or House) as something more than what the minute describes as 'a Registry of non-collegiate students'.

While it is true that an outside observer may be able to view the University's affairs with a helpful detachment which, at times, may elude those who are engaged in its day-to-day business, it is nevertheless also true that non-resident members of the University, with their welcome and continuing interest in its problems, may not always be best qualified to judge in matters of policy, simply because they lack information which those who are continuously in residence can hardly fail to acquire. It is not altogether surprising that many non-resident Fitzwilliam men, deploring as they not unreasonably did the loss of their old name, should have allowed disappointment to cloud their judgement of the merits of the recommendations of the 1924 Syndicate

[1] *Journal*, April 1928, p. 4.

as a whole. Even on the issue of the name, their Censor quickly saw that the loss of a courtesy title, highly regarded as it may have been, was more than balanced by the acquisition of a name which, for the first time, was authorized by the statutes and ordinances of the University; and, far from emphasizing still more the non-collegiate features of the place, the Syndicate had publicly affirmed the value of its corporate activities, and had afforded Fitzwilliam House the opportunity of shewing how very few were the men who desired to be non-collegiate in the full sense of the word. This – though it lay in the future – was to result in the replacement, ten years later, of the description 'Non-Coll.' by 'Fitzw.' in the class-lists, a concession which, in Mr Thatcher's own words, was to give 'immense satisfaction and pleasure to all members of Fitzwilliam House, present and past'.

Their business concluded, the members of the meeting adjourned for dinner, which, according to a notice published a year or so later in the first number of the *Journal*, was attended, a little surprisingly, by no more than eighteen of the (approximately) thirty-five who had been at the meeting earlier.[1] Whether or not both figures are correct, it is impossible not to be impressed by the spirited optimism of the few, undeterred by the apparent indifference of so many, in resolving to proceed with their plans.

From the earliest beginnings of the Society it was apparent that it could expect to achieve little unless it had a considerable membership, for subscriptions constituted its only source of revenue, and as these were for life they provided no annual income excepted what might be obtained from invested capital. The publication of an Annual Report, of an Address List, and of items of general interest, would be a drain on the Society's resources, and without substantial support its annual occasions were unlikely to be successful.

It is not therefore surprising to find the officers constantly referring to the need for new members. At the second Annual General Meeting, held on 10 December 1925, the Secretary reported that by September the number of supporters (those who had replied favourably to his letter of 28 November 1924) had risen from 177 to 242, and he did not expect that many more numbers would be found among those who were no longer in residence; moreover, of the 242 no more than 46, it seems, had then paid their subscription. By the end of September 1926 the total had increased, only, to 246, and 55 subscriptions had been paid. By December 1927, just three years after the Society's foundation, these figures stood, it appears, at 250 and 100, respectively.

[1] *Journal*, June 1926, p. 6.

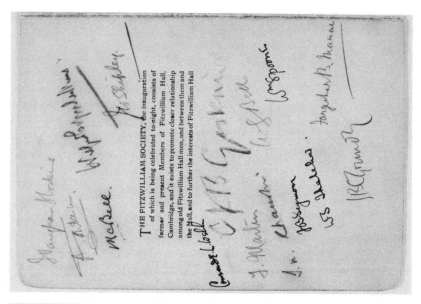

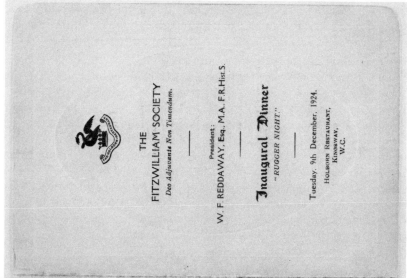

The Inaugural Dinner of the Fitzwilliam Society

The signatures are those of I. Vaughan Hoskins, R. Fontaine, Wilfred Copplestone, I.K.C. Bell, J.W. Shipley, Conrade L. Webb, C.J.B. Gaskoin, F. Martin, W.G. Bell, S.N. Chaudhuri, Wm Spooner, J.B. Seymour, W.S. Thatcher, Farquhar B. Macrae, J.B.C. Grundy. The card was G.M. Walton's

The 1927 meeting marks the end of a chapter in the Society's history, for it was then that Mr Alexander, who had done more than anybody to set it on its way, retired from the combined offices of Honorary Secretary and Treasurer. On 10 December 1925 he had presented draft Rules to his committee, which approved them for submission to a General Meeting on the same day. After discussion, they were unanimously adopted as they stood, and remained substantially unaltered for many years, except that in 1929 the list of the Society's objects was amended so as to include the holding of Reunions in Cambridge, and to leave more freedom in the choice of the date of the Annual Dinner, which was, however a year later fixed for the second Friday in January.[1]

No statements of accounts of these early years are preserved, but from the Secretary's Annual Reports it can be seen that from its foundation in December 1924 to the end of its first financial year (30 September 1925) income was £28.19.0, and expenditure £23.13.3. In the year 1925/26 income, including the first year's surplus, was £52.16.9, and expenditure £34.19.9, of which a sum of £23.6.0 was for *Magazines* supplied by the Amalgamated Clubs – a charge which appears to have been regarded as exorbitant – leaving a balance of £17.17.0. At 30 September 1927 income, including previous surpluses, was shown as £75.12.0, and expenditure £28.9.3, which left the Society at the end of its third financial year with total assets of £47.2.9.

No decision is recorded in the minutes of the Society, or of its committee, with regard to the form to be taken by its publications, but the Secretary, who had power to incur reasonable expenditure in furtherance of the Society's objects, published in June 1926, as a supplement to a *Fitzwilliam Magazine*, its first *Journal*. This contained a list of officers for the year 1925/26, the recently approved Rules, two items which were to become regular features of succeeding *Journals* – 'Fitzwilliam Society Notes', and O.FF. News', an optimistic list of 242 members of whom 187 had not then paid the subscription without which they could not be formally elected, and the names of 170 Fitzwilliam men to whom letters had been addressed and returned through the post. With his notice of the 1926 Annual Meeting, of which 246 copies had been circulated, the Secretary had also sent 214 copies of the June 1926 *Magazine*, and 91 copies of the previous *Magazine*. To this notice, which also gave particulars of the Annual Dinner, and asked recipients to say whether they would attend, he received 75 replies; and even this was an improvement on the year before, when 450 notices had elicited 77

[1] Minutes of General Meetings of 11 January 1929, and 10 January 1930.

replies. No *Journal* appeared in 1927, and in December of that year the committee of the Society decided that its 1928 *Journal* should be published independently of the *Magazine*, in view of the expense of joint publication.

Enough has been said to shew that the Society's comings and goings had assumed a pattern similar to that of other associations of the kind – annual meetings and dinners, annual choice of officers, and persistent human frailty which made subscriptions difficult to collect and an address list hard to maintain. There is little to add in filling out the tale of these three years. It was soon suggested that an alternative, or an additional, dinner should be held in Cambridge, and an attempt was made to arrange it during the Long Vacation of 1927, unsuccessful owing to the difficulty of finding a date suitable for people in Cambridge and also convenient for schoolmasters. They tried again, and at the Annual Meeting on 13 December the Chairman is asking for support for a Reunion in Cambridge, to be held at the end of July or the beginning of August 1928.

In his Annual Report for 1924/25 the Secretary announced that Mr C. Hubert Wolff (General Secretary for the year 1900/01) had proposed the foundation of a Masonic Lodge of old Fitzwilliam men, but nothing came of it. In December 1926 the committee of the Society approved a proposal by the Secretary and Treasurer that the General Meeting should be advised to invest one half of each member's life subscription, and to place the other half to the credit of the Society's current account. This recommendation appears to have been approved by the General Meeting held immediately afterwards, and effect was given to it as soon as the state of the Society's finances permitted; as soon, that is, as half the sum received from new members appeared to be capable of meeting a year's expenditure, and continuing only so long as the subscriptions of new members, augmented by such interest as might accrue from invested capital, should continue to be sufficient for the purpose.

When, on 13 December 1927, Mr Alexander had told the Annual General Meeting that, owing to pressure of other work, he did not feel able to offer himself for re-election as Honorary Secretary and Treasurer, it is not difficult to imagine that the thirty or so members present, grateful as they were for Mr Alexander's assistance over three difficult years, must have viewed the future with apprehension, for they could not know what long and devoted service they were to receive from his successor. On that day they appointed, unanimously, Mr G. M. Walton to be Secretary 'for the ensuing year'; he had been

Assistant Honorary Secretary for a twelvemonth, and was to remain their Secretary until 31 January 1966; a term of office interrupted for one year only, when in 1937/38 he took his turn as President. Until 1964 he was to be Treasurer as well.

Although at the start of its fourth year, the Society's conduct of its affairs had begun to follow a regular routine, its survival must have been in considerable doubt. Of a hundred members not more than thirty or so came to meetings; one *Journal* had been published; it had cost too much, and after missing a year the Society had resolved to issue a second, and then to debate whether it could be continued; reserves were slender, and the prospect of a healthier membership remote, for it seemed, as Mr Alexander had said, that few accessions could be expected from the older men, and the Society appeared to arouse little interest among the undergraduates. A large proportion of the men whose names had been published in the so-called Members' List in 1926 belonged to the immediate post-war years, and without new blood there was a danger that the Society might develop into a club whose members met for their annual gatherings, enjoyable enough for themselves, but limited in numbers and with little claim to represent the body of non-collegiate graduates, and with scant prospect of being, as their founders had intended, a source of influential encouragement and support for those who were directing the affairs of Fitzwilliam House in Cambridge. Something of all this must have been on the horizon when Milner Walton took over the secretaryship in December 1927 and C. J. B. Gaskoin was elected President, to be followed by Walter Harvey in January 1929; but although such fears were not without foundation, events took a different turn. Means were found of increasing the society's membership; and although we shall not now follow its fortunes year by year, we shall note the extent of this increase, observe the effects on the Society of the way in which it was achieved, and see how larger numbers enabled it to make generous contributions to the material needs of the House, and to shew in tangible ways its appreciation of the work of individuals who spent their lives in the House's service.

In his first separately published *Journal* the new Secretary made plain his view of the importance of obtaining an increase in membership, for to him the issue was simple – without more members, a great many more members, the Society would not survive; with them, he saw no reason why it should not flourish. His first move was the publication of a more realistic list of members by deleting from the first list of 'supporters' published in the *Journal* of 1926, those whose support had not included the payment of their subscription. So it is that the *Journal* of 1928 gives a 'paid-up' membership of 108, which by 1929 had risen to 156; but as the Secretary makes plain, with a creditable show rather of sorrow than of anger, there were still seventy or more recipients of two *Journals* and of a number of notices of dinners and of meetings who had given no further sign of interest, or even of life.

In the Lent term of 1929 there was a change; for attention was then directed very largely to the recruitment of new members from among the undergraduates in residence, particularly, as it would seem from the Censor's agreement that new recruits might have their subscriptions charged in their last terminal account, those in their third year. Which was cause and which effect is not now easy to determine, but this effort to find members in Cambridge coincided with the election to the committee of Henry Hugo Meyer, who, after retiring from the engineering profession at the age of fifty-five, came up in the Lent term 1928 to read law, and flung himself into undergraduate activity of all kinds, winning the respect and affection of young and old alike.[1] It was largely due to Meyer's efforts that 140 residents joined the Society in May 1929, and in 1930 its strength stood at 316, having doubled within a year. Reddaway, too, had been active among men of earlier generations. Thereafter, until the war, membership crept up to a total of about 600, the average annual increase being about 30, though with considerable variation between the years, for the 1936 *Journal* records 53, whereas two years later the figure was 4. We are told that between 1939 and 1946 gains were 68, and losses 34, figures that seem almost too neat to be true; and from then onwards there were annual increases of about 70, until at the end of the academical year 1951/52 membership is described as being 'on the thousand mark'.

At about this time, with no appreciable fall in the number of matriculations, the number of new members declined sharply, with consequential deficits in the Annual Accounts, and on 30 July 1954 a committee was appointed to recommend what should be done. The committee submitted proposals, accepted by the next Annual General Meeting, which, it was thought, might lead to the recruitment of as many as four-fifths of each year's freshmen. These proposals carried much further the device first adopted in 1929 of allowing undergraduates in the third year to have their subscriptions included in their House bills, and with the consent of the officers of the House it was agreed, as from the beginning of the Michaelmas term 1955, that the subscription, originally £1.0.0, raised to £1.10.0 in 1932, and to

[1] See also p. 366.

£2.2.0 in 1949, should be increased to £4.10.0,[1] and be charged at 10s a term on an undergraduate's terminal bill, unless, having been informed about the Society on first coming into residence, he had let it be known that he did not wish to join. That the Society was still concerned to build up its capital is evident from two other decisions: first, to revert to an earlier practice of allocating half of each year's subscriptions to the Secretary's current account, and half to its capital fund, instead of two-thirds and one-third respectively,[2] and second, that a limit of £110 should be imposed on annual expenditure on the *Journal*, and of £60, every three years, on an Address List.

As a result of these measures, membership, which in 1955, before their introduction, had stood at 1,112, rose to about 2,300 in 1969, but the committee had been optimistic in its estimate of the proportion of freshmen who would enrol, for it was never as high as four-fifths, and the average annual intake between 1955 and 1969 was about sixty per cent of the number of matriculations. Moreover, the attainment of the total membership of 2,300 was due not only to the arrangements adopted in 1955, but also to the larger numbers of students in residence in the 1960s.

This growth in membership was not, however, quite as beneficial as may have at first sight appeared. Towards the end of his time as Censor Mr Thatcher thought it right to express the hope that the Society would be strengthened by the active support of the younger generations of graduates;[3] and here he touched on an aspect of its life which was already leaving something to be desired. It is not unlikely that this has been due, at least in part and in particular since 1955, to the way in which its members have been recruited, for there has been a tendency for them to consist of men who joined not so much because they felt they ought, or because they wanted to, as from the omission of any steps to prevent their enrolment, which, as they were told on coming into residence, would be automatic in the absence of instructions to the contrary.

By their response to periodic appeals for help, Fitzwilliam men have demonstrated that active support of the Society, and attendance at its functions, is not to be regarded as a complete criterion of their concern for the well-being of their House and College, but, even so, attendances at the Annual Dinner in London, and at the Cambridge

[1] Or £4.4.0 as a single payment.
[2] The equal division adopted in 1926 had been changed at a General Meeting in 1949 'for one year, subject to review'; and had been allowed to continue.
[3] *Journal*, December 1955, p. 14.

Reunion, enjoyable as these always are, have for many years been disappointing. In 1939, when membership had reached 600, 39 came to the London dinner; corresponding figures for 1950 were 850 and 20; in 1960, about 1,500 and 41; and in 1968, over 2,000 and 54. Reunions in Cambridge have fared no better; and it did not escape notice that in 1960 and 1968, in spite of the passage of time, there were more of the men who graduated between 1920 and 1929, who therefore included founder members, than of any other ten year group; while, at the other end of the register, of the 49 who attended the 1968 Reunion, two, only, had taken their degree in or after 1960.[1]

In the pursuit of its main objective of furthering the interests of Fitzwilliam House, the Society's principal activities, from the beginning, were the holding of its Annual General Meeting and its Annual Dinner in London (to which there was added in 1928 the Annual Reunion in Cambridge), the issue of its publications from time to time, and the collection of funds. The Annual Dinner was paid for by those who attended, unless there was a deficit in any particular year, and the only expense falling on the Society's funds was the cost of dinner notices, which were posted with the notices of the Annual General Meeting, or in later years with the *Journal*. The principal single item of recurrent expenditure, assuming its publication, was the cost of the *Journal* itself; and it was the aim of the officers, and particularly of the Permanent Secretary, as he may well be called, to get together a capital sum which would bear interest sufficient to meet its cost, and would also, eventually, provide financial assistance to Fitzwilliam House in Cambridge. The first modest investment of capital was made 'as from 1 October 1928', with the purchase of £25 War Loan, and a further £45 was invested in the following year. In 1930 it was decided that investment should be with the Fitzwilliam Hall Trust, at five per cent interest, and this arrangement continued, though with falling interest rates as time went on, until 1964 when the Governors of the Trust repaid the loan. In the early years the Secretary did all he could to meet recurrent expenses without recourse to his half share of subscriptions received, and there were frequent appeals in successive issues of the *Journal* for additional contributions towards the cost of its publication, with short

---

[1] It may be added that more recently there have been some small, but encouraging, signs of change. At the Reunion of 1978, of a total of 67, six had graduated in or after 1970.

The Society's difficulties have not been exceptional. In 1969 the College instituted an Old Members' Gathering for men of selected years. In 1971, for the first time, those who were invited included a large proportion of recent graduates. Of more than 200, 19 accepted; while from more than half there was no acknowledgement. Not all will have been sent to an outdated address.

lists – very short, at times – of their amounts. Although there was no certainty that an annual publication would be possible, it was maintained, even during the Second World War, when, with somewhat smaller issues in 1940, 1941, 1944, and 1945, with *News Sheets* in 1942 and 1943, the *Journal* was printed privately for the cost of the paper.[1]

Financially, the prosperity of the Society has always turned on the size of its membership, and, except at times of special expenditure knowingly incurred, an increase in numbers has usually enabled it to shew a surplus in its annual statements of income and expenditure. We have seen how, in recruitment, less and less attention was paid to the men of earlier years (who were much harder to reach), and more and more to the enrolment of undergraduates, which was undoubtedly assisted by the collection of subscriptions by way of terminal bills, and from 1955 onwards by automatic enrolment in the absence of objection on their part. The growth of the Society's capital – also assisted by the 1955 decision to revert to the allocation of annual subscriptions equally between its capital fund and the Secretary's current account – can be ascertained from statements by the Secretary in his Annual Reports, from early *Journals* if the matter is mentioned, and, since December 1954, from audited accounts. Thus in September 1939 the fund stood at £348, and after remaining substantially unchanged during the war rose in December 1947 to 'upwards of £400', and to £890 in July 1953. In September 1955 it had fallen slightly, having been affected by a drop in recruitment, but as an immediate result of the higher subscriptions charged in October 1955, and the change in the method of their collection, it had risen again to £1,334 by June 1957. In June 1964, when the Fitzwilliam Hall Trust repaid its loan, the fund stood at £1,945, and a year later £2,033 was invested in Building Society and Unit Trust funds. At the same time, the practice of dividing the subscriptions received between the capital fund and the Secretary's current account was discontinued, with effect from 1 July 1965, and the management of investments was entrusted to a sub-committee appointed for the purpose. By June 1969 the Building Society holding (£50) had been increased to £150, and on prices at 30 June 1969 the value of the capital fund was £2,550.

It has already been said that the *Journal* was a principal item of recurrent expenditure, and its cost has all along been a source of anxiety: at the beginning, when prices were stable, because of uncertainty whether it could be met from slender capital funds, and as time

---

[1]   At Bushey, by permission of the Headmaster of the Royal Masonic School.

passed, whether investment income, assisted each year by new members' subscriptions, could match the cost of production when prices began to rise, slowly at first, but with startling rapidity as inflation set in.

Sources of information are varied, as are the terms in which it is given. There are references to the expense of the *Journal* in the Secretary's Annual Reports of earlier years, in some numbers of the *Journal* itself, and later in annual Statements of Accounts, when these began to be published; and the selection of a small number of years, usually those in which the particulars given are more precise, will serve to shew how the bill for the *Journal* increased. Of the 1928 issue – the first to appear separately – we are told that the cost was £19.19.4, but it is not clear whether this figure included postage. If it did not, the additional cost would have been small, for, as appears elsewhere, the cost of postage for all purposes in the year was little more than £4.0.0. The figures for the year 1935 are more definite, the total cost being £34.12.10, which included a charge of £3.1.2 for postage. In 1939, the year of the last pre-war issue, the amount is stated to have been £32.0.0, apparently without postage. In 1949 printing came to £52.17.6, and postage £10.19.0; ten years later the corresponding figures were £153.7.6 and £30.19.6, and in 1969 the total cost had risen to £371.12.11 (£255.2.0 and £116.10.11). This was a far cry from the limit of £110 imposed in 1955, and it brings this account to the end of the period with which it is concerned. Let it suffice to add, therefore, that although the *Journal* was now costing more than ten times the last pre-war figure, within another three years the cost had risen to over £570, a sum very nearly equal to a year's subscriptions from new members. If the *Journal* was to be saved from extinction, this was a situation that could not be allowed to continue, and special measures were taken, successfully for the immediate future, which included the Society's Jubilee appeal, and the raising of its life membership subscription from £4.50 to £9.00.

The Society's material assistance to Fitzwilliam House was of two kinds: outright gifts for a special purpose, or in commemoration of some notable event, and participation in organized attempts to raise money from sources not necessarily limited to its own membership. In 1954 the Society took a prominent part in the Friends of Fitzwilliam House Appeal, through its President of the year, in association with the Chairman of the Fitzwilliam Hall Trust, and the Censor. It gave similar support to the University's appeal on behalf of the House in 1962, and was represented on the Centenary Appeal Committee in 1969. Its first venture of the kind, however, was undertaken some years previously, and was the occasion of considerable difficulty and, it seems, unmerited discouragement. The story may now be told, at some length, as an illustration of the attitude of those in authority in the University – or of some of them – towards its non-collegiate institution.

The Fitzwilliam Society shared to the full the Censor's satisfaction at the disappearance from the class-lists, as from May 1935, of the designation 'Non-Coll.', and proposed to commemorate it by raising funds from past and present members of Fitzwilliam House to help in such rebuilding or extension of its premises as the University might feel able to undertake at some future time. The Censor's first mention of the matter was at a meeting of the Non-Collegiate Students Board on 6 November 1935, when he was asked to circulate particulars to be discussed at the Board's next meeting. The minute of that meeting reads:

> The Censor reported that the Vice-Chancellor, having been informed by him that the Fitzwilliam Society desired to issue an appeal to its members for a building fund,[1] had replied that any appeal must first be approved by the Non-Collegiate Students Board, and further that, if the appeal in any way affected the policy of the Board, the Council of the Senate must be consulted before it should be issued.
>
> The Censor submitted a statement shewing that he himself had already inaugurated a building fund and had collected £1,000, and that the aim of the new appeal by the Fitzwilliam Society was to raise a further sum of money which might be useful to the Board at some future date, if a building scheme should be taken in hand by the University.
>
> This statement was considered in connection with the Vice-Chancellor's letter, and the following minute passed:
>
> 'The Board consider that the premises known as Fitzwilliam House are inadequate to the purposes laid down in *Ordinances*, and that it is desirable that better accommodation should at some time be provided. They raise no objection to the issuing of an appeal such as the Fitzwilliam Society desires to make, provided that it is made clear that the Board have made no estimate of the sum of money which would be required if a building scheme should be undertaken by the University, and that the appeal is approved by the Council of the Senate'.

On 24 January 1936 the draft of an appeal was brought to the Board, amendments were suggested, and it was agreed that they should be incorporated in a new draft to be circulated for approval and then submitted to the Vice-Chancellor. The Council of the Senate discussed the

---

[1]   This appears to have been a slip. There are frequent other references to the Society's intention that its appeal should be addressed to all Fitzwilliam men, and not be limited to its own members.

draft on 3 February, adjourned their discussion in order to consider it at greater leisure, and on 10 February, according to a letter written that same day to the Censor by the Master of Sidney, as Vice-Chancellor's Deputy Chairman of the Board and also a member of the Council, debated the matter at some length.[1] Certain members of the Council, it appears, then objected to the proposed appeal on the grounds that it virtually, if not explicitly, committed the University to an eventual building scheme, even though the future of the non-collegiate institution was by no means clear; and the Council appointed three of their number 'to confer with the Board on the present and future policy of the University with respect to Fitzwilliam House'. A meeting was held on 15 February, but its minutes, kept by the Master of Sidney, in whose Lodge the meeting was held, are not informative; for except that they record the date and place of the meeting, and the names of those who attended it, they consist of a single sentence: 'The present and future policy of the University with regard to Non-Collegiate Students was discussed.' In March the Board put off a 'discussion on policy', at their Chairman's suggestion, as the Council had not yet reported on it; in April they were informed that the Council had not decided about their appeal 'as it was felt that this appeal affected the matter of policy', which the Council were still considering. At this point the Board were deflected from their main purpose by the news that the Council had taken exception to certain imperfections, not, it would seem, of much importance, in their Information Sheet, prepared for the benefit of applicants for admission to Fitzwilliam House, and this appears to have occupied their attention during the Easter term. In December 1936 the Board were still amending their documents for an appeal which they had sought permission to make a year earlier; and in November 1937, more than two years after the matter had first been raised, they gave their final approval on condition that the word 'Building' should not appear in any heading, and that corresponding changes should be made elsewhere.[2] In their minutes, the Board do not refer to Council consent, but there is no reason to doubt that these alterations reflected the Council's wish, as expressed by some of its members eighteen months before, to avoid any appearance of a commitment to build which might be held to arise from their consent to the making of an appeal for assistance in a possible building scheme.

That the appeal letters were finally dispatched very soon afterwards, in the name of the Fitzwilliam Society, by the Bursar of the House is

[1] Policy File 1927–42.
[2] Minutes of 11 November 1937.

not surprising, for, in all conscience, there had been ample time for the completion of every kind of necessary preparation. By July 1939 Mr Thatcher had described the appeal as a failure. The total number of subscribers was about sixty, and their contributions then amounted to £290; and by 1956, when the appeal had been overtaken by another and could so be regarded as closed, it had yielded about £1,500. Some years later Thatcher attributed this lack of success to delay in getting the appeal out, and to the 'emasculation' of its purpose. Over the two years its occasion had lost the excitement of novelty, and its aims, in becoming less specific, no longer caught the imagination.

It is not easy to understand why the Council of the Senate made so much of so little an issue. A central authority may well wish to have the last word on attempts by University departments to obtain funds from outside sources – one appeal might prejudice another of greater significance – but such a consideration could have had little weight in this instance, for an approach to present and past members of Fitzwilliam House, almost by definition men of small substance, was unlikely to divert support from any other project which the University might regard as more important. On the question of an implied commitment to build if the appeal were allowed, there would not, it seems, have been much difficulty in making it plain that though the Council hoped (if they did) that it might be possible at some time to improve the conditions in which the non-collegiate students lived and worked, their consent to the proposed appeal must not be held to commit them, or their successors, to a building programme. Be this all as it may, it is hard to find any sufficient reason why the Council should have needed two years in which to give the Board an answer, and that they in their collective wisdom should have been persuaded to think otherwise is the most disturbing feature of this dreary episode. Such treatment left the Censor disheartened and embittered; and he came to believe that there were those in high places who not only shared a widespread indifference to the affairs of the non-collegiate body, but were actively hostile to it. If it be held that he was too closely involved to form a balanced judgement, the same cannot be said of his Chairman. 'The way in which the Council deals with Fitzwilliam affairs', said Canon Weekes in a letter written to Mr Thatcher at this time, 'often produces in me a feeling of exasperation, but I feel bound to conceal it as far as possible.'[1] To any who knew Mr Weekes, this is conclusive.

In the early days of the Fitzwilliam Society Mr Thatcher, in the Diamond Jubilee number of the *Journal*, wrote of his conception of its

---

[1] Policy File 1927–42; letter of 30 April 1936.

importance for Fitzwilliam House. 'The Society fills a very real need in our life', he says, 'for Fitzwilliam House, like any similar institution, must depend for its full growth on the loyalty and support of those who have "gone down" as much as upon those of the present active members. I believe that the Society has already helped to build up and maintain such a spirit. But membership implies willingness to help and to bear some burden. We in Cambridge want to feel not only that we have the goodwill of all old members, but also that we have something more – their willingness to help in all possible ways.'[1]

Of the Society's desire to be of service to the House, and College, there has never been any doubt. There are ready to hand instances of material support and evidences of a thoughtful concern which have been a source of encouragement to the residents in Cambridge, and this has been as true of the Society as a whole as of certain of its generous members acting in their individual capacities. Such gifts and acts of kindness identify themselves, but there have been other and more indirect ways in which the Society has sought to be of assistance to the House, and of these the regular publication of its *Journal*, which has become more important than ever in the light of the recent history of the College *Magazine*,[2] and the organization of annual meetings, whether in London or in Cambridge, have been the chief. The *Journal* has helped to keep old members informed about events in Cambridge, just as London Dinners and Cambridge Reunions have afforded them opportunities of keeping in touch with Cambridge and with each other. Such knowledge and such contacts have not only been welcome in themselves, but have beyond doubt helped to maintain an interest in Cambridge affairs which has made old Fitzwilliam residents all the more ready to help the House and College when help has been needed.

In making its outright lifts the Society has never been slow to seize upon suitable occasions to show its appreciation of service rendered to its own body or to the House and College, or to supply, as far as lay in its power, needs which have become apparent from time to time. Its first recorded act of the kind was to take part in raising money for the painting of a portrait of Mr Reddaway shortly after his retirement as Censor. In October 1924 the Amalgamated Clubs had agreed that subscriptions for a Reddaway Fund should be sought from men in residence by a committee of the Captains of clubs; and it would appear

---

[1] *Journal,* April 1930, p. 15.
[2] Until 1969 the *Magazine* supplied a useful account of the doings of the undergraduate clubs and societies. Thereafter it became, rather, a record of what had befallen its contributors, and in 1975 ceased publication.

that old members were approached on 28 November, when Mr Alexander sent out his proposals for the formation of a Fitzwilliam Society. However that may be, it was the Society, according to Mr Thatcher, who commissioned the portrait from Mr Philip de Lazlo in 1926. There is no record of the contributions received, or of the cost of the portrait, save that, through the good offices of Mr Thatcher himself, the artist asked for no more than half his customary fee. The portrait was formally presented to Mr Reddaway by the Vice-Chancellor (Canon Weekes) at a ceremony held on 30 November 1926, when Mr Reddaway in his turn desired the Vice-Chancellor, as the Chairman of his Board, to accept it on behalf of Fitzwilliam House, and expressed the hope that it might in the fullness of time find a place in worthier surroundings. The portrait, with those of Reddaway's two immediate successors, is now to be seen from the stairs which lead, appropriately enough, to the lecture room which bears his name in the central block of the new college buildings.

The Society has been concerned in the presentation of two other portraits, of which the first was of Mr C. J. B. Gaskoin. In 1938, some thirty years after he had become a Director of Studies, first in Law and then in History, at Fitzwilliam Hall, a number of Mr Gaskoin's friends, on the initiative of Mr G. M. Walton, arranged for the portrait to be painted by Mr H. S. Buss, and it was duly presented by Mr Reddaway in January 1939. It had been intended that the portrait should hang in the dining hall, but, at the insistence of Mr Gaskoin himself, it was exposed to less conspicuous publicity in the Parlour. There is an account of the presentation in the *Journal* of 1939, and a list of ninety or so names of those who subscribed towards the cost of the portrait; which, with Gaskoin himself, is the subject of some engaging verses in the *Fitzwilliam Magazine*[1] which shew clearly that the portrait was regarded as a memorial, in about equal measure, of Mr Gaskoin's distinctive personality and of his special qualities as Director of Studies and as 'Actor-Manager' of the Fitzwilliam House Amateur Dramatic Society, whose performances brought the House to the favourable notice of the University over a considerable period, and created a tradition of interest in the theatre which persists in the College of today.[2]

It was at the Reunion of 1948 that the idea was first mooted of painting Mr Thatcher's portrait in commemoration of the twenty-five years of his censorship, and the President of the Society (Group Captain

---

[1] *Magazine*, April 1939, p. 8.
[2] The portrait now hangs in a room named after Mr Gaskoin, in the central block of the new College building.

J. C. C. Slater), Mr J. R. W. Alexander, Mr W. W. Williams (Assistant Censor), and Mr G. M. Walton were appointed a committee to issue an appeal for funds.

> You will be aware [said the committee's letter] of the outstanding work which Mr W. S. Thatcher has so ably and successfully discharged as Censor of Fitzwilliam House during the past twenty-five years, and you will no doubt agree that it would be opportune if past and present Fitzwilliam men and Friends of the House made him a presentation as a mark of their appreciation.
>
> The Fitzwilliam Society has, therefore, requested us to make this Appeal for contributions to a fund to provide a portrait in oils by an eminent artist, who would be selected having regard to the money available.
>
> It being desired to secure as many contributors as possible, contributions of any amount, not exceeding two guineas each, are invited. They should be sent to the Bursar at Fitzwilliam House, or to the Honorary Secretary, and will be acknowledged and report made later as to the completion of the project.[1]

Early in 1949 Mr Edward Halliday agreed to paint the portrait, which was begun in June, and finished in time for that year's Reunion in Cambridge, when it was presented by Mr Slater. The *Fitzwilliam Journal* gives the names of nearly 180 subscribers of many generations, from some who graduated in the nineteenth century to resident undergraduates.

At the same Reunion, Mr H. C. W. Barrett, who for some twenty years had in his own person constituted the office at Fitzwilliam House and, latterly, had presided over it, was given a silver inkstand as a token of appreciation of his constant helpfulness to the officers of the Society since its beginnings.

Rowing has long been distinguished for its prestige and its expense; and it is not surprising that one of the Society's most substantial monetary gifts to the House should have been for the assistance of the Boat Club which, early in 1958, was confronted with the problem of finding a clubhouse, having been given notice to quit its existing quarters by Banham the boatbuilder. By careful husbandry in the post-war years, under the guidance of Norman Walters as their Senior Treasurer, the Amalgamated Clubs had put to reserve a sum sufficient to bring the purchase of a boathouse within the realm of possibility, but the Society's offer in August 1958, of five annual payments of £200 was most welcome, and could not have been more opportunely made. By 15 December the Clubs, acting through the Fitzwilliam Hall Trust,

---

[1] *Journal*, December 1948, p. 6.

had acquired for the sum of £5,250 a boathouse of their own formerly occupied by St Catharine's College; and members of the Society may not unreasonably have felt that their help at a critical time had contributed to the startling successes of the next ten years when the Boat Club went steadily up the river until its first boats, on the Cam at least, had nowhere higher to go.

In 1962, when the House competed at Henley for the first time without being required to race in an eliminating heat, the Society expressed its own satisfaction by adding to its fourth annual contribution towards the cost of the boathouse a grant of £50 for the expenses of the Henley eight.

At the 1964 Cambridge Reunion, the second to be held in the New Buildings (in 1963, on the Friday evening of the Reunion, the new hall had first been used for dining), Mr W. J. M. Dennis, towards the end of his presidential year, handed to the Censor and Fellows on behalf of the Society and in celebration of its fortieth anniversary, a fine silver cup made in London in 1765 by Auguste le Sage, and in accordance with the Society's wish the gift was first put to ceremonial use as a Loving Cup that same evening.

In 1968 the Society invited the College to accept the sum of £500, in celebration of the forthcoming centenary of the establishment of its parent body as the non-collegiate institution of the University; and it was subsequently agreed that the money might be used to defray costs arising from the College's decision to seek a grant of arms, as nearly as might be permitted, of the pattern first appropriated by the Boat Club in 1887, and thereafter adopted for all customary purposes.

The Society has also frequently found pleasure in expressing its sense of the value of the loyal service of its own members. Among the stalwarts – the word is appropriate here if it ever was – Milner Walton held a record which may never be approached among the officers; and so it was that, at the Cambridge Reunion of 1951, 'H. T. England, as President', says the account, 'handed Guy Milner Walton a really handsome inkstand as a token of our personal affection, and of our appreciation of twenty-seven years of close attention to the tasks of Honorary Secretary, Honorary Treasurer, and Editor of the Journal.'[1] So it was, again, that on Walton's retirement from the secretaryship in 1966 Mr J. R. W. Alexander, his predecessor in office so many years before,

---

[1]   *Journal,* December 1951, p. 9. If it may be assumed – with some plausibility – that these matters had already engaged Milner Walton's attention before his appointment as Assistant Secretary in 1926, this reference to his length of service, if arithmetically a little wide of the mark, is not seriously misleading.

presented him, at that year's Reunion, with a cheque as the merest token of acknowledgement of what he had done since his appointment as Honorary Assistant Secretary in December 1926, and a year later as Honorary Secretary and Treasurer; and this without mention of the arduous tasks which fell to him as holder of the then unrecognized office of editor of the *Journal.*[1]

Although none of the Society's officers could match Walton's record, it had been nevertheless with a similar appreciation that, a year before, a presentation was made to Mr E. J. Saunders at the close of his fifteen years as Cambridge and Reunion Secretary; and there have been numerous occasions when graceful notice has been taken of what has been done for the Society or for the House. There come to mind, among others, wedding gifts to Walter Harvey and H. C. W. Barrett, presentations on their retirement to Mr Barrett (who was made an Honorary Member of the Society in 1947), and to his sister Miss E. M. Barrett, who became Censor's Secretary in 1944. The Society's sense of the fitness of things was again happily in evidence when the proximity of Mr Gaskoin's birthday to the customary date of the Cambridge Reunion was made the occasion for a celebration in 1953 of the completion of his eightieth year, when subscriptions were solicited by the Censor from men who had known Mr Gaskoin up to his retirement ten years earlier.[2]

Also most notable was the service to the Society of F. H. Taylor, for twenty years a member of its Committee, and for seven, at the end of his life, its distinguished, self-sacrificing Secretary. His last annual report was read, in his absence owing to the illness of his wife, at the General Meeting of 17 July 1976, a short while, only, before his death.

Of the many opportunities which the Society has had of expressing approval of service which has been deemed worthy of special recognition, there was one occasion above all others on which its members demonstrated unanimous and uninhibited enthusiasm. When W. S. Thatcher retired from the censorship in 1954 the Society bade him farewell at a dinner held in the hall of Pembroke College, whose Master was Chairman of the Non-Collegiate Students Board.[3] The circumstances were propitious, for the year had seen an upsurge of feeling in the House's favour, and its future was known to be under more serious consideration than for some years. Those who dined in Pembroke

[1]   *Journal,* December 1967, p. 41.
[2]   Gaskoin died on 24 March 1955. For an obituary notice (by W. S. Thatcher), see *Magazine* of June 1955, and for a tribute by H. M. B(urton), see *Journal* of the following December.
[3]   For many references to this Reunion, see *Journal,* December 1954.

College on 31 July 1954 were therefore not only applauding the courage and persistence with which their Censor had guided the fortunes of the House for thirty years, but were doing so in a new expectation, rather than their unconquerable hope, that it stood on the verge of the improvement in its status for which he and his colleagues had striven for so long. Auspicious as the occasion may have been, however, Mr Thatcher's reception as he rose to speak that evening was remarkable; and it remains an enduring testimony of his capacity for inspiring the enthusiasm and affection of his men. The President, Alderman Saville Peck, for many years the House's nearest neighbour and part owner of its premises, presented the Censor with a silver salver and a cheque for £1,000 (to which £200 was added shortly afterwards), together with a Book of Signatures bearing the names of those who had contributed to the presentation. The Reunion was attended by nearly a hundred members of the Society; twice the usual number.[1]

In this account of its origins and progress the Fitzwilliam Society may have appeared very much like many other Associations, common enough among colleges and schools up and down the country, but in one respect it has been different: in the part played by some of its individual members in the development of its parent body into a constituent College of an ancient University.[2] Later differences of opinion left the eventual achievement of collegiate status in other hands, but it remains doubtful whether, without the support of former residents in 1954, the Regent House would have given its approval then, under certain conditions, to the termination of the non-collegiate system. This indirect contribution to the life of Fitzwilliam House and College deserves a prominent place in the Society's annals; but the tale of those negotiations belongs rather to the history of the non-collegiate body itself, at a time when, more than ever before or since, former resident members of Fitzwilliam House were called upon to join in deliberations about the conduct of its affairs in Cambridge, and about its future policy.

Officers of the Society and some others

Under the first Rules, the officers were the President, the Vice-Presidents, the Honorary Secretary and Treasurer, and the Honorary Assistant Secretary. In 1946 it was decided that the latter should be responsible for the arrangements for the Annual Dinner in London, and he

---

[1]   *Journal* December 1954, pp. 8–11.
[2]   Of the Society's officers and other members, eight signed the 1954 Memorial, as such, and at the end of 1954 the President supported the Friends of Fitzwilliam House appeal launched

was described as the Honorary Assistant and Dinner Secretary from 1947 until 1967, when he became the Dinner Secretary.

Since 1947 there has also been a Cambridge Secretary, with occasional changes of title, and it appears that the committee intended that the Rules should be amended so as to create an office for him; but there is no record that this was done. The editor of the *Journal* is not mentioned in the first Rules (or, indeed, in the *Journal* itself). He is first included in the list of officers and committee members in the *Journal* for 1949, and again there is no trace of an amendment of the Rules for the creation of an office.

In the lists given below the editor of the *Journal* and the Cambridge Secretary are included, for whether or not they were officers according to the letter of the law, they performed functions of great importance for the welfare of the Society.

From 1924 until 1939 Presidents were elected for the following year at an Annual General Meeting immediately before the Annual Dinner in December or January; and they usually presided at the Annual Dinner held at the end of their year of office. Since 1947 they have been elected at the Annual General Meeting held during the Cambridge Reunion, and retiring Presidents have presided at the Saturday evening dinner, and, of recent years at least, have entertained the Society on the following morning.

In the absence of any rule governing the effective date of elections to the Presidency, it has seemed reasonable, for elections before the Second World War, to regard a new President's tenure, except for the first of all, as beginning on the day after the day of the Annual Dinner next following his election; and for elections since the war, with the exception of the year 1947, when an election was declared to have immediate effect, to date the new tenure from the Monday after the Reunion Dinner.

President	Tenure	Dinner	Chairman*
.W. F. Reddaway	9.12.'24-10.12.'25	9.12.'24	W. S. Thatcher
W. F. Reddaway	,, ,,	10.12.'25	
W. F. Reddaway	11.12.'25-14.12.'26	14.12.'26	C. J. B. Gaskoin
W. S. Thatcher	15.12.'26-13.12.'27	13.12.'27	
C. J. B. Gaskoin	14.12.'27-11.1.'29	11.1.'29	
Walter Harvey	12.1.'29-10.1.'30	10.1.'30	

*In this column are given the names of those who took the chair in the absence of the President of the year.

by the Governors of the Fitzwilliam Hall Trust; but there is no mention in the Society's minutes of the appointment of representatives to take part, on its behalf, in discussions in Cambridge or London. It seems not unlikely that the initiative came from Cambridge.

For an account of the progress of the discussions between the University authorities and the Cambridge and London members of the 'Negotiating Committee', see pp. 249-70.

Donald Baker	11.1.'30-9.1.'31	9.1.'31	W. F. Reddaway
W. F. Reddaway	10.1.'31-8.1.'32	8.1.'32	
Percy Dunsheath	9.1.'32-13.1.'33	13.1.'33	
G. F. Fyson	14.1.'33-13.1.'34	13.1.'34	
J. R. W. Alexander	14.1.'34-12.1.'35	12.1.'35	
Frank Thatcher	13.1.'35-11.1.'36	11.1.'36	
C. H. Wolff	12.1.'36-9.1.'37	9.1.'37	
G. M. Walton	10.1.'37-8.1.'38	8.1.'38	
H. D. Cochrane	9.1.'38-14.1.'39	14.1.'39	
G. G. Sharp	15.1.'39-2.8.'47	2.8.'47	
R. J. Cobb	2.8.'47-1.8.'48	9.1.'48	
J. C. C. Slater	2.8.'48-31.7.'49	6.1.'49	
F. J. Stratton	1.8.'49-6.8.'50	5.1.'50	
H. T. England	7.8.'50-5.8.'51	4.1.'51	J. R. W. Alexander
W. W. Williams	6.8.'51-3.8.'52	26.4.'52	
C. H. Watson	4.8.'52-2.8.'53	18.4.'53	
E. S. Peck	3.8.'53-1.8.'54	9.4.'54	
R. W. Haywood	2.8.'54-31.7.'55	1.4.'55	
J. W. Whitlock	1.8.'55-5.8.'56	13.4.'56	
J. W. Whitlock	6.8.'56-4.8.'57	12.4.'57	?
E. J. Saunders	5.8.'57-3.8.'58	11.4.'58	
D. W. Markwick	4.8.'58-2.8.'59	10.4.'59	
W. W. Grave	3.8.'59-31.7.'60	8.4.'60	
L. J. M. Coleby	1.8.'60-6.8.'61	14.4.'61	
F. H. Taylor	7.8.'61-5.8.'62	6.4.'62	
R. P. Thorne	6.8.'62-4.8.'63	5.4.'63	
W. J. M. Dennis	5.8.'63-2.8.'64	7.4.'64	J. R. W. Alexander
G. W. Barman	3.8.'64-1.8.'65	7.4.'65	
A. H. Morris	2.8.'65-31.7.'66	15.4.'66	J. R. W. Alexander
J. H. W. Hannant	1.8.'66-30.7.'67	7.4.'67**	
H. M. Burton	31.7.'67-28.7.'68	5.4.'68	
N. St John Stevas	29.7.'68-3.8.'69	18.4.'69	
Raymond Kelly	4.8.'69-2.8.'70	17.4.'70	

**Attended by the Master and a number of the Fellows of the College, as guests of the Society, in celebration of the achievement of collegiate status.

Secretary & Treasurer	Apptd
J. R. W. Alexander	9.8.'24
G. M. Walton	13.12.'27
H. T. England	9.1.'37
G. M. Walton	8.1.'38

Secretary	
G. M. Walton	31.7.'64
J. V. Adams	1.2.'66

Assistant Secretary	
Metford Watkins	9.12.'24
G. M. Walton	14.12.'26
R. R. Hancock	13.12.'27
H. T. England	11.1.'29
F. H. Taylor	8.1.'38

Treasurer	Apptd
R. P. Thorne	31.7.'64
L. J. M. Coleby	28.7.'67

Assistant & Dinner Secretary	
N. W. Damerell	2.8.'47
D. W. Markwick	'51
J. H. W. Hannant	31.7.'59
C. C. Hart	31.7.'64

Dinner Secretary	
J. H. W. Hannant	28.7.'67
E. H. Day	2.8.'69

Editor of Journal	Apptd
J. R. W. Alexander	9.12.'24
G. M. Walton	13.12.'27
J. V. Adams	1.2.'66
L. J. M. Coleby	27.7.'68

Cambridge Secretary	
C. H. Wolff	2.8.'47

Cambridge & Reunion Secretary	
E. J. Saunders	4.8.'50

R. H. Fairclough	30.7.'65
(Cambridge Secretary 1967)	

CHAPTER X

The Chapel

The first non-collegiate students and 'attendance on public worship' – services within the walls – appointment of first resident Chaplain (A. O. N. Lee) in 1914. Decline of chapel community between the wars. Change of direction and revival under successive undergraduate Chaplains – appointment of H. P. Schneider – chaplaincy a full-time post (1958). The chapel and the ecumenical movement – P. J. Nott and New Hall. The Fitzwilliam College statute *Of Divine Service: and of the Chaplain*. Provision for the future.

The early Reports to the Non-Collegiate Students Board by their first Censor have shown how punctiliously he sought to fulfil his obligations in regard to the attendance of his men 'on public worship'; and how, whereas at first the non-collegiate students were required to report each term on their attendance at places of worship of their choice, special services came to be instituted for them at St Michael's Church (of which at the time of his election to the censorship Mr Somerset was Vicar) and at St Paul's. We have also seen how, at Mr Huddleston's behest, the Council of King's College agreed to assign seats in their chapel to non-collegiate students, and to arrange for the registration of their attendance which, as elsewhere, was accepted as evidence of residence. It is not, however, surprising that in spite of these arrangements, made with increasing concern for their convenience, the men came to desire not only services of their own, but their own services in their own place; and there has been preserved an informative account of the events which led to the appointment of the first resident Chaplain, and the assignment of a room in Fitzwilliam Hall for exclusive use as a chapel.[1]

A new era undoubtedly began [says the anonymous author] when, in November, 1901, the Rev. T. W. Crafer was invited to supervise Students in Theology, Mr. Durnford, then Chairman, and Mr. Fitzpatrick making promises of financial guarantee. In this they were succeeded by the Rev. H. J. Carter, of Duxford, a Benefactor whose portrait is reproduced on the walls of the dining-hall. In 1905 Mr. Crafer began to hold regular services for Students in a side-chapel at King's College. These meetings were supplemented by corporate Communions, which were held terminally in

[1] *Magazine*, June 1913, p. 222.

All Saints' Church. The feeling gradually grew, however, that in spite of the beauty of the Brassie Chapel at King's, and the dignity of All Saints', our corporate worship should take place, whenever possible, within our own walls. In December, 1910, the Theological Society petitioned the Board in this sense, suggesting 'That temporary provision might be afforded in the Library.'

To this the Board assented, and further resolved, in June, 1911, that a Resident Chaplain be appointed. The next step, however, was not taken until last term, when, after the religious life of many Undergraduates had been stirred by the Church Society's Mission at Great St. Mary's, a further petition was presented to the Board. This urged, *inter alia*, 'The General need of corporate worship; the fact that there are now resident some forty professed Ordinands: that this lack is the one thing which robs us of full collegiate life: and that neither the present system of mid-day prayer in the library nor the use of various parish churches compensates the need.'

The petition was signed by more than one hundred Undergraduates, including many Nonconformists and non-Christians. The Board received it with their wonted sympathy. They discussed the possibilities of new buildings, but were of opinion that nothing at present practicable could equal in

The chapel (1913)

size, quiet and general convenience the room then used as a library. They therefore resolved unanimously that this be entirely set apart for corporate worship.[1]

It remained to equip the Chapel and to secure a Chaplain. The difficulty arising from Mr Lee's engagement at Doncaster until Christmas was surmounted by the generous offer of Mr Crafer to act as honorary Chaplain until that date. Gifts of money and furniture poured in, and before the end of the vacation enough had been provided to meet the needs of worship. The eastern portion of the Chapel is portrayed (somewhat prophetically as regards the east window) in G. H. Hewitt's sketch, and a list of subscribers and donors is added.[2]

On Wednesday, April 16, the Bishop of Ely, a former Chairman of the Board, dedicated the Chapel, many Members of the Board and other Seniors forming part of a congregation which spread far beyond the limits of the room itself. It was felt by all that no more auspicious beginning could have been made. Residents have since preached on Sunday evenings, a special and most inspiring address has been given by the Bishop of Kensington, who spoke of his heart-felt joy at the part which the Mission had played in the achievement of our Chapel.

The following course of services has been adopted for the present:–

Sundays. –	Holy Communion 9 a.m.
	Matins (sung) 11 a.m.
	Evensong (sung) with Sermon 6 p.m.
Daily. –	Evensong 6.40 p.m.
Wednesdays and Fridays. –	Litany 1.5 p.m.
Wednesdays and Holy Days. –	Holy Communion 7.30 a.m.

The altar decoration is eleventh century in type. The altar, riddel-posts, cross and candlesticks, credence-table, prayer-desk, and altar book-stand are of oak, by Philo (Cambridge). The altar frontal is of tapestry from Morris' 'Golden Bough,' handwoven in silk and linen, and the riddels of Morris' 'Tulip and Net' in handwoven wool tapestry. The altar-book is bound in white calf, with a cross of gilt on the cover. The south window, which comprises the heraldic shields of the Ely diocese, Fitzwilliam Hall, and the University, is by Leach (Cambridge). The east window will be a 'Burne-Jones' of 'Our Lord in Glory,' executed in the Morris works at Merton Abbey.[3]

---

[1] Minutes, 6 March 1913, where the signatures are ascribed to 2 Masters of Arts, 10 Bachelors, 6 advanced students, and 97 undergraduates.

[2] The dimensions of the room were 21' by 18'. Walter Harvey once referred to it as 'filled to overflowing' with about 25 people (see p. 447). The south window was the gift of Reddaway, depicting, from east to west, the arms of the diocese of Ely, of Fitzwilliam Hall, and of the University.

[3] The east window merits a mention of its own. Shown in its original position in Hewitt's sketch, and given in memory of Mr Somerset by his son-in-law Canon J. O. F. Murray, Master of Selwyn College, who dedicated it at evensong on 26 October 1913, it was (prematurely) replaced during the academical year 1930/31, in Harvey's chaplaincy, by two

The marble medallion of Mr Somerset has been removed to the Chapel.[1]
Eucharistic vessels have been lent by the Churchwardens of All Saints'.

The amount of the initial expenditure to be provided for is approximately £94, towards which £68 2s. has already been received.

There follows a list of some seventy-five persons, of whom nearly fifty were undergraduates, whose gifts in money or in kind, with a small number of later contributions, made it possible to complete the furnishing of the chapel, in its essentials at least, by the end of 1914. Many items had been given, but something like £100 had also been subscribed.

When, in December 1910, the Non-Collegiate Students Board had allowed the library to be used, temporarily, for chapel services, and, six months later, had authorized the appointment of a Chaplain, Reddaway had no intention of letting the grass grow under his feet, for in his Information Paper, prepared in July 1911 for the benefit of applicants for admission, after referring to the services conducted by Dr Crafer in the library at Fitzwilliam Hall, and to the provision made for students in King's College Chapel, he announced that his Board intended to make an appointment during the coming year; and it is not now clear why this was not done. There is no mention of unsuccessful attempts to find a Chaplain; possibly the Board saw no means of paying him, or they may have concluded that it would be better to await the ordination of the man they had in mind than to seek elsewhere. At all events, nothing had been settled when they received the undergraduates' second petition in March 1913, and, having then agreed that the library should be assigned exclusively for use as a chapel, they resolved to invite Mr A. O. N. Lee to accept appointment as Chaplain and as Steward, at a stipend for the two offices of £140 (of which £40 would be contributed by the Censor). He would be 'allotted the use of two furnished rooms throughout the year without charges for rent, rates, taxes, coals, gas, or attendance', and his appointment would date from 8 January 1914, when he would be free to leave his curacy at St

---

others in plain glass. W. S. Thatcher tells the story (*Journal*, December 1956, p. 16), adding that it went to Central Africa, where he supposed that it still was. A very tentative enquiry brought a prompt reply from Mr Hewitt (B.A. 1913). Writing from St Francis' Hospital at Katete in Zambia, on 7 March 1975, he says: 'The window is still at Fiwila. It is in the east wall of the little Chapel of St Giles, in the (Munshi wa nkumbu) "the village of mercy", which is the church in the leprosarium at Fiwila. As you will know, the treatment for leprosy has now so far advanced that mobile clinics will gradually take the place of the old leprosaria, so I will write to the Friars at Fiwila to remind them of the history of this little panel of glass, that it may duly be taken care of.'

[1] See p. 91.

George's Church in Doncaster. Mr Lee, who had graduated in 1909, with a second class in Part I of the Theological Tripos (he was in the same class in Part II a year later), was one of those people, so valuable in a small society, who could set his hand to anything. A freshman in 1906, he was in turn a Leathersellers' and a Clothworkers' Exhibitioner, was in the boat, was Secretary of the Musical Society, General Secretary of the Amalgamated Clubs, a Secretary to the Censor, and in 1910 and 1911 had been a highly successful Steward. He was ordained deacon in the diocese of York in 1912, and priest in 1913.

Mr Lee served as Chaplain until the Long Vacation of 1916, when he resigned in order to take up pastoral work in Burma. His last account of chapel activities, written for the *Magazine*, makes very clear his opinion of the value of its rôle in the corporate life of the Hall, an opinion shared to the full by the Censor, and made known to the Non-Collegiate Students Board in his Annual Report for 1915/16. 'It is difficult', he says, 'to express adequately my sense of the value of his (the Chaplain's) work under the difficult conditions of the war. All who have known him regard the idea of Fitzwilliam Hall without a resident Chaplain as now almost inconceivable. It may be convenient to mention here ... that a fund for the permanent endowment of the Resident Chaplaincy has been set on foot.'

Mr Lee's successor was the Rev. Frank Thatcher (B.A. 1912, and brother of W. S.), who was appointed on 30 November to be Chaplain and Steward, and continued in both offices until September 1924, when he left on his appointment to a living in Letchworth. Mr Thatcher, who became increasingly responsible for the financial affairs of the Hall, was also Bursar during his last three years in Cambridge. The Chaplaincy Endowment Fund to which Mr Reddaway referred was started in 1916, after Mr Lee's resignation, with an appeal addressed principally to the men of 1913 to 1916;[1] and when it was closed in 1923 it had realized a sum of £500, and, in Reddaway's words, had 'taken over No. 10 Fitzwilliam Street'.

The Fitzwilliam Hall Chapel, barely established when war broke out in 1914, did not close during the war years; and this continuity, at first sight surprising, was characteristic of the Hall itself. Its *Magazine* appeared at six-monthly intervals, though this was possible only because Reddaway took on the editorship, and wrote most of it, in order that old members in the Armed Forces should not be without Fitzwilliam news. Numbers fell, and organized games were soon dis-

---

[1] The men, that is, who were in residence during those years (*Magazine*, December 1916, p. 179.)

continued: but there were still in the Hall a larger remnant than in the colleges, and the composition of the student body may explain why this was so.

I must attempt [said Reddaway in December 1916] some picture of life in Fitzwilliam Hall during the term which is now closing, the seventh term of war. Inevitably there has been very little of the Hall left, and it is surprising that we have been able to maintain as much life as we have done. But as something like half of our 40 or 50 nominal strength lives either within the walls or just outside, those coming in from a distance have always found people about, and dinners have seldom sunk far below 20.

It may be interesting to attempt an analysis of our matriculated residents during the term. They have been at Cheshunt College 2, St Edmund's House 2, Westminster College, Ridley Hall, and Clergy Training School 0, West African Students 2, Egyptians 2, Indians 11, Cinghalese 2, Japanese 1, Russians 1, O.T.C. Cadets 1; of other British Undergraduates – engaged on work of national importance 2, Ministers of Religion 3, Anglican Ordinands 2, medically rejected 6, awaiting call to the colours 2, South African 1, Anglo-Indian 1.[1]

Small as the student company was, it contained an unusual proportion of men not required for military service; among them some who, so long as the Hall itself remained in being, might be expected to attach importance to the continued existence of the chapel; and this is borne out in a comment by Mr Frank Thatcher, then acting as Chaplain, in the Easter term of 1918. On the 'vexed question' whether chapel attendance should be voluntary or compulsory, he recalls that at Fitzwilliam Hall it has always been voluntary, adding, with especial reference to the Lent and Easter terms of 1918, that it has been 'magnificent'. However this may have been, if the Censor's Reports to the Board, the Board's minutes, and the undergraduates' *Magazine* may be taken as evidence, the chapel and the Theological Society (founded with the encouragement of Mr Crafer in 1902) appear to have played a more significant part in the corporate life of the Hall in the period before the war, and during the war, than they did thereafter for some years.[2]

Upon the resignation of Mr Frank Thatcher at the end of the academical year 1923/24, the Non-Collegiate Students Board agreed on 15 October to appoint the Rev. Walter Harvey, then Chaplain of Wellingborough School, to be Assistant Censor, Bursar and Chaplain, with effect from 1 January 1925, at a stipend of £400 with 'free rooms

[1]   *Ibid.*, p. 177.
[2]   In 1925 W. S. Thatcher described the chapel services as 'badly neglected' (*Magazine*, June 1925, p. 39).

in consideration of his Chaplain's duties'. It appears that in the interval the chaplaincy was filled, in an acting capacity, by the Rev. Frank Ranner, who had taken his degree from Fitzwilliam Hall in 1914, and was at the time curate at St Botolph's Church in Cambridge.

Harvey could not really bring himself to approve of his chapel as it was, although on occasions he appeared to regard it with a certain affection. 'We are contemplating', he writes in 1930, 'some consider-able alterations in the fabric of the Chapel. The building is damp and ill-ventilated: the lighting is defective, and the noise from the Chemistry enthusiasts down below is a discouraging element. We should like to close the windows into the adjacent court, and to open new windows to the east. We should wish to provide adequate lighting and ventilation, and to get rid of the present ugly windows. The heating arrangements are at present abominable, and it is impossible to warm the room on a really cold day. A hundred pounds may meet the cost of these alterations; they may well be carried out in the Long Vacation, if the Board agree to them, and it is thought that we might arrange for an overdraft to meet the cost.' The Board did approve of the alterations proposed, and, doubtless on the advice of the Chaplain in his bursarial capacity, they also agreed to pay for them; and for this, said the Chap-lain 'we are very much obliged'. A year later Mr Harvey declares that the recent alterations have greatly improved the chapel, which, in this more expansive mood, he describes as 'that remarkable little build-ing'.[1]

These were discouraging years for the chapel community, though they were relatively prosperous in other respects until the economic depression of 1931 brought a fall in numbers, with its threat of lower academic standards and financial insolvency. In 1930 Mr Reddaway spoke of an 'ominous shrinkage' in the number of ordinands, pre-viously an unfailing source of supply. A year later Mr Harvey takes pleasure in announcing that once a term at least the chapel is full to overflowing, when, at an early celebration, followed by breakfast in hall, there is an attendance of twenty-five; but such numbers are evi-dently exceptional. In 1934 Mr Harvey was appointed to St Peter's Horningsea, and held the living for two years; but he did not relinquish the chaplaincy, and was still in office when the Second World war brought about the virtual closure of the House.

After the war the first mention, in print, of the chapel appears to have been made by the General Secretary of the Amalgamated Clubs

---

[1] *Journal*, April 1930, p. 26; May 1931, p. 9.

(E. J. Hawkins) who, in his Notes for the year 1947/48, rejoices in the successes of the House in organized games, but deplores the relatively small numbers of those who take part, or even shew an interest, in them; and wonders how many know the whereabouts of the playing field, or, even, where the chapel is. A year later two chapel supporters, in a brief survey of the history of the Fitzwilliam chapel community, recalled how the virtually compulsory attendance at college chapels of earlier years had been succeeded by the formation of more meaningful voluntary groups (of which they mention one under the leadership of Mr Gaskoin in Fitzwilliam), which in their turn had suffered from a change in religious attitudes in recent years.[1]

The comparatively insignificant rôle of the chapel in the corporate life of the House at this time was attributed, at least in part, to the lack of a Chaplain, and the appointment in 1948 of the Rev. J. F. Sertin raised hopes of better things. Mr Sertin, who was already in orders when he came into residence as an undergraduate, served as Chaplain during his second and third years, and was succeeded by the Rev. B. D. Reed (1950/54), and the Rev. J. B. Moroney (1954/56), both Australians who had been ordained before they came to this country. Mr Reed also held a curacy at St Paul's Church during his third undergraduate year. These appointments are not without a certain interest. All three men were supported by an Ordination Candidates Training Fund whose Secretary, the Rev. H. D. Salmon, who had taken his degree from Queens' College in 1904, assiduous though he was in placing his men, can hardly have supplied any other collegiate institution with three successive Chaplains in the space of eight years. Under their guidance, the chapel in Fitzwilliam forsook its high churchmanship of the 1920s and the 1930s and took on an evangelical character. It is reasonable to suppose that, both before and after the war, the chapel community would have been more representative of the House as a whole if it had set out to accommodate men of different persuasions – in this respect the formation, in 1954, of a Society of St Michael may be relevant, for its avowed purpose was to bring into being an organization for worship and study 'outside the opportunities provided by the Chapel Services'.

Nevertheless, the chapel flourished. There are successive reports of increased attendances, and in his last year as Chaplain Mr Reed is able to announce that 'the chapel through the Parlour' has become too small, and that during the Michaelmas term, at the invitation of Canon Whittaker, Vicar of Great St Mary's, Sunday evening services have

[1] *Magazine*, June 1948, p. 11; June 1949, p. 10.

'The Chapel through the Parlour' (1950)[1]

been held in St Michael's Church. Mr Reed adds that the Bishop of Ely (Dr Wynn) also was willing for Fitzwilliam to take over St Michael's as its chapel, but that this was a matter for decision by the Non-Collegiate Students Board. The Board, however, do not appear to have been consulted, and after three years the use of St Michael's was given up, as its maintenance was beyond the resources of the chapel community in Fitzwilliam. 'Our services in St Michael's were inspiring', said the Acting Censor in April 1957, 'but in winter only the hardiest spirits were able to endure the rigours of the unheated church.'[2]

The end of Mr Reed's tenure as Chaplain in 1954 coincided with Mr Thatcher's retirement, under the age-limit, as Censor; and in his last contribution to the *Fitzwilliam Magazine* Mr Reed made grateful acknowledgement of Mr Thatcher's constant and efficacious support of the chapel, which, he says, as an undergraduate he had helped to bring into being. When, after an additional year as Senior Tutor, Censor in

---

[1]   The War Memorial Triptych was moved to the west end in 1957, and placed between the medallions of Mr Somerset and Mr Howard. See *Journal,* December 1957, facing p. 13.

[2]   *Magazine,* June 1957, p. 4.

all but name, Mr Thatcher's official connexion with the House came to its end, Mr Moroney, in his turn, paid tribute to a Censor who, he declared, had done more for the chapel than any other man.

The Michaelmas term 1956 saw a significant development in the life of the chapel in Fitzwilliam House – or, rather, the beginning of an important change in its arrangements – when the Rev. H. P. Schneider (B.A. 1952) was appointed Chaplain in succession to Mr Moroney. The full significance of this appointment was not at first realized, for Schneider had been admitted, at the same time, to the status of Research Student in the University, and as such the extent of his pastoral work would be watched with a zealous, if not a jealous, eye by the Board of Research Studies; but nevertheless his selection as Chaplain was a welcome reversion to the practice of having in the chaplaincy a more senior member of the House, instead of an undergraduate, however conscientious, whose principal objective would be the acquisition of his first degree. But although the full significance of the appointment may not have been immediately obvious, its effect soon began to appear, for it was not Schneider's pastoral work that was restricted, but his research, which was formally put aside from the beginning of the Michaelmas term 1958, when, with the concurrence of the Council of the Senate, he was given a full-time post as Chaplain for one year, subsequently renewed for a further two.

Mr Schneider brought to his work a young man's energy and resilience – he had been very close to tragedy in Czechoslovakia – and a variety of experience which enabled him to see for what they were stiffly held differences of opinion, not always on matters of the highest moment, which were coming to be regarded by many Anglicans and men of other persuasions as harmful to the health of the church at large.

Schneider's influence is already evident in a note on the chapel within a year of his arrival.[1] The activities of a newly constituted Chapel Committee; a list of preachers of widely varying allegiance; the further integration into the life of the chapel of the Saint Michael's Society; a Carol Service in 1956, which was the precursor of regular Sunday evensong in the chapel of Ridley Hall (shortly afterwards to be found on occasion too small); and a special reference to co-operation between Anglicans and Free Churchmen – these all proclaim that under Schneider's leadership the chapel community became possessed of a vigour, and an open-minded tolerance, which made it a force to be reckoned with in the corporate life of the House. In this he was greatly

[1] *Magazine,* June 1957, p. 9.

helped by R. N. Walters, a Free Churchman who had come to the House as Tutor in the Michaelmas term of 1950, at the beginning of Schneider's second undergraduate year.

Schneider's chaplaincy, consistently busy throughout, was near its beginning marked by a very special occasion, when on 27 October 1957 in the chapel of Ridley Hall a memorial service was held for Alfred Lionel Sadd (B.A. 1931), who in 1933 had gone out from Cheshunt College as a missionary to the Gilbert Islands, and was there executed by a Japanese occupying force in August 1942. The Headmaster of Sadd's school (The Leys), the Acting Censor, and the Tutor took part in the service, and the preacher was the Rev. H. W. Theobald, Sadd's contemporary at Cheshunt.[1] This was also the occasion of the dedication in Sadd's memory of altar ornaments, given by his family, for use in Fitzwilliam House Chapel. Designed in anticipation of more spacious surroundings, the cross and candlesticks are shown in a photograph of the eastern end of the little chapel in Trumpington Street with Walter Harvey's plain glass windows. On the altar step is the replica of the Warwick Vase bearing Sadd's name on its base, with the names of all Fitzwilliam men who fell in the Second World War. In a companion photograph, also taken in the Michaelmas term of 1957, shortly after the re-decoration and re-arrangement of the Chapel, the memorial of 1914–1918, moved from its earlier position over the altar, appears on the west wall between the portraits of the first Censors, with Mr Howard on the left and Mr Somerset on the right.[2]

In October 1960 Schneider left to join the staff of the Archbishop in Jerusalem as Chaplain of St Luke's Consular Church in Haifa. His success had made plain the desirability of replacing him with a full-time Chaplain of similar status; and he was followed, in turn, by F. H. Palmer and P. J. Nott. Mr Palmer, a classical exhibitioner of Jesus College (B.A. 1952), had been ordained from Wycliffe Hall in 1955, and came to the House at the beginning of the Michaelmas term 1960, from a curacy at St Mary's, Southgate, in Crawley, leaving in March 1964 on his appointment as Vicar at Holy Trinity in Cambridge. Mr Nott, a man of unusually varied experience – he had served as a regular soldier, and had been for a time in industry – read for the Certificate in Christian Theology as a member of Fitzwilliam (Westcott House), took his degree in 1961, and was ordained in that year. After serving as curate at the Church of St Nicholas in Harpenden he returned to Fitzwilliam House in 1964, and remained there as Chaplain until the Long

---

[1] Mr Theobald's sermon is given *verbatim* in the *Magazine* for 1958, pp. 14–17.
[2] *Journal*, December 1957, p. 12.

Vacation of 1969, when he went to a living in Beaconsfield. As Mr Nott's successor the Governing Body appointed, as from 1 October, the Rev. M. J. Baddeley, Master of Arts of Keble College, and Tutor of Lincoln Theological College. They were very quickly to discover how fortunate their choice had been.

Throughout Schneider's chaplaincy, and in the reigns of his successors, the policy and practice of the chapel group in the House continued along the lines which he had laid down in the beginning; and in the minutes of the Chapel Committee ecumenical co-operation, and Christian responsibility to the community at large, are recurring themes of discussion, with little disagreement on principles and much activity in their practical application. It may also be that the members of the committee, as an 'outgoing' body, were not impervious to the attractions of a critical examination, as an exercise in itself, of the merits of existing institutions, or of a challenge to accepted conventions, after the manner of their opposite numbers in other fields of undergraduate activity.

During these years a 'wind of change' swept through the chapel, and new patterns of worship were sought to replace formularies not so much hallowed by tradition, it was thought by some, as staled by custom. Already in Schneider's time there had been an experiment, once repeated, with a choral setting of Holy Communion for choir and congregation; and a persistent desire for reform led in 1966 to the appointment of a 'liturgical commission', charged with the task of recommending a new order of service for Sunday evenings. After two years or so, this body submitted proposals, much influenced by brief visits to the Protestant community at Taizé, in the Rhône valley. 'The structure of our services', said the Chapel Secretary in 1967, 'already under fire, came in for an even more radical bombardment. Morning prayer disappeared, replaced by a layman-orientated Taizé-style office. The well-established Liturgical Commission, delayed by negotiations, sharpened its teeth on the bones of Anglican Evensong, and the regular round of Evening Prayers and Offices of the week sidled themselves into the wings.' And from the wings there came another comment, possibly not far removed from the heart of the matter, to the effect that a change was as good as a holiday.

It is not surprising that the Fitzwilliam Chapel community, drawn from men of differing backgrounds and religious convictions but united in their membership of the House, should have been sympathetic to the aims of the ecumenical movement of the post-war years. Its influence was already apparent in Schneider's time, and early in the chaplaincy of his successor its spirit prompted invitations to Non-conformists to preach at evensong, or the celebration of Holy Communion after the usage of the Congregationalists, and, on one occasion, the adoption at a chapel service of the liturgy of the Church of South India. During the year 1961/62, one study group was attended by Roman Catholics, Anglicans and Free Churchmen, and the Chapel Committee included a Roman Catholic representative.

At the beginning of Mr Nott's tenure of the chaplaincy there was evidence of an open-minded receptiveness of another kind, which members of the chapel community no doubt felt to be in keeping with the ecumenical nature of their churchmanship. In 1966 Mr Nott, with the consent of those in authority, had agreed to undertake pastoral work in New Hall; and it seemed a logical and desirable consequence that New Hall undergraduates should be invited to join in the activities of Fitzwilliam House Chapel. This arrangement, which Nott was careful to assure the body of Fitzwilliam Fellows would be informal, and temporary, and which he subsequently described as 'not so much a marriage as living in righteousness together', worked most smoothly from the start, and with the passage of time seemed less and less likely to prove either temporary or unduly informal.

In the Long Vacation of 1966, the first visit of members of the chapel community to Taizé appears to have made a deep impression upon them, and to have strengthened their resolve that all that could be done should be done to remove denominational barriers within their Cambridge body; and in this frame of mind, undeterred by what earlier generations might have thought, they welcomed a ruling by the Bishop of Northampton that Roman Catholic Mass might be celebrated in Fitzwilliam House Chapel.[1]

Whilst the members of the chapel community continued to regard the House as the centre of their activities, they appeared to grow increasingly aware of wider obligations; and it became a custom to make visits, usually in the Long Vacation, to areas of particular need, or of especial interest in other ways. Of these visits the first was made by the Chaplain and six members of the House to Iona in the summer of 1961, and an account of their visit conveys something of the impact upon them by their brief association, at first hand, with a dedicated community searching for a more complete understanding of human needs, and for new ways of meeting them, in the modern world. In 1962, thirty members of the House, drawn from six religious denominations, went on a ten day mission to Stowmarket, in Suffolk, in

[1] *Magazine*, May 1967, p. 5.

support of a united campaign by the churches of the town. In the following year, at Easter, a group attended a work camp at Lee Abbey; and in the Long Vacation a visit was paid to Camberwell, to acquire and supply information on alcoholism there. These ventures, initiated by Mr Palmer, continued under Mr Nott – a visit to a Birmingham slum parish with a large immigrant population was one – and became more ambitious with the expeditions to Taizé already noted. Nearer Cambridge, work of a less exciting, but also less occasional, kind was done at Fulbourn, and with old people at Primrose Croft.

One of the unusual features of Fitzwilliam House, in comparison with the colleges of the University, was that its growth along collegiate lines was not controlled by any statutory instrument of government. Such constitution as it possessed dated from 1869, when a body of regulations had been framed for its superintendence as an institution that was not, and was not intended to become, a college, and which therefore took no account of this possibility. The ordinances of 1869 made no mention of a chapel, or, indeed, of any other building. They merely required the Censor to do what he could to ensure the attendance of his men on public worship, but not so as to embarrass those who did not belong to the Anglican Church. From the beginnings, therefore, there was an unaccustomed leniency over the matter of 'keeping chapels', which consorted well with a·policy of interdenominational co-operation when in later years this was looked upon with favour by high authority. When, therefore, in 1966 statutes came to be made for Fitzwilliam as a college of the University, the statute *Of Divine Service: and of the Chaplain* did little more than prescribe a code of practice already observed, and fully in accordance with principles on which chapel policy in Fitzwilliam House had for some years been based. Thus it was that, having laid down firmly that there should be a chapel within the precincts of the College, the statute, while it anticipated that the Chaplain would usually be a Church of England priest, allowed also for the appointment of any ordained minister of a church in full membership of the World Council of Churches, and made similar provision for the conduct of chapel services. The statute was approved, it will be remembered, by the body of Fellows, *nemine contradicente*.[1]

From the end of the Michaelmas term 1956, by courtesy of the Principal, Sunday evensong was held in the chapel of Ridley Hall, where, as the Acting Censor had said, the House was able to worship in dignity and comfort, and so continued until the end of the Easter term 1963,

[1]   *Charter and Statutes of Fitzwilliam College*, Statute XXXIII.

shortly before the move to Huntingdon Road. During the two preceding years there had been much debate about the best way of providing accommodation for a chapel, and history was repeating itself, for just as fifty years previously the undergraduates, conscious as they were of the attractions of other places available to them, had felt that their corporate worship should as far as possible take place within the walls, so now in the early 1960s it was thought very desirable that there should be some place on the new site where services might be held.

Although the architect had included it in his original Development Scheme for Fitzwilliam House, there had been no question of building a chapel, because the use of public funds for it was not permitted; and after the possible use of a music room (since habitually used by the Fitzwilliam Society for their Cambridge Reunion meetings) had been rejected on the grounds that the room was likely to be too small, it was decided not merely to divert to temporary use accommodation built for other purposes, but to try to acquire some purely temporary building and put it up on the site, on which, at that time, there was room enough and to spare. This decision had barely been announced in the Censor's Annual Letter in the *Fitzwilliam Journal* for December 1961 when an old member of Fitzwilliam Hall, as reticent as he was generous, for his name was never made public, promised a sum of money which, when added to certain previous gifts, more than covered the purchase price of two pre-fabricated huts, and the cost of erecting them during the Long Vacation of 1963. This modest building, acoustically perfect and unexpectedly comfortable, though difficult of access in wet weather, was dedicated on 13 October 1963 by the Bishop of St Edmundsbury and Ipswich, himself a Fitzwilliam man, and served its purpose admirably until, in the Easter term of 1966, on advice that planning permission for its continued use was improbable, the body of Fellows resolved to make other arrangements.

There was still no money for a chapel, and the Fellows, fully in sympathy with the desire for a place of worship on the site, reverted to the possibility of adapting some room in the new building designed for other purposes, and resolved that in view of the generous provision of accommodation for the communal use of junior members of the College they would be justified in appropriating, for the time being, a large room which had been built for amusements noisier than would (then) have been thought tolerable elsewhere. The room was furnished simply; and the very limit of its capacity, normally about sixty persons, was reached at its dedication by the Bishop of Ely on 16 October 1966.

The future prospects of the chapel community, if not its immediate present, were shortly to be transformed by a proposal from a long-standing friend of the non-collegiate institution who saluted the coming of collegiate status with an offer of funds sufficient to build a College chapel. The Governing Body took the view that the provision of a chapel should not be considered by itself, but as part of wider plans for an eventual development of the College site, and an account of their discussions of this whole matter is given in a later chapter.[1]

[1] See pp. 486–8.

CHAPTER XI

The Library

Beginnings of a reference library (1874) – to be open to members of Cavendish College – purpose-built accommodation – rules for borrowing books – gifts from University and from private persons. Frederick Paley's library – the Gibson Fund. Attempted re-organization – lack of funds prevents useful growth for many years – appointment of Senior Librarian. Impending collegiate status and capital grants for undergraduate library – individual gifts. The College Libraries Fund – library policy in the 1960s.

In their Report to the Senate of 30 April 1874, during the fifth year of their Scheme and shortly after the end of its trial period, the Non-Collegiate Students Board stated that it would be a great benefit to their men if they could have a small library, more especially of reference books, supplied by the University or by private liberality. It is unlikely that this need had not made itself felt before, and it can be no coincidence that this first mention of its occurs in a Report in which they also announced that they had been able to secure convenient rooms at 31 Trumpington Street, two at the front over a furniture shop, and one 'of considerable dimensions' at the back, which they had assigned during a large part of the day to the students themselves as a reading room and a place for meetings. It was in this reading room, which after alterations[1] in 1892 became a lecture room, and later still a Parlour for senior members of Fitzwilliam House, that the students first had recourse to their library, consisting of a small number of books purchased out of a grant of £50 from the University Chest (Grace 14 of 29 October 1874), on the application of the Censor to the Vice-Chancellor, and kept in the Censor's office, or the office of his clerk.

In 1877 the Censor was authorized to spend £50 on books, to be stamped with a Non-Collegiate Library stamp, and to deposit such of them as he might think fit at Cavendish College for the use of the non-collegiate students there; it being understood, however, that the books would all remain the property of the Board. In May 1879 the Censor was again permitted to spend £50 on books, subject to the approval of his Chairman and Deputy Chairman, part to be placed in Cavendish

---

[1] At the time of these alterations it was thought that the library might one day be housed in a large second floor room, fashioned out of two smaller rooms, to the south of the main staircase (Censor's Report to the Board of 1 March 1893). This was not done; and in due course this second floor room became the general office.

College, and part kept in 'the library at the office'; and in December
the Board agreed, subject to the same approval, to allocate a like
amount for the benefit of the men at Cavendish College. In the following May there appears to have been an unspent balance from these allocations, which was used for the purchase of the *New Encyclopaedia
Britannica* 'as cheaply as possible'.

At this time better accommodation was contrived for the library, for
in Mr Somerset's last year as Censor, and at his suggestion, there was
built on the first floor, behind the reading room, an additional room for
the library's exclusive use, until in 1911 it was also used for chapel services.

It almost begins to seem that the Non-Collegiate Students Board
were concerned lest they might be doing too little for their men at
Cavendish College, in return for the fees received from them on their
registration as non-collegiate students of the University, for in 1881,
when the Censor was again permitted to buy books, he was granted £25
for his own men, and allowed to spend up to £50 for the benefit of men
at the college, 'after consulting the Warden on his needs, if any'. This
apparent uncertainty about the urgency of the need appears to have had
some justification, for in January 1883 the Warden of the College,
which in the previous November had acquired the status of a Public
Hostel, enquired whether an unspent balance of the grant was nevertheless available for him. The Board, in this instance casting their bread
upon the waters, agreed that it was, provided that the Warden would
submit to the Censor a list of his proposed purchases; and, in reply to a
further enquiry, they resolved that in spite of their earlier cautious
stipulation, books already deposited in the College might remain there.

In March 1883 the Board, who some months earlier had received
from a majority of their students a memorial requesting permission to
borrow books from the library, approved, with effect from the beginning of the next Easter term, a set of 'rules for the use of the books
belonging to the Board'. There was to be a Librarian, appointed by the
Censor subject to the Board's approval, at a stipend of £5 a term. He
was required to be in the library for one hour on every morning in full
term, at a time to be announced by the Censor. Books could be
borrowed, one at a time for one week, only when the Librarian was
present; and there were fines for failure to return books at the proper
time (sixpence a day until the book was brought back), the heaviest
penalty (a fine of ten shillings) being prescribed for borrowing a book
without signing for it.[1]

---

[1]   This was no mere formality. On 9 February 1889 the Board agreed 'that R. Simpson should

A beginning was duly made under the new dispensation, and the first Librarian, whose name is now unknown, was appointed for the Easter term 1884, when a new catalogue was compiled, and some attempt made to improve the arrangement of the books. No Librarian is named in the Board's minutes until the Easter term of 1880, when P. W. Bradley was appointed for that term. Thereafter appointments are recorded with fair regularity, but often for unspecified periods, until November 1914, when the list ends with the name of F. S. Long, appointed for the academical year 1914/15 at a stipend of £15.[1]

That the library was on a modest scale is evident from Mr Howard's Report of June 1886, in which he states that since the Easter term of 1884, when books were first allowed to be taken out, the numbers issued in successive terms had been 36, 23, 79, 22, 53, 70, and 23. He also said that the only donation received during the last year had been a *Handbook for Victoria* presented by the Royal Commission of Victoria.

The terminal reports submitted to the Board by their undergraduate Librarians have not in general been kept, but for no obvious reason there still exist a number relating to the period between 1891 and 1917;[2] and from these it is apparent that in its early years the library continued to be of severely limited use for undergraduate study, except possibly in the early 1890s. In the Michaelmas term of 1891, 130 books (including renewals) were issued to thirty men, and in the following term the library is 'considered to be a great acquisition', especially for men reading for the Theological Tripos. In the Michaelmas terms between 1892 and 1894, 160, 118, and 167 books were borrowed, respectively, by thirty, thirty-three, and twenty-eight men; and in the Lent term of 1895 the Censor was particularly asked to convey to the Librarian (Reginald Jones) the Board's appreciation of his work in compiling a new catalogue, after the library had received an unusual number of gifts, though there is little evidence of the possibility of acquiring books by purchase,[3] which appear to have brought its total holdings to 1659 volumes, consisting, says Mr Jones, of 998 works, including some duplicates.

The library's first recorded donation was from Dr G. M. Humphry, then Professor of Anatomy in the University, who gave his three volumes on *Human Anatomy* in the Easter term of 1874. In October

---

be fined 30/- for having kept out three volumes of Beaumont and Fletcher's Works during the whole of the Michaelmas term'.

[1] He did not return into residence; and was killed in action on 26 September 1915.

[2] College Archives.

[3] In the years 1890–99, £148.10.0 was paid to undergraduate Librarians; and £19.14.9 was spent on books.

1876 the Board announced gifts from 'members of the Senate and other persons', and invited further offers, to be addressed to the Censor. In 1887 the Censor mentions a liberal gift from the University of some 180 books published by the University Press;[1] and Mr Cunningham (a Board member) had given a copy of his Hulsean Lecture. In their Report to the Senate of 12 March 1894 the Board 'acknowledge with thanks special gifts of books, maps, and pictures from the Council of Cavendish College, Sir G. M. Humphry, Mr Brandreth, Mrs S. S. Lewis, Messrs Macmillan and Bowes, Mr Rose, Mrs Somerset, and Mr Tilley'. Three of these benefactions will have been due to the closure of Cavendish College in 1891, for this will have been the occasion of the gifts from the College Council, and from Mrs Lewis, and of the presentation by Mrs Somerset of the books originally given to the College by her husband. Of the others, the Rev. Alfred Rose (Fellow of Emmanuel College since 1863, and its Bursar for twenty years) had been a member of the Board from 1884 to 1887, and was to rejoin it in 1895, and serve for a year as its Chairman from March 1900. Mr A. A. Tilley, Fellow of King's since 1876, was in turn College Lecturer in Classics (he had been second classic in 1875) and, from 1896, in Modern Languages. Mr Brandreth was probably Henry Brandreth of Trinity College, eleventh Wrangler in 1857, elected Fellow in the following year, and briefly Assistant Tutor of the College. Of Mrs Agnes Lewis much could be written, but it may be found elsewhere. She was the widow of the Rev. Samuel Savage Lewis, Librarian of Corpus Christi, antiquary, a great traveller, and, when Henry Bradshaw died in 1886, an unsuccessful candidate for election as University Librarian.[2] Mr Lewis died on 31 March 1891, and in his *Life*,[3] which she published in May 1892, his widow writes: 'During the Easter vacation (of 1888) we stayed a few days at Bournemouth with the late Dr Frederick Paley, of whose kindness in his undergraduate days Samuel had retained a vivid recollection. On Dr Paley's death in November 1888, Samuel purchased his library as a gift to Cavendish College.' It is reasonable to suppose that these books, or, as is possibly more likely, a selection of

---

[1]   Grace 16 of 9 December 1886: 'That copies of books printed at the University Press for the Syndics of the Press be granted to the Library of the Non-Collegiate Students Board'. There were similar gifts to the British School at Athens, the University College of South Wales and Monmouth at Cardiff, and to the Public Library of Newcastle-on-Tyne.

[2]   Matriculated at St John's College in 1854, he was obliged by defective eyesight to relinquish his studies for some years. On his recovery he migrated to Corpus Christi in 1865, and graduated with first class honours in Classics in 1869.

[3]   Agnes Smith Lewis, *Life of the Rev. Samuel Savage Lewis, M.A., F.S.A., Fellow and Librarian of Corpus Christi College, Cambridge* (Macmillan and Bowes, 1892), p. 142.

them, were the subject of the Board's acknowledgement, for there are some 250 of Dr Paley's books still in the College library, many of them his own publications, and some with his manuscript notes.[1]

In 1880 the provision of a separate room for the library had been warmly welcomed; and as a place for books it was far more convenient than a table in the Censor's office; but it suffered from one particular disadvantage, for access to it was through what had become the lecture room, so that it could be entered only when no lectures were being given. Reddaway lost no time in bringing this and other disadvantages of the library to the notice of his Board, who asked a committee to consider how matters might be improved. A letter of 7 February 1908, from one of the committee members, Canon F. J. Foakes-Jackson, of Jesus College,[2] gives an indication of the Board's ideas about its library, and of the condition of the library itself:

[1] Frederick Apthorp Paley was a grandson of Archdeacon William Paley, author of the *Evidences of Christianity*. He graduated from St John's College in 1838 (but not with honours, owing to his 'dislike' of Mathematics), and became a classical scholar of repute. For an account of his work, and of the circumstances in which he was required by the Master and Seniors of the College to vacate his college rooms in 1846, see *D.N.B.* XLIII, p. 99.

The closure of Cavendish College may also explain a reference by Reddaway on the subject of the meagre endowments of the non-collegiate body. 'It may occasion some surprise', he writes in the *Magazine* for May 1908, 'that, in more than a generation of existence the sole endowment that we have received is an annual sum of seven guineas, one half of which came to us by accident, for the study of the New Testament in Greek'. On 10 May 1889 the Non-Collegiate Students Board had received a letter from Mrs Margaret Gibson, offering a sum of £125 (to which she afterwards added £5 to cover the cost of investment) for the purpose of establishing her prize, first awarded in 1890. Shortly before, on 27 February, the Council of Cavendish College had approved the investment, in the name of the Master and Treasurers of the college, and of the Rev. Samuel Savage Lewis, of £125, also from Mrs Gibson, to found a prize for the same purpose, for which the first examination was to be held in the Easter term of 1890. In June 1896 the Non-Collegiate Students Board agreed to recommend that a sum of £142.5.6, 'presented to the Board by Mrs J. Y. Gibson for the purpose of increasing the annual Greek Testament Prize for Non-Collegiate Students', should be invested in London and North-Western Railway stock; and there seems no doubt that Mrs Gibson transferred to the University, for the benefit of these students, the capital, with some accrued interest, that she had given to Cavendish College, whose closure was the 'accident' to which Reddaway referred.

In 1892, the year in which she gave Dr Paley's books to the library, Mrs Lewis and Mrs Gibson (they were twins) visited the convent of St Catherine on Mount Sinai, and there discovered the Syriac manuscript of the Gospels, since known as the Sinai palimpsest. They also gave a site for Westminster College, and laid its foundation stone on 25 May 1897. They lived for many years at Castlebrae, built by Mrs Lewis and her husband in 1890.

[2] Frederick John Foakes-Jackson (1855–1941), B.A. (Trinity) 1879, and Lightfoot Scholar 1880; Fellow of Jesus College 1886–1941. A distinguished ecclesiastical historian, and an outstanding teacher whose 'chief literary output belongs to his later years when, relieved of the burden of Cambridge teaching and removed from the allurement of Cambridge society, he published a number of books in rapid succession... For many years he was one of the best-known and best-loved figures in Cambridge.' (*D.N.B.* 1941–50. P. Gardner Smith). Foakes-Jackson served on the Non-Collegiate Students Board for six years (1904–09); but

My idea is that our Library should be essentially one of reference and contain books to which students must have recourse though beyond the means of the ordinary student. It would be well to range these under heads e.g. Classical, Theological, Scientific and Historical – I don't know how many Law men you have, or books for that matter.

Perhaps re-arranging the books under heads would be a good preliminary step.

Then I think there is a good deal of really unnecessary rubbish which might be got rid of – even if it realised very little at a sale the library would be well rid of it and have a small sum in hand.

I suppose we should have to pay the librarian for extra work as his £15 is really a means of remunerating him as club secretary.[1] For an extra £5 he ought to do a good deal.

The sort of Theological additions I should suggest are the Commentaries published by Macmillan on the N.T., by Lightfoot, Westcott, Swete, Robinson &c. &c., and Hastings' *Dictionary of the Bible*.

Money is a consideration; but this will perhaps come and I take it we must consider what we could do if we got it to make the Library really useful.

Dr Foakes-Jackson was concerned principally with theological books; and so was the library; but another Board member, Mr J. H. Flather,[2] writes about the Classics:

I did something this morning [14 February], and will do more if you wish. I kept fairly good and well bound texts and editions even of rather out of way authors, and I respected the name F. A. Paley inside a book – with one or two trifling exceptions. If more were done, it would [be] going against the above mentioned principles. I forgot to look inside the Journal of Philology to see whether it was a present. If not, I think we should lose little of interest to the men if we parted with it, but it is not very saleable.

It may be worth while to weed out some of the Paley books, such as Bohn's translations, which Paley himself might not have wished to preserve.

Possibly some of Paley's books containing his *ms* notes the University Library might like to have, and Mrs Lewis might be consulted on this point ... .

his interest in student affairs was not confined to his formal membership of the Board. He audited the accounts of the Amalgamated Clubs, and was a most welcome coach of the Boat.

1 From the Easter term 1891, when this practice began under Censor Huddleston, until Reddaway's retirement in 1924, when it ceased, 23 Librarians out of a total of 35 were, or had been, General Secretaries of the Clubs.

2 James Henry Flather (1853–1928), B.A. of Emmanuel (fourteenth Classic) in 1876; Lightfoot Scholar 1877; Tutor (1878), and Master (1888) of Cavendish College until its closure in 1892. He was a member of the Non-Collegiate Students Board from 1894–96, 1900–02, and 1907–12.

Reddaway did what he could. We do not know whether he had the needs of the library particularly in mind, but on his election he moved the Censor's office from the first floor to the room immediately above it on the north side of the main staircase, and at his own expense furnished his previous office as a writing room for the men, as a memento, says the first number of the *Fitzwilliam Magazine*, of his eleven years' association with the Hall as Historical Lecturer.

By May 1908 the library had been divided into three sections: works of reference had gone to the new writing room; a number of books of everyday interest, mainly given or lent by residents, had been put in the undergraduate reading room over the dining hall, the rest being left in what came to be called 'the Library proper'.

The creation of a separately accessible reference library seems to have been much appreciated, from frequent allusions to its use in the Librarians' terminal reports; and one Librarian (A. E. Hill) in the Lent term of 1909 makes particular mention of the gift by Mr Walter Durnford, Chairman of the Board from 1901 to 1904 and later Provost of King's, of eight volumes of *The Cambridge Modern History*, an addition to the reference library which much enhanced its usefulness; but as Mr Hill also reports that only four volumes had been borrowed from the 'library proper' in the Lent term of 1909, it appears that the lending section of the library was still doing very little to supply undergraduate needs.

When, in December 1910, the Non-Collegiate Students Board, in answer to representations from the members of the Theological Society, agreed that daily services, then held in the Brassie Chapel in King's College, might temporarily at least be held in the library, they do not seem to have caused the library great inconvenience, but its arrangements were thoroughly upset by a further decision of the Board in the Lent term 1913 that the room should be given over entirely to the purposes of the chapel. At the end of that term the books were moved to the writing room, where space was limited, control more difficult, and shelving such that the catalogue was no longer serviceable. The Librarian for the following Michaelmas term (H. E. Martin) saw no reason to mince matters: the library was used principally by freshmen reading for the Previous Examination; theological students derived some benefit from it; for scientists and mathematicians it was useless. Its shelves were tottering, and supervision was impossible; another room was needed, in which non-reference books should be kept behind wire-netting doors, of which the Librarian should hold the key.

It is unlikely, however, that when the Board decided that their library should become a chapel they intended to leave it without a home, or even to relegate it all to the writing room; and it may very well be that when the change was mooted the Censor, at least, had reason to hope that alternative accommodation would soon become available in 30 Trumpington Street, which he leased from Mr George Peck for ten years in 1914. So it was that the New Library, as Redda-way himself called it, was put into a first floor room immediately over Mr Peck's corner shop, with access through a doorway built for the purpose, at Reddaway's expense, in the room then known as the read-ing room, and later as the Junior Common Room, above the dining hall.

It is hardly surprising that there should be little to tell about the library during the war years, but, like the chapel, it supplies evidence of Reddaway's determination to keep things going in every possible respect. In December 1916 – of all times, it might seem – the library is reported as being completely overhauled, and a section has been set aside for books bought from surpluses in the Gibson Prize Fund, which the Board had ruled some years previously might be used to acquire works connected with the study of the New Testament in Greek. In June 1918 the inclusion, in a list of awards, of the appointment as Librarian of a man who had recently been placed in the first class in the Oriental Languages Tripos[1] is in accordance with Reddaway's depar-ture, in three of the four war years, from his usual practice of selecting his Librarians from among the General Secretaries of the Clubs; it still suggests, however, that he regarded these appointments as a means of providing a measure of financial assistance to deserving students in return for the performance of not very exacting duties. This was also the occasion of a recourse to the Gibson Fund for a purpose a little removed, it might seem, from its object, for the balance of the fund was used to pay the Librarian's stipend for the year 1918/19, an expedient which reflects the precarious nature of the library's exis-tence during its first fifty years, for in spite of all attempts to make pro-vision for it the library was poorly housed, and with no regular income its usefulness was very severely limited.

The immediate post-war years were discouraging for the library. In November 1920, when the Censor reported that the men were trying to improve it, the Board resolved that 'all suitable facilities should be given'; but this amounted to very little; and in the years between the wars their only action in library matters was to sanction in 1922 the purchase of three additional volumes of *The Encyclopaedia Britannica*

[1] V. G. Bhat.

from a balance in the Gibson Prize Fund; to agree, on one occasion, to the appointment of a student Librarian at a stipend of £15[1]; and to decide not to pursue further a suggestion that non-collegiate students might be permitted to use the library of the University Board of Extra-Mural Studies. The Censor's Reports for the period do not refer to the library, save that for reasons that are not now apparent the appointment is mentioned of student Librarians for three years from 1930 to 1933.[2] In the *Fitzwilliam Magazine* there are recurring appeals to men going down for books they no longer need, and acknowledgements to the few who gave them. In December 1925 we are told that 'after a somewhat lengthy period of inactivity' the library is being re-organized 'on a constitutional basis', whatever that may mean, but during one term of the year 1926/27 there were fewer than a dozen borrowers; although there is here a first allusion to what in the course of time became a considerable collection of scientific books, published by Butterworth's, and given to the library through the good offices of Mr J. W. Whitlock, who had taken his degree from Fitzwilliam Hall in 1923, having, unusually, been allowed an *aegrotat* on each of his Tripos examinations.

In 1928 a change of policy is implied by the Censor, in his customary letter to the *Magazine*. 'The Reading Room, formerly the Library', he writes, 'will be in commission at the beginning of the Lent term (1929), and one hopes that it will serve a more useful purpose under the new and somewhat changed conditions.' This statement is elucidated a little by an announcemeent elsewhere in the same issue of the *Magazine* to the effect that the library is to become the reading room, it being recognized, apparently, that the creation of an undergraduates' working library was beyond the resources of Fitzwilliam House, that it was no longer so pressing a need in view of the increasing facilities in University, faculty, and departmental libraries; and that it would therefore be better to regard the library, except for its existing books and some works of reference, as a room in which the men could read and write between lectures, and meet from time to time on their various social occasions.

In the year 1933/34 an undergraduate Librarian (N. J. G. Pounds, who later became a Tutor in the House) was able to report 'continual gifts of books' from the Rev. F. A. Kirkpatrick, of Trinity College,

---

[1] In January 1924, on hearing from the General Secretary that the Board were unable 'to continue their usual payment for a librarian', a General Meeting of the Amalgamated Clubs appointed a committee of six volunteers to do the work.
[2] L. W. Day, F. J. Stratton, E. R. Reynolds.

which an editor of the *Magazine*, who had been Pounds's predecessor as undergraduate Librarian, found particularly acceptable because they supplemented an unusually inadequate literature section of the library. In spite of the change in library policy in the late 1920s, attempts were still made to obtain books, and to reduce to some kind of order those that were there, but it was virtually impossible to effect any substantial improvement in the almost complete absence of funds. After the Second World War, in a period of general reconstruction, the Non-Collegiate Students Board again authorized the appointment of an undergraduate Librarian, this time at an annual stipend of £21, whose duty it would be to issue books and ensure their return; but this was nothing more than a renewal of former practice, with some allowance for a fall in the value of money. There does, however, seem to have been a disposition to do all that could be done within the limits of such resources as were available. In 1948, when pressure of numbers made it necessary to turn the hostel into an administrative block, space was found there for a reading room and library (to be exchanged in 1952 for a ground floor room in no. 19 Fitzwilliam Street), in addition to the reading room over the chemist's shop; and in the same year, from the Censor's statement in his Annual Report to the Board that the under-graduate Librarian would be 'under Mr Pounds', it appears that the library had come to be regarded as sufficiently important to be placed in the care of a senior Librarian, and that Mr Pounds was the first holder of the post, although there is no record of his formal appoint-ment to it. He was not to remain for long, as he left to take up an Assis-tant Professorship in the University of Indiana in 1950, when Mr Anthony Hyde, of Fitzwilliam House, successor to Mr Pounds as Director of Studies in Geography, also assumed his Librarian's duties. The year 1947/48 was to prove something of a turning point, for although in June the Board's formal consent to an expenditure of £2.10.0 on books can have held out little promise of better things, even when it was preceded by their agreement to pay a sum of £10.17.3 for books bought by Mr Pounds for the reading room, a month later they resolved that the book grant should be on an annual basis. The amount was fixed at no more than £50, but it was doubled in 1952/53, and with the undergraduate Librarian's stipend of £21 brought the library's total annual subvention to the sum of £121.

The knowledge that the library could reckon on a regular income, modest though it might be, was not without immediate effect. An Accessions Book, begun by Mr Pounds in 1948 and continued by his successor, shews that between 1948 and 1963, over a period of not quite fifteen academical years, accessions were at an average annual rate of about 170, of which nearly half were gifts from senior members of the House and undergraduates. The figure would have been higher but for an unwillingness to acquire more books during the last two years of the period, when a move to the new site was imminent. Purchases on a quite different scale were made when the task was begun of building a new library in its new home. Borrowings over the period, recorded in an Entry Book, ranged from 210 in 1948/49 to 950 three years later, with an annual average of 720. A Shelf List, probably compiled in 1962, contains some 2,250 titles.[1]

There appears to have been no proposal to change the annual subvention to the library until the Council of the Senate asked for estimates of income and expenditure for the quinquennium 1962/67. The Board had reason to expect the completion of Stage I of their new buildings, including the library, early in 1963, and when they sent their estimates to the Registrary in September 1960[2] they informed the Council that, apart from the need to obtain a capital sum for initial purchases – their existing library was not only small, but in many respects out of date – provision would need to be made for the stipend of a senior part-time Librarian, for clerical assistance, and for the routine purchase of books. They therefore applied for a recurrent grant for all purposes of £1,500, with effect from the financial year 1962/63; and in the Lent term of 1962 they sought further help from the Council under arrangements then recently announced, by which, in order to relieve mounting pressure on the University Library, it was proposed to establish a College Libraries Fund from which annual grants might be made to colleges, equal in any year to one half of their library expenditure in the previous year, subject to a maximum of thirty shillings in respect of each of their undergraduates.[3] The Board asked that Fitzwilliam House should be permitted to come into this scheme, and should receive assistance at the maximum rate in 1961/62, even though such assistance would exceed the half of its expenditure in the previous year. The Council were unable, then, to approve a grant of more than £50 from the Fund, but they asked the Board to include in their annual estimates such a sum as they might judge necessary for the building up of their library stocks, on the assumption that they would receive no assistance from the College Libraries Fund until such time as Fitzwilliam House

---

1   College Archives.
2   Board papers for meeting held on 11 October 1960.
3   Report, dated 15 May 1961, of the Council of the Senate on the financial position of the Chest. (*University Reporter*, 1960–61, p. 1701).

might become an independent college. On this basis the Council agreed to recommend, with effect from the financial year 1962/63, the inclusion in the Board's annual grant from the University Chest of a sum of £2,000 for the Fitzwilliam House Library,[1] which continued until the end of the financial year 1965/66, when the House, having acquired its independence, was forthwith admitted to the scheme on the most favourable terms, even though it had not, as a college, incurred any previous expenditure to which assistance from the fund would normally have been related – a gesture by the central authorities of the University entirely in keeping with their constant readiness to help Fitzwilliam House in every possible way, during its last years as a non-collegiate institution.

The importance attached to the library, with the realization that it would soon be possible to house it more worthily, became immediately apparent in the schedule of requirements presented to the architect of the new buildings. He was asked to provide for a hundred readers' places, with space for ten thousand volumes, and to allow room for expansion.[2] The floor area allowed (2,700 square feet) was larger than for any other room, including the dining hall. The Fellows of the House, at their first meeting, appointed one of their number (A. G. Hunt)[3] to be Librarian; and under his guidance and that of his successors the library, as a repository of books and a place of study, quickly became a prominent feature in the academic life of the House and College. A number of gifts bore witness to the importance attached to it by other people. The buildings had barely been occupied when Mr J. M. Morris, Assistant Under-Librarian in the University Library, presented some 450 volumes, mainly in the field of English Literature. Early in 1964 Emmanuel College gave the *Dictionary of National Biography*, part of a bequest by a former Fellow, and passed on to Fitzwilliam House, which had no copy. At the same time, there came the first of two benefactions from the residue of the estate of Mr Francis Collingwood, placed at the disposal, for charitable purposes, of Mr J. G. Buckler of Swadlincote, father of a resident undergraduate, who remarked on the number of unoccupied shelves, and offered a sum of £1,000 to help to fill them. In the end this gift came to more than £1,500, including the

[1]   Minutes 238 of Board meeting held on 27 April 1962.
[2]   The Statement of Needs on which the building programme was based is not precise. There was to be an allowance for expansion at 'an annual rate of two hundred (volumes)', but no mention of its duration. By 1970 the library contained some fifteen thousand volumes, and the need for more space was already making itself felt.
[3]   On 1 October 1968 Mr Hunt, who had become Tutor for Admissions on 24 June, was succeeded as Librarian by Mr D. M. Thompson.

cost of such binding as was needed. A few years later, and from the same source, Mr Buckler agreed to meet the cost of a set of *Official Law Reports* (£1,200), which the College, as it had then become, could not have acquired from its own resources. In 1964, through the good offices of Mr Thomas Swan, of Emmanuel College, the library received about £350, principally from the Frank Parkinson Trust, for books connected with the study of Agriculture. In 1967, and again in 1968, the Court of the Leathersellers' Company, among the earliest benefactors of the Non-Collegiate Institution, placed the College still further in their debt with two gifts, each of £500, for books.

These benefactions were accompanied by others, no less welcome, from individual donors – from friends of the College not previously associated with it, from men in residence, or old members of Fitzwilliam Hall or House.

In May 1973 the Council of the Senate published a Report made to them at their request by a General Board Committee on Libraries 'on the operation of the College Libraries Fund',[1] and although this Report was published after the end of the period with which this narrative is concerned, it refers to matters within that period and contains a quantity of information about the libraries of the colleges, supplied by their Librarians, which is not otherwise easily available. The total number of books in the Fitzwilliam Library (14,500) was, with one exception, the lowest of all. It could hardly be otherwise, for there had been in Fitzwilliam no opportunity for the accumulation of books which had come over the years to constitute a large proportion of the holdings of older and wealthier colleges; but a comparison of the numbers of books used primarily in connexion with current undergraduate courses presents a different picture, for the Fitzwilliam total (13,550) could stand comparison with a number of others, and in scientific subjects was better than most. In a library which was building up initial stocks it was to be expected that annual expenditure would be relatively high, but, even so, it is noteworthy that the Fitzwilliam figure was exceeded by two, only, of the colleges, and that this expenditure was maintained when the University's special grant had come to an end. The number of seats for readers (104) was higher than any, but this is less remarkable in a college which did not permit books to be borrowed, except in vacations – a policy adopted from the beginning in deference to the wishes of the men themselves, who declared their preference for a system under which they might expect to find books on the shelves, and not merely find where they would have been if they had not been taken

[1] *University Reporter*, 1972–73, p. 852.

out. Although this arrangement proved lamentably less effective than had been anticipated, owing to persistent thefts on a considerable scale, it seemed, for some years at least, still to find favour with the undergraduates.

The removal of books from the shelves, deplorable though it has been, was not a problem peculiar to a single college; and the new Fitzwilliam Library emerged with no little credit from this review, by an independent body, of the resources of the Cambridge College Libraries, and of their services to undergraduates.

CHAPTER XII

Research Students

(a) Collaboration with the Universities of the Empire and foreign Universities (1919) – establishment of the degree of Doctor of Philosophy (1920) – of Master of Letters and Master of Science (1921). Large non-collegiate entry in early years – effects of foundation of new institutions – research student numbers.

(b) The first non-collegiate Doctor of Philosophy – his origins, course of research and subsequent career.

(a)

On 8 December 1917 the Senate of the University appointed a Syndicate 'to consider the means of promoting educational collaboration with the Universities of the Empire and foreign Universities'. In an interim Report, dated 8 June 1918, the Syndicate noted the widespread practice in the universities of Canada and the United States of America whereby their young graduates undertook further study partly in their own universities and partly in others, and that whereas before the war (1914–1918) the majority had gone to German universities, they now very largely wished to come to the universities of Great Britain. The Syndicate were of opinion that these students should be welcomed; they also thought that their work should receive suitable recognition, and, as they were informed that a doctor's degree had become an almost indispensable qualification for appointment to a higher teaching post in North America, they announced their intention of recommending the establishment in Cambridge of a doctor's degree, usually to be obtained after three years of supervised research. They considered it very desirable to prevent confusion between such a degree and long-standing doctorates of the University, and would propose that its holders should receive the title of Doctor of Philosophy. On 22 November 1918 the Syndicate, in a second Report, formally recommended the establishment of the Ph.D. degree, passed by the Senate on 22 February 1919 by 84 votes to 26, and the necessary alterations of University Statutes were approved by the King in Council on 11 March 1920. At the same time a Board of Research Studies was constituted, with the duty of exercising general supervision over research students, over their registration, their courses of study, and their approval for degrees. The Board quickly found that an appreciable number of applicants whom they would prefer not to reject would be unlikely to qualify for the new research degree, and on 30 September 1920 they recommended that the Council of the Senate should take necessary steps to secure a further amendment of statute for the award of the degrees, more easily obtained, of Master of Letters and Master of Science. This recommendation also was contested in the Senate, but was passed by 61 votes to 18, on November 1920, and a consequential alteration of statute was approved by the King in Council on 31 October 1921.

Most of the available information about members of the University working for a research degree is to be found in the Annual Reports of the Board of Research Studies.[1] So far as concerns non-collegiate students, some particulars are also given in the Reports of their Board, and, from the Easter term 1966, in statistical tables prepared in Fitzwilliam College. Figures obtained from these various sources rarely correspond exactly – frequently, for example, they refer to different terms in a given academical year – and alterations made in the course of time by the Board of Research Studies in the presentation of its own material hinder a ready comparison of one year with another;[2] but from these different sources a fair idea may be formed of the contribution made by the non-collegiate institution, and latterly by Fitzwilliam College, in admitting and looking after students, nearly always graduates, who have come to the University, or remained there, in pursuit of a further qualification.

The Non-Collegiate Students Board and particularly W. S. Thatcher, when he was their Censor, regarded their responsibility for research students with some uncertainty. They raised no serious problems for Reddaway, because they did not come to the University, under the new arrangements, until 1920, and Reddaway had, in effect, retired by Sep-

---

[1] Renamed 'The Board of Graduate Studies' by a statute approved by the Queen in Council on 31 January 1966.

After this note was written there came to the author's attention three articles under the heading 'The University and Research' contributed to the *Cambridge Review* (1954/55, pp. 451, 482, and 500) by the late Mr W. J. Sartain, then Assistant Secretary General of the Faculties, and then also lately Secretary to the Board of Research Studies. Mr Sartain was mainly concerned with the course of events leading up to the establishment of the degree of Doctor of Philosophy in 1920, and the degrees of Master of Science and Master of Letters in 1921, and makes, of course, no special reference to non-collegiate students, but his account is of great interest, and, not surprisingly, is admirably done.

[2] In their Annual Reports from 1921 to 1933 the Board of Research Studies shewed the total numbers of research students in the University, together with individual totals for each college. In 1933 they also included figures for the University, but not for the colleges, of students who were actually in residence, the latter usually being about two-thirds of the former. After the Second World War, they gave University and college totals under each heading until 1959, when the individual college totals of those on the Register were omitted.

tember 1923, before their numbers had become considerable. When, on 10 February 1921, the Board of Research Studies first reported on the admission of the students there were 72 on their Register. The colleges, on the whole, were being cautious, for of this total nearly half had been taken by Caius College and Fitzwilliam Hall, with 12 each, and Christ's and Emmanuel, with 9. In February 1922, out of 141 Fitzwilliam, Emmanuel, Caius, and Christ's had, respectively, 27, 21, 20, and 18; and a year later, when there were 179, Fitzwilliam was third with 27. In Thatcher's first year as Censor (1924/25) the total was 248, with Trinity (46) at the head of the list, and Fitzwilliam sixth with 16. Although the scheme had come about as a means of helping to meet the needs of young graduates from the universities of the Empire and from foreign universities (and also to ensure that the University of Cambridge should attract its share of them), there was from the beginning a substantial proportion of Cambridge graduates – 14 out of 72 in the first year, rising to 80 out of 248 in 1924/25; a proportion maintained for some years, until in the fifties it had grown to nearly half.[1] In 1922 the Board of Research Studies also drew attention to the relatively small numbers of students from Canada (11) and the United States of America (14) supposing that these numbers would increase when the new degree was better known; and mentioned the large number (24) from India in that year, very nearly equal to the combined totals of the universities of North America.

Thatcher observed these developments with mixed feelings. On the one hand, growing research student numbers meant increased revenues, as the colleges were to discover when they could bring themselves to accept more of them; on the other, research students as a group played no great part in the social or athletic life of a college, and their membership of Fitzwilliam House was unlikely to help to set it on the way to the collegiate status that Thatcher most of all desired; and there was another difficulty, to which he frequently called his Board's attention. As time passed the colleges became less unwilling to accept research students as a class, but they were for some years reluctant to admit any but the very best of those of Oriental origin. Some prejudice there may have been, but this was not the whole story, for little was known about the academic standards of some of these far-away places, or of their staffs. When Thatcher was acting for Reddaway in the year before his appointment as Censor, Fitzwilliam's total of 19 research students included half the number of the Indian research students in

---

[1] Of the research students admitted to the Register in the calendar year 1957, for example, 40.8% were from Cambridge, and 22.1% from other universities in the United Kingdom.

the University, and this he felt to be undesirable. It would, he thought, do no good to his institution if its student body came to consist so largely of men who could not find a place elsewhere, and, furthermore, the advantages of resident membership of the University for any single group would be much diminished if its members were congregated in one place. And so, as we have seen, he did not hesitate to urge his Board to impose a limit on the proportion of students of Oriental origin. The Board did not openly demur; and when Thatcher, armed with his quota, declined to admit an Oriental student *extra numerum*, there was trouble with the University authorities, who were unwilling to accept a situation in which their admission of a man to the status of research student might in effect be nullified by the refusal of every college, and of their own non-collegiate organization, to take him. That-cher's difference of opinion on the issue with the Secretary of the Board of Research Studies (R. E. Priestley, of Clare) remained friendly because they were both reasonable men, but herein lay the origin of the contention, first formally expressed by Mr Cameron's Syndicate in 1935, and not thereafter contested by the Non-Collegiate Students Board, that, except on grounds of moral unsuitability, no man accepted as a research student by the Board of Research Studies should be refused admission by Fitzwilliam House if he could not get into a college.[1]

Such were the circumstances which influenced, or even determined, the nature of the Fitzwilliam intake of men who came to the University to read for a research degree. In Reddaway's last years Fitzwilliam Hall was twice at the head of the college lists. Under Thatcher, for ten years or so, numbers remained stationary in spite of an increase in the University total from 248 in 1924 to 312 in 1933. The Cameron Syndicate reported in May 1935, and in the following Michaelmas term the Fitzwilliam total rose spectacularly; and for some thirty years thereafter, the war years excepted, Fitzwilliam was never lower than fourth among the college totals (of men on the Register, or in residence, as the case may be)[2] until in the middle sixties there came a change, principally due to the creation of new foundations, most of them set up for the reception of Fellows and graduate students, but not of undergraduates.

---

[1] By 1960, at least, experience had shewn that many of these students, especially those from the far East, were unjustifiably optimistic about finance; and it was agreed that the Censor might refuse admission to an otherwise acceptable applicant who could not supply evidence that he had adequate funds at his disposal. From time to time the amount was adjusted to keep pace with rising costs.

[2] For such provision as it was possible to make for the corporate social activities of Fitzwilliam research and graduate students, see pp. 396–8.

Of the new colleges, Churchill (1960), Darwin (1964), and University (1965) made the greatest impact on the research student entry. In the Michaelmas term 1967 they had, between them, 225 research students in residence, out of a University total of 1,578; and in that year the Fitzwilliam figure, which in 1962 had passed the hundred mark, declined to 57, and its place in the college order, third in 1962, fell to thirteenth. In 1965 the Censor and Fellows of Fitzwilliam House, then on the threshold of collegiate status, had assured the Council of the Senate that Fitzwilliam as an independent foundation would accept research students, for so long as there should be a need, as they had been accepted during the previous thirty years; but, as the Council said in their Report of 1 November 1965 on the status of Fitzwilliam House, the creation of new societies for graduates, and the willingness of the existing colleges to admit them in greater numbers, had transformed the position; and in 1965 it seemed that only very rarely would the University need to invoke the convention that an applicant who had been granted research student status should *faute de mieux* go to Fitzwilliam College.

By the Michaelmas term of 1968 – the last of the College's first hundred years – the Fitzwilliam total of research students had fallen to 53 (the decline continued until 1971, when the figure was 46, and the College's place in the list was equal twenty-first with Downing College), and its research student body, for years artificially enlarged by pressure of applications and the limits which the colleges had felt it necessary to impose on their admissions, was coming to consist, as elsewhere, of graduates of other Universities who wished to join the College in preference to any other, and of those of its own men whose undergraduate careers had given reason to suppose that they would be successful in the prosecution of research. There is no necessary relation between the number of research students in a college and the number of its matriculations, for any college, in any year, may think it desirable to have more, or fewer, students of a particular class; but at this time (1965–68), with one or two notable exceptions, there appears to be a broad correlation between the size of a college and its number of research students, and to this general pattern Fitzwilliam College was a marked exception, for whereas from 1966 to 1968 it had ranked second or third in the University in its number of matriculations, in the last of those years its number of research students stood seventeenth.[1] The reason is not far to seek; and the situation of the College was due, not

---

[1] Other exceptions, but in the opposite sense, were King's, Clare, and Corpus Christi, all with a relatively large number of research students. In each of the years 1966 and 1967

to any decision of policy by its Governing Body, but to circumstances beyond its control. As a recently autonomous institution, at the beginning of its life as a college of the University, it was in competition with established colleges, of high repute and ampler means. As time passes, the College will need to discover ways, as other colleges have done, of attracting more of the scholars and exhibitioners from whose ranks future research students may be drawn; and so become increasingly attractive as a centre of study for graduates of other universities.

Between the academical years 1920/21 and 1968/69, 477 Fitzwilliam research students were approved for the Ph.D. degree, 31 for the degree of Master of Letters, and 42 for the degree of Master of Science; and a more diligent chronicler may one day compile some record of their subsequent distinctions. It is a matter of great satisfaction that such a list would include the names of Dr Albert Szent-Györgyi and the late Sir Ernst Chain, Nobel Prizemen, respectively, in 1937 (Medicine) and 1945 (Physiology and Medicine). Both became Honorary Fellows of the College.

(b)

On 17 May 1921 Dr Peter Giles, Master of Emmanuel College and Vice-Chancellor, signed on behalf of the Board of Research Studies a notice declaring that Charles George Lewis Wolf, research student of Christ's College, had been approved for the degree of Doctor of Philosophy.[1] He was the first, and was made Doctor Designate in Philosophy at a congregation of the Senate held on 4 June.

On 16 June a similar notice was promulgated in favour of James Chadwick and Llewelyn Woosnam, research students of Gonville and Caius College, and Julius Herman, non-collegiate research student.[2] Chadwick and Herman (but not Woosnam, who waited until the next academical year) became Doctors Designate in Philosophy on 21 June; and, this being the day appointed for the purpose, all three (Chadwick, Herman, and Wolf) were thereupon created Doctors of Philosophy, their names being published in a list of Masters and Doctors who had been admitted to titles of degrees during the academical year 1920/21. Wolf, of Christ's, has by association appeared briefly in this Fitzwilliam story, and passes out of it. So does James Chadwick, but Julius

Corpus, in particular, in its number of research students was seventh among the colleges, and twenty-first in its matriculations, and in the following year ninth and twenty-second.
[1] *University Reporter*, 1920–21, p. 1099.
[2] *Ibid.*, p. 1199.

Herman found himself in good company, for Chadwick was to become Fellow of the Royal Society in 1927, Nobel Prizeman (Physics) in 1935, and, as Sir James Chadwick, Master of his College for ten years from 1948.

Herman matriculated at Fitzwilliam Hall in the Michaelmas term 1919, as Master of Arts of the University of South Africa, from Rhodes University College; and, suitably enough, took lodgings in Cambridge at 11 Kimberley Road. Having been admitted to the Register of Research Students in November, with a subject in the general field of English Drama, and with Sir Arthur Quiller-Couch as his supervisor (more good company), Herman set about submitting an application, on the basis of a book published in South Africa in 1918 under the pseudonym 'H. Skimpole', on the life and theatre of George Bernard Shaw, for permission to submit his Ph.D. thesis at the end of two years of residence instead of the three years prescribed. That the success of his application owed a good deal to advice given by his supervisor is apparent from a letter to Sir Geoffrey Butler[1] in Sir Arthur's beautiful hand – in sad contrast to Herman's own – in which he contrives not only to speak well of the book, but also to hold out hopes of a thesis which, he believes, will be even better. Of the book he says that while 'it will not compare with the thesis for knowledge, or arrangement, or mere power of writing, it is built on plenty of reading, and deals in genuine comparative criticism, not in gush'; and concludes by stating his opinion that the thesis was going to be 'a somewhat remarkable performance'; and that its author really had laid its foundations in his earlier work. In the light of this advice, it is not surprising that the Special Board for Modern and Medieval Languages ruled that Herman's work in South Africa was of sufficient calibre to exempt him from one year's residence in Cambridge. At the same time they approved as the subject of his research 'The Development of English Drama since T. Robertson down to the present day'.

From references in the *Fitzwilliam Magazine*, Herman's participation in undergraduate activities appears to have been limited to public speaking (both in domestic debates, and at the Union Society); to acting in the first production of the Fitzwilliam Hall Amateur Dramatic Society; and to writing for the *Magazine* itself. Early in his first term he is described as supporting, sincerely but with small success, a motion in favour of total prohibition; and in the following term he proposed, at some length it seems, and lost heavily, a motion 'That, in the opinion of this House, Parliamentary Government is cumbrous, unrepresenta-

[1] Secretary of the Board of Research studies.

tive, and undemocratic'. At the Union Society, he was said to be 'usually too aloof from our little world to become a popular speaker, though his contributions were always clever, eloquent, and full of sound good sense'. For the *Magazine*, his pieces, usually on literary topics, bore his earlier pen-name. Just what were the attributes of Mr Harold Skimpole that caught his fancy we are not now ever likely to know. Also in the *Magazine* there are occasional light-hearted allusions to 'J. H.', but it cannot be certain that Herman was their target, and the impression they may convey of his personality is best left to the judgement of any who may read them.

On 18 June 1921, Herman writes to the Censor: 'I have been fortunate enough to obtain my Doctorate. I shall be eternally grateful to Fitzwilliam Hall and its Censor for kindness and consideration shown towards me during my stay in Cambridge.' And in a prudent postscript he asks whether it would be possible for Reddaway to let him have a 'letter of recommendation (or otherwise), as it might prove useful in the future'. It appears that Reddaway found little difficulty in composing a 'useful' letter; for in the *Magazine* of November 1921 he quotes Herman as saying that he has 'the pleasant duty of preparing senior schoolboys for their examinations in English and History' at Graaff Reinet in Cape Province – work of no great distinction, it might seem, for a Master of Arts of the University of South Africa, also the holder of a Cambridge research degree.

CHAPTER XIII

Fitzwilliam College – the First Years

Not unsuitably, the first recorded resolution of the new Governing Body was that Friday, 9 September should be minuted as the date of the foundation of the College, being the day on which the Royal Charter had passed under the Great Seal. They also noted that the statutes had come into effect on the following day. Next, they directed that a letter should be written to former members of the Non-Collegiate Students Board, expressing their appreciation of all that the Board had done for them, especially of recent years. Thirty-five such letters were sent.

With an eye to the immediate future, the Governing Body decided that the foundation of the College should be commemorated at a New Year Dinner to be held on 11 January, 1967. When the time came, the editor of the *Fitzwilliam Journal* was generous in his allocation of space, for, in addition to printing in full the speech of the Vice-Chancellor (Mr A. Ll. Armitage, President of Queens' College, who as Deputy for earlier Vice-Chancellors had done so much for the non-collegiate institution in its last years) and the Master's reply, he had also compiled an impressive list of the friends of the College who had found time to join in its celebration.

> Among the 144 who attended [says the *Journal*] there were, in addition to the Master, Fellows and Scholars of the College and two representatives from the sister College in Oxford (St Edmund Hall), the Vice-Chancellor of the University (Mr A. Ll. Armitage, President of Queens'), the Mayor of Cambridge, Sir Maurice Bridgeman and Professor Ernst Chain, the Heads of nearly all the Colleges, the Chairman of the University Grants Committee, the Lord Bishop of Ely, the Clerk to the Privy Council, the Masters of the Clothworkers' and Leathersellers' Companies and their Clerks, the Architect (Mr Denys Lasdun), members of the Council of the Senate and of the Fitzwilliam House Building Committee, the principal University Officers, members of the Non-Collegiate Students Board as it was last constituted, the President, Secretary and no fewer than fourteen ex-Presidents of the Fitzwilliam Society, and Mrs Winifred Armstrong, the previous owner of the site on which the new buildings of the College now stand.

The absence of two other friends of the College, who had both accepted invitations, was a source of particular regret. Lord Tedder, Chancellor of the University and the College's Visitor, was obliged to withdraw at the last moment on account of illness; and Mr Thatcher, for whom the evening would have been an occasion of especial rejoicing, had died on 12 December.

The guest list itself tells something of College history. The high place assigned to the two representatives from St Edmund Hall reflects a lively satisfaction at the establishment of a friendly relationship between the two colleges, first proposed by the Principal of St Edmund Hall, and, with independence round the corner, accepted with alacrity by the Fellows of Fitzwilliam House in January 1966, against the time when the College should receive its Royal Charter. It seemed especially fitting that the sister College in Oxford should share in commemorating the recognition of Fitzwilliam as a college of the University.[1]

The Master, in his reply to the Vice-Chancellor's toast, took advantage of the occasion to announce the election of three Honorary Fellows: Sir Maurice Bridgeman, of Trinity College, with Professor Ernst Chain and Dr Albert Szent-Györgyi, of Fitzwilliam House in earlier days. Without the advice and active assistance of Sir Maurice in sponsoring the University's appeal in 1962, Fitzwilliam House could not have met the requirement that independence must be conditional upon a fair prospect of financial stability. The high distinction of Professor Chain and Dr Szent-Györgyi had long been acknowledged, and the College, honouring itself in acclaiming it at this first opportunity, was greatly complimented by the presence of Sir Maurice and Professor Chain, while regretting, but understanding, that Dr Szent-Györgyi found the distance from Massachusetts too formidable an obstacle.

There was an especial significance, too, in the presence of the Masters of the two City Companies and their Clerks. The Clothworkers' awards were approaching the centenary of their foundation. The Leathersellers' Exhibitions, begun in 1894, had ceased in 1911, but contacts with the College had been most happily, and generously, renewed in the year of its independence; and the Companies' officers were most warmly welcomed when, on this first occasion, the College found itself in a position to offer them hospitality.[2]

Armorial bearings: A resolution of the Governing Body, also at their first meeting, that authority should be sought 'for the use of the pre-

---

[1] Owing to the illness of the Principal (Dr J. N. D. Kelly), St Edmund Hall was represented by the Vice-Principal (Mr Richard Fargher) and Mr J. C. B. Gosling.

[2] For further notes on the history of the awards made by the two Companies, see pp. 532–48.

sent coat of arms' may appear to call for some explanation, for the device had been used for eighty years. There is, indeed, something of a story to tell.

At the beginning of the Michaelmas term of 1947 the Censor had received a letter, dated 21 October, from Chester Herald, of the College of Arms, to the effect that no record could be found of arms attributed to Fitzwilliam House. Mr Thatcher's information that the arms were a composite device incorporating the arms of the University with those of the Fitzwilliam family (with the consent of its reigning head) did nothing to reassure Chester Herald, because, as he said, private individuals and corporate bodies had no power to transfer their arms to others, and the issue of Letters Patent would be needed to put the matter on a proper footing.[1] There followed particulars of the not inconsiderable charges that would be incurred. At this point Mr Thatcher wisely passed the papers to the University Registrary, and on the advice of Professor H. A. Hollond, to whom the Council of the Senate frequently had recourse in case of need, Chester Herald was informed that Fitzwilliam House was not a corporation of any kind, but an association of non-collegiate students calling itself by that name. The Council did not know whether a grant of arms could be made to an 'unincorporated fluctuating body of persons', but they were not aware of any rule of law exposing to legal proceedings a body of students or other persons using a device on their notepaper or otherwise, and were in any event not disposed to recommend to the University that application for a grant of arms should be made. There followed one further exchange of letters, a rather peevish exchange, from which it was clear that the College of Arms was powerless, and the Council of the Senate, or its adviser, unmoved. Chester Herald, however, managed a creditable show of sorrow, rather than of anger; and, the time being right, the correspondence closed with reciprocal New Year greetings.

At this point two comments may not be out of place: the description of the non-collegiate body as an 'unincorporated fluctuating body of persons', though legally beyond reproach, was gall and wormwood to the Censor of the time, into whose hands it unfortunately fell. That annoyance, it is to be hoped, will soon have passed; but of more lasting effect, possibly, was an expression of opinion by Professor Hollond, who, strongly opposed as he was to the making of any application for a grant of arms at the time, nevertheless supposed that if the status of Fitzwilliam House should change 'decency would demand that a grant

[1]   See University Registry file 772/1947. For the remainder of this episode see file 'Grant of Arms' in Fitzwilliam College.

of arms should be applied for, and paid for'. It is not impossible that this observation may have remained in the mind of the University Registrary, who agreed with it, and may have exercised some influence when, after twenty years, it fell to him to bring the matter to the attention of the Governing Body of Fitzwilliam College.

It is not necessary for this account to match the lengthy, and at times leisurely, consultations between the College of Arms and the College in Cambridge which followed on the Governing Body's decision to seek authority for the continued use of its armorial bearings. At the outset it was made plain that the College, and no less the Fitzwilliam Society, hoped that the Kings of Arms would agree to license the use of an achievement very little different, if different at all, from that which had been in use for so considerable a period, and had thus acquired no small sentimental value. There was no difficulty in obtaining the Earl Marshal's warrant for a grant of arms; but it soon became apparent that the Kings of Arms would not find it possible to assign the present coat of arms to the College in the absence of some evident link with the Fitzwilliam family. In these circumstances, it seemed to the Governing Body that the College, while seeking to regularize its standing with the College of Arms, might without presumption also endeavour to establish a more formal connexion with the head of the family whose name it bore by Royal Charter; particularly as there was ready to hand a most fortunate precedent in the acceptance, some years previously, by Her Majesty Queen Elizabeth the Queen Mother of the ancient and honorific office of Patroness of Queens' College. Earl Fitzwilliam's ready acceptance of the Master's invitation to become Patron gave great pleasure; and as the Council of the Senate found no difficulty in agreeing, in view of the historical origin of the College, that the display of the arms of the University as part of the arms of the College was appropriate, the Kings of Arms were now, they said, both happy and willing to grant to the College the arms that it had used for so long.

Of a full achievement of shield, crest, helmet, mantling, supporters, and motto, the College had applied for a grant of arms (shield) and crest (including the helmet), and had signified its wish for the display of a motto of its own choosing. What may be described, in common parlance, as a small modification of the plumes in the Fitzwilliam crest created no problem, and the way was at length clear for the preparation of Letters Patent, to which an approved motto could be added at a later stage. The motto was an internal matter; and the College of Arms was content merely to state, in answer to an enquiry, that the previous use of the Fitzwilliam motto *Deo adjuvante non timendum* need not prevent

The Grant of Arms

...Know Ye therefore that We...do by these Presents grant and assign unto the Master Fellows and Scholars of Fitzwilliam College in the University of Cambridge the Arms following that is to say: Lozengy Argent and Gules a Chief Gules thereon a Cross Ermine between four Lions passant guardant Or and charged with a Bible fesseways Gules clasped and garnished Or the clasps in base And for the Crest Or a Wreath of the Colours A double Plume of Ostrich Feathers the upper plume Gules the lower Argent enfiling an ancient Crown Gules...

(From the Grant of Arms by Letters Patent of 31 December 1973)

its adoption, if that was desired. In the event, the settlement of this last question, free though it was from all external constraint, took some months, for both senior and junior members of the College became involved, and at the Master's invitation nearly thirty submissions were received. When, after a preliminary sifting the Governing Body was asked to decide by ballot from six of these, including the existing motto strongly supported by the Fitzwilliam Society, their choice fell on a joint proposal by two of the Fellows:[1] *Ex antiquis et novissimis optima.*

All obstacles now removed, the matter of the application was brought to a conclusion, and on 20 May 1974 the Master received the Letters Patent[2] at the hands of Norroy and Ulster King of Arms, who as Chester Herald had advised the College when discussions began in 1969. In this context, it is most gratifying to acknowledge a generous gesture by the Fitzwilliam Society. In April 1969 the committee of the Society agreed that a gift 'of up to £500', previously voted to the College in celebration of its forthcoming centenary, should be employed to defray the cost (two hundred and fifty guineas) of its coat of arms; and at a subsequent meeting of the Society the Chairman announced that the remainder of the £500 would be devoted to the provision of a copy to be placed on the College gates.[3]

Finance: We have seen how the body of Fellows of Fitzwilliam House had felt some apprehension, on financial grounds, as they approached the stage in their affairs when, encouraged by the Council of the Senate and prompted by their own Non-Collegiate Students Board, it seemed that full collegiate status was theirs for the asking;[4] and they did in fact obtain the Board's agreement to a postponement by one year, from 1965 to 1966, of the date by which the Board, at least, would have preferred them to seek independence.[5]

In effect, the transition was most conveniently made in two stages: when the move to Huntingdon Road took place in 1963, the House retained its non-collegiate status, and, with the undiminished financial support of the University, the Fellows had three years in which to learn how to make a living in their new surroundings; and even in 1966, with the coming of independence and the consequent loss of their annual

---

[1]   A. G. Hunt and R. W. Sharples.
[2]   See *Journal* 1975, p. 12, where, however, there are a number of errors in the transcription.
[3]   Minutes of the Fitzwilliam Society meeting held on 2 August 1969.
[4]   See p. 307.
[5]   Minutes of 15 October and 26 November 1964.

grant from the University Chest (£19,542 in the last non-collegiate year), the College was again fortunate in being relieved of the cost of the stipend of its first Master, when the Council of the Senate resolved that, for one tenure, this should be met by the University. Financially, again, the College benefited from an increase in numbers, in fulfilment of an undertaking by the Non-Collegiate Students Board, at the time of the publication of the Report of Lord Robbins's Committee, to accept more students in return for more accommodation. Higher charges were inevitable, and with an increase of some fifty per cent in the amount of establishment charges received, and with a smaller increase in tutorial fees, the College did little more than balance its first year's accounts, with an overall surplus of some £1,500 (including a loss of nearly £5,000 on the kitchens), compared with a surplus of more than £10,000 in the last non-collegiate year. This first year, however, was exceptional in that certain transfers from the University had not been completed until its very end, and in the two following years revised catering arrangements, more rooms, and a smaller loss in the Endowment Account (with a larger investment income) gave grounds for hopes that the College would not find unattainable the financial viability upon which the Council of the Senate had insisted as a condition of its recognition.

The Royal Commissioners of 1919 had declared that the conversion into a college of the University's non-collegiate institution would raise the cost of education for the men; and its seems that, at the time, they were right. They may also have been right in supposing that it might well give rise to a demand for another non-collegiate body; but circumstances had changed, for when at length Fitzwilliam House became independent a far greater national provision for higher education had done away with the need for special arrangements for any who could not afford to become members of a college, and such increased charges as were made necessary by the change of status were very largely met from public funds.

Buildings: By the end of the Long Vacation of 1967 the building programme had been completed as far as the limitations of the site seemed to allow; and the College had been most fortunate in being enabled to build rooms for some two hundred men – a number far in excess of what had been thought possible in the foreseeable future when building began. But the occupation of buildings did not leave the Governing Body free from building worries, for remedial work had been urgently necessary as early as August 1963, when rain caused flooding in the dining hall block, and in the north-east wing; and in November there was a serious blockage in the drains between the Senior Combination Room and Storey's Way, which might have been disastrous had it not been for timely assistance by the University Director of Estate Management, then fortunately living in the neighbourhood, and by the County Fire Brigade. This very troublesome episode led to the re-laying of a large part of the drainage system, and to the payment of damages of some £8,000 to the University. In 1969 one of the large windows in the dining hall cracked, and had to be replaced – no small matter with a clerestory window of plate glass three eighths of an inch thick and of an area of some sixty-five square feet. Cracks, internal and external, appeared; and there were what, it is to be hoped, will have proved to be no more than teething troubles in a number of places, notably in the College kitchens. These defects were mostly remedied, some more than once, but the acoustical properties of the dining hall are a disappointment for which no cure has yet been discovered; and matters are not much mended by the knowledge that the sister College in Oxford, so they tell us, is similarly afflicted. All in all, and quite apart from considerations of space, as in the effective limitation of the size of undergraduate rooms, there seems some reason to doubt whether those responsible for the allocation of public funds had achieved a desirable balance between permissible capital expenditure and maintenance costs.

In August 1968 the offer of a large benefaction, made for a specific purpose, caused the Governing Body to consider the lines on which its whole site might eventually be developed. Mr F. I. G. Rawlins, formerly of Trinity College, and Director in Natural Sciences at Fitzwilliam House from 1931 to 1934, offered the College a sum of £40,000 for the building of a chapel. It was a condition of this munificent benefaction that two previous gifts, each of £10,000, with interest accrued, should be put to the same purpose, and the offer was made in order that a chapel might be built forthwith, if the Master and Fellows, after receiving advice from their architect, were satisfied that the site then in their possession was suitable.

As it was essential that, wherever it might be put, a chapel by its situation and design should form an integral part of the College so far as its development could be foreseen, the Governing Body resolved to commission from the architect (Mr Denys Lasdun) a development plan of the College as it might be when the whole of the site had come into their possession.[1] The plan should make provision for

[1]   Minutes of 6 August 1968.

Fitzwilliam House, the new buildings from the south-west (1964)

(a) a chapel;

(b) a further two hundred rooms for undergraduate and graduate students, together with appropriate additional accommodation for Fellows;

(c) a block large enough to accommodate two courts for squash racquets, though it might be used for other purposes if it were to become possible to make arrangements for squash racquets elsewhere;

(d) a Master's Lodge.

To these requirements there was subsequently added the provision of a theatre, which would be needed if the room at present used (the Reddaway Room) were taken over for an extension of the library; and Mr Lasdun was also asked to bear in mind that money was likely to be made available for the building of a chapel by a benefactor who was anxious that it should be built in the near future if this could be done on that part of the site already in the College's possession.

Mr Lasdun, on being informed in September 1968 that he was likely to be offered a brief on these lines, was unwilling to propose any different site for a chapel from that which he had chosen in 1959, in his original development scheme for Fitzwilliam House. Eventually, he accepted the brief, and in his proposals, accompanied by a model and laid before the Governing Body in February 1970, a free-standing chapel building was placed within the existing confines of the College to the south-west of the Senior Combination Room. Mr Lasdun's model illustrated his proposals for the development of the site, and showed the disposition of his proposed buildings in relation to those already in being. He made no provision for a Master's Lodge.[1]

After some consideration, and after receiving the observations of the junior members of the College, the Governing Body decided that the erection of a chapel on the alternative site proposed would cause a most undesirable congestion in its neighbourhood, and agreed to take no action on the development plan for the time being.[2]

The Fitzwilliam Hall Trust: Although it occurred a little after the limit set for this tale of the first hundred years, it is not unfitting that there should be included here a brief account of the voluntary winding up of the Fitzwilliam Hall Trust. Under the terms of its Memorandum of Association it was known that an independent College would be entitled to take over the assets of the Trust upon the Association's dissolution, and, with the willing consent of the Governors, the acquisition of the Trust's 'assets and liabilities' was included in the recital of the objects of the College as these were set forth in its Royal Charter. The very considerable procedures of the liquidation were most skilfully conducted by Mr F. C. D. Swann, a Fitzwilliam graduate resident in Cambridge, and honorary secretary of the Trust for the previous seventeen years, and, after an interval which enabled the Trust to dispose satisfactorily of its trusteeship of the College Amalgamated Clubs, liquidation was completed on 7 June 1971, fifty years to the day after incorporation under the Companies Acts 1908 to 1917.[3] In the final reckoning the Governors, one of whose earliest minutes records their formal agreement that 'two garden chairs be exchanged for an armchair of the Censor's', found themselves in a position to transfer to the College assets of the order of £120,000.

---

[1] In 1962 an offer was received from Mrs R. S. Ball (see also p. 328), upon most favourable terms, of her house in Storey's Way (no. 60). It was unfortunate that it did not then seem possible to take advantage of this opportunity of acquiring a most desirable property, whether for use as a Master's Lodge, or as an investment.

[2] Minutes of 5 August 1970.

[3] Previous Secretaries had been the Rev. Frank Thatcher, until 1924 when he left Cambridge; the Rev. Walter Harvey, from 23 January 1925 until 6 January 1944; and Mr H. C. W. Barrett, who, on Mr Swann's appointment in 1954, became Clerk to the Trustees until his retirement on 30 September 1961, and was succeeded by Mr Douglas Jones.

For further details of the voluntary liquidation, see Trust minutes.

Reddaway's conception of the importance to Fitzwilliam House of the Trust's assistance in many of its corporate pursuits – of its importance to its continued corporate existence, even – was not exaggerated; and its name is perpetuated in a handsome room in the new building, regularly used for meetings of the Governing Body, and relieved of austerity by a gift from the Governors of the Trust to meet the cost of its panelling.

Admissions: During the first years of the life of the College there was a noticeable increase in its student numbers, following on the agreement of the Non-Collegiate Students Board in the Michaelmas term of 1963, in consequence of the recommendations of Lord Robbins's committee, to raise the number of admissions to Fitzwilliam House by fifteen per cent, say sixty, if suitable candidates presented themselves, and provided also that this increase did not bring about any increase in the proportion of men living in lodgings. In answer to a further enquiry, the Board also said that given satisfactory candidates for admission and suitable staff, the increase might be maintained permanently.[1] Delay in the completion of Stage II(a) of the building programme raised difficulties, but by the Michaelmas term of 1967 numbers in residence had risen to 526, an increase of forty-five since 1963, when the undertaking had been given; and, a year later, with an abnormally high figure of 559, the College had more than kept the bargain made for it. Thereafter the total was to fall a little, but, with small variations difficult to avoid altogether, the 'Robbins increase' was to be maintained.

Of the whole number of its applicants for admission in these first years, the College found itself accepting slightly less than half, and the recruitment of men of high standard continued to be difficult, a significant proportion of the intake coming from the 'pool' of creditable candidates not accepted by the other colleges in the Queens' group. Over the three years 1967–69 the proportion of applicants taken from Maintained Schools was relatively high – 55% as against 40% in the University as a whole, while from the Independent Schools the corresponding figures were 25% and 38%.

In the Entrance Scholarship Examination there were considerable grounds for encouragement, for whereas in December 1963 of three scholars and eight exhibitioners one alone had declared a first preference for Fitzwilliam, four years later, in December 1967, of fifteen winners of awards (six scholars, and nine exhibitioners) eleven had put the college first, and of the six scholars two were at the top of the

---

[1]   Minutes and papers for 28 November 1963.

whole group in their subjects (Classics and History). In that year also there were forty-five first, and sixty second, preferences for the College, figures which in the year following became seventy-four and one hundred and sixty. While Fitzwilliam could not hope to rival others on financial grounds (in December 1967 St John's College awarded twenty-five scholarships and thirty exhibitions), it remained true that its principal difficulty was not in this respect financial but was due to a comparative lack of first preference candidates of scholarship quality. In this there was no occasion for surprise, for as a new foundation the College had to make its way towards parity of esteem, and to this there could be no short cut.

The Fellows: The total of twenty-three Fellows elected in the academical year 1962/63 had risen to forty-one by the end of non-collegiate status on 9 September 1966, and those holding their fellowships on that date became, under the terms of its Charter, the first Fellows of Fitzwilliam College. By then, also, four had relinquished their fellowships – two on appointment to professorships overseas, one to a lectureship in a provincial university, and the fourth on reaching the statutory retiring age, two years, only, after his election as Fellow; for, although it was expected that the College Statutes would provide that for the purpose of determining the qualification of candidates for election to life fellowships the electors could take account of their tenure as Fellows or officers of Fitzwilliam House, there had not been for them the same opportunities of accumulating years of service as they would have had in an established college. There were to be other instances of the same kind; and it was a matter of regret that in the first years of the life of the College there should be a small number of its Fellows with such unavoidably limited tenure.

The Governing Body took an early opportunity of electing, as the College's first President, Mr W. W. Williams, Bursar and Assistant Censor under the old régime – for a tenure limited to one academical year by his express desire to retire from University and College office on 30 September 1967. For the Governing Body's choice no grounds are recorded: there seemed no need, then, to record them, for the Fellows, one and all, were doing no more – and could do no less – than express their deep sense of obligation to Mr Williams for his services to the House over a period of twenty years, and particularly for the devotion with which, as Acting Censor, he had sought to serve its best interests in times of unusual stress.

In the Easter term of his last year of residence, the Governing Body also signified their wish to commission a portrait of Mr Williams. As

William Washington Williams, M.A.
Bursar and Assistant Censor of Fitzwilliam House 1946–66;
Acting Censor 1955–58; Bursar and President of Fitzwilliam College 1966–67

they felt that many Fitzwilliam men would appreciate an opportunity of helping to acquire it, the Master was instructed to invite subscriptions from members of the Fitzwilliam Society, and to inform them that a portrait had been commissioned from Mr Andrew Freeth, whose work was well known in Cambridge. In the course of a brief stay in College, Mr Freeth executed three portraits. Two were in colour wash; but neither, to the possibly uninstructed eye of many of the Fellows, seemed quite to represent the Mr Williams they knew. A third drawing, dashed off, as they say, shortly before the artist left to catch his train, was judged much more successful, and has been regarded as a most welcome adornment of the Senior Combination Room.

Shortly after his retirement, the Governing Body elected Mr Williams into a life fellowship, and in so doing demonstrated their confident belief that – a distance of some five hundred miles notwithstanding – he would maintain his interest in the College's affairs, and would welcome this continued association with it. As President Mr Williams was succeeded by Dr B. M. Herbertson, and as Bursar by Dr Raymond Kelly. Both had come to Fitzwilliam House in the 1950s, Dr Herbertson from Magdalene College, and Dr Kelly from Trinity Hall; and both had been appointed to assistant tutorships.

By the close of 1969 the number of elections had increased to sixty-two, including two of Professors of the University,[1] in satisfaction of the quota (later to be raised to three) assigned to the college on the attainment of independence, and six to research fellowships, perforce non-stipendiary but affording the customary amenities of residence. By the same date twenty-three Fellows had retired or resigned, of the latter nearly all to assume academical appointments, including three to chairs elsewhere in the United Kingdom,[2] and one (Dr E. G. Rupp) on his election to the Dixie Professorship of Ecclesiastical History in the University, to take up in Emmanuel College the fellowship to which, as Dixie Professor, he was entitled to be admitted. Unwilling to lose Dr Rupp altogether, the College was much gratified when in 1969 he accepted an invitation to become an Honorary Fellow, as also did another Fitzwilliam graduate of high distinction, Mr Harry Lee Kuan Yew, then for ten years Prime Minister of Singapore.

Already in 1964 the Fellows of Fitzwilliam House had made an elec-

---

[1] Dr C. R. Austin, Charles Darwin Professor of Animal Embryology; and, elected on 6 August with effect from 1 October 1970, Dr S. A. de Smith, of St Catharine's College, Downing Professor elect of the Laws of England.

[2] Of the three, the last to go (Mr J. R. S. Revell, Senior Tutor and Director of Studies in Economics) was the second of a succession of four Directors of Studies in the subject who left, or were to leave, on appointment to chairs in other universities.

tion to a visiting fellowship, occupied for the academical year 1964/65 by Dr K. L. S. Gunn, Professor of Physics of McGill University; an experiment so outstandingly successful that the Fellows had no hesitation in making similar elections, usually of scholars from overseas, for periods up to a year. Of these, Dr L. M. Falicov (1961) and Dr B. H. Neumann (1935), Professors of Physics in Chicago and Mathematics at Canberra, had been non-collegiate research students. The election of Schoolmaster Fellows, also, was begun with effect from the Michaelmas term of 1967.

In the pattern of these comings and goings there had been little that was unexpected; but by the early death, on 18 June 1967, of Robert Norman Walters the College suffered a heavy blow that could not have been foreseen. Appointed Tutor in 1950, and Director of Studies in English in 1951, for much of his time he had also been Director of Studies in Classics, and Praelector; and during his last ten years of office had been in virtual charge of the conduct of admissions. There had been no corporate activity outside the range of his interest; no part of the House or College untouched by his influence.[1]

The Centenary Year: In 1969 Fitzwilliam College, founded barely three years previously, reached the hundredth anniversary of its establishment as the non-collegiate institution of the University; and it may be that the centenary celebrations lost a little from the proximity of 1966. That the year by no means passed unnoticed, however, is evident from an account written at the time for the *Fitzwilliam Journal.*[2]

On the evening of Monday, 6 January, [says the Master's Letter] most of the Fellows were at an evening party given for us by the Mistress and Fellows of Girton College, also founded (at Hitchin) in 1869. Later in the term the junior members of the College took a hand in the arrangements; for on Saturday, 1 March, the First Lent Boat set the seal on earlier success by rowing over at the head of the first division – a culmination not only of that week's spectacular achievement but of determined preparation by Boat Clubs of earlier years. The College's success was duly celebrated at a Bump Supper, and then by a decorous bonfire, the latter very suitably attended, if memory serves, by Dr E. V. Bevan, a near neighbour of the College with some interest in rowing.[3]

The undergraduate members of the College organised an athletic festival on Thursday 13 March, with matches at rugby and association football, and

---

[1]   See also *Journal* 1968, p. 13.
[2]   *Ibid.*, 1970, p. 9.
[3]   Dr Bevan was Treasurer of the Cambridge University Boat Club.

hockey, between past and present members of the College and the Hawks'
Club. Appalling weather made it impossible to play a single game, and the
festival was reduced to a reception held at the Pitt Club that same evening.
The next day the weather again did its worst to spoil the Centenary Ball,
but in spite of the inconvenience of snow-covered courts the Ball was
heavily over-subscribed and completely successful. Another undergraduate
activity was less dependent on the weather. The Fitzwilliam Theatre group
also arranged a Centenary Festival with performances of One Act Plays on
3, 4 and 5 March, and of a Revue on 10, 11 and 12 March.

In my letter last year I told how the Governing Body of the College had
decided that three events should be associated with the Centenary – in
May, June and September. The first, a Commemoration Dinner held on
Saturday, 17 May, was attended by the Vice-Chancellor and many heads of
Colleges, by the President (Mr Norman St John-Stevas) and Secretary of
the Fitzwilliam Society with a number of ex-Presidents, and by other
friends of the College, as well as by Fellows and Scholars. I myself was
privileged, in the only speech of the evening, to propose a toast which all
could honour; and the assembled company, as they wished the College
well, were very mindful of those sons of the Hall and House who had
served it in earlier years.

Posterity may like to recall that the Latin after-dinner Grace was composed and set to music, and sung, by members of the College in residence;[1] and that through the good offices of the Secretary of the Governing
Body's Wine Committee the toast was drunk in vintage Madeira of 1869.

On Wednesday, 4 June, the First Boat caught Queens' in the May
Races, and with no trouble at all on the remaining three nights became the
first Fitzwilliam Boat to go Head of the River. Notwithstanding the celebration photograph of the crew now to be seen in various College rooms,
their choice of the year 1969 for this crowning achievement is evidence of
a superb sense of timing; and is a striking and accurate reminder of the
achievements of the last fifty years also, for, as last year's *Journal* reminds
us, it was in 1919 that the May Boat first caught a representative College
Boat.[2] Once again, the young men had taken a hand.

The second function arranged by the Governing Body in the Centenary
Year was a Garden Party for all members of the College and their guests.
The date, 9 June, was skilfully chosen; for May Week, following close on
the heels of the worst Easter Term for many years, was splendidly fine.

Last year's *Journal* recorded a decision of the Governing Body that the
Centenary Year should, if practicable, be made the occasion of another
attempt to raise money for the further development of the College. In July

---

[1]   For the Grace, written by Dr R. A. O. M. Lyne and set to music by Dr Alan Brown, see *Journal* 1971, p. 18.
[2]   The Master, who should have known better, accepted too readily a statement to this effect
in the *Journal* of 1969. The first bump on a 'representative boat' was made in 1876, when
the non-collegiate boat caught Downing College on the first night of the May Races.

1968 the Governing Body resolved to seek advice from Messrs Hooker Craigmyle, who have much experience in this particular field, on the prospects of a successful Appeal. Lists were compiled and addresses verified of about 2,200 old members (together with 600 overseas), and in January and February 1969 a hundred old members of the College were visited by a Resident Appeal Director appointed by the firm with the concurrence of the Governing Body. On the results of this survey the Governing Body decided, on 19 March, to conduct an Appeal with the object of raising the sum of £100,000 from the old members of the College, and £50,000 from other sources; and during April and May literature was prepared for circulation, including a brochure giving some account of the College's early history and setting forth the Appeal's objectives. Shortly before, the College had been indebted to Mr Haywood for the revision, printing, and circulation to old members of an earlier pamphlet on the history of the College first written in the 1950's.

For the purposes of the Appeal the country was divided into fifteen regions, each with its own Committee and local Chairman. The fund raisers advised that it was essential for success that approaches should be made personally, and not by correspondence, and each local committee was supplied with lists of Fitzwilliam men in its area and asked, with helpers whom it would also recruit, to arrange for personal approaches to be made. For regions in the southern part of the country the local committees began their work in June, and in the north in October. Work is still in progress, and the present total of contributions received (15 January, 1970) is £44,000 from about four hundred and eighty contributors. Members of the College overseas have recently been approached by post. I take this opportunity of placing on record the great satisfaction that it has given me, in my visits to different parts of the country, to meet a number of Fitzwilliam men for the first time, and of making known the College's indebtedness to those who have given of their time and energy for its benefit, and also to all who have subscribed to the Appeal.[1]

The Mistress and Fellows of Girton College paid us a return visit on Monday, 16 June, and it is agreeable to record that hereabouts the College resolved to beg the acceptance by Girton of a more lasting memento of the coincidence of our centenary years. The Governing Body voted a sum of money for a piece of silver, and after much deliberation an attractive bowl was found at an appropriate price. It now bears the crests of the two Colleges, and its mark reveals that it was made in London in 1869. The Bursar and the Junior Bursar are much to be congratulated on their good fortune, and their industry, in unearthing so suitable a gift. It was received in Col-

---

[1] The outcome of this Appeal was disappointing. Gifts from former Fitzwilliam residents matched the College's own forecast of £60,000 (not the fund raisers' estimate of £100,000, which the Governing Body had from the beginning regarded as unrealistic); but attempts made on behalf of the College to raise money from other sources produced no significant result.

lege by the Mistress and four of her Fellows, with every appearance of satisfaction, on Friday, 12 December.

On the evening of 27 September there took place the third of the functions arranged by the Governing Body for the Centenary Year. When more than a year previously they decided that it should be held, they had not been able to specify its exact nature, beyond making a suggestion that it might be associated with an Appeal if one should be launched. In the event it was decided to invite to dinner in Hall all those members of the Committees who had been active, or were shortly to become active, in the conduct of the Appeal, together with as many of their helpers as could be accommodated. As space could not be found for them all, the helpers were invited by their seniority as members of the College. Visitors were given the opportunity of staying in College for the night, and advantage was taken of their presence to hold a briefing meeting on the following morning of all committees of the northern regions. For Appeal purposes this was a very convenient arrangement, but for some of us the weekend was significant also in another respect. The occupation by the College of its new buildings made it possible, for the first time, to organise an Old Members' Gathering, so described in correspondence and on menu cards, entirely on its own premises. Their common activities on behalf of the Appeal made it likely that our guests would find others of their acquaintance at the Dinner, and what was said at the time, and has been said since, makes me hope that the College will in future be able to arrange similar gatherings, based on invitations to contemporaries.

At the very end of the Long Vacation, on the evening of 30 September, the College gave a most successful Centenary Party for the members of its Assistant Staff – a function which was all the more complete because the catering for it was undertaken by an outside firm, and so needed only the minimum of help from the College Kitchen. Those responsible for the organisation of the party were much pleased to be able to welcome back former members of the staff who had retired.

With the coming of the Michaelmas Term the Governing Body turned their attention, as may seem appropriate, to more academic matters; for we then saw the first submission of essays in a competition for Centenary Essay Prizes instituted as a means of encouraging junior members to undertake substantial pieces of work, mostly in the Long Vacation, on subjects to be approved by their Directors of Studies within their fields of interest. A satisfactory number of entries have come in, and the Governing Body expects shortly to announce the awards. A successful candidate would receive, except where essays are of equal merit, a prize of £40.[1]

It is not uncommon for Colleges to establish Annual Lectures given by scholars of distinction, whether or not by their own members. The

---

[1] In this first competition prizes of £40 were awarded in the Lent term of 1970 to R. Mills, C. G. Murray, and D. G. Punter.

Governing Body, this year, have founded a Centenary Lecture;[1] and they invited Professor Sir Ernst Chain, Nobel Prize Winner in Physiology and Medicine in 1945 and formerly a Research Student of the House, now an Honorary Fellow of the College, to give the first lecture. Professor Chain chose as his subject, *"Antibiotics and Therapy in Perspective"*. His lecture was thrown open to members of the University and to others interested and was given in the University Anatomy School on 28 November. To those who know, it came as no surprise that the lecture was an outstanding success. Even the least numerate of us could hardly fail to discern something of the thrill of scientific discovery, and the Fellows, when all was over, remembered with lively satisfaction how Professor Chain was in the Senior Combination Room long after the time at which he had said he would have to set out on the long, cold, journey home.

The year has been the occasion of a number of gifts to the College. Mrs Winifred Armstrong, of The Grove, gave money for silver in celebration of the Centenary; and two most attractive salt cellars have been purchased, made in London in 1800. Sir John Stratton has, not for the first time, made us a handsome offer, with the suggestion that a piece of silver might be commissioned to commemorate the success of the Boat Club. The College Committee concerned is inviting an artist to submit proposals. Dr J. N. G. Finley, of Virginia, who visited us in 1964, has also given a substantial sum for silver. Following earlier gifts, a cup has recently come from Dr S. W. Jackman of Clare College, Professor of History in the University of Victoria (British Columbia) who was here in the Long Vacation; and at the time of the August Reunion of the Fitzwilliam Society Mr Heinz Brunner, of Düsseldorf, put before us generous proposals for the presentation of a pair of candle-sticks, to be made by a German craftsman for the Chapel. At the same time, Mr H. D. Cochrane, a most loyal supporter of the Society, brought me a most attractive silver candle-stick which made its first appearance at the Reunion Dinner, attended, in the centenary year, by an appreciably larger number of old members of the College than usual. The recital by name of so many items is not without danger, for it is all too easy to forget, but particular mention must nevertheless be made of another gift of a different kind. Mr Jek Yeung Thong, a Minister in the Government of Singapore, spent the Easter Term and Long Vacation with us, and on his departure left a charming Chinese painting on silk as a memento of a stay in the University and the College which appears to have afforded him as much pleasure and as much benefit as we, in our turn, derived from having him here.[2]

In one respect time has run ahead of commemoration, for in April the Governing Body resolved to invite Mr Sebastian Forbes to compose a piece

[1] Since changed to 'Foundation Lecture'. The original title became progressively more misleading.

[2] The approaching independence of Fitzwilliam House and the hundredth anniversary of the establishment of the non-collegiate body from which it had sprung were marked by the

of Centenary music to be performed before the end of the year. I understand that a Centenary Quartet will shortly be performed in the College by the Fitzwilliam Quartet, which includes two undergraduate members of the College.[1]

'Milestones'

I: That the provisions of the Statutes, by which all Members of the University are obliged to belong to some College or Hall, as also that by which Colleges and Halls are obliged to have all their rooms accessible through one common gate, should be annulled; and that liberty be given for the extension of the University, as well by the foundation of Halls as by permitting Members of the University, under due superintendence, to live in private lodgings, without connexion with a College or Hall.
(Report, dated 27 April 1852, of the Royal Commission on the University of Oxford)

II: Notwithstanding anything expressed or contained in the statutes of the University framed and sanctioned in accordance with the pro-

---

presentation of a number of pieces of silver by past and present members of the House, and other friends. The Fellows themselves commissioned a coffee pot and milk jug from Mr Gerald Benney; and other acquisitions were a tray, sugar bowl and cream jug given by former members of the House in Malaya, a rose water bowl from the Master and Fellows of Trinity Hall, a salver from Emmanuel College, and a water jug from Mrs Armstrong. These were all the work of Mr Benney, as were two beautiful candlesticks bought, with his ready agreement, from money given by Dr Finley. Sir John Stratton's gift, a fruit bowl of distinctive design made by Mr Brian Asquith, was formally presented, and its use inaugurated, at an annual dinner of the Billygoats' Society on 28 November 1970, when its eight slender candles afforded striking evidence of the draughts of which the dining hall is capable; for at the end of the evening its boat-shaped bowl was thick with tallow. Mr Asquith's introduction of a silver tray did, however, effect some improvement. Other generous friends who, by the centenary year, helped to celebrate the imminent, or the actual, change of status were the Governing Body of Selwyn College and the members of St Edmund's House, Messrs S. J. Bach, G. W. Barman, F. T. Bennitt (formerly of Emmanuel College), H. M. Burton, Z. K. Chojecki, H. D. Cochrane, R. R. A. Coombs (of Corpus Christi College), Sydney Dickinson, P. C. Gray, R. R. Hancock, G. F. Hickson, T. S. Lucking, N. J. G. Pounds, F. I. G. Rawlins (by bequest), and, on relinquishing their fellowships, Sydney Dickinson, K. L. S. Gunn of McGill University, and Alec Lazenby.

Another, and rather different, gift was received at this time. In 1912 members of Fitzwilliam Hall, as they were careful to call themselves, presented a silver bowl to Dr T. C. Fitzpatrick, President of Queens' College and Chairman of the Non-Collegiate Students Board, on the occasion of his marriage. On the death of Dr Fitzpatrick's widow the bowl passed to the President and Fellows of Queens' College, who felt that it might very appropriately be returned to Fitzwilliam House; and in Fitzwilliam College it remains as a reminder of the signal services rendered by two Presidents of Queens' to its earlier University governing body.

See also *Journal* 1965, p. 27; 1967, p. 18, 1970, p. 12.

[1] Mr Forbes's Quartet No. 2 was performed in the College on 1 March 1970. For the Fitzwilliam Quartet, see also p. 358–9.

visions of the Act of Parliament, 19 and 20 Vict., c.88, it shall be lawful for the University to admit as Students to matriculate and to confer degrees on persons who may not be members of any College or Hall or of any Hostel.

(Statute of the University of Cambridge approved by Her Majesty in Council on 13 May 1869)

III: The community of Non-Collegiate Students resident and nonresident shall be designated Fitzwilliam House, and Non-Collegiate Students may be described on such occasions and in such documents as the University may from time to time determine as members of Fitzwilliam House.

(Statute of the University of Cambridge approved by His Majesty in Council on 4 May 1935)

IV: That approval be given to the general proposition that steps shall be taken to terminate the present Non-Collegiate system, provided that Fitzwilliam House can be recognized as an Approved Foundation bound to limitations of the number of its undergraduate members and to the performance of certain functions now performed by it as an institution for Non-Collegiate Students.

(Recommendation contained in the Report of the Council of the Senate, approved on 27 November 1954, on the future of Fitzwilliam House)

V: Whereas a Petition has been presented unto Us by the Chancellor, Masters and Scholars of Our University of Cambridge... praying that We would be graciously pleased to grant a Charter of Incorporation for the purpose of constituting the present community of Non-Collegiate Students known as Fitzwilliam House... a Body Corporate to be called 'Fitzwilliam College in the University of Cambridge' ... Now therefore know ye that We ... do grant and declare as follows:

1. The first Master and first Fellows and all such persons as may hereafter become members of the Body Corporate hereby constituted shall for ever after be one Body Politic and Corporate by the name and style of 'The Master, Fellows and Scholars of Fitzwilliam College in the University of Cambridge'... .

(From the Royal Charter of the College, dated 9 September 1966).

Appendix A

(i) First Class Honours

In this list of men placed in the first class in one or more Tripos examinations, there have been included those who were similarly placed in the LL.B. Examination, and those who were awarded a mark of distinction in Part III of the Mathematical Tripos. In Part I of the Modern and Medieval Languages Tripos, when candidates have been required to offer two languages it has been customary, for statistical purposes, to regard a pass in each language as the equivalent of half a class; and in this list the performance of a candidate with a first class in one language only has been similarly regarded.

The Theological Training Colleges of those of their members who sat for the Theological Tripos as non-collegiate students are also indicated (1-Cheshunt College; 2-Westminster College; 3-Westcott House; 4-Wesley House).

An asterisk placed before the name of a candidate denotes distinction.

1880	Harris R. H.	Theology
1881	–	–
1882	Reid E. W.	Natural Sciences
1883	–	–
1884	–	–
1885	–	–
1886	–	–
1887	Dufton A.	Natural Sciences
1888	Whittaker W. J.	Law
1889	–	–
1890	French W.	Natural Sciences
1891	–	–
1892	–	–
1893	–	–
1894	–	–
1895	de Wet N. J.	Law
1896	Pearson H. H. W.	Natural Sciences
1897	–	–
1898	Gaskoin C. J. B.	History
1899	Staats C. W. O.	Classics
1900	Sager J. L.	Natural Sciences I
1901	–	–
1902	–	–
1903	–	–

1904	–	–
1905	–	–
1906	Bird A. L.	Mechanical Sciences
	Erith L. E. R.	Theology
1907	Curzon H. E. J.	Mathematics
1908	Taggart A. W.[1]	Theology I
1909	–	–
1910	Cowe A. E.[1]	Theology I
1911	Le Goc M.	Natural Sciences I
1912	Dunsheath P.	Mechanical Sciences
	Sullivan T. A.	History II
1913	Harris G. H.	Theology I
	Wilson J.	Mathematics I
1914	Harris G. H.	Theology II
	Long F. S.	Mathematics I
1915	Ambruzzi A.	History II
	Watt A. G.	Mod. & Med. Languages
1916	Narayana T. S.	Mathematics II
1917	Ghate V. S.	Oriental Languages
1918	Bhat V. G.	Oriental Languages
	Watkins M.	Mathematics I
1919	Inandar R. S.	Natural Sciences II
1920	Radford C. G.	Geography I
	Winckworth C. P. T.	Oriental Languages I
1921	Desai C. C.	Natural Sciences I
	Elmes R. S.	English
	Morton C. H. E.	Geography I
	Rege D. V.	Oriental Languages I & II
	Summerscale J. P.	Mod. & Med. Languages
	Valentine F. J.	Law II
	Vincent H. C. G.	Natural Sciences I
	Watkins M.	Mathematics II
	Wood H. R. B.	Geography I
1922	Elmes R. S.	English
	Honey G. D.	Mod. & Med. Languages
	Kibble W. F.	Mathematics I
	Sidhanta N. K.	English
	Stevenson W. T.	Geography I
	Sutcliffe A.	Natural Sciences II
	Sutton W. H.	Geography I
1923	Burton H. M.	English

	Cameron N. E.	Mathematics I
	Hefnawy M. T.	Natural Sciences I
	Martin T. H.	Mathematics I
	Morton C. H. E.	Geography II
	Shearer W. R.[4]	Theology IA
	Vincent H. C. G.	Natural Sciences II
	Windross R.	Mod. & Med. Languages
	Wood H. R. B.	Geography II
1924	Salter C.	Mathematics I
	Smithen F. J.	Oriental Languages I
	Wheel B. O.	Mathematics I
	Wisdom A. T. J. D.	Moral Sciences I
1925	–	–
1926	Flemington W. F.[4]	Theology II
	Nicholas E. W.[1]	Theology IB
	Turner R. R.[1]	Theology IA
	Wheel B. O.	Mathematics II
1927	Firth C. B.[1]	Theology IA
1928	Beetham T. A.[4]	Theology IA
	Brown C. J.	Mod. & Med. Languages II
	Creighton C. W.	Mod. & Med. Languages I($\frac{1}{2}$)
	Firth C. B.[1]	Theology IB
	Healey F. G.[2]	Theology II
	Sainsbury J. A. W.	Law I
1929	Jukes F. L.	Mathematics I
	Kapadia J. D.	Mathematics I
	Sainsbury J. A. W.	Law II
	Silverstone S. M.	Natural Sciences II
	Volkov N.	Mod. & Med. Languages I($\frac{1}{2}$)
	Ward A. M.[4]	Theology IA
1930	Archibald B. M.	Mechanical Sciences
	Constantine L.[4]	Theology IA
	Hodgson J.	Mod. & Med. Languages I($\frac{1}{2}$)
	Mance H. W.	Mod. & Med. Languages I($\frac{1}{2}$)
	Morgan F. W.	Geography I
	Narliker V. V.	Mathematics II
	Sainsbury J. A. W.	LL.B. Examination
	Ward A. M.[4]	Theology IB
1931	Abson W. W.	Natural Sciences I
	Booth A. L.	Theology IA
	Dewey A. A.	Mathematics I

	Harmer L. C.	Mod. & Med. Languages I($\frac{1}{2}$)
	Hodgson J.	Mod. & Med. Languages II
	Holmes E. J.	Natural Sciences I
	Kapadia J. D.	Mathematics II
	Moon J. S.[4]	Theology IA
1932	Abson H.	Mathematics I
	Blackstone B.	English I
	Bullard D. G.	Natural Sciences I
	Guy C. F.[4]	Theology IA
	Harmer L. C.	Mod. & Med. Languages I($\frac{1}{2}$)
	Liddiard F. J.	Mod. & Med. Languages I($\frac{1}{2}$)
	Moon J. S.[4]	Theology IB
	Morgan I.[4]	Theology IB
1933	Banks A. W.[4]	Theology IA
	Blackstone B.	English II
	Brandt R. B.[2]	Theology II
	Dewey A. A.	Mathematics II
	Guy C. F.[4]	Theology IB
	*Harmer L. C.	Mod. & Med. Languages II
	Hewson L. A.[4]	Theology IB
	Long G. E.[4]	Theology IA
	Turner A. K.[4]	Theology IA
	Watson P. S.[4]	Theology IA
1934	Clark G. L.	Mathematics I
	Cook A. J. T.[4]	Theology IA
	Davies R. E.[4]	Theology IA
	de Lisser K. A.	Mechanical Sciences
	Hollins T. H. B.	Mod. & Med. Languages I($\frac{1}{2}$)
	Long G. E.[4]	Theology IB
	Pounds N. J. G.	Geography I
	Sharp J. R. I.	Classics I
	Watson P. S.[4]	Theology IB
	Williams A. E.	Classics I
1935	Chandratreya G. L.	Mathematics II
	Elsden S. R.	Natural Sciences I
	Markwick D. W.	LL.B. Examination
	Rupp E. G.[4]	Theology IA
	Springett J. A.	Mathematics I
	Tolman C. F.	Natural Sciences I
1936	*Clark G. L.	Mathematics III
	Elsden S. R.	Natural Sciences II

	Measures G. F.	Mathematics I
	Rupp E. G.[4]	Theology II
	Sharp J. R. I.	English I
1937	Anderson G. W.[4]	Theology IB
	Cockerham G.	Natural Sciences I
	George A. R.[4]	Theology IB
	Phelps G. H.	English II
	Springett J. A.	Mathematics II
1938	Allwood M. S.	Moral Sciences II
	Harris W. B.[4]	Theology IB
	*Haywood R. W.	Mechanical Sciences
	Little G. E.	Natural Sciences II
	Perry S. H. H.[2]	Theology II
1939	Ajgaonkar D. N.	Mathematics II
	Cockerham G.	Natural Sciences II
	Ghyselinck A. M.	Natural Sciences I
	Grayston K.[4]	Theology IA
	Harris W. B.[4]	Theology II
	Lewy C.	Moral Sciences II
	Pulvermacher M. E.	Mathematics I
1940	*Grayston K.[4]	Theology IB
	Heathcote A. W.[4]	Theology IB
	Parikh R. K.	Mathematics II
	Williams N. E.	English II
1941	Bull G. B. G.	Geography I
	Dowse E.[4]	Theology IB
	Evans J. W.[4]	Theology IB
	Hyde A.	Geography II
	Pulvermacher M. E.	Mathematics II
	Smith S. W.	Geography I
	Valle A. S.[4]	Theology IA
1942	Bull G. B. G.	Geography II
	Underwood G. W.[4]	Theology IA
1943	Marson R. E.	Natural Sciences I
1944	–	–
1945	–	–
1946	Weil H. H.	Mod. & Med. Languages I(½)
1947	Candeland A.[4]	Theology IA
	Horvat J. A.	Mod. & Med. Languages I
	Kuper C. G.	Mathematics I
	Morris G. R.	Mathematics II

	Pepper A. T.[4]	Theology IA
	Whitaker J. J. M.	Natural Sciences I
1948	Barnes L. W. C. S.	Economics I
	Candeland A.[4]	Theology IB
	Creedy A. J.	English II
	Drewery B.[4]	Theology IB
	Goodenough G. L.	Natural Sciences I
	Lee H. K. Y.	Law I
	Lewis A. D.[2]	Theology IA
	Magee G. A.	Geography I
	Manners D. J.	Natural Sciences I
	Metcalf S. J.[4]	Theology IA
	Mohan F. L.	Mod. & Med. Languages I($\frac{1}{2}$)
	*Morris G. R.	Mathematics III
	Price E. D.	Mod. & Med. Languages I($\frac{1}{2}$)
	Stacey F. A.	History II
	Wood D. J. P.	History I
1949	Hoare E. G.	English II
	Horvat J. A.	Mod. & Med. Languages II
	Kuper C. G.	Natural Sciences II
	*Lee H. K. Y.	Law II
	Manners D. G.	Natural Sciences II
	Price E. D.	Mod. & Med. Languages II
	Turner H. D.	Mod. & Med. Languages I($\frac{1}{2}$)
	Watchman R. A.	Mathematics II
	Williams J. R.	Arch. & Anthr. II
1950	Howlings N. J. L.	English I
	Marks A. D.	Law II
	Rodd C. S.[4]	Theology I
	St John-Stevas N.	Law II
	Wilkinson P. R.	Classics I
	Williams N. E.	Arch. & Anthr. II
1951	Blackmore M.	Oriental Languages II
	Howlings N. J. L.	English II
	Long R. S.	Mathematics II
	McCarthy M. T.	Mod. & Med. Languages I
	Parry J. M.	Music I
	Watchman R. A.	Mathematics II
1952	Henry D. E.[4]	Theology I
	Ling N. R.	Natural Sciences II
	Rank H. E.	Mod. & Med. Languages I($\frac{1}{2}$)

	*Rodd C. S.[4]	Theology II
	Short R. D.	Mechanical Sciences I
	Wainwright A. W.[4]	Theology III
1953	Hoad J. W. L.[4]	Theology I
	Knowles G. W. S.[4]	Theology II
1954	Bradley J.	Mod. & Med. Languages I($\frac{1}{2}$)
	Brown J. S.	History I
	Doble P.[4]	Theology II
	Stamp H. A.	Oriental Languages I
1955	Brown J. S.	History II
	Ellingworth P.[4]	Theology II
	Morris H. V.	Arch. & Anthr. II
	Warren A. S.[4]	Theology III
1956	Aitken J. A.	Theology I
	Johnson P. D. J.	Geography II
	Russell P. W.[4]	Theology II
	Stead I. M.	Arch. & Anthr. I
1957	Howitt M. W. O.	Economics I
	Tennent I. F.	Mathematics I
1958	Anderson J. C.	Natural Sciences I
	Edwards A. V.	Natural Sciences II
	Johns A.	Mechanical Sciences I
	Ley A. J.	Mechanical Sciences I
	Marshall I. H.[4]	Theology II
	Rack H. D.[4]	Theology III
	Scott J. H.	Oriental Languages I
	Tomlinson G. K.	Mechanical Sciences I
1959	Anderson J. C.	Natural Sciences II
	Atkinson D.	Natural Sciences I
	Clegg J. B.	Natural Sciences I
	Johns A.	Mechanical Sciences II
	Jones I. H.[4]	Theology II
	Littlewood W. T.	Mod. & Med. Languages I($\frac{1}{2}$)
	Marshall I. H.[4]	Theology III
	Narlikar J. V.	Mathematics II
	Robson G.[4]	Theology III
	Sharp R. J. A.[4]	Theology II
	Slater G.[4]	Theology III
1960	Atkinson D.	Natural Sciences II
	Hudson P. D.	Mathematics I
	Jones I. H.[4]	Theology III

	Mellars P. A.	Arch. & Anthr. I
	*Narlikar J. V.	Mathematics III
	Rogers J. P. W.	English I
	Scott J. H.	Oriental Studies II
	Watson R. M.	Natural Sciences I
1961	Chapman J. H.	Natural Sciences I
	Crowson P. C. F.	Economics II
	Graves Smith T. R.	Mechanical Sciences I
	Rogers J. P. W.	English II
	Wilkinson C.	Natural Sciences I
	Yorke R. E.	Natural Sciences I
1962	Dawe R. J.	Economics II
	Graves Smith T. R.	Mechanical Sciences II
	Lee C. H.	History I
	Mellars P. A.	Arch. & Anthr. II
	Snelson J. K.	Mechanical Sciences I
	Yorke R. E.	Natural Sciences II
1963	Dunne T.	Geography I
	Philpott P. W. D.	Mod. & Med. Languages I($\frac{1}{2}$)
	Snelson J. K.	Electrical Sciences
	Webber D. W. C.	Mathematics II
1964	Batstone E. V.	Economics I
	Brooke J. H.	Natural Sciences I
	Cockroft R. D. H.	Mechanical Sciences I
	Dunne T.	Geography II
	Garcia A.	Mod. & Med. Languages I($\frac{1}{2}$)
	Hayes P. J.	Mathematics I
	Hoare R. W. N.[3]	Theology III
	Stace C.	Classics II
1965	Blunt R. F.	Natural Sciences I
	Nash G.	Natural Sciences I
	Small A. D.	Mechanical Sciences I
	Smith D. A.	Natural Sciences I
	Smith T. R.	Geography II
1966	Alexander J. S.[2]	Theology III
	Batstone E. V.	Economics II
	Bush M. E.	Natural Sciences II
	Gilchrist P. V.	Natural Sciences I
	Jones G. E.	Economics II
	Lancaster P. W.	Natural Sciences IA
	May A. N.	History II

	Scott R. H.	Natural Sciences I
	Whitfield P. J.	Natural Sciences II
	Wigglesworth J. B.	Mathematics IA
1967	Banyard S. H.	Natural Sciences IA
	Brown C. K.	Natural Sciences IB
	Catto C. J. D.	Mechanical Sciences I
	Dowling M. J.	Mod. & Med. Languages I($\frac{1}{2}$)
	Francis D. T. I.	Mathematics IA
	Gill C. J.	Agriculture I
	Hargreaves J.	Natural Sciences IA
	Johnson C. L.	Agriculture I
	Lancaster P. W.	Natural Sciences IB
	Read G.	Medical Sciences IA
	Ringrose C.	English I
	Salt P. J.	Medical Sciences IB
	Sharratt B.	English I
	Starkey D. R.	History I
	Wigglesworth J. B.	Mathematics IB
	Williams D. N.	Natural Sciences IA
1968	Andrews D. A.	Natural Sciences IA
	Ashton N. W.	Natural Sciences IA
	Barton R. D.	Natural Sciences IA
	Burman S. F.	Economics I
	Catto C. J. D.	Electrical Sciences
	Clegg W.	Natural Sciences IA
	Fisher J. A.	Medical Sciences IA
	Foss D. B.	Theology II
	Gill C. J.	Agriculture II
	Hewson A. T.	Natural Sciences IB
	Johnson C. L.	Agriculture II
	Lancaster P. W.	Natural Sciences II
	Marriott R.	Economics II
	Marrison W. P.	Economics I
	Mills R.	Economics I
	Sharratt B.	English II
	Smith B. A.[3]	Theology III
	Stapleton N. J.	Economics II
	Treadwell J. M.	English II
1969	Andrews D. A.	Natural Sciences IB
	Clegg W.	Natural Sciences IB
	Fisher J. A.	Medical Sciences IB

Healey N.[2]	Theology I
Jackson H. R.[3]	Theology II
May G. J.	Natural Sciences IB
Punter D. G.	English I
Smith R. J.	Law I
Spooner T. B.	Mechanical Sciences I
Stachulski A. V.	Natural Sciences IA
Sweet D. J.	Medical Sciences IB
Williams P. H.	Natural Sciences IA

(ii) University Scholarships

1870	T. S. Little	Whewell Scholarship for International Law
1890	J. W. Whitaker	Whewell Scholarship for International Law
1899	F. E. E. Harvey	Stewart of Rannoch Scholarship (Music)
1910	J. Rothfield	Stewart of Rannoch Scholarship (Hebrew)
1913	G. H. Harris	Crosse Scholarship (Theology)
1920	C. P. T. Winckworth	Wright Scholarship (Arabic)
1921	J. W. Barker	Gibson Spanish Scholarship
1922	K. P. Chatterji	Anthony Wilkin Studentship (Ethnology & Archaeology)
1923	R. S. Elmes	Scandinavian Studentship
1929, 1930	C. B. Firth	Bendall Sanskrit Exhibition
1930, 1931	V. V. Narliker	Isaac Newton Studentship (Astronomy & Physical Optics)
1931	A. M. Ward	Crosse Scholarship (Theology)
1933	R. B. Brandt	Burney Studentship (Philosophy of Religion)
1934	B. Blackstone	Jebb Studentship (European Literature)
1935	P. S. Watson	Burney Studentship (Philosophy of Religion)
1936	E. Bretscher	Clerk Maxwell Scholarship (Experimental Physics)
	B. C. Graves	Burney Studentship (Philosophy of Religion)
	A. M. Ward	Peregrine Maitland Studentship (Comparative Religion)
1937	W. D. Southeard	Stewart of Rannoch Scholarship (Hebrew)
	G. L. Clark	Sheepshanks Exhibition (Astronomy)
1937, 1938	G. M. Friters	Bartle Frere Exhibition

1939	R. K. Pillai	Benn Levy Studentship (Biochemistry)
1944	D. J. Davies	Burney Studentship
1945	B. Anderson	Peregrine Maitland Studentship (Comparative Religion)
1946	J. H. McD. Whitaker	Shell Scholarship (Geology)
1947	M. K. M. Aly	Sheepshanks Exhibition (Astronomy)
1949	M. F. Piercey	Pinsent Darwin Studentship (Mental Pathology)
1952, 1953	B. E. Kwaw-Swanzy	Holland Rose Studentship (History of British Empire & Commonwealth)
1954	H. Gutfreund	Imperial Chemical Industries Fellowship
1956	E. C. Hopkins	Arnold Gerstenberg Studentship (Moral Philosophy)
	P. J. Williams	Tennant Studentship (Study in Norway)
1958	A. Watanabe	Oliver Gatty Studentship (Colloid Science)
	K. S. Williams	Squire Scholarship (Law)
1959	F. L. Mann	Harold Samuel Studentship (Estate Management)
1960	J. H. Tudor	Peregrine Maitland Studentship (Comparative Religion)
	J. V. Narlikar	W. A. Meek Studentship (Scientific Research)
1961	R. S. Saini	John Stanley Gardiner Studentship (Zoology)
	B. Biswas	Oliver Gatty Studentship (Colloid Science)
	J. F. Wager	Harold Samuel Studentship (Estate Management)
1962	I. G. Solly	David Richards Travel Scholarship
1962, 1964	M. E. F. Bloch	Henry Ling Roth Research Scholarship (Ethnology)
1963	R. W. Bradnock	David Richards Travel Scholarship
	G. B. Norcliffe	David Richards Travel Scholarship
1964, 1965	A. S. Hussaini	E. G. Browne Memorial Research Studentship (Persian Studies)
1966	E. A. Mohan	Squire Scholarship (Law)
1967, 1968	R. R. Salvendran	Broodbank Fellowship (Food Preservation)
	O. Ovanessian	E. G. Browne Memorial Research Studentship (Persian Studies)
1969	R. A. Deeley	David Richards Travel Scholarship

	I. N. Lancaster	David Richards Travel Scholarship
	R. J. Smith	Squire Scholarship (Law)

(iii) University Prizes

1871, 1872	H. R. Philipps[1]	Porson Prize (Translation into Greek Verse)
1880	R. H. Harris[2]	Scholefield Prize (Greek Testament)
	R. H. Harris[2]	Evans Prize (Ecclesiastical History)
1884	G. Shirt[2]	Brotherton Sanskrit Prize
1888	W. J. Whittaker	Chancellor's Medal for English Law
1891	J. H. B. Masterman[3]	Chancellor's English Medal
1905	F. Rogers	John Winbolt Prize (Civil Engineering)
1908	S. L. Ajrekar	Brotherton Sanskrit Prize
1912	M. J. Le Goc	Frank Smart Prize (Botany)
1913	G. H. Harris	Carus Greek Testament Prize (Undergraduate)
1914	G. H. Harris	Carus Greek Testament Prize (Bachelor)
	G. H. Harris	Scholefield Prize
1919	F. F. T. Pinto	Chancellor's English Medal
1921	H. C. G. Vincent[2]	Wiltshire Prize (Geology and Mineralogy)
1923	C. C. Desai	Bhaonagar Medal (Indian Civil Service)
1925	W. F. Flemington	Carus Greek Testament Prize
1926	M. C. Desai	Bhaonagar Medal
1928	E. Evans[2]	Burney (Essay) Prize
1929	E. B. Thorpe	Hulsean Prize (Christian Religion)
1930	V. V. Narliker	Tyson Medal (Mathematics and Astronomy)
	A. M. Ward[2]	Jeremie Prize (Septuagint)
	A. M. Ward	Scholefield (Junior) Prize
1931	E. Evans	Hulsean Prize
1932	G. W. Butterfield	Drewitt Prize (Agriculture)
	A. M. Ward	Hulsean Prize
	J. S. Moon ⎱ *aeq.* I. Morgan ⎰	Scholefield (Junior) Prize
	V. V. Narliker	Rayleigh Prize (Mathematics or Natural Philosophy)
	B. Pattinson	William B. Squire Prize (Music)
1933	F. Greeves	Burney (Essay) Prize
	R. E. Davies	Jeremie Prize (Hellenistic)
1936	A. R. George	Carus Greek Testament Prize
	J. Gray[2]	Raymond Horton Smith Prize (Medicine)
	G. L. Clark	Tyson Medal
1937	J. T. Pinion	E. S. Prior Prize (Architecture)

	W. B. Harris	Jeremie Prize (Hellenistic)
	A. R. George	Scholefield (Junior) Prize
1938	S. H. H. Perry	Hebrew Prize
	S. H. H. Perry	Jeremie (Septuagint) Prize
1939	G. A. Hadjiantoniou	Jeremie (Septuagint) Prize
	K. Grayston	Scholefield (Junior) Prize
1940	E. G. Rupp	Archbishop Cranmer (Essay) Prize (Church History)
	K. Grayston	Carus Greek Testament Prize
1941	J. W. Evans	Scholefield (Junior) Prize
1943	D. J. Davies	Burney (Essay) Prize
1944	D. N. H. Roberts	Burney (Essay) Prize
1947	J. H. McD. Whitaker	Wiltshire Prize (Geology & Mineralogy)
1949	T. F. Morris	E. S. Prior Prize
1950	G. A. Clarke	E. S. Prior Prize
	C. W. Cook	Hulsean Prize
1951	B. H. Neumann	Adams Prize (Natural Philosophy)
	C. S. Rodd	Carus Greek Testament Prize
	K. E. Kirkham	T. H. Middleton Prize (Agricultural Science)
1952	C. S. Rodd	Scholefield (Junior) Prize
	E. A. Attwood	T. H. Middleton Prize
	G. E. Harris	Winchester Reading Prize
1954	A. S. Warren	Scholefield (Junior) Prize
1955	P. Ellingworth	Scholefield (Junior) Prize
	A. S. Warren	Carus Greek Testament Prize
1956	N. St John-Stevas	Yorke (Essay) Prize (Law of Property)
1958	I. H. Marshall	Carus Greek Testament Prize
	M. H. Wakelin	E. S. Prior Prize
	I. H. Marshall	Scholefield (Junior) Prize
1959	I. H. Jones	Carus Greek Testament Prize
	A. Johns ⎱ *aeq.* A. J. Ley ⎰	Charles Lamb Prize (Electrical Engineering)
	I. H. Marshall	Scholefield (Senior) Prize
	I. H. Jones	Scholefield (Junior) Prize
	V. S. Huzurbazar[2]	Adams Prize
1960	J. V. Narlikar	Tyson Medal
1961	C. J. L. Ryan	T. H. Middleton Prize
1962	J. P. W. Rogers	Members' (English Essay) Prize
	J. V. Narlikar	Smith's Prize (Mathematics or Natural Philosophy)

1964	A. de Q. Robin	Hulsean Prize
1965	T. R. Smith	Philip Lake Prize (Advanced Physiography)
	M. A. K. Omar	Yorke (Essay) Prize
1966	D. A. Pickard	Gregg Bury Prize (Philosophy of Religion)
1967	C. L. Johnson	H. E. Woodman Prize (Nutrition & Food Biochemistry)
	D. R. Cope	William Vaughan Lewis (Essay) Prize (Geography)
1968	B. Sharratt	Mrs Claude Beddington Prize (English)

[1] Herbert Rees Philipps; given wrongly in *The Historical Register* as Henry Rees Philipps. See also p. 52.

[2] Adjudged of equal merit with one other.

[3] Also 1892 and 1893, from St John's College.

Appendix B

In the lists which follow there appear the names of those non-collegiate students (however described from time to time), and of those members of Fitzwilliam College, who, over the space of one hundred years, have figured in contests between the two Universities. The inclusion of a particular name does not necessarily imply the award of a blue. The minutes of the Cambridge Blues Committee, established in 1912 and still charged with the responsibility of deciding on the entitlement of individual clubs to award blues to their members, contain much interesting information about the recognition (granted or withheld) or different clubs at different times, the number of blues or half-blues authorized, the minimum standards sometimes required, as, for example, in Athletics or Swimming, and the discretion allowed to captains; from all of which it became evident that the compilation of a complete roll of Fitzwilliam blues would, at worst, be impossible, and, at best, more time-consuming than could be contemplated. The appearance of a name in the lists, therefore, signifies no more than that its owner took part in a sufficiently well established competition with Oxford University, without regard to the question whether his club was entitled to award a full blue, a half-blue (or both), or no blue at all. On occasion, further information is given: captains and presidents are mentioned; coxswains are distinguished from the pulling men; records are noted; and in some events, as in Athletics, there are particulars of individual performances.

Incomparably the best source of collected information is *Oxford versus Cambridge 1827–1930*, by H. M. Abrahams and J. Bruce Kerr (Faber and Faber, 1931), with a supplement for one further year. Its completeness underlines the difficulties of assembling material for subsequent years, but even these experts quailed before the problems surrounding the award of blues. As with most bare records, there are colourful details which the Fitzwilliam lists do not divulge. Two men so nearly included in them may have felt, and may still feel, hardly done by: G. E. Barritt, also of Wesley House, selected for the lacrosse match of 1947, cancelled because Oxford could not raise a side; and J. D. Harrison, twelfth man for a casualty-free association football match in 1966, to whom it may almost have seemed a year later that insult had been added to absence of injury when on 4 December 1967 the Cambridge Blues Committee ruled that a chosen substitute should be awarded his full blue whether he played or not. On the other side of the medal is the unexpected emergence of two Fitzwilliam polo players, of whom the first was in the University team in 1924, and, even more surprisingly, had played for Oxford in the previous year. On both occasions he was on the losing side; and in both Universities his stay was unusually short.

But of all the colourful episodes for which there is no room in a prosaic factual narrative, the record – in more than one sense – of Ivar Vind, a Fitzwilliam freshman from Denmark in the Lent term of 1947, deserves a special mention. His academic career is best left unsung, but as the first Fitzwilliam President of the C.U.A.C. he came into his own at the Sports of 1948, when the University was overwhelmed by an unusually strong Oxford team.

> The great individual performance of the meeting ... [said the *Cambridge Review* correspondent] was that of the Cambridge President, Ivar Vind, who now joins the select company of those who have won three events in the Sports. In order to appreciate this magnificent performance, it should be realised that all three events were going on at the same time. His best effort was his leap of 6 feet three inches in the High Jump, which now stands as a record for the meeting. The previous record, which was the oldest in 'the book', was set up by the Hon. M. J. Brooks, of Brasenose, Oxford, in 1876, at Lillie Bridge. Previously authorities had been agreed that it was impossible for a man to jump 6 feet, which height Brooks surpassed by 2¼ inches. Vind's Discus throw of 131 feet, which has only been exceeded once since the event was instituted, and his win of the Pole Vault, completed a historic triple win.

Migration, usually so pervasive in its effect on the non-collegiate body, is here less prominent than might have been anticipated; furthermore, there was two-way traffic. H. E. Robinson, who in 1886 won his half-blue for Chess, played in the four succeeding years as a member of St Catharine's College; and F. W. Philpot, shown as non-collegiate by Abrahams and Bruce Kerr in athletics (1887) and cross country (1886 and 1887), had already left for St John's. There are likely to have been others who moved house before being chosen to represent the University, but Robinson appears to have been the only one who joined a college after his selection. In reverse, in addition to the polo player from Christ Church, there was in 1937 the first Fitzwilliam rugby football blue who had kept his first three terms at Magdalene; while Verhoeff (Chess, 1949) must be exceptional in having kept no term by residence, anywhere.

1881/82	Buncombe W. P.	Chess	
1882/83	Buncombe W. P.	Chess	
	Sherrard H. W.	Chess	
1883/84	Buncombe W. P.	Chess	
	Sherrard H. W.	Chess	
1884/85	Sherrard H. W.	Chess	
1885/86	Robinson H. E.	Chess	
1897/98	Wootten G. A.	Boxing & Fencing	Feather-weight
1909/10	McLaren A. D.	Billiards	
1910/11	Dubois H. A.	Athletics	High Jump
1912/13	Bombal D. L.	Fencing	Foil
1913/14	Resleure J. F.	Swimming	Records in 100 yds and 440 yds
1920/21	Lewis H. G.	Football (A)	
	Roberts E. H.	Lacrosse	
	Switzer S. le R.	Lacrosse	
1921/22	Carter W. L.	Billiards	
	Johnson S. T.	Lacrosse	
	Miller O. G.	Lawn Tennis	Doubles only. Capped for Scotland
1922/23	Chalk A. R.	Football (A)	
	Johnson S. T.	Lacrosse	
	Switzer S. le R.	Lacrosse	
1923/24	Bowker G. W.	Lacrosse	
	Johnson S. T.	Lacrosse	
	Merrill F. T.	Swimming	100 yds
	Nelson S. E.	Relay Races	One mile
	Nelson S. E.	Athletics	440 yds
	Pearce J. T.	Polo	
	Young A. E. F.	Cross Country	
1924/25	Bowker G. W.	Lacrosse	
1925/26	Bowker G. W.	Lacrosse	
	Constable P. H. C.	Billiards	
	Tan C. H.	Billiards	
1926/27	Constable P. H. C.	Billiards	Captain
	Tan C. H.	Billiards	
1929/30	Park S. J.	Badminton	
	Whitehead C.	Relay Races	Two miles
1930/31	Lane C. A.	Hockey	
	Whitehead C.	Relay Races	Two miles

1931/32	Lane C. A.	Hockey	Capped for Scotland
	Whitehead C.	Relay Races	Two miles
	Whitehead C.	Athletics	One mile
1933/34	Irfan A.	Athletics	Weight
	Wiles G. P.	Athletics	Pole Vault
	Zapoleon L. B.	Chess	
1934/35	Irfan A.	Athletics	Weight
	Nanda S. P.	Boxing	Heavy-weight
	Neumann B. H.	Chess	
	Pettit D. E. A.	Football (A)	
1935/36	Irfan A.	Athletics	Weight – 45'9½". Record
	Pettit D. E. A.	Football (A)	
1936/37	Allwood M. S.	Table Tennis	Captain
	Irfan A.	Athletics	Weight – 49'3¾". Record
	Lo K. H. C.	Lawn Tennis	Singles only
	Pettit D. E. A.	Football (A)	
1937/38	Lo K. H. C.	Lawn Tennis	Singles only
	Pettit D. E. A.	Football (A)	Captain. Capped for England
	Reed E. D. E.	Football (R)	
1938/39	Pickman D. O.	Lacrosse	
1945/46	Aly M. K. M.	Water Polo	
1946/47	Miszewski K.	Fencing	Sabre
	Vind I.	Athletics	High Jump, Pole Vault, Discus
1947/48	Jones B. M.	Swimming	Medley Relay
	Miszewski K.	Fencing	Sabre
	Telford T. M.	Badminton	
	Vind I.	Relay Races	Hurdles – 4 × 120 yds
	Vind I.	Athletics	High Jump – 6'3". Record. Pole Vault. Discus. President C.U.A.C.
1948/49	Ellis R. S.	Cross Country	
	Jones G. M.	Water Polo	
	Miszewski K.	Fencing	Sabre
	Rhodes R. G. P.	Ice Hockey	
	Telford T. M.	Badminton	Captain
	Verhoeff A.	Chess	
1949/50	Davies T. S.	Football (A)	
	Ellis R. S.	Cross Country	
	Ellis R. S.	Athletics	Three miles
	Horrell R. K.	Boxing	Middle-weight

	Jones B. M.	Football (R)	
	Jones G. M.	Water Polo	
1950/51	Brunt M. A.	Lacrosse	
	Ellis R. S.	Cross Country	Captain
	Leslie D.	Bridge	
	Williams N. E.	Football (R)	
1951/52	Honey D. G.	Relay Races	4 × 880 yds. Record
	Leigh D. C. F.	Ice Hockey	
	Leslie D.	Chess	
	Leslie D.	Bridge	
1952/53	Dewhurst T.	Football (A)	
	Heah H. A.	Badminton	
	Honey D. G.	Athletics	One mile
	Leigh D. C. F.	Ice Hockey	
1953/54	Heah H. A.	Badminton	Captain
	Leigh D. C. F.	Ice Hockey	Captain
	Rosselson L.	Chess	
	Wagg R. B. C.	Swimming	220 yds breast-stroke
1954/55	Hazzan G. C.	Squash Rackets	
	Heah H. A.	Badminton	
	Kay B. M.	Cross Country	
	Rosselson L.	Chess	
	Wagg R. B. C.	Swimming	176 yds individual medley
	Zahid N. A.	Table Tennis	
1955/56	Blane A. Q.	Basketball	
	Es-Said N.	Basketball	
	Heah H. H.	Badminton	
	Hope D. F. L.	Boxing	Bantam-weight
	Rosselson L.	Chess	
	Smith R. F.	Badminton	
	Stock J. M.	Lacrosse	
	Wagg R. B. C.	Swimming	220 yds breast-stroke
	Zahid N. A.	Table Tennis	
1956/57	Davies J.	Basketball	
	Es-Said N. A.	Basketball	
	Heah H. H.	Badminton	
	Hope D. F. L.	Boxing	Bantam-weight
	Lukshumeyah V.	Polo	
	Martel G. T.	Shooting	
	Pellow G. S.	Football (A)	
1957/58	Anderson M. C.	Swimming	

	Bannister R. F.	Boxing	Light middle-weight
	Es-Said N. A.	Basketball	Captain
	Heah H. H.	Badminton	
	Lukshumeyah V.	Polo	
	Martel G. T.	Shooting	Captain
	Meyers D. D.	Basketball	
	Warner A. C.	Gymnastics	
1958/59	Anderson M. C.	Swimming	Captain
	Bannister R. F.	Boxing	Light middle-weight
	Emery C. K.	Basketball	
	Evans M. H.	Shooting	
	Fishwick P. D.	Hockey	
	Gaposchkin E.	Basketball	
	Lukshumeyah V.	Polo	Captain
	Mackenzie P. S.	Athletics	High Jump
	Powell G.	Hockey	
	Williams K. S.	Lacrosse	
1959/60	Anderson M. C.	Swimming	
	Bannister R. F.	Boxing	Captain
	Blackburn A. L.	Basketball	
	Brodie J. B.	Cricket	
	Green J. C.	Fives (E)	
	Jones B. G.	Table Tennis	
	Mackenzie P. S.	Athletics	High jump
	Renton J. D.	Jiu-Jitsu	
	Williams K. S.	Lacrosse	
1960/61	Cox I. S.	Table Tennis	
	Green J. C.	Fives (E)	
	Houghton R. F.	Boxing	Light heavy-weight
	Jones B. G.	Table Tennis	
	Kirby P. J.	Fencing	
	Nicholas T. P.	Table Tennis	
	Renton J. D.	Jiu-Jitsu	
	Williams K. S.	Lacrosse	
1961/62	Abrahams L.	Gymnastics	
	Green J. C.	Fives (E)	
	Jones B. G.	Table Tennis	Captain
	Kirby P. J.	Fencing	Winner National Foil Championship
	Lavender J. G.	Jiu-Jitsu	
	Nicholas T. P.	Table Tennis	

	Theobald R. C.	Boxing	Middle-weight
1962/63	Abrahams L.	Athletics	
	Abrahams L.	Gymnastics	
	Kavanagh F. J.	Ice Hockey	
	Lee R. A.	Boxing	Welter-weight
	Macalpine G. A.	Golf	
	Nicholas T. P.	Table Tennis	Captain
	Thomas A. F.	Lacrosse	
	Wheeler E. F. C.	Boxing	Heavy-weight
1963/64	Akers D. F.	Football (A)	
	Bagott A. M. A.	Golf	
	Berry A. J. R.	Fencing	
	Kavanagh F. J.	Ice Hockey	
	Lee R. A.	Boxing	Welter-weight
	Nichols J. J. G. L.	Athletics	Discus
	Thomas A. F.	Lacrosse	
	Tulloch J. C.	Table Tennis	Captain
1964/65	Akers D. F.	Football (A)	
	Gesua D.	Basketball	
	Hamp-Ferguson A. J. C.	Football (R)	
	Lee R. A.	Boxing	Welter-weight
	Peacock R. D.	Hockey	
	Rahr P. V.	Bridge	
	Slater K. J. P.	Football (R)	
	Thomas A. F.	Lacrosse	
1965/66	Akers D. F.	Football (A)	
	Anderson A. A.	Boxing	Welter-weight
	Cross A. J.	Lacrosse	
	Gesua D.	Basketball	
	Hamp-Ferguson A. J. C.	Football (R)	
	Hiller G. G.	Tennis	
	Malalasekara V. P.	Cricket	
	Martin-Jenkins C. D. A.	Fives (R)	
	Noonan J. S.	Ice Hockey	
	Rahr P. V.	Bridge	
	Robson J. W.	Hockey	
	Rush J. R.	Boxing	Heavy-weight
	Thomas A. F.	Lacrosse	Captain
1966/67	Berman J. V.	Football (R)	
	Boswell P. G.	Cross Country	
	Clarke R. L.	Boxing	Middle-weight

	Evans D. W.	Basketball	
	Gesua D.	Basketball	
	Graham Young D. R.	Athletics	Pole Vault
	Jones C. D.	Relay Races	4 × 880 yds
	Malalasekara V. J.	Cricket	
	Martin D. J. P.	Fives (R)	
	Martin-Jenkins C. D. A.	Fives (R)	
	Phillips P. S.	Football (A)	
	Robson J. W.	Hockey	
	Rogers D. J.	Hockey	
	Rush J. R.	Boxing	Heavy-weight
	Stoddart K. M.	Football (A)	
	Sutcliffe H. G.	Football (A)	
	Svehlik P. J. T.	Hockey	
	Winbolt Lewis M. J.	Relay Races	4 × 110 yds; 4 × 220 yds; 4 × 440 yds
	Winbolt Lewis M. J.	Athletics	100 yds; 220 yds; 440 yds
	Winckless R. N.	Rowing	
1967/68	Burns T. C.	Football (A)	
	Cotton B. J.	Hockey	
	Findlay P.	Football (A)	
	Gill C. J.	Rowing	Coxswain
	Jorden A. M.	Cricket	
	Lilley D.	Badminton	
	Monahan J. R.	Athletics	Long Jump
	Phillips P. S.	Football (A)	
	Reddaway J. H.	Rowing	
	Robson J. W.	Hockey	
	Svehlik P. J. T.	Hockey	
	Toole M. R.	Boxing	Light welter-weight
	Winbolt Lewis M. J.	Relay Races	4 × 220 yds; 4 × 440 yds
	Winbolt Lewis	Athletics	100 yds; 220 yds; 440 yds
	Winckless R. N.	Rowing	
1968/69	Begg G. A. M.	Golf	
	Brown I. C. R.	Hockey	
	Burns T. C.	Football (A)	
	Cotton B. J.	Hockey	
	Cox D. W.	Boxing	Welter-weight
	Findlay P.	Football (A)	
	Hope A. S.	Cross Country	
	Hope A. S.	Athletics	3,000 m. steeplechase

Jorden A. M.	Cricket	Captain
Jorden A. M.	Football (R)	
Kremmel P. W.	Basketball	
McDowall J. I.	Cricket	
Marrison W. P.	Golf	
Michel K.	Football (A)	
Morgan P. D.	Football (A)	
Murison A. H.	Boxing	Light heavy-weight
Murtough C. B.	Rowing	Coxswain
Phillips P. S.	Football (A)	Capped for England
Redfern T. M.	Rowing	
Retallack C. M.	Basketball	
Roebuck J. J. O.	Pentathlon	
Shackleton I. R.	Football (R)	Capped for England
Svehlik P. J. T.	Hockey	Captain. Capped for England
Winbolt Lewis M. J.	Relay Races	4 × 440 yds; 4 × 880 yds
Winbolt Lewis M. J.	Athletics	440 yds; 880 yds; President C.U.A.C. Olympic Games Mexico City 1968.
Winckless R. N.	Rowing	President C.U.B.C.

Appendix C

Fellows of Fitzwilliam House 17.1.1963–9.9.1966 and thereafter of Fitzwilliam College until 30 September 1969

Fellowships of Fitzwilliam House were of two main classes: Class T (teaching fellowships), and Class R (research fellowships). Under the statutes of Fitzwilliam College there were five classes:

Class A: Fellowships held by College officers, or holders of University offices or posts;
Class B: Professorial fellowships;
Class C: Research fellowships;
Class D: Fellowships held by former Fellows in Class A, or by others at the discretion of the Electors;
Class E: Life fellowships.

On 9 September 1966 the existing Fellows of Fitzwilliam House became by Royal Charter Fellows of Fitzwilliam College; and on 2 November the Fellows of the College then in post were deemed, under Statute XIII of the College, to hold fellowships in the following classes: in Class A, Mr Hickson and the former Teaching Fellows of Fitzwilliam House (save for Dr New, in Class D); and in Class C, former Research Fellows of the House (save for Mr Thompson, elected Fellow in Class D with effect from 1 October).

Name, qualifications, and (first) Cambridge college	Election Date	Class	Qualifying office on election	University	Other Offices	Fitzwilliam House	1. Resignation 2. Retirement
Williams, William Washington, M.A., *Fitzw.*	17.1.1963 29.10.1967	T E	Bursar (1.1.1946-30.9.1967)	U/L Geography (1.10.1938-30.9.1967)		Assistant Censor 1.1.1946-9.9.1966) Acting Censor (1.10.1955-31.12.1958). D/S Geography (1.10.1963-30.9.1964). President (1.10.1966-30.9.1967)	1. 30.9.1967
Dickinson, Sydney, B.Sc., *Wales*; Ph.D., Minnesota; M.A., *Emm.*	17.1.1963	T	D/S Agriculture (1.10.1947-30.9.1966)	U/L Mycology (1.10.1934-30.9.1965)			2. 30.9.1965
Hickson, Geoffrey Fletcher, M.A., *Cla.*	8.2.1965		Secretary, Board of Extra-mural Studies (31.3.1928-30.9.1967)				2. 30.9.1967
Haywood, Richard Wilson, M.A., *Fitzw.*	17.1.1963	T	D/S Mechanical Sciences (1.10.1948-	U/L Engineering 1.10.1949-			
Wayper, Charles Leslie, M.A., Ph.D., *Cath.*	29.1.1963	T	D/S History (1.10.1949-	Tutor, Board of Extra-mural Studies (1.8.1946-		Junior Tutor (1.8.1948-30.9.1949) Tutor (1.10.1969-	
Wormell, Thomas Wilson, M.A., Ph.D., *Joh.*	29.1.1963	T	U/L Meteorological Physics (1.10.1950-			D/S Physical Sciences (7.6.1963-30.9.1966) D/S Natural Sciences (1.10.1966-	

Walters, Robert Norman, M.A., *Jes.*	17.1.1963	T	Tutor (1.10.1950-1.11.1966)		D/S English (1.10.1950-18.6.1967) D/S Classics (1.10.1951-18.6.1967) Praelector (1.10.1960-18.6.1967) Senior Tutor (2.11.1966-18.6.1967) Died 18.6.1967
Utting, John Edward George, M.A., *Tr.H.*	17.1.1963	T	D/S Economics (1.10.1955-12.3.1965)	Assist. Director Dept Applied Economics (1.10.1955-12.3.1965)	1. 30.4.1965
Kelly, Raymond, B.A. *Leeds*; D. U. *Lyons*; M.A., *Tr.H.*	17.1.1963	T	Assistant Tutor (1.10.1955-9.9.1966)	UAL Modern Languages (French) (1.10.1950-30.9.1955)	D/S Modern Languages (1.10.1952-23.3.1968) Domestic Bursar (1.10.1960-30.9.1967) Tutor (10.9.1966- Bursar (1.10.1967-
Herbertson, Basil Marriott, M.D., *Durham*; M.A., *Magd.*	17.1.1963	T	Assistant Tutor (1.10.1956-9.9.1966)	U/L Pathology (1.10.1953-	D/S Medicine (1.1.1951- D/S Biological Sciences (7.3.1963-20.4.1964) President (8.11.1967-
Street, John, M.A., Ph.D., *Emm.*	17.1.1963	T	Assistant Tutor (1.10.1959-9.9.1966)	U.L. Latin American Studies (1.10.1965- Director Centre Latin American Studies (1.6.1966-	D/S Modern Languages (24.3.1968- Tutor (10.9.1966-30.9.1966)
Hunt, Arthur Geoffrey, M.A., *Pet.*	29.1.1963	T	D/S Classics (1.10.1962-30.9.1968)	Senior Dept. Lecturer (Education) (1.1.1960-30.9.1968). U/L (Education) (1.10.1968-	Librarian (6.11.1963-30.9.1968) Tutor for Admissions (24.6.1968-

Name, qualifications, and (first) Cambridge college	Election Date	Class	Qualifying office on election	University	Other Offices Fitzwilliam House	1. Resignation 2. Retirement
Lazenby, Alec, M.Sc. Wales; M.A., Ph.D., Trin.	17.1.1963	T	Assistant Tutor (1.10.1962-20.7.1965)	U/L Agriculture (1.10.1958-30.9.1965)		1. 20.7.1965
Kerridge, David, M.A., Ph.D., Cai.	8.2.1963	T	ADR Biochemistry (1.10.1960-30.9.1964)	U/L Biochemistry (1.10.1964-	D/S Biological Sciences (20.4.1964-30.9.1968) Tutor for Research Students (1.1.1968-	
Nicholson, Harold, M.Eng., *Liverpool*; M.A., *Chur.*	29.1.1963	T	U/L Engineering (1.1.1961-31.12.1967)			1. 30.9.1966
Blackburn, George Michael, Ph.D., *Nottingham*; M.A. *Joh.*	29.1.1963	T	U/D Organic Chemistry (1.4.1961-30.9.1965)			1. 30.9.1965
Fleet, Stephen George, M.A., Ph.D., *Joh.*	15.2.1963	T	U/D Mineralogy (1.10.1962-30.9.1967)	U/L Mineralogy (1.10.1967-	Tutorial Bursar (25.10.1963-24.6.1967) Junior Bursar (25.6.1967- Assist. D/S Nat. Sciences (1.10.1965-	
Padley, Peter Joseph, B.Sc., *London*; Ph.D., *Jes.*	7.3.1963	T	U/D Physical Chemistry (1.10.1961-30.9.1966)		Assistant D/S Nat. Sciences (19.1.1966-30.9.1966)	1. 30.9.1966
Hall, Basil, M.A., *Fitzw.*	30.5.1963	T	D/S Theology (1.10.1961-24.3.1968)	U/L Divinity (1.10.1956-30.9.1968)		1. 30.9.1968

Name	Date				
Haggett, Peter, M.A., Cath.	22.7.1963	T	U/L Geography (1.10.1962-30.9.1966)	D/S Geography (1.10.1964-30.9.1966)	1. 30.9.1966
Hudson, Harry James, Ph.D., Sheffield; M.A., Down.	22.7.1963	T	U/L Botany (1.1.1961-		
Coles, John Morton, Ph.D., Edinburgh; M.A., Fitzw.	6.8.1963	T	UAL Archaeology (1.10.1960-30.9.1965) D/S Archaeology (1.10.1962-	U/L Archaeology (1.10.1965-	
Edwards, Anthony Vaughan, M.A., Vet.M.B., Fitzw.	1.10.1963	T	U/D Physiology (1.10.1963-30.9.1966)	U/L Physiology (1.10.1966-	Tutor (1.1.1967-
Mills, Ernest Frederick, Dip.T.P., London; M.A., Chur.	23.4.1964	T	Director Univ. Estate Management Advisory Service (30.10.1961-		D/S Land Economy (1.1.1967-
Yates, George Gilbert, M.A., Jes.	23.4.1964	T	Engineer i/c Electronic Equipment, Dept of Physics (1.1.1962- D/S Mathematics (25.2.1964-30.9.1966)	D/S Mathematics (23.10.1958-31.12.1961)	1. 30.9.1966
New, Denis Alan Trevor, M.A., Oxford; Ph.D., London; M.A., Fitzw.	23.4.1964	T	M.R.C. Research Officer, Strangeways Research Laboratory (1.9.1961-30.9.1967)	U/L Physiology (1.10.1967-	
Nicol, Alexander Douglas Ian, B.Sc., Manchester; M.A., Ph.D., Fitzw.	28.5.1964	T	Secretary, Dept of Physics (1.6.1960-30.9.1966)	Secretary, Council School of Physical Sciences (1.10.1966-	

Name, qualifications, and (first) Cambridge college	Election Date	Class	Qualifying office on election	University	Other Offices Fitzwilliam House	1. Resignation 2. Retirement
Watson, Alan John, B.A., *Oxford*; M.A., *Corp.*	28.5.1964	T	U/L Experimental Psychology (1.10.1954-		Tutor (1.10.1967-31.12.1968). Senior Tutor (1.1.1969-	
Ferrier, Robert Patton, Ph.D., *St Andrews*; M.A., *Pemb.*	28.5.1964	T	SAR Physics (1.10.1962-30.9.1966)	ADR Electron Microscopy (1.10.1966-		
Vázquez, David, Ph.D., *Madrid*	26.1.1965	R				1. 30.6.1966
Revell, John Robert Stephen, B.Sc., *London*; M.A., *Selw.*	13.3.1965	T	Senior Research Officer, Dept Applied Economics (1.10.1963-31.12.1968) Assistant Tutor (1.10.1965-23.6.1967)		D/S Economics (13.3.1965-30.9.1967) Senior Tutor (24.6.1967-31.12.1968)	1. 31.12.1968
Brown, Alan Martin, B.A., Mus.B., *Cai.*	19.3.1965	T	UAL Music (1.10.1966-		D/S Music (1.1.1967-	
Thompson, David Michael, B.A., *Qu.*	1.10.1965 1.1.1966- (Leather-sellers')	R T			Librarian (1.10.1968-Praelector (1.10.1969-	
Garratt, Peter Joseph, B.Sc., *Bristol*; Ph.D., *Columbia*	1.10.1965 1.1.1966	R T	U/D Organic and Inorganic Chemistry (1.1.1966-30.9.1966)		Assistant D/S Natural Sciences (Chemistry) (1.10.1966-30.9.1967)	1. 30.9.1967

Name	Date		Position	Position (cont.)	Note
Jakubovics, John Paul, B.Sc., Bristol; Ph.D., *Cai.*	1.1.1966	R			1. 30.9.1966
Whittington, Geoffrey, B.Sc. (Econ.), *London*	1.1.1966 R 1.10.1968 T		Research Officer, Dept Applied Economics (1.10.1964-	D/S Economics (1.10.1967-	
Kenney, Christopher Nigel, M.A., Ph.D., *Qu.*	1.2.1966	T	U/L Chemical Engineering (1.10.1966-	Tutor (1.10.1967- Assistant D/S Natural Sciences (1.10.1968-	
Jackson, John Eric, M.A., *Joh.*	28.4.1966	T	D/S Geography (1.10.1966-31.12.1968)	Geodesy and Geophysics (1.10.1948-	
Smith, Kenneth Charles Arthur, M.A., Ph.D., *Fitzw.*	28.4.1966	T	U/L Engineering (1.10.1965-		
Willis, John Raymond, B.Sc., Ph.D., *London*	28.4.1966	T	SAR Mechanics of Solids (1.9.1965-	D/S Mathematics (1.10.1966-	
Joysey, Kenneth Alan, Ph.D., *London*; M.A., *Magd.*	21.5.1966	T	Tutor (1.10.1966-30.9.1969)	U/L Zoology, and Curator of Vertebrates, Museum of Zoology (1.1.1966-	
Clarke, Malcolm Alistair, B.A., LL.B., *Joh.*	1.10.1966	C			1. 16.7.1968

Name, qualifications, and (first) Cambridge college	Election Date	Class	Qualifying office on election	Other Offices University	Fitzwilliam House	1. Resignation 2. Retirement
Walker, Geoffrey James, M.A., Ph.D., Fitzw.	15.2.1967	A	Steward (1.10.1967-	U/L Modern Languages (Spanish) (14.12.1966-		
Brooke, John Hedley, B.A., Fitzw.	26.4.1967	C				1. 30.9.1968
Mitchell, Reginald Harry, B.A., Joh.	26.4.1967	C				1. 31.8.1968
Nott, Peter John, M.A., Fitzw.	23.6.1967	A	Chaplain (25.12.1964-30.8.1969)			1. 30.8.1969
Dickens, Peter Geoffrey, B.A., Fitzw.	23.6.1967	C				
Rupp, Ernest Gordon, M.A., B.D., D.D., Fitzw.	1.9.1967	D		U/L Divinity (1.10.1952-30.9.1956)	D/S Theology (1.10.1953-30.9.1956)	1. 30.9.1968
Austin, Colin Russell, B.V.Sc., D.Sc., Sydney	1.10.1967	B	Darwin Professor of Animal Embryology (1.10.1967-			
Cross, George Alan Martin, B.A., Down.	1.10.1967	C				
Prandy, Kenneth, B.Sc. (Econ.), London; Ph.D., Liverpool	6.3.1968	A	Research Officer, Dept of Applied Economics (1.10.1967-		D/S Sociology (24.6.1969-	
Clements, Ronald Ernest, M.A., Chr.	1.10.1968	A	D/S Theology (24.3.1968-	U/L Divinity (1.10.1967-	Tutor (1.10.1968-	

Name	Date	Code	Office / Department	
Baker Smith, Malcolm Peter Dominic, M.A., *Trin.*	1.10.1968 (Leathersellers)	A	D/S English (1.9.1967-	
Robson, Brian Turnbull, M.A., Ph.D., *Cath.*	1.10.1968	A	U/L Geography (1.10.1967-	D/S Geography (1.1.1969-
Hewkin, David John, B.Sc., Ph.D., *London*	1.10.1968	D	Scientific Research Council Fellowship, Dept Organic and Inorganic Chemistry 1.10.1967-31.8.1969	1. 31.8.1969
Lyne, Richard Oliver Allen Marcus, B.A., *Joh.*	1.10.1968	C		1. 30.6.1969
Whitfield, Philip John, B.A., *Fitzw.*	1.10.1968	C		1. 30.9.1969

By 30 September 1969 the following Fellows had also been elected, with effect from the date shown

Name	Date	Code	Office / Department	
Pearl, David Stephen, B.A., LL.B., *B'ham;* LL.B., *Qu.*	1.10.1969	A	UAL Law (1.10.1967-	D/S Law (1.10.1969-
Blunden, Allen George, B.A., *Jes.*	1.10.1969	C		
Catto, Christopher John Dignet, B.A., *Fitzw.*	1.10.1969	C		
Grice, Roger, M.A., *Cath.*; Ph.D., *Harvard*	1.10.1969	A	SAR Dept Organic and Inorganic Chemistry (1.10.1969-	

Appendix D

(i) Clothworkers' Company Exhibitions

I

Never had they been so rich, never had their affairs been in such perfect order. As the great tidal wave of Victorian prosperity rolled on, bearing on its crest the cargoes from the empire, the fruits of trade that made London ever increasingly the greatest port in the world, the wealth of the Company increased with it.

So wrote Thomas Girtin, the historian of the Clothworkers' Company, in 1958,[1] and so it was that the Company, desiring that others less affluent should benefit from its prosperity, resolved on 3 June 1874 to create six exhibitions of £50 each, tenable for three years by students proceeding to any recognized National University having chartered authority to grant degrees in Arts, and instructed its Trusts and General Superintendence Committee to frame regulations for appointments to the exhibitions, and for their tenure. The committee sought the advice of Dr Edwin Abbott, of the City of London School, who emphasized 'the desirableness of encouraging the present attempt at giving a cheap University education to unattached students', and recommended that the company should offer an annual award to each of the Universities of Oxford and Cambridge for the encouragement of the study of the Natural Sciences by these students, with Classics or Mathematics as the next choice. Dr Abbott thought that in this way the Company might influence Oxford and Cambridge to promote the study of Natural Science 'which needs for its support all the outside pressure that can be brought to bear in the Universities'. Thus it came about that, in the following Michaelmas term, the Non-Collegiate Students Board, hearing from Mr Somerset of the Company's intention to award annually an exhibition of the value of £50, tenable for three years by non-collegiate students only, for the encouragement of the study of Physical Science, accepted the offer with the greatest satisfaction, and proposed that an examination should be held in the Christmas vacation, open to candidates who had not come into residence, or, being resident, had not kept more than one term. The Company agreed; and in January 1875 the first award was divided between H. J. H. Fenton and E. F. Taylor.

[1] Thomas Girtin, *The Golden Ram – a Narrative History of the Clothworkers' Company* (privately printed, 1958), p. 231.

Fenton, who matriculated in that month, kept four terms, relinquished the exhibition on his election as scholar of Christ's College, and in 1877 was placed in the first class in the Natural Sciences Tripos. Taylor was already in residence, and completed his degree course as a non-collegiate student, with a second class in the Tripos in the same year.

These arrangements continued, except that, in order to save the expense of a special examination (which was being borne by the Company), the exhibition was awarded, from December 1877, on the results of the Certificate Examination of the recently established Oxford and Cambridge Schools Examination Board, with a further modification to the effect that the best of the candidates, whether as an applicant for admission to Cambridge or to Oxford (where a similar exhibition had been established), was to be permitted to choose his University, while the remaining award would go to the candidate next in the order of merit.

In 1880 there was another change: one exhibition in Physical Science,[1] with a small increase in its value to £52.10.0, was made tenable at either University, and the other was replaced by two exhibitions of £30, one at Oxford and one at Cambridge, with no limitation of subject, tenable for three years, and awarded in November of each year to a student of one year's standing on the recommendation of his Censor (with, in Cambridge, the approval of the Non-Collegiate Students Board). Under this scheme awards were first made in 1880 – for Physical Science in July, and on the Censor's recommendation in November; and of the fifteen Physical Science exhibitions given between 1880 and 1895, when this exhibition was abandoned, thirteen were held in Cambridge.

At this time, the Company also resolved that an additional sum of £10 should be paid to a £30 exhibitioner on graduation, with a further amount of £20 if he was classed in a Tripos. In 1886 the 'honours bonus' was limited to those who were placed in the first class, and corresponding announcements were made in the University Calendar until the year 1924/25, when they ceased. Until 1890, when the Company decided that the bonuses (then defined as of £10 for graduation, with additional sums £20 for honours in the first class, and of £10 in the second) should apply to all its exhibitions, the Physical Science men did not qualify for them, and even after the Company's decision a Physical Science exhibitioner in 1896, with a first class in Natural

---

[1]   No subject prescribed; but there are subsequent references to the Physical Science Exhibition, and, with one exception (Scudamore, 1889, Moral Sciences), all the Cambridge £52.10.0 exhibitioners sat for the Natural Sciences Tripos.

Sciences, received no more than £10 in all. To the uninitiated the workings of the bonus system are not, at this distance of time, without their perplexities – in 1887 a Physical Science exhibitioner with a first class in the Tripos received nothing, while a £30 exhibitioner was paid £10 for his degree, and £20 for his second class in Theology. Doubtless there were individual circumstances to be taken into account, and there must have been persuasive reasons for the award to an Oxford non-collegiate exhibitioner, in 1886, of £10 for his B.A. degree, and of £10 for a fourth class in *Literae Humaniores*.

After the withdrawal of the £52.10.0 exhibition, the company for a time awarded one of £30 at Oxford and one at Cambridge, but in 1904 another of the same value was added at each of the two Universities, subject to a substantial change in regulations, for all the awards were to be restricted to honours candidates who were also intending to take Holy Orders in the Church of England; and it was no longer to be 'required that candidates should be of one year's standing. On their part, the Non-Collegiate Students Board sought the Company's consent to a proposal that they might assign their awards to particular dioceses, in the hope that this might help them to find suitable applicants, with possible assistance from diocesan funds. The Company raised no objection, on the understanding that no diocese should receive undue preference.

In 1924, the Oxford Censor having reported a dearth of suitable candidates, and having also enquired whether the applicants might be accepted who were not reading for Orders, or applicants from Keble College or St Edmund Hall who were, the Company reviewed its arrangements for non-collegiate awards, and concluded that as a considerable proportion were by that time financed out of its corporate funds, and relatively few by Trusts with restrictions on eligibility, the exhibitions might be thrown open to other applicants (who must, however, still produce evidence of need, and must not be members of colleges), provided only that in each University one of the six exhibitioners at any one time should have declared his intention of taking Orders in the Church of England. In 1924, also, the annual value of the exhibitions was raised from £30 to £40; and six years later the number of the awards was increased from two to three, and their tenure reduced from three years to two, appointments being made for the second and third years of residence. There is no specific evidence of the reason for this change, which was made on the initiative of the Cambridge Censor, with the concurrence of his opposite number, but it seems likely that both wished to be able to make their recommendations for awards in the light of personal knowledge of the applicants, and of work done by them at the University during their first year.

In 1935 the conditions of eligibility were again modified so that, whereas applicants were in general still required to read for honours, those who had announced their intention of taking Orders were declared admissible even though they might be poll men.[1] This concession was made at the suggestion of the two Censors, doubtless in the hope that it might lessen their difficulties in finding eligible ordinands for appointment; but within a couple of years the Cambridge Censor was obliged, on two consecutive occasions, to leave an exhibition vacant because there was no ordinand exhibitioner continuing in residence, and no suitable ordinand candidate.

At the end of 1951, at the request of the Cambridge Censor, the Company authorized a reversion to the system of awards abandoned in 1930, and the University's *Annual Register* for 1952/53 describes the (two) exhibitions as being tenable for three years, and, in its first specific mention of the Company's ruling of 1935, states that they were for 'Students who intend to read for honours in any Tripos, or who intend to take Holy Orders in the Church of England'. This announcement continued in much the same form until, in the *Annual Register* for 1956/57 the reference is to two entrance exhibitions of £40, to be awarded annually, and tenable for up to three years – this last proviso being inserted in order to allow for the possible discontinuance of an award if its holder's progress in his studies should not be satisfactory. There is here no longer any reference to ordination (or to honours, for by that time no poll degree candidate would have been considered for appointment).

In the Lent term of 1957 the exhibitions were included, with the company's consent, among the awards first offered by Fitzwilliam House on the results of an examination taken by applicants for admission in the following Michaelmas term. And, save for casual vacancies in mid-course, they continued as Entrance Awards, since 1963 made only to candidates declared to be of Open Exhibition standard in examinations conducted annually in December by the Queens' College group of colleges for the award of Open Entrance Scholarships and Exhibitions.

---

[1] In spite of this decision by the Company, and of its decision in 1924, the *University Calendar* (later the *Annual Register*) continues, up to the year 1951/52, to describe the exhibitions as being for honours men, with preference for those reading for Holy Orders.

II

Exhibitioners (Physical Science)

(*Orders
n/a: No recommendation for appointment)

Academic year of first tenure	Exhibitioner	College (on migration)
1874/75	Fenton, H. J. H.	(Christ's)
	*Taylor, E. F.	
1875/76	Scott, A.	(Trinity)
1876/77	Hooker, G. N.	
	Jones, T. R.	(St John's)
1877/78	*McCubbin, J. G.	
1878/79	Ryan, J.	(King's)
1879/80	Bowman, E.	
1880/81	Hicks, J. O.	
1881/82	*Davies, J.	(Sidney Sussex)
1882/83	Jones, E. L.	(Downing)
1883/84	Carr, J. W.	(Emmanuel)
1884/85	Dufton, A.	
1885/86	Shaw, E. A.	(King's)
1886/87	Willis, J. C.	(Caius)
1887/88	French, W.	
1888/89	n/a	
1889/90	Scudamore, W.	
1890/91	Howard, H.	
1891/92	(Oxford)	
1892/93	(Oxford)	
1893/94	Pearson, H. H. W.	(Christ's)
1894/95	Boardman, T. H.	(Peterhouse)
1895/96	Fagan, T. W.	

Exhibitioners (£30)

(*Orders
n/a: No recommendation for appointment. In 1937/38, no suitable ordinand.)

Academic year of first tenure	Exhibitioner	College (on migration)
1880/81	*Buncombe, W. P.	
1881/82	Wilson, S. B.	

1882/83	*Cole, T. E.	(Downing)
1883/84	Allnutt, J. W. F.	
1884/85	*Bickmore, C. F.	
1885/86	Morgan, J.	
1886/87	Whittaker, W. J.	(Trinity)
1887/88	*Lockett, H. J.	
1888/89	*Haigh, P.	
1889/90	Windsor, C. W.	
1890/91	*Williams, J. W. M.	
1891/92	Judd, F. H.	
1892/93	Highfield, H.	
1893/94	Potter, W. J. J.	
1894/95	Ross, P. A.	
1895/96	*Dewhurst, H.	(St Cath.)
1896/97	*Godfrey, A. R.	
1897/98	Cunnington, C. W.	
1898/99	*Cartwright, C.	
1899/1900	Payne, H. C. F. B.	
1900/01	Reynolds, R. P.	
1901/02	Wiles, J. W.	
1902/03	*Webb, E.	
1903/04	Wiles, J. W.	
1904/05	*Staley, J. E.	
	*Smith, B. T. D.	(Jesus)
1905/06	*Joyce, J. W. H.	(Christ's)
	*Richardson, F.	
1906/07	*Horton, H.	(King's)
	*Lee, H.	
1907/08	*Harvey, W.	
	*Hussey, R. L.	
1908/09	*Lee, A. O. N.	
	*Stearn, A. J. S.	
1909/10	*Bedford, H.	
	Smith, T.	(Caius)
1910/11	*Ward, R. W. A.	
	Conan-Davies, B. I.	(St Cath.)
1911/12	*Rosbotham, J.	
	*Bywaters, F. J.	
1912/13	Slawson, W. N.	
	Woods, W. A.	
1913/14	Knight, J. H.	

1913/14	Bartlett, C. W.
1914/15	Harris, F. W.
	Elliott, O. C. F.
1915/16	Sumner, E. J.
	*Cook, F.
1916/17	Flory, P. J.
	*Vincent, T. C. L.
1917/18	*Elliott, S. D.
	*Hardwick, B.
1918/19	Vincent, T. C. L.
	*Lawton, H.
	*Morris, A. H.
1919/20	*Cavendish, R. P.
	*Batchelor, K. B.
1920/21	*Lesser, N. A.
	n/a
1921/22	*Davies, L. B. Z.
	*Bishop, F. E.
	*Coles, H. A. H.
1922/23	Welch, A. H. V.
	*Beard, D.
1923/24	*Chamberlain, L. F.
	n/a
1924/25	Douglas-Smith, E. E.
	Dew, H.
1925/26	Hancock, R. R.
	Beaumont, S. P. L.
1926/27	Bates, H.
	*Oatridge, N. C.
1927/28	*Wellings, A. C. M.
	Owen, J. O. G.
1928/29	*Day, L. W.
	*Morbey, T.
1929/30	Pointon, J.
	*Alliston, C. J.
1930/31	*Fenwick, E. H.
	Lockley, W. E. E.
	Mance, H. W.
1931/32	*Cobb, R. J.
	Damerell, N. W.
	*Moore, S. E.

1932/33	*Barrand, C. N.
	*Baynham, W. B.
	Liddiard, F. J.
1933/34	*Bond, G.
	Sharp, J. R. I.
	Williams, A. E.
1934/35	Clark, G. L.
	Hollins, T. H. B.
	*Purcell, W. H. S.
1935/36	Pettit, D. A. E.
	Springett, J. A.
	*Whiting, O.
1936/37	Halford, A. E. S.
	Measures, G. F.
	Whitehead, F. S.
1937/38	Amyes, J. C. B.
	Hill, S. M.
	n/a
1938/39	Ajgaonkar, D. N.
	Hart, C. C.
	n/a
1939/40	*Alford, J. R.
	Stewart, G. L.
	Williams, N. E.
1940/41	Deighton, T.
	*Dowse, E.
	Ilsley, P. E.
1941/42	Cooper, D. R.
	*Holt, J. F.
	n/a
1942/43	Ireland, H. M.
	Stacey, F. A.
	n/a
1943/44 to 1947/48	No candidates
1948/49	St John Stevas, N.
	*Sertin, J. F.
	n/a
1949/50	*Brewster, L. A.
	n/a
	n/a

1950/51	*Reed, B. D.
	n/a
	n/a
1951/52	Cope, V.
	Stirling, J. S.
1952/53	Chesher, F. J.
	*Semper, C. M.
1953/54	Duffett, M. W.
	Hopkins, E. C.
1954/55	Cope, C. E.
	*Trotter, M. F. C.
	Warren, A.
1955/56	*Moroney, J. B.
	Gausden, M. W.
	Martel, G. T.
1956/57	Page, A. F. G.
	*Glen, R. M.
1957/58	Atkinson, D.
	*Mowbray, D.
1958/59	Crowson, P. C. F.
	Wilkinson, J. A.
1959/60	Baitup, R.
	Evans, I. F.
1960/61	Munn, B. W.
	Raffan, P. M.
	Mellars, P. A.
1961/62	*Reeve, R. P.
	Sigee, D. C.
	Walton, H. F.
1962/63	Brown, A.
	James, R. K.
1963/64	Hayes, P. J.
	Johnson, P. W. S.
1964/65	Grenfell, J. G.
	Hawker, N. H.
1965/66	Chapman, A. B.
	Clifton, R. A.
1966/67	Moore, R. H.
	Nightingale, F. R.
1967/68	Ashton, N. W.
	Venning, J. C.

1968/69	Deegan, J. L. E.
	Phillips, J. A.
	Falle, S. A. E. G.
	Mohan, E. A.
1969/70	Hann, J. G.
	Lee, G. W.
1970/71	Gore, N. D.
	Holman, J. P.
1971/72	Blake, M. C.
	Waggett, P. C.
1972/73	Collett, E. J. G.
	Lovell, A.
1973/74	Greaves, S. J.
	Moore, J. H.

III

There had been twenty-one holders of the Physical Science Exhibition when it was withdrawn in 1895, and thanks to Dr J. A. Venn more information is available about them than about many who came later. Three, only, took Holy Orders (which may have influenced the Clothworkers' Company in its subsequent decision to limit awards to candidates who had declared their intention of seeking ordination). By no means all held their exhibitions for the full term, for of the total of twenty-one eleven were taken by colleges, usually, but not always, before they proceeded to their first degree, and so forfeited awards which had been established for the benefit of non-collegiate students, and could be held by them alone. All went out in honours, seven in the first class (two of them on two separate occasions), nine in the second, and five in the third; and there was to be no lack of distinction in their subsequent careers. Not surprisingly, nearly all read Natural Sciences, the exceptions being Hooker, Jones, and Bowman, who were also the least distinguished, for they were all classed *Junior Optime*, as was Ryan, but for him Mathematics was an additional subject, over and above a full Natural Science course. Fenton had by 1899 become a Fellow of the Royal Society, and was an Honorary Fellow of Christ's College from 1911 until his death in 1929. Scott was something of a traveller, for after matriculating as a non-collegiate student in 1876, being already Bachelor of Science of Edinburgh University, he migrated to Trinity College, and graduated there with a first class in the Tripos. He was a collector of degrees, becoming Doctor of Science, first of Edinburgh (1883), and then of Cambridge (1907); and of colleges too, for in 1892 he moved again from Trinity to Peterhouse, but of neither was he Fellow. From 1896 for fifteen years he was Superintendent of the Davy-Faraday Laboratory of the Royal Institution, and from 1911 to 1938 Director of Scientific Research at the British Museum; and it was in this capacity, no doubt, that Mr Howard Carter sought his advice over the removal, and preservation, of objects found in the tomb of King Tutankhamen.

John Ryan, after four terms as an exhibitioner, went to King's College, in the Lent term of 1880, where, according to Dr Venn, he was the first Roman Catholic to be admitted since the Reformation, and was placed in the first class in Part I of the Tripos in 1882, and in Part II in the following year. After fourteen years as Professor of Physics and of Engineering at University College, Bristol, he was appointed Principal of the Woolwich Polytechnic in 1899. As a side-line he took the Cambridge degree of Master of Law in 1890, and was called to the Bar. J. W. Carr, who kept six terms before going to Emmanuel in the Michaelmas term 1885, was also in the first class in the next year, and was successively Lecturer and Professor in Biology at University College, Nottingham. H. H. W. Pearson remained non-collegiate until 1896, when he graduated with a first class in Part I, but moved to Christ's College shortly afterwards, repeated his first class in Part II, and moved again to take his M.A. degree from Caius. After a spell at Kew, he was Professor of Botany at the South African College in Cape Town from 1903 until his death in 1916, at the early age of forty-six. Shortly before he died he had been elected F.R.S.

Of those who did not migrate, Arthur Dufton and William French were both in the first class. Dufton became head of the Department of Dyeing and Chemistry at Bradford Technical College; and French, after some years in educational work at home and abroad, as teacher and administrator, turned to industry, and settled in Lancaster as Managing Director of a chemical works. In Fitzwilliam College he is remembered as a donor of silver, in 1942, and as the founder of a prize for deserving, but not necessarily distinguished, work in Chemistry, Botany or Agriculture, and (for he was a little stiff in his opinions) 'also Geology, but not Natural Sciences Tripos as such, where Physics and Mechanics play a great part'. The Censor described these benefactions as the first of the kind to be received from a former non-collegiate student.

The story of the £30 Exhibition is rather different. The first exhibitioner, appointed in 1880, read Theology, with moderate success, and

was a chess blue. He was the herald of a new era, for none of the Physical Scientists had read Theology, and relatively few had been in the
third class. Between 1880 and 1973, 165 of these exhibitioners were
appointed. For various reasons 10 did not graduate;[1] and of the
remainder 132 went out in honours, with 27½ first classes, 142½ second
classes,[2] and 55 third classes. Differing systems of examination in the
individual subjects make detailed statistical comparison unprofitable,
but it is broadly true to say that the least distinguished performances
were in the subjects with the largest numbers. In History throughout
the whole period one exhibitioner was in the first class; in Theology
there were two. Correspondingly, the proportion of men in the third
class was unusually high and as these were the subjects most frequently
offered by intending ordinands, the creation of these exhibitions for
the purpose of attracting able candidates for ordination must, with
some notable exceptions, be regarded as only moderately successful.

A striking feature of the best of these results is their chronological
distribution. In the first fifty years there were two first classes; in the
last thirty-five there were fifteen; but in the 1930s nine candidates
scored eleven and a half firsts between them. While it is true that these
were, academically, good years in the University as a whole (see
p. 411–12), the results are all the more noteworthy as having been
obtained by the non-collegiate students at a time when their Censor
was frequently expressing his uneasiness about admissions, and was
telling his Board that he did not know where his next year's freshmen
were coming from. It must seem significant, too, that the exhibitions
had then, a few years earlier, been thrown open to all comers, and were
no longer exclusively reserved for intending ordinands.

Of twenty-three £30 exhibitioners in the first period (1880–1903),
when candidature was unrestricted, at least eleven went into the
Church, and among them was Henry Highfield (1894),[3] a classic who
entered the Wesleyan Ministry, and became a distinguished Principal
of the Wesley College in Colombo. The highest academical honours in
these years went to W. J. Whittaker, top of the Law Tripos in 1888,
when he won the Chancellor's Medal for English Law. As first
Whewell Scholar in International Law in 1890, he moved to Trinity
College. From 1900 to 1908 he was Professor of English Law at University College, London, and from 1904 was for many years Reader in

[1]   Three were killed in action in the war of 1914–1918.
[2]   Candidates classed in Part I of the Modern and Medieval Languages Tripos are by conven-
      tion credited with half a class for each of the two languages they are required to offer.
[3]   Date of graduation, as with other names that follow.

the Law of Real and Personal Property to the Council of Legal Education.

J. E. Staley (1907) and B. T. D. Smith (1908) were the first exhibitioners to be appointed from applicants restricted to those who had
declared their intention of seeking Holy Orders, and both gave the new
arrangements a promising start. W. F. Reddaway, who did not hold
with filing systems, except for his own remarkable memory which
retained whatever he might wish to recall, did nevertheless occasionally
preserve, in improbable envelopes, letters to which he attached especial value. One such is from Staley, then a young curate in Peterborough, to whom Reddaway had sent a copy of his Annual Report to
the Non-Collegiate Students Board for the year 1909/10. Staley had
been Reddaway's graduate Secretary in his first years as Censor (the
Board's minutes for the years 1907/09 are in Staley's hand); he was
Reddaway's enthusiastic supporter in all that he did to foster a corporate feeling among his men, and his letter is very critical of those who
joined the non-collegiate body with the intention, avowed or not, of
leaving it in time to acquire a college name to attach to their first
degree. Staley, who died full of years and honour, was appointed
Honorary Canon of Bristol Cathedral in 1945.

Smith, after being placed in the second class in the Historical Tripos
in 1906, went as Lady Kay Scholar to Jesus College, and in 1908
became the first (former) exhibitioner to gain first class honours in
Theology. Himself a member of Westcott House, he was its Vice-Principal from 1909 to 1914. After a period as Chaplain at St John's College, which largely coincided with service as temporary Chaplain to the
Forces, he was elected Fellow of Sidney Sussex in 1918, and served
successively as Dean, Tutor, and Vice-Master. He was also University
Lecturer in Divinity from 1926 to 1940, taking his Doctor's degree in
1937. He too lived to a great age; and is still remembered as the creator
of a rock garden of great beauty.

Walter Harvey (1910) was Assistant Censor, Bursar, and Chaplain of
Fitzwilliam House from 1925 until his retirement in 1943. He died in
1978, and for some years must have been the senior among the exhibitioners.

Not long afterwards, as years go, but with a Great War in between,
came two exhibitioners who were to receive high preferment – A. H.
Morris (1920), from 1954 to 1965 Lord Bishop of St Edmundsbury and
Ipswich, who dedicated a temporary chapel in the new College buildings in 1963, and N. A. Lesser (1923), Archbishop of New Zealand
from 1961 to 1971.

Of other exhibitioners, T. H. B. Hollins (1936) was appointed Professor of Education and Director of the Institute of Education in the University of Leeds in 1967; G. L. Clark (1936), winner of the Tyson Medal in 1936, and from 1939 to 1948 Research Fellow of Trinity College, then went to Bedford College, London, as Reader in Mathematics; J. A. Springett (1937) twice in the first class in the Mathematical Tripos, became Education Officer for Essex County. D. A. E. Pettit (1937), no mean undergraduate historian, was for four years in the University Association Football side (captain in 1937), and was a member of the British Olympic Team in 1936. After a spell as a schoolmaster, he turned to industry, and as Chairman of the National Freight Corporation was knighted in 1974. F. S. Whitehead (1938) was made Reader in the Division of Education of the University of Sheffield in 1973.

There were at least four headmasters – R. R. Hancock (1928), A. E. Williams (1935), J. R. I. Sharp (1936), and C. C. Hart (1943); while Norman St John Stevas (1950, President of the Union Society, and winner of the Yorke Prize in 1957, is known as the editor of the *Collected Works* of Walter Bagehot, and as a leading member of the Conservative party, who in 1979 became Chancellor of the Duchy of Lancaster, Leader of the House of Commons, and Minister for the Arts.

Three exhibitioners, J. F. Sertin (1950), B. D. Reed (1952), and J. B. Moroney (1956), who had all taken Orders before they were admitted to an undergraduate course, also served as Chaplains during their periods of residence from 1948 to 1956.

By 1973 the Clothworkers' Company had appointed, in all, 186 exhibitioners; and in so doing had helped 176 men to qualify for a Cambridge degree, 153 of them with honours. Of the two kinds of Exhibition, those in Physical Science attracted the abler candidates, of whom in consequence a higher proportion were 'lost' to the colleges – eleven out of twenty-one, compared with eight of the forty of so £30 exhibitioners appointed before the end of the war of 1914/1918, when migration ceased to be a serious preoccupation. Rather more than one third took Orders; and in years gone by the Court of the Company may have regretted the diminishing number of ordinands, and the relatively modest attainments of some of them; but these notes, fragmentary as they are, sufficiently demonstrate that many of those who benefited from what the College Bursar felicitously described as a 'century of benevolence' went on to render yeoman service in Church and State, and that not a few achieved high distinction. For the non-collegiate body, and for the College which it has become, the Exhibitions have been of very great value, even though they have formed but a tiny part of the beneficent activity of the Company in the educational field.

(ii) Leathersellers' Company Fellowships, Scholarships, and Exhibitions

In their Report to the Senate dated 12 March 1894[1] the Non-Collegiate Students Board announced their grateful acceptance of an offer by the Leathersellers' Company to provide for the benefit of non-collegiate students four Exhibitions amounting in the aggregate to £100 a year; and at their meeting held on the same date the Board approved a Scheme of Regulations. The Exhibitions, tenable for four years from matriculation, were to be open to any student in financial need, not being a member of a college or hostel, who had resided for not less than two terms, and had passed the Previous Examination or some equivalent; and in respect of each vacancy the Board were asked 'upon the result of examination as to learning and talents, and after due enquiry' to submit to the Company the names of two candidates, in order of merit, and were also to say how many applications they had received.[2]

Awards were first made for the academic year 1894/95, and with the election of G. H. Hewitt (1912/13)[3] there had been forty-one exhibitioners, whose names, with the years of their first tenure, are given below. Of the forty-one, two – the first and the last – took an Ordinary B.A. degree; and one was given his degree by *aegrotat*. The remaining thirty-eight between them obtained fourteen first classes in a Tripos examination, thirty second, and eight third classes. The first class list furnishes clear evidence of the lure of college membership; for of the twelve men eight made a move, and of those who remained two were already at Cheshunt College training for the ministry, and one, who had once been at Caius College, returned to the University, after a lapse of some years, as a non-collegiate student. Of the other twenty-nine exhibitioners, only four migrated.

In June 1911 the Non-Collegiate Students Board were informed that the Company was reluctantly obliged to discontinue the awards – no reason being given, although in his Report for the year 1911/12 the Censor appears to suggest that the decision had been taken on financial grounds. Four similar Oxford Exhibitions were discontinued at the same time.

[1] *University Reporter*, 1893–94, p. 649–56.
[2] Minutes, 12 March 1894.
[3] See also p. 442–4.

Exhibitioners 1894–1912

Academic year of first tenure	Exhibitioner
1894/95	Smart, H.
	Ball, A.
1895/96	Pearson, H. H. W.
	Ross, P. A.
1896/97	Mitra, N.
	Gaskoin, C. J. B.
	George, S.
1897/98	Gray, W.
	Trapp, C. H.
1898/99	Thomas, P. G.
	Cartwright, C.
	Hack, J. H.
1899/1900	Staats, C.
	Sager, J. L.
	Curtis, L.
1900/01	Mills, J. T.
	Sturdee, R. J.
	Burn, R. C.
1901/02	Williams, T. C. L.
	Curzon, H. E. J.
1902/03	White, J. B.
1903/04	Langley, A. S.
	Hoisington, H. M. H.
	Clarke, J. W.
1904/05	Carmichael, E. W.
	Grear, E. L.
1905/06	Erith, E. P.
	Haggis, A. J.
	Turner, J. W.
	Bird, A. L.
1906/07	Quinney, H.
	Taggart, A. W.
	Gonne, F.
1907/08	Witney, T. C.
	McNulty, J. F.
	Lee, A. O. N.

1908/09	Cowe, A. E.
	Brookes, A.
1909/10	Thatcher, W. S.
1911/12	Swallow, J. R.
1912/13	Hewitt, G. H.

The thread was taken up again half a century later, when, at the beginning of the Easter term 1966, the Censor received, by telephone, an enquiry from Mr John Hingston, Clerk to the Company, whether he would find acceptable a suggestion that the Company should make available to Fitzwilliam College (as it was shortly to become) for a period of twenty-one years an annual sum of £3,000 for the support of teaching fellowships, with a further offer of two Entrance Scholarships annually, tenable for three years, subject to satisfactory progress by the scholars.[1] The company's offer was confirmed by letter on 9 May, and formal arrangements were speedily completed, to have effect from the beginning of the next academical year, thus most happily coinciding, within a matter of days, with the assumption by the House of its status of independent College.[2]

Under the provisions of this renewed Scheme, Mr D. M. Thompson, of Queens' College, became the College's first Leathersellers Fellow on 1 October 1966, and in the Michaelmas term of 1968 was joined by Mr M. P. D. Baker Smith, also of Queens' College – elections which afforded most welcome assistance in the teaching of History and English, respectively. Similarly, between 1966 and 1969, the following candidates in the Open Entrance Scholarships Examination were elected Leathersellers Scholars:

1966/67	Francis, D. R. I.
	Quintrell, M. D. J.
1967/68	Nolan, P. H.
	Stockton, F.
1968/69	Macbriar, I. D.
	Newman, J. T.

The College was further indebted to the company, in 1967 and 1968, for two gifts, each of £500, for books for the library.

---

[1] The College also had reason to be grateful to the Company for undertaking, in a time of rising costs, to provide annually, for seven years from 6 April 1971, an additional amount of £1,000.

[2] A more personal benefaction was the gift by Mr Hingston of a gingko tree, planted in the College grounds by Mrs Hingston on 28 November 1968.

Appendix E

31 Trumpington Street – the Keyblock

This terracotta keyblock,[1] over the southernmost ground-floor window of 31 Trumpington Street, has been a subject of speculation from time to time. When Censor Huddleston wrote about it in a report to his Non-Collegiate Board in 1893, he said that on the evidence of a rate-book of the parish of Little St Mary he was satisfied that the initials I H stood for John Halstead (or Halsted); but, he continues,

> I cannot at present offer any certain solution of the X and the Catharine Wheel... It may be a family device, or possibly it may refer to the site hav-ing been previously occupied by a house known as the Catharine Wheel, as it appears in 'The Memorials of Cambridge' by Le Keux and Cooper (Parish of St Mary the Less) that 'William Beamond, Maltster, gave in 1590 a rentcharge of three shillings and four pence, payable out of the Catherine Wheel to a learned preacher, to preach to the edification of the people that man is justified by faith only in the merits of Jesus Christ.'

Some sixty years later Mr E. S. Peck, owner of the chemist's shop next door, returned to the matter of the Cross and the Wheel.[2] He quotes a reference to the use by monastic brewers in pre-dissolution days of a double XX and a triple XXX as guarantees of quality, and to their subsequent development as trade signs; and also remarks on the use of a Saint Anthony's cross by the Wardens of the Coopers' Com-pany, as a certificate of the due inspection of beer barrels and other vessels in accordance with the requirements of legislation of the reign of Henry VIII.[3] Furthermore, among the deeds òf the property Mr Peck found John Halsted described as a brewer in an extract from his will dated 17 February 1729, and in a copy of a lease of 15 September 1769, executed by Thomas Halsted (grandson of John) he found comprehen-sive details of the property and of its use:

> All that capital messe or tenent wherein the said Thomas Halsted there dwelt, situate and being in the Parish of Little St Mary in the town of Cam-bridge afsd. tog. with all and singr. the malting office, brewing office, houses, outhouses, storehouses, granaries, stables and other edifices and buildings within the yards, gardens and house sitting next adjoining or near

---

[1] So described by the Royal Commission on Historical Monuments, in *City of Cambridge* H.M.S.O., 1969, Part I, p. 72.

[2] *Journal*, December 1951, p. 13.

[3] A.D. 1531–32. 23° Hen. VIII, c.4. 'An Acte that no Brewers of Bere or Ale shall make their barrels kylderkyns nor firkyns within them; and howmoche the same barrels &c. shall con-teyne.'

It should, however, be noted that whereas this statute prescribes the use as a distinguish-ing mark of the cross of St Anthony, the cross on the keyblock, like the cross employed by the monastic brewers, is the cross of St Andrew, still used in the trade to distinguish between beers of different quality.

thereunto with the rights privileges heredits and appurts. thereunto belonging or in any wise appurtaining.

Mr Peck mentions the rentcharge given by William Beamont in 1590, and also quotes a reference in the earliest parish registers of Little St Mary to 'A Londiner dying at ye Catherine Wheel' in 1601. 'All these facts considered', he concludes, 'I venture to suggest that this keystone may be taken to indicate the trade-sign of John Halsted, Brewer, in 1727.'

The existence, towards the close of the sixteenth century, of a Catherine Wheel, in the parish of Little St Mary, is established by the mention of William Beamont's rentcharge; but precisely what it was, more precisely where it was, and whose at different times it had been, remained unclear; and it was Mr F. A. Reeve who called attention to the inclusion, in a little volume *Cambridge Borough Documents*, Vol. 1,[1] under the heading 'Cambridge High Gable Rental', of an item

Bennet Coll. for ye Katherine Wheel ij[d]

This suggestion of Corpus ownership was quickly confirmed by Miss Mary Siraut, a former pupil of Dr Edward Miller, who, on the authority of the Bowtell Papers, was able to declare that the Catherine Wheel (however spelt) had been given to the College in 1482; and in Corpus further information was speedily forthcoming. Robert Masters, in his history of the College (1753), has a reference to it:

William Kent, clerk, A.M., and fellow of the College about 1478, made his will in 1482; wherein after recommending his soul to Almighty God, he leaves to the high altar of St Benedict's church for omission of tithes ten shillings, to the master forty pence, to each fellow three shillings: and bequeaths likewise a house he had lately purchased, called the *Kateryn Whele* in St Mary's without Trumpyngton Gatys,[d] after the decease of his mother, which was rented at 33s.4d. to be every year distributed amongst them for liveries,[e] on condition they should pray for him, and for the souls of his father and mother, in like manner as for Master Botwright. His sister Margaret, to whom he left upon marriage 6.8d. and Master Cosyn were his executors and residuary legatees. She afterwards married Robert Coope, whose claiming of the house in her right occasioned no small dispute; but

d Situated upon the King's Ditch, near Pembroke Hall.
e ...must be understood to comprehend such gowns or wearing apparel in general, as was proper for the master, fellows and scholars, according to their respective ranks.

[1] W. M. Palmer (Bowes and Bowes, 1931), p. 57.

the matter being at length referred to John Blythe, archdeacon of Richmond, and master of King's Hall, he obliged him to quit his claim and deliver up all the utensils, the College paying him 20s. per annum for twenty-five years.

This passage tells how the property came to the College, but, as will shortly appear, it is misleading on the subject of its situation,[1] and it was fortunate that the matter was brought to the notice of Mrs Catherine Hall, a colleague of University Registry days, who with the most obliging connivance of the keeper of the College Archives (Mr A. G. Woodhead) was permitted, in the course of her more general work on the College muniments, to keep a particular look-out for the appearance of a Catherine Wheel.

Mrs Hall was not long in finding a partial answer to the problem, for among the College records were papers relating to the 'dispute' (in a court of law) which give the parish (Little St Mary) and the abuttals of the property – to the west on the King's highway (Trumpington Street), and to the east on Swinecroft, named after a family who had property in the area, with the names of the occupiers at the time of tenements north and south. There was here no precise indication of the situation of *The Catherine Wheel*, but Mrs Hall was satisfied that it must have been south of properties owned by Pembroke College and Peterhouse – in modern terms between The Little Rose and Addenbrooke's Hospital, the latter most conveniently in another parish.

And so it proved. 'I find', said Mrs Hall, 'a very useful document in C.C.C.XV 140, endorsed "No. 5 for ever sold with warrant".' This document, dated June 26th, Elizabeth 28, is an indenture of sale by Corpus Christi College to Steven Payne, burgess of Cambridge, of a property described in the following terms:

> all that their tenement with all and singular thappurtenances now or late in the tenure or occupation of one Robert Norris Carpenter situate lying and

---

[1]   Bowtell, in a 'List of Antient Public Houses in Cambridge', collected from sundry old deeds and records, gives Masters as his authority for this description of the site. Dr H. P. Stokes, in *Outside the Trumpington Gates* (No. XLIV, C.A.S. Octavo Publications, 1908, p. 33) notes Masters' statement, but is more cautious, for in a note about another property said to be on the King's Ditch in St Peter's Parish, he continues 'So, the old *Katharine Wheel*, "in St Mary's without Trumpington Gate... situated upon the King's Ditch near Pembroke Hall" (according to Masters, *History* of C.C.C., p. 52), was perhaps near this, though there must be some mistake in the historian's description.'

It is possible that Masters was referring to a different Catherine Wheel, for the name was not uncommon. In his List Bowtell has another in Mill Street which, he says, 'was one of the houses pulled down to make room for the royal College built by King Henry VI'; and it is said that yet another was one of six inns in Silver Street demolished in the latter half of the nineteenth century when buildings were put up by the University Press.

being in the parish of Our Lady St Mary the Virgin without Trumpinton gates in Cambridge aforesaid

next the land called the White Channons[1] now in the tenure or occupation of John Hatcher doctor of Phisicke or his Assignes one the South side.

And the tenement of William Beamont called the Katherine Wheele one the North side. The West head thereof abutting upon the Quenes highway called Trumpinton streate

And the East head thereof abutteth upon St Thomas Leyes.[2] And it conteyneth in bredth from the South to the North at the East end twenty yardes of the Quenes Standerd and at the West end toward the Quenes highway called Trumpinton streate foure and twenty yardes. And in lengthe from the East to the West threscore and five yardes of the Quenes Standerd be it more or lesse.

The Catherine Wheel, then, was situated on the east side of Trumpington Street, with its southern boundary twenty-four yards north of the boundary between the parishes of Little St Mary and St Benedict;[3] and there can be little doubt that when John Halsted built his house in 1727 he intended that the keyblock should commemorate the previous existence on the site of the house bequeathed to Corpus Christi College by William Kent in 1482. The property of Steven Payne, or its successor, will have been demolished to make way for the western end of Fitzwilliam Street in the early 1820s.

[1] The White Canons of St Gilbert of Sempringham; who settled in Cambridge in 1291 on land made over to the Order by Cecilia of St Edmund's. The site is now occupied by (the old) Addenbrooke's Hospital. See Stokes, *op. cit.*

[2] At about this time this name came to be applied to the whole of the land immediately behind buildings on the east side of Trumpington Street, between Pembroke College and the southern parish boundary. Previously its southern part was known as Swinecroft, a name given in the fourteenth century to the whole area. Cf. maps of Cambridge by Lyne (1574) and Hammond (1592).

[3] This boundary was marked in the early nineteenth century, on a date now partially illegible, on no. 27 Trumpington Street. For references to the earlier history of this area, and to a Paternoster Hostel which may have previously occupied the site of the Catherine Wheel, see Stokes, *op. cit.*

   As a postscript to these observations on the subject of the site of the Halsted house, there may be added its curious omission from Loggan's *Cantabrigia Illustrata*. There is no building, and no empty space, between its northern and southern neighbours. The omission was repaired by William Custance in his 'new plan' of 1798.

Index